A SURVEY OF LONDON

BY JOHN STOW

REPRINTED FROM THE TEXT OF 1603

WITH INTRODUCTION AND NOTES

BY

CHARLES LETHBRIDGE KINGSFORD, M.A.

ST. JOHN'S COLLEGE

EDITOR OF 'CHRONICLES OF LONDON'

VOLUME II

OXFORD

AT THE CLARENDON PRESS

1908

HENRY FROWDE, M.A.
PUBLISHER TO THE UNIVERSITY OF OXFORD
LONDON, EDINBURGH
NEW YORK AND TORONTO

CONTENTS

VOLUME II

ILLUSTRATIONS

Queene Hithe Warde

Page 354

NEXT vnto Bredstreete Warde on the south side thereof, is Queene Hithe warde, so called of a water gate, or harborow for boates, lighters, and barges, and was of old time for shippes, at what time the timber bridge of London was drawne vp, for the passage of them to the said Hithe, as to a principall strand for landing and vnlading against the middest and hart of the Citie. This Warde beginneth in the East, in Knightriders streete, on the south side thereof, at the East end of the parish church called the holy Trinity, and runneth west on the south side to a lane called Lambert hill, which is the length of the warde in Knightriders streete, out of the which streete are diuers lanes, running south to Thames streete, and are of this warde: the first is Trinity lane, which runneth downe by the west end of Trinity Church. Then is Spuren lane, or Spooners[1] lane, now called Huggen lane. Then Bredstreete hill. Then *S. Mary Mounthaunt*: out of the which lane, on the East side thereof, is one other lane, turning East, through *S. Nicholas Olaues* church yard, to Bredstreete hill. This lane is called Finimore lane, or fiue foote lane, because it is but fiue foote in breadth at the west end: In the middest of this lane, runneth downe one other lane broader, south to Thames streete, I thinke the same to bee called Desboorne lane, for I reade of such a lane to haue beene in the parish of *Mary Summerset*, in the 22. yeare of *Edward* the third, where there is sayde to lye betweene the Tenement ⟨of⟩ *Edward de Mountacute* knight, on the East parte, and the Tenement sometime pertayning to *William Gladwine* on the west, one plot of ground, contayning in length towards Thames streete 25. foote, &c.

Queene Hithe Warde.

Knightriders streete.

Trinity lane.

Spuren lane, or Huggen lane.

Finimore or fiue foote lane.

Desborne lane

Last of all, haue you Lambart hill lane, so called of one Lambart owner thereof: and this is the furthest west part of this warde.

Lambert hill.

[1] Spooners] *1603*; Sporners *1598*

On the north side comming downe from Knightriders street, the | East side of Lambart hill is wholly of this warde: and the West side, from the north end of the Blacke-smithes Hall (which is about the middest of this lane) vnto Thames streete. Then part of Thames streete is also of this warde, to wit, from a Cooks house called the signe of King *Dauid*, three houses west from the old Swan Brewhouse in the East, vnto *Huntington* house, ouer against Saint *Peters* Church in the west, neare vnto Powles Wharffe. And on the lane side, from a Cookes house called the blew Boore, to the west end of Saint *Peters* Church, and vp Saint *Peters* hill, two houses North aboue the said Church. And these be the bounds of this ward: in which are Parrish churches seuen, Halles of companies two, & other ornaments as shall be shewed.

Page 355

Parish church of the Trinity.

First, in Knightriders streete, is the small parish church of the holy Trinity, very old, and in danger of downe falling: collections haue beene made for reparing thereof, but they will not stretch so farre, and therefore it leaneth vpon proppes, or stilts. Monuments as followeth.

Iohn Brian, Alderman in the raign of *H.* the fift, a great benefactor. *Iohn Chamber* had a Chauntrie there. *Thomas Rishby* Esquier, and *Alice* his wife, within the Chauncell. *Iohn Mirfin*, auditor of the Exchequer 1471. Sir *Richard Fowlar* of Rycote[1] in Oxfordshire, 1528. *George Cope* second sonne to sir *Iohn Cope* of Copesashby in Northamptonshire, 1572.

Parish church of S. Nicholas Cold Abbey.

Towardes the west end of Knightriders street is the parish church of *S. Nicholas Cold Abbey*, a proper church, somewhat ancient, as appeareth by the wayes raysed thereabout, so that men are forced to descend into the body of the church: it hath bin called of many *Colden*[2] *Abbey*, of some, *Cold Abbey*[2], or *Cold Bey*, & so hath the most ancient writings, as standing in a cold place, as Cold harbor, and such like. The steeple or tall tower of this church, with the south Ile, hath beene of a later building, to wit the 1. of *R.* 2. when it was ment the whole old church should haue bin new builded, as appeareth by the arching begun on the east side the steeple, vnder y[e] which, in the stone work, the armes of one *Buckland* Esquier and his wife, daughter to *Beaupere*, are cut in stone, & also

[1] Rycote] Ricks *1603*   [2] *Colden, Cold 1633*

are in the glasse windowes, wherby it appeareth he was the builder of ye steeple, & repairer of the residue. The 26. of *E.* the 3. *An⟨drew⟩ Aubery* being | Maior, *T. Frere* Fishmonger gaue one peece of ground to the said parish church of *S. Nic.* contayning 86. feete in length, & 43. feete at one end, and 34. at the other in bredth, for a Cemitorie or churchyeard. The 20. of *Richard* the second, *Thomas Barnarde-Castle*, Clearke, *Iohn Sonderash* Clearke, and *Iohn Nouncy*, gaue to the Parson and Churchwardens of the saide church and theyr successors, one messuage and one shoppe with the appurtenances in Distaffe lane and olde Fishstreete, for the reparation of the body of the saide church, the Belfrey or steeple, and ornamentes. *Page 356*

Buried in this church, *Iohn Calfe*, & *William Cogeshall*, 1426. *Waltar Turke* Fishmonger, Mayor 1349. *Richarde Es⟨g⟩astone* Fishmonger, 1330. *Nicholas Wolberge* Fishmonger, 1407. *Thomas Padington* Fishmonger, 1485. *Robert Hary*, Fishmonger, *Iohn Suring*, 1490. *Roger Darlington*, Fishmonger, 1557. *Richard Lacty*, Parson, vnder a fayre tombe on the North side the Quire, 1491. *Richard Bradbrudge*, 1497. *William Clarke*, 1501. *Iames Picman*, 1507. *Richard Farneford*, 1525. *Thomas Nicholas*, Fishmonger, 1527. *William Barde* Fishmonger, 1528.

On the North side of this church in the wall therof, was of late builded a conuenient cistern of stone and lead, for receit of Thames water, conueyed in pipes of lead to that place, for the ease and commoditie of the Fishmongers and other inhabitantes, in and aboute old Fishstreete. *Barnard Randolph*, common sergeant of the citie of London, did in his life time deliuer to the Company of Fishmongers the summe of nine hundred pound, to be imployed towardes the conducting of the said Thames water, and cesterning the same, &c. in the parishes of S. Mary Magdalen, and saint Nicholas Cold Abbay, neare vnto Fishstreete, seuen hundred pound, and other two hundred pound to charitable deedes: he deceased 1583. and shortly after this conduit with the other was made and finished. **Water conduit.**

In Trinity lane, on the west side thereof, is the Painter stayners hall, for so of olde time were they called, but now **Painter stayners hall.**

that workemanship of stayning is departed out of vse in England. Lower down in Trinity lane on the east side thereof,
Page 357
was sometime a greate | Messuage pertayning vnto *Iohn* Earle of Cornwell, in the fourteenth of *Edward* the 3. On Bredstreet hill down to the Thames on both sides, bee diuers faire houses, inhabited by Fishmongers, Cheesemongers, and Marchantes of diuers trades. On the West side whereof is the parish church of S. Nicholas Oliue, a conuenient church, hauing the monumentes of *W. Newport*, Fishmonger, one of the shiriffes, 1375. *Richard Willowes* Parson, 1391. *Richard Sturges* Fishmonger, 1470. *Thomas Lewen*, Ironmonger, one of the shiriffes, 1537. who gaue his messuage with the appurtenances, wherein hee dwelt, with foureteene Tenementes in the said parrish of saint Nicholas, to be had after the decease of *Agnes* his wife, to the Ironmongers, and they to giue stipendes appointed to Almes men, in fiue houses by them builded in the church yeard of that parrish, more to poore schollers in Oxford and Cambridge, &c. *Blitheman*, an excellent Organist of the Queens chappell, lyeth buried there with an Epitaph, 1591. &c. The next is old Fishstreete hill, a lane so called, which also runneth downe to Thames streete. In this lane, on the east side thereof, is the one end of Finimore, or Fiue foote lane. On the west side of this old Fishstreete hill, is the Bishoppe of Herefordes Inne or lodging, an auncient house and large roomes builded of stone and timber which sometime belonged to the Mounthauntes in Norfolke. *Radulphus de Maydenstone* Bishoppe of Hereford, about 1234. bought it of the Mounthauntes, and gaue it to the Bishoppes of Hereford, his successors. *Charles Booth*[1], Bishoppe of Hereforde and Chauncellour of the Marches, about the yeare 1517. repayred it, since the which time, the same is greatly ruinated, and is now diuided into many small tenementes: the Hall and principall rooms are an house to make Suger loaues, &c.

Earle of Cornwel his house.

Parish church of S. Nicholas Oliue.

Old Fishstreete hill.

Bishop of Herefords house.

Next adioyning is the parrish church of S. Mary de Monte Alto, or Mounthaunt, this is a very small church, and at the first builded to be a Chapple for the said house of the Mounthaunts, and for Tenementes thereunto belonging. The Bishop of Hereforde is Patron thereof. Monumentes in this church

Parish church of Saint Mary Monte alto.

[1] Booth] both *1603*, *1633*

of *Iohn Glocester* Alderman, 1345, who gaue Salt wharfe for two Chaunteries there, *Iohn Skip* Bishoppe of Hereford 1539. sate xii. yeares, died at London in time of Parliament, and was buried in this | church. There was sometime a fayre house in the saide parrish of Saint Mary Mounthaunt, belonging to *Roberte Belkenape*, one of the Kinges Iustices, but the saide *Belkenape* being banished this Realme, King *Richarde* the second, in the twelfth of his raigne, gaue it to *William Wickham* Bishoppe of Winchester.

Page 358

Robert Belkenape his house giuen to W. Wickham.

On the east side of this olde Fishstreete hill, is one greate House, now letten out for rent, which house sometime was one of the Halles, pertayning to the Company of Fishmongers, at such time as they had sixe Hallmotes or meeting places: namely, twaine in Bridgestreete, or new Fish streete, twaine in old Fish street, whereof this was one, and twain in Stockfishmonger row or Thames street, as appeareth by a Record, the 22. of *Richarde* the second.

One old hall of the Fishmongers.

Fishmonger Hallmotes, six in number.

Pattents.

Next westward, is one other lane called Lambard hill, the East side whereof is wholy of this Warde, and but halfe the west side, to wit, from the north end of the blacke Smithes hall.

Lambard hill.

Blacksmithes hall.

Then in Thames street of this ward, and on the north side ouer against the Queens Hith, is the parrish church of saint Michaell, a conuenient Church, but all the Monumentes therein are defaced.

Parish church of S. Michaell at Queene Hith.

I finde that *Stephen Spilman*, Gentleman, of that Family in Norfolke, sometime Mercer, Chamberlaine of London, then one of the Shiriffes and Alderman, in the yeare 1404. deceasing without issue, gaue his landes to his Family the Spilmans, and his goodes to the making or repayring of bridges and other like godly vses: And amongst others in this church he founded a chauntrie, and was buried in the Quire.

Also *Richard Marlowe*, Ironmonger, Mayor 1409. gaue twenty pound to the poore of that Warde, and ten markes to the church.

Richard Gray Ironmonger, one of the shiriffes, one thousand fiue hundred and fifteene, gaue forty pound to that church, and was buried there. At the West end of that church goeth vp a lane, called Pyellane. On the same North side, at the South end of Saint Mary Mounthaunt Lane, is the Parrish

Pyellane.

Parrish church of Saint Mary Summerset.

Page 359 Church of Saint Mary Summerset, ouer against the Bro|ken Wharfe: it is a proper church, but the monumentes are all defaced. I thinke the same to bee of olde time called Summers Hith, of some mans name that was owner of the grounde neare adioyning, as Edreds Hithe was so called of *Edred* owner thereof, and sithence called Queene Hith, as pertayning to the Queene, &c.

Summers Hithe.

Parish church of S. Peter parua by Powles wharfe.

Then is a small Parrish church of Saint *Peter*, called parua or little, neare vnto Powles wharfe: In this Church no Monumentes doe remaine. At the West ende thereof, is a Lane called Saint Peters Hill, but two houses vp that Lane on the east side is of this warde, and the rest is of Castle Baynarde warde.

Townes ende lane.

On the South side of Thames streete, beginning againe in the East, among the Cookes: The first in this warde, is the signe of *Dauid* the king: then is Townes end lane, turning downe to the Thames. Then is Queene Hith, a large receptacle for shippes, lighters, barges and such other vessels.

Edreds hith or Queene Hith.

Lib. Trinitate.

Touching the Antiquitie and vse of this gate and Hith, first I finde the same belonged to one named *Edred*, and was then called Edreds Hith, which since falling to the handes of King *Stephen*, it was by his Charter confirmed to *William De Ypre*: the Farme thereof in Fee and in Heritage, *William De Ypre* gaue it vnto the Prior and Couent of the Holy Trinitie within Aldegate, as appeareth by this Charter: To *Theobalde* by the grace of God Archbishop of Canterbury, primate of England, and Legate Apostolike, to the Bishoppe of London, and to all faithfull people, Clarkes and Laye men, *William de Ypre* sendeth greeting.

Know ye me to haue giuen and graunted to God, and to the Church of the Holy Trinitie of London, to the Prior and cannons there seruing God in perpetuall almes, Edreds Hith with the appurtenances, with such deuotion, that they shall send euery yeare twentie pound vnto the maintenance of the Hospital of S. Katherens, *which hospitall they haue in their hands, &* 100. *shillinges to the monkes of Bermondsey, &* 60. *shillinges to the brethren of the hospitall of saint* Giles, *and that which remayneth, the said Prior and Canons shall enioy*

Page 360 *to themselues: Witnesses* Richard de Lu|cie, Raph Picot, *&c.*

This Edreds Hithe after the aforesaid grantes, came againe to the Kinges handes, by what meanes I haue not read, but it pertayned vnto the Queene, and therefore was called *Ripa reginæ*, the Queenes banke or Queens Hith, and great profite therof was made to her vse, as may appeare by this which followeth.

Record.

King *Henry* the third, in the ninth of his raigne, commaunded the Constable of the Tower of London to arrest the shippes of the Cinque portes on the Riuer of Thames, and to compell them to bring their corne to no other place but to the Queens Hith onely. In the eleuenth of his raigne, hee charged the sayde Constable to destraine all fish offered to be sold in any place of this cittie, but at the Queene Hith. Moreouer in the twentie eight of the said kings raign, an inquisition was made before *William* of Yorke, Prouost of Beuerley, *Henry* of Bath, and *Hierome* of Caxton, Iustices Itenerantes, sitting in the Tower of London, touching the customs of Queen Hith, obserued in the year last before the wars betweene the king and his father, and the Barons of England, and of olde customes of other times, & what customes had beene changed, at what time the taxe and payment of al things comming thether, and between woorepath, and Anede Hith, were found and ceased, according to the olde order, as well corne and fish as of other thinges: all which customes were as well to be obserued in the parte of Downegate, as in Queen Hith, for the Kinges vse. When also it was found, that the corne arriuing between the gate of the Guild hall of the Merchantes of Colleyne, and the soke of the Archbishop of Canterbury (for he had a house neare vnto the Blacke Fryers) was not to be measured by any other quarter, then by that of the Queenes soke.

Ships of the ports arrested, and forced to bring their corne to Queene Hith.

Liberty of the Queens Hith from the Stilyeard to the Black Fryers.

Soke is court.

After this, the Baliffes of the said Hith complayned, that since the said Recognision, foureteene forraine ships laden with Fishe, arriued at Belinges gate, which shippes should haue arriued at the saide Hith: And therefore it was ordered, that if any forraine shippe laden with fish, should in forme aforesaid arriue else where then at this Hith, it should bee at the Kinges pleasure to amerce them at fortie shillinges. Notwithstanding, the shippes of the | Citizens of London

Page 361

were at libertie to arriue where the owners would appoynt them.

Queen Hith let to farme to the Maior and Comminaltie of London.

After this, the saide *Henrie* the third confirmed the graunt of *Richard* Earle of Cornwell, for the Farme of the Queene Hithe, vnto *Iohn Gisors* then Maior, and to the Comminaltie of London, and their successors for euer, as by this his Charter appeareth:

Lib. Trinitate Lon.

Henry *by the grace of God, king of England, Lord of Ireland, Duke of Guien, and Earle of Aniow, to all Archbishops, &c. Bee it knowne, that we haue seene the couenant betweene our brother* Richard *Earle of Cornwell, of the one partie, and the Maior and Comminaltie of London on the other partie, which was in this sort. In the* 30. *yeare of* Henry *the sonne of king* Iohn, *vpon the feast of the translation of S.* Edward *at Westminster, this couenant was made betweene the honorable lord* Richard *Earle of Cornwel, and* Iohn Gisors *then Maior of London, and the Commons thereof, concerning certaine exactions and demands pertaining to the Queen Hithe of London. The said Earle granted for himselfe and his heires, that the said Maior, and all Maiors insuing, and all the Commons of the citie, should haue and holde the Queene Hithe, with all the liberties, customes, and other appurtenances, repaying yearly to the said Earle, his heires and assignes,* 50. *li. at Clarken well, at two seuerall tearmes: to wit, the Sunday after Easter* 25. *pound, and at Michaelmas* 25. *pound. And for more suretie hereof, the said Earle hath set thereunto his seale, and left it with the Maior, and the Maior and Comminaltie haue set to their seale, and left it with the Earle. Wherefore we confirme and establish the saide couenant for vs, and for our heyres, Witnesses,* Raph Fitz Nichol, Richard Gray, Iohn *and* Wil. Brithem, Paulin Painter, Raph Wancia, Iohn Cumband, *and other: at Windsor the* 26. *of Februarie, the* 31. *of our reigne.*

Rob. Fabian.

The charge of this Queene Hithe was then committed to the Shiriffes, and so hath continued euer since, the profits whereof are sore diminished so that (as writeth *Robert Fabian*) it was worth in his time little aboue 20. markes, or 15. pound one yeare with an other. Now for customs of this Queene

Li. Constitut.

Hithe, in the yeare 1302. the 30. of *Edward* the first, it was found by the oath of diuerse men, that Bakers, Brewers, and others buying their corne | at Queene Hithe, should pay for measuring, portage, and carriage for euery quarter of corne whatsoeuer, from thence to west Cheap, to Saint *Anthonies* Church, to Horshew Bridge, and to Woolsey streete in the Parish of Alhallowes the lesse, and such like distances, one ob. q.: to Fleete bridge, to Newgate, Cripplegate, to Bercheouers lane, to Eastcheape and Billingsgate, one pennie. Also that the measurer (or the meater) ought to haue 8. chiefe Master Porters, euery master to haue three porters vnder him, and euery one of them to finde one horse, and seuen sackes, and he that so did not, to loose his office. This Hithe was then so frequented with vessels, bringing thither corne (besides fish, salt, fewel, and other marchandizes) that all these men, to wit, the meater, and porters, 37. in number, for all their charge of horses and sackes, and small stipend, liued well of their labors: but now the Bakers of London and other Citizens trauell into the Countries, and buy their corne of the Farmers, after the Farmers price.

Page 362

Custome of Queen Hithe.

A corne meater, 8. M. porters, and 24. porters vnder them, at queen hithe.

King *Edward* the second in the first of his raigne, gaue to *Margaret*, wife to *Peter de Gauestone*, fortie three pound, twelue shillings nine pence ob. q. out of the rent of London, to be receiued of the Queenes Hithe. Certaine Impositions were set vpon ships and other vessels comming thither, as vpon corne, salt, and other things, toward the charge of cleansing Roomeland there, the 41. of *Edward* the 3.

Liber Guild.

Romeland at Queen Hithe.

The third of *Edward* the fourth, the Market at Queene Hithe being hindred by the slackenesse of drawing vp London bridge, it was ordained, that all maner of Vesselles, Shippes, or boats, great or small, resorting to the Citie with victuall, should bee solde by retaile, and that if there came but one vessell at a time, were it salt, Wheate, Rie, or other Corne from beyond the Seas, or other graines, Garlicke, Onions, Hearings, Sprattes, Eles, Whiting, Place, Cods, Mackarell, &c. then that one vessell should come to Queene Hithe, and there to make sale: but if two vessels come, the one should come to Queene Hithe, the other to Billingsgate: if three, two of them should come to Queene Hithe, the third to Belingsgate, &c. alwaies the more to Queene Hithe: if the

Queene Hithe to be more frequented of ships & boats then Billingsgate.

vessel being great, comming with salt from the Bay, and could not come to these keyes, then the same to be conueyed by lighters, as before is ment.|

Page 363

A garner for corne & stowage-house for malt at Queene Hithe.

One large house for stowage of corne craned out of Lighters and Barges, is there lately builded: sir *Iohn Lion*, Grocer, Maior 1554. by his testament gaue an hundred pounde towardes it, but since increased and made larger at the charges of the citie, in the yeare 1565.

Corne Mill vpon barges or lighters on the Thames.

Against this Queenes Hithe, on the riuer Thames of late yeres was placed a corne Mill, vpon, or betwixt two barges or lighters, and there ground corne, as water Milles in other places, to the wonder of many that had not seene the like, but this lasted not long without decay, such as caused the same Barges and Mill to bee remooued, taken asunder, and soone forgotten. I reade of the like to haue beene in former time, as thus: In the yeare, 1525. the sixteene of *Henrie* the eight, Sir *William Bayly* being Maior, *Iohn Cooke* of Glocester, Mercer, gaue to the Maior and Comminaltie of London and theyrs[1] for euer, one great Barge, in the which two corne Milles were made and placed, which Barge and Milles were set in, and vpon the streame of the Riuer Thames, within the iurisdiction and libertie of said citie of London.

Two corne mils in one barge giuen to this citie, 1525.

And also he gaue to the Cittie all such Tymber, Bourdes, Stones, Iron, &c. prouided for making, mending, and repayring of the sayde Barge, and Milles, in rewarde whereof, the Maior gaue him fiftie pounde presently, and fiftie pounde yearely during his life, and if the sayde *Cooke* deceased before *Iohan* his wife, then shee to haue fortie Markes the yeare during her life.

Stew lane.

Timber hithe.

Brooks wharff.

Next adioyning to this Queene Hithe, on the West side thereof, is Salt Wharffe, named of Salt taken vp, measured and sold there. The next is Stew lane, of a stewe or hotte house there kept. After that is Timber Hithe, or Timber street, so called of Timber or Boordes there taken vp and wharffed: it is in the parrish of saint *Marie Somershithe*, as I reade in the fiftie six of *Henrie* the third, and in the ninth of *Edward* the second. Then is *Brookes* wharfe & broken wharfe, a watergate or key, so called of beeing broken and

[1] their heyres] theyrs *edd.*

fallen downe into the Thames. By this broken Wharffe, remayneth one large olde building of stone, with Arched Gates, which Messuage as I finde in the raigne of *Henry* | the third the 43. yeare, pertaining vnto *Hugh de Bygot*, and in the xi. of *Edward* the third, to *Thomas Brothertun* the kings brother, Earle of Norffolke, Marshall of England. In the xi. of *Henry* the sixt. to *Iohn Mowbray* Duke of Norffolke, &c.

Broken wharff.

Page 364

Bygots house by broken wharfe.

Within the gate of this house, (now belonging to the citie of London) is lately, to wit, in the yeare, 1594. and 1595. builded one large house of great height, called an engine, made by *Beuis Bulmar* Gentleman, for the conueying and forcing of Thames water to serue in the middle and West parts of the Citie. The auncient great hall of this messuage is yet standing, and partayning to a great Brew-house for Beere. West from this is Trigge lane, going downe to the Thames. Next is called Bosse lane, of a Bosse of water, like vnto that of Belingsgate, there placed by the executors of *Richard Wittington.* Then is one great messuage somtime belonging to the Abbots of Chartsey in Surrey, and was their Inne, wherein they were lodged when they repayred to the Citie: it is now called Sandie house, by what reason I haue not heard. I thinke the Lord Sands haue beene lodged there. And this is an end of this Queene Hithe ward: which hath an Alderman, and his Deputie, common Counsell sixe, Constables nine, Scauengers eight, Wardmote Inquest thirteene, and a Beedle. It is taxed to the fifteene in London twentie pound, and in the Exchequer at xix. pound xvi.s. two pence.

An engine for enforcing of Thames water.

Trigge lane.

Bosse lane.

Castle Baynard warde

THE next is Castle Bainard Warde, so named of an olde Castle there: this Ward beginneth in the East, on the Thames side, at an house called Huntington house, and runneth West by Powles Wharfe, by Baynards Castell, Puddle Wharffe, and by the South side of Blacke Friers. Then turning by the East Wall of the sayde Friers, to the Southwest ende of Creede lane. Then on the North side of Thames streete, ouer agaynst Huntington house, by Saint *Peters* Church and lane, called Peter | hill, along till ouer agaynst Puddle Wharffe: and then North vp by the great Wardrobe, to the West ende

Castle Baynard warde.

Page 365

of Carter lane. Then vp Creede lane, *Aue Mary* lane, and a peece of *Pater Noster Rowe*, to the signe of the Golden Lion, and backe againe vp Warwicke lane, all the East side thereof, to the signe of the Crowne by Newgate Market: and this is the farthest North part of this Warde.

Then out of Thames streete bee lanes ascending North to Knightriders street: the first is Peter hill lane, all of that warde (two houses excepted, adioyning to Saint *Peters* Church.) The next is Powles Wharffe hill, which thwarting Knightriders streete, and Carter lane, goeth vp to the South chaine of Powles churchyarde.

Adle streete. Then is Adlestreete, ouer against the West part of Baynards Castell, going vp by the West end of Knightriders streete, and to Carter lane. Thus much for lanes out of Thames streete. The one halfe of the West side of Lambard hill lane being of this Warde, at the Northwest ende thereof, on the South side, and at the West end of Saint *Mary Magdalens* church on the North side beginneth Knightriders streete to be of this Warde, and runneth West on both sides to the parish church of Saint *Andrew* by the Wardrope.

Then at the said East end of saint *Mary Magdalens* Church goeth vp the old Exchange, al the west side wherof vp to the south east gate of Powles churchyard, and by S. *Austens* church, is of this ward. About the midst of this olde Exchange, on the west side thereof is Carter lane, which runeth west to the east entry of the blacke Friers, and the south ende of Creed lane, out of the which Carter lane descendeth Do little lane. a lane called Do little lane, and commeth into Knightriders streete, by the Bores head Tauerne: and more West is Sermon lane, by an Inne called the Powle head. Then out of Carter lane, on the North side thereof, the south Chaine of Powles Churchyard, and the church yard it selfe on that south side of Powles church, and the church of saint *Gregorie*, the Bishoppes Palace, and the Deanes lodging, be all of this Warde: and such be the boundes thereof. The Ornaments in this Warde, be parish churches 4. Of olde time a castle: *Page 366* Diuers Noblemens | houses. Halles of Companies twaine. And such others, as shall be shewed.

In Thames street, at the south east end, is an ancient

messuage, of old time called Bewmounts Inne, as belonging to that family of Noblemen of this realme, in the 4. of *Edward* the 3. *Edward* the 4. in the 5. of his raigne gaue it to *W. Hastings*, Lord Chamberlaine, Maister of his Mints. It is now called *Huntington* House, as belonging to the Earles of *Huntington*. Next is Pauls wharfe, a large landing place, with a common stayre vpon the Riuer of Thames, at the end of a streete called powles wharfe hill, which runneth downe from Powles chaine. Next is a great Messuage called Scrupes Inne, sometime belonging to the *Scrupes*, in the 31. of *Henry* the 6. Bewmounts Inne. Paules wharfe. Scrupes Inne.

Then is one other great Messuage sometime belonging to the Abbey of *Fiscampe*, beyond the sea, and by reason of the wars, it comming to the hands of K. *Edward* the 3. the same was giuen to sir *Simon Burley*, knight of the Garter, and therefore called *Burley* house in Thames streete, betweene Baynards Castle and paules wharfe. Burley house.

Then haue you Baynards Castle, whereof this whole ward taketh the name. This Castle banketh on the Riuer Thames, and was called Baynards Castle, of *Baynard*, a Nobleman that came in with *W.* the *Conquerour*, of the which castle, and of *Baynard* himselfe, I haue spoken in another place. Baynards Castle.

There was also another tower by Baynards Castle, builded by King *Edward* the 2. *Edward* the 3. in the 2. of his raigne, gaue it to *William de Ros*[1] of *Hamelake*, in the County of *Yorke*, & his heyres, for one Rose yearely, to be payd for all seruice: the same place (as seemeth to me) was since called *Legates* Inne, in the 7. of *Edward* the fourth, where bee now diuers woodwharfes in place. Legates Inne.

Then is there a great Brewhouse, and Puddle wharfe, a water gate into the Thames, where horses vse to be watered, & therfore being filed with their trampeling, and made puddle, like as also of one *Puddle* dwelling there: it is called Puddle Wharfe. Then is there a lane betweene the blacke Fryers and the Thames, called in the 26. of *Edward* the third Castle lane. | Puddle Wharfe.

In this lane also is one great Messuage, of old time belonging to the Priory of *Okeborne*[2] in *Wilshire*, and was the Priors lodging when he repayred to London. This Prior being of *Page 367*

[1] *de Ros*] cf. i. 67: Duke *1603*
[2] *Okeborne*] *Ogbourne S. Andrew, and S. George, Wilts*

Prior of Okebornes house.

the French order, was suppressed by *H.* the 5. and with other lands and Tenements pertaining to the said Priory, was by *H.* the 6. giuen to his Colledge in Cambridge, called now the kings Colledge. About this Castle lane, was sometime a Mill, or Mils, belonging to the Templars of the new Temple, as appeareth of record: for King *Iohn* in the first yeare of his raigne, granted a place in the Fleete, neare vnto Baynards Castle, to make a mill, and the whole course of water of the Fleete, to serue the said mill.

A Mill or Mils by Baynards Castle.

I reade also that in the yeare 1274. the 2. of *E.* the 1. *Ri. Raison* and *Atheline* his wife did giue to *Nicho. de Musely* Clarke, 10 shillings of yearely free and quiet rent, out of all his tenements, with the houses thereupon built, and their appurtenances, which they had of the demise of the M. and brethren of knights Templars in England next to their mill of Fleet, ouer against the houses of *Laurence de Brooke*, in the parish of S. *Andrew* next to Baynards Castle: which tenements lyeth betweene the way, leading towards the said Mil on the west part. Also in the rights belonging to *Robert Fitzwater* & to his heyres, in the Citie of London, in the time of peace, it was declared in the yeare 1303. that the sayde *Robert* Castillon of London, and Banner bearer, had a soke (or warde) in the Citie, that was by the wall of S. *Paule*, as men go downe the streete before the Brewhouse of *S. Paule* vnto the Thames, and so to the side of the Mill, which is in the water that commeth downe from Fleete Bridge, and goeth by London wals, betwixt the Fryers preachers Church, and Ludgate, and so that warde turned backe by the house of the said Fryers, vnto the sayde common wall of the sayd Chanonry of *S. Paule*: that is all of the parish of *S. Andrew*, which is in the gift of his auncestors by seniority, as more I haue shewed in the Castles.

Soke Court or Warde pertayning to Richard Fitzwater.

Now here is to be noted, that the wall of London at that time went straight south from Ludgate, downe to the Riuer of Thames, but for building of the Blacke Fryers Church, the said wall in that place was by commaundement taken downe, and a | new wall made, straight West from Ludgate to Fleetebridge, and then by the water of Fleete, to the Riuer of Thames &c.

Page 368

In the yeare 1307. the 35. of *Edward* the first, in a Parliament at *Carlile*, *Henry Lacie* Earle of *Lincolne* complained of noyances done to the water of the Fleete: whereupon it was graunted, that the said Mill should be remoued and destroyed.

Mill by Baynards castle destroyed.

This Warde ascendeth vp by the East wall of the blacke-Fryers, to the South West end of *Creede* Lane, where it endeth on that side.

Then to beginne againe on the North side of Thames street ouer against *Huntington* house by Saint *Peters* Church and lane called *Peter* hill, and so to S. *Benet* Hude (or Hithe) ouer against Powles Wharffe, a proper parish Church, which hath the Monuments of Sir *William Cheiny* knight, and *Margaret* his wife, 1442. buried there. Doctor *Caldwell* Phisition. Sir *Gilbert Dethik*, knight, *Alias Gartar* king at Armes. West from this church, by the south end of Adlestreete, almost against Pudle Wharfe, there is one ancient building of stone and timber, builded by the Lords of *Barkley*, and therefore called *Barklies* Inne. This house is now all in ruine, and letten out in seuerall Tenements, yet the Armes of the Lord *Barkley* remaine in the stone worke of an Arched gate, and is betweene a Cheueron crosses, 10. three, three, and foure.

Parish church of S. Benet hard by Pauls wharf.

Barklies Inne.

Richard Beauchampe Earle of *Warwicke*, was lodged in this house, then called *Barklies* Inne, in the parish of Saint *Andrew*, in the raigne of *Henry* the sixt. Then turning vp towardes the North, is the parish church of S. *Andrew* in the wardrobe, a proper church, but few Monuments hath it. *Iohn Parnt* founded a chauntry there. Then is the kings greate Wardrobe, Sir *Iohn Beauchampe*, knight of the Garter, Constable of *Douer*, Warden of the Sinke Portes (sonne to *Guido de Beauchampe*, Earle of *Warwicke*) builded this house, was lodged there, deceased in the yeare 1359. and was buried on the South side of the middle Ile of Powles Church. His Executors sold the house to King *Edwarde* the third, vnto whome | the Parson of *S. Andrewes* complayning that the said *Beuchamp* had pulled downe diuers houses, in their place to build the same house, where through he was hindered of his accustomed tithes, payd by the tenants of old time, granted him 40. s. by yeare

Parish church of S. Andrew in the Wardrobe.

The Kings great Wardrobe.

Page 369

out of that house for euer. King *R.* the 3. was lodged there in the second of his raigne.

In this house of late yeres, is lodged sir *Iohn Fortescue*, knight, Maister of the Wardrobe, Chancellor and vnder Treasurer of the Exchequer, and one of her Maiesties most honourable priuy Councell. The secret letters and writings touching the estate of the Realme, were wont to be enroled in the kings Wardrobe, and not in the Chauncery, as appeareth by the records. *Claus.* 18. *E.* 4. 1. *Memb.* 13. *Claus.* 33. *E.* 1. *Memb.* 3. *Et liberat.* 1. *E.* 2. *Memb.* 4. *&c.* From this Wardrobe by the west end of Carter lane, then vp *Creede* lane, *Aue Mary* lane, a peece of *Pater Noster* Rowe, vp *Warwick* lane, all the east side, to a Brewhouse called the Crown, as I sayd

Peter hill lane. Almes houses for 6. poore widdowes.

is of this warde. Touching lanes ascending out of Thames streete, to Knightriders streete, the first is, *Peters* hill, wherein I find no matter of note, more then certaine Almes houses, lately founded on the west side thereof, by *Dauid Smith* Imbroderer, for 6. poore widowes, whereof each to haue 20. s. by the yeare.

On the East side of this lane standeth a large house, of auncient building, sometime belonging to the Abbot of *S. Mary* in *Yorke*, and was his abiding house when he came to London. *Tho. Randolfe* Esquier hath lately augmented and repaired it.

Peters Key. Paules wharfe hill. Woodmongers Hall.

At the vpper end of this lane, towards the north, the corner houses there be called *Peters* Key, but the reason thereof I haue not heard. Then is Powles wharfe hill, on the East side whereof is Woodmongers Hall. And next adioyning is *Darby* house sometime belonging to the *Stanleys*, for *Thomas Stanley* first Earle of *Darby* of that name, who maried the Lady *Margaret* Countesse of *Richmond*, mother to *Henry* the seuenth, in his time builded it.

Queene *Mary* gaue it to *Gilbert Dethike*, then *Garter* principall King of armes of englishmen, *Thomas Hawley Clarentioues* king of armes of the south partes, *William Haruy*

Page 370

Alias Norey | king of armes of the north partes, & the other Heraults and Purseuantes of armes and to their successors,

Darby house.

all the same Capital messuage or house called Darby house

with the appurtenances, scituate in the parish of saint Benet, and saint Peter, then being in the tenure of sir *Richard Sackuile* knight, and lately parcell of the landes of *Edward* Earle of Darbie, &c. To the ende that the sayde king of Armes, Heraultes and Purseuauntes of Armes, and their successors, might at their liking dwell together and at meete times to congregate, speake, conferre, and agree among themselues, for the good gouernment of their facultie, and their recordes might be more safely kept, &c. Dated the 18. of Iuly, 1555 *Philip* and *Mary* the first and third yeare.

Then higher vppe neare the south chaine of Powles Churchyeard, is the Powle head Tauerne, which house with the appurtenances was of olde time called Powles Brewhouse, for that the same was so imployed, but being since left off, and letten out. Powles Brewhouse, or Powle head Tauern.

On the west side of this streete, is one other great house builded of stone, which belongeth to Powles church, and was somtime letten to the *Blunts* Lordes *Mountioy*, but of latter time to a colledge in Cambridge, and from them to the Doctors of the Ciuill law and Arches, who keepe a Commons there, and many of them being there lodged, it is called the Doctors Commons. Doctors Commons. Aboue this on the same side, was one other great building ouer against Powles Brewhouse, and this was called Powles Bakehouse, and was imployed in baking of bread for the Church of Powles. Powles Bakehouse.

In Addle streete or Lane I find no monuments. Adlestreet.

In Lambart hill lane on the west side thereof, is the Black Smithes hall, and adioyning to the North side thereof, haue ye one plot of ground, inclosed with a bricke wall for a churchyeard, or burying plot, for the dead of S. Mary Magdalens by old Fishstreet, which was giuen to that vse by *Iohn Iwarby*, an Officer in the receipt of the Exchequer, in the 26. of King *Henry* the sixt, as appeareth by Patent. Lambert hill. Blacksmithes hall. Churchyearde of S. Mary Magdalen. *Iohn Iwarby*, &c. gaue a peece of land lying voyde in the Parrish of Saint Mary Magdalen, nigh to olde Fishstreete, betweene the Tenement of *Iohn Phi⟨l⟩pot* on the south, and the Tenement of *Bartholomewe Burwash* on the | west, and the Tenement pertayning to the Couent of the Holy Well on the North, and the way vpon Lambardes Hill on the East, for a Church yearde to the Parson and Church Wardens, &c. *Page 371*

Ouer against the North west ende of this Lambard Hill Lane in Knightriders streete, is the Parrish Church of Saint Mary Magdalen, a small Church, hauing but few monuments, *Richard Woodroffe* Marchant Taylor, 1519. *Barnard Randolph* Esquire, 1583.

Parish church of S. Mary Magdalen.

On the West side of this Church, by the Porch thereof, is placed a Conduit or Cesterne of Lead, Castelated with stone, for receite of Thames water, conueyed at the charges of the before named *Barnard Randolph* Esquier. By the East ende of Saint Mary Magdalens Church, runneth vppe the old Exchange lane, by the west end of Carter lane, to the south-east gate or chain of Powles Church yeard as is before shewed. And in this parte was the Exchange kept, and Bullion was receyued for Coynage, as is noted in Faringdon Warde within.

Conduit of Thames water.

In this Parrish Church of S. Mary Magdalen, out of Knightriders street vp to Carter lane, be two small lanes, the one of them called Do Little lane, as a place not inhabited by Artificers, or open shop keepers, but seruing for a neare passage from Knightriders street, to Carter lane.

Do little lane.

The other corruptly called Sermon lane, for Sheremoniers lane: for I find it by that name recorded in the 14. of *E.* the 1. and in that lane, a place to be called the Blacke loft (of melting siluer) with foure shops adioyning. It may therefore bee well supposed that lane to take name of Sheremonyars, such as cut and rounded the plates to bee coyned or stamped into Estarling pence, for the place of coyning was the olde Exchange, neare vnto the sayde Sheremoniars lane. Also I find that in the 13. of R. the 2. *William de la Pole* had an house there.

Sheremonyars lane.

Blacke loft of siluer melting.

In Knightriders streete, is the Colledge of Phisitions, wherin was founded in the yeare 1582. a publike Lecture in Surgery, to be read twice euery weeke, &c. as is shewed else where.

Colledge of Phisitians. Lecture in Chirurgery to be read.

In the South Churchyeard of Powles, is the south side and | west end of the saide Church: In the which west end, bee three stately gates or entries, curiously wrought of stone, namely, the middle gate, in the midst wherof is placed a massie pillar of brasse, whereunto the leaues of the said

Page 372

West gates of Powles church.

great gate are closed and fastened with lockes, boltes, and barres of yron: All which notwithstanding, on the 24. of December, in the yeare 1565. by a tempest of wind then rising from the west, these gates were blowne open, the barres, boltes and lockes broken in sunder, or greatly bended. Also on the 5. of January, in the yeare 1589. by a like Tempest of wind, then in the South west, the lesser west gate of the saide church next to the Bishoppes pallace was broken, both bolts, bars, and lockes, so that the same was blowen ouer. Gates of Pauls church blown open.

At eyther corner of this west end, is also of auncient building a strong Tower of stone, made for Bell Towers, the one of them to wit, next to the pallace, is at this present to the vse of the same pallace, the other towardes the south is called the Lowlardes Tower, and hath beene vsed as the Bishoppes prison, for such as were detected for opinions in Religion, contrary to the faith of the church. For Lowlards Tower reade M. Foxe.

The last prisoner which I haue knowne committed thereto, was in the yeare 1573. one *Peter Burchet*[1] Gentleman of the middle Temple, for hauing desperately wounded, and minding to haue murdered a seruiceable Gentleman named *Iohn Hawkins* Esquire, in the high streete neare vnto the Strand, who being taken and examined, was found to hold certaine opinions erronious, and therefore committed thether, and conuicted, but in the end by perswasion, he promised to abiure his heresies: and was by commaundement of the Councell, remoued from thence to the Tower of London, &c. where he committed as in my Annales I haue expressed. Peter Burchet.

Adioyning to this Lowlardes Tower, is the parrish Church of S. *Gregory*, appointed to the petty Canons of Powles. Monumentes of note I know none there. Parish church of S. Gregory.

The rest of that south side of S. *Paules* Church, with the chapter House, (a beautifull peece of worke, builded about the raigne of *Edwarde* the third) is now defaced by meanes of Licenses | graunted to Cutlers, Budget makers, and other, first to builde low sheddes, but now high Houses, which doe hide that beautifull side of the Church, saue onely the toppe and south Gate. *Page 373*

[1] *Burcher*] *1603*, *1633*; *Burchet*, *1598* and *Annales*

On the North west side of this Church yeard, is the Bishops pallace, a large thing for receipt, wherein diuers kinges haue beene lodged, and great housholde hath beene kept, as appeareth by the great Hall, which of late years since the rebatement of Bishops liuinges, hath not beene furnished with houshold meynie and Guestes, as was meant by the builders thereof, and was of olde time vsed.

The Bishops pallace.

The Deanes lodging on the other side, directly against the pallace, is a fayre olde House, and also diuers large houses are on the same side builded, which yet remayne, and of olde time were the Lodginges of Prebendaries and Residenciaries, which kepte great Housholdes, and liberall Hospitality, but now eyther decayed, or otherwise conuerted.

The Stacioners hall.

Then is the Stacioners Hall on the same side, lately builded for them, in place of *Peter* Colledge, where in the yeare, one thousande fiue hundred fortie and nine, the fourth of January, sixe men were slaine by the fall of earth vpon them, digging for a Well. And let this bee an end of Baynardes Castle Warde, which hath an Alderman, his Deputie, Common Councell, nine, Constables ten, Scauingers seauen, Wardmote Inquest foureteene and a Beadle. And to the Fifteene is taxed at twelue pound, in the Exchequer eleuen pound, thirteene shillinges. |

Page 374

The Warde of Faringdon

Extra, or without

The warde of Faringdon without.

THE farthest West Ward of this Cittie, being the 25. Warde of London, but without the Walles, is called Faringdon without, and was of old time part of the other Faringdon within, vntill the 17. of *Richard* the second, that it was diuided and made twaine by the names of Faringdon *infra,* and Faringdon *extra,* as is afore shewed.

The boundes of which ward without Newgate and Ludgate are these. First on the east part thereof, is the whole precinct of the late priorie of saint *Bartholomew*, and a part of Long lane on the north, towardes Aldersgate streete and Ducke lane, with the hospitall of saint *Bartholomew* on the

West, and all Smithfielde to the Barres in saint *Iohn* street. Then, out of Smithfield, Chicken lane toward Turmile brooke, and ouer that brooke by a bridge of timber into the field, then backe againe by the Pens (or folds) in Smithfield, by Smithfield pond to Cow lane, which turneth toward Oldborne: and then Hosiar lane out of Smithfield, also toward Oldborne, till it meete with a part of Cow lane. Then Cocke lane out of Smithfield, ouer against Pye corner, then also is Giltspur streete, out of Smithfield to Newgate, then from Newgate west by *S. Sepulchres* church to Turnagaine Lane: to Oldboorne Conduit, on Snor hill, to Oldboorne bridge, vp Oldboorne hill to the Barres on both sides. On the right hand or north side, at the bottome of Oldboorne hill, is Gold lane, **Gold lane.** sometime a filthy passage into the fields, now both sides builded with small tenementes. Then higher is Lither lane, **Lither lane.** turning also to the field, lately replenished with houses builded, and so to the Barre.

Now on the left hand or south side from Newgate, lieth **Old Bayly.** a street called the Old Bayly, or court of the Chamberlaine of this citty: this stretcheth downe by the wall of the Cittie vnto Ludgate: on the west side of which streete, breaketh out one other lane, called | saint Georges lane, till ye come *Page 375* to the south end of Seacole lane: and then turning towardes Fleetstreete, it is called Fleete lane. The next out of the high street from Newgate turning down south, is called the little Bayly, and runneth downe to the East of saint Georges lane. Then is Seacole lane which turneth downe into Fleete **Limeburners lane or Seacole lane.** lane: neare vnto this Seacole lane, in the turning towardes Oldboorn Conduit, is an other lane, called in record wind- **Windagaine lane.** againe Lane, it turneth downe to Turnemill Brooke, and from thence back againe, for there is no way ouer. Then beyond Old boorn bridge to Shooe lane, which runneth out **Shooelane.** of Oldboorne vnto the Conduit in Fleetestreet. Then also is Fewtars lane, which likewise stretcheth south into Fleet- **Fewtars lane.** streete by the east end of saint Dunstons church, and from this lane to the Bars be the bounds without Newgate.

Now without Ludgate, this warde runneth vp from the sayd gate to Temple barre, and hath on the right hand or north side the south end of the old Bayly, then downe Ludgate hill, to the Fleet lane ouer Fleete bridge, and by Shooe lane, and Fewters lane, and so to New streete (or Chancery lane) and vp that Lane to the house of the Rolles, which house is also of this ward, and on the other side to a lane ouer against the Roules, which entereth Ficquets field.

Shire lane.

Then hard by the Barre is one other lane called Shyre Lane, because it diuideth the Cittie from the Shire, and this turneth into Ficquets field.

From Ludgate againe on the left hand, or south side, to Fleetebridge, to bride lane, which runneth south by Bridewell, then to Water lane, which runneth down to the Thames.

Then by the White Fryers and by the Temple, euen to the Barre aforesaid, be the boundes of this Faringdon Warde without.

Giltspur or Knightriders streete.

Touching ornamentes and antiquities in this warde, first betwixt the said Newgate, and the parrish church of S. *Sepulchers* is a way towardes Smithfield, called Guilt spurre, or Knightriders streete, of the knightes and other riding that way into Smith fielde, replenished with buildings on both sides vp to Pie corner, a place so called of such a signe, sometimes a fayre Inne for receipte | of trauellers, but now diuided into tenementes, and ouer against the said Pie corner lyeth Cocke lane, which runneth downe to Oldbourne Conduit.

Page 376

Cocke lane.

West Smithfield.

Hospitall of S. Bartilmew.

Beyond this Pie corner lyeth west Smithfield, compassed about with buildinges, as first on the south side, following the right hand, standeth the large hospitall of S. *Bartilmew*, founded by *Rahere* the first Prior of S. *Bartilmewes* thereto neare adioyning, in the yeare 1102.

The first maister or Proctor of the Hospital of S. Bartilmew.

Alfune, that had not long before builded the parrish church of S. *Giles* without Criplegate, became the first Hospitelar, or Proctor for the poore of this house, and went himselfe dayly to the Shambles and other markets, where hee begged the charity of deuout people for their reliefe, promising to the liberall giuers (and that by alledging testimonies of the holy scripture) rewarde at the handes of God. *Henry* the third granted to *Katheren* late wife to *W. Hardell* xx. foot of land in length & bredth in Smithfield next to the Chappell of the Hospitall of S. Bartilmew to builde her a recluse or ankorage, commaunding the Mayor & shiriffes of London, to assign the

A recluse or ankorage by S. Bartilmewes Hospitall.

saide xx. foot to the sayd *Katheren*, carta 11 of *H.* the 3. The foundation of this hospital for the poor & diseased, their speciall sustentation, was confirmed by *E.* the third, the 26. of his raigne, it was gouerned by a Maister, and 8. brethren being priestes, for the church and 4. sisters, to see the poore serued. The Executors of *R. Whitington* sometime Mayor of London, of his goodes repayred this hospitall, about the yeare, 1423.

Sir *Iohn Wakering* priest, Mayster of this house, in the year 1463. amongst other bookes gaue to their common Library the fayrest Bible, that I haue seene, written in large velame, by a brother of that house named *Iohn Coke*, at the age of 68. years, when he had been priest 43 yeares. Since the spoyle of that Library I haue seene this booke in the custody of my worshipfull frend, M. *Walter Cope*.

Monumentes in this church of the dead, Benefactors thereunto, be these, *Elizabeth* wife to *Adam Hone* Gentleman, *Bartilmew Bildington*, *Iane* wife to *Iohn Cooke*, Dame *Alis* wife to sir *Richarde Isham*, *Alice* wife to *Nicholas Bayly*, *Iohn Woodhouse* Esquier, *Robert Palmar* Gentleman, *Ido|na* wife *Page 377* to *Iohn Walden* lying by her husband on the North side late newly builded, 1424. Sir *Thomas Malifant* or *Nanfant*, Baron of Winnow, Lord saint *George* in Glamorgan, and Lord *Ockeneton* and *Pile* in the county of Pembroke, 1438. Dame *Margaret* his wife, daughter to *Thomas Astley* Esquier, with *Edmond* and *Henry* his children. *William Markeby* Gentleman, 1438. *Richard Shepley* and *Alice* his wife, *Thomas Sauill*, sargeant at Armes, *Edward Beastby* Gentleman and *Margaret* his wife, *Waltar Ingham* and *Alienar* his wife, *Robert Warnar* and *Alice* Lady *Casne*, *Robert Caldset*, *Iohan* and *Agnes* his wiues, Sir *Robert Danuars* and Dame *Agnes* his wife, daughter to sir *Richard Delaber*, *William Brookes* Esquier, *Iohn Shirley* Esquier and *Margaret* his wife, hauing their pictures of brasse, in the habit of pilgrims, on a fayre flat stone with an Epitaph thus,

Beholde how ended is our poore pilgrimage,
Of Iohn Shirley Esquier, with Margaret his wife,
That xii. children had together in marriage,
Eight sonnes and foure daughters withouten strife,

That in honor, nurtur, and labour flowed in fame,
His pen reporteth his liues occupation,
Since Pier his life time, Iohn Shirley by name,
Of his degree, that was in Brutes Albion,
That in the yeare of grace deceased from hen,
Foureteene hundred winter, and sixe and fiftie,
In the yeare of his age, fourescore and ten,
Of October moneth, the day one and twenty.

This Gentleman, a great traueller in diuers countries, amongest other his labours, painefully collected the workes of *Geffrey Chaucer*, *Iohn Lidgate* and other learned writers, which workes hee wrote in sundry volumes to remayne for posterity. I haue seene them, and partly do possesse[1] them. *Iane* Lady *Clinton* gaue tenne pound to the poore of this house, was there buried, 1458. *Agnes* daughter to sir *William S. George*, *Iohn Rogerbrooke* Esquier, *Richard Sturgeon*, *Tho: Burgan* Gentleman,| *Elizabeth* wife to *Henry Skinard*, daughter to *Chincroft* Esquier, *William Mackley* Gentleman, and *Alice* his wife, *W. Fitzwater* Gentleman, 1466.

Page 378

This Hospitall was valued at the suppression in the yeare 1539. the 31. of *Henry* the eight, to 35. pound sixe shillinges seauen pence yearely. The church remayneth a parrish church to the tenantes dwelling in the precinct of the Hospitall, but in the yeare 1546. on the 13. of Ianuary, the Bishoppe of Rochester, preaching at Powles Crosse, declared the gift of the said king to the Cittizens for releeuing of the poore, which contayned the Church of the Gray Fryers, the church of S. *Bartilmew* with the Hospitall, the Messuages, and appurtenances in Giltspurre, *alias* Knightriders streete, Breton streete, Petar Kay, in the parrish of saint *Mary Magdalen*, in olde Fishstreete, and in the parrish of S. Benet Huda, Lymehurst, or Limehost, in the parrish of Stebunheth, &c. Then also were orders deuised for reliefe of the poore, the inhabitantes were all called to their parish churches, where, by sir *Richard Dobbes* then maior, their seuerall Aldermen, or other graue Cittizens, they were by eloquent orations perswaded how great and how many commodities would ensue

Hospital of S. Bartilmew suppressed.

[1] possesse] professe *1603*, *1633*

vnto them and their Cittie, if the poore of diuers sorts which they named, were taken from out their streets, lanes and allyes, & were bestowed and prouided for in Hospitalles abroade, &c. therefore was euery man moued, liberally to graunt what they woulde impart, towardes the preparing and furnishing of such Hospitals, & also what they would contribute weekely towardes their maintenance for a time, which they said should not be past one yeare, or twaine, vntill they were better furnished of Endowment: to make short, euery man graunted liberally, according to his hability, bookes were drawne of the reliefe in euery Ward of the City, towardes the new Hospitalles, and were deliuered by the Mayor to the Kinges Commissioners, on the 17. of February, and order was taken therein, so as the 26. of Iuly, in the yeare 1552. the repayring of the Gray Fryers house, for poore fatherlesse children, was taken in hand, and also in the latter end of the same moneth, began the repayring of this Hospitall of saint *Bartilmew*, and was of new endowed, and furnished at the charges of | the Cittizens. *Page 379*

On the east side of this hospitall, lieth Duke lane, which runneth out of Smithfield south, to the north ende of little Britaine streete. On the east side of this Ducke lane, and also of Smithfield, lyeth the late dissolued priorie of *S. Bartilmew* founded also by *Rahere*, a pleasant witted Gentleman, and therefore in his time called the kinges Minstrell. About the yeare of Christ, 1102. he founded it in a part of the oft before named morish ground, which was theretofore a common lay stall of all filth, that was to be voyded out of the citie: he placed Canons there, himself became their first Prior, and so continued till his dying day, & was there buried in a fayre monument, of late renued by pryor *Bolton*.

Priory of Saint Bartilmew.

Amongst other memorable matters, touching this priorie, one is of an Archbishops Visitation, which *Mathew Paris* hath thus. *Boniface* (sayeth he) Archbishoppe of Canterbury, in his Visitation, came to this priorie, where being receiued with procession in the most solemne wise, hee saide that hee passed not vpon the honor, but came to visite them, to whome the Canons aunswered, that they hauing a learned Bishop, ought not in contempt of him to be visited by any other:

Archbishop of Canterbury visiteth Saint Bartilmewes priorie with stripes.

Words of the Archbishop to the Prior and Canons. Suppriors cope rent and trod vnder foote, himselfe almost slaine. The Archbishop armed & ouerthrowne. The Canons beaten and trod vnder foote. The Canons complayned but could not be heard.

which aunswere so much offended the Archbishop, that hee forthwith fell on the Supprior, and smote him on the face, saying, indeed, indeede, dooth it become you English Traytors so to aunswere mee? Thus raging with oathes not to bee recited, hee rent in peeces the rich Cope of the supprior, and trode it vnder his feete, and thrust him against a pillar of the Chauncell with such violence, that hee had almost killed him: but the Canons seeing their supprior thus almost slayne, came and plucked off the Archbishoppe with such force that they ouerthrew him backwardes, whereby they might see that hee was armed and prepared to fight: the Archbishoppes men seeing theyr maister downe, being all strangers and their maisters countrimen born at Prouence, fell vpon the Canons, beat them, tare them, and trod them vnder feete, at length the Canons getting away as well as they could, ran bloody and myry, rent and torne, to the Bishoppe of London to complaine, who bad them goe to the king at Westminster, and tell him thereof, wherevpon foure of them went thether, the rest were not able, they were so sore hurt, but | when they came to Westminster, the king would neither heare nor see them, so they returned without redresse. In the meane season the whole Citie was in an vprore, and ready to haue rung the common bell, and to haue hewed the Archbishop into small peeces, who was secretly crept to Lambhith, where they sought him, and not knowing him by sight, sayd to themselues, where is this Ruffian, that cruell smiter, hee is no winner of soules, but an exactor of money, whome neyther God, nor any lawfull or free election, did bring to this promotion, but the king did vnlawfully intrude him, being vtterly vnlearned, a stranger borne, and hauing a wife, &c. But the Archbishop conueyed himselfe ouer, and went to the king with a great complaint against the Canons, whereas himselfe was guiltie. This priorie of Saint *Bartholomew* was again new builded, in the yeare 1410.

Page 380

The whole citie in an vprore against the Archbishop.

Bolton last prior of saint Bartlemew a great builder there. Canonberie.

Bolton was the last prior of this house, a great builder there: for he repayred the priorie church with the parrish Church adioyning, the offices and lodgings to the said priorie belonging, & neare adioyning: he builded of new the Mannor of Canonbery at Islington, which belonged to the Canons of this house, and is situate in a lowe ground, somewhat North from the parrish church there, but hee buylded no house at Harrow on the hill, as *Edwarde Hall* hath written, following a fable then on foote. The people (sayeth hee) being feared by Prognostications, which declared that in the yeare of Christ 1524. there should be such Eclipses in watrie signes, and such coniunctions, that by waters and flouds many people shoulde perish, people victualed themselues, and went to high groundes for feare of drowning, and especially one *Bolton*, which was prior of Saint *Bartholomewes* in Smithfield, builded him a house vppon Harrow on the hill, onely for feare of this floud, thither he went and made prouision of all things necessarie within him for the space of two Moneths, &c. but this was not so indeed, as I haue beene credibly informed: true it is that this *Bolton* was also parson of Harrow, and therfore bestowed some small reparations on the parsonage house, and builded nothing there more then a Douehouse, to serue him when he had forgone his priorie.

Edward Hall.

To this priorie king *Henrie* the second granted the priuiledge | of fayre to bee kept yearely at *Bartholomew* tide for three dayes, to wit, the Eue, the day, and next morrow, to the which the Clothiers of all England, and Drapers of London repayred, and had their Boothes and standings within the Churchyard of this priorie closed in with Walles and Gates locked euery night, and watched for safetie of mens goodes and wares, a Court of pie-powders was dayly during the Fayre holden for debts and contracts. But now notwithstanding all proclamations of the prince, and also the act of parliament, in place of Boothes within this Churchyarde (onely letten out in the Fayre time, and closed vp all the yeare after) bee many large houses builded, and the North Wall towardes Long lane taken downe, a number of Tenements are there erected, for such as will giue greate rents.

Page 381

Bartilmew fair. The forrens were licensed for three dayes, the freemen so long as they would, which was sixe or seuen dayes.

Court of Pie powdars.

Monuments of the deade in this priorie are these, of *Rahere* the first founder, *Roger Walden* Bishoppe of London, 1406. *Iohn Warton* Gentleman, and *Elizabeth* his wife, daughter to *William Scot* Esquire, *Iohn Louth* Gentleman, *Robert Shikeld* Gentleman, Sir —— *Bacon* knight, *Iohn Ludlow*, and *Alice* his wife, *W. Thirlewall* Esquire, *Richard Lancaster*

Heraulde at Armes, *Thomas Torald*, *Iohn Royston*, *Iohn Watforde*, *Iohn Carleton*, *Robert*, sonne to Sir *Robert Willowby*, *Gilbert Halstocke*, *Elanor* wife to Sir *Hugh Fenne*, mother to *Margaret* Lady *Burgauenie*, *William Essex* Esquire, *Richarde Vancke* Baron of the Exchequer, and *Margaret* his wife, daughter to *William de la Riuar*, *Iohn Winderhall*, *Iohn Duram* Esquire, and *Elizabeth* his wife, *Iohn Malwaine*, *Alice* wife to *Balstred* daughter to *Kniffe*, *William Scarlet* Esquire, *Iohn Golding*, *Hugh Waltar* Gentleman, and the late Sir *Waltar Mildmay* knight, Chancellor of the Exchequer, &c.

This priorie at the late surrender, the 30. of *Henrie* the eight, was valued at 653. li. 15. s. by yeare.

This church hauing in the bell Tower sixe Belles in a tune, those bels were sold to the parish of Saint *Sepulchres*, and then the Church being pulled downe to the Quire, the Quire was by the kings order annexed for the enlarging of the olde parish church | thereto adioyning, and so was vsed till the raigne of Queene *Marie*, who gaue the remnant of the priorie church to the Friers preachers, or black Friers, and was vsed as their couentual church vntill the first of our Soueraigne Ladie Queene *Elizabeth*, those Friers were put out, and all the saide church with the olde parrish church was wholy, as it stoode in the last yeare of *Edwarde* the sixt, giuen by parliament to remaine for euer a parrish Church to the inhabitants within the close called great S. *Bartholomewes*. Since the which time, that olde parish church is pulled downe, except the steeple of rotten Timber readie to fall of it selfe. I haue oft heard it reported, that a new steeple should bee builded with the stone, leade and tymber of the olde parish church, but no such thing was performed. The parish haue lately repayred the old woodden steeple to serue their turne.

Page 382

Long lane.

On the north side of this priorie, is the lane truly called Long, which reacheth from Smithfield to Aldersgate street. This lane is now lately builded on both the sides with tenements for brokers, tiplers, and such like: the rest of Smithfield from long lane end to the bars is inclosed with Innes, Brewhouses and large tenements, on the west side is Chicken lane downe to Cowbridge. Then be the pens or folds so called of

Chiken lane. Cowbridge. Pens in Smithfield.

sheep there parted, and penned vp to be sold on the market dayes.

Then is Smithfield pond, which of olde time in Records was called Horse-poole, for that men watered horses there, and was a great water. In the sixt of *Henrie* the fift, a new building was made in this west part of Smithfield betwixt the said Poole and the Riuer of the Wels, or Turnemill brooke, in a place then called the Elmes, for that there grew many Elme trees, and this had beene the place of execution for Offendors: since the which time the building there hath beene so encreased, that now remaineth not one tree growing.

Smithfielde pond somtime a poole.

The Elmes in Smithfield a place wherein trespassers were executed.

Amongst these new buildings is Cowbridge street, or Cow lane, which turneth toward Oldborne, in which lane, the Prior of Semperingham had his Inne, or London lodging.

The rest of that west side of Smithfield hath diuers fayre Innes and other comely buildings, vp to Hosiar lane, which also turneth downe to Oldborne, till it meete with Cowbridge streete. From this lane to Cocke lane, ouer against pie corner. |

Hosiar lane.

Cocke lane.

And thus much for encrochments and inclosure of this Smithfield, whereby remaineth but a small portion for the old vses, to wit, for markets of horses and cattle, neither for Military exercises, as Iustings, Turnings, and great triumphes which haue been there performed before the princes and nobility both of this Realm and forraigne countries.

Page 383

Iustinges in Smithfield.

For example to note: In the yeare 1357. the 31. of *Edward* the third, great and royall Iustes were there holden in Smithfield, there being present the Kings of England, France, and Scotland, with many other nobles, and great estates of diuers lands.

Fabian.

1362. The 36. of *Edward* the third, on the first fiue dayes of May, in Smithfield were Iustes holden, the King and Queene being present, with the most part of the Chiualry of England, and of France, and of other Nations, to the which came Spaniards, Cyprians, and Arminians, knightly requesting[1] the King of England, against the *Pagans* that inuaded their confines.

The 48. of *Edward* the third, Dame *Alice Perrers* (the kings Concubine) as Lady of the Sunne, rode from the Tower

Alice Perrers rode from the Tower to

[1] the ayde of *add. 1633*

Smithfield as Lady of the Sunne.

of London, through Cheape, accompanied of many Lords and Ladies, euery Lady leading a Lord by his horse bridle, till they came into west Smithfield, and then began a great Iust, which endured seuen dayes after.

Also the 9. of *Richard* the second, was the like great riding from the Tower to Westminster, and euery Lord led a Laydyes horse bridle, and on the morrow began the Iustes in Smithfield, which lasted two dayes: there bare them well, *Henry* of *Darby*, the Duke of *Lankesters* sonne, the Lord *Beamount*, sir *Simon Burley*, and sir *Paris*[1] *Courtney*.

In the 14. of *Richard* the second, after *Frosart*, royall Iustes and Turnements were proclaimed to be done in Smithfield, to begin on sunday next after the feast of saint *Michael*: many strangers came forth of other countries, namely *Valarian* Earle of *S. Paul*, that had maried King *Richards* sister, the Lady *Maud Courtney*, and *William* the yong Earle of *Ostaruant*, sonne to *Albart* of *Bauiere*, Earle of *Holland* and *Henault*. At the day appoynted, there issued forth of the tower, about the third houre of the day, 60. coursers, apparrelled for the Iusts, and vpon euery | one an Esquier of honour riding a soft pace: then came forth 60. Ladyes of honour mounted vpon palfraies, riding on the one side, richly apparrelled, and euery Lady led a knight with a chayne of gold. Those knights being on the Kings party, had their Armour and apparrell garnished with white Hartes and Crownes of gold about the Harts neckes, & so they came riding through the streetes of London to Smithfield, with a great number of trumpets and other instruments of musicke before them. The King and Queene who were lodged in the Bishops palace of London, were come from thence, with many great estates, and placed in chambers to see the Iustes: the Ladies that led the knights, were taken downe from their palfrayes, and went vp to chambers prepared for them. Then alighted the Esquiers of honour from their coursers, & the knights in good order mounted vpon them, and after their Helmets were set on their heads, and being ready in all points, proclamation made by the Haraults, the Iustes began, and

Page 384

Tower Roiall.

[1] *Paris*] *1603, 1633; i.e. Sir Peter or Piers Courtenay*

many commendable courses were runne, to the great pleasure of the beholders: this Iustes continued many dayes, with great feasting, as ye may read in Frosard.

In the yeare 1393. the 17. of *Richard* the second, certaine Lords of Scotland came into England to get worship by force of Armes, the Earle of *Mare* chalenged the Earle of *Notingham*, to iust with him, and so they rode together certaine courses, but not the full chalenge, for the Earle of *Mare* was cast both horse and man, and two of his ribbes broken with the fall, so that he was conuaied out of Smithfield, and so towards Scotland, but dyed by the way at Yorke. Sir *William Darell* knight, the Kings banner bearer of *Scotland*, chalenged sir *Percie Courtney* knight the Kings banner bearer of England, and when they had run certaine courses, gaue ouer without conclusion of victory. Then *Cookeborne* Esquier of *Scotland*, chalenged sir *Nicholas Hawberke* knight, and rode fiue courses, but *Cookeborne* was borne ouer horse and man, &c.

In the yeare 1409. the 10. of *Henry* the fourth, a great play was played at the Skinners Wel, which lasted eight daies: where were to see the same the most part of the Nobles and Gentles in England. And forthwith began a royall iusting in Smithfield, be|tween the Earle of Somerset, and the Senes- *Page 385*
hall of Henalt, sir *Io. Cornwall*, sir *Richard Arrundell*, & the sonne of sir *Iohn Cheiney*, against certaine French men. And the same yeare a battell was fought in Smithfield, betweene two Esquiers, the one called *Glaucestar* appellant, and the other *Arthure* Defendaunt, they fought valiantly, but the King tooke vp the quarrell into his hands, and pardoned them both.

In the yeare 1430. the 8. of *Henry* the 6. the 14 of Ianuary, a battell was done in Smithfield, within the listes, before the king betweene two men of Feuersham in kent, *Iohn Vpton* notary, Appellaunt, and *Iohn Downe* Gentleman, Defendaunt: *Iohn Vpton* put vpon *Iohn Downe*, that he and his compiers should imagin the Kings death, the day of his Coronation. When these had fought long, the King tooke vp the matter and forgaue both the parties.

In the yeare 1442. the twentieth of *Henry* the sixt the

thirteenth of Ianuary, a challenge was done in Smithfield, within listes, before the King, there being sir *Phillip la Beaufe* of Aragon knight, the other an Esquier of the kings house, called *Iohn Ansley* or *Anstley*, they came to the field all armed, the knight with his sword drawne, and the Esquier with his speare, which speare he cast against the knight, but the knight auoyded it with his sword, & cast it to the ground, then the Esquier tooke his axe, & smote many blowes on the knight, and made him let fall his axe, and brake vp his vmber three times, and would haue smit him on the face with his dagger, for to haue slayne him, but then the king cried hold, and so they were departed: the king made *Iohn Ansley* knight, and the knight of Aragon offered his harnesse at Windsor.

Iohn Dauy a false accuser of his master: of him was raised the by word, If ye serue me so I wil cal you Dauy.

In the yeare 1446. the 24. of *Henry* the 6. *I. Dauy* appeached his Maister *Wil. Catur* of treason, and a day being assigned them to fight in Smithfield, the Master being well beloued was so cherished by his friends, and plied with wine, that being therewith ouercome, was also vnluckily slayne by his seruant: but that false seruant (for he falsely accused his Maister) liued not long vnpunished, for he was after hanged at Teyborne for fellony. Let such false accusers note this for example, and looke for no | better end without speedy repentance.

Page 386

The same yeare, *Thomas Fitz-Thomas Prior* of *Kilmaine* appeached sir *Iames Butlar* Earle of Ormond of treasons: which had a day assigned them to fight in Smithfield, the listes were made, and the field prepared, but when it came to the point, the king commaunded they should not fight, and tooke the quarrell into his hands.

In the yeare 1467. the seuenth of *Edward* the fourth, the bastard of *Burgoigne* chalenged the Lord *Scales*, brother to the Queene, to fight with him, both on horse backe and on foote: the King therefore caused listes to bee prepared in Smithfield, the length of 120 Taylors yardes, and 10. foote, and in breadth 80. yardes, and 20. foote, double barred, 5. foote betweene the barres, the timber worke whereof, cost 200. markes, besides the fayre and costly galories prepared for the Ladyes and other: at the which martiall enterprise the King and Nobility were present. The first day they ranne together with speares, and departed with equall honour. The next day they turneyed on horse backe, the Lord *Scales* horse hauing on his Chafron a long speare pike of steele, and as the two Champions coaped together, the same horse thrust his pike into the nostrilles of the Bastards horse, so that for very payne he mounted so high that he fell on the one side with his Master, and the Lord *Scales* rode about him with his sword drawne, till the King commaunded the Marshall to helpe vp the Bastard, who sayd, I cannot hold me by the clouds, for though my horse fayle me, I will not fayle an incounter companion: but the king would not suffer them to do any more that day.

The next morrow, they came into the listes on foote, with two pole axes, and fought valiantly, but at the last, the point of the pole axe of the Lord *Scales* entered into the side of the Bastardes Helme, and by force might haue placed him on his knees: But the king cast downe his warder, and the Marshall seuered them. The Bastard required that he might performe his enterprise: but the king gaue iudgement, as the Bastard relinquished his chalenge, &c. And this may suffice for Iustes in Smithfield.

Now to returne through Giltspurre streete by Newgate, | where I first began, there standeth the fayre parish church called Saint *Sepulchers* in the Bayly, or by Chamberlaine gate, in a fayre Church yarde, though not so large as of old time, for the same is letten out for buildings, and a garden plot.

Page 387
Iohn Leyland.

This Church was newly reedified or builded, about the raigne of *Henry* the sixt, or of *Edward* the fourth: one of the *Pophames* was a great builder there, namely of one fayre chappell on the South side of the Quire, as appeareth by his Armes, and other monuments in the Glasse windowes thereof, and also the fayre Porch of the same Church towardes the South: his Image faire grauen in stone, was fixed ouer the saide Porch, but defaced and beaten downe, his title by offices was this, Chancellor of *Normandy*, Captayne of *Vernoyle, Pearch, Susan*, and *Bayon*, and Treasurer of the kings houshold: he dyed rich, leauing great treasure of strange coynes,

Pophames builders of S. Sepulchers Church.

and was buried in the Charterhouse church, by west Smithfield: the first nobilitating of these Pophames was by *Mathil⟨d⟩* the Empresse, daughter to *Henry* the first, and by *Henry* her sonne. One *Pophame*, gentleman of very fayre landes in Southampton shire, dyed without issue male, about *Henry* the sixt, and leauing foure daughters, they were maried to *Fostar*, *Barentine*, *Wodham*, and *Hamden*. *Popham Deane* (distant three miles from *Clarendon*, and three miles from *Mortisham*) was sometime the chiefe Lordship or Mannor house of these *Pophames*.

There lye buried in this Church, *William Andrew*, *Stephen Clamparde*, *Lawrence Warcam*, *Iohn Dagworth*, *William Porter*, *Robert Scarlet* Esquiers.

Next to this Church is a fayre and large Inne for receipt of trauellers, and hath to signe the Sarasens head.

There lyeth a streete from Newgate west, to the end of Turnagaine lane, and winding north to Oldborne Conduite. This Conduite by Oldborne Crosse was first builded 1498. *Thomasin* widdow to *Iohn Perciuall*, Mayor, gaue to the second making thereof 20. markes, *Richard Shore* 10.l. *Thomas Knesworth* and others also did giue towards it.

Oldboorne Conduite by Oldboorne Crosse.

But of late, a new Conduit was there builded in place of the old, namely in the yeare 1577. by *William Lamb*, somtime a gen|tleman of the Chappell to king *H*. the 8. and afterward a Citizen and Clothworker of London, the water thereof he caused to be conueyed in lead, from diuers springs to one head, and from thence to the said Conduite, and waste of one Cocke at Oldborne bridge, more then 2000. yards in length, all which was by him performed at his owne charges, amounting to the summe of 1500.l.

Page 388

From the west side of this Conduit is the high way, there called Snor hill, stretcheth out by Oldborne bridge ouer the oft named water of Turmill brooke, and so vp to Oldborne hill, all replenished with fayre building.

Without Oldborne bridge on the right hand is Gold lane, as is before shewed: vp higher on the hill be certayne Innes, and other fayre buildings, amongst the which of old time was a Messuage called *Scropes* Inne, for so I find the same recorded in the 37. of *Henry* the sixt.

Scropes Inne sometime Sergeants Inne, in Oldborne.

This house was sometime letten out to Sergeants at the law, as appeareth, and was foond by inquisition taken in the Guild Hall of London, before *William Purchase* Mayor, and Exchetor for the king *Henry* the seuenth in the 14. of his raigne, after the death of *Iohn* Lord *Scrope*, that he dyed seized[1] in his demesne of fee, by the feofment of *Guy Fairfax* knight, one of the kings Iustices, made in the 9. of the same king, vnto ⟨an⟩ Esquier, the said *Iohn Scrope* knight, Lord *Scrope* of Bolton, and *Robert Wingfield*, of one house or tenement late called Sergeants Inne, scituate against the Church of Saint *Andrew* in Oldborne in the City of London, with two gardens and two Messuages to the same tenement belonging in the sayd Citie, to hold in burgage, valued by the yeare in all reprises, x.s.

Then is the Bishop of Elies Inne, so called of belonging and pertayning to the Bishops of Elye. *William de Luda* Bishop of Elye, deceased 1298.[2] gaue this house by the name of his Mannor, with the appurtenances in Oldborne, to his successors, with condition his next successor should pay 1000. markes to the finding of three Chaplaines in the Chappell there. More, *Iohn Hotham* Bishop of Elie did giue by the name of sixe Messuages two sellars, and forty Acres of land in the Suburbs of London, in the parish of Saint *Andrew* in Oldborne, to the Prior and couent of Elie as | appeareth by patent, the 9. of *Edward* the third: this man was Bishop of Elye 20. yeares, and deceased 1336.

Elie place in Oldborne.

Page 389

Thomas Arundell Bishoppe of Elie beautifully builded of new his Pallace at Elie, and likewise his Mannors in diuers places, especially this in Oldborne, which he did not onely repaire, but rather new builded, and augmented it with a large Port, gate house, or front towardes the streete or high way: his armes are yet to bee discerned in the stone worke thereof: he sate Bishop of Elie 14. yeares, and was translated to Yorke.

In this house for the large and commodious roomes thereof, diuers great and solemne feastes haue beene kept, especially by the Sergeants at the law, whereof twaine are to be noted for posterity.

[1] dyed seized] *conj.* dyed deceased *1603*
[2] 1298] *Stubbs*; 1297 *1603*

Sergeants feast Elie house.

The first, in the yeare 1464. the fourth of *Edward* the fourth, in Michelmas tearme, the Sergeants at law held their feast in this house, to the which amongst other estates, *Mathew Phillip* Mayor of London, with the Aldermen, Shiriffes, and commons of diuers craftes being inuited, did repaire: but when the Mayor looked to keepe the state in the hall as it had beene vsed in all places within the Citie and liberties (out of the Kings presence) the Lord *Gray* of *Ruthen*, then Lord Treasurer of England, vnwitting the Sergeants and against their willes (as they sayd) was first placed: whereupon the Mayor, Aldermen, and commons departed home, and the Mayor made the Aldermen to dine with him: howbeit he & al the Citizens were wonderfully displeased, that he was so dealt with, and the new Sergeants and others were right sory therefore, and had rather then much good (as they said) it had not so happened.

One other feast was likewise there kept, in the yeare 1531, the 23. of king *Henry* the 8.: the Sergeants then made were in number 11. namely, *Thomas Audeley*, *Walter Luke*, *I. Bawdwine*, *I. Hinde*, *Christopher Iennie*, *Iohn Dowsell*, *Edward Meruine*, *Edmond Knightley*, *Roger Chomley*, *Edward Montague*, and *Robert Yorke*.

Page 390

King Henry the 8. and Q. Katherine dined at the Sergeants feastes.

These also held their feast in this Elie house for fiue daies, to wit Fryday the 10. of Nouember, Saterday, Sunday, Munday, and Tuesday. On Munday (which was their principall day) | King *Henry* and Queene *Katherine* dined there (but in two chambers) and the forraine Ambassadors in a third chamber. In the Hall at the high table, sate sir *Nicholas Lambard* Mayor of London, the Iudges, the Barons of the Exchequer, with certaine Aldermen of the Citie: At the boord on the south side, sate the Master of the Rowles, the Maister of the Chauncery, and worshipfull Citizens: On the North side of the Hall certayne Aldermen began the boorde, and then followed Merchants of the City: in the Cloistrie, Chappell and gallory, knights, Esquiers, and Gentlemen were placed: in the Halles, the Craftes of London: the Sergeantes of law and their wiues kept in their owne chambers.

It were tedious to set downe the preparation of fish, flesh, and other victuals spent in this feast, and would seeme almost incredible and (as to me it seemeth) wanted little of a feast at a coronation: neuerthelesse a little I will touch, for declaration of the change of prices. There were brought to the slaughter house 24. great Beefes, at 26. shillings 8. pence the peece from the shambles, one carkasse of an Oxe at 24.s., one hundred fat Muttons, ij.s. x.d. the peece, 51. great Veales at 4. shillings 8.d. the peece, 34. Porkes, 3. shillings 8.d. the peece, 91. pigs 6.d. the peece, Capons of Grece of one Poulter, (for they had three) 10. dozens at 20.d. the peece, Capons of *Kent* 9. dozens and sixe at 12.d. the peece, Capons course 19. dozen at 6.d. the peece, Cockes of grose 7. dozen and nine at 8.d. the peece, Cockes course 14. dozen and 8. at 3.d. the peece, Pullets the best 2.d. ob., other Pullets 2.d., Pigeons 37. dozen at x.d. the dozen, Swannes 14. dozen, larkes 340. dozen at v. d. the dozen, &c. *Edward Neuill* was Seneshall or Steward, *Thomas Ratcliffe* Controwler, *Thomas Wildon*, Clearke of the kitchin.

Next beyond this Mannor of Elie house, is Lither lane, turning into the field. Then is Furniualles Inne, now an Inne of Chauncery, but sometime belonging to sir *William Furniuall* knight, & *Thomesin* his wife, who had in Oldborne two Messuages, and 13. shops, as appeareth by Record of *Richard* the 2. in the sixt of his raigne.

Lither lane.

Furniuals Inne, an Inne of Chauncery.

Then is the Earle of Bathes Inne, now called Bath place, of late for the most part new builded, and so to the barres.

The Earle of Bathes Inne. *Page 391*

Now againe from Newgate on the left hand or south side lyeth the old Bayly, which runneth downe by the wall vpon the ditch of the Cittie called Houndes ditch to Ludgate: I haue not read how this streete tooke that name, but is like to haue risen of some court of olde time there kept, and I finde that in the yeare 1356. the 34. of *E.* the 3. the tenement and ground vpon Houndes ditch, betweene Ludgate on the south, and Newgate on the north was appointed to *Iohn Cambridge* Fishmonger, Chamberlain of London, whereby it seemeth that the Chamberlaines of London haue there kept their courts, as now they doe by the Guildehall, and till this day the Mayor and Iustices of this city kept their sessions in a part thereof, now called the Sessions hal, both for the citty of London, and shire of Middlesex. Ouer against the which house on the

Hounds ditch.

The Chamberlains house and court in the old Bayly.

The sessions hall.

S. Georges lane, an Inne of Chauncery there.

right hand turneth down saint Georges lane, towardes Fleete lane. In this S. Georges lane on the north side thereof, remayneth yet an olde wall of stone, inclosing a peece of ground vp Seacole lane, wherin by report somtime stood an Inne of Chancery: which house being greatly decayed, and standing remote from other houses of that profession, the company remoued to a common hostery, called of the signe our Lady Inne, not far from Clements Inne, which they procured from Sir *John Fineux*, Lord chiefe Iustice of the Kings bench, and since haue helde it of the owners, by the name of the new Inne, paying therefore vi.l. rent by the yeare, as tenants at their owne will: for more (as is said) cannot be gotten of them and much lesse will they be put from it. Beneath this S. Georges lane, ⟨is⟩ the lane called Fleet lane, winding south by the prison of the Fleet into Fleetstreete, by Fleete bridge. Lower downe into the Old Bayly, is at this present a standard of timber with a cocke or cockes, deliuering fayre spring water to the inhabitants, and is the wast of the water seruing the prisoners in Ludgate.

Originall of New Inne. An Inne of Chauncery.

A standard of spring water in the olde Bayly.

Next out of the high street turneth downe a lane, called the little Baylie, which runneth downe to the east ende of S. Georges lane. The next is Seacole lane, I thinke called Limeburners lane, of burning Lime there with Seacole. For I reade in record of such a Lane to haue beene in the parrish of saint Sepulcher | & there yet remayneth in this lane an Alley called Limeburners Alley. Neare vnto this Seacoale lane in the turning towardes Oldboorne Conduit is Turnagaine lane, or rather, as in a record of the fift of *Edward* the third, Windagaine lane, for that it goeth downe west to Fleete dike, from whence men must turne againe the same way they came, for there it is stopped. Then the high street turneth down Snore hill, to Oldborne Conduit, and from thence to Oldborne bridge, beyond the which bridge, on the left hand, is Shooe lane by the which men passe from Oldborn to Fleetestreet, by the Conduit there. In this Shooe lane on the lefte hande is one olde house called Oldborne Hall, it is now letten out into diuers Tenementes. On the other side at the very corner standeth the parish church of *S. Andrew*, in the which church, or neare therevnto was somtime kept a Grammer schoole, as

Page 392

Seacole lane, or Limeburners lane, somtime so called.

Windagaine lane.

Snore lane.

Shooe lane.

Oldborne hall.

Parish church of S. Andrew in Oldborne.

appeareth in an other place by a Patent, made as I haue shewed for the erection of schooles. There bee monumentes in this church of *Thomas* Lord *Writhesley* Earle of Southampton, buried 1550. *Raph Rokeby* of Lincolnes Inne Esquier, Maister of saint Katherines, and one of the Maysters of Requestes to the Queenes Maiestie, who deceased the 14. of Iune, 1596. He gaue by his Testament to Christes Hospitall in London 100.li., to the Colledge of the poore of Queene *Elizabeth* in east Greenwich, 100. pound, to the poore scollers in Cambridge, 100. pound, to the poore schollers in Oxford 100. pound, to the prisoners in the two Compters in London 200.li., to the prisoners in the Fleete 100. pound, to the prisoners in Ludgate 100. pound, to the prisoners in Newgate 100. pound, to the prisoners in the Kinges Bench 100. pound, to the prisoners in the Marshalsey an hundred pound, to the prisoners in the White Lion twenty pound, to the poore of saint Katherines twenty pound, and to euery brother and sister there, fortie shillings: *William Sydnam* founded a chauntry there. There was also of old time, (as I haue read in the thirde of *Henry* the fift) an Hospitall for the poore, which was a Cell to the house of Cluny in France, and was therefore suppressed among the Priories Aliens.

Grammer schoole in Oldborne.

Hospitall in Oldborne.

From this church of S. Andrew vp Oldborne hill bee diuers fayre builded houses, amongst the which on the left hand there | standeth three Innes of Chauncery, whereof the first adioyning vnto Crookhorn Alley is called Thaues Inne, and standeth opposite, or ouer against the said Elie house. Then is Fewtar lane which stretcheth south into Fleetestreet by the east end of S. Dunstones church, and is so called of Fewters (or idle people) lying there, as in a way leading to Gardens: but the same is now of latter yeares on both sides builded through with many fayre houses.

Page 393

Crokhorne Alley.

Thauies Inne.

Fewtars lane[1].

Beyond this Fewtars lane is Barnards Inne, *alias* Macworths[2] Inne, which is of Chauncery, belonging to the Deane and chapter of Lincolne, as sayth the Record of *H.* the 6. the 32. of his raigne, and was founded by Inquisition in the Guildhal of London before *I. Norman* Mayor the Kinges exchetre: the

Barnards Inne.

Pat. H. 6. 32.

[1] Fewtars Inne *1603* [2] Macworths *Record*; Motworths *1603*

Iury sayde, that it was not hurtfull for the king to licence *T. Atkens* cittizen of London, & one of the Executors to *Iohn Mackeworth* Deane of Lincolne, to giue one messuage in Holborn in London with the appurtenances called *Mackworthes* Inne, but now commonlie knowne by the name of Barnardes Inne, to the Deane and chapter of Lincolne, to finde one sufficient Chaplaine to celebrate diuine seruice in the chapple of S. *George* in the Cathedrall church of Lincoln, where the body of the sayde *Iohn* is buried, to haue and to hold the sayde messuage to the sayde Deane and Chapter, and to their successors for euer, in part of satisfaction of 20.li. landes and rentes, which *Edwarde* the third licensed the sayde Deane and Chapter to purchase to their owne vse, eyther of their owne fee or tenor, or of any other, so the landes were not holden of the king in capite. Then is Staple Inne, also of Chancery, but whereof so named I am ignorant: the same of late is for a great part therof fayre builded, and not a little augmented: And then at the Barre endeth this ward without newgate.

Staple Inne.

Without Ludgate on the right hand or North side from the saide gate lyeth the Old Bayly, as I sayde, then the high streete called Ludgate hill downe to Fleete lane, in which lane standeth the Fleete, a prison House, so called of the Fleet or Water running by it, and sometime flowing about it, but now vaulted ouer.

Ludgate hill.

The Fleete or Gaole in the raigne of Richard the first.

I read that *Richard* the first in the first of his raigne, confirmed to *Osbert*, brother to *William Longshampe* Chancelor of | England, and elect of Elie, and to his heyres for euer the custody of his house, or palace at Westminster, with the keeping of his gaole of the Fleet at London: also king *Iohn* by his patent dated the 3. of his raigne, gaue to S⟨imon⟩ Archdeacon of Welles the custody of the said kings house at westminster, and of his Gaole of the Fleet, together with the Wardship of the daughter and heyre of *Roberte Leueland*, &c. Then is Fleete Bridge, pitched ouer the sayd Water, whereof I haue spoken in an other place.

Page 394

Conduit in Fleetestreete.

Then also against the South end of Shooe Lane standeth a fayre Water Conduit, whereof *William Eastfield* sometime Mayor, was founder: for the Mayor and Comminaltie of London being possessed of a Conduit heade, with diuers springs of Water gathered thereinto in the Parrish of Padington, and the water conueighed from thence by pypes of leade towardes London vnto Teyborne: where it had layne by the space of sixe yeares and more: The Executors of Sir *William Eastefielde* obtayned licence of the Mayor and Comminaltie, for them in the yeare 1453. with the goodes of Sir *William*, to conueigh the sayde waters: first in pypes of leade into a pype begunne to bee laide besides the greate Conduit heade at Maribone, which stretcheth from thence vnto a separall, late before made against the Chappell of Rounseuall by Charing Crosse, and no further, and then from thence to conuay the said water into the citie, & there to make receipt or receipts for the same vnto the common weale of the comminaltie, to wit, the poore to drinke, the rich to dresse their meats, which water was by them brought thus into Fleetstreet to a standard, which they had made and finished, 1471.

The inhabitantes of Fleetestreete in the yeare 1478. obtained licence of the Mayor, Aldermen and comminaltie to make at their owne charges two cesternes, the one to be set at the said standarde, the other at Fleete bridge for the receit of the wast water: this cesterne at the standard they builded, and on the same a fayre tower of stone, garnished with images of *S. Christopher* on the top, and Angels round about lower down, with sweet sounding bels before them, whereupon by an Engine placed in the Tower, they, diuers houres of the day and night, chymed such an Hymme as was appointed.| Conduit at Fleetbridge.

This conduit or standard was againe new builded with a larger cestern, at the charges of the citie, in the yeare, 1582. *Page 395*

From this Conduit vp to Fewtars lane and further, is the parish church of S. Dunstan, called in the west, (for difference from S. Dunstone in the east) where lyeth buried *T. Duke* Skinner in S. Katherins chappel by him builded, 1421. *Nicholas Coningston*, *Iohn Knape*, and other founded chaunteries there. *Raph Bane* Bishop of Couentrie and Lichfield, 1559. and other. Parish church of saint Dunstones.

Next beyond this church is Cliffords Inne, somtime belonging to *Robert Clifford*, by gift of *Edward* the second in these words. 'The king granteth to *Robert Clifford* that messuage with the appurtenances next the Church of S. Dunstane in the West in the suburbs of London, which messuage was Cliffords Inne.

sometime *Malculines de Herley*, and came to the hands of *E.* the 1. by reason of certaine debts ⟨in⟩ which the said *Malculine* was bound at the time of his death to our sayde Father, from the time that hee was Escaetor on this side Trent: which house *Iohn* Earle of Richmount did holde at our pleasure, and is now in our possession, patent the 3. of *Ed.* the second.' After the death of this *Robert Clifford, Isabel* his wife let the same messuage to Studients of the law, as by the Recorde following may appeare.

Isabel quæ fuit vxor Roberti Clifford, Messuagium vnipartitum, quod Robertus Clifford habuit in parochia sci. Dunstoni West. in suburbio Londini, &c. tenuit, & illud dimisit post mortem dict. Roberti, apprenticiis de banco. pro x.li. annuatim, &c. Anno 18. *Eduardi tertii, inquisitio post mortem Roberti Clifford.*

This house hath since fallen into the kinges hands, as I haue heard, but returned againe to the *Cliffordes*, and is now letten to the said Studentes for foure pound by the yeare.

Somewhat beyond this Cliffordes Inne is the south ende of New streete (or Chancelar lane), on the right hande whereof is Sergeantes Inne called in Chauncery lane. And then nexte was sometime the house of the conuerted Iewes, founded by king *Henry* the third, in place of a Iewes house to him forfeited, in the yeare 1233. and the 17. of his raigne, who builded there for them a | faire Church now vsed, and called the Chappell for the custodie of Rolles and Records of Chancerie. It standeth not farre from the old Temple, but in the midway betweene the olde Temple and the new, in the which house all such Iewes and infidels as were conuerted to the Christian faith, were ordained and appoynted vnder an honest rule of life, sufficient maintenance, whereby it came to passe, that in short time there were gathered a great number of conuerts, which were baptized, instructed in the doctrine of Christ, and there liued vnder a learned Christian appointed to gouerne them: since the which time, to wit, in the yeare 1290. all the Iewes in England were banished out of the Realme, whereby the number of conuerts in this place was decayed: and therefore in the yeare 1377. this house was annexed by Patent to *William Burstall* Clearke, *Custos Rotulorum*, or keeper of the

New street or Chanceler Lane.

House of conuerts.

Page 396

Rolles of the Chauncerie, by *Edwarde* the third in the 51. yeare of his raigne: and this first Maister of the Rolles was sworne in Westminster Hall, at the Table of Marble stone: since the which time, that house hath beene commonly called the Rolles in Chancerie lane.

Rolles in Chancerie lane.

Notwithstanding such of the Iewes or other infidels, as haue in this realme beene conuerted to Christianitie, and baptised, haue beene relieued there: for I find in Record, that one *William Piers* a Iew that became a christian, was baptised in the fift of *Richard* the second, and had two pence the day allowed him during his life by the said king.

On the west side sometime was an house pertaining to the prior of *Nocton* Parke, a house of Canons in Lincolnshire: this was commonly called Hereflete Inne, and was a Brew-house, but now faire builded for the sixe Clearkes of the Chancerie, and standeth ouer against the said house called the Rolles, and neare vnto the lane which now entreth *Fickets* croft, or *Fickets* field. Then is Shere lane opening also into *Fickets* field, hard by the barres. On this north side of Fleet-streete, in the yeare of Christ 1595. I obserued, that when the laborers had broken vp the pauement, from agaynst Chancerie lanes end, vp towards Saint *Dunstons* Church, and had digged foure foote deepe, they found one other pauement of hard stone, more sufficient then the first, and therefore | harder to bee broken, vnder the which they found in the made ground, pyles of Tymber, driuen verie thicke, and almost close togither, the same being as blacke as pitch or coale, and many of them rotten as earth, which prooueth that the ground there (as sundrie other places of the Citie) haue beene a Marish or full of springs.

Prior of Nocton parke, his Inne or house of the sixe Clearks.

Fickets croft.

Shere lane.

Page 397

On the South side from Ludgate before the wall of the Citie be faire builded houses to Fleetebridge, on the which bridge a Cesterne for receite of spring water was made by the men of Fleetstreet, but the watercourse is decayed and not restored.

Conduit at Fleete bridge.

Next is Bridelane, and therein Bridewell, of olde time the kings house: for the kings of this realme haue beene there lodged, and till the ninth of *Henrie* the thirde, the Courtes were kept in the kings house wheresoeuer he was lodged, as

Bridewell the Kinges house.

may appeare by ancient records, whereof I haue seene many, but for example set forth one in the Chapter of Towers and Castles.

King *Henrie* the eight builded there a stately and beautifull house of new, for receit of the Emperor *Charles* the 5. who in the yeare of Christ 1522. was lodged himselfe at the blacke Friers, but his Nobles in this new builded Bridewell, a Gallery being made out of the house ouer the water, and through the wall of the Cittie into the Emperours lodging at the Blacke Friers: King *Henrie* himselfe oftentimes lodged there also, as namely in the yeare 1525. a Parliament being then holden in the black Friers, he created states of Nobilitie there, to wit, *Henrie Fitz Roy*, a child (which he had by *Elizabeth Blunt*) to be Earle of *Nottingham*, Duke of Richmond, and of Somerset, Lieutenant Generall from Trent Northward, warden of the East, middle, and West Marches foranenst Scotland, *Henry Courtney* Earle of Deuonshire, Coosen German to the king, to be Marques of Excester, *Henrie Brandon* a childe of two yeares olde, sonne to the Earle of Suffolke, to be Earle of Lincolne: Sir *Thomas Mannars*, Lord *Rose* to be Earle of Rutland, Sir *Henrie Clifforde* to bee Earle of Cumberland, Sir *Robert Ratcliffe* to be Vicont *Fitzwater*, and Sir *Thomas Boloine* Treasurer of the kings householde, to be Vicont Rochford.

States created at Bridewell.

In the yeare 1528. Cardinall *Campeius* was brought to the | kings presence being then at Bridewell, whither hee had called all his Nobilitie, Iudges and Councellers, &c. And there the eight of Nouember in his great Chamber hee made vnto them an oration touching his mariage with Queene *Katheren*, as ye may read in *Edward Hall*.

Page 398

In the yeare 1529. the same king *Henrie* and Queene *Katherine* were lodged there, whilest the question of their marriage was argued in the Blacke Friers, &c.

Bridewell giuen to the citie of London, to be a workehouse for the poore.

But now you shall heare how this house became a house of correction. In the yeare 1553. the seuenth of king *Edwarde* the sixt, the tenth of Aprill: Sir *George Barne*,[1] being Maior of this Citie, was sent for to the Court at White hall, and there at that time the king gaue vnto him for the Comminaltie

[1] *Barne*] Barnes *1633*

and Citizens to be a Workehouse for the poore and idle persons of the Citie, his house of Bridewell, and 700. Markes land late of the possessions of the house of the Sauoy, and all the bedding and other furniture of the said Hospitall of the Sauoy, towards the maintenance of the sayd Workehouse of Bridewell, and the Hospitall of S. *Thomas* in Southwarke.

This gift king *Edward* confirmed by his Charter, dated the 26. of Iune next following: and in the yeare 1555. in the moneth of Februarie, Sir *William Gerarde* Maior, and the Aldermen entred Bridwell, and tooke possession thereof according to the gift of the said king *Edward*, the same being confirmed by Queen *Marie*.

The Bishop of S. *Dauids* had his Inne ouer against the north side of this Bridwell, as I haue said. The Bishop of S. Dauids house.

Then is the Parish church of Saint Bridges, or Bride, of olde time a small thing, which now remaineth to be the quire, but since encreased with a large bodie and side Iles, towards the West, at the charges of *William Venor* Esquire, Warden of the Fleete, about the yeare 1480. all which he caused to be wrought[1] about in the stone in the figure of a vine with Grapes and leaues, &c. The partition betwixt the olde worke and the new, sometime prepared as a screne to be set vp in the hall of the Duke of Somersets house at Strand, was bought for eight score pound, & set vp in the yeare 1557. One wilfull bodie began to spoyle and breake the same, in the | yeare 1596. but was by the high Commissioners forced to make it vp againe, and so it resteth. *Iohn Vlsthorpe*, *William Eues-ham*, *Iohn Wigan*, and other founded Chauntries there. Parish church of S. Bride. *Page 399*

The next is Salisburie Court, a place so called for that it belonged to the Bishops of Salisburie, and was their Inne, or London house at such time as they were summoned to come to the Parliament, or came for other businesse: it hath of late time beene the dwelling, first of sir *Richard Sackuile*, and now of sir *Thomas Sackuile* his sonne, Baron of Buckhurst, Lord Treasurer, who hath greatly enlarged it with stately buildings. The Bishop of Salisburie his house.

Then is water lane running downe by the west side of a house called the Hanging sword, to the Thames. Water lane.

[1] wrought] *Thoms*; brought *1603*

White Friers. Iohn Baconthorpe.

Then was the white Friers church, called *Fratres beatæ Mariæ de monte Carmeli*, first founded (saith *Iohn Bale*) by sir *Richard Gray* knight, auncester to the Lord Gray ⟨of⟩ Codnor, in the yeare 1241. King *Edward* the first gaue to the Prior and brethren of that house a plot of ground in Fleete street, whereupon to build their house, which was since reedified or new builded, by *Hugh Courtney* Earle of Deuonshire. About the yeare 1350. the 24. of *Edward* the third, *Iohn Lufken* Maior of London, and the Comminaltie of the Citie, graunted a lane called Crockers lane, reaching from Fleetestreete to the Thames to builde in the West end of that Church. Sir *Robert Knoles* knight was a great builder there also, in the raigne of *Richarde* the second, and of *Henry* the fourth: hee deceased at his Mannor of Sculthorpe[1] in Norffolke, in the yeare 1407. and was brought to London, and honorably buried by the Lady *Constance* his wife, in the bodie of the said White Friers Church, which he had newly builded.

Crokers lane.

Robert Marshall[2] Bishop of Hereford, builded the Quire, Presbeterie, steeple, and many other partes, and was there buried, about the yeare 1420. There were buried also in the new Quire, sir *Iohn Mowbery* Earle of Nottingham, 1398. sir *Edwarde Cortney*, sir *Hugh Mongomerie*, and sir *Iohn* his brother, *Iohn Wolle*, sonne to sir *Iohn Wolle*, *Thomas Bayholt*, Esquire, *Elizabeth* Countesse of *Athole*, Dame *Iohan* wife to sir *Thomas Say* of *Alden*, sir *Pence Castle*, Baron, *Iohn* Lord | *Gray*, sonne to *Regnald* Lord *Gray* of *Wilton*, 1418. sir *Iohn Ludlow* knight, sir *Richard Derois* knight, *Richarde Gray* knight, *Iohn Ashley* knight, *Robert Bristow* Esquire, *Thomas Perry* Esquire, *Robert Tempest* Esquire, *William Call*, *William Neddow*.

Page 400

In the old Quire were buried, Dame *Margaret*, &c. *Elianor Gristles*, sir *Iohn Browne* knight, and *Iohn* his sonne and heyre, Sir *Simon de Berforde* knight, *Peter Wigus* Esquire, *Robert Mathew* Esquire, Sir *Iohn Skargell* knight, Sir *Iohn Norice* knight, Sir *Geffrey Roose* knight, *Mathew Hadocke* Esquire, *William Clarell* Esquire, *Iohn Aprichard* Esquire,

[1] Sculthorpe] Scone Thorpe *1603*
[2] Marshall] Mascall *Stubbs' Registrum*; died 1416.

William Wentworth Esquire, *Thomas Wicham* Esquire, sir ⟨*Robert*⟩ *Terwit* knight, sir *Stephen Popham* knight, Bastard *de Scales*, *Henrie Blunt* Esquire, *Elizabeth Blunt*, *Iohn Swan* Esquire, *Alice Foster* one of the heyres of sir *Stephen Popham*, sir *Robert Brocket* knight, *Iohn Drayton* Esquire, *Iohn*, sonne to *Robert Chanlowes*, and his daughter *Katherine*, *Iohn Saluin*, *William Hampton*, *Iohn Bampton*, *Iohn Winter*, *Edmond Oldhall*, *William Appleyard*, *Thomas Dabby* Esquires, sir *Hugh Courtney* knight, *Iohn Drury*, sonne to *Robert Drurie*, *Elizabeth Gemersey* gentlewoman, Sir *Thomas Townsend* knight, sir *Richard Greene* knight, *William Scot* Esquire, *Thomas Federinghey*, *I. Fulforde* Esquire, *Edwarde Eldsmere* Gentleman, *W. Hart* Gentleman, Dame *Mary Senclare*, daughter to sir *Thomas Talbot* knight, *Ancher* Esquire, sir *William Moris* knight, and Dame *Christian* his wife, sir *Peter de Mota* knight, *Richard Hewton* Esquire, sir *I. Heron* knight, *Richard Eton* Esquire, *Hugh Stapleton* Gentleman, *William Copley* Gentleman, sir *Raph Saintowen* knight, sir *Hugh Bromeflete* knight, Lord *Vessey*, principall founder of that order, the sixt of *Edward* the fourth, &c.

This house was valued at 62.li. 7.s. 3.d. and was surrendred the tenth of Nouember, the 30. of *Henrie* the eight.

In place of this Friers Church be now many fayre houses builded, lodgings for Noble men and others.

Then is the Sargeants Inne, so called, for that diuers Iudges and Sargeants at the law, keepe a Commons, and are lodged | there in Terme time. Sarieants Inne in Fleetstreet. *Page 401*

Next is the newe Temple, so called because the Templars, before the building of this house, had their Temple in Oldborne. This house was founded by the knights Templars in England, in the raigne of *Henrie* the second, and the same was dedicated to God and our blessed Ladie, by *Heraclius*, Patriarke of the church called the holy Resurrection in *Ierusalem*, in the yeare of Christ, 1185. New temple.

These knights Templars tooke their beginning about the yeare 1118. in maner following. Certaine Noble men, horsemen, religiously bent, bound by vow themselues in the handes of the Patriarke of *Ierusalem*, to serue Christ after the manner of Regular Canons in chastitie and obedience, and to renounce Original of the Templers.

their owne proper willes for euer: the first of which order were *Hugh Paganus*, and *Geffrey de S. Andromare.* And whereas at the first they had no certaine habitation, *Baldwin* king of *Ierusalem* granted vnto them a dwelling place in his pallace by the Temple, and the Canons of the same Temple gaue them the streete thereby, to build therein their houses of office, and the Patriarke, the king, the Nobles and Prelates, gaue vnto them certaine reuenues out of their Lordships.

Profession of the Templars.

Their first profession was for safegarde of the Pilgrimes comming to visite the sepulchre, and to keepe the high wayes agaynst the lying in wayte of theeues, &c. About ten yeares after they had a rule appointed vnto them, and a white Habite, by *Honorius* the second then Pope, and whereas they had but nine in number, they began to encrease greatly. Afterward in Pope *Eugenius* time, they bare crosses of red cloth on their vppermost garments, to be knowne from others: and in short time because they had their first mansion hard by the Temple of our Lord in *Ierusalem*, they were called knights of the Temple.

Many Noble men in all partes of Christendome became Brethren of this order, and builded for themselues Temples in euerie Citie or great Towne in England, but this at London was their chiefe house, which they builded after the forme of the temple nere to the sepulchre of our Lord at *Ierusalem*: they had also other temples in Cambridge, Bristow, Canterbury, Douer, Warwick.| This Temple in London was often made a storehouse of mens treasure, I meane such as feared the spoile thereof in other places.

Mathew Paris. *Page 402*

Hubert Earle of Kent, his treasure in the new Temple.

Mathew Paris noteth that in the yeare 1232. *Hubert de Burgh* Earle of *Kent* beeing prisoner in the Tower of London, the king was enformed that he had much Treasure layde vp in this new Temple, vnder the custodie of the Templars, whereupon hee sent for the Master of the Temple, and examined him straightly, who confessed that money being deliuered vnto him and his brethren to be kept, he knew not how much there was of it. The king demaunded to haue the same deliuered, but it was answered that the money being committed vnto their trust, could not be deliuered without the licence of him that committed it to Ecclesiastical protection, wherevpon the king sent his Treasurer and Iusticiar of the Exchequer vnto *Hubert*, to require him to resigne the money wholly into his hands, who answeared that he would gladly submit himselfe, and all his vnto the kings pleasure, and therevpon desired the knights of the Temple in his behalfe to present all the keyes vnto the king to doe his pleasure, with the goods which hee had commited vnto them. Then the king commaunded the money to be faithfully told and layde vp in his Treasure, by Inuentory, wherein was found (besides ready money) vessels of gold, and siluer vnprayseable, and many precious stones which would make all men wonder, if they knew the worth of them.

This Temple was againe dedicated 1240. belike also newly reedified then.

These Templars at this time were in so great glory, that they entertayned the Nobility, forraine Ambassadors, and the Prince himselfe, very often: insomuch that *Mathew Paris* crieth out on them for their pride, who being at the first so poore, as they had but one horse to serue two of them, (in token whereof they gaue in their Seale, two men riding of one horse) yet sodainly they waxed so insolent, that they disdayned other orders, and sorted themselues with Noblemen.

Mathew Paris.

Seale of the Templars.

King *Edward* the first in the yeare 1263.[1] taking with him *Robert Waleran*, and other, came to the Temple, where calling for the keeper of the Treasure house, as if he meant to see his mo|thers Iewels, that were layde vp there to be safely kept, hee entred into the house, breaking the Coffers of certaine persons that had likewise brought their money thither, and hee tooke away from thence to the value of a thousand pound.

Lib. Dunstable.

Page 403

Many Parliaments and great Counsails haue beene there kept, as may appeare by our histories. In the yeare 1308. all the Templars in England as also in other parts of Christendome were apprehended and committed to diuers prisons. In 1310. a prouinciall Counsell was holden at London against the Templars, in England, vpon herisie, and other Articles whereof they were accused, but denied all except one or two of them, notwithstanding they all did confesse that they could not

Parliament at the new Temple.

[1] 1263] 1283 *1603*; *marg. 1603* 30 Dunmow

purge themselves fully, as faultlesse, and so they were condemned to perpetuall pennance, in seuerall Monasteries, where they behaued themselues modestly.

The order of Templars condemned. Templars burned.

Phillip King of France procured their ouerthrow throughout the whole world, and caused them to be condemned by a generall Counsell, to his aduantage, as he thought, for he beleeued to haue had all their lands in France, and therefore seazed the same in his handes, (as I haue reade) caused the Templars to the number of foure and fiftie, (or after *Fabian* threescore) to bee burned at *Paris*.

Robert Fabian.

Patent. The Temple giuen to Aimer de Valence.

Edward 2. in the yeare 1313. gaue vnto *Aimor de Valence* Earle of Pembrooke, the whole place and houses called the new Temple at London, with the ground called *Ficquetes* Croft, and all the tenements and rentes with the appurtenances that belonged to the Templars in the City of London, and Suburbes thereof.

After *Aimer de Valence* (sayeth some) *Hugh Spencer* vsurping the same held it during his life, by whose death it came againe to the hands of *Edwarde* the third, but in the meane time, to wit, 1324. by a counsell holden at *Vienna*, all the landes of the Templars (least the same should be put to prophane vses) were giuen to the knightes Hospitelars of the order of Saint *Iohn Baptist*, called *S. Iohn* of *Ierusalem*, which knights had put the Turkes out of the Isle of *Rhodes*, and after wan vpon the sayd Turke dayly for a long time. |

Temple giuen to the Hospitalers of S. Iohn of Ierusalem.

Page 404

Patent 2. E. 3. Close, 18. E. 3.

The said *Edward* the third therefore granted the same to the saide knights, who possessed it, and in the eighteenth yeare of the saide kinges raigne, were forced to repaire the Bridge of the saide Temple. These knights had their head house for England by west Smithfield, and they in the raigne of the same *Edward* the third granted (for a certayne rent of x. pound by the yeare) the said Temple with the appurtenances therevnto adioyning, to the students of the common lawes of England: in whose possession the same hath euer sithence remained, and is now diuided into two houses of seuerall students, by the name of Innes of Court, to wit, the Inner Temple and the middle Temple, who kept two seuerall halles, but they resort all to the said Temple Church, in the round walke whereof (which is the West part without the Quire) there remaineth monuments of Noblemen buried, to the

The Temple granted to the students of the law and made an Inne of Court.

Monuments in the Temple.

number of 11. eight of them are Images of armed knights, fiue lying crosse legged as men vowed to the holy land, against the infidels and vnbeleeuing Iewes: the other three straight legged: the rest are coaped stones al of gray Marble: the first of the crosse legged was *W. Marshall* the elder Earle of Pembrooke, who dyed 1219. *Wil. Marshall* his sonne Earle of Pembrooke was the second, he died 1231. and *Gilbert Marshall* his brother, Earle of Pembrooke, slayne in a Turnement at Hertford, besides Ware, in the yeare 1241.

Images of knights buried crosse legged, the cause why.

After this *Robert Rose*, otherwise called *Fursan*, being made a Templar in the yeare 1245. dyed and was buried there, and these are all that I can remember to haue read of. Sir *Nicholas Hare*, Maister of the Roles, was buried there in the yeare 1557.

In the yeare 1381. the Rebelles of Essex, and of Kent, destroyed and plucked downe the houses and lodgings of this Temple, tooke out of the Church the bookes and Recordes that were in Hutches, of the apprentizes of the law, carried them into the streetes, and brent them: the house they spoyled and brent for wrath, that they bare sir *Robert Hales* Lord Prior of S. *Iohns* in Smithfield, but it was since againe at diuers times repaired, namely the gate house of the middle Temple in the raigne of *Henry* the eight, by Sir *Amias Paulet* knight, vpon occasion, as in my Annales I haue shewed. The great hall of the middle Temple was newly builded in the yeare 1572. in the raigne of our Queene *Elizabeth.* |

Recordes of the Temple destroyed and burnt.

Gate house of the Temple new builded.

Great hall of the Temple new builded.

This Temple Church hath a Maister, and foure Stipendiary Priestes, with a Clarke, these for the ministration of diuine seruice there haue stipendes allowed vnto them, out of the possessions and reuenewes of the late Hospitall and house of S. *Iohns* of Ierusalem in England, as it had beene in the raigne of *Edward* the sixt. And thus much for the said new Temple, the farthest west part of this Warde, and also of this Citie for the liberties thereof, which ward hath an Alderman, and his Deputies three. In Sepulchers parrish common Counsaile sixe, Constables foure, Scauengers foure, Wardemote inquest twelue: S. *Bridgetes* parrish, common Councellors eight, Constables eight, Scauengers eight, Wardmote inquest twentie. In Saint *Andrewes*, common Councell two, Constables two,

Page 405

Order for diuine seruice in the Temple.

Scauengers three, Wardemote inquest twelue. It is taxed to the fifteene at thirty fiue pound one shilling.

Bridge warde without, the 26. in number,

consisting of the Borough of Southwarke in the County of Surrey.

Bridge Warde without.

HAVING treated of Wardes in London, on the North side the Thames (in number 25.) I am now to crosse ouer the said Riuer into the Borough of Southwark, which is also a Warde of London, without the walles, on the South side thereof, as is Portsoken on the East, and Faringdon *extra* on the West.

This Borough, being in the County of Surrey, consisteth of diuers streetes, wayes, and winding lanes, all full of buildings, inhabited: and first to begin at the West part thereof, ouer against the west Suburbe of the Citie.

On the banke of the Riuer Thames there is now a continuall building of tenements, about halfe a mile in length to the bridge. Then from the Bridge straight towardes the South a continuall streete, called long Southwarke, builded on both sides with diuers | lanes and alleyes vp to S. Georges church, and beyond it through Blackman streete towardes New Town (or Newington) the liberties of which Borough extend almost to the parrish Church of New town aforesaid, distant one mile from London Bridge, and also southwest a continuall building, almost to Lambith, more then one mile from the said bridge.

Page 406

Then from the bridge along by the Thames Eastwarde, is saint Olaues street hauing continuall building on both the sides, with lanes and alleyes vp to Battle bridge, to Horsedowne, and towardes Rother hith: also some good halfe mile in length from London bridge.

S. Olaues streete.

So that I account the whole continual buildings on the banke of the said riuer, from the west towardes the east, to be more then a large mile in length.

Then haue ye from the entering towards the said Horsedown one other continuall streete called Bermondes eye streete, which stretcheth south, likewise furnished with buildinges on both sides, almost halfe a mile in length, vp to the late dissolued Monasterie of S. Sauiour called Bermondsey. And from thence is one long lane (so called of the length) turning west to saint Georges church afore named. Out of the which lane mentioned, Long lane, breaketh one other streete towardes the south and by east, and this is called Kentish streete for that it is the way leading into that countrie: and so haue you the bounds of this Borough.

The antiquities most notable in this Borough are these: first, for ecclesiasticall, there was Bermondsey, an Abbey of Blacke Monkes, S. Mary Oueries, a Priorie of Canons Regular, saint *Thomas* a colledge or Hospitall for the poore, & the Loke a Lazar house in Kent street. Parish churches, there haue been 6. wherof 5. do remaine, vz. S. Mary Magdalen in the priory of saint Mary Ouery, now the same S. Marie Ouery is the parrish Church for the said Mary Magdalen, and for S. Margaret on the hill, and is called S. Sauiour.

An Abbey. A Priory, A Colledge & Hospitall. A Lazar house. Parish churches.

S. Margaret on the hill being put downe, is now a Court for Iustice. S. Thomas in the Hospitall serueth for a parrish church as afore. S. George a parrish church as before it did, so doth saint Olaue, and saint Mary Magdalen by the Abbey of Bermondsey. |

There be also these 5. prisons or Gaoles.

Page 407

The Clinke on the Banke.
The Compter in the late parrish church of S. Margaret.
The Marshalsey.
The Kinges Bench.
And the white Lyon, all in long Southwarke.

Houses most notable be these.

The Bishop of Winchesters house.
The Bishop of Rochesters house.
The Duke of Suffolks house, or Southwarke place.
The Tabard an Hosterie or Inne.
The Abbot of Hyde his house.
The Prior of Lewes his house.
The Abbot of saint Augustine his house.
The Bridge house.

The Abbot of Battaile his house.
Battaile bridge.
The stewes on the Banke of Thames.
And the Beare gardens there.

The Beare gardens.

Now to returne to the West banke, there be two Beare gardens, the olde and new places, wherein be kept Beares, Buls and other beastes to be bayted. As also Mastiues in seuerall kenels, nourished to baite them. These Beares and other Beasts are there bayted in plottes of ground, scaffolded about for the Beholders to stand safe.

Liber manuscript. The Stewe on the bank side.

Next on this banke was sometime the Bordello or stewes, a place so called, of certaine stew houses priuiledged there, for the repaire of incontinent men to the like women, of the which priuiledge I haue read thus.

In a Parliament holden at Westminster the 8. of *Henry* the second, it was ordayned by the commons and confirmed by the king and Lords, that diuers constitutions for euer should bee kept within that Lordship or franchise, according to the olde customes that had been there vsed time out of mind. Amongest the which these following were some, vz.|

Page 408

That no stewholder or his wife should let or staye any single Woman to goe and come freely at all times when they listed.

No stewholder to keepe any woman to borde, but she to borde abroad at her pleasure.

To take no more for the womans chamber in the weeke then foureteene pence.

Not to keepe open his dores vpon the holydayes.

Not to keepe any single woman in his house on the holy dayes, but the Bayliffe to see them voyded out of the Lordship.

No single woman to be kept against her will that would leaue her sinne.

No stewholder to receiue any Woman of religion, or any mans wife.

No single woman to take money to lie with any man, but shee lie with him all night till the morrow.

No man to be drawn or inticed into any stewhouse.

The Constables, Balife, and others euery weeke to search euery stewhouse.

No stewholder to keepe any woman that hath the perilous infirmitie of burning, nor to sell bread, ale, flesh, fish, wood, coale, or any victuals, &c.

These and many more orders were to be obserued vpon great payne and punishment: I haue also seene diuers Patentes of confirmation, namely one dated 1345. the nineteenth of *Edwarde* the third. Also I find that in the fourth of *Richarde* the second, these stew houses, belonging to *William Walworth* then Mayor of London, were farmed by Froes of Flaunders, and spoyled by *Walter Tighler*, and other rebelles of Kent: notwithstanding I finde that ordinances for the same place and houses were againe confirmed in the raigne of *Henry* the sixt, to be continued as before. Also *Robert Fabian* writeth that in the yeare 1506. the 21. of *Henry* the seuenth, the saide stewe houses in Southwarke were for a season inhibited, and the dores closed vp, but it was not long saith he, ere the houses there were set open againe, so many as were permitted, for (as it was said) whereas before were eighteene houses, from thenceforth were | appointed to bee vsed but twelue onely. These allowed stewhouses had signes on their frontes, towardes the Thames, not hanged out, but painted on the walles, as a Boares heade, the Crosse keyes, the Gunne, the Castle, the Crane, the Cardinals Hat, the Bel, the Swanne, &c. I haue heard ancient men of good credite report, that these single women were forbidden the rightes of the Church, so long as they continued that sinnefull life, and were excluded from christian buriall, if they were not reconciled before their death. And therefore there was a plot of ground, called the single womans churchyeard, appoynted for them, far from the parish church.

Lib. S. Mariæ Eborum.

English people disdayned to be baudes. Froes of Flaunders were women for that purpose.

Robert Fabian.

Stewhouses put down by H. the 7 for a time.

Page 409

Signes on the Stewhouses.

Single women forbidden rightes of the church.

In the yeare of Christ, 1546. the 37. of *Henry* the eight, this row of stewes in Southwarke was put downe by the kings commandement, which was proclaymed by sounde of Trumpet, no more to be priuiledged, and vsed as a common Brothel, but the inhabitants of the same to keepe good and honest rule as in other places of this realme, &c.

Stewhouses put downe.

The next is the Clinke, a Gayle or prison for the trespassers in those parts, Namely in olde time for such as should brabble, frey, or breake the Peace on the saide banke, or in the Brothell houses, they were by the inhabitantes there about apprehended, and committed to this Gayle, where they were straightly imprisoned.

Winchester house.

Next is the Bishoppe of Winchesters house, or lodging when hee commeth to this Cittie: which house was first builded by *William Gifford* Bishoppe of Winchester, aboute the yeare 1107. the seuenth of *Henry* the first, vpon a plot of ground pertayning to the Prior of Bermondsey, as appeareth by a writ directed vnto the Barons of the Exchequer, in the yeare 1366. the 41. of *Edward* the 3. (the Bishops sea being voyde) for 8.l. due to the Monks of Bermondsey, for the Bishop of Winchesters lodging in Southwarke. This is a very fayre house wel repayred, and hath a large Wharfe, and landing place called the Bishop of Winchesters staires.

Rochester house.

Page 410

Adioyning to this on the south side thereof is the Bishoppe of Rochesters Inne or lodging, by whome first erected, I do not now remember me to haue read, but well I wot the same of long time | hath not beene frequented by any Bishoppe, and lyeth ruinous for lacke of reparations. The Abbot of Wauerley had a House there.

S. Mary Oueries a Priorie, and now a parish church.

East from the Bishop of Winchesters house directly ouer against it, standeth a fayre church called saint *Mary* ouer the Rie, or Ouerie, that is ouer the water. This Church or some other in place thereof was of old time long before the conquest an house of sisters founded by a mayden named *Mary*, vnto the which house and sisters she left (as was left to her by her parents) the ouersight and profites of a Crosse ferrie or trauerse ferrie ouer the Thames, there kept before that any bridge was builded. This house of sisters was after by *Swithen*, a noble Lady, conuerted vnto a colledge of Priests, who in place of the Ferrie builded a bridge of timber, and from time to time kept the same in good reparations, but lastlie the same bridge was builded of stone, and then in the yeare 1106. was this church againe founded for Channons Regular, by *William Pont de le Arche* and *William Dauncy*, Knights Normans.

Lib. Roffen. Lib. Bermondsey.

William Gifford Bishop of Winchester, was a good benefactor also, for he as some haue noted, builded the body of that church, in the yeare 1106. the seuenth of *Henry* the first.

The Canons first entered the said church, then *Algodus* was the first Prior.

King *Henry* the 1. by his Charter gaue them the Church of *S. Margaret* in Southwarke.

King *Stephen* confirmed the gift of king *Henry*, and also gaue the stone house, which was *Williams de Ponte le Arche* by Downegate.

This Priorie was burned about the yeare 1207. wherefore the Chanons did found an Hospital near vnto their Priory, where they celebrated vntill the Priory was repayred: which Hospitall was after by consent of *Peter de la Roch* Bishop of Winchester remoued into the land of *Anicius* Archdeacon of Surrey in the yeare 1228. a place where the water was more plentifull, and the ayre more holesome, and was dedicate to *S. Thomas*.

S. Thomas Hospitall.

This *Peter de Rupibus*, or *de la Roch*, founded a large chapell of *S. Mary Magdalen* in the said church of *S. Mary Ouerie*, | which Chappel was after appointed to be the parish church for the inhabitants neare adioyning.

Parish church of S. Mary Magdalen.

Page 411

This church was againe newly builded in the raigne of *Richard* the second, and king *H.* the fourth.

Iohn Gower Esquier, a famous Poet, was then an especiall benefactor to that worke, and was there buried on the North side of the said church, in the chapple of S. *Iohn*, where hee founded a chauntrie, he lieth vnder a tombe of stone, with his image also of stone ouer him: The haire of his head aburne, long to his sholders, but curling vp, and a small forked beard, on his head a chaplet, like a coronet of foure Roses, an habite of purple, damasked downe to his feet, a collar of Esses, gold about his necke, vnder his head the likenes of three bookes, which hee compiled. The first named *Speculum Meditantis*, written in French: The second *Vox clamantis* penned in Latine: The third *Confessio amantis* written in English, and this last is printed, *vox clamantis* with his Cronica tripartita, and other both in latine and French neuer printed, I haue and doe possesse, but *speculum meditantis* I neuer saw, though heard thereof to be in Kent: beside on the wall where he lyeth, there was painted three virgins crowned, one of the which was named Charity, holding this deuise.

Iohn Gower was no knight, neither had he any garland of Iuie and Roses but a Chaplet of foure Roses onely.

En toy qui es Fitz de dieu le pere,
Sauve soit, qui gist souz cest piere.

The second writing Mercie, with this deuise.

O bone Iesu fait ta mercie,
Al alme, dont le corps gist icy.

The third writing Pittie, with this deuice.

Pur ta pite Iesu regarde,
Et met cest alme en sauve garde.

His Armes a field argent, on a Cheueron azure, three Leopardes heads golde, their tongues gules, two Angels supportars, on the creast a Talbot. His Epitaph.

Armigeri scutum nihil amodo fert sibi tutum,
Reddidit immo lutum morti generale tributum,
Spiritus exutum se gaudeat esse solutum, |
Est vbi virtutum regnum sine labe statutum.

Page 412

The roofe of the middle west Ile fell downe in the yeare 1469. This Priorie was surrendered to *Henry* the eight, the 31. of his raigne, the 27. of October, the yeare of Christ, 1539. valued at 624.l. 6.s. 6.d. by the yeare.

Priory of saint Mary Ouery made a parish church.

About Christmas next following, the church of the said Priory was purchased of the king by the inhabitantes of the Borough. Doctor *Stephen Gardner* Bishop of Winchester, putting to his helping hand, they made thereof a parrish church, for the parish[1] of *S. Mary Magdalen*, on the south side of the said Quire, and of *S. Margaret* on the hill, which were made one parish of S. Sauiour.

There be monumentes in this church of *Robert Liliarde*, or *Hiliarde* Esquier, *Margaret* daughter to the Lady *Audley* wife to sir *Thomas Audley, William Greuill* Esquier, and *Margaret* his wife, one of the heyres of *William Spershut* Esquier, Dame *Katherine* wife to *Iohn Stoke* Alderman, *Robert Merfin* Esquier, *William Vndall* Esquier, Lord *Ospay Ferar*, Sir *George Brewes* Knight, *Iohn Browne*, Ladie *Brandon* wife to sir *Thomas Brandon, William* Lord *Scales, William* Earle *Warren*, Dame *Maude* wife to Sir *Iohn Peach, Lewknor*, Dame *Margaret Elrington*, one of the heires of sir *Thomas Elrington, Iohn Bowden* Esquier, *Robert S. Magil, Iohn Sand-*

[1] parish] parish church *1603*

hurst, *Iohn Gower*, *Iohn Duncell* Marchant Taylor, 1516. *Iohn Sturton* Esquier, *Robert Rouse*, *Thomas Tong*, first Norrey and after Clarentiaulx King of Armes. *William Wickham* translated from the sea of Lincolne to the Bishoprick of Winchester, in the moneth of March 1595. deceased the 11. of Iune next following, and was buried here.

Thomas Cure Esquier, Sadler to King *Edward* the sixte, Queene *Mary* and Queene *Elizabeth*, deceased the 24. of May, 1588.[1] &c.

Now passing through saint Mary Ouers Close, (in possession of the Lord *Mountacute*) and Pepper Alley into Long Southwarke, on the right hand thereof, the Market hill, where the leather is solde, there stoode the late named parrish church of Saint | *Margaret* giuen to S. Mary Oueries by *Henry* the first, put downe and ioyned with the parrish of Saint Mary Magdalen, and vnited to the late dissolued Priorie Church of saint Mary Ouery. S. Mary Ouers Close. Pepper Alley. *Page 413*

A part of this parish church of S. *Margaret* is now a Court, wherein the Assizes and sessions be kept, and the court of Admiralty is also there kept. One other part of the same church is now a prison called the Compter in Southwarke, &c. S. Margaret on the hill made a court of iustice. Court of Admiralty. Compter in Southwarke.

Farther vp on that side, almost directly ouer against Saint *Georges* church, was sometime a large and most sumptuous house, builded by *Charles Brandon* late Duke of Suffolk, in the raign of *Henry* the eight, which was called Suffolke house, but comming afterwardes into the Kinges hands, the same was called Southwarke place, and a mint of coynage was there kept for the King. Suffolk house. A mint in Southwarke.

To this place came king *Edward* the sixte, in the second of his raigne, from Hampton court, and dined in it. He at that time made *Iohn Yorke* one of the shiriffes of London knight, and then rode through the City to Westminster.

Queene *Mary* gaue this house to *Nicholas He⟨a⟩th* Archbishop of Yorke, and to his successors for euer, to be their Inne or lodging for their repaire to London, in recompence of Yorke house neare to Westminster, which King *Henry* her Father had taken from Cardinall *Wolsey*, and from the sea of Yorke.

[1] 1588] 1598 *1603*; *but v. epitaph in 1633*

Archbishop *Heth* solde the same house to a Marchant, or to Marchantes, that pulled it downe, solde the leade, stone, iron, &c. And in place thereof builded many small cottages of great rents to the encreasing of beggers in that Borough. The Archbishoppe bought Norwich house, or Suffolke place, neare vnto Charing Crosse, because it was neare vnto the Court, and left it to his successors. Now on the south side, to return backe againe towards the bridge. Ouer against this Suffolke place, is the parrish church of S. *George*, sometime pertayning to the Priorie of Barmondsey, by the gift of *Thomas Arderne* and *Thomas* his sonne, in the yeare 1122. There lie buried in this Church *William Kirton* Esquire, and his wiues, 1464.

Parish church of S. George.

Then is the white Lion, a Gaole so called, for that the same | was a common hosterie for the receit of trauellers by that signe: This house was first vsed as a Gaole within these fortie yeares last, since the which time the prisoners were once remoued thence to an house in Newtowne,[1] where they remayned for a short time and were returned backe againe to the foresaid White Lion, there to remayne as in the appointed Gaole for the countie of Surrey.

Page 414

White Lyon a Gaole for Surrey.

Kinges Bench.

Next is the Gaole or prison of the kinges Bench, but of what antiquitie the same is I know not. For I haue read that the courts of the Kinges Bench and Chauncery haue oft times beene remoued from London to other places, and so hath likewise the Gayles that serue those Courts, as in the yeare 1304. *Edwarde* the first commaunded the Courts of the kinges Bench and the Exchequer which had remayned seuen yeares at Yorke, to bee remoued to their old places at London. And in the yeare 1387. the 11. of *Richard* the 2. *Robert Trisilian* chiefe Iustice came to the city of Couentrie, and there sate by the space of a moneth, as Iustice of the Kinges Benche, and caused to be indited in that Court, about the number of two thousand persons of that Country, &c.

H. Knighton.

It seemeth therefore, that for that time, the prison or Gayle of that court was not farre off. Also in the yeare 1392. the sixteenth of the same *Richard*, the Archbishop of Yorke being Lord Chauncelor, for good wil that he bare to his City, caused

[1] Newington: *cf. p. 52*

the kings Bench and chauncery to be remoued from London to Yorke, but ere long they were returned to London.

Then is the Marshalsey, an other gayle or prison, so called as pertayning to the Marshalles of England. Of what continuance kept in Southwarke I haue not learned: but like it is, that the same hath beene remoueable, at the pleasure of the Marshalles: for I finde that in the yeare 1376, the fiftieth of *Edwarde* the third, *Henry Percie* (beeing Marshall) kept his prisoners in the Citie of London, where hauing committed one *Iohn Prendergast*, of Norwich, contrarie to the liberties of the City of London, the Citizens, by perswasion of the Lord *Fitzwalter* theyr Standard-bearer, took Armour and ranne with great rage to the Marshalles Inne, brake vp the gates, brought out the prisoner, & conueyed him away, minding to haue brent the stocks in the middest of their citty, but they first sought for sir *Henry Percy* to haue | punished him, as I haue noted in my Annales.

Marshalsey in Southwarke.

Page 415

More, about the Feast of Easter next following, *Iohn* Duke of Lancaster, hauing caused all the whole Nauie of England to be gathered together at London: It chanced a certaine Esquier to kill one of the shipmen, which act the other shipmen taking in ill part, they brought their sute into the kings court of the Marshalsey which then as chaunced (sayth mine Author) was kept in Southwarke: but when they perceyued that Court to be so fauourable to the murtherer, and further that the kinges warrant was also gotten for his pardon, they in greate fury ranne to the house, wherein the murtherer was imprisoned, brake into it, and brought forth the prisoner with his Giues on his legges, they thrust a knife to his heart, and sticked him, as if hee had beene a Hogge, after this they tyed a roape to his Giues, and drewe him to the gallowes, where when they had hanged him, as though they had done a great act, they caused the trumpets to be sounded before them to theyr ships, and there in great triumph they spent the rest of the day.

Saylers brake up the Marshalsey.

Also the rebels of Kent, in the yeare 1381. brake downe the houses of the Marshalsey, and Kinges Bench in Southwarke, tooke from thence the prisoners, brake downe the house of sir *Iohn Imworth*, then Marshall of the Marshalsey, and Kings

Rebels of Kent brake vp the Marshalsey.

Bench, &c. After this in the yeare 1387. the eleuenth of *Richard* the second, the morrow after Bartholomew day, the king kept a great Councell in the Castle of Nottingham, and the Marshalsey of the king was then kept at Lughborrow by the space of sixe dayes or more. In the year 1443. sir *Walter Man⟨n⟩y* was Marshal of the Marshalsey, the 22. of *Henry* the sixt. *William Brandon*, Esquire, was Marshall in the eight of *E*. the 4. In the yeare 1504 the prisoners of the Marshalsey, then in Southwarke, brake out, & many of them being taken, were executed, especially such as had beene committed for Felony or treason.

From thence towards London bridge on the same side, be many fayre Innes, for receipt of trauellers, by these signes, the Spurre, Christopher, Bull, Queenes head, Tabarde, George, Hart, Kinges Head, &c. Amongst the which, the most auncient is the Tabard, so called of the signe, which as we now tearme it, | is of a Iacquit, or sleeuelesse coat, whole before, open on both sides, with a square coller, winged at the shoulders: a stately garment of old time, commonly worne of Noble men and others, both at home and abroad in the warres, but then (to wit in the warres) their Armes embrodered, or otherwise depict vpon them, that euery man by his coate of Armes might be knowne from others: but now these Tabardes are onely worne by the Heraulds, and be called their coates of Armes in seruice: for the Inne of the Tabard, *Geffrey Chaucer* Esquire, the most famous Poet of England, in commendation thereof writeth thus.

The Tabarde in Southwark.

Page 416

Geff. Chaucer.

It befell in that season, on a day,
In Southwarke at the Tabert, as I lay,
Readie to wend⟨en⟩ on my Pilgrimage,
To Canterburie with full deuout courage,
That night was comen into the Hosterie,
Well nine and twentie in a companie,
Of sundrie folke, by aduenture yfall
In fellowship, and Pilgrimes were they all,
That toward Canterburie woulden ride,
The stables and ⟨the⟩ chambers weren wide,
And well we were⟨n⟩ eased at the best, &c.

Within this Inne was also the lodging of the Abbot of Hide, (by the Citie of Winchester) a faire house for him and his traine, when he came to the Citie to Parliament, &c.

The Abbot of Hide his lodging.

And then Theeues lane by S. *Thomas* Hospitall: the hospitall of Saint *Thomas*, first founded by *Richard* Prior of Bermondsey, in the Selerers ground agaynst the wall of the Monasterie, in the yeare 1213. He named it the Almerie, or house of Almes for conuarts and poore children, for the which ground the Prior ordained that the Almoner should pay ten shillings foure pence yearely to the Selerer at Michaelmas.

Hospitall of S. Thomas.

But *Peter de Rupibus*, Bishop of Winchester, in the yeare 1215 founded the same againe more fully for Canons Regular, in place of the first hospitall: he increased the rent thereof to three hundred fortie foure pound by the yeare: thus was this Hospitall | holden of the Prior and Abbot of Bermondsey, till the yeare 1428, at which time a composition was made between *Thomas Thetford*, Abbot of Bermondsey, and *Nicholas Buckland*, master of the sayde Hospitall of Saint *Thomas*, for all the landes and Tenements which were holden of the sayde Abbot and Couent in Southwarke, or elsewhere, for the olde Rent to bee payd vnto the said Abbot.

Lib. S. Mariæ Ouery. S. Thomas Hospitall the second time founded. *Page 417*

There be the Monuments in this Hospitall Church, of sir *Robert Chamber* Knight, *William Fines* Lord Say, *Richarde Chaucer*, *Iohn Gloucester*, *Adam Atwood*, *Iohn Ward*, *Michaell Cambridge*, *William West*, *Iohn Golding* Esquires, *Iohn Benham*, *George Kirkes*, *Thomas Knighton*, *Thomas Baker* Gentlemen, *Robert* sonne to Sir *Thomas Fleming*, *Agnes* wife to Sir *Walter Dennis* knight, daughter and one of the heyres of Sir *Robert Danuars*, *Iohn Euarey* Gentleman, &c.

This Hospitall was by the visitors, in the yeare 1538. valued at 266 pound seuenteene shillings sixe pence, and was surrendered to *Henrie* the eight, in the thirtieth of his raigne.

In the yeare 1552 the Citizens of London, hauing purchased the voyde suppressed Hospitall of Saint *Thomas* in Southwarke, in the Moneth of Iuly, began the reparations thereof, for poore, impotent, lame, and diseased people, so that in the Moneth of Nouember next following, the sicke and poore people were taken in. And in the yeare 1553. on the tenth of Aprill, King *Edward* the sixt, in the seuenth of his raigne,

The 3. foundation of S. Thomas Hospitall by the Cittizens of London. Gift of E. the 6 to the hospital of S. Thomas in Southwark.

gaue to the Maior, Comminaltie, and Citizens of London, to bee a workehouse for the poore and idle persons of the Citie, his house of Bridewell, and seauen hundred Markes landes of the Sauoy rentes, which Hospitall hee had impressed, with all the beddes, bedding, and other furniture belonging to the same, towards the maintenance of the said workehouse of Bridewell, and of this Hospitall of Saint *Thomas* in Southwarke. This gift, the King confirmed by his Charter, dated the twentie sixe of Iune, next following, and willed it to be called the Kings Hospitall in Southwarke.

Page 418

S. Thomas Parish church.

The Church of this Hospitall, which of olde time serued for the | tenements neare adioyning and pertaining to the saide Hospitall, remaineth as a Parish Church.

S. Olaues street and parish church.

But now to come to saint *Olaues* street: on the Banke of the riuer of Thames, is the parish church of saint *Olaue*, a faire and meetely large Church, but a farre larger Parrish, especially of Aliens or straungers, and poore people: in which Church, there lieth intombed sir *Iohn Burcettur* knight. 1466.

Prior of Lewes his Inne.

Ouer against this Parish church, on the south side the street, was sometime one great house builded of stone, with arched gates, ⟨which⟩ pertained to the Prior of Lewes in Sussex, and was his lodging when he came to London: it is now a common Hosterie for trauellers, and hath to signe the Walnut tree.

Abbot of Augustines Inne.

Wil. Thorne.

Then East from the said Parish Church of saint *Olaue* is a Key. In the yeare 1330, by the licence of *Simon Swanlond* Maior of London, ⟨it was⟩ builded ⟨by⟩ *Isabell* widow to *Hamond Goodchepe*. And next therevnto was then a great house of stone and tymber, belonging to the Abbot of saint *Augustine* without the walles of Canterburie, which was an auncient peece of worke, and seemeth to be one of the first builded houses on that side the riuer, ouer against the citie: It was called the Abbots Inne of saint *Augustine* in Southwarke, and was somtime holden of the Earles of Warren and Surrey, as appeareth by a deede, made 1281. which I haue read, and may be Englished thus:

To all to whome this present writing shall come, Iohn earle Warren sendeth greeting. Know ye that wee haue altogither remised and quiteclaimed for vs and our heires for euer, to

Nicholas Abbot of saint Augustines of Canterburie, and the Couent of the same, and their successors, suite to our court of Southwarke, which they owe vnto vs, for al that Messuage and houses theron builded, and all their appurtenances, which they haue of our fee in Southwarke, scituate vpon the Thames, between the Bridge house and church of saint Olaue. And the said Messuage, with the buildings thereon builded, and all their appurtenances to them and their successors, we haue granted in perpetuall almes to hold of vs, and our heyres for the same: sauing the seruice due to any other persons, if any such bee, then to vs: and for this remit and graunt, the sayde abbot and Couent haue giuen vnto vs fiue shillings of rent | yearly in *Page 419* *Southwarke, and haue receiued vs and our heires in al benefices which shall be in their church for euer.* This sute of court, one *William Graspeis* was bound to do to the said Earle, for the said Messuage: and heretofore to acquit in all things the church of *S. Augustine*, against the said Earle.

This house of late time belonged to sir *Anthony Sentlegar*, then to *Warham Sentlegar*, &c. And is now called *Sentlegar* house, but diuided into sundrie tenements. Next is the Bridgehouse, so called as being a storehouse for stone, timber, or whatsoeuer pertaining to the building or repairing of London bridge.

Sentlegar-house.

The Bridge house.

This house seemeth to haue taken beginning with the first founding of the bridge either of stone or timber: it is a large plot of ground, on the banke of the riuer Thames: containing diuers large buildings, for stowage of things necessary towards reparation of the said bridge.

There are also diuers Garners, for laying vp of Wheate, and other Grayners for seruice of the Citie, as neede requireth. Moreouer, there be certaine Ouens builded, in number tenne: of which sixe be very large, the other foure being but halfe so bigge. These were purposely made to bake out the bread corne of the sayd Grayners, to the best aduantage for reliefe of the poore Citizens, when neede should require. Sir *Iohn Throstone* knight, sometime an Embrotheror, then a Goldsmith, one of the Shiriffes 1516. gaue by his Testament towardes the making of these Ouens two hundreth poundes: which thing was performed by his Executors, Sir *Iohn Munday*

Garners for corne in the Bridge house.

Ouens in the Bridge house.

A Brew house builded in the Bridge house.

Goldsmith then being Mayor. There was of late, for the enlarging of the said Bridge house, taken in an old Brew-house, called Goldings, which was giuen to the City by *George Monox*, sometime Mayor, and in place thereof, is now a faire Brew-house new builded, for seruice of the Cittie with Beere.

Abbot of Battaile his Inne.

Next, was the Abbot of Battailes Inne, betwixt the Bridge-house and Battaile bridge, likewise on the banke of the Riuer of Thames: the walkes and gardens therevnto appertaining, on the other side of the way, before the gate of the said house, and was called the Maze: there is now an Inne, called the Flower de Luce, for that the signe is three Flower de Luces. Much other buildings | of small tenements are thereon builded, replenished with strangers and other, for the most part poore people.

Page 420

Battle bridge.

Then is Battaile bridge, so called of Battaile Abbey, for that it standeth on the ground, and ouer a water course (flowing out of Thames) pertayning to that Abbey, and was therefore both builded and repaired by the Abbots of that house, as being hard adioyning to the Abbots lodging.

Bermondsey streete.

Beyond this bridge is Bermondsey street, turning South, in the South end whereof was sometime a Priory, or Abbey, of saint *Sauior*, called Bermonds Eye in Suthwarkē, founded by *Alwin Childe*, a Citizen of London, in the yeare 1081.

Peter, *Richard*, *Obstert*, and *Vmbalde*, Monkes *de Charitate*, came vnto *Bermondsey*, in the yeare 1089, and *Peter* was made first Prior there, by appointment of the Pryor of the house called *Charity* in France: by which meanes, this Priory of *Bermondsey* (being a Cell to that in France) was accounted a Priory of *Aliens*.

In the yeare 1094. deceased *Alwin Childe* founder of this house. Then *William Rufus* gaue to the Monkes his mannor of *Bermondsey*, with the appurtenances, and builded for them there a new great Church.

Robert Blewet, Bishop of Lincolne (king *Williams* Chancelor) gaue them the mannor of *Charlton*, with the appurtenances. Also *Geffrey Martell*, by the graunt of *Geffrey Magnauile*, gaue them the land of Halingbury, and the tithe of Alferton, &c.

More, in the yeare 1122. *Thomas* of Arderne and *Thomas* his sonne gaue to the Monkes of *Bermonds Eye* the Church of saint *George* in Southwarke, &c.

In the yeare 1165. King *Henry* the second confirmed to them the hyde or territory of Southwarke, & Laygham Wadden, with the land of Coleman, &c.

Hide of Southwarke to the Monkes of Bermondsey.

In the yeare 1371. the Prior⟨ie⟩s of *Aliens* throughout England being seized into the kings hands, *Richard Denton*, an English man, was made Prior of *Bermondsey*: to whome was committed the custody of the said Priory, by the letters patents of king *Edward* the third, sauing to the king the aduowsons of Churches.

In the yeare 1380. the fourth of *Richard* the second, this priory was made a Denison (or free English) for the fine of 200. Markes, paid to the Kings Hanaper in the Chauncery. In the yeare 1399. *Iohn Attelborough* Prior of Bermondsey was made the first Abbot of that house by Pope *Boniface* the ninth, at the sute of king *Richard* the second.

Page 421

Bermonds Eye made an Abbey.

In the yeare 1417. *Thomas Thetford* Abbot of Bermondsey, held a Plea in Chauncery against the king, for the Mannors of *Preston*, *Bermondsey*, and *Stone*, in the county of Summerset, in the which sute the Abbot preuailed and recouered against the king.

Abbot of Bermondsey held Plea against the King, and preuailed.

In the yeare 1539. this Abbey was valued to dispend by the yeare, foure hundred seuenty foure pound, fourteene shillings foure pence halfe penny, and was surrendred to *Henry* the eight, the 31. of his raigne: the Abbey church was then pulled downe by sir *Thomas Pope* knight, and in place thereof, a goodly house builded of stone and timber, now pertayning to the Earles of Sussex.

There are buried in that church *Leofstane*, *Prouost*, shriue or Domes man of London 1115. Sir *William Bowes* knight, and Dame *Elizabeth* his wife. Sir *Tho. Pikeworth* knight, Dame *Anne Audley*: *George* sonne to *Iohn* Lord *Audley*, *Io. Winkefield* Esquier. Sir *Nicholas Blonket* knight, Dame *Bridget* wife to *William Trussell*, *Holgraue* Baron of the Exchequer, &c.

Iohn Bauow.

Next vnto this Abbey church, standeth a proper Church of saint *Mary Magdalen*, builded by the priors of Bermondsey,

Parish church of Saint Mary Magdalen.

seruing for resort of the inhabitants, (tenants to the prior or Abbots neare adioyning) there to haue their diuine seruice: this Church remayneth and serueth as afore, and is called a parish church.

The Loke a Lazer house in Kent streete.

Then in Kent streete is a Lazer house, for Leprous people: called the Loke in Southwarke: the foundation whereof I find not. Now hauing touched diuers principall parts of this Borough, I am to speake somewhat of gouernment, and so to end.

Liberties of Southwarke, farmed by Citizens of London.

This Borough vpon petition made by the Citizens of London, to *E*. the third[1] in the first yeare of his raigne, was, for diuers causes, by Parliament granted to them for euer, yeelding into the Exchequer the Fee firme of 10. li. by the yeare: which grant was confirmed by *E*. the 3. who in the 3 of his raigne, gaue them license to | take a tole towards the charge of pauing the said Borough with stone. *H*. the 4. confirmed the grant of his predecessors: so did *E*. the 4. &c.

Page 422

Liberties of Southwarke purchased.

But in the yeare 1550. King *Edward* the 6. for the summe of 647. pound two shillings and one penny, payd into his Court of Augmentations, and reuenewes of his Crowne, graunted to the Mayor and Comminalty, all his lands and tenements in Southwarke, except and reserued the capitall Messuage, two mansions called Southwarke place, late the Duke of *Suffolkes*, and all the gardens and lands to the same appertaining: the Parke and the Messuage called the Antilope. Moreouer, he gaue them the Lordship and Mannor of Southwarke, with all members & rights thereof, late pertayning to the Monastery of Bermondsey. And all messuages, places, buildings, rents, Courts, Waffes and streyes, to the same appertaining, in the County of Surrey, except as is before excepted. He also granted vnto them, his Manor & borough of Southwarke, with all the members, rights & appurtenances, late of the possession of the Archbishop of Canterbury & his sea in Southwarke. Moreover for the summe of 500. marks, he granted to the said Maior & Comminalty, and their successors, in & through the borough and towne of Southwarke: and in al the parishes of S. *Sauior*, S. *Olaue*, and saint *George*,

The Lordship and Mannor of Southwark pertaining to the Monastery of Bermondsey.

The Kings Mannor, Borough of Southwarke.

[1] third] first *1603*

and the parish of saint *Tho.* Hospitall, now called the kings Hospitall: and elsewhere in the said towne and Borough of Southwarke, and Kentish streete, Bermondsey street, in the parish of Newington, all waifes and streyes, treasure troue, all fellons goods, &c. within the parishes and precinct aforesaid, &c. The returne of writs, processes, and warrants, &c. together with a fayre in the whole towne, for three dayes: to wit, the 7. 8. and 9. of September, yearely, with a Court of *Pye powders*: A view of Franke pledge, with attachments, arrests, &c. Also to arrest all fellons, and other malefactors, within their precinct, and send them to Ward, and to Newgate. Prouided that nothing in that graunt should be preiudiciall to the Steward and Marshall of the Kinges house. The same premisses to be holden of the Mannor of East Greenwich, in the County of Kent, by fealty in free socage. Dated at Westminster the 23. day of April, in the 4. of his raigne. All which was also confirmed by Parliament, &c. And the same yeare | in the Whitson weeke, in a Court of Aldermen kept at the Guildhall of London, sir *Iohn Aylophe* knight was sworne the first Alderman of the Bridge ward without, and made vp the number of 26. Aldermen of London.

Faire in Southwarke.

Page 423

First Alderman of Southwark.

Borough of Southwarke, one of the Wards of London.

This Borough, at a subsidy to the king, yeeldeth about 1000. Marks, or 800.li. which is more then any one Cittie in England paieth, except the City of London. And also the Muster of men in this Borough doth likewise in number surpasse all other cities, except London. And thus much for the Borough of Southwark: one of the 26. wards of London, which hath an Alderman, Deputies 3. and a Bayliffe. Common Councell none. Constables 16. Scauingers 6. Wardmote inquest 20. And is taxed to the fifteene at 17.li. 17.s. 8.d.

Muster of men in Southwark.

The Suburbes without the Walles of the said Citie, briefely touched. As also without the Liberties, more at large described.

HAUING spoken of this citie, the originall, & increase, by degrees. The Walles, Gates, Ditch, Castles, Towers, Bridges, the Schools and houses of learning. Of the orders and customes, sports and pastimes. Of the honour of Citizens, and worthines of men. And last of all, how the same Citie is diuided into parts & Wards. And how the same be bounded. And what Monuments of antiquity, or ornaments of building, be in euery of them, as also in the Borough of Southwarke: I am next to speake briefly of the Suburbs, as wel without the gates, & wals, as without the liberties. And of the monuments in them.

Fitz Stephen.

Concerning the estate of the Suburbs of this Citie, in the raigne of *H.* the 2. *Fitz Stephen* hath these words. *Vpwards on the west* (saith he) *is the kings Pallace, which is an incomparable building, rising with a vawmure & bulwark. Aloft vpon the riuer, 2 miles from the wall of the city, but yet conioyned with a con|tinuall Suburb. On all sides, without the houses of the Suburbs, are the citizens gardens & orchards, planted with trees, both large, sightly, & adioyning togither. On the north side, are pastures, & plain medows, with brooks running through them, turning water mils, with a pleasant noise. Not far off, is a great forrest, a well wooded chase, hauing good couert for Harts, Buckes, Does, Boores & wild Bulles. The corne fields are not of a hungry sandie mould, but as the fruitfull fields of Asia: yeelding plentifull encrease, & filling the barnes with corne. There are near London on the north side, especiall welles in the Suburbes, sweet, holesome, and cleare. Amongst which, Holywell, Clarkenwell, and saint Clemons well, are most famous, & most frequented by schollers & youthes of the City in summer euenings, when they walke forth to take the aire.* Thus farre out of *Fitz Stephen*, for the Suburbs at that time. The 2. of *H.* the 3. the Forest of Midlesex and the Warren of Stanes were disaforested: since the which time, the suburbs about London hath bin also mightily increased with buildings: for first, to begin in the East, by the Tower of London, is the Hospitall of saint *Katheren*, founded by *Matilde* the Queene, wife to King *Stephen*, as is afore shewed in Portsoken ward, from this precinct of S. *Katheren* to Wapping in the Woze[1], the vsuall place of execution for hanging of Pirats & sea Rouers, at the

Page 424

Liber Albus.

Suburbe without the Postern by the Tower of London. Wapping in the Woze.

[1] Woze] *1598*; West, *1603*

low water marke there to remaine, till three tides had ouerflowed them, was neuer a house standing within these 40 yeares: but since the gallowes being after remooued farther off, a continuall streete, or filthy straight passage, with Alleyes of small tenements or cottages builded, inhabited by saylors victualers, along by the riuer of Thames, almost to *Radcliff*, a good mile from the Tower. On the east side, and by north of the tower, lieth East Smithfield, Hogs streete, and tower hill, and east from them both was the new abbey called *Grace*, founded by *E.* the 3. From thence Radcliffe, vp East smithfield, by Nightingall lane (which runneth south to the Hermitage, a Brewhouse so called of an Hermite sometime being there) beyond this lane to the Mannor of *Bramley* (called in record of *R.* the 2. Villa east smithfield, & Villa *de Bramley*) and to the Mannor of Shadwell, belonging to the Deane of *Pauls*, there hath been of late, in place of Elme trees many small tenements | raysed, towards Radcliffe: And Radcliffe it selfe hath beene also encreased in building eastward (in place where I haue knowne a large high way, with fayre Elme trees on both sides) that the same hath now taken hold of Lime Hurst, Lime Host, corruptly called Lime house, sometime distant a mile from Radcliffe. Hauing said this much for building, at Wapping, East Smithfield, Bramley and Shadwell, all on the south side of the high way to Radcliff: now one note on the North side, also concerning pirates. I reade that in the yeare 1440. in the lent season, certaine persons with 6. ships brought from beyond the seas fish to victuaile the city of London, which fish when they had deliuered, and were returning homeward, a number of sea theeues, in a barge, in the night came vpon them, when they were a sleep in their vessels, riding at anker on the riuer Thames, and slew them, cut their throates, cast them ouer boord, tooke their money, and drowned their ships for that no man should espie or accuse them. Two of these theeues were after taken, and hanged in chaynes vpon a gollowes set vpon a raysed hill, for that purpose made, in the field beyond East Smithfield, so that they might be seene farre into the riuer Thames. The first building at Ratcliffe in my youth (not to be forgotten) was a fayre free schoole, and Almes houses, founded by *Auice*

Nightingall lane. Hermitage. West smithfield. Bramley. Shadwell.

Page 425

Lime hurst.

Free schoole and Almes houses at Radcliffe.

Gibson, wife to *Ni. Gibson* Grocer, as before I haue noted. But of late yeares ship-wrights and (for the most part) other marine men, haue builded many large and strong houses for themselues, and smaller for Saylers, from thence almost to Poplar, and so to Blake wal. Now for Tower hil, the plaine there is likewise greatly diminished by Merchants, for building of small tenements: from thence towards Aldgate was the Mineries, whereof I haue spoken.

Tower hill without the walles.

From Aldegate east, againe lieth a large street, replenished with buildings, to wit on the north side, the parish church of *S. Bottolph*, and so other buildings to Hog lane, & to the barres on both sides.

Suburbe without Aldegate.

Also without the barres, both the sides of the streete bee pestered with Cottages, and Allies, euen vp to White chappel church: and almost halfe a mile beyond it, into the common field: all which ought to lye open & free for all men. But this common field, I say, being sometime the beauty of this City on that part, is so incroched vpon by building of filthy Cottages, and with other purprestures, | inclosures and Laystalles (notwithstanding all proclaimations and Acts of Parliament made to the contrary) that in some places it scarce remaineth a sufficient high way for the meeting of Carriages and droues of Cattell, much lesse is there any faire, pleasant or wholsome way for people to walke on foot: which is no small blemish to so famous a city, to haue so vnsauery and vnseemly an entry or passage thereunto.

Page 426

Of white chappell.

Now of white Chappell church somwhat, and then backe againe to Aldegate. This church is as it were a chappel of ease to the parrish of *Stebinhith*, & the Parson of *Stebinhith* hath the gift thereof: which being first dedicated to the name of God, and the blessed Virgin, is now called S. *Mary Matfellon.* About the year 1428 the 6. of King *H.* the 6. a deuout widow of that parish had long time cherished, and brought vp of Almes, a certayne Frenchman or Briton borne, which most vnkindly and cruelly in a night murthered the said widow sleeping in her bed, and after fled with such Iewels and other stuffe of hers as he might carry: but he was so freshly pursued that for feare he tooke the church of Saint *George* in Southwarke, and challenged priuiledge of Sanctuary there, and so

S. Mary Matfellon. A deuout widow murdered.

abiured the kings land. Then the Constables (hauing charge of him) brought him into London, intending to haue conuaied him Eastward, but so soone as he was come into the parish where before hee had committed the murther, the wiues cast vpon him so much filth and ordure of the streete, that (notwithstanding the best resistance made by the Constables) they slew him out of hand: and for this feate, it hath beene sayd, that parish to haue purchased that name of saint *Mary Matfellon*, but I finde in Record, the same to be called *Villa beatæ Mariæ de Matfellon* in the 21. of *Richard* the second.

More, we reade that in the yeare 1336. the 10. of *E.* the 3. the Bishop of Alba, Cardinall, and Parson of *Stebunhith*, Procurator generall in England, presented a Clarke to be Parson in the church of blessed *Mary* called *Matfellon*, without Aldegate of London, &c.

Now againe from Aldegate northwest to Bishops gate, lyeth Hounds ditch, and so to Bishops gate.

North and by east from Bishops gate, lieth a large street or high way, hauing on the west side therof, the parish church of *S. But*⟨*tolphe*⟩. | Suburbe without Bishops gate.

Then is the Hospitall of S. Mary of Bethelem, founded by a Cittizen of London, and as before is shewed, vp to the Barres, without the which is Norton fall gate, a libertie so called, belonging to the Deane of Powles. Thence vp to the late dissolued Priory of S. *Iohn Baptist*, called Holywell, a house of Nuns, of old time founded by a Bishop of London: *Stephen Grausend* Bishop of London, about the yeare 1318 was a benefactor therevnto, reedified by sir *Thomas Louell* knight of the Garter, who builded much there, in the raignes of *H.* the 7. and of *H.* the 8. Hee endowed this house with fayre lands, and was there buried in a large chappel by him builded for that purpose. This Priory was valued at the suppression to haue of lands 293.li. by year, and was surrendred 1539. the 31. of *H.* the 8. The church thereof being pulled downe, many houses haue been builded for the lodginges of noble men, of strangers borne and other.

Page 427

Norton fall gate.

Priory of S. John Baptist at Holywell.

From Holy well in the high streete, is a continuall building of tenementes to Sewers ditch, hauing one small side of a fielde, already made a Garden plotte. Ouer against the north corner of this field, betweene it and the Church of Saint Leonarde in Shoreditch, sometime stood a Crosse, now a Smithes Forge, diuiding three wayes: forth right the high way is builded vpon eyther side, more then a good flight shoote, towardes Kinges land, Newington, Totanham, &c.

A Crosse at Soersditch now a Smithes Forge.

On the left hand is Ealdestreete, which reacheth West to a stone Crosse, ouer against the North ende of Golding lane, and so to the ende of Goswell streete. On the right hand of this Ealdestreete, not farre from Soers ditch, but on the North side thereof, is Hoxton, a large streete with houses on both sides, and is a Prebend belonging to Powles church in London, but of Soers ditch parish.

Hoxton.

On the right hand beyond Soresditch church toward Hackney, are some late builded houses vpon the common soyle, for it was a leystall, but those houses belong to the parish of Stebunhith.

On the other side of the high way from Bishopsegate and Hounds ditch is the Dolphin, a common Inne for receipt of trauellers, then a house builded by the L. *Iohn Powlet*, then Fishers Folly, and so vp to the west ende of Berwardes Lane,| is a continuall building of small cottages, then the Hospitall called S. Mary Spittle hard within the Barres, whereof I haue spoken in Bishopsgate warde.

Page 428

From the which bars towardes Soersditch on that side, is all along a continuall building of small and base tenements, for the most part lately erected.

Soerditch so called more then 400. yeares since, as I can proue by record.

Amongst the which (I meane of the auncientest building) was one row of proper small houses with Gardens for poore decayed people, there placed by the Prior of the said Hospitall: euery one Tenant whereof paid one penny rent by the yeare at Christmas, and dined with the Prior on Christmas day: but after the suppression of the Hospitall, these houses for want of reparations in few yeares were so decayed, that it was called Rotten Rowe, and the poore worne out (for there came no new in their place): the houses, for a small portion of money, were solde from *Goddard* to *Russell* a Draper, who new builded them, and let them out for rent enough, taking also large Fines of the Tenantes, neare as much as the houses cost him purchase, and building: for hee made his bargaines so hardly

Almeshouses in Soersditch.

Rotten Row or Russel row.

with all men, that both Carpenter, Brickelayer, and Playsterer, were by that Worke vndone. And yet in honour of his name, it is now called *Russels* Row.

Now for the parrish of S. Leonards at Soersditch, the Archdeacon of London is alwayes Parson thereof, and the Cure is serued by a Vicar. In this church haue beene diuers honourable persons buried, as appeareth by monuments yet remayning: [1]sir *Iohn Elrington* with *Margaret* his wife, daughter and heyre to *Thomas* Lord *Itchingham*, widdow to *William Blount*, sonne and heyre to *Walter Blount* the first Lord *Mountioy*, which *Margaret* dyed 1481.

Parish Church of S. Leonarde at Soersditch.

Sir *Humfrey Starkie* Recorder of London, Baron of the Exchequer, *Iohn Gadde* Shereman of London, and *Anne* his wife, 1480. sir *Thomas Seymore* Mayor of London, deceased 1535. sir *Thomas Leigh* Doctor of law, 1545. Item, vnder one fayre monument lyeth buried the Lady *Katherine* daughter to *Edwarde* Duke of Buckingham, wife to *Raph Neuell* Earle of Westmerland, who dyed 1553. also *Elianor* daughter | to sir *William Paston*, wife to *Thomas Mannars* Earle of Rutland, 1551. *Margaret* daughter to *Raph Neuell* Earle of Westmerland, and wife to *Henry Mannars* Earle of Rutland, 1560. *Katherine* daughter to *Henry Neuel* Earle of Westmerland, and wife to Sir *Iohn Constable* of Holdernes, 1591. *Anne* daughter to *T. Mannars* Earle of Rutland, sir *T. Mannars* 4. son to *Thomas* Earle of Rutland, 1591. *Oliuer Mannars*, 5. son to *Thomas* Earle of Rutland, 1563. all vnder one monument. *Richard* and *Harry Yong* 1545. [1]

Page 429

Notwithstanding that of late one Vicker there, for couetousnes of the brasse which he conuerted into coyned siluer, plucking vp many plates fixed on the graues, & left no memory of such as had beene buried vnder them: A greate iniurie both to the liuing and the dead, forbidden by publike proclamation, in the raigne of our soueraigne Lady Queene *Elizabeth*, but not forborn by many, that eyther of a preposterous zeale, or of a greedy minde spare not to satisfie themselues by so wicked a meanes.

One note of Shoreditch, and so an ende of that suburbe. I reade that in the year 1440. the 18. of *H.* the 6. a Fuller of Shorditch appeached of treason many worthy Esquiers and

[1] Sir J. Elrington . . . Richard and Harry Yong 1545] *om. 1598*

A Fuller of Shoreditch for falsely accusing hanged and quartered.

Deut. 16.

The reward of a false brother.

Gentlemen of Kent, but he being proued false, was attaint, condemned and had iudgement to be drawne, hanged and quartered, which was done, his head set on London bridge, and his quarters on the gates: this iustice was done, according to the 16. of Deuteronomie. 'The iudges shall make diligent inquisition, and if the witnes bee founde false, and to haue giuen false witnes against his brother, then shall they doe vnto him, as he had thought to doe vnto his brother,' &c. I reade of the Kinges Mannor Vocatus[1] Shorditch place in the parrish of Hackney, but how it tooke that name I know not, and therfore I wil turn backe from Shoreditch Crosse to Bethelem-Crosse, and so passe through that Hospitall into the More fielde, which lyeth without the Posterne called Moregate.

Bethlem crosse.

This fielde of old time was called the More. As appeareth by the Charter of *William* Conqueror to the Colledge of S. *Martin* declaring a running water to passe into the Citie from the same More. Also *Fitzstephen* writeth of this More, saying thus: *When* | *the great Fenne or More, which watereth the walles on the north side is frozen*, &c. This Fen or More field stretching from the wall of the City betwixt Bishopsgate and the posterne called Cripples gate to Fensbery, and to Holy well, continued a wast and vnprofitable ground a long time, so that the same was all letten for foure markes the yeare, in the raigne of *Edward* the 2: but in the yeare 1415. the 3. of *Henry* the 5. *Thomas Fawconer* Mayor, as I haue shewed, caused the wall of the Citty to be broken toward the said More, and builded the Posterne called Moregate, for the ease of the Cittizens to walke that waye vppon Causeyes towardes Iseldon and Hoxton: moreouer he caused the ditches of the Citie, and other the ditches from Soers ditch to Deepe ditch, by Bethelem into the More ditch, to be new cast and cleansed, by meanes whereof the sayde Fenne or More was greatly dreyned and dryed: but shortly after, to wit in 1477, *Raph Ioceline* Mayor, for repayring the Wall of the Cittie, caused the sayde More to bee searched for Clay and Bricke to bee brente there, &c. by which meanes this fielde was made the worse for a long time.

Page 430

Fensbery fields & More-fieldes an vnprofitable ground.

In the yeare 1498. all the Gardens which had continued time out of mind, without Moregate, to witte, aboute and

[1] Vocatus] Vocator *1603*

beyonde the Lordship of Finsbery, were destroyed. And of them was made a playne field for Archers to shoote in. And in the yeare 1512. *Roger Atchley* Mayor caused diuers dikes to be cast, and made to drein the waters of the sayde More fields, with bridges arched ouer them, and the groundes about to bee leuelled, whereby the sayd fielde was made somewhat more commodious, but yet it stoode full of noysome waters: Whereupon in the yeare 1527. sir *Thomas Semor* Mayor caused diuers sluces to be made, to conuey the sayd waters ouer the Towne ditch, into the course of Walbrooke, and so into the Thames: and by these degrees was this Fenne or More at length made main and hard ground, which before being ouergrowne with Flagges, sedges and rushes, serued to no vse, since the which time, also the further groundes beyonde Fensbury Court haue been so ouerheightned with Laystalles of dung, that now three windmilles are thereon set: the ditches be filled vp, and the bridges ouerwhelmed. |

Gardens without Moregate, destroyed and made plaine ground.

Ditches east to dreine the Morefield.

Slewces to conuey the standing water out of the More.

Morefield raysed, and wind mils set thereon.

And now concerning the inclosures of common grounds about this cittie, whereof I mind not much to argue, *Edwarde Hall* setteth downe a note of his time, to wit in the fift or sixte of *Henry* the eight: before this time sayth hee, the inhabitantes of the Townes aboute London, as Iseldone, Hoxton, Shorsditch and others, had so inclosed the common fieldes with hedges, and ditches, that neyther the yong men of the City might shoote, nor the auncient persons walke for theyr pleasures in those fieldes, but that either their bowes and arrowes were taken away or broken, or the honest persons arrested or indighted: saying, that no Londoner ought to goe out of the City, but in the high Waies. This saying so grieued the Londoners, that suddainlie this yeare a great number of the Citie assembled themselues in a morning, and a Turner in a fooles coate came crying through the Citty, shouelles and spades, shouelles and spades: so many of the people followed, that it was a wonder to behold, and within a short space all the hedges about the City were cast down, and the diches filled vp, and euery thing made plaine, such was the diligence of these workmen: the kinges councell hearing of this assembly came to the gray Fryers, & sent for the Mayor and councell of the city to know the cause, which declared to

Page 431

Edward Hall.

Hedges pulled downe and ditches filled vp.

them the iniurie and annoying done to the citizens, and to their liberties, which though they wold not seeke disorderly to redresse, yet the comminalty & yong persons could not be stayed thus to remedy the same. When the kings councell had heard their answere, they dissimuled the mater & commanded the Mayor to see that no other thing were attempted, but that they should forthwith call home the yonger sort: who hauing speedily atchieued their desire, returned home before the Kings Councell, and the Mayor departed without more harme: after which time (sayeth *Hall*) these fieldes were neuer hedged: but now wee see the thing in worse case than euer, by meanes of inclosure for Gardens, wherein are builded many fayre summer houses, and as in other places of the Suburbes, some of them like Midsommer Pageantes, with Towers, Turrets, and Chimney tops, not so much for vse or profite, as for shewe and pleasure, bewraying the vanity of mens mindes, much vnlike to the disposition of the ancient Cittizens, who delighted in | the building of Hospitals, and Almes houses for the poore, and therein both imployed their wits, and spent their wealthes in preferment of the common commoditie of this our Citie.

Banqueting houses like Banqueroutes bearing great shew and little worth.

Page 432

Suburbe without Criplegate.

But to come backe againe to Moregate, and from thence west through a narrow lane called the Posterne, because it hath at eyther end a doore to be shut in the night season, betwixt the More ditch inclosed with bricke for Tenter yardes, and the Gardens of the sayd More fielde, to More lane, a part of the Suburbe without Creplesgate: without this Posterne called Cripplesgate also lay a part of the sayde More euen to the Riuer of the Wels, as in another place I haue shewed, and no houses were there builded till the latter end of the raigne of *William* the Conqueror, and of his sonne *William Rufus*: about which times some fewe houses being there builded along East and West, thwart before the said gate, one *Alfune* builded for the inhabitants a Parish Church, which is of Saint *Giles*, somewhat west from the sayde gate, and is now on the banke of the towne ditch, and so was there a street since called Forestreet, as standing before the gate.

Parish church of S. Giles.

This *Alfune*, in the raigne of *Henrie* the first, became the first Hospitaler of S. *Bartlemewes* Hospitall in Smithfield, as in an other place I haue noted. And this Parish Church of S. *Giles* being at the first a small thing, stood in place where now standeth the Vicarage house: but hath beene since at diuerse times much enlarged, according as the Parish hath increased, and was at the length newly builded in place where now it standeth. But the same new church being large, strongly builded, and richly furnished with ornaments, was in the yeare 1545. by casualtie of fire sore burnt and consumed, notwithstanding it was againe within a short space of time repayred, as now it sheweth.

Some little distance from the east end of this Church, standeth a fayre Conduit castellated in Forestreet. Then had yee a Bosse of sweet water in the wall of the churchyard, lately made a pompe, but already decayed.

Then had yee a fayre Poole of sweete water neare to the Church of saint *Giles*, wherein *Anne of Lodbery* was drowned, as I haue before declared.

In the East ende of Forestreete is More lane: then next is | *Page 433* Grubstreete, of late yeares inhabited for the most part by Bowyers, Fletchers, Bowstring makers, and such like, now little occupied, Archerie giuing place to a number of bowling Allies, and Dicing houses, which in al places are increased, and too much frequented. Grubstreet.

This street stretcheth North to Euerades Well street, which thwarteth it to White Crosse streete. The next from Forestreete North is White Crosse street, likewise extending it selfe vp to the West ende of Euerades Well streete, and from the end thereof to Ealdstreete. Euerades Well streete.

From the west end of Forestreete lyeth Red crosse street, from the which Crosse on the right hand East lyeth Beech lane, and reacheth to the White crosse streete. From Red Crosse north lyeth Golding lane, which stretcheth vp to a Crosse in Ealdestreet, which Golding lane on both the sides is replenished with many tenements of poore people. Golding lane.

On the left hand and west of the Red Crosse lyeth a streete of old time called Houndes ditch, and of later time named Barbican, of such cause as I haue before noted. And thus haue you all the Suburbe without Creplegate, being almost altogither in the Parish of S. *Giles*, which hath more then 1800. Householders, and aboue 4000. Communicants.

Suburbe without Aldersgate.

Without Aldersgate on the left hand is the Parish Church of S. *Buttolph*, on the North side of the which church lyeth a way called little Britane streete, towardes the Priorie of Saint *Bartholomew* in Smithfield, but the high way without Aldersgate runneth straight North from the said gate vnto Houndes ditch or Barbican streete on the right hand, and Long lane on the left hand which runneth into Smithfield.

Then from the farther ende of Aldersgate streete, straight North to the Barre, is called Goswell street, replenished with smal tenements, cottages, and Allies, Gardens, banquetting houses, and bowling places.

Ealdstreete.

Page 434

Beyond these bars, leauing the Charterhouse on the left hand or the west side, the way stretcheth vp towards Iseldon, and on the right hand, or East side, at a Red Crosse turneth into Ealdstreete, so called, for that it was the old high way from Aldersgate streete | for the Northeast parts of England before Bishopsgate was builded, which streete runneth East to a Smithes Forge, sometime a Crosse before Shoreditch Church, from whence the passengers and Carriages were to turne North to Kings land, Tottenham, Waltham, Ware, &c.

Hospital without Aldersgate.

There was sometime in this suburbe without Aldersgate an Hospitall for the poore, but an Alien of Clunie, a French order, and therefore suppressed by king *Henrie* the fift, who gaue the house with lands and goods to the parish of saint *Buttolph*, and a brotherhoode of the Trinitie was there founded, which was afterwards suppressed by *Henry* the 8. or *Edward* the sixt.

The Mount.

There is at the farthest north corner of this Suburbe a windmill which was sometime by a Tempest of winde ouerthrowne, and in place thereof a Chappell was builded by Queene *Katherine* (first wife of *Henrie* the eight,) who named it the Mount of Caluerie, because it was of Christs passion, and was in the end of *Henry* the eight pulled downe, and a Windmill newly set vp as afore.

Suburbe without Newgate.

Without Newgat lyeth the West and by North Suburbe, on the right hand or Northside whereof betwixt the said gate, and the Parish of saint *Sepulchre* turneth a way towards west

Smith field, called as I haue shewed Giltspurre streete, or Knightriders street, then is Smithfield it selfe, compassed about with buildings as I haue before declared in Faringdon ward without.

And without the barre of West Smithfield lyeth a large street or way, called of the house of *S. Iohn* there, *S. Iohns* streete, and stretcheth towards Iseldon, on the right hand whereof stoode the late dissolued Monasterie, called the Charterhouse, founded by sir *Walter Manny* knight, a stranger borne, Lord of the towne of Manny in the Dioces of Cambrey, beyond the seas, who for seruice done to king *Edward* the third was made knight of the Garter. This house he founded upon this occasion. A great Pestilence entring this Iland, began first in Dorsetshire, then proceeded into Deuonshire, Somerset shire, Glocester shire, and Oxforde shire, and at length came to London, and ouerspred all England, so wasting the people, that scarce the tenth person of all sortes was left aliue, and Churchyards were not sufficient to receiue the dead | but men were forced to chuse out certain fields for burials, wherevpon *Raph Stratford* Bishop of London in the yeare 1348. bought a peece of ground called *no mans land*, which he inclosed with a wall of Bricke and dedicated for buriall of the deade, builded therevpon a proper Chappell, which is now enlarged and made a dwelling house, and this burying plot is become a fayre Garden, retaining the old name of Pardon Churchyard.

S. Iohns street.

Charterhouse.

Page 435

No mans land.

Pardon church yard by the Charterhouse.

About this in the yeare 1349. the said sir *Walter Manny* in respect of daunger that might befal in this time of so great a plague and infection, purchased thirteene Acres and a rode of ground adioyning to the said *no mans land*, and lying in a place called Spittle Croft, because it belonged to S. Bartilmewes Hospitall, since that called the new Church Haw, and caused it to be consecrated by the said Bishop of London to the vse of burials.

In this plot of ground there was in that yeare more then 50000. persons buried, as I haue reade in the Charters of *Edward* the third: Also I haue seene and read an Inscription fixed on a stone Crosse, sometime standing in the same churchyard and hauing these wordes: *Anno Domini* 1349. *regnante magna pestilentia, consecratum fuit hoc Cœmiterium, in quo & infra septa presentis monasterii, sepulta fuerunt mortuorum corpora plusquam quinquaginta millia, præter alia multa abhinc vsque ad presens, quorum animabus propitietur deus Amen.* In consideration of the number of Christian people here buried, the sayd sir *Walter Manny* caused first a Chappell to be builded, where for the space of twentie three yeares offerings were made, and it is to be noted that aboue 100000. bodies of Christian people had in that Churchyard beene buried, for the

Charterhouse churchyard prepared for buriall of the poore, so to remaine for euer.

sayde knight had purchased that place for the buriall of poore people, trauailers and other that were diseased to remaine for euer, whervpon an order was taken for the auoyding of contention betweene the parsons of Churches and that house, to wit, that the bodies should be had vnto the Church where they

Bull of Pope Clement.

were Parishioners, or died, and after the funerall seruice done, had to the place where they should be buried. And the yeare 1371. hee caused there to bee founded an house of Carthusian Monks, which he willed to be called the Salutation, and that

Page 436

one of the Monkes should be called | Prior, and he gaue them the saide place of thirteene Acres and a Rode of land, with the Chappell, and houses there builded for their habitation: he also gaue them the three Acres of land lying without the walles on the North part betwixt the landes of the Abbot of Westminster, and the lands of the Prior of S. *Iohn*, (which three Acres were purchased, inclosed, and dedicated by *Raph Stratford* Bishop of London, as is afore shewed,) remained till our time, by the name of Pardon Churchyard, and serued for burying of such as desperately ended their liues, or were

Vse of the Fraerie Cart.

executed for Felonies, who were fetched thither vsually in a close cart, bayled ouer and couered with blacke, hauing a plaine white Crosse thwarting, and at the fore end a Saint *Iohns* Crosse without, and within a Bell ringing by shaking of the cart, whereby the same might be heard when it passed, and this was called the Fraerie Cart, which belonged to Saint *Iohns*, and had the priuiledge of Sanctuarie. In this Charter house were the Monuments of the sayd sir *Waltar Manny*, & *Margaret* his wife, *Marmaduke Lumley*, *Laurence Brumley* knight, sir *Edward Hederset* knight, sir *William Manny* knight, Dame *Iahan Borough*, *Iohn Dorewentwatar* knight[1], *Robert*

[1] Dore, Want Water] *1598, 1603*

Olney Esquire, *Katherine* daughter to sir *William Babington* knight, *Blanch* daughter to *Hugh Waterton*, *Katherine* wife to *Iohn* at *Poole*, daughter and heyre to *Richard de Lacie*, *William Rawlin*, sir *Iohn Lenthaine*, and Dame *Margaret* his wife, daughter to *Iohn Fray*, *Iohn Peake* Esquire, *William Baron*, and *William Baron* Esquire, sir *Thomas Thwaites* knight, *Philip Morgan* Bishop of Ely, 1434.

In the Cloystrie, *Bartholomew Rede* knight, Maior of London, buried 1505. sir *Iohn Popham*, &c.

This Monasterie at the suppression in the 29. of *Henrie* the 8. was valued at 642.l. 4.d. halfepenny yearely.

A little without the Barres of west Smithfield is Charter-house lane, so called, for that ⟨it⟩ leadeth to the sayd plot of the late dissolued Monasterie, in place whereof, first the Lord *North*, but since *Thomas Howarde* late Duke of Norffolke, haue made large and sumptuous buildinges, both for lodging and pleasure. At the gate of this Charter house is a faire water Conduit, with | two cockes seruing the vse of the neighbours to their great commoditie.

Charter house lane.

Conduit by the Charter-house.

Page 437

Saint Iohns streete from the entring this lane is also on both the sides replenished with buildinges vp to Clarken Well. On the left hand of which street lyeth a lane called Cow crosse, of a crosse sometime standing there, which lane turneth downe to another lane called Turnemill streete, which stretcheth vp to the West side of Clarken Well, and was called Turnemill streete for such cause as is afore declared.

Cow Crosse.

One other lane there is called S. *Peters* lane, which turneth from saint *Iohns* streete to Cow crosse.

On the left hand also stoode the late dissolued Priorie of saint *Iohn* of Ierusalem in England, founded about the yeare of Christ 1100. by *Iorden Briset* Baron, and *Muriell* his wife, neare vnto Clarkes well besides west Smithfield, which *Iorden*[1] hauing first founded the Priorie of Nunes at Clarks well bought of them ten Acres of land, giuing them in exchange ten Acres of land in his Lordship of Welling hall in the Countie of Kent, saint *Iohns* Church was dedicated by *Eraclius* Patriarke of the holy resurrection of Christ at Ierusalem, in

Priorie of S. Iohn of Ierusalem.

[1] Brian] *1603*

the yeare 1185. and was the chiefe seate in England of the religious knights of *S. Iohn* of Ierusalem, whose profession was, besides their dayly seruice of God, to defende Christians agaynst Pagans, and to fight for the Church, vsing for their habite a blacke vpper garment, with a white Crosse on the fore part thereof, and for their good seruice was so highly esteemed, that when the order of Templars was dissolued, their lands and possessions were by parliament graunted vnto these, who after the losse of Ierusalem recouered the Isle of Rodes from the Turke, and there placed themselues, beeing called thereof for many yeares knights of the Rhodes, but after the losse thereof, 1523. they remooued to the Isle of Malta, manfully opposing themselues agaynst the turkish inuasions.

The Rebels of Essex and of Kent, 1381, set fire on this house, causing it to burne by the space of seauen dayes togither, not suffering any to quench it, since the which time the Priors of that house haue newe builded both the Church and houses therevnto appertaining, which church was finished

Page 438 by *Thomas Doc|wrey* late Lord Prior there, about the yeare 1504, as appeareth by the inscription ouer the gate house, yet remayning. This house at the suppression in the 32. of *H.* the 8. was valued to dispend in lands 3385.li. 19.s. 8.d. yearely, sir *W. Weston* being then Lord Prior, dyed on the same seuenth of May, on which the house was suppressed, so that great yearely pensions being granted to the knights by the king, and namely to the Lord Prior during his life 1000.li. hee neuer receiued penny.

The king tooke into his hands all the lands that belonged to that house and that order wheresoeuer in England and Ireland, for the augmentation of his Crowne.

This Priory church and house of saint *Iohn* was preserued from spoyle, or downe pulling so long as king *Henry* the eight raigned, and was imployed as a storehouse for the kings toyles and tents, for hunting, and for the warres, &c. but in the third of king *Edward* the sixt, the Church for the most part, to wit, the body and side Iles with the great Bell Tower, (a most curious peece of workemanshippe, grauen, guilt, and inameled to the great beautifying of the Cittie, and passing all other that I haue seene) was vndermined and blowne up with Gunpowder, the stone thereof was imployed in building of the Lord Protectors house at the Strand: that part of the Quire which remayneth, with some side Chappels, was by Cardinall *Poole* in the raigne of Queene *Mary*, closed vp at the west end, and otherwise repaired, and sir *Thomas Tresham* knight was then made Lord Prior there, with restitution of some lands, but the same was againe suppressed in the first yeare of Queene *Elizabeth.*

There was buried in this Church, brethren of that house, and knights of that order. *Iohn Botell*, *William Bagecore*, *Richard Barrow*, *Iohn Vanclay*, *Thomas Launcelen*, *Iohn Mallory*, *William Turney*, *William Hulles,—Hils* or *Hayles*, *Iohn Weston*, *Redington*, *William Longstrother*, *Iohn Langstrother*, *William Tong*, *Iohn Wakeline*. Then of other: *Thomas Thornburgh* Gentleman, *William West*, Gentleman, *Iohn Fulling*, and *Adam Gill* Esquiers, sir *Iohn Mortimor*, and Dame *Elianor* his wife, *Nicholas Siluerston*, *William Plompton* Esquier, *Margaret Tong*, and *Isabel Tong*, *Walter Bellingham alias* | *Ireland*, king of Armes of Ireland, *Thomas* *Page 439* *Bedle* Gentleman, *Katheren* daughter of *William Plompton* Esquier, *Richard Turpin* Gentleman, *Iohan* wife to *Alexander Dikes*, *Iohn Bottle* and *Richard Bottle* Esquiers, *Rowland Darcie*, *Richard Sutton* Gentleman, *Richard Bottill* Gent. Sir *W. Harpden* knight, *Robert Kingston* Esquier, and *Margery* his wife, *Iohn Roch*, *Richard Cednor* Gentleman, *Simon Mallory* 1442. *William Mallory*, *Robert Longstrother*, *Ralph Asteley*, *William Marshall*, *Robert Sauage*, *Robert Gondall* Esquiers, and *Margery* his wife, *William Bapthorpe* Baron of the Exchequer, 1442.

Priory of Clerken well.

North from the house of S. *Iohns*, was the Priory of Clarken well, so called of Clarkes well adioyning, which Priory was also founded about the yeare 1100. by *Iorden Briset* Baron, the sonne of *Ralph*, the sonne of *Brian Briset*: who gaue to *Robert* a Priest, fourteene Acres of land lying in the field next adioyning to the said Clarkes well, thereupon to build an house of religious persons, which he founded to the honour of God, and the Assumption of our Lady, and placed therein blacke Nuns. This *Iorden Briset* gaue also to that house one peece of ground thereby, to build a wind mill vpon, &c. He and *Muriell* his wife were buried in the Chapter house there: more buried in this Church, *Iohn Wikes* Esquier, and *Isabell* his wife, Dame *Agnes Clifford*, *Ralph Timbleby*, Esquier, Dame *Iohan* Baronnesse of *Greystocke*, Dame *Iohan*, Lady *Ferrars*. And of later time in the parish Church, *Constances*[1] *Bennet*, a Greeke borne, he gaue two houses, the one in saint *Iohns* streete, the other in Turnmill street, the rents of them to be distributed in Coales euery yeare against Christmas, to the poore of that parish.

William Herne, a Maister of defence, and yeoman of the gard, 1580. gaue lands and tenements to the Clothworkers in London, they to pay yearely for euer, fourteene pound to the Churchwardens of Clarken well, and fourteene pound to the Churchwardens of *S. Sepulchers*, towards reparations of these Churches, & reliefe of the poore men, more, he gaue after the death of one man, yet liuing, eight li. the yeare for euer, to the mending of high wayes.

Page 440

Thomas Sackeford Esquier, one of the masters of requests, gaue | to the poore of that parish 40. shillings the yeare for euer, out of his Almes house at Woodbridge in Suffolke, where he is buried. *Henry Stoke*, Gardiner, buried there, gaue 20.s. the yeare for euer, towards reparation of that church. This Priory was valued to dispend 262.li. 9.s. by yeare, and was surrendred the 30. of *H.* the 8. Many faire houses are now builded about the Priory, namely by the high way towards Iseldon.

So much of the Church which remaineth, (for one great Ile thereof fell downe) serueth as a parish Church of Saint *Iohn*, not onely for the Tenementes, and neare inhabitantes, but also (as is afore sayde) for all vp to Highgate, Moswell &c.

Neare vnto this Church besides Clarkes well lane, diuers other welles, namely Skinners well, Fags well, Tode[2] well, Loders well, Rede well &c. now dammed vp.

Now to returne agayne to Giltspurre street, where I first began with this Suburbe, there standeth the Parrish Church of Saint *Sepulchre* in the Bayly, as is before shewed, from this streete to Turnagaine lane by Hosiar lane, Cow lane & Holdborn Conduite downe Snore hill to Oldborne bridge,

[1] *Constantius 1633* [2] Gode *1603*

and vp Oldborne hill, by Gold lane on the right hand, and Lither lane beyond it, to the Barres, beyond the which Barres on the same side, is *Porte Poole*, or Grayes Inne lane, so called of the Inne of Courte, named Grayes Inne, a goodly house there scituate, by whome builded or first begun I haue not yet learned, but seemeth to be since *Edward* the thirds time, and is a prebend to *Paules* Church in London.

Portpoole, in Greyes Inne lane, Greyes Inne an Inne of Court.

This lane is furnished with faire buildings, and many tenements on both the sides, leading to the fieldes, towards Highgate and Hamsted.

On the high streete haue ye many fayre houses builded, and lodgings for Gentlemen, Innes for trauellers, and such like vp almost (for it lacketh but little) to saint *Giles* in the fieldes: amongst the which buildinges for the most part being very new, one passeth the rest in largenesse of roomes, lately builded by a Widdow sometime wife to *Richard Alington* Esquier, which *Richard Alington* deceased in the yeare 1561. And thus much for that north side of Oldborne. |

Widow Alington her building.

Page 441

Now from Newgate on the left hand or south side lyeth the old Bayly, and so downe by Seacole lane end to Oldborne bridge, vp Oldborne hill, by Shooe lane and Fewters lane to the barres.

South side of Oldborne.

Beyond the barres had ye in old time a Temple builded by the Templars, whose order first began in the yeare of Christ 1118. in the 19. of *Henry* the first. This Temple was left and fell to ruine since the yeare 1184. when the Templars had builded them a new Temple in Fleet streete, neare to the Riuer of Thames. A great part of this old Temple was pulled downe but of late in the yeare 1595. Adioyning to this old Temple, was sometime the Bishop of Lincolnes Inne, wherein he lodged when he repayred to this City. *Robert de Curars*[1] Bishop of Lincolne, builded it about the yeare 1147. *Iohn Russell* Bishop of Lincolne, Chauncellor of England in the raigne of *Richard* the third, was lodged there. It hath of late yeares belonged to the Earles of Southampton, and therefore called Southampton house. *Master Ropar* hath of late builded much there, by meanes whereof part of the ruines of the old Temple were seene to remaine builded of Cane stone,

Old Temple.

The Bishop of Lincolns Inne.

Southampton house.

Curars: Robert de Chesney, cons. 1148

round in forme as the new Temple by Temple barre and other Temples in England. Beyond this old Temple, and the Bishoppe of Lincolnes house, is New streete, so called in the raigne of *H.* the 3. when he of a Iewes house founded the house of Conuerts, betwixt the old Temple and the new.

New streete.

The same street hath sithence beene called Chauncery lane, by reason that king *E.* the 3. annexed the house of Conuerts by patent to the office of *Custos Rotulorum*, or maister of the Rolles, in the 51. of his raigne.

New streete or Chancery lane.

In this streete the first faire building to be noted on the east side, is called the Coursitors office, builded with diuers fayre lodgings for Gentlemen, all of Bricke and timber, by sir *Nicholas Bacon* late Lord keeper of the great Seale.

Coursitors office in Chancery lane.

Neare vnto this Coursitors office, be diuers faire houses & large gardens, builded and made in a ground, sometime belonging to one great house on the other side the street, there made by *Ralph Neuel* Bishop of Chichester. This ground he had by the gift of *H.* the 3. as appeareth. *The king granteth to Ralph Bishop of Chichester Chancellor, that place with the Garden which Iohn Herlison* | *forfeyted in that street, called Newstreete, ouer against the land of the sayde Bishoppe in the same streete, which place with the garden and appurtenance was the kinges exchete by the libertie of the cittie of London, as it was acknowledged before the king in his court at the tower of London, in the last pleas of the crown of that Cittie, cart.* 11. *H.* 3.

Page 442

Then was the house of conuertes, wherein now the Rowles of Chancery be kept. Then the Sergeants Inne, &c.

On the West side of Newstreete, towardes the North ende thereof, was of olde time the church, and house of the Preaching Friers: the which house I finde that in the yeare of Christ, 1221. the Friers Preachers 13. in number came into England, and hauing to their Prior one named *Gilbert de Fraxineto* in company of *Peter de la Roche* Bishoppe of Winchester, came to Canterbury, where presenting themselves before the Archbishop *Steuen* ⟨*Langton*⟩, hee commaunded the sayde Prior to preach, whose sermon he liked so well, that euer after hee loued that order. These Fryers came to

Black fryers Church in Oldborne.

London, and had their first house without the Wall of the Cittie by Oldborne, neare vnto the old Temple.

Hubert de Burgo Earle of Kent was a great benefactor vnto these Fryers, and deceasing at his Mannor of Bansted in Surrey, or after some writers, at his Castle of Barkamsted in Hartfordshire, in the yeare 1242. was buried in their Church, vnto the which church he had giuen his place at Westminster, which the sayde Fryers afterward solde to *Walter Grey* Archbishop of Yorke, and he left it to his successors in that sea, for euer to be their house when they should repaire to the Cittie of London. And therefore the same was called Yorke place, which name so continued vntill the yeare 1529. that king *Henry* the eight tooke it from *Thomas Wolsey* Cardinall and Archbishop of Yorke, and then gaue it to name White hall.

Earle of Kent buried in the Blacke Fryers.

Margaret sister to the King of Scottes, Widdowe to *Gilbert*[1] Earle Marshall, deceased 1244. and was buried in this church.

In the yeare 1250. the Fryers of this order of preachers thorough Christendome and from Ierusalem, were by a conuocation assembled together, at this their house by Oldborne, to entreat | of their estate, to the number of 400. hauing meat and drink found them of almes, because they had no possessions of their owne. The first day the king came to their Chapter, found them meate and drinke, and dined with them. An other day the Queene founde them meate and drinke: afterward the Bishop of London, then the Abbot of Westminster, of S. Albons, Waltham, and others. In the yeare 1276. *Gregory Rokesley* Mayor and the Barons of London graunted and gaue to *Robert Kilwerbie* Archbishop of Canterbury, two lanes or wayes next the street of Baynards Castle, and the Tower of Mountfichet to be destroyed. On the which place the sayde *Robert* builded the late new church, with the rest of the stones that were left of the sayde Tower. And thus the blacke Fryers left their church and house by Oldborne, and departed to their new. This olde Fryer house, (*iuxta* Holborne sayeth the Patent) was by king *Edwarde* the first, in the 16. of his raigne, giuen to *Henry Lacy* Earle of Lincolne.

Conuocations of Black Fryers in Oldborn.

Page 443

[1] Gilbert] Geffrey *1603*

Bishop of Chichesters Inne.

Next to this house of Fryers, was one other great House, sometime belonging to the Bishop of Chichester, whereof *Mathew Paris* writeth thus: *Raph de noua villa*, or *Neuill, Bishop of Chichester and Chauncellor of England, sometime builded a noble house, euen from the grounde, not farre from the newe Temple and house of Conuertes, in the which place hee deceased in the yeare* 1244.

Lincolns Inne.

In this place after the decease of the sayde Bishoppe, and in place of the house of Blacke Fryers, before spoken of, *Henry Lacy* Earle of Lincolne, Constable of Chester, and Custos of England, builded his Inne, and for the most parte was lodged there: hee deceased in this house in the yeare 1310. and was buried in the new worke, (whervnto he had beene a great benefactor) of saint Pauls church, betwixt our Lady chappell and saint Dunstones Chappell. This Lincolnes Inne sometime pertayning to the Bishops of Chichester, as a part of the sayde great house, is now an Inne of Court, retayning the name of Lincolnes Inne as afore, but now lately encreased with fayre buildinges, and replenished with Gentlemen studious in the common lawes. In the raigne of *H.* the 8. sir *Thomas Louell* was a great builder there, especially he builded the gate house and forefront towardes the east, placing thereon aswell the *Lacies* | armes as his owne: hee caused the *Lacies* armes to bee cast and wrought in leade, on the louer of the hall of that house, which was in the 3. Escutcheons a Lyon rampart for *Lacie*, 7. Mascules voyded for Quincie, and 3. Wheat sheaues for Chester. This Louer being of late repayred the sayde Escutcheons were left out. The rest of that side euen to Fleetstreete is replenished with fayre buildings.

Page 444

Lincolns Inne an Inne of Court.

Hospitall of S. Giles founded.

Now the high Oldborne street, from the north end of Newstreet, stretcheth on the left hand in building lately framed, vp to S. Giles in the field, which was an Hospitall founded by *Matilda* the Queene, wife to *Henry* the first, about the yeare 1117. This Hospitall, sayeth the record of *Edward* the third, the 19. yeare, was founded without the barre *veteris Templi London & conuersorum*.

This Hospitall was founded, as a sell to *Burton Lager* of Ierusalem, as may appeare by a deed dated the 24. of *H.* the 7. in these wordes: *Thomas Norton knight, Mayster of*

Burton Lager of Ierusalem in England, and the Bretheren of the same place, keepers of the Hospitall of saint Giles without the barres of the olde Temple of London, haue solde to Geffrey Kent Cittizen & Draper of London a messuage or house with two sollars[1] *aboue edified in the parrish of Alhallowes Hony lane in west Chepe, adioyning to the west part of a tenement called the Gote on the Hope, pertayning to the Drapers of London, for xxx.li.*

Burton Lagar an Hospitall in Leycester-shire.

At this Hospitall, the prisoners conuayed from the City of London towardes Teyborne, there to be executed for treasons, fellonies, or other trespasses, were presented with a great Bowle of Ale, thereof to drinke at theyr pleasure, as to be theyr last refreshing in this life.

S. Giles bowle.

Now without Ludgate lyeth the south end of the olde Bayly, then down Ludgate hill by Fleet lane, ouer Fleet bridge, vp Fleetestreete by Shooe lane, Fewtars lane, Newstreet or Chauncerie lane, and to Shire lane by the Barre on the right hand. And from Ludgate on the left hand or south side by Bride lane, Water lane, Crokers lane, Sergeants Inne, and the new Temple by the barre: all which is of Faringdon Ward as is afore shewed. |

Suburbe without Ludgate.

Liberties of the Dutchie of Lancaster

Page 445

NEXT without the Barre, the new temple, and Liberties of the Citty of London, in the Suburbes, is a libertie pertayning to the Dutchie of Lancaster, which beginneth in the east, on the south side or left hand by the riuer Thames, and stretcheth west to Iuie bridge where it endeth, and againe on the north side or right hand, some small distance without Temple barre in the high streete from a payre of stockes there standing, stretcheth one large middle row or troupe of small tenementes, partly opening to the south, partly towardes the north, vp west to a stone crosse, now headles, ouer against the Strand, and this is the boundes of that libertie, which sometime belonged to *Briane Lisle*, since to *Peter* of Sauoy, and then to the house of Lancaster, as shall be shewed: *Henry* the third in the 30. yeare of his raigne did graunt to his vnckle *Peter* of Sauoy all those houses vpon the Thames, which sometimes pertayned to *Briane de Insula*, or *Lisle*, without the Walles

Liberties of the Dutchie without temple barre, the bounds thereof.

[1] sollars] *1633*; sellars *1603*

Strand street Rotum cartar. Petri de Sabaud.

of his Cittie of London, in the way or streete called the Strand, to hold to him and to his heyres, yeelding yearely in the Exchequer at the feast of S. *Michaell* Tharchangell, three barbed arrowes for all seruices. Dated at Reding, &c. This *Peter* of Sauoy builded the Sauoy.

Monuments of Strand street. Excester house since Paget house, Lester house, and Essex house.

But first amongst other buildinges memorable for greatnes on the riuer of Thames, Excester house, so called for that the same belonged to the Bishoppes of Excester, and was their Inne or London lodging: who was first builder thereof I haue not read, but that *Walter Stapleton* was a greate Builder there in the raigne of *Edward* the second is manifest, for the Cittizens of London when they had beheaded him in Cheape neare vnto the cathedrall Church of S. *Paule*, they buried him in a heape of Sand or rubbish in his owne house without Temple barre, where | he had made great building. *Edmond Lacie* Bishoppe of Excester builded the great hall in the raigne of *Henry* the 6, &c. The same hath since beene called *Paget* house, because *William* Lord *Paget* enlarged and possessed it. Then *Leycester* house, because *Robert Dudley* Earle of Leycester of late new builded there, & now *Essex* house of the Earle of Essex lodging there.

Page 446

Chaple of the Holy Ghost.

Then west was a Chapple dedicated to the Holy Ghost, called saint Spirite, vppon what occasion founded I haue not read.

Milford lane.

Next is Milford lane downe to the Thames, but why so called I haue not read as yet.

Bishoppe of Bathes Inne, or Arundell house.

Then was the Bishop of *Bathes* Inne, lately new builded, for a great part thereof, by the Lord *Thomas Seamer* Admirall, which house came sithens to bee possessed by the Earle of Arundel, and thereof called Arundell house.

Parrish church of S. Mary at the Strand.

Next beyond the which on the street side was somtime a faire cemitorie or churchyeard, and in the same a parrish Church called of the Natiuity of our Lady and the Innocents of the Strand, & of some by meane of a Brotherhood kept there, called of S. *Vrsula* at the Strand.

Chesters Inne, or Strand Inne, an Inne of Chancery.

And neare adioyning to the sayd church betwixt it and the riuer of Thames, was an Inne of Chancery commonly called Chesters Inne, (because it belonged to the Bishop of *Chester*,) by others named of the scituation *Strand Inne*.

Then was there an house belonging to the Bishop of *Landaffe*, for I find in record the 4. of *Edwarde* the 2. that a vacant place lying neare the church of our Lady at Strand, the sayde Bishop procured it of *Thomas* Earle of *Lancaster* for the enlarging of this house.

The Bishop of Landalph his Inne.

Then had yee in the high streete a fayre bridge called Strand bridge, and vnder it a lane or way down to the landing place on the banke of Thames.

Strand bridge.

Then was the Bishoppe of *Chester* (commonly called of *Lichfield* and *Couentrie*) his Inne or London lodging : this house was first builded by *Walter Langton* Bishoppe of Chester, treasurer of England in the raigne of *Edward* the first.

Bishop of Chester his Inne.

And next vnto it adioyning was the Bishop of *Worcesters* | Inne : all which, to wit the parrish of Saint Mary at Strande, Strand Inne, Strand Bridge with the lane vnder it, the Bishop of Chesters Inne, the Bishoppe of Worcesters Inne, with all the tenementes adioyning, were by commandement of *Edward* Duke of Sommerset vncle to *Edward* the sixt, and Lord Protector pulled downe, and made leuell ground, in the yeare 1549. In place whereof he builded that large and goodly house, now called Somerset house.

Page 447

Somerset-house.

In the high street neare vnto the Strande, sometime stoode a crosse of stone against the Bishoppe of Couentrie or Chester his house, whereof I read that in the yeare 1294. and diuers other times, the Iustices Itenerantes sate without London, at the stone Crosse ouer against the Bishop of Couentries house, & somtime they sate in the Bishops house, which was hard by the strand as is afore sayd.

Stone crosse at Strand.

Then next is the Sauoy, so called of *Peter* Earle of Sauoy and Richmond, sonne to *Thomas* Earle of Sauoy, brother to *Boniface* Archbishop of Canterbury, and vncle vnto *Heleanor* wife to king *H.* the third.

Sauoyhouse, first builded by Peter earle of Sauoy and Richmond.

He first builded this house in the yeare 1245. And here is occasion offered mee, for satisfying of some Denyers thereof, to proue that this *Peter* of Sauoy was also Earle of Sauoy. Wherfore out of a booke of the Genealogies of all the whole house of Sauoy, compiled of *Phillebert Pingonio*, Baron of Suzani, remayning in the handes of *W. Smith*, *alias Rouge-dragon*, officer of Armes, I haue gathered this. *Thomas* Earle

Thomas Earle of Sauoy his pedegree by occasion.

of Sauoy had issue by *Beatrix*, daughter to *Aimon* Earle of Geneva, 9. sons & 3. daughters: *Amadis* his first son succeeded Earle of Sauoy in the yeare 1253. *Peter* his second son, Earle of Sauoy & of Richmond, in 1268. *Philip* his third sonne, Earle of Sauoy and Burgundie, 1284. *Thomas* the 4. Earle of Flaunders and prince of Piemont, *Boniface* the eight, Archbishop of Canterbury, *Beatrix* his daughter maried to *Reymond Beringarius* of Aragon, Earle of Prouince and Narbone, had issue & was mother to fiue Queenes: The first, *Margaret*, wife to *Lewes* king of Fraunce, 2. *Elianor* wife to *Henry* the 3. king of England, 3. *Sanctia*, wife to *Richard* king of Romaines, 4. *Beatrix* wife to *Charles* | king of Naples, 5. *Iohanna* wife to *Philip* king of Nauarre.

Beatrix sister to Peter earle of Sauoy, mother to five Queenes.

Page 448

Fratres de monte Iouis or priory de Cornuto by Hauering at the Bowre.

To return again to the house of Sauoy, Queene *Eleanor*, wife to king *Henry* the third, purchased this place afterwards of the Fraternitie or Brethren of Montioy, vnto whome *Peter* of Sauoy, as it seemeth, had giuen it, for her sonne *Edmonde* Earle of Lancaster, (as M. *Camden* hath noted out of a Register booke of the Dukes of Lancaster). *Henry* Duke of Lancaster repayred or rather new builded it with the charges of 52,0CO. Markes, which money he had gathered together at the Town of Bridgerike.[1]

H. Knighton.

Iohn the French king was lodged there, in the yeare 1357. and also in the yeare 1363. for it was at that time the fayrest Mannor in England.

H. Knighton.

Sauoy brent, blown vp with Gunpowder. Rebels, more malitious then couetous, spoyle all before them.

In the yeare 1381. the rebelles of Kent and Essex burnt this house, vnto the which there was none in the realme to bee compared in beauty and statelines, (sayth mine Author). They set fire on it round about, and made proclamation that none, on payne to loose his head, should conuert to his own vse any thing that there was, but that they should breake such plate and vessell of Gold and siluer as was founde in that house (which was in great plentie) into small peeces, and throw the same into the riuer of Thames: Precious stones they should bruse in mortars, that the same might bee to no vse, and so it was done by them: One of their companions they burned in the fire, because he minded to haue reserued one goodly peece of plate.

[1] Bergerac

They found there certaine barrels of Gunpowder, which they thought had beene golde or siluer, and throwing them into the fire, more suddenly then they thought, the Hall was blowne vppe, the houses destroyed, and themselues very hardly escaped away.

Liber manuscript. French.

This house being thus defaced, and almost ouerthrown by these rebelles for malice they bare to *Iohn of Gaunt* Duke of Lancaster, of latter time came to the kings hands, and was again raysed and beautifully builded, for an Hospitall of *S. Iohn Baptist*, by king *Henry* the seuenth, about the yeare 1509. for the which Hospitall, retayning still the old name of Sauoy, he purchased lands to be imployed vpon the releeuing of an hundred poor people. This | Hospitall being valued to dispend 529 pound, fifteene shillings, &c. by yeare, was suppressed the tenth of Iune, the seuenth of *Edward* the sixt, the beddes, bedding and other furniture belonging thereunto with seuen hundred markes of the said landes by yeare, hee gaue to the Cittizens of London, with his house of Bridewell, to the furnishing thereof to be a workehouse for the poore and idle persons, and towards the furnishing of the Hospital of S. *Thomas* in Southwarke lately suppressed.

Sauoy builded for an hospital.

Page 449

Hospitall of Savoy suppressed.

This Hospitall of Sauoy was againe new founded, erected, corporated and endowed with landes by Queene *Mary*, the thirde of Nouember: in the fourth of her raigne one *Iackson* tooke possession, and was made maister thereof in the same moneth of Nouember. The Ladies of the Court, and Maydens of honour (a thing not to be forgotten) stored the same of new with beddes, bedding and other furniture, in very ample manner, &c. and it was by patent so confirmed at Westminster, the 9. of May, the 4. and 5. of *Philip* and *Mary*.

Hospitall of Sauoy: a new foundation thereof.

The Chappell of this Hospitall serueth now as a Parish church to the Tenements thereof neare adioyning and others.

Parrish church of S. Iohn in the Sauoy.

The next was sometime the Bishoppe of *Carliles* Inne, which now belongeth to the Earle of Bedford, and is called Russell or Bedford house. It stretcheth from the Hospitall of Sauoy, west to Iuie bridge, where sir *Robert Cecill*, principall Secretary to her Maiestie, hath lately raysed a large and stately house of brick and timber, as also leuiled and paued the high way neare adioining, to the great beautifying of that

Bishop of Carlile his Inne, or Bedford house.

street, and commoditie of passengers. *Richard* the 2. in the 8. of his raigne, granted licence to paue with stone the high way called Strand street from Temple barre to the Sauoy, and tole to be taken towards the charges, and again the like was granted in the 24. of *H.* the 6.

Iuie bridge in the high street which had a way vnder it, leading downe to the Thames, the like as somtime had the Strand bridge, is now taken downe, but the lane remayneth as afore, or better, & parteth the Liberty of the Dutchie, and the City of Westminster on that south side.

Now to beginne againe at Temple Barre ouer against it. In the high streete as is afore shewed, is one large Middle *Page 450* Rowe of | houses and small Tenementes builded, partly opening to the South, partlie towardes the north. Amongst the which standeth the parrish Church of saint *Clement Danes*, so called because *Harolde* a Danish king and other Danes were buried there. This *Harolde* whome king *Canutus* had by a Concubine, raigned three yeares, and was buried at Westminster, but afterwarde *Hardicanutus* the lawfull sonne of *Canutus*, in revenge of a displeasure done to his mother, by expelling her out of the Realme, and the murder of his brother *Allured*, commaunded the body of *Harolde* to bee digged out of the earth, and to bee throwne into the Thames, where it was by a Fisherman taken vppe and buried in this Churchyeard: but out of a fayre leager Booke, sometime belonging to the Abbey of Chartsey, in the Countie of Surrey, is noted as in *Francis Thin*, after this sorte. *In the raigne of king Etheldred, the Monastery of Chartsey was destroyed.* 90. *Monkes of that house were slayne by the Danes, whose bodyes were buried in a place next to the Olde Monastery. William Malmseberie sayeth, they burnt the Church together with the Monkes and Abbot. But the Danes continuing in their fury (throughout the whole lande) desirous at the length to returne home into Denmarke, were by the iust iudgement of God all slayne at London in a place which is called the Church of the Danes.*

Parish church of S. Clement Danes.

Liber Chartsey.

W. Malmes.

Danes slaine at S. Clement Dane.

Headles crosse by the Strand.

This sayde middle row of houses stretching west to a Stone Crosse, now headles, by or against the Strand, including the sayd parrish Church of S. *Clement*, is also wholy of the libertie and Dutchie of Lancaster.

Thus much for the Boundes and antiquities of this libertie, wherein I haue noted Parrish Churches twaine, sometime 3. houses of name 6. to wit, the Sauoy, or Lancaster house, now an Hospitall, Somerset house, Essex house, Arundell house, Bedford or Russell house, and sir *Robert Cecils* house, besides Chesters Inne or Strand Inne, sometime an Inne of Chancerie, &c. This liberty is gouerned by the Chanceler of that Dutchie, at this present Sir *Robert Cecill* knight, principall Secretary to her Maiestie, & one of her Maiesties most honorable priuie Councellers. There is vnder him a Steward that keepeth court | and Leete for the Queene, giueth the charge and taketh the oathes of euerie vnder Officer: then is there 4. Burgesses, and 4. assistants to take vp controuersies, a Bayliffe which hath 2. or 3. vnder Bailiffes, that make arrests within that libertie, 4. Constables, 4. Wardens that keepe the lands and Stocke for the poore, 4. wardens for high wayes, a Iury or Inquest of 14. or 16. to present defaults, 4. Alecunners, which looke to Assisse of weightes & measures &c. 4. Scauengers and a Beadle, and their common Prison is Newgate. There is in this liberty 50. men which is alwayes to be at an howers warning, with all necessary furniture to serue the Queene, as occasion shall require. Their charge at a Fifteene is 13.s. 4.d. Thus much for the Suburbe in the libertie of the Dutchie of Lancaster.

Chancelor of the dutchie of Lancaster.

Page 451

The Citie of Westminster with the Antiquities, Boundes, and Liberties thereof

NOW touching the City of Westminster, I wil beginne at Temple Barre, on the right hand or North side, and so passe vppe West, through a Backe lane or streete, wherein doe stande three Innes of Chancery, the first called Clements Inne, because it standeth neare to saint Clements church, but nearer to the fayre fountaine called Clements well: the second, New Inne, so called as latelier made of a common hostery, and the signe of our Lady, an Inne of Chancery for Students, then the other, to wit about the beginning of the raigne of *Henry* the 7. and not so late as some haue supposed, to wit, at the pulling downe of

Clements Inne of Chancerie. Clements well. New Inne of Chancery.

Strand Inne, in the raigne of king *Edward* the sixt, for I read that sir *Thomas More*, sometime Lord Chancellor, was a Student in this new Inne, and went from thence to Lincolnes Inne, &c.

Lyons Inne of Chancery.
Druery lane.

The thirde is Lyons Inne, an Inne of Chancery also. This street stretcheth vppe vnto Drury lane, so called, for that there is a house belonging to the Familie of the *Druries*. This lane turneth North towarde S. | *Giles* in the field. From the south end of this lane in the high street are diuerse faire buildings, Hosteries, and houses for Gentlemen, and men of honor, amongst the which *Cicile* house is one, which sometime belonged to the Parson of S. *Martins* in the fielde, and by composition came to Sir *Thomas Palmer* knight in the raign of *Edward* the sixt, who began to builde the same of Bricke and Timber, very large and spacious, but of later time it hath beene farre more beautifully encreased by the late sir *William Cicile* Baron of Burghley, Lord Treasurer, and great counseller of the estate.

Page 452

Cicill house.

Bedford house.

Parish church of S. Martin in the field.

From thence is now a continuall new building of diuers fayre houses, euen vp to the Earle of Bedfords house lately builded nigh to Iuy Bridge, and so on the north side to a lane that turneth to the parish Church of S. *Martins* in the field, in the liberty of Westminster. Then had ye an house wherein somtime were distraught and lunatike people, of what antiquity founded, or by whom I haue not read, neither of the suppression, but it was said that sometime a king of England, not liking such a kind of people to remaine so neare his pallace, caused them to be remoued farther of, to Bethlem without Bishops gate of London, and to that Hospitall the said house by Charing crosse doth yet remaine.

An house belonging to Bethlem.

The Meuse by Charing crosse.

Then is the Mewse, so called of the kinges Faulchons there kept by the kinges Faulconer, which of olde time was an office of great account, as appeareth by a Recorde of *Richard* the second, in the first yeare of his raigne: Sir *Simon Burley* knight was made Constable for the castles of Windsor, Wigmore, and Guilford, and of the Manor of Kenington, and also master of the kings Faulcons at the Mewse neare vnto Charing crosse by Westminster. But in the yeare of Christ 1534. the 26. of *H.* the 8. the king hauing faire stabling at Lomsbery (a Manor in the farthest west part of Oldborne) the same was fiered and burnt, with many great horses, and great store of Hay. After which time, the forenamed house called the Mewse by Charing crosse was new builded, and prepared for stabling of the kings horses, in the raigne of *Edward* the sixt and Queene *Mary*, and so remaineth to that vse, and this is the farthest building West on the North side of that high streete. |

The Mewse new builded for stabling of the kings horses.

On the southside of the which street, in the liberties of Westminster (beginning at Iuie Bridge), first is Durham house, builded by *Thomas Hatfielde* Bishop of Durham, who was made Bishop of that sea in the yeare 1345. and sat Bishop there 36. yeares.

Page 453

The Bishop of Durhams house.

Amongst maters memorable concerning this house, this is one. In the yeare of Christ 1540. the 32 of *Henry* the eight, on May day, a great and triumphant Iusting was holden at Westminster, which had been formerly proclamed in France, Flanders, Scotland and Spaine, for all commers that woulde vndertake the challengers of England, which were sir *Iohn Dudley*, sir *Thomas Seymer*, sir *Thomas Po⟨y⟩nings*, and sir *George Carew* knights, and *Anthonie Kingston*, and *Richarde Cromwell* Esquiers, all which came into the Lists that day richly apparelled and their horses trapped al in white Veluet: there came against them the sayde day 46. Defendants, or Vndertakers, vz. the Earle of *Surrey* formost, Lorde *William Howard*, Lord Clinton, and Lord Cromwell, sonne and heyre to *Thomas Cromwell* Earle of Essex, and Chamberlaine of England, with other, and that day, after the Iustes performed, the Chalengers rode vnto this Durham house, where they kept open household, and feasted the King and Queene, with her Ladies, and all the Court: the second day *Anthonie Kingston* and *Richard Cromwell* were made knights there: the thirde day of May the said Chalengers did Turney on horsebacke with swordes, and against them came 49. Defendants: sir *Iohn Dudley*, and the Earle of *Surrey*, running first, which at the first course lost their Gauntlets, and that day sir *Richarde Cromwell* ouerthrew maister *Palmer* and his horse in the field, to the great honor of the chalengers, the fift of May the Chalengers fought on foote at the Barriers, and against them came 50. Defendants, which fought valiantly: but sir *Richard Cromwell* ouerthrew that day at the Barriers master *Culpepper* in the

Iusting feast at Durham house.

field, and the sixt day the Chalengers brake vp their houshold.

In this time of their housekeeping they had not onely feasted the King, Queene, Ladies, and all the Court, as is afore shewed: but also they cheared all the Knightes and Burgesses of the com|mon house in the Parliament, and entertained the Maior of London with the Aldermen and their wiues at a dinner, &c.

Page 454

Pencioners.

The king gaue to euery of the said chalengers, and their heyres for euer, in reward of their valiant actiuitie, one hundred markes, and a house to dwell in, of yearely reuenue, out of the landes pertayning to the Hospitall of S. *Iohn* of Jerusalem.

The Bishop of Norwich his house.

Next beyond this Durham house is another great house somtime belonging to the Bishop of Norwich, and was his London lodging, which nowe pertaineth to the Archbishop of Yorke by this occasion. In the yeare 1529, when Cardinall *Wolsey* Archbishop of Yorke was indited in the Premunirey, whereby King *Henry* the eight was entituled to his goodes and possessions: hee also seazed into his hands the said Archbishops house, commonly called Yorke place, and changed the name thereof into White hal: whereby the Archbishops of Yorke being dispossessed, and hauing no house of repayre about London, Queene *Marie* gaue vnto *Nicholas Heth* then Archbishop of Yorke, and to his successors, Suffolke house in Southwarke, lately builded by *Charles Brandon*, Duke of Suffolke, as I haue shewed.

This house the said Archbishop sold, and bought the aforesayd house of old time belonging to the Bishops of Norwich, which of this last purchase is now called Yorke house: the Lord Chauncellors or Lord Keepers of the greate Seale of England haue beene lately there lodged.

Hospitall of S. Mary Rounciuall.

Then was there an Hospitall of *S. Marie Rounciuall* by Charing Crosse (a Cell to the Priorie and Couent of *Rounciuall* in *Nauar* in *Pampelion* Dioces) where a Fraternitie was founded in the 15. of *Edward* the 4. but now the same is suppressed and turned into tenements.

Hermitage with a Chappell of Saint Katherine. Charing crosse.

Neare vnto this Hospitall was an Hermitage, with a chappell of S. *Katherine*, ouer against Charing crosse, which crosse, builded of stone, was of old time a fayre peece of worke there made by commandement of *Edward* the first, in the 21. yeare of his raigne, in memorie of *Helianor* his deceased Queene, as is before declared.

West from this Crosse stoode sometime an Hospitall of saint *Iames*, consisting of two hydes of lande with the appurtenances | in the parish ⟨of⟩ *S. Margaret* in Westminster, and founded by the Citizens of London, before the time of any mans memory, for 14. sisters maidens that were leprouse, liuing chastly and honestly in diuine seruice.

Hospitall of Saint Iames.

Page 455

Afterwards diuers Citizens of London gaue sixe and fifty li. rent therevnto, and then were adioyned eight brethren to minister diuine seruice there. After this also sundry deuout men of London gaue to this Hospitall foure Hides of land in the field of Westminster, and in Hendon, Calcote, and Hampsted, eighty acres of land and Woode, &c. King *Edward* the first confirmed those giftes, and granted a Fayre to be kept on the Eue of saint *Iames*, the day, the morrowe, and foure dayes following, in the eighteenth of his raigne.

S. Iames Fayre for 7. dayes.

This Hospitall was surrendred to *Henry* the eight, the three and twentieth of his raigne, the sisters being compounded with were allowed Pensions for tearme of their liues, and the king builded there a goodly Mannor, annexing thereunto a Parke, closed about with a wall of bricke, now called saint *Iames* Parke, seruing indifferently to the said Mannor, and to the Mannor or Pallace of White Hall.

S. Iames parke.

South from Charing crosse on the right hand, are diuers fayre houses lately builded before the Parke, then a large Tilt yard for Noblemen and other to exercise themselues in Iusting, Turn⟨ey⟩ing[1], and fighting at Barryers.

Tylt yarde at Westminster.

On the left hand from Charing Crosse bee also diuers fayre Tenements lately builded, till ye come to a large plotte of ground inclosed with bricke, and is called Scotland, where great buildings hath beene for receipt of the kings of Scotland, and other estates of that countrey: for *Margaret* Queene of Scots and sister to King *Henry* the eight, had her abiding there, when she came into England after the death of her husband, as the kings of Scotland had in former times, when they came to the Parliament of England.

Scotland, a plot of ground so called.

[1] Turneying] *1633*; Turning *1598*, *1603*

White hall. Then is the said White Hal sometime belonging to *Hubert de Burgh* Earle of Kent, and Iusticier of England, who gaue it to the blacke Fryers in Oldborne, as I haue before noted. King *H.* the eight ordayned it to be called an Honor, and builded there a | sumptuous Gallery and a beautifull Gate house, thwart the high streete to saint *Iames* Parke, &c.

Page 456

In this Gallory the Princes with their Nobility vse to stand or sit, and at Windowes to behold all triumphant Iustings, and other military exercises.

Beyond this Gallery on the left hand is the garden or orchyard belonging to the said White Hall.

Tennis courts, Bowling Allies, and Cocke pit. On the right hand be diuers fayre Tennis courtes, bowling allies, and a Cocke pit, al built by king *Henry* the eight, and then one other arched gate with a way ouer it thwarting the street from the kings gardens to the said parke.

Long ditch. S. Stephens Ally. From this gate vp Kings streete, to a bridge ouer Long ditch (so called for that the same almost insulateth the City of Westminster) neare which bridge is a way leading to Chanon Row, so called for that the same belonged to the Deane and Chanons of *S. Stephens* chappell, who were there lodged, as now diuers Noblemen and Gentlemen be: Whereof one is belonging to sir *Edward Hobby*, one other to *Iohn Thine* Esquier, once stately builded by *Anne Stanhop* Dutches of Somerset, mother to the Earle of Hartford, who now enioyeth that house. Next, a stately house now in building by *William* Earle of Darby, ouer against the which is a fayre house builded by *Henry Clinton* Earle of Lincolne.

From this way vp to the Woolestable and to the high Tower, or gate which entreth the pallace court, all is replenished with buildings and inhabitantes.

T. Clifford. Touching this Woolestable, I reade that in the raigne of *E.* the first, the Staple being at Westminster, the parrishioners of *S. Margaret* and Marchants of the Staple builded of new the said church, the great Chancell excepted, which was lately before new builded by the Abbot of Westminster.

Record. No siluer to be transported. Moreouer that *Edward* the third, in the 17. of his raigne, decreed that no siluer bee carried out of the Realme on paine of death. And that whosoeuer transporteth wooll, should bring ouer for euery sacke foure nobles of siluer Bullion.

In the 25. of his raigne he appointed the Staple of Wooll to be kept onely at Canterbury, for the honour of *S. Thomas.* But in the 27. of the same king *E.* the Staple of Wooll, before kept at *Bruges* | in Flanders, was ordayned by Parliament to be kept in diuers places of England, Wales and Ireland, as at New Castle, Yorke, Lincolne, Canterbury, Norwich, Westminster, Chichester, Winchester, Excester, Bristow, Carmardyn, &c. to the great benefit of the king, & losse vnto strangers & marchants. For there grew vnto the king by this meanes (as it was said) the summe of 1000 a hundred and two pounds by the yeare, more then any his predecessors before had receiued: the Staple at Westminster at that time began on the next morrow after the feast of *S. Peter Ad vincula.* The next yeare was granted to the king by Parliament towardes the recouery of his title in France, fifty shillings of euery sacke of wool transported ouer seas, for the space of sixe yeares next ensuing, by meanes whereof the king might dispend daily during those yeares more then a thousand markes starling. For by the common opinion there were more then 100000. sackes of Wooll yearely transported into forraine landes, so that during sixe yeares the said grant extended to fifteene hundred thousand pound starling.

Page 457

Wool staple at Westminster.

Robert de Auesbury.

In the 37. of *Edward* the third it was granted vnto him for two yeares to take sixe and twenty shillings eight pence, vpon euery sack of Wool transported, and the same yeare the staple of wooll (notwithstanding the kings oath and other great estates) was ordained to be kept at Callis, and sixe and twenty Marchants, the best and wealthiest of all England, to be farmers there, both of the Towne and Staple, for three yeares, euery Marchant to haue sixe men of Armes, and foure Archers at the kings cost. He ordained there also two Maiors, one for the towne, and one for the Staple, and he tooke for *mala capta*, commonly called *Maltorth,* twenty shillings, and of the said Marchants Gardians of the Towne forty pence, vpon euery sacke of Wooll.

Staple at Callis let to farme.

In the 44. of *Edward* the third, Quinborough, Kingston vpon Hull, and Boston, were made Staples of Wooll, which matter so much offended some that in the 50. of his raigne, in a Parliament at London, it was complained that the staple of

Record. Wooll was so remoued from Callis to diuers townes in England, contrary to the statute appointing that citizens and Marchants should keepe it there, and that the king might haue the profits and customes with the exchange of gold and siluer that was there made, by al the Marchants | in Christindome (esteemed to amount to 8000.li. by yeare the exchange onely): and the Citizens and Marchants so ordred the matter that the king spent nothing vpon souldiers neither vpon defence of the towne against the enemies, whereas now he spent 8000.li. by yeare.

Page 458

In the 51. of *Edward* the third, when the Staple was setled[1] at Callis, the Maior of the Staple did furnish the Captaine of the towne vpon Enirode[2] with 100. Bilmen, 1200. Archers of Marchants and their seruants, without any wages.

Manuscript. In the yeare 1388. the twelfth of *Richard* the second, in a Parliament at Cambridge, it was ordayned that the Staple of Wooles should be brought from Middlebrough in Holland to Callis.

French Wooll staples at Middle-borough.

In the fourteenth of his raigne there was granted 40.s. vpon euery sacke of wooll, and in the 21. was graunted 50.s. vpon euery sacke transported by english men, and three pound by strangers, &c. It seemeth that the Marchants of this Staple be the most ancient Marchants of this Realme, and that all commodities of the realm are Staple Marchandizes by law and Charter, as Wooles, Leather, Wool-fels, Lead, Tyn, cloth, &c.

Staple Marchants the most ancientst of this realme.

King *Henry* the sixt had sixe wooll houses within the staple at Westminster: those he granted to the Deane and Cannons of saint *Stephen* at Westminster, and confirmed it the 21. of his raigne. Thus much for the Staple haue I shortly noted.

And now to passe to the famous Monastery of Westminster: at the very entrance of the Close thereof, is a lane that leadeth toward the west, called Theeuing lane, for that theeues were led that way to the Gate house, while the sanctuary continued in force.

Theeuing lane.

This Monastery was founded and builded by *Sebert* king of the East Saxons, vpon the perswasion of *Ethelbert* king of

[1] setled] *1633;* sealed *1603*
[2] Enirode] *1603;* any Rode, *1633*

Kent, who hauing embraced christianity, and being baptized by *Melitus* Bishop of London: immediately (to shew himselfe a christian indeed) built a church to the honour of God and *S. Peter*, on the west side of the city of London, in a place (which because it was ouergrowne with thornes, and enuironed with water) the *Saxons* called *Thorney*, and now of the Monastery and west scituation thereof is called Westminster. | *Page 459*

Foundation of Westminster by Sebert, a Christian king not onely in word, but in deed.

In this place (saith *Sulcardus*) long before was a Temple of *Apollo*, which being ouerthrowne, king *Lucius* built therin a church of Christianity.

Sulcardus.

Sebert was buried in this church, with his wife *Athelgoda*, whose bodies many yeares after, to wit in the raigne of *Richard* the second (saith *Walsingham*) were translated from the old church to the new, and there enterred.

Walsingham.

Edgar king of the west Saxons repayred this Monastery about the yeare of Christ, 958. *E.* the Confessor builded it of new, whereupon *T. Clifford* writeth thus.

Without the walles of London (saith hee) vpon the Riuer of Thames, there was in times passed a little Monastery, builded to the honour of God and Saint Peter, *with a few* Benedict *Monkes in it, vnder an Abbot, seruing Christ: very poore they were, and little was giuen them for their reliefe. Here the King entended (for that it was neare to the famous Cittie of London and the Riuer of Thames, that brought in all kinde of Marchandizes from all partes of the worlde) to make his Sepulcher. Hee commaunded therfore that, of the tenthes of all his rentes, the worke should bee begunne in such sort as should become the Prince of the Apostles.*

T. Clifford.

At this his commandement the worke is nobly begun, euen from the foundation, and happily proceedeth till the same was finished: the charges bestowed, or to bee bestowed, are not regarded. Hee graunted to this church great priuiledges, aboue all the churches in this land, as partly appeareth by this his Charter.

Edpeard Cyng gret willm biscope ⁊ leofstane ⁊ Alfsie Port gerefen ⁊ ealle minne burhþegn on Lū-den freondlice: And ic cyþe eop ꝥ hæbbe seo gifta gyfen ⁊ vnnam Christ ⁊ S. Peter þam haligan Apostel into westminster: fulra freodome ofer ealle þa land þe longaþ into þære haligan stow, &c.

Page 460 *Edwarde, King, greets William, Bishop, and Leofstane and Aelfsie Portreeues, and all my Burgesses of London friendly, and I tell you that I haue this gift giuen and granted to Christ and S. Peter the holy Apostle, at Westminster, full freedome ouer all the land that belongeth to that holy place, &c.*

Parish church of S. Margaret. He also caused the parish church of *S. Margaret* to be newly builded without the Abby church of Westminster, for the ease & commodity of the Monks, because before that time the parrish Church stood within the old Abbey church in the south Isle, somewhat to their annoyance.

Mathew Paris. King *Henry* the third, in the yeare of Christ 1220, and in the fift of his raigne, began the new worke of our Ladies Chappell, whereof he layd the first stone in the foundation, and in the yeare 1245. the walles and steeple of the old Church (builded by king *Edward*) were taken downe, and inlarging the same Church, he caused them to bee made more comely, for the furtherance whereof, in the yeare 1246. the same king (diuising how to extort money from the Citizens of London towards the charges) appointed a Mart to bee kept at Westminster, the same to last fifteene dayes, and in the meane space all trade of Marchandise to cease in the City, which thing the Citizens were faine to redeeme with two thousand pound of siluer.

A Mart at Westminster.

The worke of this church, with the houses of Office, was finished to the end of the quire, in the yeare 1285. the 14 of *E.* the first. All which labour of 66. yeares, was in the yeare 1299. defaced by a fire kindled in the lesser Hall of the kinges Pallace at Westminster, the same with many other houses adioyning, and with the Queenes chamber, were all consumed, the flame thereof also (being driven with the wind) fired the Monastery, which was also with the pallace consumed.

Westminster with the palace burned.

Then was this Monastery againe repaired by the Abbots of that church, king *Edward* the first and his successors putting to their helping hands.

Edward the second appropriated vnto this Church the patronages of the churches of Kelueden and Sabritsworth[1] in *Essex* in the Diocesse of London.

Simon Langham Abbot (hauing beene a great builder there in | the yeare 1362.) gaue 400.li. to the building of the body of the church: but (amongst others) Abbot *Islip* was in his time a great builder there, as may appeare in the stone worke and glasse windowes of the church. Since whose decease that worke hath staied as he left it, vnperfected, the church and steeple being all of one height. *Page 461*

King *Henry* the seuenth, about the yeare of Christ 1502. caused the chappel of our Lady, builded by *Henry* the third, with a Tauern also called the White Rose neare adioyning, to be taken downe: in which plot of ground, on the 24. of Ianuary, the first stone of the new chappell was laid by the hands of Abbot *Islip*, sir *Reginald Bray*, knight of the Garter, Doctor *Barnes*, Maister of the Rolles, Doctor *Wal*, Chaplen to the king, Maister *Hugh Aldham*, Chaplen to the Countess of Darby and Richmond (the Kinges mother), sir *Edward Stanhop* knight, and diuers other: vpon the which stone was engrauen the same day and yeare, &c.

New chappell at Westminster.

The charges in building this chappell amounted to the summe of 14000. pound. The stone for this worke (as I haue beene informed) was brought from Huddlestone Quarrie in Yorkeshire.

The Altar and sepulture of the same king *Henry* the seuenth, wherein his body resteth in this his new chappel, was made & finished in the yeare 1519. by one *Peter* a Painter of Florence: for the which he receiued 1000. pound starling for the whole stuffe and workmanship, at the hands of the kings executors, *Richard* Bishop of Winchester, *Richard* Bishop of London, *Thomas* Bishop of Durham, *Iohn* Bishop of Rochester, *Tho.* Duke of Norfolke, Treasurer of England, *Charles* Earle of Worcester the kinges Chamberlaine, *Iohn Fineux* knight, chiefe Iustice of the kinges Bench, *Robert Reade* knight, cheife Iustice of the Common place.

This Monastery being valued to dispend by the yeare 3470. pound, &c. was surrendrd to *Henry* the eight, in the yeare 1539. *Benson*, then Abbot, was made the first Deane: and not

⟨[1] Sawbridgeworth *in Herts*⟩

Westminster a Bishops Sea.

long after it was aduanced to a Bishoppes Sea, in the yeare 1541. *Thomas Thurlby* being both the first and last Bishop there, who when he had impouerished the church, was translated to Norwich | in the yeare 1550. the fourth of *Edward* the sixt, and from thence to Elie, in the yeare 1554. the second of Queene *Mary*. *Richard Cox* Doctor in Diuinity (late Schoolemaister to king *Edward* the 6.) was made Deane of Westminster, whome Queene *Mary* put out, and made Doctor *Weston* Deane, vntill the yeare 1556, and then he being remoued from thence on the 21. of Nouember, *Iohn Fekenham* (late Deane of *Paules*) was made Abbot of Westminster, and tooke possession of the same, being installed, and fourteene Monks more receiued the habite with him that day of the order of saint *Benedict*: but the said *Iohn Feckenham*, with his Monkes, enioyed not that place fully three yeares, for in the yeare 1559. in the Moneth of Iuly they were all put out, and Queene *Elizabeth* made the said Monastery a Colledge, instituting there a Deane, twelue Prebends, a Schoolmaister, and Usher, 40. schollers called commonly the Queenes schollers, 12. Alms men, & so it was named the Collegiat church of Westminster, founded by Queene *Elizabeth*, who placed Doctor *Bil* first Deane of that new erection, after whome succeeded Doctor *Gabriel Goodman*, who gouerned that church forty yeares, and after Doctor *L. Andrewes*.

Page 462

Westminster made a Collegiat church.

King and Q. crowned at Westminster.

Kings and Queenes crowned in this church: *William* surnamed *Conqueror*, and *Matilde* his wife, were the first: and since them all other Kings and Queenes of this realme haue been there crowned.

Kings and Q. buried at Westminster.

Kinges and Queenes buried in this Church are these: *Sebert* king of the East Saxons, with his wife *Athelgade*, *Harold* surnamed *Harefote*, king of the West Saxons: *Edward* the simple, surnamed Confessor, sometime richly shrined in a Tombe of siluer and Gold, curiously wrought by commaundement of *William* the Conqueror: *Egitha* his wife was there buried also. *Hugolyn* Chamberlaine to *Edward* the Confessor. K. *Henry* the third, whose sepulture was richly garnished with precious stones of Iasper, which his sonne *Edward* the first brought out of France for that purpose: *Elianor* wife to *Henry* the third: *Edward* the first, who offered to the

S. Edwards shrine at Westminster.

shrine of *Edward* the Confessor the chaire of Marble, wherein the Kinges of Scotland were Crowned, with the Scepter and Crowne also to the same King belonging. | He gaue also to that church landes to the value of 100. *Page 463* pound by the yeare, 20. pound thereof yearely to be distributed to the poore for euer: then there lyeth *Eleanor* his wife, daughter to *Ferdinando* king of Castile, 1293. *Edward* the third by Queene *Phillip* of Henault: *Richard* the second and *Anne* his wife, with their images upon them which cost more then foure hundred marks for the guilding: *Henry* the fift with a royall image of siluer and guilt, which *Katherine* his wife caused to bee laid vpon him, but the head of this image being of massie siluer is broken off, and conuayed away with the plates of siluer and guilte that couered his body: *Katherin* his wife was buried in the old Lady chapel, 1438. but her corps being taken vp in the raign of *Henry* the 7. when a new foundation was to be laid, she was neuer since buried, but remayneth aboue ground in a coffin of boordes behinde the East end of the Presbyterie [1]: *Henry* the seuenth in a sumptuous Sepulture and Chappell before specified, and *Elizabeth* his Wife, *Edwarde* the sixt in the same Chappell without any Monument, Queene *Mary* without any Monument, in the same Chappell: *Matilde* daughter to *Malcolme* king of Scottes, wife to *H.* the first, dyed 1118. lyeth in the Reuestrie: *Anne* wife to *Richarde* the 3. *Margaret* Countes of Richmond and Darby, mother to *H.* the seuenth. *Anne* of Cleue, wife to *Henry* the eight. *Edmond* second son to *Henry* the third, first Earle of Lancaster, Darby, and Leycester, and *Aueline* his wife, daughter and heyre to *William de Fortibus* Earle of Albemarle. In S. *Thomas* chappell lie the bones of the children of *Henry* the third, and of *Edward* the first, in number nine. In the Chapter house, *Elianor* Countesse of Barre, daughter to *Edward* the first, *William* of Windsore and *Blaunch* his sister, children to *Edward* the thirde, *Iohn* of Eltham Earle of Cornewell, sonne to *Edward* the second, *Elianor* wife to *Thomas* of Woodstocke, Duke of Glocester, *Thomas* of Woodstocke by king *Edward* the third his Father, *Margaret* daughter to *Edward* the fourth, *Elizabeth* daughter to *Henry* the seuenth, *William de Valence* Earle of Pembrooke,

[1] Her body now lieth in a small place by her husband, unburied *1633*

A⟨y⟩mer de Valence Earle of Pembrooke, *Margaret* and *Iohn* sonne and daughter to *William de Valence*, *Iohn Waltham* Bishop of Sarum, Treasurer of England, *Thomas Ruthal* Bishop | of Durham, 1522. *Giles* Lord *Dawbeny*, Lord Lieutenant of Callice, Chamberlaine to king *Henry* the seuenth, 1508. and *Elizabeth* his wife of the Family of the Arundelles in Cornwal, 1500. *Iohn Vicount Welles* 1498. The Ladie *Katherine*, daughter to the Dutches of Norfolke: sir *Thomas Hungerford* knight, Father to sir *Iohn Hungerford* of Downampney knight: a sonne and daughter to *Humfrey Bohun* Earle of Hereford and Essex, and *Elizabeth* his wife: *Philip* Dutches of Yorke, daughter to the Lord *Mohun*, thrice married, to the Lord *Fitzwalter*, sir *Iohn Golofer*, and to the Duke of Yorke: *William Dudley* Bishoppe elect of Durham, sonne to *Iohn* Baron of Dudley, *Nicholas* Baron *Carow*[1], 1470. *Walter Hungerford*, sonne to *Edward Hungerforde* knight, Sir *Iohn Burley* knight, and *Anne* his wife, daughter to *Alane Buxhull* knight, 1416. sir *Iohn Golofer* knight, 1396. *Humfrey Burcher*, Lord *Cromwell*, sonne to *Bourchier* Earle of Essex, slayne at Barnet, *Henry Bourchier* sonne and heyre to *Iohn Bourchier*, Lord *Barners* also slayne at Barnet, 1471. Sir *William Trussell* knight, Sir *Thomas Vaughan* knight, *Francis Brandon* Dutchesse of Suffolke, 1560. *Mary Gray* her daughter, 1578. Sir *Iohn Hampden* Knight, Sir *Lewes Vicount Robsart* knight, Lord *Bourchere* of *Henalt*, 1430. and his wife daughter and heyre to the Lord *Bourchere*: *Robert Brown* and *William Browne* Esquers: The Lady *Iohane Tokyne* daughter of *Dabridge court*: *George Mortimer* Bastarde, *Iohn Felbye* Esquier, *Anne* wife to *Iohn Watkins*, *William Southwike* Esquier, *William Southcot* Esquier. *Raph Constantine* Gentleman, *Arthur Troffote* Esquier, *Robert Hawley* Esquier, slaine in that Church, sir *Richarde Rouse* knight, sir *Geffrey Maundeuile* Earle of Essex, and *Athelarde* his wife, Sir *Foulke* of Newcastle, Sir *Iames Barons* knight, Sir *Iohn Salisbery* knight, *Margaret Dowglas* Countesse of Lineaux[2], with *Charles* her sonne, Earle of Lineaux, *Henrie Scogan*, a learned Poet, in the Cloyster: *Geffrey Chaucer*, the most famous Poet of England, also in the Cloyster, 1400. but

Page 464

[1] Carow] *1598;* Carew *1603* [2] Leuenox *1633*

since *Nicholas Brigham* Gentleman raysed a Monumente for him in the South Crosse Ile of the Church: his workes were | Page 465 partly published in Print by *William Caxton* in the raigne of *Henry* the sixt, increased by *William Thinne* Esquier, in the raigne of *Henry* the eight: corrected and twise encreased through mine owne paynefull labors, in the raigne of Queene *Elizabeth*, to witte in the yeare 1561. and againe, beautified with notes by me collected out of diuers Recordes and Monuments, which I deliuered to my louing friend *Thomas Speight*, and hee hauing drawne the same into a good forme and Methode, as also explayned the olde and obscure wordes, &c. hath published them in *Anno* 1597.

Anne Stanhope Dutches of Sommerset, and *Iane* her daughter, *Anne Cecill* Countesse of Oxford, daughter to the Lorde *Burghley*, with *Mildred Burghley* her Mother, *Elizabeth Barkley* Countesse of Ormonde, *Frauncis Sidney* Countesse of Sussex, *Francis Howard* Countesse of Hertford, 1598. *Thomas* Baron *Wentworth*, *Thomas* Baron *Wharton*, *Iohn* lord *Russel*, sir *Thomas Bromley* Lord Chauncellor, sir *Iohn Puckering* Lord Keeper, Sir *Henry Cary* Lord *Hunsdon*, and Lord *Chamberlayne*, 1596. to whose memory his sonne sir *George Cary* lord Hunsdon and lord Chamberlaine, hath erected a stately monument.

This church hath had great priuiledge of Sanctuary within the precinct therof, to wit, the church, churchyard and close, &c. from whence it hath not beene lawfull for any prince or other, to take any person that fled thether for any cause: which priuiledge was first granted by *Sebert* king of the East Saxons, since increased by *Edgare* king of the West Saxons, renewed and confirmed by king *Edward* the Confessor, as appeareth by this his Charter following.

Sanctuary at Westminster.

Edward by the grace of God, King of Englishmen: I make it to be known to all generations of the world after me, that by speciall commandement of our holy father Pope Leo, I haue renewed and honored the holy church of the blessed Apostle S. Peter of Westminster, and I order and establish for euer, that what person of what condition or estate soeuer hee be, from whence soeuer he come, or for what offence or cause it be, either for his refuge into the said holy place, he be assu|red of his life, Page 466 *liberty and lims: And ouer this I forbid vnder the paine of euerlasting damnation, that no Minister of mine or of my successors intermeddle them with any the goods, lands or possessions of the said persons taking the said sanctuary: for I haue taken their goodes & liuelode into my speciall protection, and therefore I grant to euery each of them, in as much as my terrestriall power may suffice, all maner freedom of ioyous libertie, and whosoeuer presumes or doth contrary to this my graunt, I will hee lose his name, worship, dignity & power, and that with the great traytor Iudas that betrayed our Sauiour, he be in the euerlasting fire of hell, and I will and ordayne that this my graunt endure as long as there remayneth in England, eyther loue or dread of christian name.*

More of this sanctuary ye may read in our histories, and also in the statute of *Henry* the 8. the 32. yeare.

Parish church of S. Margaret.

The parish church of *S. Margaret* sometime within the Abbey, was by *E.* the *Confessor* remoued, and builded without, for ease of the Monks. This church continued till the daies of *E.* the 1. at what time the marchants of the staple and parishioners of Westminster builded it all of new, the great chancell excepted, which was builded by the Abbots of Westminster, and this remaineth now a fayr parish church, though sometime in danger of down pulling: In the south Ile of this church is a fayre marble monument of Dame *Mary Billing*, the heyre of *Robert Nesenham* of Conington in Huntingtonshire, first married to *William Coton*, to whose issue her inheritance alone discended, remayning with *Rob. Coton* at this day, heyre of her and her first husbandes familie: her second husband was sir *Thomas Billing* chiefe Iustice of England, & her last, whom likewise she buried, was *Thomas Lacy*, erecting this monument to the memory of her 3. husbands, with whose armes she hath garnished it, and for her own burial, wherein she was enterred in the yeare 1499.

In the raigne of E. the 6.

Next to this famous Monastery, is the kings principall Pallace, of what antiquity it is vncertain: but *Edward* the *Confessor* held his court there, as may appeare by the testimony of sundrie, and namely of *Ingulphus* as I haue before told you. The said king had his pallace, and for the most

Page 467

remayned there: where hee al|so ended his life, and was

buried in the Monastery which hee had builded. It is not to be doubted, but that king *William* the first, as hee was crowned there, so he builded much at this Pallace, for he found it far inferior to the building of princely pallaces in France. And it is manifest by the testimonie of many authors, that *W. Rufus* builded the great Hall there, about the year of Christ 1097. Amongst others, *Roger* of *Windouer*, and *Mathew Paris*, doe write, that king *William* (being returned out of Normandy, into England) kept his feast of Whitsontide very roially at Westminster, in the new hall which he had lately builded, the length whereof (say some) was 270. foote, and seuenty foure foot in bredth, and when he heard men say, that this Hall was too great, he answered and said: this hall is not bigge inough by the one halfe, and is but a Bedde chamber in comparison of that I meane to make: a diligent searcher (saith *Paris*) might find out the foundation of the hal, which he had supposed to haue builded, stretching from the riuer of Thames euen to the common high way. This Pallace was repaired about the yeare 1163. by *Thomas Becket* Chauncelor of England, with exceeding great celerity and speede, which before was ready to haue fallen downe. This hath beene the principall seat and Pallace of al the kings of England since the conquest: for here haue they in the great hall kept their feasts of coronation especially, and other solemne feasts, as at Christmas and such like most commonly: for proofe whereof, I finde Recorded that in the yeare 1236. and the twentieth of *Henry* the third, on the 29. of December, *William de Hauerhull*, the kinges Treasurer, is commanded that vpon the day of circumcision of our Lord he cause 6000. poore people to be fed at Westminster, for the state of the king, the Queene, and their children, the weake and aged to be placed in the great hall, & in the lesser, those that were most strong and in reasonable plight in the kinges chamber, the children in the Queenes, and when the king knoweth the charge he would allow it in the accounts.

Great hall at Westminster. Mathew Paris.

Liber Woodbridge.

Pallace repayred. W. Fitzstephen.

Record Tower.

The vse of great Hall was to feed the poore.

In the yeare 1238. the same king *Henry* kepte his feast of Christmas at Westminster in the great Hall, so did he in the year 1241. where he placed the Legate in the most honorable

Mathew Paris. Great Feastes in Westminster hall.

place of the Table, to wit in the midest, which the Noblemen took in euill | part: the king sate on the right hand, and the Archbishop on the left, and then all the Prelates & Nobles according to their estates: for the king himselfe set the Guests. The yeare 1242, he likewise kept his Christmas in the hall, &c. Also in the yeare 1243. *Richard* Earle of Cornewall, the kings brother, maried *Cincia*, daughter to *Beatrice* Countesse of Prouince, and kept his mariage feast in the great Hall at Westminster, with great royalty and company of noble men: insomuch, that there were told (*triginta milia*) 30000 dishes of meates at that dinner.

Page 468

H. the 3. sate in the exchequer & amerced the Shiriffes.

In the yeare 1256. king *Henry* sate in the Exchequer of this Hall, and there set downe order for the appearance of Shiriffes, and bringing in of their accounts: there was fiue Markes set on euery Shiriffes head for a fine, because they had not distrained euery person that might dispend fifteene pound land by the yeare, to receyue the order of Knighthoode, as the same Shiriffes were commaunded. Also the Maior, Aldermen, and Shiriffes of London, being accused of oppression and wrongs done by them, and submitting themselues in this place before the king sitting in judgement vpon that matter, they were condemned to pay their fines for their offences committed, and further euery one of them discharged of assise and warde.

Translation of E. the Confessor.

In the yeares 1268. and 1269. the same king kept his Christmas feasts at Westminster as before: and also in the same 1269. he translated, with great solemnitie, the bodie of king *Edward* the Confessor into a new Chappell, at the backe of the high Altar: which Chappell he had prepared of a maruelous workemanship, bestowing a new Tombe or Shrine of Golde, and on the day of his translation he kept a royall feast in the great Hall of the Palace: thus much for the feasts of old time in this hall.

Marshes about Woolwich drowned.

Wheries rowed in Westminster hall.

We read also, that in the yeare 1236. the riuer of Thames ouerflowing the bankes, caused the Marches about Woolwich to be all on a Sea, wherein Boats and other vesselles were carried with the streame, so that besides cattell, the greatest number of men, women and children, inhabitants there, were drowned: and in the great Palace of Westminster, men did row with wheryes in the middest of the Hall, being forced to ryde to theyr chambers. |

Moreouer in the yeare 1242, the Thames ouerflowing the bankes about Lambhithe, drowned houses and fieldes, by the space of sixe miles, so that in the great hall at Westminster, men tooke their horses, because the water ran ouer all. This Palace was (in the yeare 1299. the 27. of *Edward* the first) burnt by a vehement fire, kindled in the lesser hall of the kings house: the same with many other houses adioyning, and with the Queenes chamber, were consumed, but after that repayred.

Page 469

T. Walsing. Pallace at Westminster burnt.

In the yeare 1303. the 31. of *Edward* the first, the kings treasurie at Westminster was robbed, for the which *Walter*, Abbot of Westminster, with 49. of his brethren, and 32. other, were throwne into the Tower of London, and indighted of the robbery of an hundred thousand pound, but they affirming themselues to be cleare of the fact, and desiring the king of speedie iustice, a commission was directed for inquiry of the truth, and they were freed.

The kings treasurie at Westminster robbed. The Abbot & Monks sent to the Tower.

In the yeare 1316. *Edward* the second did solemnize his feast of Penticost at Westminster, in the great hall, where sitting royally at the table with his Pears about him, there entred a woman adorned like a Minstrell, sitting on a great horse, trapped as Minstrels then vsed, who rode round about the Tables, shewing pastime, and at length came vp to the kings Table, and laide before him a letter, and forthwith turning her horse, saluted euery one, and departed. The letter being opened, had these contents: 'Our Soueraigne Lord the King hath nothing curteously respected his knights, that in his fathers time, and also in his owne, haue put forth their persons to diuers perils, and haue vtterly lost, or greatly diminished their substance, for honor of the said king, and he hath inriched aboundantly such as haue not borne the waight as yet of the busines,' &c.

E. the 2. keeping his feasts at westm. hall, was presente with a complaint of not rewarding souldiers.

This great hall was begun to be repayred in the yeare 1397. by *Richard* the second, who caused the walles, windowes, & roofe, to be taken downe, and new made, with a stately porch, and diuerse lodgings of a maruellous worke, and with great costs: all which he leuied of strangers banished, or flying out

Great hall at westminster repayred.

of their Countryes, who obtayned license to remaine in this land by the Kinges Charters, which they had purchased with great summes of money, *Iohn Boterell* being then Clarke of the workes. |

Page 470

Great feasts in Westminster hall.

This hall being finished in the yeare 1399. the same King kept a most royal Christmas there, with dayly Iustings, and runnings at Tilt, whereunto resorted such a number of people, that there was euerie day spent twentie eight, or twentie sixe Oxen, and three hundred sheepe, besides fowle without number: he caused a Gowne for himselfe to be made of Golde, garnished with Pearle and precious Stones, to the value of 3000. Marks: he was garded by Cheshire men, and had about him commonly thirteene bishops, besides Barons, Knights, Esquires, and other more then needed: insomuch, that to the houshold, came euery day to meate 10000. people, as appeareth by the Messes tolde out from the Kitchen to 300. seruitors.

Ro. Iuelefe.

Thus was this great hall for the honour of the Prince oftentymes furnished with guests, not onely in this kings time (a prodigall Prince) but in the time of other also, both before and since, though not so vsually noted. For when it is said, the king held his feast of Christmas, or such a feast at Westminster, it may well be supposed to be kept in this great hall, as most sufficient to such a purpose.

Ro. Fabian.

King Henry the 7. feasted the Maior of London, &c.

I find noted by *Robert Fabian* (sometime an Alderman of London) that king *Henrie* the seuenth in the ninth of his raigne (holding his royall feast of Christmas at Westminster) on the twelfth day, feasted *Raph Austry*, then Maior of London, and his brethren the Aldermen, with other commoners in great number, and after dinner dubbing the Maior knight, caused him with his brethren to stay and behold the disguisings and other disports, in the night following shewed in the great hall, which was richly hanged with Arras, and staged about on both sides: which disportes being ended in the morning, the king, the Queene, the Ambassadors, & other estates, being set at a table of stone, 60. knights, and Esquires serued 60. dishes to the kings Messe, and as many to the Queenes (neither flesh nor fish) and serued the Maior with twentie foure dishes to his messe, of the same maner, with sundrie wines in most plenteous wise: and finally, the King and Queene, being conueyed with great lights into the Pallace, the Mayor with his companie in Barges returned and came to London by breake of the next day. Thus much for building of this great hall, | and feasting therein. *Page 471*

It moreouer appeareth that many Parliaments haue beene kept there: for I find noted, that in the yeare 1397. the great hall at Westminster, being out of reparations, and therefore, as it were, new builded by *Richard* the second (as is afore shewed) the same *Richard* in the meane time hauing occasion to hold a parliament, caused for that purpose a large house to be builded in the middest of the Palace Court, betwixt the clocke Tower, and the gate of the olde great hall: this house was very large and long, made of tymber, couered with Tyle, open on both the sides, and at both the endes, that all men might see and heare what was both sayde and done. Parliament kept in Westminster hall.

The Kinges Archers (in number 4000. Cheshire men) compassed the house about with their Bowes bent, and Arrowes nocked in their handes, alwayes readie to shoote: they had bouch of Court (to wit, meate and drinke) and great wages, of six pence by the day. Bouch of Court.

The olde great Hall being new builded, Parliaments were againe there kept as before: namely, one in the yeare 1399. for the deposing of *Richard* the second. A great part of this Palace at Westminster was once againe burnt in the yeare 1512. the 4. of *Henry* the eight, since which time, it hath not beene reedified: onely the great Hall, with the offices neare adioyning, are kept in good reparations, and serueth as afore, for feastes at Coronations, Arraignments of great persons charged with treasons, keeping of the Courts of iustice, &c. But the Princes haue beene lodged in other places about the city, as at Baynards Castle, at Bridewell, and White hall, sometime called Yorke place, and sometime at S. *Iames*. I find of record the 50. of Ed. the 3. that the Chapter house of the Abbot of Westm. was then the vsual house for the commons in Parliament.

This great hall hath beene the vsuall place of pleadings, and ministration of Iustice, whereof somewhat shortly I will note. In times past, the courts and benches followed the king, wheresoeuer he went, as well since the conquest, as before, which thing at length being thought combersome, painfull, Magna Carta. Common place[1] in westminster hall.

[1] pleas *1633*

and chargeable to the people, it was in the yeare 1224. the 9. of *H.* 3. agreed that there should be a standing place appointed, where matters should be heard and iudged, which was in the great hall at Westminster. |

Page 472

In this hall he ordayned three iudgement seates, to wit, at the entry on the right hand, the common place[1], where ciuill matters are to ⟨be⟩ pleaded, specially such as touch lands or contracts: at the vpper end of the Hall, on the right hand, or Southest corner, the Kings bench, where pleas of the Crowne haue their hearing: and on the left hand or South-west corner, sitteth the Lord Chancellor, accompanied with the master of the Rowles, and other men, learned for the most part in the Ciuill lawe, and called maisters of the Chauncerie, which haue the Kings fee. The times of pleading in these courts are foure in the yeare, which are called Tearmes, the first is Hillarie Terme, which beginneth the 23. of Ianuary, if it be not Sunday, and endeth the 12. of February. The second is Easter Terme, and beginneth 17. dayes after Easter day, and endeth four dayes after Ascen-sion day. The third Terme beginneth 6. or seuen dayes after Trinitie Sunday, and endeth the Wednesday fortnight after. The fourth is Michaelmas Terme, which beginneth the 9. of October, if it be not Sunday, and endeth the 28. of Nouember.

T. Smith.

Court of the Chancerie.

And here is to be noted, that the Kings of this Realme haue vsed sometimes to sit in person in the Kings Bench: namely King *Edward* the fourth, in the yere 1462. in Michael-mas Terme sate in the Kings Bench three dayes togither, in the open Court, to vnderstand how his lawes were ministred and executed.

Kings of this Realme haue sate on the Kings Bench in West. hall.

Within the Port, or entrie into the Hall, on eyther side are ascendings vp into large Chambers without the Hall adioyning thereunto, wherein certaine Courts be kept: namely, on the right hand, is the court of the Exchequer, a place of account for the reuenewes of the Crowne: the hearers of the account haue Auditors vnder them, but they which are the chiefe for accounts of the prince, are called Barons of the Exchequer, whereof one is called the chiefe Baron. The greatest officer of

Court of the exchequer.

[1] pleas *1633*; place *1603*

al is called the high treasurer. In this Court be heard those that are delators, or informers, in popular and penall actions, hauing thereby part of the profite by the law assigned vnto them. Informers.

In this Court, if any question bee, it is determined after the order of the common law of England by twelue men, and all subsidies, Taxes and Customes, by account: for in this office, the | Shiriffes of the Shire do attende vpon the execution of the commandements of the Iudges, which the Earle should do, if he were not attending vpon the Princes in the warres, or otherwise about him: for the chiefe office of the earl was, to see the Kings iustice to haue course, and to bee well executed in the Shire, and the Princes Reuenewes to bee well aunswered and brought into the Treasurie. *Page 473*

If any fines or amerciaments be extracted out of any of the sayde Courts vpon any man, or any arrerages of accounts of such thinges as is of customes, taxes and subsidies, or other such like occasions, the same the Shiriffe of the Shire doth gather, and is aunswerable therefore in the Exchequer. As for other ordinarie rents of patrimoniall landes, and most commonly of taxes, customes, and subsidies, there be particular receyuers and collectors, which doe aunswere it into the Exchequer. This Court of the Exchequer hath of olde time, and as I thinke, since the Conquest, beene kept at Westminster, notwithstanding sometimes remoued thence by commaundement of the king, and after restored againe, as namely in the yeare 1209, King *Iohn* commaunded the Exchequer to be remoued from Westminster to Northhampton, &c.

On the left hand aboue the staire is the Duchie chamber, wherein is kept the Court for the Duchie of Lancaster, by a Chancellor of that Duchie, and other officers vnder him. Then is there in an other chamber, the office of the receits of the Queenes reuenewes for the Crowne: then is there also the Starre Chamber, where in the Terme time euery weeke once at the least, which is commonly on Frydayes and Wednesdayes, and on the next day after the Terme endeth, the Lord Chancellor and the Lords, and other of the priuy Councell, and the chiefe Iustices of England, from 9. of the clocke till it be 11. do sit. Dutchy court. Office of receit. Star chamber.

This place is called the Starre Chamber, because the roofe

thereof is decked with the likenes of Stars guilt: there be plaints heard, of ryots, rowts, and other misdemeanors, which if they bee found by the kings Councell, the partie offender shall be censured by these persons, which speake one after another, and hee shal bee both fined and commaunded to prison. |

Page 474

Then at the vpper end of the great hall by the Kings bench, is a going vp to a great Chamber, called the White hall, wherein is now kept the court of Wards and Liueries: and adioyning thereunto is the Court of Requests. Then is S. *Stephens* Chappell, of old time founded by king *Stephen.* King *Iohn* in the 7. of his raign graunted to *Baldwinus de London* Clarke of his Exchequer, the Chappleship of Saint *Stephens* at Westminster, &c. This Chappell was againe since, of a farre more curious workemanship, new builded by king *Edward* the third, in the yeare 1347. for thirtie eight persons in that Church to serue God, to wit, a Deane, 12. secular Canons, thirteene Vicars, foure Clarkes, sixe Choristes, two Seruitors, to wit, a Verger, and a keeper of the Chappell. He builded for those from the house of receit, along nigh to the Thames, within the same Pallace, there to inhabite, and since that, there was also builded[1] for them, betwixt the Clocke-house and the Wooll-staple, called the Wey house. He also builded to the vse of this Chappell (though out of the Pallace Court) some distance west, in the little Sanctuarie, a strong Clochard of stone and timber, couered with Lead, and placed therein three great Bels, since vsually rung at coronations, triumphs, funerall of Princes, and their obits. Of those Bels men fabuled, that their ringing sowred all the drinke in the towne. More, that about the biggest Bell was written,

The court of Wardes and Liueries. Court of Requests. S. Stephens Chappell.

Little Sanctuarie.

King Edward made me,
Thirtie thousand and three,
Take me downe and wey me,
And more shall ye find me.

But these Bels being taken downe indeed, were found all three not to wey 20. thousand. True it is, that in the Citie of Roane in Normandie, there is one great Bell, that hath such inscription as followeth.

[1] were also buildings *1633*

Ie suis George de Ambois,
Qui trente sinq mille pois:
Mes lui qui me pesera,
Trente six mill me trouera.

I am George of Ambois,
Thirtie fiue thousand in pois:
But he that shall weigh me,
Thirtie six thousand shall find me. |

The said king *Ed.* endowed this chappell with lands, to the yearly value of 500.l. Doctor *Iohn Chambers* the kinges Phisitian, the last Deane of this Colledge, builded thereunto a cloyster of curious workmanship, to the charges of 11000. marks. This chappell, or colledge, at the suppression, was valued to dispend in lands by the yeare 1085. pound. 10.s. 5.d. and was surrendred to *Edward* the sixt, since the which time, the same Chappell hath serued as a Parliament house.

Page 475

Cloyster of S. Stephens chappel builded.

Parliament house.

By this chappel of S. *Stephen*, was sometime one other smaller chappel, called our Lady of the Piew, to the which Lady great offerings were vsed to be made. Amongst other things I haue read that *Richard* the 2. after the ouerthrow of *Wat Tilar* and other his rebels in the 4. of his raigne, went to Westminster, and there giuing thanks to God for his victorie, made his offering in this Chappell, but as diuerse haue noted, namely *Iohn Piggot*, in the yeare 1452.[1] on the 17. of February, by negligence of a Scholler appoynted by his Schoolemaister to put foorth the lightes of this Chappell, the Image of our Ladie richly decked with iewels, precious stones, pearles, and rings, more then any Ieweller could iudge the price, for so sayth mine Author, was with all this apparell, ornaments, and Chappell it selfe burnt, but since againe reedified by *Anthonie* Earle *Riuers*, Lord *Scales*, and of the Isle of Wight, Vncle and gouernour to the Prince of Wales, that should haue beene king *Edward* the fifth, &c.

Chappel of our Ladie in the piew.

The sayd Pallace, before the entrie thereunto, hath a large Court, and in the same a Tower of stone, containing a clocke, which striketh euery houre on a great Bell, to bee heard into the Hall in sitting time of the Courts, or otherwise: for the same Clocke, in a calme, will be heard into the Citie of

Clocke house at westminster.

[1] 1452] 1252 *1603*

London. King *Henrie* the sixt gaue the keeping of this clocke with the Tower, called the Clocke house, and the appurtenances vnto *William Walsby* Deane of Saint *Stephens*, with the wages of sixe pence the day out of his Exchequer. By this Tower standeth a fountaine, which at Coronations and great triumphes is made to runne with wine out of diuerse spoutes.

Fountain in the pallace Court.

On the East side of this Court, is an Arched Gate to the riuer of Thames, with a fayre Bridge and landing place, for all | men that haue occasion. On the North side is the South ende of Saint *Stephens* Alley, or Canon Row, and also a way into the old wooll staple: & on the West side is a verie faire gate begun by *Richard* the third, in the yeare 1484. and was by him builded a great height, and many faire lodgings in it, but left vnfinished, and is called the high Tower at Westminster. Thus much for the monasterie and pallace may suffice. And now will I speake of the gate house, and of Totehill streete, stretching from the west part of the Close.

Page 476

Westminster bridge or common landing place.

High tower at Westminster.

The Gate-house is so called of two Gates, the one out of the Colledge court toward the North, on the East side whereof was the Bishop of Londons prison for Clarkes conuict, and the other gate, adioyning to the first but towards the west, is a Gaile or prison for offenders thither committed. *Walter Warfield* Celerer to the Monastery, caused both these gates with the appurtenances to be builded in the raigne of *Edward* the third.

Gate house at Westminster.

On the Southside of this gate, king *H.* the 7. founded an almes house for 13. poore men: one of them to be a priest, aged 45. yeres, a good Gramarian, the other 12. to be aged fiftie yeares, without wiues, euery Saturday the priest to receyue of the Abbot, or prior, foure pence by the day, and each other two pence halfe penny by the day for euer, for their sustenance, and euery yeare to each one a gowne and a hood ready made: and to three women that dressed their meat, and kept them in their sicknes, each to haue euery Saturday 16.d. and euery yere a gowne ready made. More, to the 13. poore men yearly 80. quarters of cole, and 1000. of good fagots to their vse: in the hall and kitchen of their mansion, a discreete Monke to be ouerseer of them, and he to haue 40.s. by the yeare, &c. and

Almeshouse of Henry the 7.

hereunto was euery Abbot and Prior sworne. Neare vnto this house westward, was an old chappel of S. *Anne*, ouer against the which the Lady *Margaret* mother to king *H.* the 7. erected an Almeshouse for poore women, which is now turned into lodgings for the singing men of the colledge: the place wherein this chappell and Almeshouse standeth, was called the *Elemosinary* or Almory, now corruptly the Ambry, for that the Almes of the Abbey were there distributed to the poore. And therein *Islip* Abbot of Westmin. erected the first Presse of booke printing that euer was in England | about the yeare of Christ, 1471. *William Caxton* Cittizen of London, mercer, brought it into England, and was the first that practised it in the sayde Abbey, after which time, the like was practised in the Abbyes of S. Augustine at Canterbury, S. Albons and other monasteries. From the west gate runneth along Totehil streete, wherein is a house of the Lord *Gray* of Wilton, and on the other side at the entrie into Totehill fielde, Stourton house, which *Gyles*, the last L. *Dacre* of the south, purchased and builte new, whose Lady and wife *Anne* sister to *Thomas* the Lorde *Buckhurst*, left money to her Executors to builde an hospitall for twentie poore women, and so many children to be brought vp vnder them, for whose maintenance she assigned landes to the value of one hundred pound by the yeare, which Hospitall her Executors haue new begun in the field adioyning. From the entry into Totehill field, the streete is called Petty France, in which, and vpon S. Hermits hill, on the south side thereof, *Cornelius van Dun* (a Brabander borne, Yeoman of the Guard to king *H.* the 8. king *E.* the 6. Queene *Mary* and Queene *Elizabeth*) built 20. houses for poore women to dwell rent free, and neare hereunto was a chappell of Mary Magdalen, now wholy ruinated.

Chappell of Saint Anne.

Almeshouse founded by Lady Margaret.

Almory at Westminster.

Page 477

Printing of bookes at Westm. the first in England.

Totehill street.

Hospital founded by Lady Anne Dacre.

Petty France.

Almeshouses for poor women.

Chappell of Mary Magdalen.

In the yeare of Christ 1256. the 40. of *H.* the third, *Iohn Mansell*, the kings Counceller and a priest, did inuite to a stately dinner the kings and Queens of England and Scotland, *Edward* the kinges sonne, Earles, Barons and knightes, the Bishop of London and diuers cittizens, whereby his guestes did grow to such a number, that his house at Totehill could not receiue them, but that he was forced to set vppe tentes and pauillions to receiue his guestes, whereof there was such

Mathew Paris. 700. messe of meat at one dinner in Totehill.

a multitude that 700. messe of meate did not serue for the first dinner.

Gouernement of Weminster Citty.

The Cittie of Westminster for ciuill gouernment is diuided into twelue seuerall Wardes, for the which the Deane of the collegiate church of Westminster, or the high Steward doe elect 12 Burgesses, and as many assistantes, that is, one Burgesse, and one Assistant for euery Warde, out of the which twelue Burgesses, two are nominated yearely, vpon Thursday in Easter weeke, for chief Burgesses to continue for one yeare next following, who | haue authority giuen them by the Act of Parliament, 27. *Elizabeth*, to heare, examine, determine and punish according to the lawes of the Realme, and lawfull customes of the Cittie of London, matters of incontinency, common scoldes, inmates, and common annoyances, and likewise to commit such persons as shall offend against the peace, and therof to giue knowledge within foure and twentie houres to some Iustice of Peace in the County of Midlesex.

Page 478

Gouernors of the Cittie of London, and first of Ecclesiastical Bishops, and other Ministers there.

HAUING thus run through the description of these Cities of London and Westminster aswell in their originall foundations, as in their increases of buildinges and ornaments, together with such incidentes of sundrie sortes as are before, both generally and particularly, discoursed: It remaineth that somewhat bee noted by me, touching the pollicie and gouernment, both Ecclesiastical and ciuill, of London: as I haue already done for Westminster, the order whereof is appointed by the late statute, euen as that of London is maintained by the customes thereof, most laudably vsed before all the time of memory.

W. Malmsbery. Antiquities of Glasto.

And first to beginne with the Ecclesiasticall iurisdiction, I read that the Christian faith was first preached in this Iland (then called Britaine) by *Ioseph* of Arimathea, and his brethren disciples of Christ, in the time of Aruiragus, then Gouernor here, vnder the Romaine Emperour, after which time, *Lucius* king of the Britaines sent his Ambassadors *Eluanus* and *Meduuanus*, two men learned in the scriptures, with letters to

Lib. consti. Eleutherius died in the yeare 186. when he had sitten Bishop 15. yeares.

Eleutherius Bishop of Rome, desiring him to send some deuout and learned men, by whose instruction he and his people might be taught the faith and religi|on of Christ. *Eleutherius* baptized those messengers, making *Eluanus* a Bishoppe and *Meduuanus* a Teacher, and sent ouer with them into Britaine two other famous Clearkes, *Faganus* & *Deruuianus*, by whose diligence *Lucius* and his people of Britaine were instructed in the faith of Christ and baptized, the temples of Idols were conuerted into cathedral churches, & Bishops were placed where *Flammines* before had bin, at London, Yorke and Carleon vpon Vske were placed Archbishops, saith some. The Epistle said [1] to be [1] sent by *Eleutherius* to king *Lucius*, for the establishing of the faith, ye may read in my Annales, Sommaries and Chronicles, truely translated & set down as mine author hath it, for some haue curtoled and corrupted it, and then fathered it vppon reuerend *Bede*, who neuer wrote word thereof, or otherwise to that effect, more then this as followeth. *Page 479* Liber custom.

In the yeare 156. *Marcus Aurelius Verus* the 14. Emperor after *Augustus*, gouerned the Empire with his Brother *Aurelius Comodus*, In whose time *Elutherius*, a Holy man, being Pope of the Church of Rome, *Lucius* king of Britaines wrote vnto him, desiring that by his commaundement hee might bee made Christian : which his request was graunted him, whereby the Britaines receiuing then the faith, kept it sound and undefiled in rest and peace, vntill *Dioclesian* the Emperours time : thus farre *Bede*, which may suffice to proue the Christian Faith there to be receiued here. And now of the London Bishops as I find them. Bede.

There remaineth in the Parish Church of S. *Peter* vppon Cornhill in London, a table wherein is written that *Lucius* founded the same Church to be an Archbishops see, and Metropolitane or chiefe church of his kingdome, and that it so endured the space of foure hundred yeares, vntill the comming of *Augustine* the Monk & others from Rome, in the raigne of the Saxons. The Archbishops names, I finde onely to be set downe by *Ioceline* of Furnes, in his book of Brittish Bishoppes, and not else where. *Thean* (sayeth hee) was the first Archbishoppe of London in the time of *Lucius*, who builded the said church of S. *Peter*, in a place called Cornhill Ioceline of Furnes.

1–1 *corr. 1633*

in London, by the aide of *Ciran*, chiefe Butler to king *Lucius.* |

Page 480 2. *Eluanus* was the second, and he builded a Library to the same church adioyning, and conuerted many of the Druides, (learned men in the Pagan law) to the Christian faith.

3. *Cadar* was the third, then followed,
4. *Obinus.*
5. *Conan.*
6. *Paludius.*
7. *Stephen.*
8. *Iltute.*
9. *Dedwin.*
10. *Theodred.*
11. *Hillary.*
12. *Guidelium.*[1]
13. *Vodimus* slaine by the Saxons.

14. *Theanus*, the foureteenth, fledde with the Britaines into Wales, about the yeare of Christ, 587. Thus much out of *Ioceline* of the Archbishops: the credit whereof I leaue to the iudgement of the learned, for I reade of a Bishop of London (not before named) in the yeare of Christ 326. to be present at the 2. councell, holden at Arles, in the time of *Constantine* the great, who subscribed thereunto in these wordes, *Ex prouincia Britaniæ Ciuitate Londinensi Restitutus Episcopus*, as plainely appeareth in the first Tome of the Councelles: hee writeth not himselfe Archbishop, and therefore maketh the matter of Archbishops doubtful, or rather ouerthroweth that opinion. 1. Tome Conc.

The Saxons being Pagans, having chased the Britons with the Christian preachers into the mountaines of Wales and Cornewall: and hauing diuided this kingdome of the Britons amongst themselues, at the length, to wit, in the yeare 596. Pope *Gregory* moued ⟨of⟩ a godly instinction (sayeth *Bede*) in the 147. yeare after the arriual of the Angles or Saxons in Britaine, sent *Augustine, Melitus, Iustus* and *Iohn* with other Monks to preach the gospel to the saide Nation of the Angles: these landed in the Ile of *Thanet*, and were first receiued by *Ethelbert*, King of Kent, whome they conuerted

*⟨*Heading sometimes Spiritual Governments* and *Government Spiritual in 1603*⟩

[1] or Guiteline, *add. 1633*

to the faith of Christ with diuers other of his people in the 34. yeare of his raigne, which *Ethelbert* gaue vnto *Augustine* the Citty of Canterbury. |

This *Augustine* in the yeare of Christ 604, consecrated *Melitus* and *Iustus* bishops, appointing *Melitus* to preach vnto the East Saxons, whose chiefe citie was London: and there K. *Sebert* Nephew to *Ethelbert* by preaching of *Melitus* receiued the word of life: and then *Ethelbert*, king of Kent builded in the Citie of London S. *Paules* Church, wherein *Melitus* began to bee Bishop in the yeare 619. and sate fiue yeares. *Ethelbert* by his charter gaue lands to this Church of S. *Paul*: so did other kings after him. King *Sebert* through the good life, and like preaching of *Melitus*, hauing receiued Baptisme, to shew himself a Christian builded a Church to the honour of God and S. *Peter*, on the west side of London, which Church is called Westminster, but the successors of *Sebert*, being Pagans, expelled *Melitus* out of their kingdomes.

Page 481

Saint Paules Church in London first founded.

1. Melitus first Bishop of London, 619.

Iustus the second, Bishop for a time, and then *Melitus* againe: after whose decease, the seate was voyde for a time: at length *Sigebert*, sonne to *Sigebert*, brother to *Sebert*, ruled in Essex: he became a Christian, and tooke to him a holy man named *Cedde*, or *Chadde*, who wan many by preaching and good life to the Christian religion.

2. Iustus, 624.

Cedde, or *Chad*, was by *Finan* consecrated Bishop of the East Saxons, and he ordred Priests and Deacons in all the parts of Essex, but especially at *Ithancaster*, and *Tilberie*.

3. Cedde, B. of London, 658: Ithancaster, and Tilberie. Raphe Cogshall.

This Citie of *Ithancaster* (sayth *Raph Cogshall*) stood on the banke of the riuer *Pante* that runneth by *Maldun* in the hundred of *Danesey*, but now is drowned in *Pante*, so that nothing remaineth but the ruine of the Citie in the Riuer. *Tilberie* (both the West and East) standeth on the Thames side, nigh ouer agaynst Grauesend.

Wina, expelled from the Church of Winchester by *Cenewalche* the king, was adopted to be the 4. Bishop of London, in the raigne of *Wolferus* king of Mercia, and sat 9. yeares.

4. Wina, 666.

Erkenwalde, borne in the castle, or towne of Stallingborough in Lindsey, first Abbot of Crotesey[1], was by *Theodore* archbishop of Canterburie, appointed to be Bishop of the East

5. Erkenwald, 680.

[1] Crotesey] Crotese or Chartesey, *1633 in marg.*

Saxons, in the Citie of London. This *Erkenwald* in the yeare of Christ 677. before he was made Bishop, had builded two Monasteries, one | for himselfe, being a Monke in the Isle of Crote in Surrey, by the riuer of Thames, and another for his sister *Edilburge*, being a Nun, in a certain place called Berching in Essex: he deceased at Berching in the yeare 697. and was then buried in *Pauls* church, and translated into the new Church of saint *Paule* in the yeare 1148.

Page 482

Crotesey, or Chattesey.

6. Waldhere 697. King Sebba became a Monke in Paules Church.

Waldhere was Bishop of London. *Sebba*, king of the East Saxons, at his hands receyued the habite of Monke, for at that time there were Monkes in *Pauls* church, as writeth *Radulphus De Diceto*[1], and others. To this Bishop he brought a great summe of money, to bee bestowed and giuen to the poore, reseruing nothing to himselfe, but rather desired to remaine poore in goodes, as in Spirit, for the Kingdome of Heauen: when hee had raigned thirty yeare, hee deceased at *Paules*, and was there buried, and lyeth nowe in a coffin of stone on the North side of the Isle next the Quire.

7. Ingwaldus, 716.

Ingwaldus, Bishop of London, was at the consecration of *Tatwine*, Archbishop of Canterbury: he confirmed the foundation of Crowland in the yeare 716. sayth *Ingulfus*, and deceased in the yeare 744. as sayth *Houeden*.

746. *Engulfe*, Bishop of London.

754. *Wichet*, or *Wigerus*, Bishop of London.

761. *Eadbrightus*, or *Edbrithe*, Bishop of London.

768. *Eadgain*, or *Eadgarus*, Bishop of London.

773. *Kenewallth*, Bishop of London.

784. *Eadbaldus*, Bishop of London.

795. *Heatbright*, Bishop of London, deceased 802. saith *Houeden*.

813. *Osmond* Bishop of London: he was witnesse to a Charter made to *Crowland* in the yeare 833. saith *Ingulfus*.

835. *Ethelnothe*, Bishop of London.

838. *Elbertus*, or *Celbertus*[2] Bishop of London.

841. *Deorwulf*,[3] Bishop of London.

850. *Swithulfus*, Bishop of London: he likewise was witnesse to a Charter of *Crowland* 851.

[1] De Diceto] Dedicato *1603*, *1633*
[2] *Ceolberht*, *Stubbs' Reg.*
[3] *Caulfe*, *1603*; *Ceorulf*, *1633*.

860. *Edstanus* Bishop of London, witnesse to a Charter to *Crowland*, 860.
870. *Vlfsius* Bishop of London.
878. *Ethelwardus*, Bishop of London.
886. *Elstanus* Bishop of London, died in the yeare 900. saith *Asser*: and all these, sayth the Authour of *Flores Historiarum*, were buried in the old church of saint *Paule*, but there remayneth now no memorie of them.
900. *Theodricus* Bishop of London: this man confirmed king *Edreds* Charter, made to Winchester in the yere 947. wherby it seemeth that he was Bishop of London of a later time then he is here placed.
922. *Welstanus* Bishop of London.
941. *Brithelme* Bishop of London.
958. *Dunstanus* Abbot of Glastonberie, then Bishop of Worcester, and then Bishop of London: he was afterward translated to Canterburie, 960.
960. *Ealfstanus* bishop of London, the 28. in number.
981. *Edgare* bishop of London: he confirmed the graunts made to Winchester, and to Crowland, 966, and againe to Crowland 970. the Charter of *Etheldred*, concerning *Vlfrunhampton*, 996.
1004. *Elphinus* bishop of London.
1010. *Alwinus* bishop of London.
1012. *Alfhune* bishop of London: he was sent into Normandie in the yeare 1013. sayth *Asser*.
1044. *Robert* a Monke of Gemerisins[1] in Normandie, bishop of London 7 yeares, afterward translated from London to Canterberie.
1050. *Specgasius* elected, but reiected by the king.
1051. *William*, a Norman, Chaplaine to *Edward* the Confessor, was made bishop of London, 1051. sate 17. yeares, and deceased 1070. He obtained of *William* the Conqueror the charter of liberties for the citie of London, as I haue set downe in my Summarie, and appeareth by his Epitaph in *Paules* church.
1070. *Hugh de Orwell* bishop of London: hee died of a leprosie when he had sitten fifteene yeares.

[1] Gemet. = Gemeticensis (of Jumièges) *1598*

1085. *Mauricius* bishop of London: in whose time, to wit, in | Page 484 the yeare 1086. the Church of S. *Paule* was burnt, with the most part of this Citie, and therefore he laid the foundation of a new large Church, and hauing sitten 22. yeares, hee deceased 1107, saith *Paris.*

1108. *Richard Beame*, or *Beamor*, Bishop of London, did wonderfully encrease the worke of this church begunne, purchasing the streetes and lanes adioyning of his owne money: and hee founded the Monasterie of S. *Osyth* in Essex: he sate bishop 19. yeares, and deceased 1127.

1127. *Gilbertus Vniuersalis*, a Canon of *Lions*, elected by *H.* the first: he deceased 1141. when he had sitten xiiii. yeares.

1142. *Robert de Sigillo*, a Monke of Reading, whom *Mawde* the Empresse made Bishop of London, where he sate xi. yeres. *Geffrey de Magnauile* tooke him prisoner at Fulham, and he deceased 1152.

1153. *Richard Beames*, Archdeacon of Essex, bishop of London ten yeares, who deceased 1162.

1163. *Gilbert Foliot* Bishop of Hereford, from whence translated to London, sate 23. yeares, and deceased 1186.

1189. *Richard Fitz Nele* the kings Treasurer, Archdeacon of Essex, elected Bishop of London at Pipwel, 1189: he sate nine yeares, and deceased 1198. This man also tooke great paines about the building of *Paules* Church, and raised many other goodly buildings in his Diocesse.

1199. *William S. Mary Church*, a Norman, bishop of London, who was one of the three Bishops that by the Popes commaundement executed his interdiction or curse vpon the whole realme of England, but he was forced with the other Bishops to flie the Realme in 1208. and his Castell at Stortforde[1] in Essex, was by commaundement of king *Iohn* ouerthrowne, 1210. This *William* in companie of the Archbishop of Canterburie and of the Bishop of Elie went to Rome, and there complained agaynst the king 1212. and returned, so as in the yeare 1215. King *Iohn* in the Church of Saint *Paule*, at the handes of this *William* tooke vpon him the Crosse for the holy land: hee resigned his Bishopricke of his owne voluntarie, in the yeare, 1221. sayth *Cogshall.* |

[1] Stortforde] *1598;* Stratford *1603*

1221. *Eustachius de Fauconbridge*, Treasurer of the Exchequer *Page 485* (saith *Paris*) Chancellor of the Exchequer (sayth *Taxtor*, and *Cogshall*) bishop of London, 1223. whilest at Chelmesforde he was giuing holy Orders, a great tempest of winde and raine annoyed so many as came thither, whereof it was gathered, how highly God was displeased with such as came to receyue Orders, to the ende they might liue a more easie life of the Stipende appoynted to the Church men, giuing themselues to banketting, and so with vncleane and filthie bodies, (but more vncleane soules) presume to minister vnto God, the Authour of puritie and cleannesse. *Falcatius de Breut* was deliuered to his custodie in the yeare 1224. This *Eustachius* deceased in the yeare 1228. and was buryed in *Paules* Church, in the South side without or aboue the Quire.

1229. *Roger Niger* Archdeacon of Colchester, made Bishop of London. In the yeare 1230. sayth *Paris*, vpon the feast day of the conuersion of S. *Paul*, when he was at Masse in the Cathedrall Church of S. *Paule*, a great multitude of people being there present, suddenly the weather waxed darke, so as one could scantly see another, and an horrible thunderclap lighted on the Church, which so shooke it that it was like to haue fallen, and therewithal out of a darke cloude proceeded a flash of lightning, that all the Church seemed to be on fire, whereupon such a stench ensued, that all men thought they should haue died: thousands of men and women ran out of the church, and being astonied fell vpon the ground voyd of all sence and vnderstanding, none of all the multitude tarried in the Church, saue the Bishop and one Deacon, which stood still before the high Aultar, awayting the will of God: when the ayre was cleansed, the multitude returned into the Church, and the bishop ended the seruice.

This *Roger Niger* is commended to haue beene a man of worthy life, excellently well learned, a notable Preacher, pleasant in talke, milde of countenance, and liberall at his table. He admonished the Vsurers of his time to leaue Mathew Paris. such enormities, as they tendered the saluation of theyr soules, and to doe penaunce for that they had committed:

but when hee sawe they laughed him to scorne, and also
Page 486 threatned him, the bishop generally excommuni|cated and accursed all such, and commaunded streightly that such Usurers should depart farther from the Citie of London, which hither towardes had beene ignoraunt of such mischiefe and wickednesse, least his Dioces should be infected there-withall. He fell sicke, and dyed at his Mannor of Bishops hall, in the lordship and parish of Stebunheth, in the yeare 1241, and was buried in *Pauls* Church, on the north side of the Presbiterie, in a faire tombe coped, of gray Marble.

1241. *Fulco Basset* Deane of Yorke, by the death of *Gilbert Basset* possessed his lands, and was then made bishop of London, deceased on the xxi. of May, in the yere 1259. as saith *Iohn Taxtor*, and was buried in *Paules* Church.

1259. *Henry Wingham* Chancelor of England, made bishop of London, deceased in the yeare 1262. sayth *Taxtor*, and was buryed in *Paules* Church, on the South side without or aboue the Quire, in a Marble Monument, close at the heade of *Fauconbridge*.

1262. *Richard Talbot* Bishop of London, streghtwayes after his consecration deceased, saith *Euersden*.

1262. *Henry Sandwich*, bishop of London, deceased in the yeare 1273, as the same Author affirmeth.

1273. *Iohn Cheshul* Deane of *Paules*, treasurer of the Exchequer, and keeper of the great seale, was bishop of London, and deceased in the yeare 1279. saith *Euersden*.

1280. *Fulco Louel* Archdeacon of Colchester, elected bishop of London, but refused the place.

1280. *Richard Grauesend* Archdeacon of Northampton, Bishop of London. It appeareth by the Charter warren graunted to this bishop, that in his time there were two woods in the parish of Stebunhith pertaining to the said bishop: I haue since I kept house for my self, knowne the one of them by Bishops hal, but now they are both made plain of wood, and not to be discerned from other grounds. Some haue fabuled that this *Richard Grauesend* bishop of London, in the yeare 1392. the 16. of *Richard* the 2. purchased the Charter of liberties to this City: which thing hath no

Fable of Richard Grauesend reproued.

possibility of truth, as I haue proued, for he deceased in the yeare 1303. almost 90. yeares before that time. |

1307. *Raph Baldocke* Deane of Powles, Bishop of London, consecrated at Lyons by *Peter* Bishoppe of Alba, in the yeare 1307: he was a great furtherer of the new work of Powles, to witte, the East end called our Lady Chappell, and other adioyning: this *Raph* deceased in the yeare 1313. and was buried in the said Lady Chappell, vnder a flat stone. *Page 487*

1313. *Gilbert Segraue* was consecrated Bishop of London, and sate 3. yeares.

1317. *Richard Newport*, Bishop of London, sate 2. years, and was buried in *Paules* church.

1318. *Stephen Grauesend*, Bishoppe of London, sate twentie yeares.

1338. *Richard Bentworth* Bishop of London and chancelour of England, deceased the yeare 1339.

1339. *Raph Stratford* Bishoppe of London: he purchased the peece of ground called No mans land beside Smithfield, and dedicated it to the vse of buriall, as before hath appeared: hee was borne at Stratford vpon Auon, and therefore builded a chappel to Saint *Thomas* there: he sate fourteene yeares, deceased at Stebunhith.

1354. *Michaell Norbroke*, Bishop of London, deceased in the yeare 1361. sayth *Mirimouth*, sate 7. yeares.

1362. *Simon Sudbery* Bishoppe of London, sate 13. yeares, translated to bee Archbishoppe of Canterbury in the yeare 1375.

1375. *William Courtney* translated from Hereford to the Bishopricke of London, and after translated from thence to the Archbishopricke of Canterbury, in the yeare 1381.

1381. *Robert Breybrooke* Chanon of Lichfield, Bishoppe of London, made Chancellour in the 6. of *R.* the 2. sate Bishoppe 20. yeares, and deceased in the yeare 1404: hee was buried in the saide Lady chappell at Powles.

1405. *Roger Walden* Treasurer of the Exchequer, Archbishop of Canterbury, was deposed, and after made bishop of London: he deceased in the yeare 1406. and was buried in Powles church, ⟨by⟩ Alhallowes aultar.

1406. *Nicholas*[1] *Bubwith* Bishoppe of London, treasurer of the |

[1] Richard *1603*

Page 488 Exchequer, translated to *Salisbury*, and from thence to Bathe, and lyeth buried at Wels.

1407. *Richard Clifford*, remoued from Worcester to London, deceased 1422. as saith *Thomas Walsingham*, and was buried in *Paules*.

1422. *Iohn Kempe* fellow of *Martin*[1] Colledge in Oxford, was made Bishop of Rochester, from whence remoued to Chichester, and thence to London: he was made the kings Chancellor in the yeare 1425. the 4. of *Henry* the 6. and was remoued from London to Yorke, in the yeare 1426. He sate Archbishop there 25. yeares, and was translated to Canterbury, hee was afterwards made Cardinall in the yeare 1452. In the Bishop of Londons house at Fulham he receiued the Crosse, and the next day the Pall at the hands of *Thomas Kempe* Bishop of London: he deceased in the yeare 1454.

1426. *William Gray* Deane of Yorke, consecrated Bishop of London, who founded a Colledge at Thele in Hartfordshire for a Maister and foure Chanons, and made it a cell to Elsing spittle in London, it had of old time beene a Colledge, decayed & therefore newly founded: he was translated to Lincolne 1431.

1432. *Robert Fitzhugh* Archdeacon of Northampton, consecrated Bishop of London, sate 5. yeares, deceased in the yeare 1435, and was buried on the south side of the Quire of Powles.

1435. *Robert Gilbert* Doctor of Diuinity, Deane of Yorke, consecrated Bishop of London, sate 12. yeares, deceased 1448.

1449. *Thomas Kempe*, Archdeacon of Richmond, consecrated Bishop of London at Yorke house, (now White hall) by the hands of his vncle *Iohn Kemp*, Archbishop of Yorke, the eight of February, 1449. He founded a chappell of the Trinity in the body of saint Pauls church on the north side, he sate Bishoppe of London 39. yeares, and 48 dayes, and then, deceased in the yere 1489. was there buried.

1489. *Iohn Marshal* bishop of London, deceased in the year 1493.

1493. *Richard Hill* bishop of London, deceased 1495, and was buried in the body of saint *Paules* church.

[1] *Merton*

1496. *Thomas Sauage* first bishop of Rochester, then bishop of London 5. yeares, was translated to Yorke 1501. where hee | sate Archbishop seuen yeares, and was there buried in the yere 1507. *Page 489*

1502. *William Wareham* Bishop of London, made keeper of the great Seale, sate two yeares, was translated to Canterbury.

1504. *William Barons* Bishop of London, sate 10. moneths, and 11. dayes, deceased in the yeare 1505.

1505. *Richard Fitz Iames* fellow of Martin[1] Colledge in Oxford, in the raigne of *Henry* the 6. was made Bishop of Rochester, after Bishop of Chichester, and then Bishop of London. He deceased 1521. and lyeth buried hard beneath the Northwest pillar of the Steple in *Paules*, vnder a faire tombe of marble, ouer the which was builded a faire Chappell of timber, with stayres mounting thereunto: this chappell was burned with fire from the steeple 1561. and the tombe was taken downe.

1521. *Cuthbert Tunstal*, Doctor of law, Master of the rowles, Lord priuie Seale, and Bishop of London, was thence translated to the Bishopricke of Durham in the yeare 1529.

1529. *Iohn Stokesley*[2] Bishop of London, sate 9.[3] yeares, deceased in the yeare 1539. and was buried in the Lady chappel in *Paules*.

1539. *Edmond Boner* Doctor of the ciuill law, Archdeacon of Leycester, then Bishop of Hereford, was elected to London in the yeare 1539. whilest he was beyond the seas, Embassadour for king *Henry* the eight. On the first of September 1549. he preached at *Paules* Crosse, for the which sermon he was charged before the counsell of king *Edward* the 6. by *William Latimer* Parson of saint *Lawrence Poltney*, and *Iohn Hoper*, sometime a white Monke, and being conuented before certain Commissioners at Lambith, was for his disobedience to the kings order, on the 20. day of the same month sent to the Marshalsey and depriued from his bishopricke.

1550. *Nicholas Ridley* Bishop of Rochester, elected Bishop of London, was installed in *Paules* church on the 12. of Aprill.

[1] *Merton* [2] ⟨Consecrated Nov. 27, 1530; d. Sept. 8, 1539⟩. [3] 13 *1603*.

This man by his deede dated the 12. day after Christmas, in the 4. yeare of *Edward* the sixt, gaue to the king the Mannors of Branketrie and Southminster, and the patron-
Page 490 age of the church | of Cogshall in Essex, the Mannors of Stebunheth and Hackney, in the County of Middlesex, and the Marsh of Stebunheth, with al and singular messuages, lands, and tenements to the said Mannors belonging, and also the aduowson of the viccarage of the parish church of Cogshall in Essex aforesaid : which grant was confirmed by the Deane and Chapter of *Paules* the same day and yeare with exception of such lands in Southminster, Stebunheth and Hackney, as onely pertayned to them. The said king *Edward* by his letters patents, dated the 16. of Aprill, in the said fourth yeare of his raigne, granted to sir *Thomas Wentworth*, Lord *Wentworth*, Lord Chamberlaine of the kings houshold, for and in consideration of his good and faithfull seruice before done, a part of the late receiued gift, to wit, the Lordshippes of Stebunheth and Hackney, with all the members and appurtenances thereto belonging in Stebunheth, Hackney way, Shorditch, Holiwell streete, White chappell, Stratford at Bow, Poplar, North streete, Limehouse, Ratliffe, Cleue streete, Brockstreet, Mile end, Bleten hall green, Oldford, Westheth, Kingsland, Shakelwell, Newinton streete, alias Hackney street, Clopton, Churchstreete, Welstreet, Humbarton, Grouestreet, Gunston street, *alias* Morestreet, in the county of Middlesex, together with the Marsh of Stebunhith, &c. The Mannor of Hackney was valued at lxi.li. ix.s. 4.d. by yeare: and the Mannor of Stebunhith at cxl.li. 8.s. 11.d. ob. by yeare, to be holden in chiefe, by the seruice of the twenti⟨e⟩th part of a knights fee. This Bishop *Nicholas Ridley*, for preaching a sermon at *Paules* crosse, on the 16. of Iuly in the yeare 1553. was committed to the Towre of London, where he remained prisoner till the 10. of Aprill, in the yeare 1554. and was thence sent to Oxford, there to dispute with the Diuines and learned men of the contrary opinion, and on the 16. of October 1555. he was burned at Oxford for opinions against the Romish order of sacraments, &c.

1553. *Edmond Boner* aforesaid, being released out of the

Marshalsey, was restored to the Bishoprick of London, by Q. *Mary* on the 5. of August in the yeare 1553. and againe deposed by Q. *Elizabeth*, in the moneth of Iuly *An.* 1559. and was eftsoones committed to the Marshalsey, where he died on the 5. of September 1569. and was at midnight buried amongst other prisoners in *S. Georges* churchyard. |

1559. *Edmond Grindal* bishop of London, being consecrated *Page 491* the 21. of December 1559. was translated to Yorke, in the yeare 1570. and from thence remoued to Canterbury, in the yeare 1575. He died blind 1583. on the 6. of Iuly, and was buried at Crodowne in *Surrey*.

1570. *Edwine Sands*, being translated from Worcester to the bishopricke of London, in the yeare 1570. was thence translated to Yorke in the yeare 1576. and died in the yeare 1588.

1576. *Iohn Elmere* bishop of London, deceased in the yere 1594 on the 3 of Iune at Fulanham, & was buried in *Paules* church before saint *Thomas* chappell.

1594. *Richard Fletcher*, bishop of Worcester, was on the 30. of December in *Paules* church elected bishop of London, and deceased on the 15 of Iune 1596. Hee was buried in *Paules* church, without any solemne funerall.

1597. *Richard Bancroft* Doctor of Diuinity, consecrated at Lambith on Sunday the eight of May, now sitteth bishop of London, in the yeare 1598. being installed there.

This much for the succession of the Bishops of London, whose diocesse containeth the citie of London, the whole shires of Middlesex and Essex, and a part of Hartfordshire. These Bishops haue for Assistants in the Cathedrall church of saint *Paules*, a Deane, a chaunter, a chauncelor, a Treasurer, 5. Archdeacons, to wit, London, Middlesex, Essex, Colchester, and saint *Albons*, and 30. prebendaries: there appertaineth also to the said churches for furniture of the Quire in diuine seruice, and ministration of the sacraments, a Colledge of 12. pety Chanons, 6. vickars choral, & Queristers, &c.

This Diocesse is diuided into Parishes, euery parish hauing his Parson, or vicar at the least, learned men for the most part, and sufficient Preachers to instruct the people. There were in this citty and within the suburbes thereof in the raigne of *Henry* the second (as writeth *Fitz Stephens*) 13. great conuentuall churches, besides the lesser sort called parish churches, to the number of 126, al which conuentuall churches, and some others since that time founded, are now suppressed and gone, except the Cathedrall church of saint *Paule* in London, and the colledge of saint *Peter* at Westminster : | of all which parish churches, though I haue spoken, yet for more ease to the Reader, I will here againe set them downe in manner of a Table, not by order of Alphabet, but as they be placed in the wardes and suburbes.

Page 492

Parish Churches

IN Portsoken ward, parish churches 3.

The Hospitall of saint *Katheren* serueth for that libertie.

Trinity in the Minories, for precinct thereof.

S. *Bottolphe* by Aldegate, the onely parish church for that ward.

2. In Tower streete warde. 4.

In the Tower, saint *Peter*, for the Inhabitants there.

Alhallowes Barking by the Tower.

S. *Olaue*, in Hart streete.

S. *Dunstone* in the East.

3. In Aldegate ward. 3.

S. *Katheren* Christs church.

S. *Andrewes* vndershafte.

S. *Katheren* Colman church.

4. In Limestreet ward none.

There was saint *Mary* at the Axe, and saint *Augustine* in the wall, both sup⟨p⟩ressed, and vnited, the one to Alhallowes in the wall, in Brodestreete ward, the other to saint *Andrewe* vndershaft in Limestreete warde.

5. In Bishops gate warde. 3.

S. *Bottolphes* without Bishopsgate.

S. *Ethelburge* within the Gate.

S. *Helens* adioyning to the Nuns Priory.

6. In Brodestreete ward. 6.

Alhallows by the wall.

S. *Peters* the Poore.
S. *Martins Oteswitche.*
S. *Benet Fynke.*
S. *Bartilmew* by the Exchange.
S. *Christopher* by the stockes market.

7. In Cornhill warde. 2. |

S. *Peter* vpon Cornehill. *Page 493*
S. *Michaell* vpon Cornehill.

8. In Langborne ward 7.

S. *Gabriel* Fenchurch.
S. *Dyones* Backchurch.
Alhallowes in Lombardstreete.
S. *Edmond* in Lombardstreete.
Alhallowes Staning at Mart lane end.
S. *Nicholas Acon* in Lombardstreete.
S. *Mary Wolnoth* in Lombardstreete.

9. In Billinsgate ward 5.

S. *Buttolph* by Billinsgate.
S. *Mary* on the Hill.
S. *Margaret* Pattens.
S. *Andrew* Hubert in Eastcheape.
S. *George* in Buttolph lane.

10. In Bridgeward within 4.

S. *Magnus* at the bridge foote.
S. *Margaret* bridgestreete.
S. *Leonard* Milkchurch, Fishstreete hill.
S. *Benet* Grasse church.

11. In Candlewike streete 5.

S. *Clements* Eastcheape.
S. *Mary* Abchurch.
S. *Michael* in crooked lane, somtime a Colledge.
S. *Martins* Orgars.
S. *Laurence* Pountney, sometime a colledge.

12. In Walbrooke warde 5.

S. *Swithen* by London stone.
S. *Mary* Woolchurch.

S. *Stephen* by Walbrooke.
S. *Iohn* vpon Walbrooke.
S. *Mary* Bothaw.

13. In Downegate ward 2.

Alhallowes Hay wharfe, in the Roperie.
Alhallowes the lesse, in the Roperie.

14. In the Vintrie ward 4. |

Page 494 S. *Michael Paternoster* in the Royall, sometime a colledge.
S. *Thomas* Apostles.
S. *Martin* in the Vintrie.
S. *Iames* at Garlicke Hith.

15. In Cordwainer streete ward 3.

S. *Anthonies* in Budge row.
Alde Mary church. New *Mary* Church, or *Mary le Bow.*

16. In Cheape Warde 7.

S. *Benet* Sorhoge, or Syth.
S. *Pancrate* by Sopars lane.
S. *Mildred* in the Poultrie.
S. *Mary* Colchurch.
S. *Martin* Pomerie in Ironmonger lane.
Alhallowes in Honie lane.
S. *Laurence* in the Iury.
The chappell of Guildhall, somtime a colledge.

17. In Colemanstreete ward 3.

S. *Olaue* Vpwell in the old Iurie.
S. *Margaret* in Lothburie.
S. *Stephen* in Colemanstreet.

18. Bassings hall ward 1.

S. *Michael* at Bassings hall.

19. In Cripplegate ward 6.

S. *Mary* Aldermanburie.
S. *Alphage* sometime an hospitall of *Elsing*.
S. *Mary Magdalen* in Milkstreete.
S. *Albons* in Woodstreete.
S. *Michael* in Hugen lane.
S. *Giles* without Cripplesgate.

20. In Aldersgate warde 6.

S. *Iohn Zacharie.*
S. *Mary Staining.*
S. *Olaue* in siluerstreete.
S. *Leonard* in Foster lane.
S. *Anne* by Aldersgate.
S. *Buttolph* without Aldersgate.[1] |

21. In Faringdon ward within, the Cathedrall Church of saint *Paule*, and parish Churches 9. *Page 495*

S. *Peters* at the Crosse in Cheape.
S. *Fauster* in Foster lane.
Christ Church made a parish Church of the gray Friers church, and of two parish Churches, saint *Nicholas*, and saint *Ewin*, and also an Hospitall for poore children.
S. *Mathew* in Fryday street.
S. *Augustine* by *Paules* gate.
S. *Faith* vnder *Paules* Church.
S. *Martins* at Ludgate.
S. *Anne* at the blacke Friers.
S. *Michael* at corne by *Paules.*
Chappell of saint *Iames* by Cripplesgate.

22. In Bredstreete ward 4.

Alhallowes in Bredstreete.
S. *Mildreds* in Bredstreete.
S. *Iohn Euangelist* in Fryday streete.
S. *Margaret Moses* in Fryday streete.

23. In Queene hithe ward 7.

S. *Trinitie* in Trinity lane.
S. *Nicholas* Cold Abbey.
S. *Nicholas* Olaue.
S. *Mary Mounthaunt.*
S. *Michael* at Queene hithe.
S. *Mary* at *Sommers* hithe.
S. *Peters* at *Paules* wharfe.

[1] Aldersgate] *1598;* Aldgate *1603*

24. In Castle Baynards warde 4.

S. *Benet* Hude, or Hith, by *Paules* wharfe.
S. *Andrewe* by the Wardrobe.
S. *Mary Magdalen* in old Fishstreete.
S. *Gregorie* by *Paules* Church.

25. In Faringdon ward without 7.

S. *Sepulchers* without Newgate.
S. *Andrew* in Oldburne.
S. *Dunstone* in the west.
S. *Bartlemew* by the Priorie. |
Page 496 S. *Bartlemew* the Hospitall.
S. *Briget* or *Brides* in Fleetstreet.
S. *Parnell* in the Temple for the studentes there.

26. In the Borough of Southwarke, and Bridge Warde without, 4.

S. *Sauiours* in Southwarke made of twaine, *vz. S. Mary Magdalen*, and *S. Margaret.*
S. *George* the Marter.
S. *Thomas* the Hospitall.
S. *Olaue* in Southwarke.
} *Dioces of Winchester.*

Thus haue yee in the 26. Wards of London and Borough of Southwarke, parrish Churches to the number of 114.

And in the suburbes adioyning, parrish Churches 9. as followeth.

S. *Mary Magdalen* at Bermondsey in the borough of Southwarke, Dioces Winton.
S. *Mary Matfelon* White chappell.
S. *Leonard* Shorditch.
S. *Iohn Baptist* Clearken well.
S. *Giles* in the field, sometime an Hospitall.

In the Dutchie of Lancaster.

S. *Clement Danes* without Temple barre.
S. *Iohn Baptist Sauoy*, an Hospitall.

In the Citty of Westminster, that Liberty as followeth.

The Colledge of *S. Peter* called Westminster.

Parish Churches twaine.

S. *Margaret* a parrish church by Westminster.

S. *Martin* in the field by Charing Crosse.

Thus haue yee in the Wards of London and in the suburbs of the same cittie, the borough of Southwarke, and the Cittie of Westminster, a Cathedral church of *S. Paule*, a Collegiate church of *S. Peter* in Westminster, and Parish churches, 123. |

Hospitals in this Cittie, and Suburbes thereof, that haue beene of old time, and now presently are, I reade of these as followeth.

Page 497

HOSPITAL of saint *Mary* in the parish of Barking church, that was prouided for poore priests, and others, men and women in the City of London, that were fallen into frensie or losse of their memory, vntill such time as they should recouer, was since suppressed and giuen to the Hospitall of saint *Katherine* by the Tower.

An hospital for frensie people in Tower street ward.

S. Anthonies, an Hospitall of 13. poore men and colledge, with a free schoole, for poore mens children, founded by Cittizens of London, lately by *Iohn Tate*, first a Brewer & then a Mercer, in the Warde of Brodestreete, suppressed in the raigne of *Edward* the sixt, the schoole in some sorte remayning, but sore decayed.

S. Anthonies in Brodestreete warde.

S. Bartlemew in Smithfield, an Hospitall of great receipt, and reliefe for the poore, was suppressed by *Henry* the eight, and againe by him giuen to the Citty, and is endowed by the Cittizens beneuolence.

S. Bartilmew in Smithfielde.

S. Giles in the fieldes was an Hospitall for leprose people out of the City of London and shire of Middlesex, founded by *Matilde* the Queene, wife to *Henry* the 1, and suppressed by K. *Henry* the eight.

S. Giles in the fields.

S. Iohn of *Ierusalem* by Westsmithfield, an Hospitall of the Knightes of the Rhodes, for maintenance of soldiers against the Turkes and Infidels, was suppressed by King *Henry* the 8.

S. Iohn of Ierusalem for defence of the Rhodes.

S. Iames in the field was an Hospitall for leprouse virgines of the citty of London, founded by cittizens for that purpose, and suppressed by king *Henry* the 8.

S. Iames in the field.

S. Iohns at Sauoy.

S. Iohn at *Sauoy*, an Hospitall for reliefe of one hundreth poor people, founded by *Henry* the seuenth, suppressed by *Edwarde* the sixt. Againe new founded, indowed and furnished by Queene *Mary*, and so remayneth.

Page 498
S. Katheren by the Tower.

S. Katherine by the Tower of London, an Hospitall with a Maister, Brethren, and sisters and Almes women, founded by *Matilde* wife to King *Stephen*, not suppressed, but in force as afore.

Elsing Spittle.

S. Mary within Criplesgate, an Hospitall founded by *William Elsing*, for an hundred blind people of the cittie, was suppressed by king *Henry* the eight.

S. Mary Bethlem.

S. Mary Bethelem without Bishopsgate was an Hospitall, founded by *Simon Fitzmary* a Cittizen of London to haue beene a Priory, and remayneth for lunaticke people, being suppressed and giuen to Christs Hospitall.

S. Mary Spittle.

S. Mary without Bishopsgate was an Hospitall and Priorie, called *S. Mary Spittle,* founded by a cittizen of London, for reliefe of the poore, with prouision of 180. beddes there for the poore: it was suppressed in the raigne of King *Henry* the eight.

S. Mary Rounsiuall.

S. Mary Rounceuall by Charing crosse, was an Hospital suppressed with the Priories Aliens, in the raigne of king *Henry* the fifte, then was it made a brotherhoode in the fifteenth of *Edward* the fourth, and again suppressed by king *Edward* the sixt.

S. Thomas of Acon.

S. Thomas of *Acres* in Cheape was an Hospitall for a Master and brethren (in the Record called *Militia*): it was surrendred and sold to the Mercers.

S. Thomas in Southwarke.

S. Thomas in *Southwarke* being an Hospitall of great receite for the poore, was suppressed, but againe newly founded and indowed by the beneuolence and charitie of the cittizens of London.

Hospital without Aldersgate.

An Hospitall there was without Aldersgate, a cell to the house of *Cluny*, of the French order, suppressed by King *Henry* the fift.

Hospitall without Criplesgate.

An Hospitall without Criplesgate, also a like Cell to the saide house of Cluny, suppressed by king *Henry* the 5.

Hospitall in Oldborne.

A third Hospitall in Oldborne, being also a Cell to the saide house of *Cluny*, suppressed by king *Henry* the 5.

The Hospitall or Almes house called Gods house, for thirteene poore men, with a colledge called Whitington colledge, founded by *Richard Whitington* Mercer, and suppressed: but the poor re|maine, and are paid their allowance by the Mercers. Gods house at Whittington Colledge. *Page 499*

Christs Hospitall in Newgate market of a new foundation in the Grey Fryers church by king *Henry* the eight: poor fatherless children be there brought vp and nourished at the charges of the cittizens, to the number of——. Christs Hospitall.

Bridewell, now an Hospitall (or house of correction) founded by king *Edward* the sixt, to be a Workehouse for the poore and idle persons of the City, wherein a great number of vagrant persons be now set a worke, and relieued at the charges of the cittizens. Of all these Hospitals, being twenty in number, you may reade before in their seuerall places, as also of good and charitable prouisions made for the poore, by sundrie well disposed Cittizens. Hospitall of Bridewell.

Now of Leprose people, and Lazar houses.

IT is to be obserued, that leprose persons were alwayes, for auoiding the daunger of infection, to be separated from the sound, &c. God himselfe commaunding to put out of the Host euery leaper. Whereupon I reade that in a prouinciall Synode holden at Westminster by *Hubert* Archbishoppe of Canterbury, in the yeare of Christ 1200. the second of king *Iohn*, it was decreed according to the institution of the Lateran Counsaile, that when so many leprose people were assembled, that might bee able to builde a Church with a Churchyeard for them-selues, and to haue one especiall priest of their owne, that they should bee permitted to haue the same without contradiction, so they bee not iniurious to the olde Churches, by that which was graunted to them for pitties sake. And further it was decreede, that they bee not compelled to giue any Tithes of their Gardens or increase of cattell. Leuiticus 15. Numbers 5. Leprose persons to be separated from the sound.

I haue moreouer heard, that there is a writte in our Law, *de leproso amouendo*, and I haue read that king *Edward* the third in the 20. yeare of his raigne, gaue commaundement to the mayor and Shiriffes of London, to make proclamation in Leprouse persons to be voided the Citty.

euery Ward of the citty and suburbes, that all leprose persons inhabiting there should auoid within fifteen dayes next, and that no man suffer any | such leprose person to abide within his house, vpon paine to forfeite his said house, and to incurre the kinges further displeasure: And that they should cause the said Lepers to be remoued into some out places of the fieldes, from the haunt or company of sound people: whereupon certaine Lazar houses, as may be supposed, were then builded without the cittie some good distance, to wit, the locke without Southwarke in Kent street, one other betwixt the Miles end and Stratford Bow, one other at Kingsland, betwixt Shoreditch and Stoke Newington, and an other at Knightes bridge, west from Charing crosse. These foure I haue noted to bee erected for the receit of Leprouse people sent out of the citty. At that time also the cittizens required of the Gardian of saint *Giles* hospitall, to take from them, and to keepe continually, the number of foureteene persons leprous, according to the foundation of *Matilde* the Queene, which was for leprous persons of the cittie of London and the shire of Middlesex, which was granted: more, the Wardens or Keepers of the Portes, Gates or Posternes of this citty were sworne in the Mayors court before the Recorder, &c. That they should well and faithfully keepe the same Portes and Posternes, and not to suffer any leprous person to enter the sayde citty.

Page 500

Lazar houses builded. The locke in Kentstreet, one other beyonde the Miles end, one other at Kingesland, one other at Knightsbridge. W. Dunthorn.

Portars of the gates of London sworn.

John Gardener Porter of the Postern by the Tower his oth before the Mayor and Recorder of London, on Monday after the feast of saint *Bartlemew*, the 49. of *Edward* the third: *That the Gates and Posterne be well and faithfully kept in his office and Baylywicke, and that he should not suffer any leapers or leaper to enter the citty, or to remaine in the suburbes, and if any leaper or leapers force themselues to enter by his Gates or Posterne, hee to binde them fast to horses, and send them to bee examined of the superiors*, &c.

Portars of the gates and Posterns sworne.

Finally, I read that one *William Pole* Yeoman of the crowne to king *Edward* the fourth, being striken with a leprosie, was also desirous to build an Hospitall, with a chappell to the honour of God and saint *Anthony*, for the reliefe and harborow of such leprous persons as were destitute in the kingdome, to the end they should not be offensiue to other in their passing to and fro: for the which cause *Edward* the 4. did by his charter dated the | 12. of his raigne, giue vnto the said *W.* for euer, a certaine parcell of his land, lying in his high way of Highgate, and Haloway, within the Countie of Middlesex, containing 60. foote in length, & 34. in breadth. *Page 501* Lazar house at Holoway.

The temporall Gouernment of this City, somewhat in briefe manner.

THIS Citie of London being vnder the gouernment of the Britons, Romaines, and Saxons, the most ancient and famous City of the whole realme, was at length destroied by the Danes, and left desolate: as may appeare by our histories. But *Aelfred* king of the west Saxons, hauing brought this whole realme (from many parts) into one Monarkie, honourably repayred this Citie, and made it againe habitable, and then committed the custody thereof to his sonne in law *Adhered* Earle of Mercia: after whose decease the Citie with all other possessions, pertayning to the saide Earle, returned to king *Edward* surnamed the Elder, &c. And so remained in the kings hands, being gouerned vnder him by Portgraues (or Portreues) which name is compounded of the two saxon words, *porte*, and *gerefe* or *reue*. *Porte* betokeneth a Towne, and *Gerefe* signifieth a Gardian, ruler or keeper of the towne. Patent. Aserius Meneuen. Florencius Wigorn. Marianus Scotus. Portgraues. RobertFabian.

These Gouernors of old time (saith *Robert Fabian*) with the lawes and customes then vsed within this citie, were registred in a booke called the Doomes day, written in the saxon tongue: but of later dayes when the said lawes and customes were changed, and for that also the said booke was of a small hand, sore defaced, & hard to be red or vnderstood, it was lesse set by, so that it was imbeseled, & lost. Thus farre *Fabian.*

Notwithstanding I haue found by search of diuers old Registers and other record abroad, namely in a booke sometime appertayning to the Monastery of saint *Albons*, of the Portgraues, & other Gouernors of this citie, as followeth. Li. S. Albanie.

First, that in the raigne of king *Edward* the last before the con|quest, *Wolfegare* was Portgraue: as may appeare by the Charter of the same king, in these words. *Edward king,* *Page 502*

Cittizens of London called Burgesses.

greeteth Alfward Bishop, and Wolfgar my Portgraue, & all the Burgesses of London. And afterward that in another charter, king *Edward* greeteth *William* Bishop, and *Swetman* my Portgraue. And after that in another charter to the Abbey of Chertsey, to *William* Bishop, and *Leofstane*, and *Alssy* Portgraues. In the raigne of *William* Conqueror, *William* Bishop of London procured of the said Conqueror his Charter of liberties, to the same *William* Bishop, & *Godfrey* Portgraue, in saxon tongue, and corrected in English thus:

Charter of W. Conquerour.

William king greet W. Bishop, & Godfrey Portgraue, & all the Burgeses within London, French and English. And I graunt that they be all their law worth, that they were in Edwards dayes the king. And I will that each child bee his fathers heire. And I will not suffer that any man do you wrong, and God you keepe. And then in the raigne of the said Conqueror & of *W. Rufus*, *Godfrey de Magnauile* was Portgraue, (or shiriffe) as may appeare by their Charters, and *Richard de Par* was Prouost.

Prouost.

In the raigne of king *Henry* the first, *Hugh Buche* was Portgraue, and *Leofstanus* Goldsmith Prouost, buried at Bermondsey.

Leyland.

After them *Aubery de Vere* was Portgraue, and *Robert Bar Querel* Prouost. This *Aubery de Vere* was slaine in the raigne of K. *Stephen.* It is to be noted also that K. *H.* the first granted to the Citizens of London the Shriuewicke thereof, and of Middlesex, as in another place is shewed.

Shiriffes.

In the raigne of king *Stephen*, *Gilbert Becket* was Portgraue, and *Andrew Bucheuet* Prouost.

After him, *Godfrey Magnauile*, the sonne of *William*, the sonne of *Godfrey Magnauile*, by the gift of *Maulde* the Empresse, was Portgraue or shiriffe of London and Middlesex, for the yearely farme of three hundred pound, as appeareth by the Charter.

In the time of king *H.* the second, *Peter Fitz Walter* was Portgraue: after him, *Iohn Fitz Nigel* was Portgraue: after him *Ernulfus Buchel* became Portgraue: and after him,

William Fitz Isabel. These Portgraues are also in diuers recordes called Vice|counties, Vicounties, or shiriffes, as being vnder an Earle, for that they then, as since, vsed that office as the shiriffes of London do till this day. Some Authors do call them Domesmen, Eldermen, or Judges of the kings Court.

Page 503

Portgraues, since called Shiriffes, and Iudges of the Kings Court, & haue therefore vnder Shiriffes men learned in the law, to sit in their Courts.

William Fitz Stephen, noting the estate of this Citie, and gouernment thereof, in his time vnder the raigne of king *Stephen*, and of *Henry* the second, hath these words.

Domesmen of Iudges of the kings Court.

This Cittie (saith he) *euen as Rome, is diuided into wardes, it hath yearely shiriffes insteade of Consuls, it hath the Dignity of Senators and Aldermen, it hath vnder Officers, & according to the quality of lawes, it hath seueral Courts, and general assemblies vpon appointed dayes.* Thus much for the antiquity of shiriffes, and also of Aldermen, in seuerall Wardes of this Cittie, may suffice. And now for the name of Bailiffes, and after that, of Maiors as followeth.

In the first yeare of king *Richard* the first, the Citizens of London obtained to be gouerned by two Bailiffes, which bailiffes are in diuers ancient deeds called shiriffes, according to the speech of the lawe, which called the shire *Balliua*, for that they, like as the Portgraues, vsed the same office of shriuewicke, for the which the City paid to fee farme three hundreth pounds yearely as before, since the raigne of *Henry the* first, which also is yet paid by the Citie into the Exchequer vntill this day.

Bailiffes of London.

They also obtained to haue a Maior, to be their principall Gouernour and Lieftenant of the citie, as of the kings Chamber.

1189. The names of the first Bailiffes, or Officers, entring into their office at the feast of Saint *Michael* the Archangell; in the yeare of Christ 1189. were named[1] *Iohn Herlison*, *Roger Duke*, *William de Hauerhill*,[1] bailiffes or sheriffes.

Their 1. Maior was *H. Fitz Alwin Fitz Liefstane*, Goldsmith, pointed by the said king, and continued maior from

First Maior of London.

[1-1] *O.*; Stow *has* Henry Cornhill and Richard Reynere, *who vacated office on this date, having been sheriffs since Easter* 1187; Stow *consequently puts the sheriffs a year too late down to* 1206. *L. has only* Johannes Herlisun *and* Roger le Duc. *F. has the same error as* Stow. (*For abbreviations see Note on pp.* 384–5 *below.*)

the first of *Richard* the first, vntill the fifteenth of king *Iohn*, which was 24. yeares and more.

1190. The 2. of Richard I, shiriffes *William de Haverhill*, *Iohn Bucuinte.*[1] Maior *Henry Fitz Alwin.*[2]

1191. The 3. shiriffes *Nicholas Duket*,[3] *Peter filius Neuelon.*[4] Maior *Henry Fitz Alwin.* |

Page 504 1192. The 4. *Roger le Duc*, *Roger Fitz Alan.*[5] Maior *Henry Fitz Alwin.*

1193. The 5. *William Fitz Isabel*, *William Fitz Alulf.*[6] Maior *Henry Fitz Alwin.*

1194. The 6. *Robert Besaunt*, *Iukel.*[7] Maior *Henry Fitz Alwin.*

1195. The 7. *Godard de Antioche*,[8] *Robert filius Durand.*[9] Maior *Henry Fitz Alwin.*

1196. The 8. *Nicholas Duket*, *Robert Blund.*[10] Maior *Henry Fitz Alwin.*

1197. The 9. *Constantine Fitz Alulf*,[11] *Robert de Bel.*[12] Maior *Henry Fitz Alwin.*

1198. The 10. *Arnold Fitz Alulf*,[13] *Richard Blunt.*[14] Maior *Henry Fitz Alwin.*

King Iohn began his raigne the sixt of Aprill 1199.

1199. The 1. of King Iohn, shiriffes *Roger de Deserto*,[15] *Iames the Alderman*[16]; Maior *H. Fitz Alwin.*

King *Iohn* granted the shiriffewicke of London, and Middlesex, to the cittizens thereof, as king *H.* the first before had done, for the summe of 300. pound yearly. Also he gaue them authority to chuse and depriue their shiriffes at their pleasure.

[1] Bokointe, *L*; Bucknote, *S.* [2] *See* p. 384.
[3] *A.*, *L.*, *O.*; Duke, *S.*
[4] Petrus filius Neulun, *Anc. Deeds* A. 2383; Petrus Nevelun, *L.*; Peter Newlay, *S.*
[5] Ricardus filius Aleyn, *H.*; Richard Fitz Alwin, *S.*
[6] Fitz Arnold, *S.*; filius Athulfi, *L.*
[7] Jukelis Aldermannus, *L.*; Ioke de Iosue, *S.*; Jokel le Jeofne, *F.*
[8] *A.*, *L.*; Gerad de Anteloche, *S.* [9] Robert Durant, *A.*, *S.*
[10] Roger Blunt, *S.*; Rogerus le Blund, *H.*
[11] filius Athelhulphi, *L.*; Fitz Arnulph, *F.*; Fitz Arnold, *S.*
[12] Le bel, *L.*; Robert le Beel, *F.*; Richard de Beaco, *S.*
[13] Arnulphus filius Athulfi, *L.*; Arnald Fitz Arnulph, *F.*; Arnold Fitz Arnold, *S.*; Ern. Ruf., *A.*
[14] Ricardus filius Bartholomei, *L.*; Richard Fitz Bartilmew, *S.*
[15] *A.*, *L.*; Roger Desert, *F.*; Roger Dorsit, *S.*; Robert de Deserto, *O.*
[16] James Fitz Bartholomew, Alderman, *F.*; Iames Bartilmew, *S.*

1200. The 2. shiriffes *Simon de Aldermanbury, William Fitz Alis.*[1] Maior *Henry Fitz Alwin.*

1201. The 3. *Norman Blund,*[2] *Iohn de Cayo* or *Cay*[3]; M. *Henry Fitz Alwin.*

1202. The 4. *Walter Brun,*[4] *William Chamberleyn.*[5] Maior *Henry Fitz Alwin.*

Walter Brune, and *Rose* his wife, founded the Hospitall of saint *Mary* without Bishopsgate, commonly called saint *Mary* Spittle.

1203. The 5. *Thomas Haverel, Hamond Brond.* Maior *Henry Fitz Alwin.*

1204. The 6. *Iohn Walran,*[6] *Richard Winchester.*[7] Maior *Henry Fitz Alwin.*

1205. The 7. *Iohn filius Elinandi,*[8] *Edmund Fitz Gerard.*[9] M. *Henry Fitz Alwin.*|

1206. The 8. *Henry of St. Alban's, Serlo the Mercer.*[10] Maior *Henry Fitz Alwin.* *Page 505*

1207. The 9. *William Hardel,*[11] *Robert Winchester.*[12] Maior *Henry Fitz Alwin.*

1208. The 10. *Peter Duke,*[13] *Thomas Nele.*[14] Maior *Henry Fitz Alwin.*

The King, by his letters Patents, graunted to the Citizens of London, libertie and authoritie yearely to chuse to themselues a Maior.

1209. The 11. *Peter Neuelun,*[15] *William Blund.*[16] Maior *Henry Fitz Alwin.*

[1] *L., O., F.*; Robert Fitz Alis, *Anc. Deeds* A. 2119; Walter Fitz Alis, *S.*
[2] Blundel, *S.*
[3] *Anc. Deeds* A. 1951, 2550, *and L.*; John de Caike, *O.*; John de Ely, *H., F.*; Iohn de Glie, *S.* (Ely, *in Summary*).
[4] Browne, *S.* [5] *Anc. Deeds* A. 2493; Camerarius, *O., L.*
[6] *Anc. Deeds* A. 2180; Walerain, *O.*; Walraven, *F., L.*; Walgraue, *S.*
[7] de Wintona, *O., L.*
[8] *O.*; Holyland, *F.*; Heliland, *L.*; filius Elinant, *Anc. Deeds* A. 2332; Holland, *S.*
[9] *S., F., O.*; Edmond de la Hale, *L.*; Edmund de Angulo, *Anc. Deeds* u. s.; Edm. fil. Ger., *A.*
[10] *By omitting these Sheriffs* Stow *gets his next entries correct.*
[11] *O., L.*; Edmond Hardle, *S., F.*
[12] Roger Winchester, *S., F.*; Robert de Wintona, *O., L.*
[13] le Duc, *O., L.*; Buke, *H., F.*
[14] Thomas Aldermannus, *O.*; Thomas filius Nigelli, *L.*; Thomas Fitz Neel, *F.*
[15] *O.*; Petrus Junior, *L.*; Peter Jeofne, *F.*; Peter le Iosue, *S.*; *probably a son of the sheriff of* 1191. [16] Willelmus Wite, *A., L.*

1210. The 12. *Adam de Withebi*,[1] *Stephen le Gras*.[2] Maior *Henry Fitz Alwin.*

1211. The 13. *Ioce*[3] *Fitz Peter, Iohn Garland.* Maior *Henry Fitz Alwin.*[4]

This *Henry Fitz Alwin* deceased, and was buried in the priorie of the holy Trinitie, neare vnto Aldgate.

1212. The 14. *Ralph Helyland*,[5] *Constantine Fitz Alulf.*[6] Maior *Roger Fitz Alan.*[7]

1213. The 15. *Martin Fitz Alis, Peter Bate.*[8] Maior *Roger Fitz Alan.*[9]

This yeare the ditch about London was begun to bee made of 200. foote broad, by the Londoners.

1214. The 16. *Salomon Basing, Hugh Basing.* Maior *Serle Mercer.*[10]

1215. The 17. *Iohn Travars, Andrew Neuelun.*[11] Maior *William Hardel.*

King Henry the third began his raigne the 19. of October, 1216.

1216. The 1. shiriffes, *Benet Senturer*,[12] *William Blund.*[13] Maior *Iames Alderman* for part, and *Salomon Basing* for part.[14]

1217. second, *Thomas Bokerel, Ralph Eiland.*[15] Maior *Serle Mercer.*[16]

1218. The third, *Iohn Viel, Ioce le Spicer.*[17] Maior *Serle Mercer.*

[1] Wyteby, *L.*; Whiteby, *F.*; Whitley, *S.*

[2] Crassus, *L.*; le Grace, *S.* [3] Iohn, *S.*

[4] *Henry Fitz Alwin died Sept.* 19, 1212. *See* p. 315 below.

[5] Elylond, *H.*, *F.*; Randolf Eiland, *S.*; Ralph Holmant, Helmer, *or* Holin, *Anc. Deeds* A. 2562, 2624, 11609; Elinant, *A.*

[6] *Anc. Deeds* u. s.; Constantine Josue, *S.*; *There are no names for this year in O.*

[7] *Anc. Deeds* u. s., *L.*, *F.*; Henry Fitz Alwin, *S.*

[8] Bath, *L.* [9] *L.*; Fitz Alwin, *S.*; Serlo le Mercer, *F.*

[10] Serlo le Mercer, *L.*; William Hardel, *F.*

[11] *L.*; Newelond, *F.*; Newland, *S.*; *O. has no names for this or the next year.*

[12] *S.*; Benedict Campanarius, *L.*, *Anc. Deeds* A. 1476; Benedict le Seynturer, *F.*

[13] *L.*, *Anc. Deeds* u. s.; Willelmus Albus Trauers, *A.*; Blund Travers, *H.*; le Blounditravers, *F.*; Blome Travers, *G.*; Bluntinars, *S.*

[14] *S.*, *L.* [15] Helylaunde, *L.*; Elylond, *H.*; Elinant, *O.*

[16] Serlo le Mercer factus est Maior Londoniarum, qui duravit per quinque annos, *L.*

[17] *F.*; Josce, *Anc. Deeds* A. 2388; Joce Ponderator, *L.*, *O.*; Iohn le Spicer, *S.*

The Forrest of Middlesex, and the warren of Stanes were this yeare disaforrested. |

1219. The fourth, *Richard Wimbledon, Iohn Viel.*[1] Maior *Serle Mercer.* Page 506

1220. The fifth, *Richard Renger, Ioce le Ieofne.*[2] Maior *Serle Mercer.*

1221. The sixt, *Richard Renger, Thomas Lambart.* Maior *Serle Mercer.*

Constantine Fitz Alulf raised great troubles in this citie, and was hanged with his Nephew and other.

1222. The seuenth, *William le Ioynour,*[3] *Thomas Lambart.* maior *Richard Renger.*[4]

1223. The eight, *Iohn Trauars, Andrew Bokerel.* Maior *Richard Renger.*

1224. The ninth, *Iohn Trauars, Andrew Bokerel.* Maior *Richard Renger.*

The king graunted to the comminaltie of London to haue a common seale.

1225. The tenth, *Roger Duke, Martin Fitz William.* maior *Richard Renger.*

1226. The eleuenth, *Roger Duke, Martin Fitz William.* maior *Richard Renger.*

This yeare the king confirmed to the citizens of London, free warren or libertie to hunt a certaine circuite about the citie, in the waren of Stanes, &c. And also that the citizens of London should passe tol-free throughout all England, & that the keddles, or weres in the riuer of Thames, and Midway should be plucked vp and destroyed for euer, &c. patent xi. *Henry* 3.

1227. The twelfth, *Stephen Bokerel, Henry Cocham.*[5] Maior *Roger Duke.*[6]

The liberties and franchises of London were ratified, and the king granted that either shiriffe should haue two Clarks and two sergeants, also that the Citizens should haue a common seale.

[1] Vitalis, *O.*

[2] *F.*; Joceus Junior, *L.*; Joceus Juvenis, *Anc. Deeds* A. 13423; Joce son of William, *id.* A. 1647, *O.*; Iohn Viel, *S.*

[3] *O., L., F.*; Richard Renger, *S.*

[4] Hoc anno factus est Maior Londoniarum Ricardus Renger qui duravit per v. annos, *L.*; Serle Mercer, *S.*

[5] de Cokham, *L.*, *Anc. Deeds* A. 1489; de Cobham, *F.*

[6] qui duravit per iiij. annos, *L.*

1228. The thirteenth, *Stephen Bokerell, Henrie Cocham.* maior *Roger Ducke.*

1229. The fourteenth, *Walter de Winchester,*[1] *Robert Fitz Iohn.* Maior *Roger Duke.*

1230. The fifteenth, *Richard Fitz Walter,*[2] *Iohn de Woborne.* Maior *Roger Ducke.* |

Page 507 1231. The xvi. *Michael de St. Helena,*[3] *Walter le Bufle.*[4] Maior *Andrew Bokerel*[5] Pepperer.

1232. The xvii. *Henry de Edmonton,*[6] *Gerard Bat.* Maior *Andrew Bokerel* Pepperer.

1233. The xviii. *Simon Fitz Mary, Roger Blunt.*[7] Maior *Andrew Bokerel* Pepperer.

1234. The xix. *Ralph Ashwye,*[8] *Iohn Norman.* Maior *Andrew Bokerel* Pepperer.

1235. The xx. *Gerard Bat, Robert Hardel.*[9] Maior *Andrew Bokerel* Peperer.

1236. The xxi. *Henry Cocham,*[10] *Iordan of Couentrie.* Maior *Andrew Bokerel* pepperer.

1237. The xxii. *IohnToloson,*[11] *Geruais* the Cordwainer.[12] Maior *Andrew Bokerel*[13] pepperer, [and then *Richard Renger*][13].

1238. The xxiii. *Iohn de Codres,*[14] *Iohn de Wylhale*[15]; M. *Richard Renger,* [and then *William Ioyner*].[16]

This *William Ioyner* builded the Quire of the Gray Friers church in London, and became a lay brother of that house.

[1] *L., F., Anc. Deeds,* A. 1626.; William Winchester, *S.*
[2] *O., L., F.*; Richard Walter, *S.*
[3] Michael S. Helan, *S.*
[4] *Anc. Deeds* A. 1485, B. 2348; le Bufler, *O.*; le Busle, *L.*; Walter de Buffell, *S.*
[5] duravit per vij. annos, *L.* [6] Edelmeton, *O. L., F.*
[7] Blund, *O.*
[8] Eswy, *Anc. Deeds* A. 1791; Radulfus Elwy, Mercer, *L.*
[9] *L., F., Anc. Deeds* A. 1807; Richard Hardle, *S.*
[10] Cokham, *L.*; Cobham, F.
[11] de Tulesan, *L., O.*: Tolosane, *F.*
[12] Gervasius Chordewaner, *G.*; Gervasius Camerarius, *L.*
[13] Hoc anno obiit Andreas Bukerel, et factus est Maior Ricardus Renger, *L.*
[14] *O.*; de Koudres, *L.*; Coundres, *F.*; Codras, *S.*
[15] *O., L.*; Wilhal, *S.*
[16] Hoc anno obiit predictus Ricardus Renger Maior, et factus est Maior Willielmus Joynier, *L.*; Richard Renger, *S.*

1239. The xxiiii. *Reiner*[1] *de Bongey*, *Ralph Ashwy.*[2] Mayor *Gerard Bat.*[3]

1240. The xxv. *Iohn de Gisors, Michael Touy.*[4] Maior *Reginald Bungeye.*[5]

This yeare, Aldermen of London were chosen, and chaunged yearely, but that order lasted not long. *Gerard Bat* was againe elected Maior for that yeare to come, but the king would not admit him, being charged with taking money of the victualers in the precedent yeare.

1241. The xxvi. *Thomas Duresme,*[6] *Iohn Viel.*[7] M. *Rolph Ashwy.*[8]

1242. The xxvii. *Robert Fitz Iohn,*[9] *Ralph Ashwye.*[10] Maior *Ralph Ashwye.*[11]

1243. The xxviii. *Hugh Blunt*, *Adam Basing.*[12] Maior *Ralph Ashwye.*

1244. The xxix. *Ralph de Arcubus* spicer,[13] *Nicholas Bat.* Maior *Michael Touy.*[14]

1245. The xxx. *Robert of Cornehil*, *Adam of Bentley.*[15] Maior *Iohn Gisors* Pepperer.[16]

1246. The xxxi. *Simon Fitz Mary*, *Laurence Frowicke.* Maior *Peter Fitz Alan.*[17] |

Simon Fitzmary founded the Hospitall of Mary called Bethelem without Bishopsgate. Queene Hith let to farme to the cittizens of London. *Page 508*

[1] *F.*, *Anc. Deeds* A. 2017; Reginaldus, *L.O.*; Roger, *S.*

[2] Radulfus Eswy, Mercer, *L.*; Aswy, *O.*

[3] *Owing to a dispute with the King there was no Mayor till Jan.* 13, 1240, *when* Bat *was admitted*, *L.*; William Ioyner, *S.*

[4] *Anc. Deeds* A. 140, *L.*, *F.*; Tony, *S.*

[5] *L.*; Bat *was elected as stated by* Stow, *but not admitted.*

[6] de Durham, *L.*

[7] John son of John Viel, *L.*, *Anc. Deeds* A. 7824.

[8] *Anc. Deeds*, u. s.; Radulfus Elwy [mercer] qui duravit per tres annos, *L.*; Reginald Bongey, *S.*, *F.*

[9] *L.*, *O.*; Iohn Fitz Iohn, *S.*, *F.*

[10] Radulfus Eswy, Aurifaber, *L.*

[11] Ralph Haswy *occurs as Mayor in June*, 1243, *ap. Anc. Deeds*, D. 240; Reginald Bongey, *S.*, *F.*

[12] *O.*, *F.*, *S.*; de Giseburne, *L.*

[13] *L.*; Ralph Spicer, *F.*; Raph Foster, *S.*

[14] Tony, *S.*

[15] de Benetlega, *O.*

[16] *For this year see L.* Nicholas Bat *and* Adam de Benetley *were chosen sheriffs*; Bat *was rejected, and succeeded first by* John de Gisors, *then by* Robert de Cornehill. Michael Tovy *was elected Mayor; the King refused to admit him: and on Jan.* 12., 1246, John de Gisors *was chosen in his place.* Cf. *Anc. Deeds*, A. 1987.

[17] *L.*, *Anc. Deeds* A. 1892, 2506; Iohn Gisors, *S.*

1247. The 32. *William Vyel,*[1] *Nicholas Bat.* Mayor *Michael Touy.*[2]

1248. The 33. *Nicholas Fitz Iosey,*[3] *Geffrey Winchester.* M. *Michael Touy.*[4]

1249. The 34. *Ralph Hardel,*[5] *Iohn de Tolesane.*[6] M. *Roger Fitz Roger.*

1250. The 35. *Humfrey le Feure,*[7] *William Fitz Richard.* Mayor *Iohn Norman.*

1251. The 36. *Laurence Frowike, Nicholas Bat.* Mayor *Adam Basing.*

1252. The 37. *William Durham, Thomas Wimborne.* M. *Iohn Tolason* Draper.

The king graunted that the Mayor should bee presented to the Barons of the Exchequer, and they should admit him.

1253. The 38. *Iohn Northampton, Richard Pickard.* Mayor *Nicholas Bat.*[8]

1254. The 39. *William Ashwy,*[9] *Robert de Linton.*[10] Mayor *Ralph*[11] *Hardel* Draper.

The liberties of this city were seized, the Mayor charged that hee looked not to the assize of bread.

The Maior, diuers Aldermen, and the shiriffes of London, were depriued, and other placed in their roomes.

1255. The 40. *Mathew Bukerel, Iohn le Mynur.*[12] M. *Ralph*[13] *Hardel* Draper.

1256. The 41. *Richard Ewel,*[14] *William Ashwie.*[15] Mayor *Ralph*[16] *Hardel.*

[1] *O., L.*; John Viel, *S., F.*
[2] *Anc. Deeds* A. 1470, *L.*; Peter Fitz-Alan, *F.*; Peter Fitz Alwin, *S.*
[3] filius Iosce, *O.*; filius Jocey, *L.*
[4] Tonny, *S.*
[5] Richard Hardell, *S.*
[6] Iohn Tholason, *S.*
[7] *O., L.*; Faber, *Anc. Deeds* A. 2042; Bas, *S.*; Bat, *F.*
[8] *L., Anc. Deeds* A. 1605; Richard Hardell, draper, *S.*
[9] William Eswy, Mercer, *L.*; Ralph Ashwie, *F., S.*
[10] *L., F.*; Robert of Limon, *S.* Ashwy *and* Linton *were removed for neglect regarding the gaols* (see vol. i, p. 36 *above*), in Feb. 1255, *and* Henry de Walemunt *and* Stephen de Oystergate (*or* Doo) *appointed in their place. L.*
[11] Richard, *S.*
[12] Stow *gives* Doo *and* Walmond (*see above*), *as sheriffs for* 1255–6. *Consequently he gives the sheriffs for* 1255–6 *under* 1256, and those *for* 1256–7 *under* 1257.
[13] Richard, *S.*
[14] Owel, *S.*
[15] William Eswy, Drapparius, *L.*
[16] Richard, *S.*

1257. The 42. *Thomas Fitz Thomas, William Grapefige.* Mayor *William Fitz Richard.*[1]

The king caused the walles of this Cittie to bee repayred and made with bulwarks.

1258. The 43. *Iohn Adrian, Robert Cornhill.* Mayor *Iohn Gisors* Peperer.[2]

1259. The 44. *Adam Bruning,*[3] *Henry de Coventry.* Mayor *William Fitz Richard.* |

1260. The 45. *Iohn Northampton, Richard Picard.* Mayor *William Fitz Richard.* *Page 509*

1261. The 46. *Philip le Tayllur,*[4] *Richard Walbrooke.* Mayor *Thomas Fitz Thomas.*[5]

1262. The 47. *Robert de Mountpiler, Osbert de Suffolke.* Mayor *Thomas Fitz Thomas.*[6]

1263. The 48. *Gregory Rokesley, Thomas de Ford.*[7] Mayor *Thomas Fitz Thomas.*[8]

The cittizens of London fortified the Cittie with iron chaines drawne thwart their streetes.

1264. The 49. *Edward Blund, Peter Angar.* Mayor *Thomas Fitz Thomas.*[9]

1265. The 50. bailiffs, *Iohn Adrian, Walter Hervi,* till 28. Nov., and then *Sir Iohn de la Linde* and *Iohn Walrauen*; custos *Hugh Fitz Otho.*[10]

The chaines and postes in London were plucked vp, the Mayor and principall Cittizens committed to Ward, and

[1] *The year began with* Ralph Hardel *mayor, and* Thomas Fitz Thomas *and* Robert de Catelonie, *sheriffs.* Robert *died, and* Matthew Bukerel *succeeded him on Oct* 19. *On Feb.* 1, 1258, *all were removed, and a custos appointed with* Michael Tovy *and* John Adrian *to act as sheriffs. Finally on Feb.* 13, Fitz Thomas, Grapefige, *and* Fitz Richard *were appointed as above. L.*, cf. *Ann. Lond.* 50. Stow *has none of these.*

[2] *The above is* Stow's *entry for* 1259. *Under* 1258 *he gave* Cornhill *and* Adrian *as sheriffs and* Richard Hardle *as mayor. The repetition of* Cornhill *and* Adrian *puts the sheriffs and mayors for* 1259 *to* 1264 *a year too late in* Stow's *list.*

[3] Browning, *S.*

[4] *O., L.*; Iohn Tailor, *S.* [5] Thomas Fitz Richard, *S.*

[6] T. Fitz T. Fitz Richard, *S.*

[7] *L.*; de la Forde, *O.*; de Lafford, *F.*; de Deford, *S.*

[8] Thomas Fitz Thomas Fitz Richard, *S.*

[9] Thomas Fitz T. Fitz Richard, *S.*

[10] *So L. O. agrees, except for reading* Lynde *and* Walerand. *On May* 6, 1266, William Fitz Richard *became sheriff and held office till Nov.* 11, *L., O. S. has the sheriffs and mayor for* 1264–5.

Othon Constable of the Tower, was made Custos of the Citty, &c.

1266. The 51. *Iohn Adrian, Lucas de Batencourt*[1]; custos *Alan de la Souche.*[2]

This *Alen de la Souch* being a Baron of this Realme, and also chiefe Iustice, was in the yeare 1270. slayne in Westminster hall by *Iohn Warren* Earle of Surrey.

The Earle of Glocester entered the Citty with an Armie, and therein builded bulwarkes, cast trenches, &c.

1267. The 52. [bailiffs][3] *Iohn Adrian, Lucas de Batencourt*; Custos[4] *Alen de la Souch.*

Thomas Fitz Theobald and *Agnes* his wife founded the Hospitall of S. *Thomas* of Acon in Westcheape.

1268. The 53. *Walter Haruy, William Duresme.*[5] Custos *Sir Stephen de Edeworth.*[6]

A varience fell in London betweene the Goldsmithes and the Taylors, where through many men were slayne.

1269. The 54. *Thomas Basing, Robert Cornhill*; C. *Hugh Fitz Ottonis*, custos of London and constable of the Tower.[7]

1270. The 55. *Gregory Rocksley, Henry Waleys.* M. *Iohn Adrian*, Vintoner.[8] |

Page 510 The steeple of Bow church in Cheape fell downe, and slew many people.

1271. The 56. *Richard Paris, Iohn de Bodele.*[9] M. *Sir Walter Haruy.*

[1] Adrian *and* Batencourt *appointed Nov.* 11, *L.*

[2] *Appointed June* 23, 1267, *L. S. gives* John Hind *and* John Walrauen *as sheriffs*, William Richards *as mayor.*

[3] *Held office till April* 7, 1268, *when* William de Durham, *and* Walter Harvy *succeeded, L., O.*

[4] Mayor, *S. Succeeded by* Thomas de Eppegrave *on April* 7, 1268, *and on July* 26 *by* Sir Stephen de Edeworth, *L.*

[5] *S. adds* T. Wimborne. Harvy, *and* Duresme, *or* Durham *were succeeded as bailiffs on May* 3 1269 *by* Robert de Cornhill, *and* Thomas Basing, *L.*

[6] Mayor, Sir Stephen Edward, *S.* Edeworth *was succeeded in Feb.* 1269 *by* Hugh Fitz Otho.

[7] *So S.* Basing, Cornhill, *and* Fitz Otho held *office till July* 6, 1270, *when by the King's consent the citizens chose* John Adrian, Draper, *Mayor, and* Philip le Tailur *and* Walter le Poter *sheriffs, L.*, cf. *O. and Anc. Deeds* A. 2013.

[8] Stow, *by giving* Walter Potter, Philip Tailor, *and* John Adrian, *makes all his names a year too late till* 1298, *when his error is rectified by omitting* William *and* John de Storteford, *the sheriffs of* 1297–8.

[9] *O.*; Buddele, *L.*; Wodeley, *S.*

1272. The 57. *Iohn Horne*, *Walter Potter*.[1] Mayor *Sir Walter Haruy*;[2] Custos *Henry Frowike*, Peparar, for part of that year.[2]

King Edward the first beganne his raigne the 16. of Nouember, 1272.

1273. The first, Shiriffes *Nicholas Winchester*, *Henry Couentrie*.[3] M. *Henry Walles*.

1274. The 2. *Lucas Bate⟨n⟩corte*, *Henry Frowike*. M. *Gregory Rocksley*: chiefe Say-maister of all the kings Mints throughout England, and Keeper of the Kinges Exchange at London.

1275. The 3. *Iohn Horne*, *Raph Blunt*. Mayor *Gregory Rocksley*.

1276. The 4. *Robert de Araz*,[4] *Raph Le Feure*.[5] Mayor *Gregory Rocksley*.

1277. The 5. *Iohn Adrian*, *Walter Langley*.[6] Mayor *Gregorie Rocksley*.

1278. The 6. *Robert Basing*, *William le Mazerer* or *Mazeliner*.[7] M. *Gregorie Rocksley*.

1279. The 7. *Thomas Box*,[8] *Raph de la More*.[9] M. *Gregorie Rocksley*.

1280. The 8. *William Farindon*, *Nicholas Winchester*. M. *Gregorie Rocksley*.

This *W. Farindon* Goldsmith, one of the shiriffes, was father to *Nicholas Farindon*: Of these two, Farindon Ward took that name.

1281. The 9. *William le Mazerer* or *Maseliner*,[10] *Richard Chigwel*. M. *Henry Walleis*.

This *Henry Walleis* builded the Tun vpon Cornhill to bee a prison, and the Stockes to be a Market house.

1282. The 10. *Anketel de Betevil*,[11] *Walter le Blund*.[12] M. *Henry Walleis*.

[1] le Poter, *O*.

[2–2] Stow *places this correctly under* 1272. Harvy's *election was disputed, and* Frowike *was custos from Nov.* 10, 1272, *to Jan.* 13, 1273. *L.*

[3] Peter Cosyn, *and* Robert de Melleburne *were elected, but removed on Nov.* 30 *for taking bribes from bakers, L., and Anc. Deeds* A. 6250.

[4] Arar, *S.*

[5] *Or* Faber; L. Fewre, *S.*

[6] le Engleys, *Anc. Deeds* A. 2009; Longeleys, *F.*; le Cornwaleis, *O.*

[7] *O.*; Maraliuer, *S.*

[8] Fox, *S.*

[9] Delamere, *S.*; atte More, *F.*

[10] Maraliuer, *S.*

[11] Anketrin de Betanil, *S.*

[12] *O.*, *F.*; Raph Blund, *S.*

1283. The 11. *Iordaine Goodcheape*, *Martin Box.* Mayor *Henry Walleis.* |

Page 511 *Laurence Ducket* Goldsmith, murdered in Bow Church, and the murtherers hanged.

1284. The 12. *Stephen Cornhill*, *Robert Roksley.* Mayor *Gregory Roksley*,[1] Custos *Raph Sandwitch.*[2]

It was ordained, that Millars should haue but one half peny for a quarter of Wheat grinding, and the great water Conduit in Cheape was begun to be made.

1285. The 13. *Walter le Blunt*,[3] *Iohn Wade.* C. *Raph Sandwitch.*[4]

1286. The 14. *Walter Hawtoune*,[5] *Thomas Cros.*[6] C. *Raph Sandwitch.*

Wheate was solde at London for sixteen pence, and for twelue pence the quarter.

1287. The 15. *William Hereford*, *Thomas Stanes.* C. *Raph Sandwitch.*

1288. The 16. *William Betain*,[7] *Iohn Canterbury.* C. *Raph Sandwitch*, *Raph Barnauars* and Sir *Iohn Britaine.*[8]

1289. The 17. *Salomon le Cutiller*,[9] *Folke S. Edmond.* C. Sir *Iohn Briton* knight.

This yeare a subsidie was graunted, for the reparations of London Bridge.

1290. The 18. *Thomas Romain*, *William de Leyre.*[10] C. *Ralph Sandwitch.*[11]

1291. The 19. *Raph Blunt*, *Hamo Box.* C. *Raph Sandwitch.*[12]

1292. The 20. *Henry Bole*, *Elias Russel.* C. *Raph Sandwitch.*

Three men had their right hand cut off, at the Standarde in Cheape, for rescuing of a prisoner, arrested by a Sergeant of London.

[1] *Till June* 29, 1285, *F.*

[2] *F.*; Custos, Raph Sandwitch and John Briton, *S.*

[3] le Withe, *Anc. Deeds* A. 2653.

[4] *According to F.* Sir John Breton *was Custos from Feb.* 2, 1286, *till July* 20, 1287.

[5] Hauteyn, *O.* [6] *S.*, *F.*, *Anc. Deeds* A. 2331; Gros, *O.*

[7] de Betoyne, *O.*; de Bettune, *Anc. Deeds* C. 286.

[8] *See note on* p. 385 *below.*

[9] *O.*; de Laufare, *F.*, cf. *Cal. Wills* i. 227, *for* Salomon de Lauvare, cutler; Salamon le Sotel, *S.*

[10] de Lier, *S.* [11] *Anc. Deeds* A. 2010; Sir Iohn Briton, *S.*

[12] Sir Iohn Briton, knight, Raph Sandwitch, *S.*

1293. The 21. *Robert Rokesley* the yonger, *Martin Amersbury.*[1] C. Sir *Raph Sandwitch.*[2]

1294. The 22. *Henry Box, Richard Gloucester.* C. Sir *Iohn Briton.*[3]

1295. The 23. *Iohn Dunstable, Adam de Halingbery.* C. Sir *Iohn Briton.*[4]

1296. The 24. *Thomas* of *Suffolke, Adam* of *Fulham.* C. Sir *Iohn Briton.*[5]

This yeare all the liberties of the Citty were restored, the maioralty excepted. |

1297. The 25. *William de Storteford, Iohn de Storteford.*[6] C. Sir *Iohn Briton.* *Page 512*

Certaine Cittizens of London brake vp the Tunne vppon Cornhill, and took out prisoners, for the which they were grieuously punished.

1298. The 26. *Richard Refham,*[7] *Thomas Sely.*[8] Mayor *Henrie Walleis.*

1299. The 27. *Iohn de Armenters,*[9] *Henry de Fyngrye.*[10] Mayor *Elias Russel.*

1300. The 28. *Lucas de Hauering, Richard Champs.* Mayor *Elias Russell.*

1301. The 29. *Robert Callor, Peter de Bosenho.* Mayor, Sir *Iohn Blunt* knight.

1302. The 30. *Hugh Pourt, Simon Paris.* Maior, Sir *Iohn Blunt.*

1303. The 31. *W. Combmartin, Iohn Bureford.*[11] C. Sir *Iohn Blunt.*

1304. The 32. *Roger Paris, Iohn de Lincolne.* C. Sir *Iohn Blunt.*

Geffrey Hertilepole, Alderman, was elected to bee Recorder

[1] de Ambresbery, *O.*

[2] *S.*; *according to F.* Breton *became Custos on June* 11, 1294, cf. *Anc. Deeds* C. 152, *and Mun. Gild.* II. i. 242.

[3] *Anc. Deeds* C. 12; Sir Raph Sandwitch, *S.*

[4] Johannes le Blount, *Mun. Gild.*

[5] Johannes le Blount, *Mun. Gild.*

[6] Stow *by omitting these names at last gets his dates right*: *see note on* 1270 *above.*

[7] le Mercer, *Anc. Deeds* B. 2238; Lefham, *S.*

[8] Saly, *Anc. Deeds* B. 2238.

[9] Armenter, *S.*

[10] Fingene, *S.*

[11] Buckford, *S.*

of London, and tooke his oath, and was appointed to weare his apparrell as an Alderman.

1305. The 33. *William Cosine, Reginald Thunderley.* C. Sir *Iohn Blunt.*

1306. The 34. *Geffrey Cundute,*[1] *Simon Bolet.*[2] C. Sir *Iohn Blunt.*

Seacole was forbidden to be burned in London, Southwark, &c.

Edward the second began his raigne the 7. of Iuly, the yeare of Christ, 1307.

1307. The first, shiriffes, *Nicholas Pigot, Nigellus Drury.* M. Sir *Iohn Blunt.*

1308. The second, *W. Basing, Iames le Boteler.*[3] Mayor *Nicholas Faringdon* Goldsmith.

1309. The third, *Roger le Paumer, Iames* of S. *Edmond.* Maior *Thomas Romaine.*

1310. The fourth, *Simon de Corpe, Peter Blakeney.*[4] Mayor | *Richard Reffam*, Mercer.

Page 513

The king commaunded the Mayor & Comminaltie to make the wall of London from Ludgate to Fleetbridge and from thence to the Thames.

1311. The 5. *Simon Merwod, Richard Wilford.* Mayor, Sir *Iohn Gisors*, Pepperar.

Order was taken, that Marchant straungers should sell their wares within forty dayes after their arriuall, or else the same to be forfeited.

1312. The sixt, *Iohn Lambin, Adam Lutkin.*[5] Maior, Sir *Iohn Gisors*, Peperar.

1313. The seuenth, *Robert Burdeyn,*[6] *Hugh de Garton.* Maior *Nicholas Farindon*, Goldsmith.

Prices set on victuals, a fat stalled oxe, 24.s. a fat mutton, 20.d. a fat goose two pence halfe penny, a fat capon two pence, a fatte henne one penny, two chickens one penny, three pigeons one penny, twentie foure egges one penny, &c.

[1] atte Condut, *O.* [2] Bilet, *S.*

[3] Botenar, *S.*

[4] *Died in Aug.* 1311, *and was succeeded by* Iohn Cambridge; *Ann. Lond.* 175.

[5] Ludekyn, *Anc. Deeds* B. 1988; *he succeeded* Wilford, *who was re-elected but died in office, Letter Book* D. 19–20.

[6] *O., F.*; Gurden, *S.*; Adam Burton, *G.*

1314. The eight, *Stephen Abingdon, Hamond Chigwel.* Mayor, Sir *Iohn Gisors*, Pepperar.

Famine and mortality of people, so that the quicke might vnneath bury the dead: Horse flesh, and dogs flesh was good meat.

1315. The ninth, *Hamond Goodchepe, William Bodelay.* Mayor *Stephen Abendon.*

1316. The 10. *William Caustone,*[1] *Raph Belancer.* Mayor *Iohn Wingraue.*

An earely Haruest, a Bushell of Wheate that had beene sold for ten shillinges, was now sold for ten pence, &c.

1317. The eleventh, *Iohn Prior, W. Furneis.* Mayor *Iohn Wingraue.*

Such a murren of kine, that dogs and rauens that fed on them were poysoned.

1318. The twelfth, *Iohn Pontel,*[2] *Iohn Dalling.* Mayor *Iohn Wingraue.*

1319. 13. *Simon Abindon, I. Preston.* M. *Hamond Chickwel*, Pepperar.

Iohn Gisors, late mayor of London, and many other cittizens fled the city for thinges laid to their charge.

1320. The 14. *Renauld* at *Conduit, W. Produn.*[3] Mayor | *Nicholas Farendon*, Goldsmith. *Page 514*

1321. The 15. *Richard Constantine, Richard Hackney.* M. *Hamond Chickwell*, Peperar.

1322. The 16. *Iohn Grantham, Richard Elie.* M. *Hamonde Chickwell*, Peperar.

Fish and flesh market established at the stockes in the midst of the Citty.

1323. The 17. *Adam* of *Salisbury, Iohn* of *Oxford.* M. *Nicholas Farindon*, Goldsmith.

Of this *Nicholas Farindon*, and of *William Farindon* his father, reade more in Farindon Warde.

1324. The 18. *Benet* of *Fulsham,*[4] *Iohn Cawson.*[5] M. *Hamonde Chickwell*, Peperar.

1325. The 19. *Gilbert Mordon, Iohn Cotton.* M. *Hamond Chickwell*, Peperar.

[1] Canston, *S.*
[2] Poyntel, *O., F.*; John Pulteney, *G.*
[3] Prudhomme, *F.*
[4] *O., F.*; Fulham, *S.*
[5] de Caustone, *O., F.*

The Cittizens of London tooke the Bishoppe of Excester, & cut off his head at the Standard in Cheape.

1326. The 20. *Richard Rothing*, *Roger Chaunteclere.* Mayor *Richard Betoyne*,[1] Goldsmith.

This *Richard Rothing* is said to new build the Parish church of S. *Iames* at Garlicke Hith.

Edward the third beganne his raigne the 25. of Ianuary, the year, 1326.

This king *Edward* granted, that the Mayor should be Justice for the Gaole deliuery at Newgate, that the Cittizens of London should not be constrained to goe out of the Citty of London to any warre. More he granted, that the liberties and franchises of the citty should not after this time, for any cause, bee taken into the kinges hands, &c. More hee graunted by his letters Patents, dated the sixt of March, that no Escheter should be in the Citty, but the Mayor for his time.

1327. The first, shiriffes, *Henry Darcie, Iohn Hauton.* Mayor *Hamond Chickwell*, Peperar.

This yeare the Walles of London were repayred.

1328. The second, *Simon Francis, Henry Combmartin.* M. *Iohn Grantham.* |

Page 515 1329. The 3. *Richard le Lacer*,[2] *Henry Gisors.*[3] Maior, *Simon Swandland.*

This yeare, the king kept a greate Iusting in Cheape, betwixt Sopars lane, and the great Crosse.

1330. The 4. *Robert of Elie*, *Thomas Harewolde* or *Harrewode.*[4] Mayor, Sir *Iohn Pultney*, Draper.

1331. The 5. *Iohn Mocking, Andrew Auberie.* Mayor, Sir *Iohn Pultney*, Draper.

1332. The 6. *Nicholas Pike, Iohn Husbond.* Mayor *Iohn Preston*, Draper.

This yeare was founded Elsinges Spittle, by *W. Elsing*, Mercer, that became first Prior of that Hospitall.

1333. The 7. *Iohn Hamond, William Hansard.* Mayor, Sir *Iohn Pultney*, Draper.

1334. The 8. *Iohn Hingstone*,[5] *Walter Turke.* Mayor *Reginald* at *Conduit*, Vintoner.

[1] *F.*; Britaine, *S.* [2] Lazar, *S.* [3] William Gisors, *S.*
[4] Horwold, *F.*; Whorwode, *S.* [5] Hyunston, *O.*; Kingston, *G.*

1335. The 9. *Walter de Moredon,*[1] *Ralph de Vpton.*[2] Mayor *Reginald* at *Conduit.*[3]

1336. The 10. *Iohn Clarke,*[4] *W⟨illiam⟩ Curtes.*[5] Mayor, Sir *Iohn Pultney*, Draper.

This Sir *Iohn Pultney* founded a colledge in the parish church of S. *Lawrence* by Candlewicke streete.

1337. The 11. *Walter Nele, Nicholas Crane.* Mayor *Henry Darcy.*

Walter Nele, Bladesmith, gaue lands to the repayring of the high wayes about London.

1338. The 12. *William Pomfret, Hugh Marberer.*[6] Mayor *Henry Darcy.* The king graunted that the Sergeantes of the Mayor and shiriffes of London, should beare mases of siluer and guilt with the kings armes.

1339. The 13. *William Thorney, Roger Forsham.*[7] Mayor *Andrew Aubery*, Grocer.

1340. The 14. *Adam Lucas, Bartlemew Deumars.*[8] Mayor *Andrew Aubery*, Grocer.

1341. The 15. *Richard de Barking*, *Iohn de Rokesly.* Mayor *Iohn* of *Oxenford,*[9] Vintoner.

1342. The 16. *Iohn Louekin, Richard Kyslyngbury.*[10] Mayor *Simon* | *Francis*, Mercer. *Page 516*

The price of Gascoyn wines at London, 4.d. & Reinish wine, sixe pence the Gallon.

1343. The 17. *Iohn Syward,*[11] *Iohn Aylesham.* M. *Iohn Hamond.*

1344. The 18. *Geffrey Wichingham, Thomas Leggy.*[12] Mayor *Iohn Hamond.*

1345. The 19. *Edmond Hemenhall, Iohn* of *Glocester.* Mayor *Richard Leget.*

1346. The 20. *Iohn Croyden, William Claptus.*[13] M. *Geffrey Wichingham.*

[1] Motdon, *S.* [2] Richard Vpton, *S.*
[3] *F.*; Nicholas Woton, *S.*, *in the Summarie*, Richard Wotton.
[4] John le Clerk of North halle, *O.*; John de Northalle, *F.*, *G.*
[5] William Curteys of Briklesworth, *O.*; William de Brikelesworth, *F.*, *G.*
[6] Marbeler, *S.* [7] Frosham, *S.*
[8] *F.*; Deux Mars, *O.*; Maris, *S.*; Mareys, *G.*
[9] *He died in office on June* 18, *and was succeeded by* Simon Francis, *F.*
[10] Rislingbury, *S.*
[11] Steward, *S.* [12] Leg, *S.* [13] *O.*, *F.*; Cloptun, *S.*, *G.*

1347. The 21. *Adam Brabasoun,*[1] *Richard Bas⟨ingstoke⟩.* M. *Thomas Leggy*, Skinner.

King *Edward* wonne Callis from the French.

1348. The 22. *Henry Picard, Simon Dolsely.*[2] Mayor *Iohn Loueken*, Fishmonger.

A great pest. Sir *Walter Mannie*, knight, founded the Charterhouse by Smithfield, to be a buriall for the dead.

1349. The 23. *Adam of Bury, Raph de Lenn.*[3] M. *Walter Turk*, Fishmonger.

1350. The 24. *Iohn Notte, W. Worcester.* Mayor *Richard Kyslyngbury.*[4]

1351. The 25. *Iohn Wroth, Gilbert Stayndrop.*[5] Maior *Andrew Aubury*, Grocer.

1352. The 26. *Iohn Peche, Iohn Stodeye.*[6] M. *Adam Frauncis*, mercer.

This mayor procured an act of Parliament, that no knowne whore should weare any hoode, or attire on her head, except reied or striped cloth of diuers colours, &c.

1353. The 27. *W. Welde,*[7] *Iohn Little.* Mayor *Adam Francis*, mercer.

This *Adam Francis* was one of the founders of the Colledge in Guildhall chappell, &c. *Henry Frowike* was the other.

1354. The 28. *William de Todenham,*[8] *Richard Smelt.* Mayor *Thomas Leggy*, Skinner.

Aldermen of London, were vsed to be changed yearely, but now it was ordayned, that they should not be remoued, without some speciall cause. |

Page 517 1355. The 29. *Walter Forester,*[9] *Thomas Brandon.* Maior *Simon Francis*, mercer.

1356. The 30. *Richard Notingham, Thomas Dolsely.*[10] Maior *Henry Picard*, Vintoner.

This *H. Picard* feasted the Kings of England, of France, Cipres, and Scots, with other great estates, all in one day.

1357. The 31. *Stephen Cauendish,*[11] *Bartholomew Frestlynges.*[12] Maior, sir *Iohn Stody* Vintoner.

[1] Brapsen, *S.* [2] Dolseby, *S.* [3] of Lym, *S.*
[4] Killingbury, *S.* [5] Gilbert of Stenineshorpe, *S.*
[6] Stotley, *S.* [7] Wilde, *S.* [8] Tudenham, *F.*; Totingham, *S.*
[9] Forster, *F.*, *S.* [10] Dossel, *S.* [11] Candish, *S.*
[12] Frestlyng, *F.*; Bartilmew Frostling, *S.*

This *Iohn Stody* gaue tenements to the Vintoners in London, for reliefe of the poore of that Company.

1358. The 32. *Iohn Barnes, Iohn Buris.* Maior *Iohn Louekin*, Stockfishmonger.

1359. The 33. *Simon* of *Benington, Iohn* of *Chichester.* Maior *Symon Dolsely,*[1] Grocer.

1360. The 34. *Iohn Denis, Walter Berny.* Maior *I. Wroth*, Fishmonger.

1361. The 35. *William Holbech, Iames Tame.* Maior *I. Peche*, Fishmonger.

1362. The 36. *Iohn* of S. *Albons, Iames Andrew.* Maior *Stephen Cauendish,*[2] Draper.

1363. The 37. *Richard Croyden, Iohn Hiltoft.*[3] Maior *Iohn Not*, Pepparer.

1364. The 38. *Iohn de Mitford, Simon de Mordon.* Maior *Adam* of *Bury*, Skinner.

1365. The 39. *Iohn de Briklesworth,*[4] *Thomas Ireland.* Maior *Iohn Louekin*, Fishmonger, and *Adam* of *Bury*, Skinner.[5]

1366. The 40. *Iohn Warde, Thomas of Lee.* Maior *Iohn Lofkin*, Fishmonger.

This *Iohn Lofkin* builded the parish church of saint *Michael* in Crooked Lane.

1367. The 41. *Iohn Turngold, William Dikeman.* Maior *Iames Andrew*, Draper.

1368. The 42. *Robert Girdelere,*[6] *Adam Wimondham.* Maior *Simon Mordon*, Stockfishmonger.

This yeare Wheate was sold for 2.s. 6.d. the bushell.

1369. The 43. *Iohn Piel, Hugh Holbech.*[7] Maior *Iohn Chichester*, Goldsmith. |

1370. The 44. *William Walworth, Robert Geyton.* Mayor *Iohn Barnes*, mercer. *Page 518*

1371. The 45. *Adam Stable,*[8] *Robert Hatfield.* Maior *Iohn Barnes*, mercer.

This *Iohn Barnes* gaue a chest with three lockes, and one thousand marke to be lent to poore yong men.

[1] Dolseby, *S.* [2] *F.*; Gondish, *S.*
[3] Litoft, *S.* [4] Bryklisworth, F.; Bukulsworth, *S.*
[5] Bury *was mayor till Jan.* 28, 1366, *when* Lovekin *succeeded, F.*
[6] Gurdeler, *F.*; Cordeler, *S.* [7] Holdich, *S.* [8] Staple, *S.*

1372. The 46. *Iohn Philpot, Nicholas Brembar.* Maior *Iohn Piel*, Mercer.

1373. The 47. *Iohn Aubury, Iohn Fifhyde.*[1] Maior *Adam* of *Bury*, Skinner.

1374. The 48. *Richard Lions, William Woodhouse.* Maior *William Walworth*, Fishmonger.

1375. The 49. *Iohn Hadley, W. Newport.* Maior *Io. Ward*, Grocer.

1376. The 50. *Iohn Northampton, Robert Laund.* Maior *Adam Stable*, mercer.

The Londoners ment to haue slaine *Iohn* Duke of Lancaster: *Adam Stable* maior put downe, and *Nicholas Brembar* elected. Also the Aldermen were deposed, & other set in their places.

Richard the second began his raigne the 21. of Iune, in the yeare 1377.

1377. The first, shiriffes, *Nicholas Twiford, Andrew Pikeman.* Maior, sir *Nicholas Brembar*, Grocer.

Iohn Philpot a Citizen of London, sent shippes to the sea, and scoured it of Pirates, taking many of them prisoners.

1378. The 2. *Iohn Boseham, Thomas Cornwalis.* Maior, sir *Iohn Philpot*, Grocer.

This Sir *Iohn Philpot* gaue to the Citie lands for the finding of thirteene poore people for euer.

1379. The 3. *Iohn Helisdon, William Barrat.* Maior *Io. Hadley*, Grocer.

1380. The 4. *Walter Doget, William Knightcoate.* Maior *W. Walworth*, Fishmonger.

This *William Walworth* arrested *Wat Tiler* the rebel, & was knighted. He increased the parish church of Saint
Page 519 *Michael* in | Crooked lane, and founded there a colledge. Other Aldermen were also knighted for their seruice in the field.

1381. The 5. *Iohn Rote, Iohn Hend.* Mayor *Iohn Northampton*, Draper.

1382. The 6. *Adam Bamme, Iohn Sely.* Mayor *Iohn Northampton*, Draper or Skinner, as I find in record.

1383. The 7. *Simon Winchcombe, Iohn More.* Mayor, Sir

[1] Fyffide, *F.*; Fished, *S.*

Nicholas Brembar, Grocer. *Iohn Northampton*, late Mayor of London, was committed to perpetuall prison, and his goods confiscated.

1384. The 8. *Nicholas Exton*, *Iohn Fressh.*[1] Mayor, Sir *Nicholas Brembar*, Grocer, knighted with *William Walworth.*

1385. The 9. *Iohn Organ*, *Iohn Churchman.* Mayor, Sir *Nicholas Brembar*, Grocer: the foresaid *Iohn Churchman* new builded the custome house neere to the Tower of London, and did many other works for the commodity of this Citie.

1386. The 10. *W. Standone*,[2] *W. More.* Maior *Nicholas Exton*, Fishmonger. This yeare the Citizens of London, fearing the French, pulled downe houses neare about their City, repaired their walles, and clensed their ditches, &c.

1387. The 11. *William Venor*, *Hugh Fastolf.*[3] Maior *Nicholas Exton*, Fishmonger. Sir *Nicholas Brember*, late Maior of London, was this yeare beheaded.

1388. The 12. *Thomas Austin*, *Adam Carlhul.* Maior *Nicholas Tuiford*, Goldsmith, knighted with *W. Walworth.*

1389. The 13. *Iohn Walcot*, *Iohn Louenay.*[4] Maior *William Venor*, Grocer.

1390. The 14. *Iohn Francis*, *Thomas Viuent.* Maior *Adam Bamme*, Goldsmith: this *Adam Bamme* prouided from beyond the seas Corne in great aboundance, so that the Citie was able to serue the countrie.

1391. The 15. *Iohn Shadworth*, *Henry Vanner.*[5] Maior *Iohn Hend*, Draper: this mayor was for displeasure taken, sent to Windsor Castle, and the king made Warden of the Citty, &c.

1392. The 16. *Gilbert Maghfield*, *Thomas Neuton.*[6] maior *William Stondone*, Grocer. |

1393. The 17. *Drew Barintin*, *Richard Whitington.* mayor *Iohn Hadley*, Grocer: Faringdon Warde was by Parliament appointed to be diuided into two Wardes, to wit, *infra*, *& extra*. *Page 520*

[1] French, *S.*
[2] Staundone, *F.*; Staman, *O.*
[3] Forstalfe, *S.*
[4] Loveye, *F.*; Loneye, *O.*
[5] Vamer, *S.*
[6] Newington, *S.*

1394. The 18. *William Brampton,*[1] *Thomas Knoles.* mayor *Iohn Froshe,*[2] mercer.

1395. The 19. *Roger Elles, William Shyryngham.*[3] maior *William More*, Vintner.

1396. The 20. *Thomas Wilford, William Parker.* maior *Adam Bamme*, Goldsmith.

1397. The 21. *Iohn Wodcoke, William Askam.* maior *Richard Whitington*, mercer.

1398. The 22. *Iohn Wade, Iohn Warnar.* maior *Drew Barentin*, Goldsmith.

Henry the fourth began his raigne the 29. of Septemb. the yeare 1399.

1399. The 1. shiriffes, *William Waldern, William Hyde.*[4] mayor *Thomas Knoles*, Grocer.

1400. The 2. *Iohn Wakel, William Enote.*[5] maior *Iohn Francis*, Goldsmith.

1401. The 3. *William Venor, Iohn Fremelyngham.*[6] maior *Iohn Shadworth*, mercer: the Conduit vpon Cornhill was this yere made of an old prison house called the *Tunne.*

1402. The 4. *Richard Marlow, Robert Chicheley.* maior I. *Walcote*, Draper.

1403. The 5. *Thomas Falconer, Thomas Poole.* maior *W. Ascham*, Fishmonger.

1404. The 6. *William Louthe,*[7] *Stephen Spilman.* maior *Iohn Hend*, Draper: this *Iohn Hend* was a new builder of the parish church of Saint *Swithen* by London stone.

1405. The 7. *Henry Barton, William Crowmere.*[8] maior *Iohn Wodcocke*, mercer: this maior caused all the Weres in the riuer of Thames, from Stanes to the riuer of Medwey, to bee destroyed, and the trinkes to be burned, &c.

1406. The 8. *Nicholas Wooton, Gefferey Brooke.* maior | *Richard Whittington*, mercer. This year a great pestilence in London tooke away more then 30000. people.

Page 521

[1] Bramston, *S.* [2] Fresshe, *F.*
[3] Seuenoke, *S.* [4] Hende, *S.* [5] Menot, *F.*; Ebot, *S.*
[6] Iohn Fremingham, *S.*
[7] Bouth, *S.* [8] Crome, *S.*

1407. The 9. *Henry Pontfrackt*, *Henry Halton*, Mercer. Maior *William Stondon*, Grocer.

1408. The 10. *Thomas Duke*,[1] *William Norton*. Maior *Drew Barentine*, Goldsmith. This *Drew Barentine* builded a part of the Goldsmith Hall, and gaue them lands.

1409. The 11. *Iohn Lane*,[2] *William Chichley*. M. *Richard Marlow*, Ironmonger. A great play at Skinners well, which lasted eight dayes, and was of matter from the creation of the world: the most part of all the great Estates of England were there to behold it.

1410. The 12. *Iohn Penne*, *Thomas Pike*. Maior *Thomas Knoles*, Grocer. This *Thomas Knoles* began anew to build the Guild hall in London, &c.

1411. The 13. *Iohn Rainwel*, *William Cotton*. Maior *Robert Chichley*, Grocer.

1412. The 14. *Ralph Lobenham*,[3] *William Seuenocke*. Maior *William Waldren*, Mercer.

Henry the fift began his raigne the 20. of March, the yeare 1412.

1413. The 1. shiriffes, *Iohn Sutton*, *Iohn Micholl*.[4] Maior *William Cromar*, Draper. Sir *Iohn Oldcastle* assembled a great power in Fickets field by London, which power was ouercome and taken by the king and his power.

1414. The 2. *Iohn Michell*, *Thomas Alen*. M. *Th. Falconer*, mercer: this maior caused the Posterne called Moregate to bee builded, and he lent to the king 10000. marks upon Jewels, &c.

1415. The 3. *William Cambridge*, *Alen Euerard*. maior *Nicholas Wotton*, Draper.

1416. The 4. *Robert Whittington*, *Iohn Couentrie*. M. *Hen. Barton*, Skinner: this *Henrie Barton* ordayned Lanthornes with lights to bee hanged out on the Winter euening betwixt Hallontide and Candlemasse.

1417. The 5. *H. Read*, *Io. Gidney*.[5] M. *Ri. Marlow*, Ironmonger.

[1] Ducke, *S.* [2] Law, *S.* [3] Lovinhinde, *S.*
[4] Michell, *S*; Nichole, *G.* [5] Gedney, *O.*

1418. The 6. *Iohn Brian, Raph Barton, Iohn Parnesse.*[1] maior *William Seuenoke*: this *William Seuenoke*, sonne to *Wil|liam Rumsched* of *Seuenoke* in Kent, was by his father bound an Apprentise with *Hugh de Bois* Citizen and Ferrer of London, for a terme of yeares, which being expired in the yeare 1394. the xviii. of *Richard* the 2. *Iohn Hadley* being maior of London, and *Stephen Spilman* Chamberlaine of the Guild-hall: he alledged that his maister had vsed the trade or mystery of a Grocer, and not of a Ferrer, and therefore required to bee made free of the Grocers companie, which was graunted: this *William Seuenoke* founded in the towne of Seuenoke a free schoole, and almes houses for the poore.

Page 522

1419. The 7. *Robert Whityngham*,[2] *Iohn Butler.*[3] Maior *Richard Whittington*, Mercer: this maior founded Whittington Colledge.

1420. The 8. *Iohn Butler*,[4] *Iohn Wells.* Maior *William Cambridge*, Grocer.

1421. The 9. *Richard Gosseline, William Weston.* Maior *Rob. Chichley*, Grocer. This maior gaue one plot of ground thereupon to build the parish church of S. *Stephen* vpon Walbrooke.

Henrie the sixt began his raigne the 31. of August, the yeare 1422.

1422. The 1. shiriffes, *William Eastfield, Robert Tatarsall.* Maior *William Waldern*, mercer. This yeare the west gate of London was begun to be builded by the Executors of *Richard Whittington.*

1423. The 2. *Nicholas Iames, Thomas Wandesford.*[5] Maior *William Cromer*, Draper.

1424. The 3. *Simon Seman, Iohn Bywater.*[6] Maior *Iohn Michel*, Fishmonger.

1425. The 4. *William Melreth, Iohn Brokle.*[7] Maior *Iohn Couentrie*, mercer.

1426. The 5. *Iohn Arnold, Iohn Higham.* M. *Iohn Reinwell*, Fishmonger. This maior gaue tenements to the Citie for the discharge of three wards in London for fifteenes, &c.

[1] Pernys, *F.*; Purveys, *O.*
[2] Whittington, *S.*
[3] Botiller, *O.*; Boteler, *F.*
[4] Boteler, *O.*, *F.*
[5] Waynesford, *F.*; Windford, *S.*
[6] Bythewater, *O.*
[7] Brokell, *S.*

1427. The 6. *Henrie Frowicke, Robert Oteley.* Maior *Iohn Gidney*, Draper.

1428. The 7. *Thomas Duffehouse, Iohn Abbot.* Maior | *Henry Barton*, Skinner. Page 523

1429. The 8. *William Russe, Raph Holland.* Maior *William Eastfield*, mercer. *Raph Holland* gaue to impotent poore 120 pound, to prisoners 80. pound, to hospitals 40. pound, &c.

1430. The 9. *Waltar Chartsey, Robert Large.* Maior *Nicholas Wotton*, Draper. *Waltar Chartesey*, Draper, gaue to the poore 100.li. beside 20.li. to the Hospitals, &c.

1431. The 10. *Iohn Hatherley,*[1] *Stephen Browne.* Maior *Iohn Wels*, Grocer. This *Iohn Wels*, a great benefactor to the new building of the Chappell by the Guild hall, and of his goods the standard in west Cheape was made.

1432. The 11. *Iohn Olney, Iohn Paddesley.* M. *Iohn Parneis*, Fishmonger.

1433. The 12. *Thomas Chalton, Iohn Ling.* Maior *Iohn Brokle*, Draper.

1434. The 13. *Thomas Barnewell, Symon Eyre.* Maior *Robert Oteley*, Grocer.

1435. The 14. *Thomas Catworth, Robert Clopton.* Maior *Henry Frowicke*, Mercer.

1436. The 15. *Thomas Morsted, William Gregorie.* Maior *Iohn Michel*, Fishmonger.

1437. The 16. *William Hales, William Chapman.* Maior, Sir *William Eastfield*, mercer: this sir *William Eastfield* knight of the Bath, a great benefactor to the water Conduits.

1438. The 17. *Hugh Dyke,*[2] *Nicholas Yoo.* Maior *Stephen Browne*, Grocer. Wheate solde for three shillings the Bushell: but this man sent into *Prusia*, & caused to be brought from thence certaine ships laden with Rie, which did great reliefe.

1439. The 18. *Philip Malpas, Robert Marshal.* Maior *Robert Large*, Mercer. *Philip Malpas* at his decease gaue 120.li. to poore prisoners, and euery yeare for fiue yeares 400. shirts and smocks, 40. payre of sheetes, and 150. gowns of frise to the poore, to poore maides marriages 100. markes, to

[1] Atherle, *F.*; Aderley, *S.*

[2] Diker, *S.*

high wayes, 100. markes, and to 500. poore people in London euery one six shillings eight pence, &c.

1440. The 19. *Iohn Sutton*, *William Wetinhale.* Maior *Iohn Paddesley,* Goldsmith, mayster of the Workes of money in | Page 524 the tower of London.

1441. The 20. *William Combes*,[1] *Richard Rich.* M. *Robert Clopton*, Draper.

1442. The 21. *Thomas Beamont*,[2] *Richard Nordon.*[3] M. *Iohn Hatherley*, Ironmonger.

1443. The 22. *Nicholas Wyfold*,[4] *Iohn Norman.* Maior *Thomas Catworth*, Grocer.

1444. The 23. *Stephen Forstar*, *Hugh Witch.* Maior, *Henrie Frowicke*, mercer : this yeare Powles steeple was fiered with lightning and hardly quenched.

1445. 24. *Iohn Darby*, *Godfrey Filding.*[5] Mayor *Simon Eyre*, Draper: this *Simon Eyre* builded the Leaden Hall in London, to bee a common garner for the citty, &c.

1446. The 25. *Robert Horne*, *Godfrey Bolaine.*[6] Maior *Iohn Olney*, mercer.

1447. The 26. *William Abraham*, *Thomas Scot.* Mayor *Iohn Gidney*,[7] Draper.

1448. The 27. *William Cantelowe*,[8] *William Marrow.* Mayor *Stephen Browne*, Grocer.

1449. The 28. *William Hulin*, *Thomas Caninges.* Mayor *Thomas Chalton*, mercer: this yeare *Iacke Cade* a Rebell of Kent came to London, entered the Citty, &c.

1450. The 29. *I*[*ohn*] *Middleton*, *William Deere.* Mayor *Nicholas Wyfold*,[9] Grocer. Souldiers made a fray against the maior the same day he tooke his charge at Westminster.

1451. The 30. *Mathew Philip*, *Christopher Warter.*[10] Mayor *William Gregory*, Skinner.

1452. The 31. *Richard Lee*, *Richard Alley.* Mayor *Godfrey Filding* mercer, of counsell to *H.* the 6. and *E.* the fourth: this yeare was a great fray at the wrastling.

[1] Combis, *S.*; Combys, *G.* [2] Beaumond, *O.*
[3] Morden, *S.*; Northeyn *Chron. Lond.* 150. [4] Wilforde, *S.*
[5] Feldyng, *F.* [6] Boleyn, *F.* [7] Gedney, *F.*
[8] Catlow, *S.* [9] *F.*; Wilforde, *S.* [10] Warton, *S.*

1453. The 32. *Iohn Walden,*[1] *Thomas Cooke*. Mayor *Iohn Norman*, Draper: this *Iohn Norman* was the first Maior that was rowed to Westminster by water, for before that time they rode on horsebacke.

1454. The 33. *Iohn Field*, *W. Taylor*. Mayor *Stephen Forstar*, Fishmonger: this *Stephen Forstar* enlarged Ludgate for the ease of prisoners there, &c. |

1455. The 34. *Iohn Yong*, *Thomas Olgraue.*[2] M. *William* *Page 525*
Marrow, Grocer. The Mercers seruants in London made a riote vpon the Lombards and other strangers.

1456. The 35. *Iohn Styward,*[3] *Raph Verney*. Maior *Thomas Caning*, Grocer.

1457. The 36. *William Edwards*, *Thomas Reiner*. Maior *Godfrey Boloine*, mercer. This *Godfrey Boloine* gave 1000 pound to poore housholders in London, &c.

1458. The 37. *Raph Ioceline*, *Richard Nedeham.*[4] Maior *Thomas Scot*, Draper.

1459. The 38. *Iohn Plommar*, *Iohn Stockar.*[5] Maior *William Hulin*, Fishmonger.

1460. 39. *Richard Fleming Iohn Lambard*. Maior *Richarde Lee*, Grocer.

Edward the fourth began his raigne the fourth of March in the yeare 1460. after the account of the Church of England.

1461. The first, shiriffes, *George Ireland*, *Iohn Locke*. Maior *Hugh Witch*, mercer.

1462. The 2. *William Hampton*, *Bartholomew Iames*. M. *Thomas Cooke*, Draper, made knight of the Bath in the fift of *Edward* the fourth, and had great troubles after.

1463. The 3. *Robert Basset,*[6] *Thomas Muschampe*. Maior *Mathew Philip*, Goldsmith, made knight of the Bath, the fift of *Edward* the fourth, and after in the field the tenth of *Edward* the fourth.

1464. The 4. *Iohn Tate*, *Iohn Stone*. Maior *Raph Ioceline*, Draper, knight of the Bath, and also in the field.

1465. The 5. *Henrie Wauer*, *William Constantine*. Maior

[1] Waldron, *S*. [2] Oulegreve, *O*.; Holgrave, *G*.
[3] Steward, *S*. [4] Medham, *S*. [5] Stokker, *F*.; Stokkes, *O*. [6] Baslet, *S*.

Raph Verney, mercer. *Henrie Wauer* one of the shiriffes, made knight of the Bath.

1466. The 6. *Iohn Bromer*,[1] *Henry Brice*.[2] Mayor *Iohn Yong*, Grocer, made knight in the field. This yeare began the troubles of sir *Thomas Cooke*, and of other Aldermen, as yee may read in my Summarie.

1467. The 7. *Thomas Stalbroke*, *Humfrey Heyford*. Maior *Thomas Oldgraue*, Skinner. |

Page 526 1468. The 8. *Symon Smith*, *William Hariot*. Maior *William Tayler*, Grocer. This Maior gaue tenementes to discharge Cordwayner streete ward of fifteenes.

1469. The 9. *Richard Gardener*, *Robert Drope*. Maior *Richard Lee*, Grocer. This yeare the tower of London being deliuered to the Maior and his brethren, they deliuered king *H.* from thence.

1470. The 10. Sir *Iohn Crosbie*, *Iohn Ward*. Maior Sir ⟨*Iohn*⟩ *Stockton*, Mercer. *Thomas* the Bastard Fauconbridge with a riotous companie set vpon this Citie, at Aldgate, Bishopsgate, the Bridge, &c. and xii. Aldermen with the Recorder were knighted in the field by *Edward* the 4. to wit, *Iohn Stokton* Maior, *Raph Verney* late maior, *Iohn Yong* late maior, *William Tayler* late maior, *Richard Lee* late maior, *Mathew Philips* late maior, *George Ireland*, *William Stoker*, *William Hampton* since maior, *Thomas Stalbroke*, *Iohn Crosbie*, *and Bartlemew Iames* since maior, with *Thomas Vrswike* Recorder.

1471. The 11. *Iohn Allin*, *Iohn Shelley*. Maior *Willey Edward*, Grocer: the water Conduit at Aldermanburie, and the standard in Fleetstreet were finished.

1472. The 12. *Iohn Browne*, *Thomas Bledlow*. Maior, Sir *William Hampton*, Fishmonger: this sir *William Hampton* punished strumpets, and caused stockes to be set in euery ward to punish vagabonds.

1473. The 13. Sir *William Stokar*, *Robert Belisdon*.[3] Maior *Iohn Tate*, mercer: this yeare the Shiriffes of London were appoynted each of them to haue sixteene Sergeants, euerie

[1] Browne, *S.*
[2] Brice, *died June* 20, 1467, *and was succeeded by* Iohn Stokton, *F.*
[3] Billesdon, *O.*, *F.*

Sergeant to haue his yeoman, and six Clearkes, to wit, a Secondarie, a Clearke of the Papers, and foure other Clearkes, besides the vnder shiriffes Clearkes.

1474. The 14. *Edmond Shaw*, *Thomas Hil.* Maior *Robert Drope*, Draper: this *Robert Drope* increased the water conduit vpon Cornehill, &c.

1475. The 15. *Hugh Brice*, *Robert Colwich.* Maior *Robert Basset* Saltar: this *Robert Basset* corrected the Bakers, and other victualers of this Cittie. |

1476. The 16. *Richard Rawson*, *William Horne.* Maior, sir *Raph Ioceline*, Draper, knight of the Bath: by the diligence of this Maior, the walles of the Cittie were repayred. *Page 527*

1477. The 17. *Henry Collet*, *Iohn Stoker*, Maior *Humphrey Hayford*, Goldsmith.

1478. The 18. *Robert Harding*, *Robert Bifield*, Mayor *Richard Gardener*, mercer. *Robert Bifield* shiriffe was fined by the Maior, and payd 50.li. toward the water Conduits.

1479. The 19. *Thomas Ilam*, *Iohn Warde.* Maior, Sir *Bartholomew Iames*, Draper, made knight in the field, by *E.* the 4. *T. Ilam* newly builded the great Conduit in west Cheape.

1480. The 20. *Thomas Daniel*, *William Bacon.* Maior *Iohn Browne*, Mercer.

1481. The 21. *Robert Tate*, *William Wiking.*[1] Mayor *William Hariot*, Draper.

1482. The 22. *William White*, *Iohn Mathew.* Maior *Edmond Sha* Goldsmith. This *Edmond Sha* caused the Posterne called Cripplesgate to be newly builded, &c.

Edward the fift began his raigne the 9. of April, in the yeare 1483.

Richard the third began his raigne the 22. of Iune, in the yeare 1483.

1483. The 1. shiriffes, *Thomas Norland*[2], *William Martin.* M. *Robert Bilisden*, Haberdasher.

1484. The 2. *Richard Chester*, *Thomas Brittaine*, *Raphe Austrie.* M. *Tho. Hill*, Grocer, sir *William Stocker*, Draper,

[1] Wiking *died Oct.* 19, 1481, *and*, Richard Chawry *was chosen in his place*, *F.*

[2] Northland, *O.*; Northlond, *F.*

Ioh. Ward, Grocer: three shiriffes and three Maiors this yeare by means of a sweating sickness, &c. *Thomas Hil* appointed by his testament the water Conduit in Grasse-street to be builded.

Henrie the seuenth began his raigne the 22. of August, in the yeare 1485.

1485. The 1. shiriffes, *Iohn Tate, Iohn Swan.* Maior *Hugh Brise*[1], Goldsmith. This *Hugh Brise* was keeper of the kings mints at London.

1486. The 2. *Iohn Perciuall, Hugh Clopton.* Maior *Henry* | *Collet* mercer: the crosse in Cheape was new builded in beautifull manner. Page 528

1487. The 3. *Iohn Fenkell, William Remington.* Maior, Sir *William Horne*, Saltar: this *William Horne* made knight in the field by *Henry* the 7. gaue to the repayring of high wayes betwixt London and Cambridge 500. marks, and to the preachers at Paules Crosse, &c.

1488. The 4. *W. Isaack, Raph Tilney.* Maior *Robert Tate*, Mercer.

1489. The 5. *William Caple, Iohn Brocke.* Maior *W. White*, Draper.

1490. The 6. *Henry Cote, Robert Reuell*[2], *Hugh Pemberton.* Maior, *Iohn Mathew*, mercer.

1491. The 7. *Thomas Wood, William Browne.* Maior *Hugh Clopton*, mercer. *Hugh Clopton* builded the great stone bridge at Stratford vpon Hauen in Warwicke shire.

1492. The 8. *William Purchase, William Welbecke.* Maior *William Martin*, Skinner. A riot made vpon the Esterlings by the Mercers seruants and other.

1493. The 9. *Robert Fabian, Iohn Winger.* Maior, Sir *Raph Astrie*, Fishmonger, made knight by *H.* the seuenth: *Robert Fabian*, Alderman, made *Fabians* Chronicle, a paineful labour, to the honor of the Cittie, and the whole realme.

1494. The 10. *Nicholas Alwine, Iohn Warner.* Maior, *Richard Chawry*, Salter.

1495. The 11. *Thomas Knesworth, Henry Somer.* Maior, *Henry Colet*, mercer.

[1] Brice, *F.*

[2] *d. Feb.* 23, 1491.

1496. The 12. Sir *Iohn Sha*, Sir *Richard Haddon.* Maior Sir *Iohn Tate* the yonger, mercer, the king made this maior, *Robert Shefield* Recorder, and both the shiriffes knightes, for their good seruice against the rebels at Black Hith field.

1497. The 13. *Bartlemew Read*, *Thomas Windout.* Maior *W. Purchase*, Mercer. All the Gardens in the Morefielde were destroyed and made playne ground.

1498. The 14. *Thomas Bradbury*, *Stephen Ienings.* Maior Sir *Iohn Perceuall*, made knight in the fielde by king *Henrie* | the seuenth. Page 529

1499. The xv. *Iames Wilford*, *Thomas Brond.* Maior *Nicholas Alwin*, Mercer. This *Nicholas Alwyn* gaue to three thousand poore people in London, twelue pence the peece, and to three thousand in the towne of Spalding the like, &c.

1500. The xvi. *Iohn Hawes*, *William Steede.* Mayor, *W. Remington*, Fishmonger.

1501. The xvii. *Laurence Ailmer*, *Henry Hede.* Mayor, Sir *Iohn Sha*, Goldsmith, made knight in the fielde by *Henry* the seuenth: this sir *Iohn Sha* caused his Brethren the Aldermen to ride from the Guildhall vnto the waters side, where hee tooke his Barge to Westminster, hee was sworne by the Kinges councell, hee commonly in the afternoones kepte a Court alone, called before him many matters, and redressed them.

1502. The xviii. *Henry Kebel*, *Nicholas Nines.*[1] Mayor *Bartlemew Reade*, Goldsmith.

1503. The xix. *Christopher Hawes*, *Robert Wats*, *Thomas Granger.* M. Sir *William Capell*, Draper, made knight by *Henry* the seuenth. This sir *William* caused a Cage in euerie Warde to be set for punishing of vagabondes.

1504. The xx. *Roger Acheley*, *William Brown.* Mayor, *Iohn Winger*, Grocer.

1505. The xxi. *Richard Shore*, *Roger Groue.* Mayor *Thomas Knesworth*, Fishmonger: this *Thomas Knesworth* appointed the water Conduit at Bishopsgate to bee builded, &c.

1506. The xxii. *William Copenger*, *Thomas Iohnson*[2], *William*

[1] Nynys, *O.*; Nynes, *F.* [2] *The king refused to admit* Iohnson.

Fitzwilliams, Marchant taylor, after of Counsell to *Henrie* the eight. Mayor Sir *Richard Haddon*, Mercer.

1507. The xxiii. *William Butler*, *Iohn Kirkby*. Mayor *William Browne*[1], Mercer, for part *Laurence Ailmer*, Draper.

1508. *The* 24. *Thomas Exmew*, *Richard Smith*. Mayor *Stephen Ieninges*, Marchant taylor: this *Stephen Ieninges* builded the greatest part of S. *Andrewes* church called Vndershaft. He builded a free schoole at Vlfrunehampton in Staffordshire, &c. |

Page 530 Henry the 8. began his raigne the 22. of April, the yeare 1509.

1509. The first. Shiriffes, *George Monoxe*, *Iohn Doget*. M. *Thomas Bradbury*[2], Mercer, for parte Sir *William Caple*, Draper.

1510. The second. *Iohn Milborne*, *Iohn Rest*. Mayor *Henrie Keble*, Grocer. This *Henry Keble* gaue one thousand pounde toward the new building of his parrish church of Aldermary.

1511. The 3. *Nicholas Shelton*, *Thomas Mirfine*. Mayor *Roger Acheley*, Draper. This *Roger Acheley* prouided corn for seruice of this Cittie in great plentie: Hee caused the same to be stowed vppe in the common Garner called Leaden Hall.

1512. The 4. *Robert Aldarnes*, *Robert Fenrother*. Mayor, sir *William Copinger*.[3], Fishmonger, for part, *Richard Haddon*, Mercer, for the rest. Sir *W. Copinger* gaue halfe his goodes to his wife, and the other halfe to the poore that had most need.

1513. The 5. *Iohn Dawes*, *Iohn Bridges*[4], *Roger Basford*.[5] Mayor, *W. Browne*, Mercer, and *Iohn Tate*, Mercer, this *Iohn Tate* new builded the church of S. *Anthonies* Hospital in London.

1514. The 6. *Iames Yarford*, *Iohn Monday*. Mayor *George Monoux*, Draper.

[1] *d. March* 22, 1508.
[2] *d. Jan.* 1510.
[3] *d. Feb.* 7, 1513.
[4] Brugges, *O.*; Bruge, *F.*
[5] Bafford *S.*

1515. The 7. *Henry Warley*, *Richarde Grey*, *W. Bayly*. Mayor, Sir *William Butler*, Grocer.

1516. The 8. *Thomas Seimer*, *Iohn Thurstone*. Mayor *Iohn Rest*, Grocer.

1517. The 9. *Thomas Baldrie*, *Raph Simondes*. Mayor, Sir *Thomas Exmew*, Goldsmith. Sir *Thomas Exmew* made the water conduit in London wall by Moregate, &c.

1518. The 10. *Iohn Allen*, *Iames Spencer*. Mayor, *Thomas Mirfin*, Skinner.

1519. The eleuenth, *Iohn Wilkenson*, *Nicholas Partrich*. M. Sir *Iames Yarford*, mercer. From this time the mayors of London, for the most part, haue beene knighted by curtesie of | the kinges, and not otherwise. *Page 531*

1520. The 12. Sir *Iohn Skeuinton*, *Iohn Kyme*. Mayor, Sir *Iohn Bruge*, Draper.

1521. The 13. *Iohn Breton*, *Thomas Pargetor*. M. Sir *Iohn Milborne*, Draper. This Sir *Iohn Milborne* founded foureteene Almes houses by the Crossed Fryers church, &c.

1522. The 14. *Iohn Rudstone*, *Iohn Champneis*. Mayor, Sir *Iohn Mundy*, Goldsmith.

1523. The 15. *Michaell English*, *Nicholas Ienines*. Mayor, Sir *T. Baldry*, mercer.

1524. The 16. *Raph Dodmer*, *William Roche*. M. Sir *W. Bayly*, Draper.

1525. The 17. *Iohn Caunton*, *Christopher Askew*. Maior, Sir *Iohn Allen*, Mercer.

1526. The 18. *Stephen Peacocke*, *Nicholas Lambert*. M. Sir *Thomas Seamer*, Mercer.

1527. The 19. *Iohn Hardy*, *William Holles*.[1] M. Sir *Iames Spencer*, Vintner.

1528. The 20. *Raph Waren*, *Iohn Long*. M. Sir *Iohn Rudstone*, Draper.

1529. The 21. *Michel Dormer*, *Walter Champion*. Mayor, Sir *Raph Dodmer*, Mercer. This yeare it was decreed that no man should be mayor of London more then one yeare.

1530. The 22. *William Dauntsey*, *Richard Choppyn*.[2] M. Sir *T. Pargitor*, Saltar.

[1] Howle, *O.*; Holyes, *F.*

[2] Choppyng, *F.*; Champion, *S.*

1531. The 23. *Richard Gresham, Edward Altham.* Mayor Sir *Nicholas Lambard*, Grocer.

1532. The 24. *Richard Reynoldes, Nicholas Pinchon, Iohn Martin, Iohn Preste.*[1] Mayor, Sir *Stephen Pecocke*, Haberdasher.

1533. The 25. *William Forman*, Sir *T. Kitson.* Maior, Sir *Christopher Askew*, Draper.

1534. The 26. *Nicholas Leuison*[2], *W. Denham.* Mayor, Sir *Iohn Champneis*, Skinner.

1535. The 27. *Humfrey Munmoth, Iohn Cootes.* M. Sir *Iohn Allen*, Mercer, by the kings appointment hee was of his councell. A man of great wisedome, and also of great charity. | The fore named Shiriffes, *Munmouth* and *Cootes*, put away xii. Sergeants, and xii. Yeomen, but were by a common councell forced to take them againe.

Page 532

1536. The 28. *Robert Paget, William Boyer.*[3] Maior, Sir *Raph Waren*, Mercer.

1537. The 29. Sir *Iohn Gresham, Thomas Lewen.* Maior, Sir *Richard Gresham*, Mercer.

1538. The 30. *William Wilkenson, Nicholas Gibson.* Maior *William Forman*, Haberdasher.

1539. The 31. *Iohn Feiry*[4], *Thomas Huntlow.* Maior, Sir *W. Holles*, Mercer.

1540. The 32. Sir *William Laxton, Martin Bowes.* Maior, Sir *William Roch*, Draper.

1541. The 33. *Rowland Hill, Henry Suckley.* Maior, Sir *Michael Dormer*, Mercer.

1542. The 34. *Henry Habberthorne*[5], *Henry Amcotes.* Maior *Iohn Cootes*, Salter.

1543. The 35. *Iohn Toleus*[6], *Richard Dobbes.* Maior, Sir *W. Bowyer*, Draper: For parte, Sir *Raph Waren*, Mercer.

1544. The 36. *Iohn Wilford, Andrew Iude.* Maior, Sir *W. Laxton*, Grocer.

1545. The 37. *George Barnes*[7], *Ralph Alley.* Maior, Sir *Martin Bowes*, Goldsmith.

[1] Prist, *S.*; *he succeeded* Martin *on Sept.* 18, 1533; Martin *succeeded* Pinchon *on Mar.* 12, 1533.

[2] Laveson, *O.*; Lewson, *F.*

[3] Bowyer, *F.*, *O.*

[4] Feyerey, *O.*; Fayrey, *F.*

[5] Hobberthorne, *F.*, *O.*

[6] Tolus, *O.*

[7] Barons, *O.*; Barne, *F.*

1546. The 38. *Richard Iarueis, Thomas Curteis.* Maior, Sir *Henry Hubbarthorne*, marchant taylor.

Edward the sixt began his raigne the 28. of Ianuary, in the yeare 1546.

1547. The 1. Shiriffes *Thomas White, Robert Charsey.*[1] Maior, Sir *Iohn Gresham*, Mercer.

1548. The 2. *William Locke*, Sir *Iohn Ailife.* Maior, Sir *Henry Amcotes*, Fishmonger.

1549. The 3. *Richard Turke, Iohn Yorke.* Maior *Rowland Hill*, Mercer.

1550. The 4. *Augustine Hind, Iohn Lyon.* Maior, Sir *An|drew Iud*, Skinner. Page 533

1551. The 5. *Iohn Lamberd, Iohn Cowper.* Maior, Sir *Richard Dobbes*, Skinner.

1552. The 6. *William Gerard, Iohn Maynard.* Maior, Sir *George Barnes*, Haberdasher.

Queene Mary began her raigne the 6. of Iuly the yeare 1553.

1553. The 1. shiriffes, *Thomas Ofley, William Huet.* Maior, Sir *Thomas White*, Marchant taylor. This *Thomas White* founded Saint *Iohns* Colledge in Oxford. Hee gaue to the Citie of Bristow two thousand pound.

1554. The 2. *Dauid Woodrofe, William Chester.* Maior, Sir *Iohn Lion*, Grocer.

1555. The 3. *Thomas Leigh, Iohn Machil.*[2] Maior, Sir *William Gerard*, Haberdasher.

1556. The 4. *William Harper, Iohn White.* Maior, Sir *Thomas Ofley*, Marchant taylor.

1557. The 5. *Richard Malorie, Iames Aitham.*[3] Maior, Sir *Thomas Curteis*, Fishmonger.

1558. The 6. *Iohn Halse, Richard Champion.* Maior, Sir *Thomas Leigh*, Mercer.

Queene Elizabeth began her raigne the 17. of Nouember, in the yeare of Christ 1558.

1559. The 1. shiriffes *Thomas Lodge, Roger Martin.* Maior, Sir *William Huet*, Clothworker.

[1] Chertesey, *O.*, *F.* [2] Macham, *O.* [3] Altham, *O.*

1560. The 2. *Christopher Draper*, *Thomas Row*. Maior, Sir *William Chester*, Draper: this yeare the Marchant taylors of London founded their notable free schoole for poore mens children, &c.

1561. The 3. *Alexander Auenon* [1], *Humfrey Baskeruile*. Maior, Sir *William Harper*, Marchant taylor.

1562. The 4. *William Alin*, *Richard Chamberlaine*. Mayor, |
Page 534 Sir *Thomas Lodge*, Grocer.

1563. The 5. *Edward Bankes*, *Rowland Heyward*. Maior, Sir *Iohn White*, Grocer.

1564. The 6. *Edward Iackeman*, *Lionel Ducket*. Maior, Sir *Richard Malorie*, Mercer.

1565. The 7. *Iohn Riuers*, *Iames Hawes*. Maior, Sir *Richard Champion*, Draper.

1566. The 8. *Richard Lambert*, *Ambrose Nicholas*, *Iohn Langley*. Maior, Sir *Christopher Draper*, Ironmonger.

1567. The 9. *Thomas Ramsey*, *William Bond*. Maior, Sir *Roger Martin*, Mercer.

1568. The 10. *Iohn Oleph*, *Robert Harding*, *Iames Bacon*. Maior, Sir *Thomas Row*, marchant taylor.

1569. The 11. *Henry Becher*, *William Dane*. Maior *Alexander Auenon*, Ironmonger.

1570. The 12. *Francis Bernam* [2], *William Box*. Maior, Sir *Rowland Heyward*, Clothworker.

1571. The 13. *Henry Miles* [3], *Iohn Braunch*. Maior, Sir *William Allin*, Mercer.

1572. The 14. *Richard Pipe*, *Nicholas Woodrofe*. Maior, Sir *Lionel Ducket*, Mercer.

1573. The 15. *Iames Haruy*, *Thomas Pullison*. Maior, Sir *I. Riuers*, Grocer.

1574. The 16. *Thomas Blanke*, *Anthony Gamage*. Maior *Iames Hawes*, Clothworker.

1575. The 17. *Edward Osborne*, *Wolstane Dixie*. Maior *Ambrose Nicholas*, Salter.

1576. The 18. *William Kimpton*, *George Barne*. Maior, Sir *Iohn Langley*, Goldsmith.

1577. The 19. *Nicholas Backhouse*, *Francis Bowyer*. Maior Sir *Thomas Ramsey*, Grocer.

[1] Avernon, *O*. [2] Barneham, *O*. [3] Mylles, *O*.

1578. The 20. *George Bond, Thomas Starkie.* Maior, Sir *Richard Pipe*, Draper.

1579. The 21. *Martin Calthrope*[1], *Iohn Hart.* Maior, Sir *Nicholas Woodrofe*, Haberdasher.

1580. The 22. *Ralph Woodcock, Iohn Alate.*[2] Maior, Sir *Iohn Branch*, Draper. |

1581. The 23. *Richard Martin, William Webbe.* Maior, Sir *Iames Haruie*, Ironmonger. *Page 535*

1582. The 24. *William Roe, Iohn Haydon*[3], *Cuthbert Buckle.* Maior, Sir *Thomas Blancke*, Haberdasher.

1583. The 25. *William Masham, Iohn Spencer.* Maior *Edward Osborne*, Clothworker.

1584. The 26. *Stephen Slany, Henry Billingsley.* Maior, Sir *Thomas Pullison*, Draper.

1585. The 27. *Anthony Radclife, Henry Pranell.*[4] Maior, Sir *Wolstane Dixie*, Skinner.

1586. The 28. *Robert House, William Elkin.* Maior, Sir *George Barne*, Haberdasher.

1587. The 29. *Thomas Skinner, Iohn Katcher.* Maior, Sir *George Bond*, Haberdasher.

1588. The 30. *Hugh Ofley, Richard Saltenstall.* Maior, Sir *Martin Calthrope*[5], Draper, for part, and *Richard Martin*, Goldsmith, for the rest of that yeare.

1589. The 31. *Richard Gurney, Stephen Some.* Maior, Sir *Iohn Hart*, Grocer.

1590. The 32. *Nicholas Mosley, Robert Broke.* Maior *Iohn Allot*[6], Fishmonger, for part, Sir *Rowland Heyward*, Clothworker, for the rest.

1591. The 33. *William Rider, Benet Barnham.* Maior, Sir *W. Web*, Salter.

1592. The 34. *Iohn Garrard, Robert Taylor.* Maior, Sir *W. Roe*, Ironmonger.

1593. The 35. *Paule Banning, Peter Hauton.*[7] Maior, Sir *Cuthbert Buckle*[8], Vintner, for part: Sir *Richard Martin*, Goldsmith, for the rest.

[1] Calthorpe, *O.*
[2] Allott, *O.*
[3] *d. Nov.* 24, 1582.
[4] Humphrey Praunell, *O.*
[5] *d. May* 3, 1589.
[6] *d. Sept.* 1591.
[7] Houghton, *O.*
[8] *d. July* 1, 1594.

1594. The 36. *Robert Lee*, *Thomas Benet*. Maior, Sir *I. Spencer*, Clothworker.

1595. The 37. *Thomas Low*, *Leonard Holiday*. Maior, Sir *Stephen Slany*, Skinner.

1596. The 38. *Iohn Wattes*, *Richard Godard*. Maior, *Thomas Skinner*[1], Clothworker: for part, Sir *Henry Billingsley*, Haberdasher. |

Page 536 1597. The 39. *Henry Roe*[2], *Iohn More*. Mayor, Sir *Richard Saltenstall*, Skinner.

1598. The 40. *Edward Holmeden*, *Robert Hampson*. Mayor, Sir *Stephen Some*, Grocer.

1599. The 41. *Humfrey Welde*, Grocer, *Roger Clarke*, Salter. Mayor, Sir *Nicholas Mosley*, Clothworker.

1600. The 42. *Robert Cambell*, Ironmonger, *Thomas Smith*, Haberdasher, *William Crauen*, Marchant taylor. Mayor, Sir *William Rider*, Haberdasher.

1601. The 43. *Henry Anderson*, Girdler, *W. Glouer*, Dier. Maior, Sir *Iohn Garrard*, Haberdasher.

1602. The 44. *Iames Pemberton*, Goldsmith. *Iohn Swinerton*, Marchant taylor. Mayor, *Robert Lee*, Marchant taylor.

Thus much for the chiefe & principal gouernours of this famous Citie, of whose publike gouernment, with the assistants of inferior Officers, their charges for keeping of the peace, seruice of the Prince, and honour of this Citie, much might haue beene said, and I had thought to haue touched more at large: but being informed that a learned gentleman (*Iames Dalton*) a Citizen borne, minded such a labour, and promised to performe it, I haue forborne, and left the same to his good leysure: but hee being now lately deceased without finishing any such worke (a common fault, to promise more then to performe) and I heare not of any other that taketh it in hand, I haue beene diuers times minded to adde certayne Chapters to this booke, but being (by the good pleasure of God) visited with sicknes, such as my feete (which haue borne mee many a mile) haue of late yeares refused, once in foure or fiue

[1] *d. Dec.* 30, 1596.

[2] Henry Awmond, *O.*

monethes to conuay me from my bed to my study, and therefore could not do as I would.

At length remembring I had long since gathered notes to haue Chaptered, am now forced to deliuer them vnperfected, and desire the Readers to pardon me, that want not will to pleasure them. |

Aldermen and Shiriffes of London.

Page 537

THERE bee in this Citie, according to the number of Wardes 26. Aldermen, whereof yearely, on the feast day of Saint *Michael* the Archangell, one of them is elected to be Mayor, for the yeare following, to begin on the 28. of October, the other Aldermen his brethren, are to him Assistants in Counsails, Courtes, &c.

Recorder of London.

More, there is a Recorder of London, a graue and learned Lawyer, skilfull in the Customes of this Citty, Also assistant to the Lord Maior: Hee taketh place in Counsels, and in Courts before any man that hath not beene Mayor: and learnedly deliuereth the sentences of the whole Court.

Shiriffes of London.

The shiriffes of London, of old time chosen out of the Commonalty, Commoners, and oftentimes neuer came to bee Aldermen, as many Aldermen were neuer shiriffes, and yet aduanced to bee Mayor, but of late (by occasion) the shiriffes haue beene made Aldermen, before, or presently after their election.

Nicholas Faringdon was neuer shiriffe, yet foure times Maior of this Cittie, and so of other, which reproueth a bye worde, such a one will be Maior, or he be shiriffe, &c.

Then is there a Chamberlaine of London.
A Common Clarke, or Towne Clarke.
A Common Sergeant.

Officers belonging to the Lord Mayors house.

SWORD bearer.
Common Hunt.
Common Crier.
Water Bailiffe.
} Esquiers. 4. |

Page 538 Coroner of London.
Sergeant Caruers. 3.
Sergeants of the Chamber. 3.
Sergeant of the Chanell.
Yeoman of the Chanell.
Yeomen of the water side. 4.
Vnder water Bailiffe.
Yeomen of the Chamber. 2.
Meale weighers. 3.
Yeomen of the Wood wharfes. 2.

The Sword bearers man. Common Hunts men. 2. Common Criers man. Water Bailiffes men. 2. The Caruers man.	Gentlemens men 7.

Whereof nine of these haue Liueries of the Lord Mayor, viz. The sword bearer and his man, the three Caruers and the foure Yeomen of the water side. All the rest haue their Liueries from the Chamber of London.

Thus farre after my notes deliuered by an Officer of the Lord Maiors house, but vnperfect: for I remember a Crowner, an vnder Chamberlaine, and foure Clarkes of the Maiors Court, and others.

The Shiriffes of London their Officers

THE Shiriffes of London, in the yeare 1471. were appointed each of them to haue 16. Sergeants, euery Sergeant to haue his Yeoman. And 6. Clarkes, to wit, a Secondary, a Clarke of the Papers, and 4. other Clarkes, besides the vnder shiriffes Clarkes, their Stewards, Butlers, Porters, and other in household many. |

Page 539 *Of the Maiors and Shiriffes Liueryes somewhat.*

TO follow president of former time, the Clarkes of Companies were to enquire for them of their companies that would haue the Maiors Lyuery, their money as a beneuolence giuen, which must be xx s. at the least put in a purse, with theyr names that gaue it, and the Wardens to deliuer it to the Mayor by the first of December, for the which euery man had then sent him foure yeardes of broade Cloath rowed or striped thwart, with a different colour to make him a Gowne, and these were called rey Gownes, which was then the Liuery of the Mayor, and also of the Shiriffes, but each differing from others in the colours.

Of Older times I reade, that the Officers of this Cittie ware Gownes of partie colours, as the right syde of one colour, and the left syde of an other: as for example, I reade in Bookes of accountes in the Guildhall, that in the 19. yeare of *Henrie* the sixt, there was bought for an Officers Gowne two yeards of Cloath, coloured Mustard villars (a colour now out of vse) and two yeardes of Cloath coloured blew, price two shillinges the yeard, in all eight shillings. More, paied to *Iohn Pope*, Draper, for two Gowne clothes, eight yeards of two colours *eux ambo deux de roug* (or red) *medley brune* and *porre* (or purple) colour, price the yeard 2. s. These Gownes were for *Piers Rider*, and *Iohn Bukles*, Clarkes of the Chamber.

More, I reade that in the yeare 1516. in the seuenth of *Henrie* the 8. it was agreed by a common Councell in the Guildhall, that the shiriffes of London should (as they had beene accustomed) giue yearely Reyed Gownes, to the Recorder, Chamberlaine, common Sergeant, and common Clarke, the Sworde bearer, Common hunt, Water Bayly, common Crier, like as to their owne Officers, &c.

1525. More, in the 16. of *Henrie* the eight, sir *William Bayly* then being Maior, made a request for that clothes of Ray (as hee alledged) were euill wrought, his Officers might bee permitted (contrarie to custome) for that yeare to weare Gownes of | one colour, to the which in a common Councell *Page 540* one answered and said, yea, it might be permitted, and no man said nay, and so it passed. Thus much for partie coloured, and Ray Gownes haue I read. But for beneuolence to the Maior, I find that of later time, [that] each man giuing fortie shillings towards his charges, receyued foure yeards of broade cloath to make him a Gowne, for *Thomas White* performed it in the first of Queene *Mary*, but sir *Thomas Lodge* gaue in stead of foure yeards of broad cloth, three yards of Satten to make them Dublets, and since that the three yeards of Satten is turned into a siluer spoone, and so it holdeth.

The dayes of attendance that the fellowships doe giue to the Maior at his going to Paules were seuen, as followeth.

1. Alhallowen day.
2. Christmasse day.
3. Saint *Stephens* day.
4. Saint *Iohns* day.
5. New years day.
6. Twelfe day.
7. Candlemasse day.

The 23. of Henrie the eight, these companies had place at the Maiors feast, in the Guild hall in order as followeth, I speake by president, for I was neuer feast-folower.

1. Mercers, the wardens and 17. persons, fiue messe.
2. Grocers, the wardens and 16. persons, foure messe.
3. Drapers, the wardens and 12. persons, foure messe.
4. Fishmongers, the wardens and 12. persons, foure messe.
5. Goldsmiths, the wardens and 10. persons, three messe.
6. Skinners, the wardens and 8. persons, three messe.
7. Marchant Taylers, the wardens and 9. persons, three messe.
8. Vintoners, the wardens and 6. persons, two messe.
9. Ironmongers the wardens and ⟨1⟩4. persons 4. messe & a halfe.
10. Marchant Haberdashers, the wardens and 14. persons, foure messe and a halfe. |
11. Saltars, the wardens and eight persons, two Messe and a halfe. *Page 541*
12. Dyars, the Wardenes, and 6. persons 2. messe.
13. Lethersellars, the Wardens, and 8. persons, 3. messe.
14. Pewterers, the wardens and 5. persons, 2. messe.
15. Cutlers, the wardens and 5. persons, 2. messe.
16. Armorers, the Wardens and three persons, one messe.
17. Waxechandlers, the wardens and 6. persons, two messe.

18. Tallow Chandlers, the wardens and three persons, two messe.
19. Sheremen, the wardens and 5. persons, 2. messe.
20. Fullars, the wardens and 9. persons, 2. messe.
21. Sadlers, the Wardens and 4 persons, 2. messe.
22. Bruers, the wardens and 12 persons, 4. messe.
23. Scriueners, the wardens and 6. persons, 2. messe.
24. Butchers, the wardens and 7. persons, 3. messe.
25. Bakers, the wardens, and 4. persons, 2. messe.
26. Poultars, the wardens and one person, one messe.
27. Stacioners, the wardens and two persons, one messe.
28. Inholders, the wardens, and 4. persons, 2. messe.
29. Girdlars, the wardens and 4. persons, two messe.
30. Chirurgions, the wardens and two persons, one messe.
31. Foundars, the wardens and one person, one messe.
32. Barbars, the wardens, and 4. persons, two messe.

No Clothing. Vpholders, the wardens and 2. persons, one messe.

34. Broyderars, the Wardens and two persons, one messe.
35. Bowiers, the wardens and two persons, one messe.
36. Fletchers, the wardens and 2. persons, one messe.

No Clothing. Turnars, the wardens and 2. persons, one messe.

38. Cordwainers, the wardens and 4. persons, 2. messe.
39. Painters stayners, the wardens and 5. persons, 2. messe.
40. Masons, the wardens and one person, one messe.
41. Plummers, the wardens, and two persons, one messe.
42. Carpentars, the wardens and 4. persons, 2. messe.
43. Powch makers, the wardens and 2. persons, one messe.
44. Joynars, the wardens and two persons, one messe.
45. Coopers, the wardens andone person, one messe. |

No Clothing. Glasiars, the wardens and two persons, one messe. *Page 542*

No Clothing. Linnendrapers, the wardens and two persons, one messe.

No Clothing. Woodmongers, the wardens, and two persons, one messe.

49. Coriars, the wardens and two persons, one messe.

No Clothing. Foystors, the wardens and two persons, one messe.

No Clothing. Grey Tanners, the wardens and two persons, one messe.

52. Tilars, the wardens, and one person, one messe.

53. Weuers, the wardens and one person, one messe.

54. Blacksmithes, the wardens, and one messe.

No Clothing. Lorimars, the wardens and two persons, one messe.

56. Spurriars, the wardens and two persons, one messe.

57. Wiresellars, the wardens and one person, one messe.

No Clothing. Fruterers, the wardens and two persons, one messe.

No Clothing. Ferrers, the wardens and two persons, one messe.

60. Bladesmithes, the wardens and two persons, one messe.

These Companies seuerally at sundry times purchased the kinges fauour and licence by his Letters Patentes, to associate themselues in Brotherhoodes with maister and Wardens for their gouernment, many also haue procured Corporations with Priuileges, &c. but I reade not of licence by them procured for Liueries to be worne, but at their Gouernours discretion to appoint as occasion asketh, some time in triumphant manner, some time more mourning like, and such Liueries haue they taken vppon them, as well before as since, they were by licence associated into Brotherhoods or Corporations. For the first of these companies that I reade of to bee a Guild, Brotherhoode or Fraternitie in this Cittie were the Weauers, whose Guild was confirmed by *Henry* the second. The next Fraternity, which was of saint *Iohn Baptist*, time out of minde called of Taylors, and Linnen Armorers of London, I find that king *Edwarde* the first, in the 28. of his raigne, confirmed that Guild by the name of Taylors and
Page 543 Linnen Armorers, and gaue to the Brethren | there of authority, yearely to chuse vnto them a Gouernour or Maister with Wardens, &c. The other Companies haue since purchased licence of societies, Brotherhoodes, or Corporations in the raignes of *Edwarde* the thirde, *Richard* the second, *Henry* the fourth, *Henry* the fift, *Henry* the sixt, and *Edward* the fourth, &c.

Somewhat of Liueries worne by Cittizens of London, in time of triumphes, and other wayes.

1236. THE twentieth of *Henry* the third, The Mayor, Aldermen, Shiriffes and Cittizens of London rode out to meete the King and his new wife, Queen *Elianor,* daughter to *Reymond Beringarius* of Aragon, Earle of Prouince and Narbone. The Cittizens were clothed in long garments, embroydered about with gold, and silke of diuers colours, their horses finelie trapped, to the number of three hundred sixtie, euerie man bearing a golden or siluer cuppe in his hande, the kinges Trumpets before them sounding, &c. as yee may reade in my Annales.

1300. The 29. of *Edward* the first, the saide king tooke to wife *Margaret* sister to *Philip Le Bew* king of Fraunce, they were married at Canterbury. The Queene was conuayed to London, against whome the Cittizens to the number of sixe hundred rode in one Liuerie of red and white, with the cognisances of their misteries embroydered vpon their sleeues, they receiued her foure miles out of London, and so conueyed her to Westminster.

1415. The 3. of *Henry* the fift, the said king arriuing at Douer, the mayor of London with the Aldermen and craftes men riding in red with hoods red and white, met with the king on the Blacke Hith, comming from Eltham with his prisoners out of France.

1432. The 10. of *Henry* the sixt, hee being crowned in France, returning into England, came to Eltham towardes London, and the Mayor of London *Iohn Welles,* the Aldermen, with the comminalty rode against him on Horsebacke, the Mayor in Crimson | veluet, a great veluet *Page 544* hat furred, a girdle of golde aboute his middle, and a Bawdrike of gold about his necke trilling down behind him, his three Henxemen, on three great coursers following him, in one sute of red, all spangled in siluer, then the Aldermen in Gownes of scarlet, with sanguine hoodes, and all the Comminaltie of the citty cloathed in white gownes, and scarlet hoods, with diuers cognizances embrodered on their sleeues, &c.

1485. The first of *Henrie* the seuenth, The Mayor, Aldermen, Shiriffes and Comminality, all cloathed in Violet (as in a mourning colour) mette the king at Shorditch, and conuayed him to Powles Church, where hee offered his Banners.

Thus much for liueries of Cittizens in auncient times, both in triumphes and otherwise, may suffice, whereby may be obserued that the couerture of mens heads was then hoodes, for neyther Cappe or hat is spoken of, except that *Iohn Wels* Mayor of London to were a hat in time of triumph, but differing from the hattes lately taken in vse, and now commonly worne for Noble mens Liueries. I reade that *Thomas* Earle of Lancaster in the raigne of *E.* the second gaue at Christmas in Liueries, to such as serued him, 159. broade cloathes, allowing to euery garment furres to furre their hoodes: more nearer our time, there yet remeyneth the counterfeites and pictures of Aldermen, and other that liued in the raignes of *Henrie* the sixte and *Edwarde* the fourth, namely Alderman *Darby* dwelled in Fenchurch street over against the parrish church of S. *Diones*, left his picture, as of an Alderman in a gowne of skarlet on his backe, a hoode on his head, &c. as is in that house (and else where) to bee seene: for a further monument of those late times, men may beholde the glasse Windows of the Mayors court in the Guild hall aboue the stayrs, the mayor is there pictured, sitting in habite, party coloured, and a hoode on his head, his Swordebearer before him with an hatte or Cappe of maintenance: the Common Clearke, and other officers bare headed, their hoodes on their shoulders: and therefore I take it, that the vse of square bonets worne by Noble men, Gentlemen,
Page 545 Cittizens and others, tooke beginning in this | Realm by *Henry* the seuenth, and in his time, and of further antiquitie I can see no counterfeyte or other proofe of vse. *Henry* the eight (towards his latter raigne) ware a round flat cap of scarlet or of veluet, with a bruch or Jewell, and a feather, diuers Gentlemen, Courtiers, and other did the like. The youthfull Cittizens also tooke them to the new fashion of flatte caps, knit of woollen yearne blacke, but so light that

they were forced to tye them vnder their chins, for else the wind would be maister ouer them. The vse of these flat round cappes so far increased (being of lesse price then the French Bonet) that in short time some yong Aldermen tooke ⟨to⟩ the wearing of them, Sir *Iohn White* ware it in his Maioralty, and was the first that left example to his Followers, but now the spanish felt, or the like counterfeyte, is most commonly of all men both spirituall and temporall taken to vse, so that the French Bonet or square cappe, and also the round or flat cap, haue for the most parte giuen place to the spanish felte, but yet in London amongst the grauer sort, (I meane the Liueries of Companies) remayneth a memory of the hoodes of olde time worne by their predecessors: These hoodes were worne, the Roundelets vpon their heads, the skirts to hang behind in their neckes to keep them warme, the tippet to lye on their shoulder, or to wind about their neckes, these hoodes were of olde time made in colours according to their gownes, which were of two colours, as red and blew or red and purple, murrey, or as it pleased their Masters and wardens to appoint to the Companies, but now of late time, they haue vsed their gowns to be al of one colour, and those of the sadest; but their hoodes being made the one halfe of the same cloath their gownes be of, the other halfe remayneth red as of old time.

And so I end, as wanting time to trauell further in this Worke. |

NOW since that I haue given you an outward view of this City, it shall not be impertinent to let you take an insight also of the same, such as a Londoner borne discoursed aboue twenty yeares agone, for aunswere (as it seemeth) to some obiections, that then were made against the growing greatnes thereof. The author gaue it me, & therefore, howsoeuer I conceale his name (which it selfe pretendeth not), I thinke I may without his offence impart it to others, that they may take pleasure in the reading as I doubt not but he did in the writing. Long may they (that list) enuie, and long may wee and our posterity enioy the good estate of this Cittie. | *Page 546*

Page 547 A Discourse of the names and first causes of the institution of Cities and peopled townes. And of the commodities that doe growe by the same: and namely of the Cittie of London. Written by way of an Apologie (or defence) against the opinion of some men, which thinke that the greatnes of that Cittie standeth not with the profit and securitie of this Realme.

CITTIES and well peopled places bee called *Oppida*, in Latine, eyther *ab ope danda*, or *ab opibus*, or *ab opponendo se hostibus.* They be named also *Ciuitates a coeundo*, and *vrbes* either of the word *vrbare*, because the first inclosure of them was described with the draught of a plow, or else *ab orbe*, for the rounde compasse that they at the first had.

In the Greeke a cittie is tearmed πόλις, eyther of the worde πολὺς, *multus*, or of πολεύω, πολεύειν, *id est*, *habitare*, *alere*, *gubernare.*

In the Saxon (or old English) sometimes Tun, which wee now call towne, deriued of the word Tynan, to inclose or tyne, as some yet speake. But for as much as that worde was proper to euery village, and inclosed dwelling, therefore our auncesters called their walled townes buꞃh or biꞃiᵹ, and wee now *Bury* and *Borow*, of the Greeke word πύργος, (as I thinke) which signifieth a Tower or a high building.

The walles of these townes had their name of *vallum*, because at the first they were but of that earth which was cast out of the trench or ditch wherewith they were enuironed.

But afterward, being made of matter more fitte for defence, they were named *a muniendo mænia.* By the Etimologie of |
Page 548 these names, it may appeare that common Weales, Citties and townes, were at the first inuented to the end that men might lead a ciuill life amongst themselues, and bee saued harmeles againe theyr enemies: whereupon *Plato* saith, *Ciuitates ab initio vtilitatis causa constitutæ sunt. Aristotle*, 1. *Politicorum*, 2. saith, *Ciuitas a natura profecta est: homo enim animal aptum est ad cœtus, et proinde ciuitatis origo ad viuendum, institutio ad*

bene viuendum refertur. And *Cicero, lib. primo de inuentione.* in the beginning saith: *Fuit quoddam tempus cum in agris homines passim bestiarum more vagabantur, &c., quo quidem tempore, quidam (magnus viz. vir et sapiens) dispersos homines in agris, & tectis siluestribus abditos, ratione quadam compulit in vnum locum, atque eos in vnamquamque rem induxit vtilem & honestam. Vrbibus vero constitutis fidem colere, & iustitiam retinere discebant, et aliis parere sua voluntate consuescebant &c.* The same man discourseth notablie to the same effect, in his Oration *pro Sestio,* a little after the middest thereof, shewing that in the life of men dispersed, *vis* beareth all the sway: but in the ciuill life and societie, *ars* is better maintained, &c. This thing well saw king *William* the Conqueror, who in his lawes, fol. 125. saith, *Burgi et Ciuitates fundatæ & edificatæ sunt, ad tuitionem gentium & populorum Regni, & idcirco obseruari debent cum omni libertate, integritate & ratione.* And his predecessors, king *Ethelstane,* and king *Canutus* in their lawes, *fol.* 62, and 106. had commaunded thus: *Oppida instaurentur, &c.*

Seeing therefore that as *Cicero,* 2. *officior.,* saith, *Proxime et secundum Deos, homines hominibus maxime vtiles esse possunt.* And that men are congregated into Citties and commonwealthes, for honestie and vtilities sake, these shortly bee the commodities that do come by citties, comminalties, and corporations. First, men by this nearenes of conuersation are withdrawn from barbarous feritie and force to a certaine mildnes of manners and to humanity and iustice: whereby they are contented to giue and take right, to and from their equals and inferiors, and to heare and obey their heades and superiors. Also the doctrine of God | is more fitly deliuered, *Page 548* and the discipline thereof more aptely to bee executed, in peopled townes then abroad, by reason of the facilitie of common and often assembling. And consequently, such inhabitantes be better managed in order, and better instructed in wisedome: whereof it came to passe that at the first, they that excelled others this way, were called *astuti* of the Greeke worde ἄστυ, which signifieth a Citty, although the tearme bee now declined to the worst part, and doe betoken euil, euen as *Tyrannus, Sophista,* and some such other originally good wordes are fallen: And hereof also good behauiour is yet called *Vrbanitas*, because it is rather found in Citties, then else where. In summe, by often hearing, men be better perswaded in religion, and for that they liue in the eye of others, they bee by example the more easily trayned to iustice, and by shamefastnesse restrayned from iniurie.

And whereas commonwealthes and kingdomes cannot haue, next after God, any surer foundation, then the loue and good will of one man towardes another, that also is closely bred and maintayned in Citties, where men by mutual societie and companying together, doe grow to alliances, comminalties and corporations.

The liberall sciences and learninges of all sortes, which bee *lumina reipublicæ*, doe flourish onely in peopled towns, without the which a realme is in no better case then a man that lacketh both his eyes.

Manual artes or Handy crafts, as they haue for the most part beene inuented in townes and citties, so they cannot any where else be eyther maintained or amended. The like is to bee sayde of Marchandize, vnder which name I comprehend all manner of buying, selling, bartering, exchaunging, communicating of thinges that men need to and fro. Wealth and riches, which are truely called *subsidia belli, et ornamenta pacis*, are increased chiefly in Townes and Citties both to the prince and people.

The necessity of the poore and needy is in such places both sooner to be espied, and hath meanes to be more charitably relieued.

The places themselues bee surer refuges in all extremities of forraine inuasion, and the inhabitantes be a ready hand & strength of men with munition to oppresse intestine sedition.

Moreouer, for as much as the force of the warres of our |
Page 550 time consisteth chiefly in shot, all other souldiers being either horse men or footemen armed on lande, or Mariners at the sea, it seemeth to me that Citizens and Townesmen be as fit to be imploied in any of these seruices, that on horsebacke onely excepted, as the inhabitants that be drawne out of the countrey.

Furthermore, euen as these societies and assemblies of men in Cities and great Townes, are a continuall bridle against tyranny, which was the cause that *Tarquin*, *Nero*, *Dionisius*, and such others haue alwayes sought to weaken them, So, being wel tempered, they are a strong forte and bulwarke not onely in the *Aristocritie*, but also in the lawfull kingdome or iust royalty.

At once the propagation of Religion, the execution of good policie, the exercise of Charity, and the defence of the countrey, is best performed by townes and Cities: and this ciuill life approcheth nearest to the shape of that misticall body whereof Christ is the head, and men be the members: whereupon both at the first, that man of God *Moyses*, in the commonwealth of the Israelites, and the Gouernours of all Countries in all ages sithence haue continually maintayned the same. And to chaunge it were nothing else but to *Metamorphose* the world, and to make wilde beastes of reasonable men. To stand longer vpon this it were, *in re non dubia*, *vti oratione non necessaria*: and therefore I will come to London.

The singularities of the City of London.

WHATSOEVER is said of Cities generally, maketh also for London specially: Howbeit these thinges are particularly for our purpose to bee considered in it. The scituation: the former estimation that it hath had: the seruice that it hath done: the present estate and gouernment of it, and such benefites as do grow to the realme by the maintenance thereof.

This Realme hath onely three principall Riuers, whereon a royall Cittie may well be scituated: Trent in the north,| Seuerne, in the southwest, and Thames in the southeast: of *Page 551* the which, Thames both for the streight course in length reacheth furthest into the bellie of the land, and for the breadth and stilnesse of the water is most nauigable vp and downe the streame: by reason whereof London standing almost in the middle of that course, is more commodiously serued with prouision of necessaries, then any towne standing vpon the other two Riuers can be, and doth also more easily communicate to the rest of the Realme the commodities of her owne entercourse and trafficke.

This Riuer openeth indifferently vpon France and Flaunders, our mightiest neighbours, to whose doings wee ought to haue a bent eye, and special regard: and this Citie standeth thereon in such conuenient distance from the sea, as it is not onely neare enough for intelligence of the affayres of those Princes, and for the resistance of their attempts: but also sufficiently remoued from the feare of any sodaine daungers that may be offered by them: whereas for the Prince of this Realme to dwell vpon Trent, were to turne his backe, or blind side to his most daungerous borderers: and for him to rest and dwell vpon Seuerne, were to be shut vp in a cumbersome corner: which openeth but vpon Ireland onely, a place of much lesse importance.

Neither could London be pitched so commodiously vpon any other part of the same riuer of Thames, as where it now standeth. For if it were remoued more to the west, it should lose the benefit of the ebbing and flowing: and if it were seated more towardes the East, it should be nearer to daunger of the enemie, and further both from the good ayre, and from doing good to the inner parts of the Realme: neither may I omit that none other place is so plentifully watered with springs, as London is.

And whereas, amongst other things, Corne and Cattell, Hay and Fuell be of great necessitie: of the which Cattell may be driuen frome afarre, and corne may easily be transported.

But Hay and Fuell, being of greater bulke and burthen, must be had at hande: onely London, by the benefit of this scituation and Riuer, may be sufficiently serued therewith. *Page 552* In which respect | an Alderman of London reasonably (as me thought) affirmed, that although London receiued great nourishment by the residence of the Prince, the repaire of the Parliament, and Courtes of Justice, yet it stoode principally by the aduantage of the scituation vpon the Riuer: for whenas on a time it was told him by a Courtier, that Queene *Mary*, in her displeasure against London, had appointed to remoue with the Parliament and Terme to Oxford, this playne man demaunded, whether she meant also to diuert the Riuer of Thames from London, or no? and when the Gentleman had answered no, then, quoth the Alderman, by Gods grace wee shall do well enough at London, whatsoeuer become of the Tearme and Parliament. I my selfe being then a young scholler at Oxford, did see great preparation made towards that Tearme and Parliament, and do well remember that the common opinion and voyce was, that they were not holden there because prouision of Hay could not be made in all the Countrey to serue for ten whole dayes together, and yet is that quarter plentifully stored with Hay for the proportion of the shire it selfe.

For proofe of the ancient estimation of London, I will not vse the Authoritie of the Brittish Historie, nor of such as follow it, (although some hold it credible enough that London was first *Trinobantum ciuitas*, or *Troia noua*, that famous Citie in our Histories, and then *Ludstoune*, and by corruption London, as they report) because they bee not of sufficient force to drawe the gaynesayers. Neither will I stand much vpon that honourable testimony which *Geruas. Tilberiens.* giueth to London in his booke *de otiis Imperialibus*, saying thus, concerning the blessing of God towards it,

In Vrbe London, exceptione habet diuulgatum id per omnes æquè gentes Lucani prouerbium:
Inuida fatorum series summisque negatum
Stare diu:
Nam ea annis 354. *ante Romam conditam numquam amisit principatum nec bello consumpta est.*

But I will rather vse the credite of one or two auncient forraine writers, and then descend to latter histories. *Cornel. Tacitus lib.* 14. *Annal.* sayth, *Londinum copia negociatorum et comme|atuum maxime celebris*; and *Herodian* in the life of *Seuerus* the Emperour sayth, *Londinum vrbs magna et opulenta.* *Page 553* *Beda, lib. Hist. Ecclesiastic.* 1. *Cha.* 29. sheweth that Pope *Gregory* appointed two Archbishops Seas in England, the one at London, the other at Yorke; king *Ethelstane* in his lawes appointing how many Mint maisters should be in each Citie, allotteth eight to London, and not so many to any other

Citie. The Penner of those lawes that are said to be made by *Edward* the Confessor, and confirmed by *William* the Conqueror saith, *London est caput Regni et Legum.* King *Henry* the first, in the third Chapter of his lawes, commaundeth that no Citizen of London should be amerced aboue 100 s. for any pecuniarie paine. The great Charter of England, that *Helena* for which there was so long and so great warre and contention, in the ninth chapter saith, *ciuitas London habeat omnes suas Libertates antiquas &c.* About the time of King *I.* London was reputed *regni firmata Columna*, as *Alexander Necham* writeth, and in the beginning of the raigne of *Richard* the second it was called *Camera regis*, as *Thomas Walsingham* reporteth. I passe ouer the recitall of the Saxon Charter of king *William* the Conqueror, the latine Charters of *Henry* the first & second, of *Richard* the first, of *Iohn*, and of *Edward* the first, all which gaue vnto the Citizens of London great Priuiledges, and of *Edward* the third, who reciting al the grants of his predecessors, not onely confirmed but also increased the same, and of the latter kings who haue likewise added many things thereunto. Onely I wish to be noted by them, that during all this time, all those wise and politique Princes haue thought it fit, not onely to maintaine London in such plight as they found it, but also to adorne, increase and amplifie it with singular tokens of their liberall fauour and good liking. And whether there be not now the same or greater causes to draw the like or better estimation and cherishing, let any man be iudge, that will take the paines to compare the present estate of London, yet still growing to better, with the former condition of the same.

It were too much to recite particularly the Martiall seruices that this city hath done from time to time: neither do I think that they be all committed to writing, only for a tast as it were, I will note these few following. |

Page 554 Almost 60. yeares before the Conquest, a huge armie of the Danes (whereof king *Sweyne* was the leader,) besieged king *Etheldred* in London (then the which as the storie sayeth then he had none other refuge), but they were manfully repulsed, and a great number of them slaine.

After the death of this *Sweyne*, his sonne *Canutus* (afterwarde king of England) besieged London, both by land and water: but after much labour finding it impregnable, he departed; and in the same yeare repayring his forces, he girded it with a new siege, in the which the Citizens so defended themselues, and offended him, that in the end he went away with shame.

In the dissention that arose betweene king *Edward* the Confessor & his father in law Earle *Goodwin* (which was the mightiest subiect within this land that euer I haue read of) the Earle with a great armie came to London, and was for all that by the countenance of the Citizens resisted, till such time as the Nobilitie made reconciliation betweene them. About 70. years after the Conquest, *Maude* the Empresse made warre vpon king *Stephen* for the right of the Crowne, and had taken his person prisoner, but by the strength and assistance of the Londoners and Kentishmen, *Maude* was put to flight at Winchester, and her brother *Robert*, then Earle of Glocester, was taken in exchange, for whome King *Stephen* was deliuered. I dispute not whose right was better, but I auouch the seruice, seeing *Stephen* was in possession.

The Hystorie of *William Walworth* the Maior of London is well knowne, by whose manhoode and policie, the person of king *Richarde* the second was rescued, the Citie saued, *Wat Tilar* killed, and all his straglers discomfited, in rewarde of which seruice, the Maior and other Aldermen were knighted.

Iacke Cade also hauing discomfited the kinges Armie, that was sent agaynst him, came to London, and was there manfully and with long fight resisted, vntill that by the good policie of the Citizens his company was dispersed.

Finally, in the tenth yeare of the raigne of king *Edwarde* the fourth, and not many dayes before the death of *Henrie* the sixt, | *Thomas Neuell*, commonly called the bastard of *Page 555* *Fauconbridge*, armed a great companie agaynst the king, and being denied passage through London, he assaulted it on diuerse parts: but he was repulsed by the Citizens, and chased as farre as Stratford with the losse of a great many.

Thus much of certaine their principall, and personall seruices, in war onely, for it were infinite to repeate the particular aides of men and money which London hath ministered: and I had rather to leaue it to be coniectured at, by comparison to be made between it and other Cities, whereof I will giue you this one note for an example. In the 12. yeare of the raigne of king *Edward* the 2. it was ordered by Parliament, that euery City of the realme should make out souldiers agaynst the *Scots*: at which time London was appoynted to send 200. men, and Canterburie, being then one of our best Cities, 40. and no more. And this proportion of fiue[1] to one, is now in our age increased, at the least fiue[1] to one, both in souldiers and subsidie. As for the other seruices that London hath done in tymes of peace, they are to be measured by consideration of the commodities, whereof I will speake anon. In the meane season let the estate and gouernment of this City be considered to the end that it may appeare that it standeth well with the policie of the Realme.

Cæsar in his Commentaries is witnes, that in his time the Cities of Britaine had large territories annexed vnto them, and were seuerall estates of themselues, gouerned by particular kings or Potentates, as in Italie and Germany yet be: and that *Mandubratius* was king of the Trinobants, whose chiefe citie London is taken to haue beene. And I find not that this gouernment was altered, either by *Cæsar*, or his successors, notwithstanding that the Countrie became tributarie vnto them: but that it continued vntill at length the Britons themselues reduced all their peoples into one Monarchie, howbeit that lasted not any long season: for vpon *Vortiger* their king came the Saxons our Auncestors, and they draue the Britons into Wales, Cornwall, and Britaine in France, and in processe of Warre diuided the Country amongst themselues into an Eptarchie, or seauen kingdomes, of the which one was called

Page 556 the Kingdome of the East Saxons, | which hauing in maner the same limits that the Bishoprike of London now inioyeth, contayned Essex, Middlesex and a part of Hertfordshire, and so included London. Again, it appeareth that in course of time and about 800. yeares after Christ, *Egbert* (then K. of the west Saxons) *Vt pisces sæpe minutos magnus comest*, ouercame the rest of the kings, and once more erected a Monarchie,

[1] fiue *1603;* ? twenty-five, *or* -sixe.

the which till the comming in of the Normans, and from thence euen hitherto, hath continued.

Now I doubt not (whatsoeuer London was in the time of *Cæsar*) but that vnder the Eptarchie and Monarchy it hath beene a subiect, and no free City, though happily endowed with some large priuiledges. For king *William* the Conqueror found a Portreeue there, whose name was *Godfrey* (by which name he greeteth him in his Saxon *Charter*[1], and his office was none other then the charge of a Bayliffe, or Reeue, as by the selfe same name continuing yet in Grauesend, and certain other places, may well appeare. But the Frenchmen vsing their own language, called him somtime a Prouost, and sometime a Bayliffe: whatsoeuer his name and office were, he was *perpetuus Magistratus*, giuen by the Prince, and not chosen by the Citizens, as it seemeth, for what time king *Richard* the first needed money towardes his expedition in the Holy land, they first purchased of him the Libertie to choose yearly from amongst themselues two Bayliffes: and king *Iohn* his successor, at their like sute changed their Bayliffes into a Maior, and two shiriffes. To these *Henrie* the third added Aldermen, at the first elegible yearely, but afterward by king *Edward* the third made perpetuall Magistrates, and Iustices of the peace within their wards, in which plight of government it presently standeth. This shortly as I could, is the Historical and outward estate of London: now come I to the inward pith and substance.

The estate of this Citie is to be examined by the quantitie, and by the qualitie.

The quantitie therefore consisteth in the number of the Citizens, which is very great, and farre exceedeth proportion of *Hippodamus*, which appoynted 10000. and of others which haue set downe other numbers, as meete stintes in theyr opinions to bee well gouerned, but yet seeing both reason and experience haue | freed vs from the law of any definite *Page 557* number, so that other things be obserued, let that bee admitted: neither is London, I feare me, so great as populous: for well sayth one, *Non idem est magna Ciuitas & frequens, magna est enim quæ multos habet qui arma ferre possunt*, whatsoeuer the number bee, it breedeth no feare of sedition: for as much as the same consisteth not in the extreames, but in a verie medio-

[1] *Charter*] Chre *1603*

critie of wealth and riches, as it shall better appeare anone. And if the causes of English rebellions be searched out, they shall bee found in effect to bee these twaine, *Ambition* and *Couetousnes*, of which the first raigneth in the mindes of high and noble personages, or of such others, as seeke to be gracious and popular, and haue robbed the hearts of the multitude, whereas in London, if any where in the worlde, *honos vere onus est*, and euery man rather shunneth then seeketh the Maioraltie which is the best marke amongst them, neyther hath there been any strong faction, nor any man more popular then the rest, forasmuch as the gouernment is by a Paterne, as it were, and alwayes the same, how oftensoeuer they chänge their Magistrate. *Couetousnesse*, that other Syre of sedition, possesseth the miserable and needy sort, and such as be naughty packes, vnthrifts, which although it cannot be chosen, but that in a frequent City as London is, there shall be found many, yet beare they not any great sway, seeing the multitude and most part there is of a competent wealth, and earnestly bent to honest labour, I confesse that London is a mighty arme and instrument to bring any great desire to effect, if it may be woon to a mans deuotion: wherof also there want not examples in the English Historie. But forasmuch as the same is by the like reason seruiceable and meete to impeach any disloyall attempt, let it rather be well gouerned then euil liked therefore, for it shall appeare anon that as London hath adhered to some rebellions, so hath it resisted many, and was neuer the author of any one. The qualitie of this Citty consisteth eyther in the law and gouer⟨n⟩ment thereof: or in the degrees and condition of the Citizens, or in their strength and riches.

It is besides the purpose to dispute, whether the estate of the gouernement here bee a *Democratie*, or *Aristocratie*, for whatsoeuer it bee, being considered in it selfe, certayne it is, *Page 558* that in re|spect of the whole Realme, London is but a Citizen, and no Citie, a subiect and no free estate, an obedienciarie, and no place indowed with any distinct or absolute power, for it is gouerned by the same law that the rest of the Realme is, both in causes Criminall, and Ciuill, a few customes onely excepted, which also are to bee adiudged or foriudged by the common law. And in the assembly of the estates of our Realme (which we call Parliament) they are but a member of the Comminaltie, and send two Burgesses for theyr Citie, as euerie poore Borough doth, and two knights for their Countie as euery other shyre doth, and are as straightly bound by such lawes as any part of the Realme is, for if contribution in subsidie of money to the Prince bee decreed, the Londoners haue none exemption, no not so much as to assesse themselues: for the prince doth appoint the Commissioners.

If Souldiers must be mustered, Londoners haue no law to keepe themselues at home, if prouision for the Princes houshold bee to bee made, their goods are not priuiledged. In summe, therefore, the gouernment of London differeth not in substance, but in ceremonie from the rest of the realme, as namely, in the names and choise of their officers, and in their Guildes and Fraternities, established for the maintenance of Handicrafts, and Labourers, and for equitie and good order, to be kept in buying and selling. And yet in these also are they to be controlled by the generall law: for by the statutes 28. *E.* 3. *Chap.* 10. and 1. *H.* 4. *Chap.* 15. the points of their misgouernment are inquirable by the inhabitants of the Forren shyres adioyning and punishable by such Iusticiars as the Prince shall thereunto depute. To conclude therefore, the estate of London for gouernement is so agreeable a Symphony with the rest, that there is no feare of daungerous discord to ensue thereby.

The multitude (or whole body) of this populous Citie is two wayes to bee considered, generally and specially: generally, they bee naturall Subiects, a part of the Commons of this Realme, and are by birth for the most part a mixture of all countries of the same, by bloud Gentlemen, Yeomen and of the basest sort, without distinction, and by profession busie Bees, and trauellers for their liuing in the hiue of this common wealth, but specially con|sidered, they consist of these three *Page 559* parts, Marchantes, Handicrafts men, and Labourers. Marchandise is also diuided into these three sortes, Nauigation, by the which Marchandizes are brought, and carried in and out ouer the Seas: Inuection by the which commodities are gathered into the Citie, and dispersed from thence into the Countrey by lande: and Negotiation, which I may call the keeping of a retayling or standing shop. In common speech they of the first sort be called Marchantes, and both the other Retaylers. Handicrafts men bee those which do exercise such artes as require both labour and cunning, as Goldsmithes, Taylors, and Haberdashers, Skinners, &c. Labourers and Hirelings I call those *quorum operae non artes emuntur*, as *Tullie* sayeth, of which sort be Porters, Carmen, Watermen, &c. Againe these three sortes may be considered, eyther in respect of their wealth, or number: in wealth Marchants, and some of the chiefe Retaylers haue the first place: the most part of Retaylers, and all artificers, the second or meane place: and Hyrelings the lowest roome: but in number they of the middle place be first, and doe farre exceede both the rest: Hyrelings be next, and Marchantes bee the last. Now, out of this, that the estate of London, in the persons of the Citizens, is so friendly enterlaced, and knit in league with the rest of the Realme, not onely at their beginning by birth and bloud as I haue shewed, but also verie commonly at their ending by life and conuersation (for that Marchantes and rich men, being satisfyed with gaine, doe for the most part marry theyr Children into the Countrey, and conuey themselues after *Ciceroes* counsell, *veluti ex portu in agros & possessiones*): I doe inferre[1] that there is not onely no danger towardes the common quiet thereby, but also great occasion and cause of good loue and amitie; out of this, that they be generally bent to trauell, and doe flie pouertie, *per mare, per saxa, per ignes*, as the Poet sayeth, I draw hope, that they shall escape the note of many vices, which idle people do fall into. And out of this, that they bee a great multitude, and that yet the greatest part of them be neyther too rich nor too poore, but doe liue in the mediocritie, I conclude with *Aristotle*, that the Prince needeth not to feare sedition by them, for thus sayth hee: *Magnæ vrbes magis sunt a seditione liberæ, quod in eis dominetur* | *Page 560* *mediocritas, nam in paruis nihil medium est, sunt enim omnes vel pauperes vel opulenti.* I am now to come to the strength and power of this Cittie, which consisteth partly in the number of the Cittizens themselues, whereof I haue spoken before, partly in their riches, and in their warlike furniture, for as

[1] inferre] referre *1603*

touching the strength of the place[1] it selfe, that is apparant to the eye, and therefore is not to be treated of.

The wealth and warlicke furniture of London is eyther publicke or priuate, & no doubt the common treasure cannot be much there, seeing that the reuenew which they haue hardly sufficeth to maintaine their bridge and Conduits, and to pay their Officers and seruantes. Their Tolle doth not any more then pay their Fee Farme, that they pay to the Prince. Their Issues for default of Appearances be neuer leuied, and the profites of their Courtes of Iustice do goe to particular mens handes. Argumentes hereof be these two, one that they can do nothing of extraordinarie charge without a generall contribution: an other that they haue suffered such as haue borne the chiefe office amongst them, and were become Bankrupt, to depart the Cittie without reliefe, which I think they neyther would nor could haue done, if the common tresure had sufficed to couer their shame, hereof therefore we need not be afraide. The publike armour and munition of this Citty remayneth in the Hals of the Companies, as it doth throughout the whole Realme for a great part in the Parrish churches, neyther is that kept together, but onely for obedience to the law, which commandeth it, and therefore if that threaten daunger to the estate it may by another law bee taken from them, and committed to a more safe Armourie.

The priuate riches of London resteth chiefly in the handes of the Marchantes and Retaylers, for Artificers haue not much to spare, and Labourers haue neede that it were giuen vnto them. Now how necessarie and seruiceable the estate of Marchandise is to this realme, it may partly appeare by the practise of that peaceable, politike and rich Prince king *Henry* the seauenth, of whome *Polidore* (writing his life) sayeth thus: *Mercatores ille sæpenumero pecunia multa data gratuito iuuabat, vt mercatura ars vna omnium cunctis æque mortalibus tum commoda, tum* | *necessaria, in suo regno copiosior esset.* But *Page 561* chiefly by the inestimable commodities that grow thereby: for who knoweth not that we haue extreame neede of many thinges, whereof forraine Countries haue great store, and that wee may spare many thinges whereof they haue neede: or

[1] place] peece *1598, 1603*

who is ignorant of this, that wee haue no mines of siluer or golde within our realme: so that the encrease of our coyne and Bulloine commeth from else where, and yet neverthelesse we be both fed, clad, and otherwise serued with forraine commodities and delightes, as plentifull as with our domesticall: which thing commeth to passe by the meane of Marchandise onely, which importeth necessaries from other Countries, and exporteth the superfluities of our own. For seeing wee haue no way to encrease our treasure by mines of gold or siluer at home, and can haue nothing without money or ware from other countries abroad, it followeth necessarily, that if wee follow the counsel of that good olde husband *Marcus Cato*, saying, *Oportet patrem familias vendacem esse, non emacem*, and doe carrie more commodities in value ouer the seas, then we bring hether from thence, that then the Realme shall receiue that ouerplus in money: but if we bring from beyond the seas marchandise of more value, then that which we do send ouer may counteruaile, then the Realme payeth for that ouerplus in ready money, and consequently is a looser by that ill husbandrie: and therefore in this part great and heedefull regard must be had that *Symmetria* and due proportion be kept, least otherwise eyther the Realme bee defrauded of her treasure, or the subiectes corrupted in vanitie, by excessive importation of superfluous and needles Marchandize, or els that wee feele penurie, euen in our greatest plentie and store, by immoderate exportation of our own needfull commodities. Other the benefites that marchandise bringeth, shall hereafter appeare in the general recitall of the commodities that come by London, and therefore it resteth that I speake a word of Retaylors, and finally shewe that much good groweth by them both. The chiefe part of Retayling, is but a handmaide to marchandise, dispersing by peecemeale, that which the marchant bringeth in grosse: of which trade be Mercers, *Page 562* Grocers, Vinteners, Haberdashers, Ironmongers, | Millayners, and al such as sell wares growing or made beyond the seas, and therefore so long as Marchandise it selfe shalbe profitable and such proportion kept as neyther we loose our treasure thereby nor be cloyed with vnnecessary forrain wares, this kind of Retailing is to be retayned also.

Now that Marchantes and Retaylors of London be very rich and great, it is so farre from any harme, that it is a thing both prayseworthy and profitable: for *Mercatura* (sayeth *Cicero*) *si tenuis est, sordida putanda est, sin magna est et copiosa non est vituperanda.* And truely Marchants and Retaylars doe not altogether *intus canere*, and profit themselues only, for the prince and realme both are enriched by their riches: the realme winneth treasure, if their trade be so moderated by authority, that it breake not proportion, & they besides beare a good fleece, which the prince may sheare when shee[1] seeth good.

But here before I conclude this part, I haue shortly to aunswere the accusation of those men, which charge London with the losse and decay of many (or most) of the auncient Citties, Corporate Townes and markets within this Realme, by drawing from them to her selfe alone, say they, both all trade of traffique by sea, and the retayling of Wares, and exercise of Manuall Artes also. Touching Nauigation, which I must confesse, is apparantly decayed in many port townes, and flourisheth onely or chiefly at London, I impute that partly to the fall of the Staple, the which being long since a great trade, and bestowed sometimes at one town and sometimes at another within the realme, did much enrich the place where it was, and being now not onely diminished in force, but also translated ouer the seas, cannot but bring some decay with it, partly, to the empayring of hauens, which in many places haue empouerished those townes, whose estate doth ebbe and flow with them, and partly to the dissolution of religious houses, by whose wealth and haunt, many of those places were chiefly fedde and nourished. I meane not to rehearse particular examples of euery sort: for the thing it selfe speaketh, and I hast to an ende: As for Retaylers therefore, and Handicraftes men, it is no maruaile if they abandon Countrie Townes, and resort to London: for | not onely the *Page 563*
Court, which is now a dayes much greater & more gallant then in former times, and which was wonte to bee contented to remaine with a small companie, sometimes at an Abbey or

[1] shee] he *1633*

Priorie, sometimes at a Bishops house, and sometimes at some meane Mannor of the kings own, is now for the most part either abiding at London, or else so neare vnto it, that the prouision of thinges most fit for it, may easily be fetched from thence: but also by occasion thereof, the Gentlemen of all shires do flie and flock to this Citty, the yonger sort of them to see and shew vanity, and the elder to saue the cost and charge of Hospitality, and house keeping. For hereby it commeth to passe that the Gentlemen being eyther for a good portion of the yeare out of the Countrie, or playing the Farmours, Grasiars, Brewers or such like, more then Gentleman were wont to doe within the Countrie, Retaylers and Artificers, at the least of such thinges as pertayne to the backe or belly, do leaue the Countrie townes, where there is no vent, and do flie to London, where they be sure to finde ready and quicke market. And yet I wish, that euen as many Townes in the Low countries of king *Philips* doe stand some by one handy arte, and some by an other: so also that it might be prouided here that the making of some things, might (by discreete dispensation) be allotted to some speciall townes, to the end, that although the daintinesse of men cannot be restrayned, which will needes seeke those things at London, yet other places also might be relieued, at the least by the Workemanship of them.

Thus much then of the estate of London, in the gouernment thereof, in the condition of the Cittizens, and in their power and riches. Now follow⟨s⟩ the enumeration of such benefites, as redound to the Prince and this Realme by this Citty: In which doing I professe not to rehearse all, but onely to recite and runne ouer the chiefe and principall of them.

Besides the commodities of the furtherance of Religion, and Iustice: The propagation of Learning: The maintenaunce of artes: The increase of riches, and the defence of Countries (all which are before shewed to grow generally by Citties, and be common to London with them) London bringeth singularly
Page 564 these good | thinges following.

By aduantage of the scituation it disperseth forraine Wares, (as the stomacke doth meat) to all the members most commodiously.

By the Benefite of the riuer of Thames, and greate trade of Marchandize, it is the chiefe maker of Marriners, and Nurse of our Nauie, and ships (as men know) be the wooden Walles for defence of our realme.

It maintaineth, in flourishing estate, the countries of Norfolke, Suffolke, Essex, Kent and Sussex, which as they lie in the face of our most puissant neighbour, so ought they, aboue others, to bee conserued in the greatest strength and riches: and these, as it is well knowne, stand not so much by the benefite of their owne soile, as by the neighbourhood and nearnes which they haue to London.

It releeueth plentifullie, and with good policie, not onely her owne poore people, a thing which scarsely any other Towne or shire doth, but also the poore that from each quarter of the Realme doe flocke vnto it, and it imparteth liberally to the necessitie of the Uniuersities besides. It is an ornament to the realm by the beautie thereof, and a terror to other countries by reason of the greate welth and frequencie. It spreadeth the honour of our Countrie far abroad by her long nauigations, and maketh our power feared, euen of barbarous Princes. It only is stored with rich Marchants, which sort onely is tollerable: for beggarlie Marchantes do byte too neare, and will do more harme then good to the Realm.

It onely of any place in this realme is able to furnish the sodaine necessity with a strong armie. It auayleth the prince in Tronage, Poundage and other her custómes, much more then all the rest of the realme.

It yeeldeth a greater Subsidie then any one part of the realme, I meane not for the proportion of the value of the goodes onelie, but also for the faithfull seruice there vsed, in making the assesse, for no where else bee men taxed so neare to their iust value as in London: yea many are found there, that for their countenance and credite sake, refuse not to bee rated aboue their abilitie, which thing neuer hapneth abroade in the | country. I omit that in ancient time, the inhabitants of London & other Cities, were accustomably taxed after the tenth of their goods, when the countrie was assessed at the fifteenth, and rated at the viij. when the countrie was set at *Page 565* the xii. for that were to awake a sleeping Dogge, and I should be thought *dicenda, tacenda locutus*, as the Poet said.

It onely doth and is able to make the Prince a readie prest or loane of money.

It onely is found fit and able to entertaine strangers honourablie, and to receiue the Prince of the Realme worthily.

Almightie God (*qui nisi custodiat ciuitatem, frustra vigilat custos*) grant, that her Maiestie euermore rightly esteeme & rule this Citie, and he giue grace, that the Citizens may answere duty, aswell towards God and her Maiestie, as towards this whole realme and countrey, *Amen.*

An Appendix contayning the examination of such causes as haue heretofore moued the Princes, either to fine and ransome the Citizens of London, or to seize the Liberties of the Citty it selfe

THESE all may be reduced to these few heads: for eyther the Citizens haue adheared, in aide or armes, to such as haue warred vpon the Prince: or they haue made tumult, and broken the common peace at home: or they haue misbehaued themselues in point of gouernment and iustice: or finally, and to speake the plaine truth, the princes haue taken hold of small matters, and coyned good summes of money out of them.

To the first head I will referre whatsoeuer they haue done either in those warres that happened betweene king *Stephen* and *Maude* the Empresse, being competitors of the crowne: *Page 566* or bee|tweene king *Iohn* and his nobles, assisting *Lewes* the French kings sonne when he inuaded the Realme: for it is apparent by all Histories, that the Londoners were not the mouers of these wars, but were onely vsed as instruments to maintayne them. The like is to be said of all the offences that king *Henry* the third, whose whole raigne was a continuall warfare, conceiued against this City, concerning the bearing of Armour against him: for the first part of his raigne was spent in the continuation of those warres that his father had begun with *Lewes.* And the rest of his life he bestowed in that contention, which was commonly called the Barons warres. In which Tragedy London, as it could not be otherwise, had now and then a part, and had many a snub at the kings hand for it. But in the end when he had triumphed ouer *Simon Mountford* at Euesham, London felt it most tragicall: for then hee both seysed their liberties, and sucked themselues drie: and yet *Edictum Kenelworth*, made shortly after, hath an honourable testimonie for London, saying, *Te London laudamus, &c.* As for the other offences that he tooke against the Londoners, they pertaine to the other parts of my diuision.

Next after this, against whom the Londoners did put on armes, followeth king *Edward* the second, who in the end was depriued of his kingdome, not by their meanes but by a generall defection, both of his owne wife and sonne, and almost of the whole Nobility and Realme besides. In which trouble, that furious assault and slaughter committed by them vpon the Bishop of Excester, then Treasurer of the Realme, is to be imputed, partly to the sway of the time wherewith they were carried, and partly to a priuate displeasure which they had to the Bishop.

Finally commeth to hand King *Richard* the second: for these three onely in all the Catalogue of our kings, haue beene heauie Lordes to London, who also had much contention with his Nobilitie, and was in the end deposed. But whatsoeuer countenance and aide the Citie of London brought to the warres and vprores of that time, it is notoriously true that London neuer led the dance, but euer followed the pipe of the Nobilitie. To close vp this first part therefore I affirme, that in all the troublesome actions during the raigne of these three kings, as also in all that heauing in, & hur|ling out, that after- *Page 567* ward happened betweene king *H.* the sixt, and king *Edward* the fourth, the City of London was many times a friend and fautor, but neuer the first motiue or author of any intestine warre or sedition.

In the second room I place a couple of tumultuous affrayes that chaunced in the daies of king *R.* the first, the one vpon the day of his Coronation against the Iewes, which contrary to the kings owne proclamation, would needes enter the Church to see him sacred, & were therefore cruelly handled by the common people. The other was caused by *William* with the long beard, who after that he had inflamed the poore people against the richer sort, and was called to answere for his fault, tooke Bow church for Sanctuary, and kept it Castle like, till he was fiered out.

Here is place also for the stoning to death of a Gentleman, seruant to the halfe brother of king *Henry* the third, which had before prouoked the Citizens to fury, by wounding diuers of them without any cause, 1257: for the riotous fray betweene the seruantes of the Goldsmithes and the Taylors, 1268: for the hurly burly and bloodshed betweene the Londoners and the men of Westminster, moued by the young men vpon an occasion of a wrestling on Saint *Iames* day, 1221, and made worse by one *Constantine* an ancient Citizen: for the braule and businesse that arose about a Bakers loafe at Salisbury place 1391: for the which and some other misdemeanors king *Richard* the 2. was so incensed by euill counsell against the Londoners that he determined to destroy them, & raze their Citie: and for the fight that was betweene the citizens & sanctuary men of *S. Martins* 1454, vnder king *Henry* the sixt: and finally for the misrule on euill May day 1519. and for such other like if there haue beene any.

To the third head may be referred the seiser of their liberties, for a false iudgement giuen against a poore widdow, called *Margaret Viel*, 1246. the 2. seueral seisers in one yeare 1258. for false packing in collections of money, and other enormities: and finally the seiser made by king *Edward* the first for taking of bribes of the Bakers 1285. But all this security in seising and resuming of the liberties, which was in old time the *Page 568* onely ordinarie punishment, | was at length mitigated by king *Edward* the third and king *Henry* the fourth in their statutes before remembred.

In the last place stand those offences, which I repute rather taken then giuen, and do fall within the measure of the adage, *vt canem cædas, cito inuenias baculum*: for king *Iohn* in the tenth of his raigne deposed the Bailiffes of London, because they had bought vp the wheate in the market, so that there was not to serue his Purueyers. King *Henry* the third his sonne compelled the Londoners to pay him 5000.li. because they had lent to *Lewes* the French the like summe, of a good mind to dispatch him out of their Citie and the realme, at such time as the Protector and the whole Nobilitie fell to composition with him for his departure. And the same king fined them at three thousand markes, for the escape of a prisoner out of Newgate, of whom they tooke no charge: for he was a Clarke, prisoner to the Bishop of London, vnder the custody of his owne seruants, and as for the place, it was onely borrowed of the Londoners to serue that turne. Hitherto of these things to this end, that whatsoeuer misdemeanor shall bee obiected out of Historie against London, the same may herein appeare, both in his true place, and proper colour. |

Page 569

The Author to the Reader.

BECAUSE amongst other mine Authors I haue oftentimes alledged Fitz-Stephens, *as one more choice then other, namely for the auncient estate of this Citie, more then* 400. *yeares since: and also the said Author being rare, I haue in this place thought good by impression to impart the same to my louing friends, the learned Antiquaries, as the Author wrote it in the Latine tongue. And first to note in effect, what* M. Bale *in commendation of the said Author writeth.*

William Stephanides, *or* Fitzstephen, *a Monke of Canterbury, borne of worshipfull parentes in the Citie of London, wel brought vp at the first vnder good Maisters, did more and more increase in honest conditions and learning: for euer in his young yeares there appeared in him a certaine light of a Gentlemanlike disposition, which promised many good things, afterward by him performed. Such time as other spent in braules, and idle talke, he employed in holesome exercises for the honour of his countrie, following therein the example of* Plato: *and was very studious both in humanity and diuinity.*

The City of London his birth place, the most noble of all other Cities of this land, and the Princes seate, scituated in the south part of the Iland, he loued aboue all the other, so that at length hee wrote most elegantly in latine of the sites and rites of the same. Leland *in diuers of his bookes commendeth him for an excellent writer. He liued in the raigne of king* Stephen, *wrote in the raigne of* Henry *the second, and deceased in the yeare of Christ* 1191. *in the raigne of* Richard the first. |

Descriptio Nobilissimae Ciuitatis Londoniae.* *Page 570*

De Situ Eiusdem.

Inter nobiles vrbes orbis[1], quas fama celebrat, ciuitas Londonia[2], regni Anglorum sedes, vna est quæ famam sui latius diffundit, opes et merces longius transmittit, caput altius extollit. Felix est aeris salubritate, Christiana religione, firmitate munitionum, natura situs, honore ciuium, pudicitia matronali. Ludis etiam quam[3] iocunda, et nobilium est[4] fœcunda virorum. Quæ singula semotim libet inspicere.

De Clementia Aeris.[5]

Ibi siquidem—

'Emollit animos hominum clementia cœli';

non vt sint in Venerem putres[6] †, sed ne feri sint et bestiales, potius[7] benigni et liberales.

De Religione.

Est ibi, in ecclesia Beati Pauli, Episcopalis Sedes. Quondam fuit Metropolitana, et adhuc futura creditur, si remeauerint ciues in insulam: nisi forte Beati Thomæ Martyris titulus Archiepiscopalis dignitatem illam Cantuariæ, vbi nunc est, conseruet perpetuam. Sed cum vtramque vrbium harum[8] Sanctus Thoma illustrauerit, Londoniam ortu, Cantuariam occasu, ipsius Sancti intuitu, cum iustitiæ accessu, habet altera aduersus alteram quod amplius alleget. Sunt etiam, quod ad Christianæ fidei cultum pertinet[9], tum in Londonia tum in suburbano, tresdecim maiores ecclesiæ Conuentuum, præter minores Parochianas[10] centum viginti sex.

De Firmitate Vrbis.

Habet ab Oriente arcem palatinam, maximam et fortissimam, cuius et area et muri a[11] fundamento profundissimo

[1] orbis vrbes, *L.* [2] Londoniae, *L.* [3] etiam est, *L.* [4] est, *om. S.* [5] Caeli, *C.* [6] putres, *om. C.* [7] sed potius, *C.* [8] harum vrbium, *L.* [9] pertinent, *L.* [10] parochitanas, *L.* [11] et, *C.*

* For a Note on the Text here given see p. 387 below.

† Persius, *Sat.* 5. 58: 'In Venerem putret.'

exurgunt[1]; cæmento cum sanguine animalium temperato. |
Page 571 Ab Occidente duo[2] castella munitissima; muro vrbis alto et magno, duplatis heptapylæ[3] portis, intercontinuante, spatio turrito ab Aquilone per intercapedines. Similiterque, ab Austro Londonia murata et turrita fuit; sed fluuius maximus piscosus Thamensis[4], mari influo refluoque, qui illac allabitur, mænia illa tractu temporis alluit[5], labefactauit, deiecit. Item, sursum ab Occidente palatium regium eminet super fluuium eundem, ædificium incomparabile, cum antemurali et propugnaculis, duobus millibus ab vrbe, suburbano frequenti continuante.

De Hortis.

Vndique extra domos suburbanorum horti ciuium, arboribus consiti, spatiosi et speciosi, contigui habentur.

De Pascuis et Sationalibus.

Item, a Borea sunt agri pascui[6], et pratorum grata planities, aquis fluuialibus interfluis; ad quas molinorum versatiles rotæ citantur cum murmure iocoso. Proxime patet foresta ingens[7], saltus nemorosi, ferarum latebræ, ceruorum, damarum, aprorum, et taurorum[8] siluestrium. Agri vrbis sationales non sunt ieiunæ glareæ, sed pingues Asiæ campi, qui 'faciant[9] lætas segetes'*; et suorum cultorum repleant horrea 'Cerealis mergite[10] culmi'.†

De Fontibus.

Sunt etiam[11] circa Londoniam ab Aquilone suburbani fontes præcipui, aqua dulci, salubri, perspicua, et 'per claros riuo trepidante lapillos'. Inter quos Fons Sacer, Fons Clericorum, Fons Sancti Clementis, nominatiores habentur; et adeuntur celebriore[12] accessu et maiore[13] frequentia scholarium, et vrbanæ iuuentutis in serotinis æstiuis ad auram exeuntis. Vrbs sane bona, cum[14] bonum habeat dominum. |

[1] exsurgunt, *L. H.* [2] duo sunt, *C.* [3] eptafile, *L.* [4] Thamesis, *L.* [5] abluit, *L.* [6] agri, pascue, *L.* [7] ingens foresta, *L.* [8] vrsorum, *L.* [9] faciunt, *C.* S. [10] iugere, *S.* [11] et, *S.* [12] celebriori, *S.* [13] maiori, *S.* [14] si, *L.*

* Vergil, *Georgics*, i. 1. † Id., ib. ii. 517.

De Honore Ciuium. Page 572

Vrbs ista viris est honorata, armis decorata, multo habitatore populosa; vt tempore bellicæ cladis, Rege[1] Stephano, bello apti ex ea exeuntes qui ostentatui[2] haberentur, viginti millia armatorum equitum[3] et[4] sexaginta millia[5] peditum æstimarentur. Ciues Londoniæ, vbicumque locorum, præ omnibus aliis ciuibus ornatu morum, vestium, et mensæ, locutione[6] spectabiles et noti habentur.[7]

De Matronis.

Vrbis matronæ ipsæ Sabinæ sunt.

De Scholis.

In Londoniis tres principales ecclesiæ; videlicet, Sedes Episcopalis ecclesia Sancti Pauli, ecclesia Sanctæ Trinitatis, et ecclesia Sancti Martini[8], scholas celebres habent[9] de[10] priuilegio et antiqua dignitate. Plerumque tamen fauore personæ alicuius[11], vel aliquorum doctorum, qui secundum philosophiam noti et præclari habentur[12], et aliæ sunt ibi scholæ de gratia et permissione.[13]

Diebus festis, ad ecclesias festiuas magistri conuentus celebrant.[14] Disputant[15] scholares, quidam demonstratiue, dialectice alii; alii recitant[16] enthymemata, hii melius perfectis[17] vtuntur syllogismis. Quidam ad ostentationem exercentur disputatione, quæ est inter colluctantes; alii ad veritatem, ea quæ est perfectionis[18] gratia. Sophistæ simulatores agmine et inundatione verborum beati iudicantur; alii paralogizant.[19] Oratores aliqui quandoque orationibus rhetoricis aliquid dicunt apposite[20] ad persuadendum, curantes artis præcepta seruare et ex contingentibus nihil omittere. Pueri diuersarum scho-

[1] sub Rege, *S.*; iubente Rege, *L.* [2] ostentatui ostentui, *L.* [3] millia equitum armatos, *C.* [4] et, *om. S.* [5] mille, *S.* [6] lautiorum, *L.* [7] *After* habentur *L. adds*: Habitatores aliarum vrbium ciues, huius barones dicuntur. Eis est finis omnis controuersiæ sacramentum. [8] videlicet . . . Martini, *om. S. L. H.* [9] habent celebres, *C.* [10] et, *C.* [11] personæ *om. C.* [12] habeantur *H*; noti habeantur et præclari, *C.* [13] favore personali alicuius notorum secundum philosophiam plures ibi scholæ admittuntur, *L.* [14] celebrantur, *S.*; magistri celebrant cum discipulis suis conventus, gratia exercitationis, *C.* [15] Disputant ibidem, *C.* [16] hii rotant, *L.* [17] perfectis melius, *L.* [18] perspectionis, *L.* [19] paralogizantur, *C. H.* [20] apposite, *om. L.*

larum inter se versibus[1] conrixantur: aut[2] de principiis artis[3] grammaticæ, aut de[4] regulis præteritorum vel futurorum[5] contendunt. Sunt alii qui in[6] epigrammatibus, rhythmis, et metris, vtuntur uetere illa triuiali dicacitate; licentia Fescennina socios, suppressis nominibus, liberius lacerant; lœdorias iaculantur et scommata*; salibus Socraticis sociorum, vel forte maiorum, vitia tangunt; vel mordacius dente rodunt Theonino[7].† Auditores

'—— multum ridere parati,
Ingeminant tremulos naso crispante cachinnos'.‡ |

Page 573 *De Dispositione Vrbis.*

Singulorum officiorum exercitores[8], singularum rerum venditores, singularum operarum suarum locatores, cotidiano[9] mane per se sunt locis distincti omnes, vt officiis. Præterea est in Londonia, super ripam fluminis, inter vina et nauibus et cellis vinariis venalia, publica coquina. Ibi quotidie, pro tempore, est inuenire cibaria, fercula, assa[10], frixa, elixa, pisces, pisciculos, carnes grossiores pauperibus, delicatiores diuitioribus, venationum, avium, avicularum. Si subito veniant ad aliquem ciuium amici fatigati ex itinere, nec libeat ieiunis expectare, vt noui cibi emantur et[11] coquantur,

'Dent[12] famuli manibus lymphas panesque'[13] §,

interim ad ripam curritur; ibi præsto sunt omnia desiderabilia. Quantalibet militum vel peregrinorum infinitas intrat[14] vrbem, qualibet diei vel noctis hora, vel ab urbe exitura, ne vel hii nimium ieiunent, vel alii impransi exeant, illuc, si placet[15],

[1] versibus inter se, *S. H.* [2] et, *S.* [3] artis, *om. L.* [4] aut de, *om. S. H.*; vel, *L.* [5] supinorum, *L.* [6] in, *om. S.* [7] ne mordacius dente rodant Theonino, audacibus dithirambis, *L.*; ne mordacius dente rodant procaciori, audacioribus conuitiis, *C.* [8] exercitatores, *C.* [9] quotidiano, *S.* [10] assa, *om. C.*; *D. and H. agree with S.*; assa, pista, frixa, *L.* [11] et, *om. S. H.* [12] dant, *S.* [13] panesque canistris, *L.* [14] intrant, *C.*; intrans, *L.*; intrarit, *D. H.* [15] placeat, *S. H.*

---

* Macrobius, *Saturnalia*, vii. 3.
† Horace, *Epist.* i. 18. 82: 'Dente Theonino.'
‡ Persius, *Sat.* 3. 86, 87: 'His populus ridet, multumque torosa iuuentus Ingeminat tremulos naso crispante cachinnos.'
§ Vergil, *Aeneid*, i. 701: 'Dant famuli manibus lymphas, Cereremque canistris.'

diuertunt, et se pro modo suo singuli reficiunt. Qui se curare volunt molliter, accipiunt anserem, vel Afram auem, vel attagen Ionicum *; non opus ut quid quærant [1], appositis, quæ ibi inueniuntur, deliciis. Hæc equidem publica coquina est, et ciuitati plurimum expediens, et ad ciuilitatem [2] pertinens. Hinc est, quod legitur in 'Gorgia' Platonis †, iuxta medicinam esse coquorum officium simulacrum [3], et adulationem quartæ particulæ ciuilitatis.[4]

[5] Est ibi extra vnam portarum, statim in suburbio, quidam planus campus, re et nomine. Omni sexta feria, nisi sit maior festiuitas præceptæ solemnitatis, est ibi [6] celebre spectaculum [7] nobilium equorum venalium: spectaturi vel empturi veniunt, qui in vrbe assunt [8], Comites, Barones, Milites, ciues plurimi. Iuuat videre gradarios, succussatura nitente [9], suauiter ambulantes; pedibus lateraliter simul erectis, quasi a subalternis, et demissis: hinc, equos qui armigeris magis conueniunt, durius | incedentes, sed expedite tamen, qui quasi a contradictoribus [10] *Page 574* pedes simul eleuant et deponunt: hinc, nobiles pullos iuniores [11], qui, nondum fræno bene [12] assueti,—

'Altius incedunt, et mollia crura reponunt:' ‡

hinc, summarios, membris validis et vegetis: hinc, dextrarios pretiosos, elegantis formæ, staturæ honestæ, micantes auribus, ceruicibus arduis, clunibus obesis. In horum incessu spectant emptores; primo, passum suaviorem, postea motum citatiorem, qui est quasi a contrariis pedibus, anterioribus simul solo amotis et admotis, et posterioribus similiter. Cum talium sonipedum cursus imminet, et aliorum forte, qui similiter sunt in genere suo ad vecturam validi, ad cursuram vegeti, clamor attollitur,

[1] molliter, accipenserem vel aliam auem, vel attagen Ionicum non quærant, *S. H.*; *so also L., but reading* Affram, *for* aliam. [2] ciuitatem, *S. H.* [3] simulantium, *S.* [4] ciuitatis, *C.* [5] *C. begins a fresh chapter headed* De Smethefelde. [6] ibidem, *L.* [7] spectaculorum, *S.* [8] adsunt, *S.* [9] succussatura intente et, *L.*; cute succo satura, pilo connitente, *C.* [10] contradictoriis, *L.* [11] minores, *L.* [12] bene, *om. L.*

---

* Horace, *Epod.* 2. 53–5: 'Non Afra avis descendat in ventrem meum, Non attagen Ionicus Iucundior.'

† *Gorgias*, 464E.

‡ Vergil, *Georg.* iii. 76: 'Altius ingreditur, et mollia crura reponit.' *For the next few lines* cf. id. ib. iii. 77–85.

vulgares equos in partem ire[1] præcipitur. Sessores alipedum pueri tres[2] simul, aliquando bini ex condicto et bini[3] certamini se præparant, docti equis imperitare indomitorum 'lupatis temperant frænis ora'*: hoc maxime præcauent[4], ne alter alteri cursum[5] præripiat.

Equi[6] similiter, pro modo suo,[7] ad certamen cursus illius se[8] attollunt; tremunt artus, moræ impatientes, stare loco nesciunt; facto signo, membra extendunt; cursum rapiunt, agilitate peruicaci feruntur. Certant sessores laudis amore, spe[9] victoriæ, equis admissis subdere calcaria, et nec minus vrgere eos virgis et ciere clamoribus. Putares omnia in motu esse, secundum Heraclitum, et falsam omnino Zenonis sententiam, dicentis quoniam non contingit moueri neque stadium pertransire.

Parte alia stant seorsum[10] rusticorum peculia, agrorum instrumenta, sues longis lateribus, vaccæ distentis vberibus,—

'Corpora magna boum, lanigerumque pecus.' †

Stant ibi aptæ aratris, trahis, et bigis equæ; quarundam ventres fœtibus[11] protument[12]; alias editi fœtus obeunt, pulli lasciuiores, sequela inseparabilis. Ad vrbem hanc[13], ex omni natione quæ sub cœlo est, navalia gaudent[14] institores habere commercia;—

'Aurum mittit Arabs; species et thura Sabæus;
Arma Scythes; oleum palmarum diuite silua,
Page 575 Pingue solum Ba|bylon; Nilus lapides pretiosos;
Seres purpureas vestes: Galli sua vina;
Norwegi, Rusci[15], varium, grisium, sabelinas.' ‡

Vrbe Roma, secundum Chronicorum fidem, satis antiquior est. Ab eisdem quippe patribus Troianis, hæc prius a Bruto condita est quam illa[16] a Remo et Romulo; vnde et adhuc

[1] iræ, *S.* [2] quadraginta, *L.* [3] ex condicto et bini, *om. C.*
[4] præcauerit, *C.* [5] concursum, *S.* [6] Etqui, *S.* [7] se *before* ad, *L.*
[8] se, *om. S. L. H.* [9] et spe, *L.* [10] seorsim, *S.* [11] fœtibus, *om. L.*
[12] tument, *S. H.* [13] Ad hanc vrbem, *L.* [14] gaudem, *S.*
[15] Russi, *S. H.* [16] illa, *om. S.*

* Horace, *Od.* i. 8. 6, 7.

† *This line seems to be made up of two separate 'tags' from Ovid and Vergil.*

‡ *These lines are of unknown authorship, but are based on Vergil,* Georgics, i. 57 *and* ii. 115–17.

antiquis eisdem vtuntur legibus et communibus institutis. Hæc[1], similiter illi, regionibus est distincta; habet annuos, pro Consulibus, Vicecomites; habet Senatoriam dignitatem et[2] magistratus minores; eluuiones et aquæductus in vicis; ad genera causarum, deliberatiuæ, demonstratiuæ, iudicialis, loca sua, fora singula; habet sua diebus statutis Comitia.[3]

Non puto vrbem esse in qua sint probabiliores consuetudines, in ecclesiis visitandis, ordinatis Dei honorandis, festis feriandis, eleemosynis dandis, in hospitibus suscipiendis, in desponsationibus firmandis, matrimoniis contrahendis, nuptiis celebrandis, conuiuiis ornandis, conuiuis hilarandis; etiam, in exequiis curandis et cadaueribus humandis.

Solæ pestes Londoniæ[4] sunt immodica[5] stultorum potatio[6] et frequens incendium. Ad hæc, omnes fere Episcopi, Abbates, et magnates Angliæ, quasi ciues et municipes sunt vrbis Londoniæ; sua ibi habentes ædificia præclara, vbi se recipiunt, vbi diuites impensas faciunt, ad concilia, ad conuentus celebres in vrbem[7] evocati a Domino Rege, vel Metropolitano suo, seu propriis tracti negotiis.

De Ludis.

Amplius et ad ludos vrbis veniamus, quoniam non expedit vtilem tantum et seriam vrbem esse, nisi dulcis etiam sit et iocunda.[8] Vnde et in sigillis summorum Pontificum, vsque ad tempora Leonis[9] Papæ, ex altera parte bullæ, sculpto[10] per impressionem piscatore Petro, et supra eum claue, quasi manu[11] Dei de cœlis ei porrecta, et circa eum versu;—

'Tu pro me nauem liquisti, suscipe clauem.' | *

Ex altera parte impressa erat vrbs, et scriptura ista;— *Page 576*

'Aurea[12] Roma.' †

Item ad laudem Cæsaris Augusti et Romæ, dictum est;—

'Nocte pluit tota, redeunt spectacula mane;
Diuisum imperium cum Ioue, Cæsar, habes.' ‡

[1] Hec etiam, *L.* [2] et, *om. L.* [3] sua die ius statuendi Comitia, *C.*; sua diebus statutis Commercia, *L.* [4] Londini, *S.* [5] immoderata, *S. H.* [6] putatio, *C.* [7] in urbem, *om. L.* [8] iucunda, *S.* [9] ultimi Leonis, *L.* [10] scripto, *C. L.*; sculpto, *D.* [11] in manu, *C.* [12] Aulæa, *L.*

* Cf. Ciaconius, *De Vitis Pontificum*, i. 807.
† Ausonius, *De Claris Vrbibus*, 1.
‡ Donatus, *Vita Virgilii*, ap. Heyne's *Virgil*, vol. v, p. 343.

Londonia, pro spectaculis theatralibus, pro ludis scenicis, ludos habet sanctiores, repræsentationes Miraculorum quæ sancti Confessores operati sunt, seu repræsentationes Passionum quibus claruit constantia Martyrum.

Præterea, quotannis, die quæ dicitur 'Carniuale[1]', vt a puerorum ludis[2] incipiamus,—omnes enim pueri fuimus—scholarum singuli[3] pueri suos apportant magistro suo gallos gallinaceos pugnatores[4]; et totum illud antemeridianum datur ludo puerorum, vacantium spectare in scholis suorum pugnas gallorum.

Post prandium, exit in campos omnis[5] iuuentus vrbis ad lusum[6] pilæ celebrem. Singulorum studiorum scholares suam habent pilam; singulorum officiorum vrbis exercitores[7] suam [8] singuli pilam[9] in manibus.[10] Maiores natu, patres, et diuites vrbis, in equis, spectatum ueniunt certamina iuniorum, et modo suo iuuenantur[11] cum iuuenibus; et excitari videtur in eis motus caloris naturalis, contemplatione tanti motus et participatione gaudiorum adolescentiæ liberioris.

Singulis diebus Dominicis in Quadragesima, post prandia[12], exit in campos[13] iuuenum recens examen* in equis bellicosis[14], 'in equis certamine primis' †, quorum quisque[15]—

'Aptus et in gyros[16] currere doctus equo.' ‡

Erumpunt a portis cateruatim filii ciuium laici, instructi lanceis et scutis militaribus; iuniores hastilibus[17], ferro dempto[18], præfurcatis; simulacra belli cient[19] §, et agonisticam exercent militarem[20]. Adueniunt et plurimi aulici, Rege in vicino posito, et de familiis[21] Consulum et Baronum ephebi, nondum cingulo donati militiæ, gratia concertandi. Accendit[22] singulos spes victoriæ; equi feri adhinniunt; tremunt artus,

[1] Carnilevaria, *H. L.*; Carnivelaria, *C.* [2] a ludis puerorum London, *L.* [3] singularum, *L.* [4] pugnaces, *L.* [5] vadit in suburbanam planitiem, *L.* [6] ludum, *L.* [7] exercitatores, *C.* [8] fere *before* singuli, *L.* [9] polam, *C.* [10] pilam in manibus, *om. L.* [11] inueniuntur, *S. H.* [12] prandium, *C.* [13] campum, *C.* [14] et *after* bellicosis, *C.* [15] sit *after* quisque, *C.* [16] est *before* currere, *L.* [17] hastalibus, *S.* [18] ferro dempto, *om. L.* [19] campestria prælia ludunt, *after* cient, *L.* [20] militiam *C.* [21] Episcoporum, *after* familiis, *L.* [22] accedit, *C.*

* Horace, *Od.* i. 35. 30, 31: 'iuuenum recens Examen.'
† Horace, *Ars Poetica*, 84: 'equum certamine primum.'
‡ Ovid, *Art. Am.* iii. 384: 'In gyros ire coactus equus.'
§ Vergil, *Aeneid*, v. 674.

frænos mandunt, | impatientes moræ stare loco nesciunt. Cum Page 577 tandem sonipedum rapit vngula cursum *, sessores adolescentes, diuisis agminibus, hii præcedentibus [1] instant, nec assequuntur [2]; hii socios [3] deiiciunt et præteruolant.

In feriis Paschalibus ludunt quasi prælia naualia. In arbore siquidem mediamna [4] scuto fortiter innexo, nauicula, multo [5] remo et raptu fluminis cita, in prora [6] stantem habet iuuenem, scutum illud lancea percussurum. Qui si, scuto illi lanceam illidens, frangat eam, et immotus persistat [7], habet propositum, voti compos est [8]. Si vero lancea integra fortiter percusserit, in profluentem amnem [9] deiicitur [10]; nauis motu suo acta præterit. Sunt tamen hinc inde secus scutum [11] duæ naues stationariæ, et in eis iuuenes plurimi, vt eripiant percussorem flumine absorptum [12], cum primo emersus comparet, vel 'summa rursus cum bullit in vnda'.† Supra Pontem, et in [13] solariis supra fluuium, sunt qui talia spectent [14], 'multum ridere parati.'‡

In festis tota æstate iuuenes ludentes exercentur in saliendo, in [15] arcu, lucta [16], iactu lapidum, amentatis missilibus vltra metam expediendis, parmis duellionum. Puellarum Cytherea [17] ducit choros, et 'pede libero pulsatur tellus', vsque imminente luna. §

In hyeme, singulis fere festis, ante prandium, vel apri spumantes pugnant pro capitibus, et verres, fulmineis [18] accincti dentibus‖, addendi succidiæ, vel pingues tauri cornupetæ [19], seu vrsi immanes, cum obiectis depugnant canibus.

Cum est congelata palus illa magna quæ mœnia vrbis Aquilonalia alluit, exeunt lusum super glaciem densæ iuuenum

[1] hiis præcedentibus, *C.* [2] assectuntur, *L.* [3] consequuntur *after* socios, *L.* [4] mediamne, *C.* [5] multo, *om. S.*; malo, *H.* [6] celsa in puppi, *L.* [7] et immotus persistat, *om. L.* [8] est, *om. L.* [9] fluuium, *L.* [10] deiicietur, *C.* [11] scutum, *om. C.* [12] absortum, *L.* [13] in, *om. C.* [14] spectant, *L.* [15] in saliendo, in, *om. L.* [16] cursu, saltu, *before* lucta, *L.*; in lucta, *S. H.* [17] cithara, *L.* [18] prominentibus, *C.* [19] cornipete, *L.*

---

* Horace, *Sat.* i. 1. 114.
† Persius, *Sat.* 3. 34: 'Demersus summa rursus non bullit in vnda.'
‡ cf. *above* p. 222.
§ Horace, *Odes* i. 4. 5: 'iam Cytherea choros ducit Venus imminente Luna'; *and* i. 37. 1, 2: 'nunc pede libero Pulsanda tellus.'
‖ Phaedrus, i. 21. 5; 'Aper fulmineis ad eum venit dentibus.'

turmæ. Hii, ex cursu motu captato [1] citatiore, distantia pedum posita [2], magnum spatium, latere altero prætenso [3], perlabuntur. Alii quasi magnos lapides molares de glacie sedes sibi faciunt; sessorem vnum trahunt plurimi præcurrentes, manibus se tenentes. In tanta citatione motus [4] aliquando pedibus lapsi [5] cadunt omnes proni. Sunt alii super glaciem ludere doctiores, | *Page 578* singuli pedibus suis aptantes, et sub talaribus suis alligantes ossa, tibias scilicet animalium; et palos, ferro acuto supposito [6], tenentes [7] in manibus, quos [8] aliquando glaciei illidunt [9], tanta rapacitate feruntur quanta auis volans, vel pilum balistæ. Interdum autem [10], magna [11] procul distantia, ex condicto, duo aliqui ita ab oppositis veniunt, concurritur [12], palos erigunt, se inuicem percutiunt; vel alter vel ambo cadunt, non sine læsione corporali, cum post casum etiam vi motus feruntur ab inuicem procul; et qua parte glacies caput tangit [13], totum radit, totum decorticat. Plerumque tibia cadentis, vel brachium, si super illud ceciderit, confringitur: sed ætas auida gloriæ iuuentus, cupida victoriæ, vt in veris prœliis fortius se habeat [14], ita in simulatis exercetur [15].

Plurimi ciuium delectantur, ludentes in auibus cœli, nisis, accipitribus, et huiusmodi [16]; et in canibus militantibus in siluis. Habentque [17] ciues suum ius venandi in Middelsexia, Hertfordscira, et tota Chiltra, et in Cantia vsque ad aquam Crayæ [18]. Lundonienses, tunc 'Trinouantes *' dicti, Caium Iulium Cæsarem, qui nullas nisi sanguine fuso vias habere † gaudebat [19], reppulerunt. Vnde Lucanus,—

'Territa quæsitis ostendit terga Britannis.' ‡

Ciuitas Londonia peperit [20] aliquot [21], qui regna plurima et Romanum sibi subdiderunt imperium; et plurimos alios, quos

[1] aptato, *L.* [2] composita, *L.* [3] praetenso, *om. L.* [4] citatione lubrici motus, *L.* [5] lapsis, *L.* [6] superposito, *S.* [7] tenent, *L.* [8] quos cum, *L.* [9] allidunt, *S. D.* [10] a, *L.* [11] permagna, *S.* [12] curritur, *C.* [13] excipit, *L.* [14] habeant, *S. H.* [15] exercentur, *S.* [16] nisis . . . huiusmodi, *om. L.* [17] Habent, *L.* [18] Graiæ, *S. H.*; Craie, *D.* [19] gaudebat habere vias, *C.* [20] repperit, *S. D.* [21] aliquos, *S.*

* Geoff. Monmouth, *Hist. Britt.* iv. 3–9.
† Lucan, *Pharsalia*, ii. 439.
‡ Id. ib. ii. 572.

mundi 'dominos' virtus 'euexit ad Deos'*; vt fuerat in Apollinis Oraculo Bruto promissum ;—

'Brute, sub occasu[1] solis, trans Gallica regna,
 Insula in Oceano est, vndique clausa mari.
Hanc pete ; namque tibi sedes erit illa perennis ;
 Hic[2] fiet natis altera Troia tuis.
Hic de stirpe tua reges nascentur ; et ipsis
 Totius terræ subditus orbis erit.' †

Et[3] temporibus Christianis nobilem illum edidit Imperatorem Constantinum[4], qui vrbem Romam et imperialia insignia omnia Deo donauit, et Beato Petro, et Siluestro, Papæ Romano[5]; cui et stratoris exhibuit officium, et se non amplius Imperatorem, sed Sanctæ Romanæ Ecclesiæ defensorem, gauisus est vocari ; et ne pax Domini Papæ, occasione præsentiæ eius, sæcularis strepitus tumultu concuteretur, ipse ab vrbe, Domino Papæ collata, omnino[6] discessit, et sibi ciuitatem Bizantium ædificauit. ‡ *Page 579*

Lundonia et modernis temporibus Reges illustres magnificosque peperit, Imperatricem Matildem, et Henricum Regem Tertium §; et Beatum Thomam, Archiepiscopum[7], Christi Martyrem gloriosum,

' ——Quali non candidiorem
Ipsa[8] tulit, nec quo fuerit deuinctior alter' ||

omnibus bonis[9] totius orbis Latini.

[1] occasum, *Geoff. Mon.* [2] Sic, *Geoff. Mon.*; Haec, *S. H.* [3] In, *S. H.* [4] Helene regine filium, *after* Constantinum, *L.* [5] Romano, *om. S.* [6] omnino, *om. S.* [7] archiepiscopum, *om. L.* [8] ipsa, *om. S. H.* [9] nec qui fuerat deiunctior alter in omnibus hominibus, *L.*

* Horace, *Od.* i. 1. 6 : 'Terrarum dominos euehit ad deos.'
† Geoff. Monmouth, *Hist. Britt.* i. 11, iii. 9.
‡ *Pseudo-Constantine Donation*, ap. Migne, *Patrologia*, viii. 567.
§ i. e. *The young king, son of Henry II.*
|| Horace, *Sat.* i. 5. 41, 42 : 'quales neque candidiores Terra tulit neque quis me sit deuinctior alter.'

THE VARIATIONS OF THE FIRST EDITION OF THE SURVEY IN 1598 FROM THE TEXT OF 1603

Passages or phrases which did not appear in the edition of 1598 are denoted by an asterisk

VOLUME I

PAGE **xcvii,** l. 2. *Robert Lee, Lord Mayor*] the Lord Mayor

xcviii, ll. 18–28. *which some other . . . any other*] but I trust hereafter that shalbe supplied, and I professe (if more touching this worke come vnto me) to afforde it, in all dutie. In the meane time I recommend this to your view, my laboures to your consideration, and my selfe to your seruice (as I haue professed during life) in this or any other.

1, ll. 1–15. *As the . . . greater maiestie.*] As Rome the chiefe Citie of the world to glorifie it selfe, drew her originall from the Gods, Goddesses, and demy Gods, by the Troian progeny. So this famous Citie of London for greater glorie, and in emulation of Rome, deriueth it selfe from the very same originall. For (as Jeffery of Monmoth, the Welche Historian reporteth) Brute descended from the demy god Eneas, the sonne of Venus, daughter of Iupiter, aboute the yeare of the world 2855, the yeare before Christes natiuitie 1108, builded a Citie neare vnto a riuer now called Thames, and named it Troynouant, or Trenouant.

l. 16. **as . . . noteth*

ll. 17, 18. *also . . . faire*] also added fayre

3, l. 27. *hauing*] which hath

l. 29. *whereof*] which

4, l. 8. *Fastnes*] Paces

l. 18. *confederates*] leager fellowes

5, l. 2. *this Citie*] this our Citie

l. 14. *inwalled this Citie*] inwalled it

7, l. 27. *ignorant of building*] ignorant of the Architecture or building.

ll. 30–32. *artificers . . . wodden buildings.*] Masons and Workemen in stone into this Iland amongst the Saxons, (he I say) brought hyther Artificers of stone houses, Paynters and Glasiers, artes before that time vnto the Saxons vnknowne, who before that time vsed but wodden buildinges.

l. 32 to page 8, l. 2. **And to this . . . diuine seruice.*

8, ll. 8, 9. *of the . . . Londennir,*] of the olde Saxons Londonceaster, Londonbeig,

l. 22. *whereof William*] whereof I haue read some, namely William

9, ll. 1–12. **By the Northside . . . landside.*

ll. 19, 20. *then brake . . . purses*] and then they brake into the houses of the Jewes, and searched their coffers

9, l. 23. *of this Citie*] of the Citie of London

ll. 26–30. **hauing graunted . . . he also*

ll. 34, 35. **along behinde the houses*

l. 39 to page 10, l. 2. **1328 . . . repaired.*

10, ll. 9, 10. *and Bricke . . . burnt:*] and willed brick to be made and brent there,

ll. 18, 19. *the Posterne . . . repayred*] the Posterne. A greate part of the same wal called Moregate was repayred

ll. 20, 21. *in two . . . fixed*] standing in two places there

11, l. 5. **for defence thereof.*

ll. 19–22. **All which sayde . . . name of Wel.*

12, ll. 9, 10. *That . . . proued thus,*] That the Riuer of the Wels, in the West parte of the Citie, was of old time so called: it may be prooued thus,

ll. 18, 19. *this water . . . continued,*] this water hath beene since that time called Turnemill Brooke: yet then called the riuer of the Wels, which name of Ryuer continued:

14, l. 6. *in a Booke*] in an olde writing[1] booke

l. 16. *to scowre*] to couer

15, ll. 21, 22. *is faire . . . full.*] is thereof yet fayre curbed square with harde stone, and is alwaies kepte cleane for common vse: it is alwaies ful, and neuer wanteth water.

ll. 24–26. *west ende . . . incloseth it:*] west ende of this Clarkes well Church, without the stone wall that incloseth the Church,

ll. 26–38. **the sayd Church . . . Gentiles in England, &c.*

l. 39 to page 16, l. 9. *Other smaller . . . discerned.*] the other smaller wells that stood neare vnto Clarkes wel, to wit Skinners wel, Fagges well, Todwell, Loderswell, and Redwell, are all decayed and so filled vp, that their places are now hardly discerned:

16, l. 21. *is called Smithfield pond.*] is but fowle: and is called Smithfielde Ponde.

17, ll. 15–18. *Water . . . an other place.*] Water procured to the Standarde in West Cheape aboute the yeare 1431.

ll. 23–6. **The Conduit . . . other Conduits.*

18, l. 13. *Bulmer*] Bulman

ll. 26, 27. **neare . . . Lothbery*

ll. 28–30. *Eastfield . . . Cripplegate.*] Eastfielde conueyed water from Teyborne and from Highbery.

19, l. 5. *Wodrooffe*] Wodren

l. 10. *900 li.*] 700 li.

l. 12. **The towne Ditch without the Wall of the citie.*

20, ll. 7–13. **namely . . . XCV. li. iij. s. iiij. d.*

ll. 19–23. **And againe . . . viii. CXIIIJ. pound, xv. s. viij. d.*

l. 23. *Before the which*] At which

l. 36. **for I cannot helpe it.*

[1] *Writen*, Tanner MS. 464.

23, ll. 1–4. *liberality . . . was builded.*] liberality of diuers persons 215 yeares before the bridge of stone was finished.

ll. 22, 23. *foure years . . . 1205.*] foure yeares before this worke was finished, and was buried in the Chappell builded on the same bridge in the yeare 1205.

ll. 29–32. *foure Clearks . . . erected,*] foure Clarkes and other. There was also a Chantrie for Iohn Hatfielde &c. So that in the yeare 23 of Henry the 6 there was 4 Chaplens in the saide Chappell; after that example sundry houses were thereupon shortly after erected.

l. 32 to page 24, l. 9. **and many . . . on this Bridge.*

24, ll. 10, 11. *The first . . . foure yeares*] The first action on this bridge was lamentable, for within 3 yeres

ll. 12–14. *the Borough . . . there*] a maruelous terrible chance happened, for the citie of London vpon the south side of the riuer of Thames, as also the Church of our Ladie of the Canons in Southwarke

l. 37 to page 25, l. 3. **1381, a great . . . Annales.*

25, ll. 27–34. **In the yeare 1450 . . . in number.*

l. 35. *common siege*] common stage

l. 38. to page 26, l. 7. **In the year 1553 . . . Annales.*

26, ll. 16, 17. **vz. wardens, as aforesaid, and others*

l. 25. **sometime about the Fleete.*

27, ll. 13–15. **as before . . . vpon Walbrooke*

ll. 17, 18. *should clense . . . extended.*] should vaulte or bridge and clense the same so farre as his landes extended.

ll. 20–4. *Also . . . discerned.*] In the thirde of Henry the fift, this watercourse hauing had many bridges (as ye haue hearde) I haue reade of one by the name of Horshew bridge, by the Church of S. Iohn Baptist now called S. Iohns vpon Walbrooke, which hath beene since vaulted ouer with bricke, and the Streetes or Lanes where through it passed so paued, that the same watercourse or brooke is now hardly discerned.

l. 27. **in this Citie*

28, ll. 2–5. *Tower of London . . . builded,*] Tower of London, which then serued as a Posterne for Passengers out of the East: from thence through Towerstreete, Eastcheape, and Candelweekestrete, to London-stone, the midle point of that high way: then through Budgerow, Wathelingstreete, and leauing Paules Church, on the right hand, to Ludgate in the West, the next be Aldgate, Bishopsgate, Criplegate, Aldersgate, Ludgate, and the Bridgegate, ouer the Thames. Since the which time hath been builded Newgate

l. 10. **or reasonable coniecture*

ll. 12–19. *For the first . . . gate and posterne*] The first was the Posterne gate next vnto the Tower of London which at the length fell downe in the yeare 1440, the 18 of Henry the 6, and was neuer reedified againe of stone, but an homely cotage with a narrow passage made of timber, lath, and loame, hath beene in place thereof set vp, and so remaineth. The ruine of the said Posterne

28, l. 23. **to the white tower,*

ll. 25, 26. *outer wal.*] utter wal of the Tower.

ll. 28–33. *Thames . . . reedified.*] Thames, to haue flowed aboute it. By meanes of this ditch the foundation of that gate being loosed and greatly weakened, fell at the length, as ye haue hearde and so remaineth.

l. 33 to page 29, l. 7. **Such was . . . Communaltie, &c.*

29, ll. 10–16. **This is one . . . antiquitie of the gate*

ll. 18, 19. **as ye . . . Portsoken*

l. 27 to page 31, l. 2. **More, I reade . . . thus much for Aeldgate.*

31, l. 4. *The third and next*] The next

l. 12. *Blethenhall greene*] Blethenhal green now called Bednal-greene

l. 36. INSERTS *after Chanons regular*: the 19 of Henry the thirde.

32, ll. 1-3. *Thus much . . . repayring the same*] Thus much for Antiquitie, now for repayring of this gate.

l. 4. *confirmed*] graunted or confirmed

33, l. 1. **seemeth to me that*

ll. 8, 9. **but since . . . Monke of Bery*

ll. 25, 26. *More, I read that*] Besides this

34, l. 16. *This is . . . hath*] This gate hath

35, l. 3. **and is the fift principall gate*

ll. 4, 5. *about . . . Stephen*] about the raigne of Henry II or Richard I.

ll. 12–14. **a kind of . . . that time, &c.*

37, l. 7. *Thomas Knowles . . . London,*] Lastly Thomas Knowles Mayor,

ll. 14–38. **Tuesday next . . . them in irons.*

38, l. 2. **and sixt principal gate*

ll. 35, 36. *defaced . . . Idoll*] defaced by vnaduised folkes

39, l. 37 to page 40, l. 2. **38 foot . . . in bredth*

40, l. 19. **three broad Arrow heades*

l. 31. **Thus much for gates in the wall.*

l. 32 to page 41, l. 6. *Water gates . . . Ripa Reginæ*] Of the Water-gates of name, on the banke of the riuer of Thames. The first from the West towards the East is called Ripa Reginae

41, l. 11. *so called*] so called, as may be supposed

42, l. 1. *The next*] The next after Downgate (of old time)

ll. 23, 24. **and is the . . . Fitzstephen*

l. 25. *newe made*] weakely made

43, l. 17. INSERTS after *now*: the largest water gate on the Riuer of Thames, and therefore

l. 35. INSERTS after *Customers key*: which is now of late most beautifully enlarged and built

44, l. 8. *said Riuer:*] said Riuer, and therefore concerning Gates let this suffice.

ll. 8–16. **now for . . . Francigenarum*

45, ll. 13–20. **Ye haue . . . Tower*

ll. 21, 22. *which . . . white tower,*] This was the great square Tower, which was then builded,

45, ll. 28–33. **and also . . . at Westminster.*

46, ll. 9–15. **In the yeare 1153 . . . repayred.*

l. 38 to page 47, l. 7. **It is also to be noted . . . good likings.*

47, l. 7 to page 48, l. 1. *But Mathew Paris . . . Lion Tower.*] Aboute the yeare 1239 King Henry the third caused the Tower of London to be fortified with bulwarkes, which after they were builded fell downe, and therefore he caused it to be reedified more strongly, to his cost of more then twelue thousand markes.

In the yeare 1274 King Edward the first commaunded the Treasurer and Chamberlaine of his Exchequer, to deliuer out of his Treasorie, vnto Giles of Andwarp 200 markes, of the fines taken of diuers Marchants, or vsurers of London, towardes the worke of the ditch about the Tower of London.

48, ll. 1–34. **I find also . . . John Bowre.*

l. 35. *Edward the fourth . . . London*] Edward the fourth fortified this Tower and made it strong.

l. 35 to page 49, l. 6. **and inclosed . . . somewhat.*

49, ll. 7–28. **and other parts . . . vsually opened.*

ll. 28–31. *And thus much . . . in the same*] Thus much for the foundation and building, increase and maintenance of this Tower. Now somewhat of accidents in the same.

l. 39 to page 50, l. 7. **In 1214 . . . Tower: Likewise*

50, ll. 8, 9. **and again . . . Iusticers.*

ll. 18, 19. *brought . . . hanged.*] brought him to the gallowes, and there hanged him and other twaine.

ll. 29, 30. **as ye . . . Gates.*

51, ll. 12–14. **E. 2 . . . their dyet.*

ll. 27, 28. **and kept . . . her sonne.*

52, ll. 2–4. **I finde . . . Buckles bury.*

53, l. 38 to page 54, l. 1. *Thus . . . money matters*] Thus haue I set downe according to my small reading in antiquitie, these money matters

54, ll. 10–13. **first poynted . . . were not vsuall.*

ll. 32–5. **King Edward . . . forbidden.*

55, ll. 13–31. **In the yeare 1411 . . . money for them.*

l. 32. *In the yeare 1465*] In the yeare 1464

56, l. 3 to page 57, l 27. **saith the Record . . . siluer in the middest thereof.*

58, ll. 15–26. **In the yeare 1426 . . . Queenes, and others.*

ll. 31–4. *entered the same . . . murdered.*] entered the same, and deliuered king Henry, but the next yeare hee was againe sent thether, and there murthered.

l. 36. **with Malmesey*

ll. 37, 38. *were said to be murthered there.*] were murdered in the Tower.

l. 39 to page 59, l. 5. **In the yeare 1485 . . . before the king.*

59, ll. 12–26. **In the yeare 1546 . . . Easterweeke.*

62, ll. 16–22. **The yeare 1216 . . . owne Lord, &c.*

l. 30 to page 65, l. 28. **and sware . . . out of an olde Recorde.*

65, ll. 38, 39. **in the yeare 1428 . . . that same*

66, ll. 5–28. **In the yeare 1460 . . . scepter in his hand.*

l. 29. *Edward the fourth . . . leauing*] and true it is, that his sonne King Edwarde the fourth being dead, and leauing

ll. 30–5. *Richard, D. of Glocester . . . in my Annales.*] there Richarde, Duke of Glocester, then Protector, practised for the Crowne, and as it were by election of the Commons, made in the Guild hall of London, tooke upon him there the title of the Realme, as offered and imposed vpon him; as yee may reade set downe and penned, by Sir Thomas Moore.

ll. 36, 37. *Henry . . . raigne*] King Henry the 7 aboute the yeare 1501 the 3 of his raigne

67, l. 2. *In the seauenteenth*] In the 7

ll. 10–29. **The 20 of the saide . . . Katheren Queene of England; &c.*

l. 31 to page 68, l. 3. **Next adioyning . . . the 7 of E. the fourth.*

68, l. 8. *since named*] surnamed

l. 22. *a Charter . . . wherein*] a Charter, the 10 of June, the 4 of Edwarde the 1, remayning of Recorde in the Tower, wherein

l. 28. *One other Tower*] A third Tower

71, ll. 1, 2. **king Stephen was there lodged*

l. 20. *More*] The rest

ll. 23–7. **Sernes Tower . . . at Westminster.*

75, ll. 1, 2. *St. Anthonies schoole . . . were*] St. Anthonies Schoole, howsoeuer the same be now fallen, both in number and estimation, were

ll. 4–9. **the schollers . . . following him: and*

l. 9. *mindfull*] the children mindful

ll. 15–24. **with the decay . . . of Canterburie, &c.*

76, l. 22. *whose names were*] whose names be

77, l. 20. *the old Temple*] the old Temple in Oldborne

ll. 22–6. **in the libertie of Westminster . . . St. Andrewes Church.*

l. 27. *There was also . . . of Chancerie*] One other Inne of Chauncery sometime there was

l. 30. **in Strand streete, and*

ll. 31, 32. **in the libertie . . . Inne of Chancerie*

l. 32. *with other houses*] The which and other dwelling houses

ll. 34, 35. *that large . . . vnfinished,*] that beautiful (but yet vnperfect house)

81, l. 22. **and the Stockes Market*

ll. 35–7. *Pater noster makers . . . Paules Church yarde*] Pater-noster Beademakers and Text Writers are gone out of Pater Noster Rowe into Stationers of Paules Churchyard:

82, l. 14. **to confirme his opinion*

83, l. 4. **or rather is mightily encreased*

l. 14. *or baked tyle*] bricke or tyle

l. 16. *often consuming*] often consuming and deuouring

83, l. 22. *a Booke*] a booke (as I heare)

ll. 23–5. **which Booke . . . this matter.*

ll. 30–3. **The Coach man . . . him home.*

84, l. 5. **because she was sicke and weake*

ll. 17, 18. **for the world . . . on foote.*

85, l. 9. **Great families of old time kept.*

l. 11 to page 87, l. 27. **by noble men, and great estates . . . kept. Nearer to our time*

88, ll. 7–19. **Richard Redman . . . which were many.*

l. 37. **and great reliefe at his gate.*

89, ll. 2, 3. **yet their . . . sit vpon them.*

ll. 4–15. *Edward Duke of Sommerset . . . left shoulder.*] These, as all other of these times gaue great reliefe to the poore, and I haue oft seene at that Lorde Cromwels gate, more then two hundred persons serued twice euery day with breade, meate, and drinke.

Edward Duke of Sommerset was not inferior in keeping a number of tall Gentlemen and Yeomen. These (I say) and all other men of honour and worshippe then lodging in this Citie, or within the liberties therof, did without grudging, beare their part of charges with the citizens, according to their estimated estates, without the which those musters of old time could not haue beene so great.

And thus I end touching vsuall Orders and Customes of this Citie.

l. 17 to page 91, l. 27. **These as all other . . . through the Citie to Westminster.*[1]

93, l. 33. INSERTS after *publike places*: as the Theater, the Curtine &c.

94, ll. 1–33. *The marching forth . . . well dowked.*] The youthes of this citie time out of mind haue left off to practise the disarmed launce, and shielde on horsebacke in the fieldes, but I haue seene some few vpon the Riuer of Thames rowed in boates, with staues flat at the foreend, runing one against another, and for the most part eyther one, or both ouerthrowne and well ducked.

95, ll. 15–17. **namely in Bearegardens . . . stand vpon.*

96, l. 7. *One other shew*] Of one other shew ye may reade

97, ll. 6–8. **The like was . . . great thanks.*

ll. 25–39. **Against the feast of Christmas . . . great tempests.*

99, l. 3. *Monke of Bery*] monke of Bray

ll. 27, 28. *and therefore . . . in the night.*] And therefore to speake of watches and shewes in the nightes.

l. 29 to page 101, l. 2. **Of watches in this Citie . . . enormities in the night,*

101, ll. 2–4. *I reade . . . to bee kept,*] First I reade that in the yeare of Christ, 1253, watches in Cities and Borough towns were commanded by King Henry the thirde,

[1] The whole section *Of Charitable Alms in old times given* is thus an insertion in the edition of 1603, being expanded from the original conclusion of the previous section as given above. Some part of it appeared elsewhere in 1598. Cf. p. 265 below.

101, ll. 31–8. **euery mans doore . . . Then had ye.*

105, ll. 20–7. **and Thomas the Archbishop . . . of Canterburie, &c.*

ll. 27–30. *Unto this . . . other matters.*] thus far FitzStephen: whereunto may be added innumerable persons of honor, borne in London, and actions done by worthie citizens, whereof I will onely note a few best knowne to the comminalty.

ll. 31–3. **The Citizens . . . of their Citie.*

l. 34. *1197*] 1235

l. 36. **Domus Dei, or*

106, ll. 11–14. **He also . . . London bridge.*

ll. 19–30. **Sir Iohn Poultney . . . poore people, &c.*

l. 37. *effect*] intent

l. 38 to page 107, l. 10. **Iohn Lofken . . . stone and glasse.*

108, ll. 4–8. **Iohn Churchman . . . to sit, &c.*

l. 9. *Adam Bamme . . . 1391*] In the yere 1391 Adam Bamme, Maior,

ll. 16–27. **Thomas Knoles . . . glasse windowes*

l. 28. *Thomas Falconar . . . 1414*] In the yere 1415, Thomas Faulconer Maior,

l. 30 to page 109, l. 2. **More he made . . . with his goods*

109, ll. 2–8. *founded . . . Newgate, &c.*] In the yeare 1420 Richarde Whitington Maior founded Whitingtons Colledge for the poore, with diuinitie lectures to be reade there for euer: Hee also builded Newgate &c

ll. 9–24. **Iohn Carpenter . . . Walbrooke, &c.*

ll. 28–30. **a great builder . . . to be*

ll. 32–6. *William Eastfield . . . Cripples gate, &c.*] In the yeare 1438 William Eastfielde Maior, conueyed water to the Conduite in Fleete-streete to Alderman-berry and to Criplesgate.

ll. 37, 38. *Stephen Browne . . . thence*] In the yeare 1439 Stephen Browne Maior sent into Prussia, and caused corne to be brought thence to London in great quantitie

110, ll. 3–18. **Philip Malpas . . . Hodsdon in Hertfordshire.*

l. 21. *to charitable vses.*] to be bestowed in charitable actions for releefe of the poore.

ll. 22–34. **Godfrey Bollein . . . of his owne charges.*

l. 35. INSERTS: In the yeare 1471 Iohn Stockton Maior, and 11 Aldermen of London, with the Recorder were all made knightes in the fielde, by Edwarde the fourth, for their good seruice done vnto him.

ll. 35, 36. *Edmond Shaw . . . goods, &c.*] In the yeare 1483 Edmond Shaa Maior, builded Criplesgate.

ll. 37, 38. **Thomas Hill . . . to be builded.*

l. 39 to page 111, l. 3. *Hugh Clopton . . . Summarie.*] In the yeare 1491, Hugh Clopton Maior, builded the great stone arched bridge at Stratford vpon Auon.

111, l. 9 to page 113, l. 15. **Sir Iohn Perciuall . . . in coales for euer.*

113, l. 19. **as in my Summarie.*

113, ll. 20–37. **Edward Hall . . . and also buried.*

l. 38 to page 114, l. 3. *Sir Thomas Gresham . . . for the poore.*] In the yere 1566 Sir Thomas Gresham, Mercer, builded that stately Exchange Royal in London, and left his dwelling-house in Bishopsgate streete, to be a colledge of readings &c. as in my summary.

114, ll. 4–19. **William Patten . . . gift for euer.*

ll. 24–8. **Sir T. Offley . . . trust in them.*

l. 29. *Iohn Haydon, Shiriffe, 1583.*] In the yeare 1582 Iohn Haydon, Alderman,

l. 32. *900li.*] 906*l.*

l. 35. *in charitable actions*] in deedes of charity.

l. 37 to page 116, l. 26. *more then of other . . . Coopers set in place.*

116, ll. 27–33. *Margaret Danne . . . 30 yeares after.*] About the yeare 1570 Margaret Dan, widowe to William Dan, late one of the Sheriffes of London, gaue by her testament more then 2000 pound to charitable actions.

117, ll. 2–4. *I haue . . . erected.*] I haue expressed, and as farith by monumentes erected in Christes Hospitall: which gift she afterward in her widowhode confirmed and greatly augmented.

118, l. 15. *I haue discoursed.*] I haue at large discoursed

ll. 22–24. **not Galus brooke . . . fabuled, but*

l. 34. *taketh name*] taketh his name

119, l. 11. *This Citie was*] The city thus

120, l. 18. *Bridge ward without.*] The Bridge warde without, in the Brugh of Southwarke.

l. 22. *which soundeth*] which soundeth as much as

124, l. 19. **and his two wiues*

126, ll. 3–6. **a plague . . . in their house.*

ll. 36, 37. *whereby . . . shallow.*] Whereby the ditch is filled vp and made shallow enough.

127, l. 7. **Henrie Iorden . . . Chaunterie there*

l. 21. *within these fortie yeares*] within these fortie foure yeares last,

l. 31. *towards*] in

l. 37 to page 128, l. 6. **Amongst the which . . . was finished.*

128, l. 39 to page 129, l. 1. **which houses . . . and such like.*

129, ll. 11, 12. **the filth . . . into the ditch*

l. 17. *a Beedle*] a Beadle, to attend vpon them all

l. 18. *foure pound ten shillings.*] ix pound

130, l. 26. INSERTS after *Chicke lane*: and to Berwardes lane,

ll. 35, 36. **some haue written . . . this chappell was*

l. 38. **his cosen*

131, l. 3. **and auotion . . . Stretham*

l. 8. *new builded*] new builded this Chappell

ll. 9, 10. **Hamond de Lega . . . chapple*

ll. 10, 11. *London . . . colledge.*] London in the yeare 1488, when he deceased 1501 was buried there. This Chappell and Colledge

131, ll. 23, 24. *of the Greene . . . Houshold*] in houshold
ll. 27, 28. *Sir Richarde . . . Chartley*] Lord Ferrers.
l. 32. **or M. of the Heance men*
ll. 34–6. **Iohn Crolys . . . Chantery there 1388.*
ll. 37, 38. **now corruptly called Sything lane*

132, l. 12. *King of Armes*] Herralde
l. 17. INSERTS after *Marchant, &c.*: Woodroffe lane towardes the Tower is in this Parish.
ll. 23, 24. **Cokedon hall . . . I reade of.*
l. 26. *Mincheon*] Mincheon or Minion
ll. 26–8. **so called . . . Bishopsgate streete*
l. 38. *fourth of Henry the fift . . .*] thirde of Henry the fift, by the name of halfe pence of Genoa forbidden to pass as vnlawfull payment amongst the English subiectes.
l. 38 to page 133, l. 4. **it was . . . the other halfe*

133, l. 6. INSERTS after *stronger*: There was at that time also forbidden certaine other coynes called Seskaris, and Dodkins, with all Scottish monies.
l. 15. **Alderman of London*
l. 33. *for Harpe Lane,*] or Harpe Lane
l. 36 to page 134, l. 2. *who was . . . children.*] who was brother to Chichley the archbishop: he had 24 children.

137, l. 24. INSERTS after *antiquitie*: but I leaue euery man to his owne iudgement, and passe to other matters.

138, l. 5. *to the fifteene at sixe and twentie pounds.*] to the fifteene at 46*l.* and accounted in the Exchequer at 45*l.* 10*s.*

139, l. 22. **to Crowched Friers, and then Woodroffe lane*

142, l. 18. **about the Citie*
l. 33. **seuen in number.*
l. 37. *Rowles*] Rowalles [1]

144, ll. 4–9. *I haue oft . . . towardes the North.*
l. 20. *as he tearmed it*] as he poor man tearmed it.[2]
l. 38. *reproach*] the reproch

145, l. 1. **amongst them*
l. 9. *builded the whole*] builded the one halfe, to wit, the whole,
ll. 21, 22. *Buried in this Church . . . Shiriffes 1439. Sir Robert*] The monuments of the dead buried in this Church are these: Philip Malpas, one of the Sheriffes in the yeare 1439, was buried in the old church: this man gaue by his testament to the poore prisoners 125 pound: to other poore, euery yeare for fiue yeares together foure hundred shirtes and smockes, an hundred and fiftie gownes, and fortie paire of sheetes, to poore maydes marriages an hundred markes, to high wayes an hundred markes, and to fiue hundred poore people in London euery one sixe shil-

[1] *Harley MS.* 538, Lord of Rowels.
[2] *Harley MS.* 538, 'as they tearmed it'; see p. 292 below.

linges eyght pence, besides twentie markes the yeare to a graduate, to preach abroad in the countries: twentie shillings the yeare, for twentie yeares to the preachers at the Spittle, the three Eastre holydayes.[1] Sir Robert

145, ll. 31–3. **Stephen Woodroffe . . . weekely for euer.*

ll. 33–5. **he bequeathed . . . thereby.*

ll. 37–8. **William Hanbury, Baker.*

146, ll. 8, 9. *lately . . . Beale*] lately builded, by M. Beale.

ll. 31, 32. *Thomas . . . son*] Sir Thomas Henage the father and the sonne.

147, ll. 4, 5. **the south . . . Woodroffe lane*

ll. 36, 37. **Sir Rice Grifith . . . 1531.*

148, ll. 20–6. **more he appoyntea . . . continued for euer.*

margin. **These poyntes . . . wronged.*

149, l. 33. *Blanch apleton*] the Blanch Chapleton

150, l. 1. *long since discontinued*] now long time since discontinued

ll. 9–13. **with three . . . Ironmongers hall.*

l. 16. *fifteene . . . pound*] fifteene in London at 46*l.* and amounted in the Exchequer to 45*l.* 10*s.*

151, l. 28. *out but one*] out one

l. 32. **the contrarie.*

152, l. 8. **and againe new buildeth it.*

l. 28. INSERTS after *Mutas*: a Seruiceable Gentleman

154, ll. 5–12. **Within the sayde . . . H. the sixt.*

l. 12. *He was buried in the*] hee deceased in the yeare 1459, and was buried in his

l. 15. *prisons*] prisoners

l. 23. INSERTS before *one Maister with*: three Schoolemaisters, with an Usher, to wit,

l. 39. INSERTS after *learne*: flying tales haue I hearde, but not of credit, to auouch, and therefore I ouer passe them;

157, ll. 31–4. **I reade also . . . size appoynted.*

160, ll. 18, 19. *Britain . . . Tile*] Britaine (or Romayne) tyle as they call it

l. 22. **made their prall*

ll. 23–6. **which pumpe . . . yeare 1600.*

ll. 36, 37. **Against the east . . . pumpe.*

161, ll. 2, 3. **or the poore . . . Ed. the 3.*

l. 11. INSERTS after *a dwelling house*: reseruing the Church yarde for a garden plot.

162, l. 18. **and withholden*

163, ll. 17, 18. **but now lately . . . other meane people.*

l. 34. *fifteene at . . . ob. q.*] fifteene at 40 shillings, or thereabout.

164, ll. 15, 16. **an Ancris . . . London.*

[1] See i. 110 above.

164, ll. 35–7. **Stephen Geninges . . . Testament 1523.*

165, ll. 23–9. **and is called . . . for euer.*

l. 30. *Iohn Powlet.*] the Lord Iohn Powlet.

l. 36. *Sir Roger Manars.*] M. Cornewallos.

l. 38. **wealth, (for he was indebted to many)*

166, ll. 5, 6. **by Citizens . . . pleasure.*

l. 21. *Hospitall, commonly*] hospital of our blessed Ladie commonly

ll. 23–38. * *Walter Archdeacon . . . of his raigne.*

167, ll. 4, 5. *Sir . . . 1452.*] There lyeth buried Sir Henry Plesington, Knight, 1452.

ll. 14–16. **which chappell . . . buried,*

l. 20. *stood . . . Prelates, now*

168, l. 2. **continued vntill this day.*

l. 10. INSERTS after *yeare 1439*: the 18 of Henry the sixt

169, l. 7. **what so euer it was at the first*

171, l. 26. *Henrie the third.*] Henry the thirde, as I haue founde in Recordes.

172, ll. 3–28. *these monuments*, &c. [The list in the 1603 edition has been rearranged, and some dates and names added.]

l. 7. *Seamer*] Somer

l. 21. *Liade*] Lynd

173, l. 19. *Germain Cioll*] Ierome Serall

l. 22. *1576*] 1567

l. 24. *Denmarke*] Germany

174, ll. 8, 9. **in the Chapter . . . learning.*

ll. 20–35. **Alice Smith . . . charitable mind.*

175, l. 11. *fifteene at thirteene pound.*] fifteene at xxii*l.* in London, and in the Exchequer xxi*l.* x*s.*

176, l. 10. **Robert Beele Esquire 1601.*

l. 38. *was . . . grauited*] is letten

177, ll. 11, 12. *amongst . . . which is in*] which is the backe part of Gresham house in

l. 15. **which be now*

178, ll. 2–4. **Lucie . . . Epitaph,*

l. 6. *Brekenake*] Pembrooke

l. 9. *Atcourt*] Courtney

ll. 12, 13. **beheaded . . . 1463.*

l. 19. *Rodlegate*] Dadlegate

ll. 22, 23. * *The Lorde Barons . . . 1471.*

179, ll. 12, 13. **sir Iames Tirell . . . 1502.*

ll. 14, 15. **Edward . . . Huntington*

l. 29. *and an house*] he had also an house

l. 39. INSERTS after *causeth them*: in some matters

180, l. 8. *Gartier*] gartier or principall

l. 24. *the free schoole*] there a large Free Schoole

ll. 26–9. *whereof . . . Pumpe*] in this Schoole hath beene many good schollers trained vp. Now in three needle street, on the south part therof, the first monument at y[e] east end by the wel with 2 buckets or pump

180, ll. 30, 31. *of Martin . . . founders thereof.*] of William Oteswich, and Iohn Otoswich his sonne new founders thereof.

182, ll. 7–10. **This was . . . Cordwayner streete.*

ll. 11, 12. *Thomas . . . Armes*] Thomas Clarentius principall king of Herraldes

183, l. 31. **whereon . . . free schoole*

ll. 33–5. *breadth, whereon . . . his raigne*] breadth in the parish of S. Bennet Finke: this was giuen to the Mayster of the Hospitall, to the enlarging of their Church and house to the same belonging, for a maister, fourteene priests &c., in the seuenth of Henry the Sixt. Moreouer king Henry the Sixt, in the twentieth of his raigne

l. 39. *Burnworth*] Turnworth

184, ll. 12–14. *Hee also . . . in Windsore.*] This Hospitall was annexed, vnited, and appropriated vnto the Colegiate Church of S. George in Windsor, aboute the yeare 1485, (as was reported) by Sir Anthonie Baker, (maister of the saide Hospitall) to Sir Iohn Wolsborne knight, and other commissioners in the seauen and thirtith of Henry the eight.

ll. 15–30. **The Procters . . . vse of the Hospitall.*

l. 31. *In the yeare 1499*] since the saide annexing, to wit in the yeare 1499, the foureteenth of Henry the seuenth

ll. 36–9. **and finished . . . and other.*

l. 39. INSERTS: This goodly foundation hauing a free schoole and Almeshouses for poore men, (builded of hard stone) adioyning to the west end of the Church, was of olde time confirmed by Henry the Sixt in the yeare 1447. The outward worke of this new church was finished in the yeare 1501. The saide Iohn Tate deceased about the yeare 1514, and was there buried in a monument by him prepared, as appeareth by an indenture tripartite, made betweene the saide Iohn Tate, the Deane of Windsor, and William Milborne, Chamberlaine.

185, l. 12. **performed*

l. 22. *builded this Church*] builded this Church and was there buried

ll. 23–5. **was buried . . . Edward the fourth.*

l. 28. **was also buried there*

l. 31. **a Sermon*

ll. 34, 35. **Iohn Dent . . . Anne his wife.*

186, ll. 5–10. **This Gidney . . . he and she.*

ll. 13, 14. **hee dwelt . . . 8. pence*

l. 15. **a Batchler*

l. 18. *Iohn Broke*] Iohn Becke

187, l. 9. INSERTS after *bounds*: of this ward

l. 13. *It appeareth*] yet it appeareth

l. 16, 17. *and it . . . beefe not aboue*] and shortly after it was enacted, that the said Butchers & others should sel their beefe and mutton by weight, to wit beefe not aboue

187, l. 31. *same act . . . Grasiers*] same to raise in price; by meane that euery Grazier

l. 34. INSERTS after *raysing his price*: but the true causes of enhansing the prices both of those and other victualls are not to bee disputed here.

ll. 34–7. **The number . . . 720 Oxen weekly.*

188, l. 2. **on the north side*

l. 5. *stalles*] stalles on the north side of that streete

l. 13. *German*] German or Dutch man borne

ll. 20–2. *with foure . . . wayes*] with foure spoutes runneth foure waies

ll. 25, 26. **but now . . . I know not.*[1]

l. 34 to page 189, l. 13. **To this prison . . . 25. of our raigne.*

189, ll. 14–18. *More . . . brake*] Also without the West side of this Tunne, was a fayre well of springing water, curbed round with hard stone. In the yeare 1298 certaine principall Citizens of London brake

l. 21. *great fines.*] great fines, as in another place I haue shewed.

l. 21 to page 190, l. 38. **It cost the citizens . . . hard stone: but*

191, ll. 5, 6. **and this was for night walkers.*

l. 9. *scoulds . . . offenders.*] and scolds &c.

ll. 9–34. **As in the . . . to be reformed.*

ll. 35–7. *The foresaid . . . increased*] In the yeare 1475, R. Drope Mayor, dwelling in that warde, inlarged

192, l. 17. *foure great horses*] and were vsed to haue foure great horses

l. 19. *backe againe*] backe again; now three horses serue the turn.

193, l. 13. **through threeneedle streete*

ll. 30–2. **besides the . . . were kept*

194, l. 1. *that for winning*] but of late for winning

l. 9. *fame reporteth*] some reporteth

l. 17. *sea Metropolitane*] sea, and made it the Metropolitane

ll. 36–8. **in the yeare 1425 . . . there: and*

195, l. 4. *Monumentes . . . defaced.*] The monuments of the dead in this Church be these

ll. 4–17. **I reade . . . buried there*

ll. 20, 21. **Thomas Gardener . . . Smith*

l. 21. *and other.*] and diuers other that be defaced.

ll. 22–37. **for the antiquity . . . yet remayneth.*

196, ll. 1, 2. **since . . . the sixt*

ll. 8–15. *a sixt Bell . . . 100. Markes.*] One Russe a Draper gaue a sixt Bell, which he named Russe after his owne name, to be nightly rung at eight of the clocke: which bell vsually rong by one man more then 100

[1] For reading of *Harley MS.* 538 see p. 302 below.

yeares, of late ouer hayled by 4 or 5 at once, hath beene thrice broken, and therefore not rong as heretofore.

196, ll. 15–37. **And here a Note . . . founded Chaunteries there*

197, l. 1. *poore maides . . . parrish*] maides marriages.

ll. 2, 3. *and gownes . . . 100. &c.*] gownes of brodecloth to the poore 100, to prisons, Hospitals and Lazare houses liberally; hee also gaue his house in Cornhill to be sold, and the price thereof to be spent on the amendment of high wayes

ll. 3, 4. *matching . . . Vicecount*] afterwardes Vice Countesse

ll. 6–21. **and her great . . . Drope and Lady Lisle*

ll. 21, 22. *notwithstanding . . . Tombe*] notwithstanding the tombe of them both

ll. 25, 26. *was buried there, 1511.*] 1511 lyeth there

l. 34. *His . . . Garnam*] His monument is gone. Elizabeth Peak widow gaue ye patronage or gift of the benefice to the Drapers, and lyeth buried in the belfrey 1518. Richard Garneham

l. 35. *Smith*] Smith my Godfathers

l. 36. *his wife, buryed*] his wife my Godmother did lie

l. 37 to p. 198, l. 1. *Thomas Stow . . . father, 1559.*] Thomas Stow and Thomas Stow my grandfather and father

198, l. 10. **G. Barne, and other*

ll. 15–17. **Thomas Houghton . . . William Towerson.*

ll. 22–6. **the Church yarde . . . Iohn Rudstone*

ll. 28–31. *Sermons . . . and other.*] lands for sermons to be preached there, but that is gone, and his Tombe of marble before the pulpit is taken away, amongst others, namely of Doctor Yaxly one of the Phisitions to King Henry the eight, that was buried there with his wife, vnder a Tombe of marble.

ll. 31–7. **The Quire . . . kingdome of heauen.*

199, ll. 17, 18. **for that was allowed free.*

l. 23. *Leopards passant, gardant*] Lyons passant

l. 33. *Some say*] Others say

200, l. 5. **or sixe*

201, ll. 5–11. **of what originall . . . the second.*

l. 12. *The meeting . . . continued*] which manner continued

ll. 14–17. *meetings at . . . Exchange.*] meeting in Cornehill at the Burse, since by her Maiestie named the Royall Exchange.

l. 19. **on both the sides*

l. 23. *At the . . . standeth*] At Limestreet corner is

ll. 25–9. **in the raigne . . . buried. Also*

ll. 33–5. **The Ladie Wich . . . Sermons, &c.*

ll. 37, 38. **Henrie Trauers . . . about 1504.*

202, l. 3. *Clothworker, Maior, &c.*] Clothworker mayor 1583, buried there.

ll. 4–6. **by the foure . . . on the West.*

202, ll. 10, 11. *broder . . . incrochments.*] larger in breadth.

ll. 26–32. **Next is a common . . . night watches.*

203, ll. 4, 5. **Matilde . . . Chaunterie there, &c.*

l. 11. **Knight banaret, and yet*

l. 33. INSERTS after *Stockes market*: and these be the bounds of this warde

l. 36 to page 204, l. 1. **as may bee supposed . . . of stone.*

204, l. 5. *it would . . . downe.*] it would not haue remained there so long

l. 10. INSERTS after *his wife*: Alice, William and Iohn, wife and sonnes to Thomas Clarell, Agnes daughter to Thomas Niter Gent., William Atwell, Felix daughter to Sir Thomas Gisers, and wife to Trauers, Thomas Mason Esquire, Edmond Wartar Esquire, Ioane wife to Iohn Chamberlaine Esquire, daughter to Roger Lewkner Esquire, William Frier, Iohn Hamburger Esquire, Hugh Moresby, Gilbert Prince, Alderman, Oliuer Chorley, gentleman, Sir Iohn Writh (or Writhesley) alias Garter, principall king at Armes, sometime laid vnder a faire tombe in the quire, now broken downe and gone. Ióane wife to Thomas Writhesley, sonne to Sir Iohn Writhesley, Gartar, daughter and heire to William Hall Esquire, Iohn Writhesley the yonger, sonne to Sir Iohn Writhesley and Alienor, Eleanor seconde wife to Iohn Writhesley, daughter and heire to Thomas Arnalde, and Agnes his second wife, Iohn Writhesley sonne of Thomas, Agnes Arnold, first maried to William Writhesley, daughter of Richard Warmeforde, Barbara Hungerford, daughter to Sir Iohn Writhesley, wife to Anthonie Hungerford, son to Sir Thomas Hungerford of Dennampney in the countie of Glocester.

ll. 16–19. **And here I am to note . . . leaue them.*

ll. 20–3. *By this Church . . . alley.*] [In the 1598 edition placed before the list of monuments.]

l. 29. *Iulian, wife to Iohn Lambart Alderman.*] Iulian, wife to Iohn Lambard Alderman, mother of William Lamberd, yet liuing

l. 33. **Goldsmith*

205, l. 3. INSERTS after *Peach*: Hugh Acton, Taylor

l. 4. **he founded a Chanterie there*

ll. 5–11. **he gaue . . . Woolnoths church.*

ll. 26, 27. *It is taxed . . . 20l. 9s. 8d.*] It is taxed to the fifteene in London at xxi pound. In the Exchequer at xx*l*. x*s*.

206, l. 25. *Belinsgate in the*] this Billinsgate, I haue not read in any recorde, more then that in the

l. 27. *standage*] strandage

207, 5. *defaced and gone*] defaced and cleane gone

208, l. 9. **bad and*

l. 24. *for the stranger will not*] for they will not

209, l. 14. **Richard Goslin, shiriffe, 1422.*

210, l. 32. *Mumforde*] Mounforde[1]

l. 35. **Roger Delakere founded a Chauntrie there.*

212, l. 4. **Iohn Blund Mayor, 1307*

l. 11. **Mauritius Griffeth . . . 1559*

l. 12. *Blanch*] Branch[2]

ll. 14–20. *Maoraltie . . . raysed on him*] mayoralty, deceased, 1571, in the parish of S. Christopher, but was buried there, as in the parish where he was borne[3]

213, l. 5. **Haberdasher*

ll. 5, 6. **Philip Cushen . . . 1600.*

l. 33 to page 215, l. 19. **of whose antiquitie I reade . . . Those Stockfishmongers, and Saltfishmongers*

215, l. 22. *sir Iohn Cornwall . . . Ampthull*] the Lord Fanhope

ll. 23–6. *Crooked lane . . . why, or when*] Crooked lane, whereas before they had seueral halles, in Thames Street twaine, in new fishstreet twain, & in old fish street twaine, in all six seueral halls. This company was so great as I haue read in the recordes of the Tower: now worne out of knowledge to the company, who bee not able so much as to shewe the reason, why

ll. 27–37. **Neither to say . . . other places.*

216, ll. 18, 19. *taxed . . . 47l.*] taxed to the fifteene in London at fifty pound, and in the exchequer at 49 pound ten shillings.

l. 35. *Tauerns, but*] Tauernes, for they dressed not meates to be sold, but

217, l. 6. **after the watch was broken vp*

l. 36, 37. **so called . . . Oueries, and other*

218, ll. 25, 26. **William Chartney . . . Chaunterie there.*

ll. 33–5. **Simon de Winchcomb . . . Hondon an other*

219, ll. 8–10. **It is now . . . Rhenish wine.*

ll. 15, 16. **William de Burgo . . . 1317.*

ll. 26, 27. *Iake Straw, but Iacke*] Iack Straw in Smithfield, and there to haue been therefore knighted by the king, but that is not trew, for Iack

221, ll. 33, 34. *Crosse, and sworde . . . Walworth.*] crosse and sword as now &c.

223, l. 5. INSERTS before *Iohn Bold*: Winslow, Gent.

224, ll. 5, 6. **Thomas Aylesbourgh . . . Chaunteries, and*

l. 9. **and other.*

l. 30. *is none*] is there none

226, ll. 8, 9. **In the yeare 1507 . . . pence. And*

l. 16. **in all 82 li. 3s.*

227, ll. 7, 8. **Anne Cawode . . . Chauntrie there, &c.*

228, ll. 30, 31. *Horshew Bridge, in Horshew bridge streete.*] Horshew Bridge, a Bridge ouer the Brooke in Horsebridge lane.

[1] The better form: see *Cal. Wills*, ii. 650–1.
[2] See p. 311 below.
[3] See pp. 311–2 below.

228, l. 38. **I haue lerned*

229, l. 18. *Huytley*] Huntley

l. 19. **since, Lancelot Bathurst, &c.*

ll. 26, 27. *It is taxed . . . shillings.*] It is taxed to the fifteene in London to forty pound, and in the Exchequer to thirty nine pound.

230, l. 1. **when I come to them.*

l. 24 to page 231, l. 7. **This companie of Skinners . . . for what is done.*

231, l. 7. *Then lower downe was*] Then was there

l. 35. *Mariner.*] Warrier

232, l. 14. *William Cosin was*] William Cosin, dwelling there, was

l. 15. INSERTS after *1306*: the 34 of Edwarde the 1.

l. 20. *Steleyard*] Stele house or Stele yarde

234, l. 31, 32. **or the Flemish Geld*

235, l. 10. *graue stones*] graue stones on these persons

ll. 20, 21. **Nicholas Louen . . . Chaunteries there*

l. 24. *vsed it, and*] vsed it, and so doth

236, ll. 37, 38. **it was then counted . . . stately house*

237, l. 2. INSERTS after *raigne*: and not otherwise

238, l. 12. *it is taxed . . . pound.*] It is taxed to the fifteene in London at 36 pound, and in the Exchequer at 34*l.* 10*s.*

239, l. 6. *a Brewhouse*] a Brewhouse on the Thames side.

240, ll. 19–24. *The Vintners . . . great Burdeous Marchants*] These Vintners, as well Englishmen as strangers borne, were of old time great Burdeaux merchants

l. 31. INSERTS after *Gallon*: William More Vintner Mayor, in the raigne of Richard the Second.

l. 31 to page 241, l. 18. **I reade of sweet wines . . . therewith, I reade that*

241, l. 19. *T. Duke of Clarence, and I. Duke of Bedford*] Thomas Duke of Clarence and Iohn Duke of Bedford

l. 32. *in like meeter*] of verse

242, ll. 1, 2. **the raigne . . . confirmed*

l. 2. INSERTS after *Henry the 6*: Hauing thus much not without trauaile & some charges noted for the antiquitie of these Vintners, about two yeares since or more I repayred to the common hall of that company, and there shewed, and read it in a court of Assistance, requiring them as being one of the principall companies in this cittie (of whome I meant therefore to write the more at large) if they knew any more which might sound to their worship or commendation, at their leysure to send it me, and I wold ioyne it to my former collection: at which time I was answered by some that tooke vpon them the speech, that they were none of the principall, but of the inferiour companies, and so willing me to leaue them I departed, and neuer since heard from them, which hath somewhat discouraged me any farther to trauail amongst the companies to learn ought at their hands.

IN MARGIN: The Vintoners one of the 12 principall companies. The readiest to speak not alwaies the wisest men.

242, l. 10. *is the royall streete and*] in the royall streete is

ll. 11–18. **I thinke of olde . . . Walbrooke water. Then is*

l. 28. *These were bounde*] These were (as the manner was then) bound

243, ll. 22, 23. **borne in Almayne . . . the sixt dayes.*

244, l. 38 to page 245, l. 10. *Richard de Wilehale . . . Saint Mary Ouery, 6.s.*

245, l. 10. *This house*] which

l. 30. *to shew actiuities*] to shew their actiuities

l. 36. *H. Causton*] Henry Causton

l. 38. *T. Roman Maior 1310*] Thomas Romaine

246, ll. 18, 19. **William Shipton . . . Chauntries there*

247, ll. 27–31. **On the other side . . . Apostles in London, &c.*

248, ll. 8, 9. **sometime called Saint Martin de Beremand church.*

249, ll. 1, 2. **William Stoksbie . . . Chantries there.*

ll. 9–14. **I read . . . 20.s. and 3.d. by yeare.*

l. 15. *Whitthorne*] Withers

ll. 15, 16. **and before . . . Chantrie there.*

l. 33. INSERTS after *Harbert*: the Lord Strange

l. 34. *Worcester*] Glocester

ll. 37, 38. **Richard Plat . . . there, 1601.*

250, ll. 2, 3. *It is taxed . . . 4. pence.*] It is taxed to the fifteene in London, at six and thirty pound, and in the Exchequer at thirty fiue pound, fiue shillings

251, l. 11. *against . . . wholy*] against that lanes end: and this place is wholly

ll. 17–25. **I haue not read . . . halfe pennie the pounde.*

252, ll. 33, 34. **Iohn Grantham . . . Chanteries there.*

253, ll. 7, 8. **and yet not . . . Chauntrie there.*

ll. 9–11. *gaue . . . Kirion lane*] gaue lands to that church,

ll. 27–31. *Sir William Laxton . . . later buried*] Sir William Laxton, Grocer, Mayor, deceased 1556, was buried in the vault, prepared by Henry Keble principall founder of that church for himself, but now his bones are vnkindly cast out, his monuments pulled downe, and the bodies of the said Sir William Laxton, and of Sir Thomas Lodge Grocer Mayor, are laid in place, with monuments ouer them for the time, till an other giue money for their place, and then away with them.

ll. 31, 32. **William Blunt . . . buried there, 1594. &c.*

l. 34 to page 254, l. 7. *This Church in the reigne . . . I cannot learne.*] called de Arcubus, of the stone Arches or Bowes on the top of the Steeple, or bell Tower thereof, which arching was as well on the old steeple, as on the new, for no other part of the church seemeth to haue beene arched at any time, yet hath the said church neuer beene knowne by any other name, then S. Mary Bow, or le Bow: neither is that Church so called of the court there kept, but the said Court taketh name of the place wherein it is kept, & is called the court of the arches, but of what antiquitie or continuation I cannot declare.

254, l. 19. **and a marish ground.*

margin. INSERTS after *hanged*: God amend or shortly send such an end to such false brethren.

255, ll. 9–11. **Iordan Goodcheape . . . attainted*

l. 39 to page 256, l. 7. **This Bell . . . at your will.*

256, l. 37. INSERTS after *1499*: deceased 1505.

257, l. 8. **Hawley . . . chauntries there.*

ll. 13–18. *King Edward . . . pleasures.*] This building was made by K. Edward the third vpon this occasion. In the raigne of the sayde King diuers iustings were made in London betwixt Sopars Lane and the Crosse in Chepe: for the standard stoode not then in place where now it is, namely one great iusting was there in the yeare 1330, the fourth of Edward the third, whereof is noted thus. About the feast of S. Michael there was a great and solemne iusting of all the stout Earles, Barons and nobles of the realme, at London in West Cheape, betwixt the great crosse and the great conduit, nigh Sopars Lane, which iusting lasted three daies; where Queene Philip with many Ladies fell from a stage of timber, notwithstanding they were not hurt at all: wherefore the Queene toke great care to saue the Carpenters from punishment, and through her prayer (which she made on her knees) she pacified the King and counsaile, and thereby purchased great loue of the people. After which time the King caused this silde or shede to bee made, and strongly to bee builded of stone, for himself, the Queene, and other estates to stand in, and there to behold the iustings and other shewes at their pleasure [1].

ll. 22, 23. * *to Stephen Spilman . . . Seldam, shed or building*

l. 25. *or Tamarsilde*] and in the 8 of the same H. called *Tamarside*

l. 27. INSERTS after *London*: and a certaine shop in the said parish, betweene the same shed and the kings high way of west Cheape, annexed to the said shed, with two shops, sellers and edifices whatsoeuer, as well builded or any way being ouer the said shop, as ouer the entry of the said shed, which were holden of him in burgage, as all the Cittie of London is, and which were worth by yeare in all issues, according to the true value of them, vij pound xiij*s*. and iiij*d*. as was founde by inquisition thereof before Thomas Knowles Mayor, and Eschetor in the said Citie.[2]

258, ll. 26, 27. *at 52 li. . . . 52. pound, 6.s.*] at 72.l. 16.*s*. in the Exchequer at 72. pound

ll. 29, 30. **and taketh . . . this warde*

l. 30. *also*] which also

260, ll. 1–6. **in the 18 . . . the yeare. And*

l. 6. *he gaue the same Tower*] of his raigne did grant

[1] For the longer account in the edition of 1603 see vol. i. p. 268.
[2] Compare vol. i. p. 270 above.

260, ll. 8, 9. *name of . . . in London.*] name of his Tower called Seruesse[1] Tower at Bucklesbery

l. 38 to page 261, l. 3. *Edward Hall . . . in this church.*

261, l. 22. INSERTS after *morning*: the 13th of Nouember

l. 39. INSERTS after *high streete*: which is the maine body of this warde : first ouer against the parish church of S. Mildred, on the south side of the Poultrie, vp to the great Conduite, haue yee diuers fayre houses, sometimes inhabited by Poulters, now by Grocers, Haberdashers, and Vpholders, at the west end of this Poultrie, on the south side, haue ye the great Conduite, which is the beginning of west Cheape. This Conduite was the first sweete water that was conueyed by pipes of lead vnder ground, to this place in the Citie, from Padington ; it was castellated with stone and cesterned in lead, which was begunne in the yeare 1285. Henry Wales being then Maior. This Conduite was againe new builded by Thomas Ilame one of the Sheriffes in the yeare 1479. Beyond this Conduite, on the south side of Cheap be now faire and large houses, for the most part possessed of Mercers vp to the north corner of Cordwainer streete, corruptlie called Bow lane, which houses in former time were but shedes (or shops) with solars ouer them, as of late one of them remained at Sopars lane end, wherein a woman solde seedes, rootes, and herbs, but those sheddes or shops, by incrochmentes on the high streete, are now largely builded on both sides outward, and also vpwarde towarde heauen, some three, foure, or fiue stories on high. &c.[2]

l. 39 to page 262, l. 1. *called . . . side thereof*] On the north side of the Poultrie

262, l. 14. *Scalding wike*] of Skalding house or Skalding wike

ll. 18, 19. **Salomon Lanuare . . . one other.*

l. 27. *Tho. Tusser*] Thomas Tusser Gentleman

263, ll. 1, 2. *Some foure . . . is a prison*] Of the name of this streete called the Poultrie, I haue before spoken as also of the lane called Skalding house or Skalding wike &c. On this north side some foure houses west from Saint Mildred Church, is a prison

l. 6. *was . . . Corpus Christi*] was sometime a proper Chappell of Corpus Christi

l. 9. *in which Chappel*] where

264, ll. 1–5. **Henrie Ady . . . there buried.*

l. 16 to page 269, l. 3. **More I reade of Bordhangly . . . saint Mary Cole church where we left.*[3]

269, l. 4. INSERTS after *or Acars*: near to the great Conduit in Cheape

l. 19. INSERTS after *Parliament*: there is also a preaching in the Italian tongue to the Italians and others on the Sondaies.

l. 21. *1428*] the eight of Henry the sixt

[1] *In the margin*, Seruice Tower by Walbrook.
[2] Compare the parallel passages of the 1603 edition on i. 264, 268.
[3] Much of this passage appears elsewhere in the first edition, see pp. 249–51, 254.

269, l. 36. *this Hospital*] this Chappell

270, ll. 1–3. *remoued . . . letten out for rent.*] remoued into the great olde Chappell, and his Chappell is made into shops, and letten out for rent, by his successors the Mercers.

ll. 3–5. *enabled . . . Richard the 2.*] enabled to be a Company the 20 of Richarde the second

ll. 5–17. **They had three . . . Eschetor in the said Citie.*[1]

ll. 22–5. **In the yeare 1536 . . . being Maior.*

ll. 27, 28. *whereof . . . raigne*] in the 8

271, ll. 9–15. **I find that Iohn Norman . . . no farther.*

l. 15. INSERTS: Without this lane is the Standarde in Cheape, which Iohn Wels Grocer Maior 1430 caused to be made with a small cesterne for fresh water, hauing one Cocke continually running, when the same is not turned nor lockt; this was finished by his executors, Thomas Knoles, and Iohn Chichley, they purchased licence of Henry the sixt, to conuey water, to make the Conduite. Now whether the Standarde in West Cheape, so oft spoken of in former times, be the same and stoode iust in this place, or else where, or that the same were remoueable, may be some question: for it is manifest that in the raigne of Edwarde the thirde, and at other times when the great iustinges, and other running on horsebacke were practised betwixt the great Crosse, and the great Conduite at Sopars lane end, there was no such Standarde, or other Obstacle betweene them, neither was that streete paued with hard stone as now it is. We read that in the yeare 1293, three men had their right hands stricken off at the Standard in Cheape for rescuing of a Prisoner; it is verie likelie therefore that the olde Crosse in Cheape (which was then newlie builded) was also the Standarde.

In the yeare 1326 the Citizens tooke Walter Stapleton, Bishop of Excester, and beheaded him with other at the Standarde in Cheape. In the yeare 1399 King Henry the fourth caused the Blanch Charters made by Richarde the second, to bee burnt at the Standarde in West Cheape. In the yeare 1381. Wat Tylar beheaded Richarde Lions and others in Cheape. In the yeare 1461. Iohn Dauie had his hand striken off at the Standarde in Cheape, also Iacke Cade the Rebell beheaded the Lorde Say at the Standarde in Cheape &c. Thus much for the Body of Cheape warde may suffice[2].

ll. 16, 17. *Now for . . . Catteten streete*] Then followeth Catte streete (so called in Recordes the 24 of Henry the sixt, now corruptlie Catteten street)

272, l. 37. *Sir Iohn Sha*] Edmond Shaw

l. 38 to page 273, l. 9. **who was the first . . . worke was finished*

273, ll. 14–17. **How this gift . . . then they performe.*

275, ll. 13, 14. *because of olde time . . . there about.*] because of olde time

[1] See, however, the parallel passage in the 1598 edition on p. 249 above.

[2] This differs a good deal from the parallel passage in the 1603 edition: see i. 264–5.

since the raigne of William Conqueror (that first brought Iewes from Roan into this realme) many Iewes inhabited there about, vntill that in the yeare 1290. the 18. of Edward the first they were wholly and for euer by the said king banished this realme, hauing of their owne goodes to beare their charges, till they were out of his dominions. The number of the Iewes at that time banished were 15060 persons, whose houses being sold, the king made of them a mightie masse of money.[1]

275, l. 16. *70. yeares*] 60. yeares

276, l. 11. *Angell his wife*] Angell his wife, 1517.

ll. 13–15. *The wife of a Maister . . . Chester*] a Countesse of Cornewall and Chester, but her name and time is not there apparent

l. 18. **Samuell Thornhill, 1597.*

l. 23. **eleuen shillinges.*

277, l. 12. *disdainely*] disdainfully

278, l. 27 to page 281, l. 25. **Then is the olde Iurie . . . thus much for the Iewes.*[2]

281, l. 26. *In this . . . olde Iury*] In the Olde Iurie,

ll. 27–31. **Vpwell, so . . . King confirmed*

ll. 31, 32. *In this . . . Parishioners*] in which to the commendation of the parishioners.

282, l. 12. **Iohn Brian*

l. 18. **made in place of Iewes houses*

283, l. 5. INSERTS after *yeare 1399*: This may bee some argument, which I ouerpasse.

ll. 5–8. **Hugh Clopton . . . Chaunteries there.*

ll. 30, 31. **two fifteenes . . . charges thereof*

l. 32. INSERTS after *springes*: without the North wall of the Cittie

l. 38 to page 284, l. 4. **sometime belonging . . . deceased, 1509.*

284, ll. 6, 7. **Alderman Bennet now possesseth it.*

ll. 14–17. **which companie of Armourers . . . the sixt.*

l. 20. INSERTS after *defaced*: there is one Tombe on the South side the Quire but without inscription.

ll. 20–7. **notwithstanding, I find . . . the 17. of Henrie the sixt.*

ll. 27–31. *Thomas Bradberie . . . buried there.*] I read that Thomas Bradbury, Mercer, Maior, in the yeare 1509. was buried there, his Tombe is on the north side the Quire, & also one Edmond Harlocke Curriar to bee a great benefactor, Sir Iohn Garme, Skirringham, 1468, Richard Hamney 1418, Richard Colsel &c.

ll. 32–5. **This Church . . . a parish church.*

285, ll. 5, 6. *It is taxed . . . xv.l. xvi.s. ix.d.*] It is taxed to the fifteene, in London, at 19*l.* and in the Exchequer at 19*l.*

l. 17. *Monuments on*] Monumentes of building on,

286, ll. 21–4. **Richard the second . . . Edward the third.*

[1] In the 1603 edition this is expanded into the long account of the Jewry under Coleman Street Ward: see i. 278–81.

[2] Cf. the passage at the top of this page.

288, ll. 9–13. *onely I read . . . where they dwelt*] onely I read of a branch of this family of Bassinges to haue spread it self into Cambridgeshire, near vnto a water or bourne, and was therefore for a difference from other of that name, called Bassing at the bourn, and more shortly Bassingborne. But this family is also worne out, and hath left the name to the place, where they dwelt.

ll. 32–6. **In the 21 . . . forfeyture thereof.*

290, ll. 1–4. **Thus haue you . . . Coopers hall.*

l. 8. **seuen pound.*

291, ll. 38–9. *to be noted*] meete to be noted

292, l. 5. *to be short*] to be short and plaine

293, l. 5. *I doubt*] I haue some doubt

294, l. 6. INSERTS after *Cripplegate*: obtaining first the kinges licence of Mortmaine, vnder the great seale of England

295, ll. 2–4. *Sir Rowland Heyward . . . there 1593*] The Lord William of Thame was buried in this Church, and so was his successor in that house Sir Rowland Heyward Mayor &c.

l. 4. **Richard Lee . . . 1597.*

l. 5. *sold there*] sold there (as is supposed)

ll. 7, 8. *Rokesley . . . dwelled*] Rokesley chiefe say maister of the kings mints, and Mayor of London in the yeare 1275. the third of Edward the first (in which office he continued 7. yeares together) dwelled

l. 11. *without other charge*] without being bounden to reparations or other charge:

296, ll. 21, 22. **Thomas Chalton, Mercer, Mayor 1450.*

297, l. 3. INSERTS after *Mirley, Knight*: Iohn Collet

l. 10. *for at this present it is*] but it is at this present

l. 12. INSERTS after *decayed*: and not worth a pinne,

298, l. 4. *to William Lambarde*] to my louing friend William Lambarde

l. 21. *Maister Glasier*] at this present mayster Glasier.

299, l. 31. INSERTS after *following*: to be buried there, to wit,

l. 31 to page 300, l. 4. **Alice, William & Iohn . . . Writhesley & Alianor*[1]

300, ll. 4, 5. *Alionor . . . Thomas Arnolde*] Elianor wife to Iohn Writh, Esquire, daughter to Thomas Arnald, Esquire,

ll. 6, 7. *Margaret with her daughter*] Margaret Writh her daughter.

l. 10. *1409*] 1439

l. 13. *Iohn Baronie*] Frauncis Baromi

l. 17. *King at Armes*] Herrald at Armes

301, ll. 11–14. **by the name of . . . the 15. yeare*

302, ll. 15–26. *Then in Golding lane . . . of the Almes people.*] Then in Golding Lane be also Almes houses, 13. in number, and so many poore people placed in them Rent free, and euery one hath two pence by the weeke for euer. Of the foundation of Thomas Hayes, Chamberlaine of

[1] On this see i. 204 and ii. 245 above.

London, in the latter time of Henry the eight, he left faire lands about Iseldonne, to maintaine his foundation: Maister Ironmonger hath the Order of them.

303, l. 12. INSERTS after *forty pound*: and in the Exchequer at thirtie nine pound ten shillings.

304, ll. 12, 13. *which stone wall . . . Faringdon ward.*] which is also of this ward.

305, ll. 9–11. **of Thomas Lichfield . . . 14 of E. the 2.*

l. 24. INSERTS before *Iohn Hewet*: Thomas Leichfield

306, ll. 21–3. **The men of this mistery . . . Richard the second.*

307, ll. 19–21. **William Gregory . . . remayneth.*

l. 27 to page 308, l. 37. **This colledge claymed . . . in the leafe 299*

309, ll. 1–10. *the Colledge church . . . saint Mathewes Gospel.*] the Colledge church was pulled downe and in place thereof many houses foorthwith builded, highly prised, and letten to strangers borne, and other such as claime the benefit of ye priuiledges, which were at the first granted only to ye church, and to the Deane, Prebends & Canons, seruing God according to ye foundation.

ll. 16 17. **it is now a Printing house.*

l. 32. *R. Cawod and T. Smith*] Robert Cawod and Thomas Smith

ll. 37–9. **Thomas Bilsington . . . Helmet vpon Cornhill.*

310, l. 5. *I. Hartshorne*] Iohn Hartshorne

l. 12. **the Clothworkers . . . ouersight thereof.*

ll. 16, 17. *and in the Exchequer, 6.l. 19.s*] and likewise in the Exchequer.

312, l. 22. *to the east . . . Augustines church*] to the gate

ll. 23–5. **which arch . . . yere 1361*

313, l. 36. *in West Cheape streete*] in Westcheape

l. 38. **as before . . . west Cheape streate*] vpon this occasion.

l. 39. INSERTS here the account of the founding of Cheap cross as on i. 265–6 above, from *Queene Elianor* to *let of cariages*, but omitting the words *in the yere 1533 against the coronation of Queen Anne.* The first edition then continues:

'In the yere 1581. the 21. of Iune in the night, the lowest Images about the said Crosse, were broken and defaced.

Whereupon proclamation was made, that who so wold bewray the doers therof, shuld haue fortie crownes: but nothing came to light. The Image of the blessed virgin at that time robbed of her son, and her armes broken by which shee staied him on her knees, her whole bodie also was strained with ropes so as it was readie to fall: But was in the yere 1595. again fastened and repaired. In the yeare 1596. about Bartholomewtide, a new Sonne mishapen (as borne out of time) was laide in her armes. The other Images remaining broken as before.

On the east side of the same Crosse, the steppes being taken thence, vnder the Images of Christes resurrection, was set vp a curious wrought frame of grey Marble, and in the same an Image in Alabaster of a woman (for the most part naked), and Thames water prilling from her breasts: but the same is oft times dried vp.[1]

314, l. 15. **Sir Alexander Auenon, Maior, 1570.*

ll. 18–21. *yeelding . . . yeres since.*] for thirtie shillings foure pence the yeares rent, but now increased much.

315, l. 1. *Iohn Standelfe*] Iohn Standelfe and Iohn Standelfe

ll. 4–20. **both of Ealdersgate street ward . . . common seale at that time.*

ll. 20–8. *At the north end . . . said Elizabeth.*] at the North end whereof, is one great house builded of stone, commonly called the Lord Windsor's house, but I haue read it by the name of Neuells Inne in siluer street, and at the ende of Monkes well streete.

l. 29 to page 316, l. 3. *This companie . . . hall in that street, &c.*] whom obtained their incorporation in the yeare one thousand sixtie and foure, the second of Edward the fourth, since the which time they builded theyr Hall.

316, l. 26. INSERTS after *for the Butchers*: and there is the Butchers Hall.

ll. 35, 36. **in the middest whereof the church stoode.*

l. 38 to page 317, l. 2. **and there is . . . wals of the citie.*

318, ll. 16, 17. **their Conduit head . . . Henrie the third, &c.*

l. 31. *by Pattents*] by pattent of

319, l. 37. *Monuments*] [The list in the 1603 edition has been rearranged, with some additions.]

322, l. 33. *This church hath*] a proper church, and hath,

l. 38. *Anthony Cage*] — Cage

l. 39 to page 323, l. 3. **Allen at Condit . . . in the same streete.*

323, l. 36. *H. Reade*] Henry Reade

326, ll. 19–21. **Also the new . . . yeare 1256.*

327, ll. 23–6. **In the yeare 1408 . . . other easements.*

l. 37. *at the dispence*] painted about the Cloyster: at the speciall request and dispence

328, l. 32. **neare vnto a Carpenters yard.*

329, l. 26. *in the yeare . . . remaineth.*] then their former church was, and so it still remaineth to that vse.

330, l. 2. INSERTS before *Robert*: In this chapell were buried

l. 3. *were*] and were

l. 4. **or coped*

l. 5. **before the said Chappell*

l. 11. *citie . . . milles.*] citie, to beare three winde-milles.

l. 22. INSERTS after *because hee*: was borne in London and

l. 28. *heard*] heard off,

l. 32. INSERTS after *downe*] and broken also.

331, ll. 22, 23. **This Pulpit . . . defaced.*

[1] The paragraph *In the yeare* 1599, &c., (i. 267) is of course an addition of the 1603 edition.

332, ll. 20–4. *before Aprill . . . collected.*] But concerning the steeple litle was done, through whose default God knoweth: it was said that the money appointed for newe building of the steeple, was collected, and brought to the hands of Edmond Grindall then Bishop of London.

ll. 36–7. *new buried . . . shewed*] now buried in the West Ile, with an Epitaph, as in another place I haue shewed.

333, ll. 2–4. **Martin . . . Pateshull 1240.*

ll. 7, 8. *Bishop . . . Quire, 1262*] B. 1262

ll. 8–15. **Geffrey de Acra . . . Middlesex, 1309.*

ll. 24, 25. *new worke . . . church*] newe woorke of Powles,

335, ll. 8–10. **Sir Raph . . . Quire, 1308.*

l. 11. *Guildford . . . Apostles, 1313.*] Gylford, L. Marshall was buried in the Postles chapell, 1313.

ll. 12–28. * *William Chateleshunte . . . north doore, 1353.*

l. 32. **proper chapple, and*

336, l. 1. INSERTS after *call him*: Sir Raphe de Hingham, cheefe Iustice of both Benches successiuely, buried in the side of the North walke, against the Quire, 1308. Sir Iohn Pulteney, Draper, Mayor, 1348, in a faire chapell by him builded, on the North side of Powles, wherein he founded 3. chaplains. Richard de Plesseys in the North walke before Saint Georges chapell, 1361. Sir Symon Burley, constable of Douer, and Chamberlaine to Richard the second, knight of the Garter, beheaded, lyeth buried in the North walke against the Quire. Adam de Bery, Mayor, in the yeare 1364, buried in a Chapel of Saint Mary Magdalen: or of the holy Ghost, called Holmes Colledge.

Roger Holmes Chauncelor and Prebend of Powles, was buried there 1400.

ll. 1–8. **Michael Norborow, . . . doore of Pauls, 1390.*

ll. 10–20. **sir Richard Burley . . . Beauchampe, 1423.*

l. 22 to page 337, l. 27. * *Walter Sherington . . . shrine; and of later time*

337, l. 29. * *Thomas Linicar, Doctor of Phisicke*

l. 31. **Iohn Dowman Canon of Paules, 1525.*

338, l. 11. *where a merry*] whereof a mery

l. 14. *saint Thomas*] S. Georges

ll. 17, 18. *to bee buried there.*] and so an end for Paul's church.

l. 31. *namely, A.B.C.*] namely A.B.C. Or Absies

339, l. 11. *and belongeth*] and belonged

l. 23. *here hath beene*] here, be

l. 24. * *William Seuenoake Maior, 1418.*

ll. 26, 27. *Sir Roger Cholmley*] Sir Roger Cholemly, some say William Seuen-Oake, Maior &c.

ll. 27, 28. **Iohn Went . . . Chanteries there.*

340, l. 5. **and from thence to Leycester.*

ll. 22–3. *in my Annales I haue*] in other places hath beene

l. 28. *were buried*] are interred, or buried

340, l. 36. INSERTS after *Brewes*: Dame Iahu, daughter to Thomas, wife to Syr Gnight

341, ll. 12–14. **The Countesse of Huntington . . . buried here 1443*

l. 23. *Nicholas Eare*] Nicholas Carre, Esquire

l. 30. *Carden*] Cardin, alias Carden

342, l. 3. *new builded*] first builded

l. 5. *1361.*] 1361, which was the 35 of Edward the third

l. 16. *I. Oxney*] Iohn Oxney

ll. 17, 18. **Iohn Leiland the famous Antiquary*

l. 20. **Barber Chirurgion*

ll. 20, 21. **Iohn Mundham . . . E. the second.*

ll. 34, 35. *Prebend houses*] Prebend almes houses

343, ll. 17, 18. INSERTS after *Mountgodard streete*: by all likelihood; and after *Goddards*: or Pots

l. 21. **of olde time*

344, l. 2. *the fifteene 50. pound.*] the fifteene in London at 54. pound, and in the Exchequer at 53. pound 6. shillings, 8. pence.

l. 33. *Then is Fryday streete*] Then is there one other streete, which is called Friday streete

345, ll. 12–27. **at Breadstreet corner . . . Next to be noted*

ll. 27–28. *frame of . . . the Walles*] frame and front of faire houses, and shops, that be within all the walles

l. 33. *It contayneth*] It continueth

346, l. 9. INSERTS after *present*: as of olde time also

l. 22. *stalles*] stables

ll. 26–9. **Walter Turke . . . the other iiii.s.*

l. 38. **Robert Basset, Salter, Mayor 1476.*

347, ll. 6–14. **In the 23. of Henry the eight . . . through Cheape, Cornehill &c.*

ll. 14–6. *More . . . steeple of stone.*] The steeple of this church had sometime a faire speere of stone, but taken downe vpon this occasion

ll. 17, 18. *about mid day . . . lightning*] about noone or midday, fell a great tempest at London, in the ende whereof, happened a great lightening

l. 35. **to that parish*

348, l. 13. *same side*] same East side

l. 15. *name of . . . the twenteeth*] name I haue not read: other then that in the 20

l. 20. *Basing*] any Basing

ll. 23, 24. *Arched Vaultes . . . The same is now*] Arched Vaultes of stone, and with Arched Gates, now

349, ll. 2–4. **for the most part . . . placed*

ll. 5–7. **as the labours . . . Vniuersity of Oxford*

ll. 7–9. *he writing . . . here to touch.*] wherein the Authour writing a Chapter of Gyaunts, and hauing beene deceiued by some Authours, too much crediting their smoothe speeche, hath set downe more matter then troth, as partly (and also against my will) I am enforced to touch.

349, l. 10. **as he tearmeth it*

ll. 16–19. **The errour . . . or shin bone.*

l. 19. *Notwithstanding, it*] Wherevnto [1]

350, l. 7. *set vp*] set vp in the streete

l. 8. *principall house*] principall Hall or house.

351, l. 5. *Note that*] Such

ll. 13, 14. **Wil. de Auinger . . . Ed. the 3.*

ll. 19–21. **There was of . . . chauntries there.*

ll. 28–37. **Of these Cordwayners . . . to pay xxx. s.*

352, l. 7. *36. li. 18. s. 2. d.*] at thirtie sixe *pound tenne shillings.*

VOLUME II

2, l. 19. *as followeth.*] are therein none.

ll. 20–5. *John Brian . . . Northamptonshire, 1572.*

l. 27. *proper*] comely

ll. 28, 29. **so that . . . the church :*

ll. 30, 31. *of some . . . Bey*] of some Colde Abbey

l. 31 to page 3, l. 13. *as standing . . . ornamentes.*] but I could neuer learne the cause why it should bee so called, and therefore I will let it passe. There bee monuments in this Church, of Andrew Aubery, Grocer, Mayor, and Thomas Fryar, Fishmonger, in the year 1351. who gaue to this church and parish one plot of ground, containing fiftie six foote in length, and fortie three foote in breadth at both endes, to be a buriall place for the dead of the said Parish, the twentie sixt of Edward the third. Also Thomas Madesley, Clarke, and Iohn Pylor gaue to the Wardens of that Parish one shop and a house in Distar lane, for the continual repairing of the bodie of that church, the belles and Ornaments, the twentieth of Richard the 2.

3, l. 14. *in this church*] there

l. 16. *Nicholas Wolberge*] Richard Walberge

ll. 18–23. *John Suring . . . Barde, Fishmonger, 1528.*] and others.

5, ll. 2–4. **Iohn Skip . . . in this church.*

l. 30. *in this church*] to this church

l. 31. **he founded a chauntrie*

6, l. 9. INSERTS after *little* : vpon the Thames.

9, l. 17. INSERTS after *but now* : that case is altered.

11, l. 27. *Exchequer . . . pence*] Exchequer at twentie pound.

13, ll. 22–8. *There was also . . . woodwharfes in place.*] There was also a messuage by Baynardes Castle, called Legates Inne, in the 7. of Edward the fourth, where be now diuers Wood Wharfes.

[1] Cf. p. 353 for the original draft of the story of Gerard the Giant.

13, ll. 31, 32. *and made . . . Puddle Wharfe.*] and made Puddle like, it is (as I suppose) called Puddle Wharfe.

15, ll. 14, 15. **Doctor Caldwell . . . king at Armes.*

ll. 28, 29. **Iohn Parnt founded a chauntry there.*

l. 29. INSERTS after *Wardrobe*: I haue not read by whom the same was builded, neither when, or for what cause, but only that

ll. 32, 33. *builded . . . deceased*] was lodged there: this house then bearing the name of the King's Wardrobe, in the 5 of E. the 3. The saide Iohn Beauchampe deceased

l. 34 to page 16, l. 2. **His Executors . . . second of his raigne.*

16, ll. 20–4. **On the East side . . . repaired it.*

l. 28. *is Darby house*] Garter House, so called of the Office there kept by Garter king of Heraults, and other Heraults. This house was

18, ll. 4, 5. **Richard Woodroffe . . . Randolph Esquire, 1583.*

ll. 18–20. **as a place . . . to Carter lane.*

ll. 21–30. *The other . . . house there.*] The other Sermon Lane, or Sheremoniers Lane, the reason of their names so giuen, I haue not learned, but I finde Sermon Lane or Sheremoniers Lane, so called in the foureteenth of Edward the first, and a place there, to be called the blacke loft, with foure shops adioyning. I finde also that in the thirteenth of Richard the second, William de la Pole had an house there; it may bee supposed that lane to take name of such as cutte and rounded the plates to be coyned into Esterling pence, for the place of coyning was in the olde Exchaunge neare vnto this.

19, l. 28. *as in my Annales I haue expressed.*] as in another place I haue at large reported.

20, ll. 15–18. **in place of Peter Colledge . . . for a Well.*

ll. 22, 23. **in the Exchequer . . . shillinges.*

21, ll. 16, 17. **lately replenished with houses builded*

22, l. 35 to page 23, l. 4. **Henry the third granted . . . E. the third the 26. of his raigne*

23, ll. 4–7. *it was gouerned . . . the yeare 1423.*] this Hospital was since repayred about the yeare 1423, of the goodes and by the executors of Richarde Whittington, sometime Maior of London, and was gouerned by a Maister, and eight brethren, being Priestes for the church, and foure Sisters to see the poore serued.

l. 21. **or Nanfant*

l. 22. *Lord saint George*] Lord Sir George

l. 34 to page 24, l. 13. **thus:*

Beholde how ended is . . . .

. . . *and partly do possesse them.*

24, l. 16. *Sturgeon*] Surgeon

25, l. 31. **pryor*

26, ll. 32–4. * *This priorie . . . in the yeare 1410.*

27, ll. 27, 28. **notwithstanding . . . of parliament*

l. 33. **for such as will giue greate rents.*

28, l. 9. INSERTS after *late*: wise and worthy

l. 18. *gaue the remnant of the priorie church*] gaue it

ll. 21, 22. *were put out . . . parrish church*] were once more put out and then all the saide church

l. 31. *was performed.*] is performed.

l. 31. INSERTS after *performed*: for it is more easie to pul downe then to set vp and builde.

ll. 31, 32. **The parish haue . . . serue their turne.*

29, l. 25 to page 33, l. 22. **For example to note: . . . for Iustes in Smithfield.*

33, l. 27. **and a garden plot.*

34, ll. 14, 15. **Next to this Church . . . Sarasens head.*

ll. 29, 30. *owne charges . . . 1500. l.*] owne onely charges, (amounting to the summe of 1500. pound) and by him finished.

ll. 38, 39. *for so I find, . . . the sixt.*] about the 37. of Henry the sixt.

35, ll. 1–14. **This house was . . . all reprises, x.s.*

ll. 15, 16. *so called . . . of Elye.*] commonly called Ely place, for that it pertaineth vnto the Bishops of Ely

ll. 16–20. **William de Luda . . . Chappell there.*

l. 20. *More*] the which

ll. 21–4. *by the name . . . appeareth by patent*, by the name of his Mannor and sixe tenements in Oldeborne to the Church and couent of Ely, as appeareth by pattent of Record

36, l. 22. *Robert Yorke.*] Roger Yorke

39, ll. 3, 4. *Thomas Lord Writhesley . . . buried 1550.*] an Earle of Southampton buried there

l. 18. **William Sydnam . . . chauntry there.*

l. 34. *which is of Chauncery*] which is the second Inne of Chauncerie

l. 36 to page 40, l. 15. **and was founded . . . the king in capite.*

40, l. 15. *also of Chancery*] the thirde Inne of Chauncery

ll. 33, 34. **whereof I haue spoken in an other place.*

41, l. 15. INSERTS after *1471*: neere vnto Shooe lane.

ll. 32, 33. **Nicholas Coningston . . . chaunteries there.*

l. 36 to page 42, l. 7. **by gift . . . patent the 3. of Ed. the second.*

42, l. 7. *After . . . Robert Clifford*] after whose death

l. 17. **but returned againe to the Cliffordes*

45, ll. 15–21. *Saint Bridges . . . Grapes and leaues. &c.*] S. Bridget or S. Bride (as they terme it) now a fayre church, the which William Venor, Esquier, Warden of the Fleete aboute the yeare 1480, increased with a large body, and side Isles from the Quire (which of olde time was the whole Church) downe to the west end, all through this Church builded of his charges is wrought in the stone worke, round about both within and without, the figure or likenes of a vine, with Clusters of Grapes amongst the leaues &c.

ll. 21–8. **The partition . . . Chauntries there.*

l. 35. *Lord Treasurer*] one of her Maiesties most honorable Counsaile.

45, l. 35. **who hath . . . stately buildings.*

46, l. 21. *were*] lye

l. 32. *were buried*] lye

48, l. 26. INSERTS after *Warwick*: & others in other places

49, l. 20. *riding of*] riding vpon

51, l. 9. INSERTS after *Ware*: twentie miles from London, was the thirde, he died

52, l. 2. *fifteene . . . one shilling.*] fifteen in London at 35 *l.*, and in the Exchequer at 34 *l.* 10 *s.*

56, ll. 20, 21. **The Abbot of Wauerley had a House there.*

57, l. 22. *Iohn Gower . . . Poet*] Iohn Gower a learned Gentleman and a famous Poet (but no knight as some haue mistaken it)

ll. 24, 25. **in the chapple . . . chauntrie, he lieth*

l. 33. *written*] set forth

l. 33 to page 58, l. 16. **and this last . . . fell downe in the yeare 1469.*

58, ll. 29, 30. *William Greuill . . . his wife*] Margaret wife to William Greuell Esquire, and

59, l. 1. INSERTS after *Gower*: Poet,

l. 1. **Iohn Duncell, Marchant Taylor, 1516*

ll. 2–9. **Thomas Tong . . . deceased the 24. of May, 1598. &c.*

60, l. 1. *solde*] hath solde

l. 2. *or to Marchants*] or to certaine Merchants

61, l. 39. *Immorth*] Imworth

62, ll. 7, 8. **William Brandon . . . E. the 4.*

l. 27. INSERTS after *thereof*: in the raigne of E. the 3.

63, l. 4. *And then*] Then next haue yee

l. 4. **Theeues lane by S. Thomas Hospitall*

ll. 11, 12. *But . . . Canons Regular*] This Hospitall was againe new founded, by Peter de Rupibus, Bishop of Winchester, for Cannons Regular

l. 21. INSERTS after *Abbot*: and Couent

l. 30. INSERTS after *This Hospitall*: beeing in the yeare 1220 made to dispend three hundred fortie foure pound by the yeare

64, l. 13. *remaineth as*] remaineth now as it was before

67, ll. 31, 32. **Leofstane . . . London 1115*

70, l. 36. *to Wapping in the west*] To Wapping in the Woze, and Wapping it selfe

71, ll. 11–13. *which runneth south . . . this lane to*] (which runneth South by the Hermitage to Wapping) to

ll. 15–22. *and to the Mannor of Shadwell . . . mile from Radcliffe.*] Not farre from thence, of very late where of old time stoode the Mannor of Shadwell, belonging to the Deane of Powles, there haue beene raised many small Tenements towards Radliffe; and Radliffe itselfe hath bin so increased in building Eastward (in place where I haue knowne faire hedges, long rowes of Elme, and other trees) that the same haue now taken hold of Limehurst (or Lime hoste itselfe), commonly called Lime house, sometime distant a mile from Radliffe &c.

71, l. 22 to page 72, l. 5. **Hauing said this much . . . and so to Blake wal.*

72, ll. 6-8. *diminished by Merchants . . . whereof I haue spoken.*] diminished, by incrochments for building of small tenements, and taking in of garden plots, timbaryars or what they list.

From this Tower Hill towards Aldegate (being a long continuall streete) amongst other buildings, was that Abbey of Nunnes, called the Minorities, or Minories, whereof I haue spoken. And on the other side of that streete, lyeth the Ditche, without the wall of the Citie, from the Tower vnto Aldegate.

l. 19. *other purprestures*] other prepesterous like

73, ll. 7, 8. *this feate . . . purchased*] this fact, that parish purchased

ll. 9–15. **but I finde in Record . . . Aldegate of London, &c.*

ll. 22, 23. *vp to the Barres . . . Norton fall gate*] Thence vp to the Barres and to Norton fall gate

ll. 27, 28. **Stephen Grausend . . . benejactor therevnto*

ll. 28, 29. *Louell knight of the Garter*] Louell, brought vp in Lincolnes Inne

l. 36. INSERTS after *and other*: And neare therevnto are builded two publique houses for the acting and shewe of Comedies, Tragedies, and Histories, for recreation. Whereof the one is called the Courtein, the other the Theatre: both standing on the Southwest side towards the field.

l. 38. *Sewers ditch*] Sors Ditche, or Sewers Ditche

74, l. 7. *Golding lane*] Grubstreete

l. 15. *but those houses belong*] belonging

ll. 19, 20. *a house builded . . . Berwardes Lane*] a fayre house lately builded by the Lorde Iohn Powlet. Next to that, a large house, with gardens of pleasure, builded ⟨by⟩ Iasper Fisher. From this vp to the West ende of Hog Lane

l. 21. *then the*] Then was the

l. 35. **for a small portion of money*

ll. 38, 39. *neare as much . . . purchase*] which some thinke to be neare as much, as the houses cost him in the purchase

75, ll. 8–27. *sir Iohn Elrington . . . Harry Yong 1545.*[1]

l. 33. *Queene Elizabeth*] the Queene that now is

l. 36 to page 76, l. 12. **One note of Shoreditch . . . Bethelem-Crosse*

76, l. 12. *and so . . . that Hospitall*] Now will I passe through the Hospitall of S. Mary Bethelem

ll. 30, 31. *other the ditches . . . More ditch*] other ditches thereabout

77, l. 19. **whereof I mind not much to argue*

78, ll. 11, 12. *worse case . . . inclosure*] worse case then euer before it was, by the meanes of inclosure

79, l. 8. **by casualtie of fire*

82, ll. 8–16. **and it is to be noted . . . should be buried.*

l. 22. *he also gaue them the three Acres*] But the three acres

[1] This insertion in the text of 1603 explains the ungrammatical sentence 'Notwithstanding that,' &c.

83, l. 7. **Philip Morgan Bishop of Ely, 1434.*

85, l. 10. **Iohn Botell*

86, ll. 5–23. **And of later time . . . reparation of that church.*

l. 25. *houses . . . namely*] houses for Gentlemen and others, are now builded aboute this Priorie, especially

l. 33. **now dammed vp.*

87, l. 3. *Porte Poole*] Porte Poole lane

ll. 29, 30. *Adioyning . . . sometime*] The same was after

ll. 31, 32. **Robert de Curars . . . yeare 1147.*

88, ll. 2, 3. *this old . . . Lincolnes*] this Southampton

l. 14. INSERTS after *Seale*: deceased in the yeare 1578.

ll. 18–27. **This ground he had . . . Cittie, cart. 11. H. 3.*

90, l. 20. INSERTS after *common lawes*: this house was greatly increased with new buildinges.

l. 36. INSERTS after *conuersorum*: Moreouer (saith the same Recorde) in the 20 of Edward the third, the saide king sent commandement vnder his great seale, to the Mayor and Sheriffes of London, willing them to make proclamations in euery Ward of the Citie and suburbes, that all leprous persons, within the saide Citie & suburbes should auoid within fifteen daies, and that no man suffer any such leprose person to abide within his house, vppon paine to forfeite his saide house, and to incur the King's farther displeasure. And that they should cause the saide Lepers to be remoued into some out places of the fieldes, from the haunt or company of all sound people: wherevpon it followed that the citizens required of the Gardian of Saynt Giles Hospitall, to take from them and to keepe continually the number of foureteene persons, according to the foundation of Matilde the Queen, which was for Leprose persons of the Citie of London and the shire of Middlesex.

IN MARGIN: Hospitall of S. Giles founded for Leprose persons of the Citie of London and shire of Middlesex. *Pattent.* All leprose people to be voided the citie & suburbs. *W. Dunthorne.*

l. 37 to page 91, l. 7. **This Hospitall was founded . . . Drapers of London, for xxx.li.*

91, ll. 8–12. *prisoners . . . this life.*] prisoners conueyed towards Tyborne, there to be executed, were saluted with a Bowle of Ale, thereof to drinke as their last refreshing in this life.

l. 21. **of Lancaster.*

l. 22 to p. 92, l. 7. *Next without the Barre . . . Excester house*] Next without the barre and libertie of the citie of London and the liberties of the Dutchy of Lancaster, on the said south side or left hande neere vnto the Riuer of Thames, amongst other buildings memorable for greatnesse, the first was Excester house

92, ll. 9–17. **who was first builder . . . raigne of Henry the 6, &c.*

l. 21. *of the Earle of Essex lodging there.*] of the late Earle of Essex there inhabiting

l. 26. *I haue not read as yet.*] I haue not heard nor can coniecture

93, ll. 1–5. **Then was there . . . enlarging of this house.*

ll. 9, 10. *(*commonly . . . Couentrie*) his*

ll. 10–12. **this house . . . Edward the first.*

l. 34. **mee, for satisfying of some Denyers thereof*

95, l. 36 to page 96, l. 1. **where sir Robert Cecill . . . commoditie of passengers.*

96, ll. 1–10. *Richard the 2 . . . on that south side.*] And thus far on this South side the high streete is of the libertie of the Dutchy of Lancaster.

Iuie bridge in the high streete hath a way or low going doune vnder it, stretching to the Thames: the like as sometime had the Strand bridge before spoken of.

This whole streete from Temple Bar to the Sauoy was commanded to be paued, and Tole to be taken towards the charges thereof in the 24. yeare of Henry the sixt.

l. 12. OMITS **as is afore shewed, is.* INSERTS: standeth a pair of Stockes and then

ll. 25–26. **but out of . . . of the Danes.*

97, ll. 1–7. **Thus much . . . Chancerie, &c.*

ll. 20–3. **There is in . . . is 13. s. 4. d.*

98, l. 17. *the estate.*] the estate of England.

l. 19. INSERTS after *Bedfords house*: which is a goodly house.

l. 20. INSERTS after *Iuy Bridge*: ouer against the olde Bedforde house, namely called Russell house and Dacres house, now the house of Sir Thomas Cecile Lorde Burghley,

ll. 22–9. *in the liberty . . . doth yet remaine.*] and stretcheth to S. Giles in the fielde. Then had ye the Chappell of our Lady called the Pew, with an house wherein sometime were distraight and Lunatike people.

Amongst other thinges of this Chappel I haue read that on the 17. of Februarie in the yeare of Christ 1452. by negligence of a scholler appointed by his Scholemaister, to put forth the lights of this Chappell, the Image of our Lady, richly decked with Iewels, pretious stones, pearles, and ringes (more then any Ieweller could iudge the price) (for so sayth mine Author) was with all this apparrell, ornamentes and Chapple itselfe brent.[1]

IN MARGIN: Chappell of our Lady in the Pew, an house belonging to Bethlem. Chappell of our Lady the Pew brent. *Iohn Piggot.*

l. 37 to page 99, l. 5. *But in the yeare . . . to that vse*] Of later time king Henry the eight hauing fayre stabling for horses there in the yeare 1534. and the 28. of his raigne, it was burned with many great houses and much hay therein: but it was againe reedified in the raignes of king Edwarde the sixt, and Queene Marie

102, ll. 21–7. **Whereof one . . . Earle of Lincolne.*

l. 36 to page 103, l. 3. **Edward the third, in the 17. . . . honour of S. Thomas. But*

[1] Cf. corresponding passage of 1603 edition on ii. 121.

103, l. 33. INSERTS after *Maltorth*: I thinke Custome

104, ll. 11–14. **In the 51 . . . without any wages.*

106, l. 13. INSERTS after *their annoyance*: This church of S. Margaret (which that king Edward builded) continued till the daies of king Edward the first, at what time the staple of Woolles was at Westminster, and then the parishioners and Merchantes of the Staple builded it all of new, the great chancell excepted, which was done by the Abbots of Westminster as is afore shewed.[1]

l. 16. **whereof . . . in the foundation*

107, ll. 34, 35. **kinges Bench . . . Iustice of the*

108, ll. 23, 24. *who gouerned . . . L. Andrewes.*] now Resident.

l. 35. **Hugolyn . . . the Confessor.*

110, l. 4. INSERTS after *Dawbeny*: Earle of Bridgewater OMITS *Lord Lieutenant of Callice*

l. 14. **elect*

l. 15. **sonne to Iohn Baron of Dudley*

l. 16. *Edward Hungerforde knight*] Edmond

ll. 17, 18. **daughter to Alane Buxull knight, 1416.*

ll. 19, 20. **sonne to Bourchier . . . Barnet*

l. 21. *Iohn Bourchier . . . Barnet, 1471*] the Lord Barons, and both slain at Barnet

l. 23. **Gray*

ll. 31, 32. *Robert Hawley Esquier*] Robert Hall knight

111, l. 17. *Francis Howard Countesse of Hertford, 1598*] Elizabeth Countesse of Hertford

ll. 20–3. **Sir Henry Cary . . . stately monument.*

112, ll. 16–33. **The parish church of S. Margaret . . . in the yeare 1499.*[2]

113, l. 36. INSERTS after *in the accounts*: The like commaundement, the said king Henry gaue to Hugh Gifford and William Browne, that vpon Fryday next after the Epiphany, they should cause to be fed in the great Hal of Windsor, at a good fire, all the poore and needy children that could be found, and the kings children, being waighed and measured, their weight and measure to be distributed for their good estates.[3]

114, ll. 18–24. **Also the Maior . . . assise and warde.*

116, ll. 3, 4. **Iohn Boterell . . . workes.*

l. 24. INSERTS after *Fabian*: the Chronickler

119, l. 1. *high treasurer.*] high Treasurer of England

120, ll. 11–13. **King Iohn . . . Westminster, &c.*

ll. 26–9. **since vsually rung . . . in the towne.*

l. 29. *More, that . . . written*] about the biggest of which (as I haue beene informed) was written

l. 34 to page 121, l. 8. **But these Bels . . . Thirtie six thousand shall find me.*

[1] Cf. vol. ii. p. 112, for parallel passage in 1603 edition.
[2] Cf. parallel passage above.
[3] Cf. vol. i. p. 90 above.

121, ll. 17–33. **By this chappel of S. Stephen . . . Edward the fifth, &c.*[1]

123, l. 9. INSERTS before *erected*: first practized and

ll. 11–15. **William Caxton . . . monasteries.*

l. 32 to page 124, l. 2. **In the yeare of Christ . . . the first dinner.*

125, l. 11. **saith some.*

ll. 17–27. **more then this as followeth . . . receiued here.*

ll. 27–9. *And now . . . There remaineth*] But to my matter of our London Bishops as I finde it written: First, there remaineth

126, l. 17. *the foureteenth, fledde*] the fourteenth and the last for he fled

128, l. 4. INSERTS before *in the Isle*: at Crotsey

l. 9. INSERTS after *Paule*: on the eighteenth kallendes of December

l. 30. *Heatbright*] Hutbright

129, ll. 7, 8. *but there . . . of them.*] but there remaineth memories there

ll. 27, 28. *Robert . . . 7 yeares*] Robert Bishop of London, 7 yeares a monk of Gemet, in Normandie:

ll. 35, 36. *and appeareth . . . Paules church.*

131, l. 14. **or aboue*

l. 37 to page 132, l. 7. **He admonished . . . infected therewithall.*

132, l. 10. **coped*

ll. 17, 18. **or aboue*

ll. 18, 19. **close at . . . Fauconbridge.*

l. 33. **since I kept house for*

133, l. 15. *Bentworth*] Wentworth or Bentworth

l. 31. *Chancellour*] Lord Chancellour

l. 34. *Treasurer of the Exchequer*] Treasurer of England

l. 37. *in Powles . . . aultar.*] at S. Bartilmewes Pryorie in Smithfield.

134, ll. 8, 9. *the kings Chancellor*] Lord Chancellour

135, l. 17. **and the tombe was taken downe.*

136, l. 5. INSERTS after *Stebunheth*: otherwise called Stebinhith

l. 6. INSERTS after *Stebunheth*: or Stebinhith

ll. 6, 7. **with al and singular . . . belonging*

ll. 16, 17. *for . . . seruice*] for his good seruice

ll. 18–20. *with all . . . Hackney way*] and the landes in

ll. 29–31. **to be holden . . . knights fee.*

137, l. 18. *saint Thomas*] S. Georges

ll. 23–5. *consecrated . . . yeare 1598*] nowe sitteth Bishop of London in this yeare 1598

140, l. 14. Alde Mary church. New Mary Church, or Mary le Bow.]
St. Mary Aldmary Church.
S. Mary Bow at the North corner of Cordwayner street

l. 25. **Vpwell*

141, l. 20. *by Paules*] by Paules gate

143, ll. 6, 7. **a Cathedral church . . . Westminster and*

145, l. 9. **to the number of —.*

[1] See p. 264 above.

146, ll. 15–33. **also the cittizens*[1] . . . *of the superiors, &c.*

l. 37. **God and*

148, ll. 8–15. *Godfrey Portgraue . . . God you keepe.*] Godfrey Portgraue and to all the Burgesses of the Citie of London, in as large forme as they enioyed the same in the time of K. Edward before the conquest.

ll. 20, 21. **buried at Bermondsey.*

149, l. 18. *of Maiors as followeth.*] of Maior I finde as followeth.

151, ll. 7–9. **Walter Brune . . . saint Mary Spittle.*

153, l. 29. **patent xi. Henry 3.*

ll. 32–5. **The liberties . . . common seale.*

154, l. 16. INSERTS under date *1235*: This yeare Walter Brune citizen of London, and Rosia his wife, founded S. Mary Spittle without Bishopsgate.

155, ll. 6–9. **Gerard Bat was . . . precedent yeare.*

ll. 23, 24. **Queene Hith . . . of London.*

158, ll. 5–7. **This Alen . . . Earle of Surrey.*

ll. 18, 19. *C. Hugh . . . Tower.*] M. Hugh Fitz Thomas.

159, l. 10. **at London.*

164, ll. 14–17. **More hee graunted by his letters . . . for his time.*

165, ll. 12–14. **The king graunted . . . kings armes.*

ll. 23, 24. *The price . . . Gallon.*] The price of Gascone Wines at London, not to bee solde aboue foure pence the gallon, and Renish wine sixe pence the gallon.

168, l. 37. **or Skinner, as I find in record.*

171, ll. 32, 33. *Winter . . . Candlemasse.*] Winter eueninges.

172, ll. 2–11. **this William Seuenoke . . . which was graunted*

177, l. 1. **euerie Sergeant to haue his yeoman*

179, ll. 2–5. **the king made . . . Black Hith field.*

ll. 22–5. **hee was sworne . . . redressed them.*

180, l. 1. **Marchant taylor, after of Counsell to Henrie the eight.*

182, ll. 13–15. **The fore named Shiriffes . . . them againe.*

186, ll. 12–20. **1599. The 41 . . . Robert Lee, Marchant taylor.*

l. 26. **Iames Dalton*

l. 29, to page 195, l. 26. *but hee being now . . . to trauell further in this Worke.*

204, ll. 23–5. *in rewarde . . . were knighted*] in memory and reward of which seruice the Cittie had a Daggar added to their shielde of Armes, and the Maiors haue beene most commonly sithens knighted.

IN MARGIN: After the common opinion of men of late times.[2]

218, l. 4. *400 yeares*] three hundred yeares

[1] In the 1598 edition there is no stop at 'city' and a full stop after 'at that time'.

[2] The explanation of Stow's tampering with his friend's original text is to be found on i. 221 above. The marginal note was no doubt Stow's own.

NOTES

For a list of abbreviations used in the citation of authorities see p. 389 below.

PAGE **1**, ll. 1–25. *As the Romane writers, &c.* The original draft in *Harley MS.* 538, f. 1, preserves a version which differs from either of the printed editions:

'The foundacion of the Citie of London.'

'Aftar the common opinion, and as writithe Geffrey Monmouthe, Brute the first kynge of the Britaynes in this Ysle about the yere of the worlde 2855, the yere before Christes natiuite 1108, builded a citie nere vnto a riuar now called Thames, and named it Trenouantum, or new Troy. Kynge Lud repayred this Citie with fayre buildings, Towres, and Walls, and named it Cair Lud, or Lud's Towne, more he builded on the west parte of this citie a stronge gate naming it Lud gate, and this he did about the yere before Christes birthe 66. This Lud had yssue two sons, &c.'

The text of the early part of the *Survey* as now contained in *Harley MS.* 538 is much disordered. The third chapter, 'Of Riuers, Brooks, &c.,' is in a fragmentary state; this is to be explained no doubt by the existence of a revised draft in *Tanner MS.* 464—see note below. The text of the early chapters in the *Harley MS.* agrees fairly closely with the edition of 1598, but with some occasional variations: e.g. p. 6, l. 20, 'faynt and cowardous hartes'; and p. 7, ll. 5–7, 'was naythar man of his handes nor good of counsel, but gyven to unlawfull &c.'

5, l. 14. *the first that inwalled this Citie.* For notices of the most recent discoveries on the Roman wall see articles in *Archaeologia*, lii. 615 (at Aldersgate), lix. 125–40 (at Newgate), lx. 169–250 (at various points between Moorgate and the Tower). Discoveries on the last occasion indicated that the wall was built about the end of the second century (lx. 183). Stow's citation of Simeon of Durham is an error; the reference to Helena is found only in Henry of Huntingdon, *Hist. Anglorum*, 30.

9, l. 8. *the wall on the southside.* There is good reason to believe that Thames Street marks the line of the most ancient walls, and that the street was outside on the river-bank; the gates and wharves below have been recovered from the river. See Lethaby, *London before the Conquest*, 90.

11–21. *Of Auncient and present Riuers, &c.* A revised draft of this chapter is bound up with Stow's transcripts of Leland's *Collections* in *Tanner MS.* 464 (1), ff. 155–63. In its characteristics it is exactly similar to the principal portion of the original in *Harley MS.* 538. It supplies some variations of interest and importance, viz.:—

Title: 'Of Rivars, brokes, bournes, pooles, wells, and conduits of freshe watars servinge the citie. As also of the ditchē 200 foote brode compassinge the wall of the same citie.'

Page 11, ll. 9–11. 'A runninge wattar called Walbrooke of running from the northe walle thrughe the midste of the city into the riuar of Thamis served the harte of the Citie.'

ll. 14–16. 'had his falle into the river of the Wells or Turnmill broke. Then was there among many other fayre waters thre principall fountaynes or wells in the subarbes.' l. 18. 'Riuilus [*Rivulus*] de Fags Well.' l. 27. 'served of swete and holsom waters.' l. 31. 'Thames the most excellent and famous Rivar of England.'

Page 12, ll. 7–10. '3000 pore men be put a worke. The River of the Wells in the West parte of this Citie, that it was of olde tyme so called may be proved thus.'

Page 13, ll. 33–6. 'the wirke fayled, and no good was done, so that the broke by menes of incrochementes vpon the banques, gitinges over it, and castinge in of fullage is now worse than ever it was.'

l. 39–*Page* 14, l. 2. 'any ditche by the walls thereof betwene Bishopsgate . . . entred the walle and therefore was of the wall called Walbrooke.'

Page 14, l. 6. 'an olde writen booke.' ll. 24–5. 'so that the course of Walbrooke is now hardly knowne. ll. 31–4. 'Shareborne lane, devidinge into dyvers rills or rillets . . . called Langbourne Warde, and of the borne devidinge into shares Share-borne Lane toke that name.' l. 37. 'the names afore shewed.' l. 38. 'Olde borne or Holeborne.'

Page 15, ll. 19–22. 'The fountayne at S. Clement Danes . . . alwayes full and never wantithe.'

Page 16, l. 6. 'Riuulus de Fags Well.' ll. 20–1. 'the land water falling into the small portion remayninge, inclosed with brike, is but a fowle water and is cawled Smithfild ponde.'

Page 17, ll. 34–5. *omits* 'again . . . Lambe 1577'.

Page 19, l. 12. *The separate title is omitted as in the* 1598 *edition.*

ll. 20–22. 'Which ditche beinge made for defence of the Citie hath at all tymes since, bene clensed and mayntayned as nede required.' ll. 24–8. 'stopped up for garden plottes, and houses builded thereon, even to the very wall and on many places upon both ditch and wall. I can but wishe that reformation might be hadde.'

12, l. 19. *the riuer of the Wels.* The name is simply Stow's translation of the *rivulus foncium* of William's Latin charter. But since, as Mr. W. H. Stevenson points out, this in its turn is 'a mere translation of the O. E. *wylriðe* of the Old-English original, it cannot have been more than a small stream (*riðe*) issuing from a spring or springs'. It is not clear that the words of the charter are intended to distinguish the *rivulus foncium* near the north corner (*aquilonare cornu*) of the wall from the running water which entered the city. Mr. Lethaby (*London* *before the Conquest*, 45–7) has argued that they were identical, and that the Well-brook is Walbrook itself (see further note below). If there was a brook draining west from the Moor, it must either have joined the Fagswell brook (see p. 272 below) or have run through the site of St. Bartholomew's Hospital, which before Rahere's time was but a marsh (*Cotton MS.*, Vespasian, B. ix, f. 7vo); if so the Well-brook might be the stream running through the Hospital to Holborn Bridge, which was covered in by licence from Edward I 'on account of the too great stench proceeding from it'. (Morley, *Bartholomew Fair*, 70.) In any case Stow's identification of the Well-brook with Turnmill-brook is an untenable conjecture; the latter was clearly the upper course of the Fleet, or that part of the Holeburn which ran parallel with Turnmill street.

Both the English and Latin texts of William's charter were edited by Mr. Stevenson in *Engl. Hist. Rev.* xi. 731–44: see also xii. 105–10.

l. 22. *Booke of Parliament recordes:* see *Rot. Parl.* i. 200. The original reads 'Holeburne', not 'Oldborne', and does not mention the river 'of Wells' as Stow's marginal note implies. The date should be 1306.

13, l. 13. *a fayre Register booke.* The fifteenth-century cartulary of the Hospital of St. John, *Cotton MS.*, Nero, E. vi, ff. 22–3, deeds relating to land in 'Trillemelstrete'.

14, l. 2. *of the wall called Walbrooke.* William's Charter (see p. 270 above) has simply 'usque in aquam currentem que ingreditur ciuitatem'. The stream is called Walebroc in 1114–33 (*Chron. Ramsey*, 248; *Cartul. de Rameseia*, i. 139, Rolls Ser.). Mr. Lethaby has suggested that Walbrook is really the Well-brook or *Rivulus Foncium.* It may have received a stream from the west, but the main stream came from the north-east, and there seems to be no proof of the use of the name outside the wall. The course of Walbrook is shown by a dotted line on the map at the end of this volume. For another map, and documents illustrating its history, see J. E. Price, *Roman Pavement in Bucklersbury*, pp. 48–55. For notes on recent excavations see *Archaeologia*, lx. 178–83, 230–3. For the legend of Gualo see p. 286 below.

l. 16. *to scowre.* The reading of 1598, viz. 'to couer', seems the better. See *Memorials*, 43, and *Letter-Book* C, 71.

l. 20. *Iohn de Beuer* called John le Benere in *Letter-Book* B, 216, C, 70, 72. See also *Cal. Wills*, i. 196. His name is printed as John de Bever or le Bevere in *Mun. Gild.* II. i. 95, 97.

l. 26. *Langborne water*, see note on p. 307.

l. 31. *Shareborne lane*, see note on p. 307.

l. 38. *Oldborne, or Hilborne.* Stow usually writes Oldborne; here he gives Hilborne as an alternative. Neither of his suggested derivations can be maintained. If Oldborne were correct the original form would be Ealdborne. But in early documents it is always Holeburne or Holeborne (as Stow himself wrote in his MS., see p. 270); Holeburne, the stream, occurs in *Domesday*, i. 127, and in a charter of Henry II (*Mon. Angl.* iv. 85), and

Holeburn strate in 1251 (*Hist. MSS. Comm.* 9th Rep. 3). The meaning is no doubt the burn in the hollow or hole (Isaac Taylor, *Words and Places*, 186–7); compare the neighbouring Hockley in the Hole. This is accepted by the best authorities. But the notorious, though later, association of Holborn with the hill has suggested support for Stow's second form. For a prolonged discussion see *Notes and Queries*, 8th ser. ix, x, xii, 9th ser. i, and 10th ser. ii and v. See also a paper by F. G. Waller on *The Holeburne* in *Trans. Lond. and Midd.* iv. 97–123, with a map.

15, l. 32. *Skinners well, neare vnto Clarkes well.* Stow's authority for the history of all these wells is the Cartulary of the Priory of the Nuns at Clerkenwell (*Cotton MS.*, Faustina, B. II). The most important document is one, dated April 1197, relating to the donations of Lecia de Montigny, widow of Henry Foliot, and daughter of Jordan Briset the founder; this is printed in *Monasticon*, iv. 83, and appears in another form in *Feet of Fines*, 7 and 8 Ric. I, No. 136, Pipe Roll Soc. 20. Skinners well is there described as lying in the valley between the Nuns' Priory and the Holeburn. It is traditionally said to have been on the west side of the Church of St. James, Clerkenwell. The Clerkes Well was fifty years ago still marked by a pump at the south-east corner of Ray Street (*London Past and Present*, i. 418, iii. 252). The two wells can have been only a little distance apart. So the Clerks' plays are described commonly as held at Skinnerswell. There does not seem to be any authority for the statement that the Skinners held plays. In Aug. 1385 the performance of the play that was customarily held at 'Skynneres welle' was forbidden (*Letter-Book*, H, 272). For other references to the plays see Malvern's continuation of Higden, ap. *Polychronicon*, ix. 47, 259; Nicolas, *Lond. Chron.* 91; Devon, *Issue Rolls of the Exchequer*, 244; Chambers, *Mediaeval Stage*, ii. 380.

16, l. 6. *Fagges well.* In 1197 certain lands are described as lying between the Garden of the Hospitallers and Smithfield Bar 'super rivulum de Fackeswell', and other lands as between that brook and 'Chikennelane'. (*Feet of Fines*, u. s.) This fixes the position of Faggeswell brook as approximately at the boundary of the City.

l. 7. *Todwell.* This is clearly a misreading by Stow of *Cotton MS.*, Faustina, B. II, f. 27, where certain land is described as 'inter Skinners well et Godewelle subtus viam usque in Holeburn'; Stow has written 'Skinnerswell' in the margin. In *Feet of Fines*, u. s., Godewell is described as between the Priory and the Holeburne; apparently somewhat to the south, and on the far side of the valley.

l. 7. *Loders wel.* About 1200 Muriel de Montigny gave the 'fons qui vocatur Loddereswell' to the Nuns of Clerkenwell with a right of way thereto from the Priory (*Cartulary*, f. 32 vo.).

l. 8. *Radwell.* This comes from the same source, 'terram quam Osbertus tenuit in Redwell' (*Cartulary*, ff. 6, 39). The reference is apparently to Radwell in Hertfordshire.

l. 11. *Dame Annis the cleare.* 'A spring called Dame Annis de Cleare, called by the name of a rich London widow, called Annis Cleare, who, matching herself with a riotous courtier in the time of Edward I, who vainely consumed all her wealth, and leaving her in much povertie, there she drowned herself, being then but a shallow ditch or running water.' *The Pleasant walks of Moore Fields: a dialogue between a Country Gentleman and a Citizen*, 1607.

This well was neare Paul Street, Finsbury, in the neighbourhood of which there is still a St. Agnes Terrace. The name St. Agnes Clair Fields continued till a hundred years ago.

l. 13. *Perillous pond.* The site is in Baldwin Street, City Road. As 'Peerless Pool' it continued as a public bath till well into the last century; see for an account of it in 1831 *Gent. Mag. Library*, xvi. 213–14. For the pond in Stow's time see Dekker and Middleton, *The Roaring Girl*, Act II. sc. i: 'Push! let your boy lead his water-spaniel along, and we'll show the bravest sport at Parlous Pond.'

19, l. 14. *was begun to be made.* So in vol. i. p. 13, Stow writes of Walbrook 'before there was any ditch'. If he meant that there was no ditch before 1213 he was in error. Recent excavations have shown clearly that there was a ditch of Roman work. See *Archaeologia*, lii. 615, and lx. 203–7, and 212–3. The Roman ditch was, however, smaller than the great ditch of the thirteenth century. On the obstruction of the ditch see further vol. i. p. 164, and notes on pp. 297 and 369 below.

20, l. 4. *to be clensed.* The draft in *Harley MS.* 538, f. 5, then proceeds: 'and dyvars tymes sens, lyghtly once in xx yeres the same hath been observed, as myself have sene, but now of late no suche mattar, that charge is saved and greate profit made by suffringe or rather forsynge the decay thereof; a matter manifest to all, and nathelesse for me to write.' This passage takes the place of the whole remainder of vol. i. p. 20.

21, l. 2. *by report of Bartholomew Linsted, alias Fowle.* Stow's friend, William Lambarde, rejected the story, calling Prior 'Fowler' an obscure man, and his story 'without date of time or warrant of writing' (*Dictionarium Angliae Topographicum*, 176: first published in 1730, but written before 1585). See *Chronicles of London Bridge*, 33–8.

l. 20. *the Timber Bridge.* The earliest proof is in the record of the drowning of a witch at 'Lundene brigce' in King Edgar's time (Kemble, *Cod. Dipl.* dxci). The date of Swein's siege was 1013.

22, l. 25. *Joseph Holland.* One of Stow's associates in the old Society of Antiquaries. He was a native of Devon, and a herald and genealogist. Some of his manuscript collections are preserved in the British Museum and at the College of Arms (Hearne, *Curious Discourses*, ii. 436). A paper of his was included in John Dodderidge's *Opinions of certain learned antiquaries on The Antiquities of Parliaments*: London, 1658 and 1670, from *Harley MS.* 305.

23, l. 9. *more towardes the west.* Stow is in error. The Roman bridge was on the same place as the mediaeval bridge, just east of the existing bridge. This was shown by discoveries when the bridge was building about 1830. See Roach Smith, ap. *Archaeological Journal*, i. 112.

24, margin. *William Packenton*, Treasurer of Edward the Black Prince, and author of a Chronicle in French from 1208 to 1333. Leland (*Collectanea*, ii. 455) translates some extracts, which tend to show that this Chronicle was the second edition of the *Brute*. See Sir E. M. Thompson's edition of *Chronicon Galfridi le Baker*, pp. 183-4, and *Dic. Nat. Biog.* xliii. 95. Stow probably quotes from Leland.

25, l. 4. *In the yeare 1395*. The date is wrong. David Lindsay, Earl of Crawford, had licence to come to England for the tournament on Jan. 22, 1390, and was here till the end of May (*Rotuli Scotiae*, ii. 103). Stow's authority was Hector Boece (*Scot. Hist.* 335, ed. 1575, where there is no date), as shown in his MSS. An earlier account is given by Andrew Wyntoun. See *Chronicles of London Bridge*, 187-203.

26, l. 8. *To conclude of this bridge.* With Stow's account may be compared that of Lyly in *Euphues and his England* (ii. 192, ed. Bond): 'Among all the straunge and beautifull showes, mee thinketh there is none so notable as the Bridge which crosseth the Theames, which is in manner of a continuell streete, well replenyshed with large and stately houses on both sides, and situate upon twentie arches, whereof each one is made of excellent free stone, everye one of them being three score foote in hight, and full twentie in distaunce one from another.' See for more exact dimensions *Chronicles of London Bridge*, 81.

29, l. 9. *Aeldgate.* Stow's derivation is wrong. If correct the old form should be Ealdgate. But it appears as 'Ealsegate' in the *De Miraculis S. Edmundi* of Hermann, written about 1095 (*Memorials of St. Edmunds*, i. 43, Rolls Ser.), and the normal forms throughout the Middle Ages are 'Alegate' and 'Algate'. Aldgate is the Eastgate of the English Chronicle (*sub anno* 1052), though the gate by the Tower is said by Stow (vol. i. p. 28) to have been the chief gate on that side till 1190. Norman, the first prior of Trinity (1108-47), rebuilt Aldgate from the foundation (*Guildhall MS.* 122, f. 13). Mr. Stevenson suggests that Algate was derived from Ealh, an owner or builder. The east gate of Gloucester was known as 'Ailesgate' from 'Æðel' (*Engl. Hist. Rev.* xii. 491).

31, l. 23. *The eldest note*, &c. However, it occurs in *Domesday* (i. 128): 'Canonici S. Pauli habent ad portam Episcopi x. cotarios.' Gilbert Foliot (*d.* 1187) refers to his gate called 'Bissupesgate' (*Hist. MSS. Comm.* 9th Rep. 25).

32, l. 28. *there builded a Posterne.* The record from *Letter-Book*, I (ap. *Memorials*, 614) shows that what was done in 1415 was the enlargement of 'the little Postern, built of old in the wall of the said city'. The gardens, destroyed in 1498 (ii. 76-7), were laid out at the same time. For Moorfield, see further notes on pp. 369-70.

33, l. 5. *Cripplegate.* Abbo of Fleury does not describe the bringing of St. Edmund to London. Hermann, who does, says that the procession came in at Ealsegate (*Memorials of St. Edmund's Abbey*, i. 43). In the *Nova Legenda Angliae* (ii. 596–9, ed. Horstman) the gate is Algate. Lydgate, however, writes in his *Legend of St. Edmund and St. Fremund* (ap. Horstman's *Sammlung Altenglischer Legenden*, p. 436):

He kam to London toward eue late
At whos komyng blynde men kauhte syht,
And whan he was entred Crepylgate
They that were lame be grace they goon upryht.

The change was no doubt due to the fancied derivation of Cripplegate from cripples, who begged there, which appears in *Liber S. Bartholomaei* (*Cotton MS.*, Vesp., B. ix, f. 15): 'Ad portam, que lingua Anglorum *crepelsgate*, Latine vero *porta contractorum* vocatur.' (This is the passage relating to Alfune which Stow quotes lower down: but the *Liber* was not written till about 1180; both here and in the English version on f. 54 there are notes of Stow's in the margin.) For later instances of this derivation see Baldwin's humorous version below, and Ben Jonson in *Every Man in his Humour*, 'As lame as Vulcan, or the founder of Cripplegate.' But 'cripple' in Cripplegate is connected with O.E. 'crepel', a burrow. So Cripplegate would mean the sunk, or covered, or perhaps the narrow (cramped) gate. Cripplegap is used in the north of England of a small hole left in walls for the sheep to pass through. There was a postern at Shrewsbury called Crepulgate, and connected with the Severn by a lode (O.E. *lad*) called Crepul-lode. (*N. and Q.* 9th Ser. i. 2.)

Cripplegate is one of the three gates named in the Laws of Ethelred about 1000 (Thorpe, *Ancient Laws and Institutes*, p. 127). 'Crepelgate' is the most usual form of the name in early London wills and documents.

l. 26. *Alfune.* See above, and note on p. 360 below.

l. 36. *I. de Blackwell.* John de Bauquell, who was a prominent citizen at the time, ancestor of the later Blackwells. See pp. 336–7 below.

34, l. 1. *Fabians Manuscript.* This notice does not appear in the printed Chronicle of Fabyan. See further, *Introduction*, p. xxxv.

Margin. *In a booke called Beware the cat.* A most scarce and curious tale, published under the initials G. B., but now known to have been written by William Baldwin (see vol. i. p. x). Only two copies, one printed in 1570, the other in 1584, are known; but ten copies were reprinted privately by J. O. Halliwell-Phillips in 1864. For its history see further *Catalogue of the Huth Library*, i. 80, and J. P. Collier, *Bibliographical Account of Early English Literature*, i. 43–7.

Beware the Cat is a tale professed to be told by one of Baldwin's friends, when they were keeping Christmas, 1552, in John Day's office at Aldersgate. It is a quaint medley of folk-lore, fairy-story, and broad jest, mingled with satire on popery, which opens thus:—

'Being lodged, as I thank him I have been often, at a friend's house of mine, which were rowmish within than garnish without, standing at

Saint Martin's Lane end, hangeth partly upon the town-wall that is called Alder's Gate, either of one Aldrich, or els of elders, that is to say ancient men of the citie, which among them builded it, as bishops did Bishopsgate, or els of elder trees, which bischaunce, as they doe in the Gardines now there about, so while the comon there was vacant, grew abundantly in the same place where the gate was after builded, and called thereof Eldergate, as Moorgate took the name of the field without it, which hath been a very moore, or els because it is the most ancient gate of the cittie, was thereof in respect of the other, as Newgate, called the Elder Gate, or els as Ludgate taketh the name of Lud, who builded it, so most part of Haroldes (I know) will soonest assent Aleredus builded this, but they are deceived, for he and his wife Algag builded Algate, which thereof taketh the name, as Cripple gate doth of a Cripple, who begged so much in his life as (put to the silver weather-cock which he stole from Powles steeple), after his death builded it.'

'But whereof soever this gate, Aldersgate, took the name (which longeth chiefly to Historyes to know), &c.'

The whole passage reads like a piece of grave fooling, which proved too delicate for Stow's simplicity.

Stow himself is at fault in his derivation. Aldersgate is a corruption of Ealdredesgate, or Ealdred's gate, by which name it is mentioned about 1000 (Thorpe, *Ancient Laws*, &c., p. 127). Later forms are Aldredesgate in 1275, and Aldrichegate in 1243 and 1372 (*Cal. Wills*, i. 25, ii. 162; *Mun. Gild.* I. 106).

ll. 25–6. *John Day . . . a late famous Printer.* Dibdin (*Typ. Antiq.* iv. 41) writes of him thus: 'There are very few of our earlier printers to whom both literature and typography are more deeply indebted.' Day, who died 1584, had been a printer at Aldersgate from 1549, and published about 230 volumes. See *Dict. Nat. Biog.* xiv. 233.

35, l. 2. *Newgate, as latelier builded.* Recent excavations revealed extensive remains of the Roman wall and gate at Newgate (*Archaeologia*, lix. 125–40). This was no doubt also the Westgate of Saxon London—'Westgetum' in a charter, dated 857, of Burhred of Mercia, ap. Thorpe, *Diplomatarium*, 118. Probably the new gate was built after one of the great fires early in the twelfth century; but the *Vita Arkenwaldi*, which is quoted here and in vol. i. p. 69, describes only the buildings of Maurice and Richard about St. Paul's (*Nova Legenda Angliae*, i. 395–6, ed. Horstman). Saward de 'Nova Porta' is mentioned in a deed about 1162 (*Hist. MSS. Comm.* 9th Rep. 5), and Newgate is referred to as a prison in the Pipe Roll for 1190. Its earlier name was Chamberlain Gate: see note on pp. 361–2. See also R. R. Sharpe, *Memorials of Newgate Gaol.*

ll. 21–3. *the high and large street . . . so crossed and stopped vp.* The greatest change appears to be that described in Wren's *Parentalia*, p. 272. 'Upon demolishing the ruins [of St. Paul's] and searching the foundations of the Quire, the Surveyor [Wren] discovered nine wells in a row, which no doubt had anciently belonged to a street of houses that lay aslope from the High Street [Watling Street] to the Roman causeway [Cheapside], and this street, which was taken away to make room for the new Quire [of 1256], came so near to the old [Norman] Presbyterium that the church could not extend further that way at first.' It has been argued from this that a Roman road ran diagonally to Newgate; but the theory is doubtful: see Lethaby, *London before the Conquest*, 150–2.

36, l. 19. *Iohn Offrem.* His real name was John de Frome. See *Ann. Lond.* 46, *Lib. de Ant. Legg.* 22, and *Hist. MSS. Comm.* 9th Rep. 14 *b.*

l. 38. *In the yeare* 1414, &c. Probably this refers to the occurrence in 1419, when, through the abuse of the privileges of Ludgate by persons 'more willing to take up their abode there . . . than to pay their debts,' the Mayor and Sheriffs abolished that prison, and removed the prisoners to Newgate. This was in June. In November following, since many persons, 'by reason of the fetid and corrupt atmosphere that is in the hateful gaol of Newgate,' had died, Whittington ordered the use of Ludgate to be restored (*Memorials*, 673, 677).

38, l. 4. *Ludsgate, or Fludsgate.* Camden, *Britannia* (ii. 80, ed. Gough), 'Ludgate or Fludsgate, as Leland thinks, from the rivulet there.' Geoffrey of Monmouth (*Hist. Brit.*) speaks of it as 'the gate which to this day is called in the British tongue Porth-Lud, and in the Saxon Luddesgata'. The tradition may be old, and Mr. W. H. Stevenson (*Eng. Hist. Rev.* xii. 491) has suggested again that the name is due to an owner called Ludd or Ludda. But 'ludgeat' is given in O.E. dictionaries as meaning a postern, and 'lidgate' is used of a swinging gate between a meadow and the highway (*N. E. D.*) See also Lethaby, *London before the Conquest*, 84-6.

l. 11. *Luds gate for the West.* The chief gate on the west was Newgate, see note above. But the postern at Ludgate was no doubt ancient.

l. 24. *Hebrewe caracters.* The Hebrew should probably be read—
הן מצב הר׳ משה בן הרבן יצחק

41, l. 11. *Downe gate, so called of the sodaine descending.* 'Downe,' and its explanation, seem to be guesses of Stow's. A wharf 'apud Duuegate' is mentioned in an alleged charter of William I (*Cotton Charter*, vi. 3), which, though a fabrication, probably dates from the reign of Henry I. Stephen granted to St. Mary Overy the stone house of William de Pont de l'Arche 'contra seldas de Dovegata' (*Mon. Angl.* vi. 172). In a charter of Henry II to Rouen, 1150–1, there is mention of the port of 'Duuegate' at London (*Cal. French Documents*, 34–5, ed. Round). 'Duuesgate' occurs in an early deed in the Clerkenwell Cartulary (*Cotton. MS.*, Faustina, B. ii, f. 75; where Stow has written 'Dunesgate', but the third letter is certainly *u*). 'Douegate', or 'Douuegate', is the regular mediaeval form. In the sixteenth century it is 'Dow Lane' and 'Dovegate'. 'Duvegate' looks like a compound (O.E. **Dūfangeat*) of *Dove*, probably a woman's name. Camden (*Britannia*, ii. 80) writes: 'Dourgate, vulgarly Dowgate, or the Water gate'; this is an impossible derivation.

ll. 30–31. *Guild hall of the marchants of Cullen.* The Emperor's men are mentioned in the Laws of Ethelred II (978–1016), and the house of the merchants of Cologne appears in a charter of Henry II in 1157. (Lappenberg, *Urkundliche Geschichte des Stahlhofes*, II. 3). Probably this was identical with the *Gilda Aula Teutonicorum* (see p. 319 below), for in 1235 certain property in All Hallows Hay-wharf is described as between the Guildhall of the Cologne merchants and Wancelines-lane (? Wyndgos-lane—*Anc. Deeds*, A. 1791). Riley (*Mun. Gild.* I. p. xcvi) thought that the two were distinct; but the *Gilda Aula Teutonicorum* is first mentioned in 1260, and no notice of the Guildhall of the Cologne merchants occurs after that date.

42, l. 1. *Wolfes gate.* Probably a mere misprint for 'Wolses gate'; but the error has been perpetuated in all editions. In the *Liber Albus* (*Mun. Gild.* I. 242, 697) it appears as 'Wolsiesgate in Corderia', and as 'Wolsyesyate'. Stow himself on i. 235 has 'Wolses gate'. So also 'Wolsis lane', ap. *Cal. Wills*, i. 220.

43, l. 2. *W. rex Angliæ, &c.* The charter is contained in *Cotton MS.*, Faustina, A. iii, f. 63vo, where, however, it reads 'terra *Alunodi* de porta Sancti Bothulphi'.

52, l. 5. *here to digresse a little.* In Hearne's *Curious Discourses* (ii. 318, 2nd ed.) there is a note on sterling money which Stow had contributed to the old Society of Antiquaries. It is, however, very brief, and does not represent this long digression.

58, l. 7. *In the yeare 1414.* Oldcastle's escape was in Oct. 1413; the parliament of Leicester in May 1414.

60, l. 26. *large summes of monies.* The draft in *Harley MS.* 538. f. 15 then continues: 'both presently in theyr lyves and also by theyr testaments at theyre deseace. Amonge the whiche by testament Robar Large, maior of London, in anno Christi 1439, gave 100 markes. Sir Stephen Forstar, maior in anno 1454, gave 20 li., Sir John Crosby, shryve, who deceased anno 1475, gave 100 li. to the wirkes of the newe towre of stone at the sowthe ende of London bridge. Richard Gardinar, maior in 1478, gave 100 li. to the buylding up of the voyd place upon London bridge. John Mathew, maior anno 1490, gave 10 markes, &c. This gate and towre was then both strongly and beautifully builded, and sens of late repayred.'

62, l. 33. *The rights that belonged to Robert Fitzwalter*, &c. The French original is in the *Liber Custumarum* (*Mun. Gild.* II. i. 147–51). Stow's translation is not quite accurate. Read—p. 63, l. 12: 'the feet, hands and head, argent, with a sword in the hands of the said image'; l. 16: 'shall salute the mayor as his companion and peer'; ll. 19, 20: 'to bear, to carry, and to gouern'; l. 20: 'to your power'; ll. 34–5: 'chosen forthwith of the host of the City of London'; ll. 36–9: 'command the mayor and burgesses of the city to cause to be rung the common bell of the said city; and all the commons shall go follow the banner of St. Paul, and the banner of the said Robert; which banner of

St. Paul the same Robert shall bear in his own hand as far as Algate'; p. 64, ll. 2–5: 'think good, if so be they must make any issue forth of the city. Then also must the said mayor, the said Robert, and two of the most sage persons of each ward dismount to foresee'; l. 31: 'it is lawfull'; p. 65, l. 6: 'at Wodewharf'[1]; l. 13: 'his great Council.' Though omitted in the edition of 1598, 'The Rights of Robert FitzWalter' appear in the draft in *Harley MS.* 538.

The second Robert FitzWalter had licence in 1275 to transfer Baynard's Castle and the Tower called Montfichet to Archbishop Kilwardby for the founding of Blackfriars (see i. 68), but with a reservation of all his franchises and privileges in the City. (*C. P. R.* Edw. I, i. 96.) It was in pursuance of this reservation that in 1303 he claimed his privileges. The claim was renewed by him in 1321, before the King's Justices, who refused to entertain it. It was for the last time advanced by John FitzWalter in 1347, but peremptorily rejected by the Mayor and Common Council. (*Letter-Book* F, 169.) See Riley's *Introduction* to *Mun. Gild.* II. i. pp. lxxvi–lxxxiv; and *Memorials*, p. 236. On the soke of Robert FitzWalter and the jurisdiction of the Lord of Castle Baynard on the Thames see *Eng. Hist. Rev.* xvii. 485–6, with a document edited there by Miss Bateson from *Add. MS.* 14252.

65, l. 29. *This Robert deceased.* Stow is in error in his genealogy. Robert FitzWalter, the baronial leader, died in 1234, and his son Walter in 1258. Robert II was an infant when his father died, and lived till 1325. He was succeeded by Robert III, who died in 1328. John, son of Robert, died in 1361. The male line of FitzWalter became extinct in 1432. Nicolas, *Historic Peerage*, 199; G. E. C., *Complete Peerage*.

l. 34. *More of the Lord FitzWaltar.* In the draft in *Harley MS.* 538, f. 17vo there follows a long account of the intervention of Walter, Lord FitzWalter, in defence of the City in their quarrel with John of Gaunt in 1377. FitzWalter offered his help as 'being by ancient inheritance standard-bearer to the city'. The passage, which is given in the *Annales*, p. 433, ed. 1605, is a translation from the *Chronicon Angliae*, pp. 121–3.

l. 36. *how this honour of Baynards Castell fell*, &c. The later Baynard Castle was not on the site of the old house of the FitzWalters at Blackfriars, but some distance to the east near Paul's Wharf. In a declaration made about 1446 it is stated that a certain deed was sealed 'in the duc of Yorkys place besyde Paulys warfe, in a chambyr in the est parte of the courte, were that my lord of Glowsetir lyith now' (Lappenberg, II. 71; the date of the deed seems to have been 1417). This enables us to identify the later Baynard Castle with the 'Hospice called le Old Inne by

[1] The Woodwharf was apparently near to, if not identical with, the later Paul's Wharf. In the thirteenth century, and as late as 1349, St. Bennet Hithe was called St. Benedict at Woodwharf (*Hist. MSS. Comm.* 9th Rep. 4, 5; *Cal. Wills*, i. 8, 59, 562). In 1320 it appears as St. Benedict at Wodewharf near St. Paul's Wharf, and after 1349 as St. Benedict at Paul's Wharf (*id.* i. 287, 605; ii. 111). In the original draft in *Harley MS.* 538 Stow wrote 'at a wood wharf'.

Pauls Wharfe', which appears amongst the possessions of Edward, Duke of York, who was killed at Agincourt (*Cal. Inq. p. m.* iv. 14). After the death of Humphrey of Gloucester it fell, with the rest of his property, to the crown (*Rot. Parl.* v. 132), but soon reverted to Richard, Duke of York. It is called 'Baynardis Castell' as Richard's house in 1457 (*Chron. Lond.* 168). It is possible that Edward, Duke of York, may have acquired the 'Old Inne' through his marriage to Philippa, widow of Walter FitzWalter (*d.* 1386)—see ii. 110 above.

67, l. 6. *King of the Romaines.* In *Harley MS.* 538, f. 19, 'fabian writer' is put in the margin. The notice does not occur in the printed Continuation, but see *Chron. London*, pp. 259, 260.

68, l. 33. *as appeareth by their grantes.* A longish explanation is inserted in *Harley MS.* 538, f. 19vo:—'Edward the first, the tenthe yere of his reigne, graunted to the maior and citizens of London to take toward the makynge of the wall and inclosure of the Citie certayn customes, as apperith by the graunt. Also Kyng Edward the second sent his writ commaundinge the Citizens of London to make the walle alle redy begon, and the Towre at the ende of the same walle within the watar of Thames, nere to the house of the Blake friars, of the profites rising of the customes before to them graunted; this writ was dated the 18 of Julii the 4 of E. the second. The wall was then finished, &c.'

69, ll. 1, 2. *An other Tower . . . the King.* In place of this sentence *Harley MS.* 538, f. 19vo, has:—'A Towre or Castle there was in the west parte of the Citie, as William fitz Stevens hathe noted in these words: "The Citie of London saythe he (who wrote in the reigne of Henry the second) *habet ab occidente arcem palatinam, ab oriente duo castella munitissima.* It hath in the west a princely tower or castle. And in the cast two towres or castles. Now for the first, to wite in the west, which was a princely Towre or Castle in the reigne of H. the second as the same FitzStephen notithe. It hath bene of longe since distroyed, and no monument thereof remayninge, wherefore I could nevar lerne where the same was situate, more than on the west parte of the Citie. I read that, &c."'

l. 5. *foundation of a new Church.* In *Harley MS.* 538 Stow then inserts: 'a wirke that men iudged would nevar have bene finished, it was to them so wonderfull for largenes.' And four lines lower, after *successor*: 'dyd also wonderfully increase the same chirche, purchasynge of his owne cost the large stretes about it.' The next paragraph—*This Tower or Castle* to *large Chronicles*—is omitted.

70, l. 35. *Base court.* See note on p. 340.

71, l. 1. *Tower Royall . . . king Stephen was there lodged.* Stow was no doubt misled by finding Stephen at the *turris regia*, which, however, meant the Tower of London (cf. Round, *Geoffrey de Mandeville*, 336). The derivation of Tower Royal was quite different—see p. 324 below.

l. 8. *the Queenes Wardrobe.* According to the City record (*Memorials*, 450) it was to the Great Wardrobe in Castle Baynard that Richard went.

l. 23. *Sernes Tower.* See note on p. 329.

72, l. 18. *The three principall Churches,* &c. See FitzStephen's text on ii. 221 above, where the churches are named as St. Paul's, Trinity, and St. Martin's. But Stow's copy (see note *ad loc.*) did not name the churches. The schools at St. Mary Arches (*de Archa*) and St. Martin-le-Grand are mentioned in a deed, probably before 1141, of Henry of Blois (*d.* 1171), bishop of Winchester (Round, *Commune of London*, 117). The School at St. Paul's was as old as the reign of Henry I (Dugdale, *St. Paul's*, 6).

l. 27. *Ingulphus . . . writeth thus.* This passage (Gale, *Scriptores*, i. 62, 73) is one of the most noted in the spurious fifteenth-century chronicle falsely ascribed to Ingulph. The story is of course quite unwarranted.

73, l. 15. *Our Ladie of Rounciuall.* See note on p. 374.

l. 27. *foure other Grammer schooles.* See i. 194 and note on p. 321.

74, l. 11. *Mannor of the Rose.* See note on p. 322.

l. 39. *reuiued in . . . Christs Hospitall.* In the *Annales* sub anno 1555, Stow describes a disputation held here before the Mayor on St. Bartholomew's Eve, when the prizes were three silver pens, and the first was won by a scholar of St. Anthony's.

78, l. 12. *Boltas Mootes.* This appears in all editions of the *Survey.* But no doubt the true reading should be 'Boltes, Mootes, and putting of cases'. It is often difficult to distinguish *a* from *e* in Stow's handwriting. This will then agree with 'meetings, boltinges, and other learned exercises' a few lines lower down. Boltinges (or boltes) were discussions inferior to Moots. The holding of Moots has been of late years after long disuse revived: see Douthwaite, *Gray's Inn*, 80–7, and Fletcher, *Pension-book of Gray's Inn.*

79, l. 21. *common cookerie or cookes row*—see note on p. 322.

81, l. 21. *the friendly water of Thames.* Nash looks at the matter differently when he writes in *Pierce Penilesse* of 'Brewers that by retayling filthy Thames water come in few yeres to be worth fortie or fiftie thousand pound.' (*Works*, ii. 33.)

ll. 26–7. *the Shoomakers . . . to Saint Martins Le Grand.* So Dekker in *The Guls Hornbooke* (*Works*, ii. 223): 'If thy quicksiluer can runne so farre on thy errant as to fetche thee bootes out of S. Martens.'

l. 37. *Stationers of Paules Church yarde.* In the sixteenth century the principal booksellers and publishers were gathered there. References in contemporary literature are of course common, e.g. 'Paul's Churchyard the peruser of every man's works, and Exchange of all Authors.' (Nash, *Strange Newes*, &c., ap. *Works*, ii. 207.) For a list of booksellers in St. Paul's Churchyard in 1582 see Arber's *Transcript of Stationers' Registers.*

82, l. 16. *Thomas Clifford.* This and the other quotation from Clifford (on ii. 105) clearly come from the 'Life of Edward the Confessor,' which was written for Queen Eadgyth within a few years of her husband's death.—See Luard, *Lives of Edward the Confessor*, 417. In the *Annales* (p. 128, ed. 1605) Stow makes the same quotation from 'T. Clifford', but a little earlier (on p. 123) refers to the *Vita Edwardi Regis* as dedicated to Eadgyth by a nameless writer. On ii. 102 Clifford is cited for events in the reign of Edward I. Possibly Clifford was a friend who supplied Stow with information.

83, ll. 3, 4. *quaffing . . . is mightily increased.* Nash in 1592 writes thus: 'Superfluitie in drink, a sinne, that ever since we have mixt ourselves with the Low Countries is counted honourable; but before we knew their lingring warres, was held in ye highest degree of hatred that might be. Then if we had seene a man goe wallowing in the streetes, or line sleeping under the boord we would have spet at him as a toade, and warnd all our friends out of his company; now he is nobody that cannot drinke *super nagulum*, &c. He is reputed a pesaunt and a boore that will not take his licour profoundly' (*Pierce Penilesse*, ap. *Works*, ii. 78).

Margin. *W. Patten.* He was son of Richard Patten (*d.* 1536), clothworker of London, and was Lord of the Manor of Stoke Newington. He was a lawyer by profession, and a member of the old Society of Antiquaries as late as Feb. 1590 (*Stowe MS.* 1045, f. 2). His only known work is an account (reprinted in *Tudor Tracts*, ed. A. F. Pollard) of 'The expedicion into Scotland' in 1548, in which he had taken part. See *Dict. Nat. Biog.* xliv. 50, and vol. i, p. 114, above.

84, l. 2. *I read that.* Stow clearly follows the *Anominalle Chronicle* (517) for the erroneous statements that Richard's mother accompanied him in a whirlicote, and that Buckingham was present (see Oman, *Great Revolt of* 1381, pp. 63, 197: however, the City record—*Memorials*, 449—also gives the former). On the *Anominalle Chronicle*, see Introduction, p. xxiii, and note on p. 366 below.

l. 14. *the vse of coatches.* In the *Annales* (p. 867, ed. 1631) there is a notice added by Howes, which, however, reads like an expansion of the present passage, and may perhaps have come from Stow's collections: 'In the yeare 1564 Guilliam Boonen, a Dutchman, became the Queene's Coachman, and was the first that brought the use of coaches into England. . . . Then little by little they grew usuall among the Nobilities, and others of Sort, and within twentie yeeres became a great trade of Coachmaking. About that time began long Waggons to come in use, such as now come to London from Canterbury, Norwich, Ipswich, Glocester, &c., with passengers and commodities. Lastly, even at this time, 1605, began the ordinary use of Caroaches.' 'Caroach' was used of a town-carriage as distinguished from 'coach', a country-carriage.

Stow himself in the *Summary Abridged* (p. 260, ed. 1604), under date 1555, writes: 'This yeare Walter Ripon made a coach for the Earle of Rutland, which was the first coach (saith he) that euer was made in England. Since, to wit, in anno 1564, the said Walter Ripon made the first hollow turning coach, with pillers and arches, for her maiestie, being then her seruant. Also in anno 1584, a Chariot Throne, with foure pillars behind to beare a Canapie with a crowne imperiall on the toppe, and before two lower pillars, whereon stood a Lion and a Dragon, the supporters of the arms of England.'

S. Rowlands, in 1612, writes in *Knave of Hearts*, p. 7:

Such Carting ne'er was seen before,
A Coach must carry to Church dore
An Asse that's with foure Horses drawne:
And Mistress Easie to the Pawne
Must passe upon two paire of Wheeles,
As though the poxe were in her Heeles.

85, l. 13. *an account made by H. Leicester.* A copy of this '*Record of Pontefract*' was in possession of J. Watson Reid, F.S.A., who intended to publish it. See J. G. Nichols's *Illustrations of Manners and Expenses*, pp. ix, x, where a fragment is printed. See also Nichols's *Leicestershire*, i. 223. Stow's transcript seems to be faulty (cf. i. 86, l. 23); the first sum totals only 4,560*l.* 16*s.* 8½*d.*, instead of 5,230*l.* 17*s.* 7½*d.*; the second is correct, and the third and fourth are only a few pence out.

87, l. 27, margin. *Rob. Fabian's manuscript.* The quotation does not correspond so well with the printed Fabyan, pp. 632–3, as with the Vitellius Chronicle (*Chron. Lond.* 168). Fabyan's manuscript may have followed more closely the common original.

91, l. 19. *sir Thomas Cromwel.* Wriothesly writes in his *Chronicle*, i. 96: 'My Lord Cromwell had among them one m. men of gunners, morris pykes, and bowemen, goeing in jerkins after the socheners fashion, and his gentlemen goeinge by, to sett them in array, in jerkins of buffe leather, dublets and hose of white satten and taffata sarsenet, which he did for the honour of the citye.'

96, l. 7. *One other shew*, &c. The original of this narrative is contained in two fragments amongst Stow's *Collections*, ap. *Harley MS.* 247, derived apparently from a continuation of Higden's *Polychronicon.* They are printed at the end of Sir E. M. Thompson's *Introduction* to the *Chronicon Angliae* (pp. lxvii and lxxxii). Stow has somewhat altered his original, which, for instance, in ll. 25–7 has 'with black vizerdes like deuils nothing amiable, seeming like legates'. 'From some forain Princes' is a gloss.

100, l. 5. *Roger Houeden.* Hoveden (ii. 131) has only a brief note. Stow's source is the *Gesta Henrici Secundi* (i. 155). The real date was June or July 1174. Mr. Round has shown by reference to the Pipe Roll for 1175, giving account 'de catallis Johannis Vetuli suspensi', that in John Senex we have an elegant Latinization of the well-known London surname 'Viel' (*Commune of London*, 112; cf. *Hist. MSS. Comm.* 9th Rep. 25).

101, l. 29. *the vertue that a great fire hath.* In his account of the great pestilence of 1563 Stow relates that on July 9 every householder was ordered 'to lay owt woodd and make bonfyers in ye stretes and lanes to that intent they should therby consume ye corrupte ayers, which othar wyse myght infecte ye sitie with ye plage ... it wase commaundyd to contynew ye same iij tymes a weke'. (*Memoranda*, p. 123.)

101, l. 30. *On the Vigil*, &c. The Hanse merchants made provision in their expenses for 1400 for the hanging out of lamps on St. John's eve and on St. Peter's eve, and also for furnishing two torches for the Corpus Christi procession (cf. i. 230 above). See Lappenberg, *Stahlhof*, II. 27.

103, l. 13. *a great muster.* Some contemporary notices for 1538–9, apparently written by a citizen, and preserved amongst Stow's *Collections* (*Harley MS.* 530, f. 119), include the following:

'Memorandum. That on Thorsday the viij day of May, in the yere of our Lord M. vc. xxxix, was made a muster in London, suche a mouster seyn in no kynges day y^t^ eny man can tell of: for ther was in nomber xxxvj M. men in harnys, wythe morys pykys, and handgonys, and bowys; w^t^ all ye alldermen one horsebak, w^t^ ye shreffes in blake velvet, & chaynes of gold abowȝt ther neckes. And the fyrst settyng owt of euery warde was commaundyd to goo owt at Algat to myllend grene, & the ffeylde ther abowȝt; and browȝt forthe ageyn & set v in aray of all maner of wepons; & so forthe a longste throwȝ Chepsyde & throwȝ powlles chirche yard, & throwȝ ffleyt stret, & so to Westmyster throwȝ Kyng Stret, & ye seyntwary; and so Rounde abowȝt ye kynges parke, & by sent James, & so over ye feldes by ye condyt hede, & so forthe to holborne, and in at new gat, & so euery man home.

'God save the Kyng.

'Master Wyllm. fforman then beyng meare of London.'

See other accounts in Wriothesley's *Chronicle*, i. 95–7, and *Letters and Papers*, xiv. 940.

l. 20. *forbad the marching watch.* Wriothesley adds to a similar account, that the sheriffs had made their preparations, 'and had noe knowlege till two dayes afore Midsommer that y^t^ should not be kept, which was a great losse to pore men' (*Chronicle*, i. 100; and ii. 3 for Gresham's revival). Another contemporary, after mentioning that there was to be no solemn watch on Midsummer night, continues: 'at which some of the citizens of London are not a little dissatisfied.' *Letters and Papers*, xiv. 1144.

l. 32. *some attemptes.* Stow describes one such, made in 1564, in his *Summarie* for 1566 (f. 275) thus: 'This yeare, thorough the earnest sute of the Armorers, there was on the Vigile of Sainct Peter a certayne kynde of a watche in the Citie of London, whiche dyd onely stande in the hyghest streetes of Cheape, Cornhyll, and so foorthe towardes Algate: whyche was to the commons of the same citie (for the most parte) as chargeable as when in tymes paste it was most commendably done, where as this beyng to very small purpose was of as small a number well lyked.' This is somewhat fuller than the notice as finally incorporated in the *Annales.* There were other watches in 1566 on St. John's eve, and in 1567 on St. Peter's eve. These appear to be the last which Stow records.

l. 33. *a book.* John Mountgomery's book is still preserved in the

City archives at the Guildhall. It is a thin folio of twenty leaves. See i. 83 for a similar instance of a book presented by W. Patten.

108, l. 33. *William Seuenoke.* For various wills see *Cal. Wills*, ii. 462, and *C.P.R.* Henry VI, ii. 216.

109, l. 12. *monument of death.* See note on p. 346.

112, l. 12. *a Cawsey.* Norden refers to it in 1594; see *Description of Essex* (Camd. Soc.). It is described as 'now broken down', in 1735, by Farmer in his *History of Waltham Abbey*, p. 193.

l. 28. *a rich coller of golde*, &c. 'Att this Court [27 Oct. 1545] my lorde Mayer brought in and delyvered here in the Court to the handes of Mr. Chamberleyn the Coler of Esses lately gevyn to this Cittie by Sir John Aleyn, Knyght and Alderman, to be used alweyes and worne by the Lorde Mayer of this Cittie for the tyme beyng.' (Repertory 11, f. 238, ap. *Cal. Wills*, ii. 695.) This was at the end of Laxton's year. Sir Martin Bowes, who was mayor 1545-6, left at his death in 1566 'a goodly cross of gold set with "perell" and stone to hang at the collar of gold which the Mayor wears at high feasts' (*id. ib.*).

114, l. 31. *Barnard Randolph.* His donation was made to enable Peter Morris or Morice to bring water by means of his engine from London Bridge to Old Fish Street, as he had already done to Leadenhall. See *Remembrancia*, p. 553—date Dec. 1582; and i. 188 and ii. 3, 11 above.

115, l. 20. *the Hole, or two penny wardes.* The two lowest wards in the Counters, occupied by the poorest prisoners, were so called. See Jo. Cook in Greene's *Tu Quoque* (Hazlitt, *Old Plays*, xi. 257): '*Holdfast.* "If you have no money, you'd best remove into some cheaper ward." *Spendall.* "What ward should I remove in?" *Holdfast.* "Why, to the Two-penny ward; it's likeliest to hold out with your means; or if you will you may go into the hole, and there you may feed for nothing."'

The two higher wards were the Master's side and the Knight's side. So Webster, *Westward Ho!* Act III. sc. ii: 'Which is the dearest ward in prison, Sergeant? The Knight's ward?' 'No! Sir; the Master's side.' And *Appius and Virginia*, Act III, sc. iv: 'It is thought she shall lie neither on the Knight-side, nor in the Two-penny ward; for if he may have his will of her, he means to put her in the Hole.'

l. 35. *One worthy citizen*, &c. This no doubt refers to Robert Dowe's charity (see *Introduction*, p. xxiv above). But Dowe provided for thirteen almsmen, who received £6 13*s.* 4*d.* apiece, with a gown, costing £2 3*s.* 4*d.*, every third year. Clode, *Early History of the Merchant Taylors*, i. 162-3.

117, l. 15. *Hauing thus in generality handled*, &c. Stow originally arranged his narrative otherwise. In *Harley MS.* 538, f. 24, he writes: 'Havyng spoken of the Walls and gates, the ditche, the Castles and Towers, and last of all of the bridges, all which for the moaste parte are but the outmoste inclosure of this Citye, I am next to towche of the Suburbes withoute the walls, and then returninge and enteringe the gates, whereof I have spoken, there to view how the sayde citie is and hath of old tyme bene devided into wardes, parishes, stretes, and lanes, of principall governors, inferior maiestrates, other officers, and matters as occasyon offerith.' Accordingly he treated first of the suburbs and of the Ward of Farringdon Without before he came to Portsoken. See also note on p. 365.

118, l. 24. *as some haue fabuled.* A reference to Richard Grafton's *Manuell*, f. xi, where this legend is given under date 235 A.D. The legend comes from Geoffrey of Monmouth. See note on p. 271 above as to the course of Walbrook.

119, l. 15. *wardes*, &c. The earliest list of Wards giving the names now in use is one for 1285–6 in *Letter-Book* A, 209. Farringdon (the undivided ward) there appears as 'Lodgate and Neugate'; Langborne as 'Langeford'; and Broad-Street as 'Lodingeberi'. A list of 1293 (*Letter-Book* C, 12) gives 'Langeburne' and 'Lotheberi' with the addition *modo vocatur Bradestrate.* A list of 1320 (*Letter-Book* E, 124–5) has 'Bradestrate' and 'Farndon'. (See also *Cal. Wills*, i. 702–4.) In earlier lists the wards are usually called by the names of the aldermen holding them. There is a list of this kind for 1275 in the Hundred Rolls, giving, however, 'Bassingeshol,' 'Warda Fori,' Colemannestrate, Portsokne, Langeburne, Douegate, Walebrok, and Cornhull. A list for 1230 is given in Madox, *Hist. Exchequer*, i. 708–9 with a reference to one of 1228; the whole number of twenty-four already appear, Portsoken and Bassushage are alone described by name. A list of about twenty wards, mostly under the names of the aldermen, is contained in a document at St. Paul's; *Warda Fori* (Cheap), Alegate, the Bishop's Ward, and 'Brocesgange' (Walbrook) already appear; the document can be dated about 1130 (*Hist. MSS. Comm.* 9th Rep. 66; Round, *Geoffrey de Mandeville*, 435–6). The last list is printed in facsimile in Price's *Account of the Guildhall*, p. 16 *sqq.* 'Langebrod' also occurs in the twelfth century (see p. 307 below). The division of the wards into a western and eastern group by the Walbrook is given in a list of 1346 (*Letter-Book* F, 143–4).

120, l. 23. *a Guild.* The Knighten guild of London is known to us only through the gift of its soke to Trinity, and the consequent preservation of the documents in the Priory Chartulary. Its true character is uncertain, and its bearing on the history of municipal institutions in London has been disputed. See Round, *Geoffrey de Mandeville*, 307–9, and *Commune of London*, 97–105, 221; and Gross, *The Gild Merchant*, i. 186–8. The documents have been printed in *Trans. Lond. and Midd.* v. 477–93, and in *Letter-Book* C, 73–5, 216–25. See also a deed, ap. *Chron. de Rameseia*, 241, Rolls Ser.

ll. 23–4. *in the dayes of king Edgar.* The *Guildhali MS.* 122 has 'temporibus Edgari', which supports Stow. But *Letter-Book* C, 216 reads 'temporibus Knwti'. Similarly lower down (p. 121, l. 20) C reads 'Knyty, Edgari, et Edredi'.

121, l. 28. *William king of England*, &c. In this charter C reads *G. de Magn.* (sc. Magnavilla) *et R. Delpare*, and *Henrico de Both* as *testes.*

122, l. 3. *insomuch that in the yeare 1115.* The date should be 1125. The names of the members of the Knighten Guild should be 'Radulfus filius Algodi, Wlwardus le Doverisshe, Orgarus le Prude, Edwardus Upcornhill, Blacstanus et Alwynus cognatus ejus, Ailwinus et Robertus frater eius filii Leostani, Leostanus Aurifaber, et Wyzo filius eius, Hugo filius Wulgari, Algarus, Secusenne, Orgarus filius Deremanni, Osbertus Drinchepyn, Adelardus Horneþitesinne'. In the list of witnesses for 'John prior of Derland' read 'John prior de Landa'. *Letter-book* C, pp. 219–20.

123, l. 2. *Geffrey Clinton the Chauncellor.* The copy in *Letter-Book* C, 220-21 reads 'Gaufrido Çancellario et Gaufrido de Clinton'. Geoffrey the Chancellor is Geoffrey Rufus, who was chancellor from 1124 onwards.

124, l. 1. *Helianor the queene wife to king Edward the first.* St. Katherine's fell under the priory of Holy Trinity by the deed of William of Ypres (quoted in vol. ii. p. 6). In 1255 Eleanor of Provence, the queen of Henry III, recovered control, and it was she who refounded it in 1273 (*Mon. Angl.* vi. 694–6).

l. 14. *inhabitants, English and strangers.* There were many aliens there. Ben Jonson in *The Devil is an Ass*, Act I. sc. i, writes:

To Shoreditch, Whitechapel, and so to St. Katherns,
To drink with the Dutch there and take forth their patterns.

125, l. 13. *sir Arthur Darcie.* He had a grant of New Abbey, 24 Aug. 1542 (*Letters and Papers*, xvii. p. 399). Stow has preserved, in *Harley MS.* 544, f. 101, a list of burials at the Abbey from a visitation by Clarencieux in 1533.—'In the Chaple of our Lady liethe buried sir T. Mongomerye and his twoo wives; William Belknap, esquier; one of the heires of Rafe Butler Lord of Sudeley and treasurer of England; more, in a tomb one of the dowghters of ye sayd mongomery which was married to one of the mortimeres. Also Alice Spice, sister and heyre to the seyde sir Thomas, which had two husbands, first Clement Spice of Blake notley in Essex.

'On the south syde the quier sir Nicholas Loveyn, svme tyme lord of East Smithfield, and besyde hym on the flore his wyfe, doughter to Sir William Poultney[1]. . . . Before the high altar lyeth dame Elizabethe, one of the doughters to Edward late Duke of Buckyngham, she was wyfe to Robert lord Fitzwatar, Earle of Sussex; and besydes his brother George Ratclyffe, second sonn to the sayde lord and lady, which died without ysshew; and ryht before the high altar vnder a stone lieth dame Jane Stafford doughtar to Humphrey duke of Bokyngham, and wyfe to sir William Knyvet, knight. Also there lyes on the north syde the qwire in a tombe Lewes John, esquier, and his wyfe doughter to the Earl of Oxforde. And besydes his tombe lyeth Eleanor dowghter to Lewes John, which had foure husbands, to wite John White, sir William Tirell, sir Henry Fitz Lewes, and Thomas Garthe, esquier, treasurer to Edward, late Duke of Bokyngham. In a chaple without the qwire on the southe syd lieth sir

[1] An error: see p. 321 below.

Thomas Charles, sometyme Lyvetenaunt of the Tower. Also at the qwire dore lay Walter Hayward, secretary to the lord treasurer. Also Elizabeth Rowley, gentlewoman. In a tombe in S. Annes Chaple on the south syde sir John Mongomery, eldar brother to Sir Thomas; in the same chaple lyeth sir Andrew Cavendysshe and dame Rose his wyfe. On the north syde lieth Richard or John Walden, esquire, and Elizabeth his wife.'

126, l. 22. *Goodman . . . Farmers there.* Rowland Goodman seems to have been a considerable farmer in the eastern suburbs during the reign of Henry VIII. Besides Goodman's Fields here referred to, he had on 20 Jan. 1535 a lease from the Convent of St. Helen's of lands in St. Botolph without Bishopsgate; at the dissolution in 1543 he obtained a grant by purchase from the king (Cox, *Annals of St. Helens*, 16, 34). At his death in Sept. 1547 he also held lands in St. Botolph, late the property of the Hospital of St. Mary without Bishopsgate (*Inq. p. m. London*, i. 95).

127, l. 7. *Henrie Jorden*, &c. He was a bell-founder of Billiter Lane, and founded a chantry here by will dated 15 Oct. 1468, and proved Nov. 1470. See Stahlschmidt, *Surrey Bells and London Bell-founders*, 56–71, and *Cal. Wills*, ii. 543.

l. 8. *John Romeny, Ollarius*, &c. John Romenye, Ollarius, by his will dated 23 April, 1349, left money for St. Botolph's. He and his wife Agnes both died in that year (*id.* i. 425, 555, 623; *Letter-book* F, 187). 'Olarie' in the text of 1603 is Stow's translation of *Ollarius*, a potter; but till late in the fourteenth century *Ollarius* or Poter is the invariable description of a bell-founder, which was probably Romany's business. See Stahlschmidt, *u. s.*, pp. 2 and 20 (giving the will in full).

ll. 28–9. *Garden plottes, teynter yardes.* This alludes to the enclosure about 1574 by Benedict Spinola, a prominent Italian merchant, of eight acres of land to form twenty tenter-yards and certain gardens. In 1584 it was presented as an annoyance to the archers and others. But it was shown in reply that the ground had never been commonly used for archers, and that Hog Lane was so foul and filthy that none could pass there; Spinola had, moreover, spent much money, and the tenter-yards were of great use to the cloth-workers. (Strype, *Survey*, Bk. II, ch. ii.) The gardens were no doubt the 'Spinilas' pleasure' of vol. i. p. 166. The tenter-yards by Houndsditch are shown plainly in Agas's map of London.

128, l. 33. *Gunfounders surnamed Owens.* In the *Annales* (p. 571, ed. 1631) Howes inserted under date 1535: 'John Owen began to make brasse Ordinance . . . He was the first Englishman, that ever made that kind of Artillerie in England; issue of his name, and the name of Pit have continued unto the dayes of King James most ready and excellent gun-makers.'

Robert and John Owen were at work at Houndsditch before 1531; they had a grant of the 'Belfounders house' there in 1540. (*Letters and Papers*, v. 664, xvi. p. 717.)

129, l. 1. *Brokers*, &c. For brokers in Houndsditch see Beaumont and Fletcher, *The Woman's Prize*, Act II. sc. ii :—

More knavery and usury,
And foolery, and brokery than Dog's ditch.

And Rowlands, *Letting of Humours Blood in the Head Vaine*, p. 45 :—

But into Houndsditch to the Brokers row.

See also note on p. 361 below. Houndsditch and its neighbourhood are still the haunt of brokers and second-hand clothes dealers.

131, l. 18. *Monumentes . . . Alhallowes Barking.* See a paper thereon by G. R. Corner in *Trans. London and Middlesex*, ii. 224–58. It is there suggested that Studenham is an error for Sir Thomas Tudenham, who was executed in 1462; but he was buried at Austinfriars (see i. 178 above). Sir John Stile, draper, was alive in 1526. A John Style, mercer, who died about 1505, was a benefactor of All Hallows Barking. In *Harley MS.* 538, f. 44[vo], John Bolt is styled 'grocer and merchant of the Staple'. See also Maskell's *Hist. of All Hallows Barking.*

l. 35. *John Crolys and Thomas Pike.* John Croke (see vol. i. 131, l. 3) founded a chantry here in 1477. Pike is an error for Thomas Pilk, who founded a chantry in 1351 (*Cal. Wills*, i. 645; Maskell, *u. s.* 16).

l. 37. *Sydon lane.* 'Shyvethenestrat' in 1257 (*Anc. Deeds*, C. 1202), 'Syvidlane' in 1259, 'Sivendestrete' in 1291, 'Syvethenelane' in 1329, 'Sivedenelane' in 1334, and 'Syvedonlane' in 1516 (*Cal. Wills*, i. 2, 101, 352, 400, ii. 630). In a patent of 1312 it is called 'Sevyng lane' (*C.P.R.* Edw. II, i. 481). It is now Seething Lane.

132, l. 10. *Richard Cely and Robert Cely.* They were merchants of the Staple in the time of Edward IV. Their business correspondence is preserved in the Record Office, and has been in part published by the Royal Historical Society. Richard Cely the elder was patron of St. Olave's; he died in 1481; Richard the younger (*d.* 1494) and Robert were his sons. They lived in Mark Lane, in St. Olave's parish. A present of a vernicle, or copy of St. Veronica's handkerchief, to St. Olave's Church by Robert is recorded (*Cely Papers*, pp. xlviii and 4; Povah, *Annals of St. Olave*, p. 22).

l. 12. *John Clarentiaulx.* Probably Sir John Arundell.

l. 16. *Chapone.* Peter Capony, or Capponi, died of the plague, Oct. 27, 1582, aged 32. His monument, with a kneeling effigy, describes him as 'Petrus Caponius. Florentinus' (Povah, *Annals of St. Olave*, 94). Referred to as 'Piero Capony a gentleman of Florence' in *Acts of Privy Council*, x. 67.

l. 23. *Cokedon hall.* It occurs in 1316 and 1342 (*Cal. Wills*, i. 262, 468).

l. 39. *Galley halfe pence.* In a churchwardens' account book *sub anno* 1521, appears the entry 'Resaved for ij vnces of galy-halfepenys sold this yere vj*s.* iiij*d.*', *N. and Q.*, 4th ser. ii. 344. Stow's authority is *Letter-Book* I, f. clx.

l. 30. *Sporiar lane, of old time so called.* 'Sporieres lane' in 1295 and 1354, 'Water lane' in 1459, and 'the lane sometime called Sporyers lane now called Water lane' in 1513 (*Cal. Wills*, i. 122, 619, ii. 619).

134, l. 34. *Edwaters.* Strype corrects to 'Edward Waters'.

135, l. 3. *John Tate.* In *Harley MS.* 538, f. 46, 'son to Sir John Tate, sometyme maior of London, was theyre buried in the sayd chaple of W. Hariot, vnder a tombe in the northe wall now defaced, sir Christopher Draper, Ironmonger, maior of London, 1566, deceased 1580.'

l. 21. *Passekes wharffe.* 'Pesokes wharf' and a tenement called 'Horneres keys' appear as the property of William Harendon in 1448 (*Cal. Inq. p. m.* iv. 236).

137, ll. 25–6. *Hospitall . . . founded by Robert Denton.* It was founded as stated, but proving impracticable, was changed in July, 1378, to a bequest for a Chantry-priest at St. Katherine's by the Tower (*Mon. Angl.* vi. 708–9; *Cal. Inq. p. m.* ii. 307). Stow here follows Leland (*Collectanea*, i. 110); he is more accurate in his own note on vol. ii. p. 143.

l. 32. *Cobhams Inne.* As belonging to Sir John Oldcastle in right of his wife, who died seized of it in 1434 (*Cal. Inq. p. m.* iv. 38, 155).

138, l. 21. *Mistresse Cornewallies.* 'Principall Place' in St. Katherine, Christchurch, which had formerly belonged to Evesham Abbey, was granted to Edward and Alice Cornwallis by Henry VIII, in Sept. 1540 (*Letters and Papers*, xvi. p. 55). Alice Cornwallis died seized thereof on Jan. 8, 1556. Her son, Thomas, sold it in 1562 to Nicholas Throckmorton, who died there on Feb. 12, 1571 (*Inq. p. m. Lond.* i. 143, ii. 143). The puddings are not mentioned in the grant, but the story is illustrated by items of Henry's expenditure, e.g. on Oct. 26, 1530—'To the wife that made the King podings at Hampton Corte, vj*s.* viij*d.*' (*Letters and Papers*, v. p. 752, cf. also pp. 749, 750, 758).

l. 29. *Belzettars lane.* Stow is right as to the older form, but wrong as to the derivation. Belzeters means bell-founders; the first person to be described as 'belyeter' is William Burford of St. Botolph without Aldgate in 1390 (*Cal. Wills*, ii. 301). But the lane is called 'Belzeters-lane' in 1298, and 'Belleyeterslane' as late as 1468 (*id.* i. 134, ii. 543). See also Stahlschmidt, *Surrey Bells and London Bellfounders*, pp. 2, 3, 37; and notes on p. 288 above.

139, l. 29. *Thus much for the bounds.* In the foregoing description Stow has in part followed a statement in the Trinity Cartulary (*Guildhall MS.* 122, f. 13): 'Praeterea sciendum est quanta sit ista Soka, cujus fines tales sunt. A porta de Algate usque ad portam Bally Turris, que nuncupatur Tungate, et tota venella vocata Chykenlane versus Berkynchurche usque ad cimiterium, excepta una domo viciniore cimiterio, et iterum redditur eadem via usque ad ecclesiam Sancti Olavi, et tunc redditur per viculum qui tendit ad ecclesiam de Colemanschurche, deinde versus Fenchurch usque ad domum brasineam, ubi nunc habetur signum Columbe. Extitit itaque ibi olim viculus, per quem ibatur usque ad domum Teol filii Ivonis Aldermanni in Lymestrete, qui viculus nunc obstructus est quia suspectus erat pro furibus nocturnis, et ideo, quod non ibi patet via, redditur iterum per viculum versus capellam Sancti Michaelis, et sic versus Lymstratam ad domum Ricardi Canel, et deinde itur per vicum juxta ecclesiam Sancti Andree usque ad ecclesiam Sancti Augustini juxta murum Trinitatis. Deinde usque ad portam de Algate.'

'Teol' should be 'Theobald'. 'Trinitatis' in the last line is probably an error for 'ciuitatis'.

140, l. 12. *in the parishes of*. Stow translates from the Trinity Cartulary, ff. 25–6: 'In parochiis sancte Marie Magdalene, sancti Michaelis, sancte Katerine, et beatissime Trinitatis, que nunc una est parochia, scilicet Sanctissime Trinitatis, que antiquissime extitit Sancte Crucis.'

For supposed ruins of St. Michael's in 1789 see *Gent. Mag. Library*, xvi. 56–7.

l. 16. *The Priorie was builded*, &c. Stow has fallen into a confusion. The deed which he quotes does not relate to the site of the Priory, but to a plot of land on the opposite side of Aldgate Street. By this deed, dated July 7, 1314, the Prior and Convent 'confirmaverunt Johanni de la Marche civi London. quandam placeam terre cum pertinenciis in parochia Sancte Katerine versus Algate London., que quidem placea terre jacet in longitudine inter vicum regium, quo itur versus Algate, juxta capellam sancti Michaelis versus Aquilonem et terram Johannis Page versus austrum, et continet in eadem longitudine iiij^{xx} iij ulnas et dimidium et j quartarium, et dimidium quartarii unius ulne de ulnis ferreis domini Regis; et jacet in latitudine inter murum cimiterii dicte capelle versus occidentem et terram Willelmi Manhale versus orientem, et continet in eadem latitudine in capite Aquilonis xv ulnas et unum quartarium unius ulne et tres polices, et continet in capite australi a terra domini Johannis Cokermuth versus orientem usque ad venellam vocatam Bellezeterlane versus occidentem xlviij ulnas unum quartarium et dimidium quartarii unius ulne.' The rent was to be 53*s*. 4*d*. annually. This is from the Trinity Cartulary, *u. s.* f. 44.

141, l. 7. *according to their estates*. In *Harley MS.* 538, f. 48, Stow continues: 'In so moche that as eny man mowght come into theyr church to prayer, so mowght they enter the hall at meale tymes and fill theyr bellyes, and at all tymes of the day come to the buttre and sellar and have breade and drinke, or to the kitchen in the fore none and require of the coke a peace of befe, which shuld be given hym roste or sod on his knife or dagger's poynt, and so to beare it abrode, whither he would for himselfe and his frinds. The liberalite of this house, as I have hard and partely sene, is rather to be wondered at than reviled of them that have not sene the lyke.'

l. 8. *monuments*. There are lists in *Harley MSS.* 6033 and 6069. The former reads for 'Heningham' Hemmyngham, and for 'Charcam' Charchand de Mille; the latter Mannyngham, and Charthano de Mille. Both have Nycke for 'Nucke'. For 'Beringham' Bermyngham or

Bernyngham. In 6069 Margaret Chenie's second and third husbands are called Thomas Breus and William Burcestur (Berners and Burcestur, ap. *Anc. Deeds*, A. 7356); for 'Halling' read Helmyng; and for 'Auesey', Anestie. Stow has copied a list in *Harley MS.* 544, f. 66vo.

l. 24. *Henrie Fitzalwine . . . 1213.* See note on p. 315.

l. 37. *gaue to sir Thomas Audley.* On April 9, 1534. (*Letters and Papers*, vii. 587 (10).)

142, l. 36. *Monuments.* A list in *Harley MS.* 6069, f. 30, supplies the variants: 'Sir Thomas Fleming, knight, Lord of the Rowles in Essex'; 'John Good'; and 'Sanche' for 'Sewch' (p. 143, l. 4).

143, l. 12. *S. Andrew Vndershaft.* In deeds of Prior Norman (*d.* 1147) the Church is St. Andrew 'ad sanctam Trinitatem' (*Anc. Deeds*, A. 2338, 7285). Later it was usually called St. Andrew, Cornhill. In 1361 it is called St. Andrew Aneknappe (atte Knappe), or 'on the hill', from *knap*, O.E. *cnaep*, the top of a hill. St. Andrew 'atte Shafte' occurs in 1477 (*Cal. Wills*, ii. 30, 583). For the history of the church see a paper by Mr. Philip Norman in *Transactions of the St. Paul's Ecclesiological Society*, vol. v.

margin. *Chaucer. chance of dice.* No such poem appears in Stow's own edition, nor amongst Chaucer's accepted works. Professor Skeat has, however, identified this verse with the sixth stanza of an anonymous poem entitled *Chance of the Dice* in *Fairfax MS.* 16, f. 194. He says further: 'the poem is certainly not Chaucer's, but it may be Lydgate's.' The *Fairfax MS.* supplies the following corrections: line 2, 'floon' (=arrows) for 'flying'; line 4, 'when that' for 'when'; line 6, 'crokke' (=crock, a round paunch) for 'croke'; line 7, 'clokke' (=cluck) for 'cloke'. 'Crowdeth' in line 6 means presses forward. See *The Chaucer Canon*, p. 126.

144, ll. 11, 12. *neighbours and Tenants.* In *Harley MS.* 538 the text continues: 'of the sayd houses and alley, over whose dores and gate . . . dined, gathered to them more strengthe,' &c.

l. 20. *as he tearmed it.* Stow, in *Harley MS.* 538, wrote 'as they termed it'.

l. 25. *the Baylife of Romfort.* Wriothesley has 'taylor of Raynesford in Essex' (*Chronicle*, ii. 19). But the Greyfriars Chronicle has simply 'one that came from Romford' (*Monumenta Franciscana*, ii. 221).

145, l. 37. *Hugh Offley.* 'Deceased 1594', *Harley MS.* 538. He died Nov. 26, 1594 (*Inq. p. m. Lond.* iii. 224).

146, l. 3. *one faire greate house.* It came to Sir Edward Wotton with his wife Hester, daughter of William Pickering the younger (*Inq. p. m. London*, iii. 240–3). Sir William Pickering the elder had a grant of the site from Henry VIII in 1538 (*Letters and Papers*, xiii. Pt. ii. 491 (18)).

l. 9. *Robert Beale.* A member of the old Society of Antiquaries. He died in 1601, and was buried at All Hallows on the Wall. See i. 176.

l. 12. *The Papey.* The original documents show that the Hospital of le Papey was really founded (or refounded—for the brethren of St.

Augustine are mentioned in 1365, *Anc. Deeds*, A. 2273) in 1442 by Thomas Symmineson or Symson, William Cleve ('Oliver' is a misreading, derived, as it would seem, from Leland, *Collectanea*, i. 111), William Barnaby, and John Stafford, priests. It was for the benefit of priests disabled by age or sickness. A contemporary refers to: 'Pappy Chyrche on the Wall betwyne Algate and Bevysse Markes. And hyt ys a great Fraternyte of prestys and othyr seqular men. And there ben founde of almys certayne prestys, both blynde and lame, that be empotent; and they have day masse, and xiiij*d*. a weke, barber and launder, and one to dresse and provyde for hyr mete and drinke' (*Collections of a London Citizen*, p. viii. Camd. Soc.). The patronage of the church belonged to the soke, which Queen Matilda gave to Trinity Priory; in the fourteenth century document, where this is recorded, it is called 'ecclesia sancti Augustini Pavie super murum' (*Lansdowne MS*. 448, f. 8). St. Augustin de Pavy occurs in 1417 (see p. 297 below). Trinity was a priory of Augustinian Canons, and St. Augustine's relics were preserved in the church of San Pietro at Pavia (Papia)—held by the Augustinian canons of Mortara from 1221. This probably explains the name 'Papey' as used to distinguish St. Augustine on the Wall from the church of St. Augustine of Canterbury by Paul's Gate. In 1170–87 the church is simply St. Augustine 'super murum': in 1252–3 we get 'Parochia Sancti Augustini Pappay' (*Guildhall MS*. 122, f. 508). For an account of the Papey by T. Hugo see *Trans. Lond. & Midd.* v. 183–221. For the 'Liber Papie' see note on p. 297.

l. 30. *Buries Markes, corruptly Beuis markes.* A Bury chronicler refers to the abbot's house at 'Burys markys' about 1470 (*Memorials oj St. Edmunds*, iii. 299). But 'Bewesmarkes' occurs in 1407, and 'Bevys Marke' in 1450 (*Cal. Wills*, ii. 372, 518). It was granted to Sir Thomas Heneage in 1541 (*Letters and Papers*, see xv. 942 (118), xvi. p. 715).

147, l. 21. *Thomas Mollington*, Lord of Wem in Shropshire in the time of Henry IV. See Eyton, *Shropshire*, ix. 178. A list in *Harley MS.* 6069, f. 25 has 'Thomas Molington, baron of Wem'. The same list gives John Tyrrell for 'Tirres' (l. 20); Brosted for 'Brosked' (l. 28); and Condorow for 'Couderow' (l. 29).

ll. 33, 34. *Skeuington* and *Milborne.* In *Harley MS.* 538 the dates of death, viz. 1524 and 1539, are given.

148, margin. *These poyntes not performed.* Munday (*Survey*, p. 157, ed. 1633) says that Stow was mistaken, and that Milborne's will contained no bequest of bread and coal, but provided for Almshouses only. See also Strype, ii. ch. iv.

l. 34. *Lord Lumleyes house.* Crutched Friars was granted to Sir Thomas Wyatt on July 10, 1540 (*Letters and Papers*, xv. 942 (49); for his messuage called 'Pekes Gardeyn' in 1540, see *Anc. Deeds*, A. 12598). John, sixth Lord Lumley, who died at Lumley house in 1609, was a member of the old Society of Antiquaries. The Navy Office was here in Pepys's time.

149, l. 7. *Monte Joues or Monasterie Cornute.* Hornechurch Priory or Monasterium Cornutum was founded by Henry II as a cell to the Hospital de Monte Jovis, on the Great St. Bernard. Richard II granted it to William of Wykeham for New College, Oxford. (*Mon. Angl.* vi. 652–3.) Stow follows the Trinity Cartulary (*Guildhall MS.* 122, f. 35) for the grant of this site.

l. 15. *made into bowling Alleys.* In Dec. 1553 'the Lord Maior and the sheriffes went to these three common bowlinge allies, that is to say, Northumberland alley by Algate, St. Nicholas shambles alley, and an alley in the Old Baylie; and with mattockes did breake and digge up all the said alleys' (Wriothesley's *Chronicle*, ii. 105). Three years before the Mayor and Sheriffs 'rode to the bowlinge allyes and play-houses at Pawles wharfe and by Aldgate', and broke up the tables, and sent the players to the Counters (*id.* ii. 43). See more on bowling alleys on p. 368. This Northumberland House is to be distinguished from another in Aldersgate (p. 343).

l. 36. *Blanch apleton.* 'Blanches appeltuna' in the soke of Robert de Valoniis (de Vaux) occurs in 1177 (*Anc. Deeds*, A. 7295). A part of the manor came to the family of Ros of Hamelake with one of the co-heiresses of John de Vaux in 1288 (*Cal. Inquisitions*, ii. p. 404—new ed.). Another part belonged to the Bohuns, Earls of Hereford. The name was finally corrupted into Blind Chapel Court, through the intermediary Blanch Chapulton.

150, l. 3. *Mart lane.* It appears as 'Marthe lane' from the beginning of the thirteenth century down to 1280; for the next two hundred years 'Marte lane' is the usual form. 'Marke' is a corruption of the sixteenth century. (*Anc. Deeds*, A. 2679, 7354, 7820; *Cal. Wills*, i. 50, ii. 613, 689.)

l. 5. *Basket makers*, &c. By order of the Court of Common Council on October 12, 1464. See *Archaeologia*, xxxii. 131, quoting, somewhat inaccurately, City Record, ap. *Jor. Cooke*, No. 7, f. 43.

l. 19. *Limestreete, of making or selling of Lime.* This is confirmed by the occurrence of Ailnoth the lime-burner of 'Lim Strate' in the twelfth century (*Anc. Deeds*, A. 11559).

l. 37. *diuerse fayre houses.* Lime Street was in Stow's time a good residential quarter. See quotation on p. 338 below.

151, l. 2. *the king's Artirce.* I am unable to identify the reference or explain the word. It is 'Artirce' in *Harley MS.* 538. Possibly it may be an error for 'Artirie'.

l. 6. *belonging to the Lord Neuill*, see note on p. 295.

l. 13. *Benbriges Inne.* In Holand's will called Penbridge's Inn (*Cal. Wills*, ii. 525). Probably the house which Sir Richard de Pembridge or Pembrugge held in 1375 (*Cal. Inq. p. m.* ii. 348).

l. 33. *Lord Sowches Messuage.* The lords Zouch of Harringworth had a hospice in St. Andrew parish 'juxta Lymestrete', 1381–1415 (*Cal. Inq. p. m.* iii. 43, 192, iv. 15).

152, ll. 35, 36. *a faire house*, &c. In *Harley MS.* 538, f. 52vo: 'a fayre large house for an alderman or other of good worship, wherein, &c.'

l. 9. *the greene gate.* It fell to the crown in 1391 by the death of Michael, son of Simon Pistoye (*Cal. Inq. p. m.* iii. 140), and was granted on December 24 to Roger Croppehulle and Thomas Brounflete (*P. R. C.*, Richd. II, v. 12). Henry IV granted it on March 1, 1408, to Thomas Walsyngham (*id.* Henry IV, iii. 409). Malpas by his will—proved May 8, 1468—left his great place in Cornhill and Lime Street to his daughter Elizabeth and her husband, Sir Thomas Cooke. Cooke by his will—proved June 1, 1478—left 'Greene Gate' to his wife, with remainder to his son Philip (Orridge, *Illustrations of Jack Cade's Rebellion*, 11, 18). Possibly, however, 'The Green Gate' had been forfeited through Cooke's troubles in the reign of Edward IV, for on April 28, 1486, Henry VII granted it to John Forester (Campbell, *Materials Hist. Henry VII*, i. 417). Sir William de Ryvers was a Breton in the service of Henry VII, and Master of the King's hawks. (*Chron. Lond.* 202, 249, 251.) John Mutas or Meautys was French secretary to Henry VIII; for the sack of his house in 1517, see *Letters and Papers*, ii. 3204. David Woodroffe was seized of 'The Greene Gate' at his death in 1563 (*Inq. p. m. Lond.* ii. 12).

153, l. 1. *Leaden Hall.* The earliest mention is in 1296 as 'La Ledene halle' (*Cal. Wills*, i. 128). It occurs as 'la sale de plom' in 1302 (*Lib. de Ant. Legg.* 249; 'aula plumbea' in *Ann. Lond.* 127), and in 1321 when inspectors were appointed for the poultry-market there (*Mun. Gild.* II. i. 305). In 1345 there is reference to 'Ledenhalle gardyn' belonging to Sir John Neville (*Letter-Book* F, 86), and in the will of William de Kyngeston (see below) in 1375 there is a note of a tenement called 'le ledenhall' formerly belonging to Sir John Nevill (*Cal. Wills*, ii. 173; translation in Strype, ii. ch. viii).

l. 32. *The Horsemill.* Apparently a building which included tenements belonging to several persons. In 1353 Peter de Blithe disposed of rents issuing from tenements called 'le Horsmelne'; in 1370 William Bysshop bequeathed shops belonging to 'le Horsmille'; a share in the Horsemill was included in the lands which William de Kyngeston gave to St. Peter's Cornhill in 1375; and in 1413 William Baret left his share in a tenement, 'le Horsmelle,' to the church of St. Dunstan in the East (*Cal. Wills*, i. 674; ii. 139, 173, 396).

156, l. 32. *Carts of Stratford.* The London Chronicle, ap. *Harley MS.* 540, f. 7, has the following under 1527, with reference to another time of dearth: 'Ye bread cartes y^t came from Stratford to London were mett by ye way at Myll ende by ye citisens of London, y^t ye mayr and ye shrives were fayne to goo and reskue them, and se them brought to ye markytes apoynted.' This is reproduced by Stow in his *Annales*, p. 904, ed. 1605.

157, l. 5. *comfort of the Citizens.* In *Harley MS.* 538, f. 55vo, Stow adds: 'He dyd more than ryde about the market and away.'

l. 21. *a Baker named John of Stratforde.* See *Letter-Book* D, 311, and compare for bakers of Stratford, *Mun. Gild.* I. 241–2, III. 412–29.

l. 26. *I read in the visions of Pierce Plowman.* Stow's version, written as prose, is inaccurate. The text as given by Professor Skeat, *Piers Plowman*, vol. i. p. 402, ll. 266–71, is as follows:—

There was a carful comune · whan no carte come to toune
With bake bred fro Stretforth · tho gan beggeres wepe,
And werkmen were agaste a litel · this wil be thouȝte longe.
In the date of owre dryȝte · in a drye Apprile,
A thousande and thre hondreth · tweis thretty and ten,
My wafres there were gesen [1] · whan Chichestre was maire.

The reference to John Chichester fixes the date as 1369–70. John Malvern, whose name Stow puts in the margin, was author of a continuation of Higden's *Polychronicon* from 1346 to 1394 (*Dict. Nat. Biog.* xxxvi. 8). The description of him as author of *Piers Plowman* is an error due to the obvious connexion of William Langland with Malvern.

160, l. 29. *S. Marie at the Axe.* It occurs as St. Mary del Ax about 1200, and this is the regular form throughout the thirteenth century (*Anc. Deeds*, A. 2416, 2425, 2447). In the *Rotuli Hundredorum* it is called Sancta Maria apud Ax, atte Ax, atten Ax, atte Nax. As S. Mary de Ax it was in the patronage of the Nuns of St. Helen's in 1303 (*Mun. Gild.* II. i. 236). In 1514 the parishioners in a petition to the king declared that 'the Churche ys in soo great decaye that y[t] ys lyke every day to fall downe', and 'the parson ys departyd frome the same Churche where it pleasethe hym and left the parishyns withoute any maner of devyne service'. They begged for assistance on account of their poverty, and because the 'said poore Church ys honored by kepyng of an holly relyke an axe, oon of the iij. that the xj.m[l]. Virgyns were be hedyd w[t] all, the whiche holly relyke as yett remayneth in the said Churche' (Bills signed 5 Hen. VIII, No. 79, ap. *Gent. Mag. Library*, xvi. 45-6; cf. *Letters and Papers*, i. 4993). After the suppression of St. Helen's the decay grew worse, and ultimately on March 3, 1561, St. Mary Axe was united to St. Andrew Undershaft (Hennesey, *Novum Repertorium Lond.* 94). It is impossible to reject Stow's statement that there was a house with the sign of the Axe close by; but the house may have borrowed its name from the Church; or it may be that the name was the cause and not a consequence of the relic. An alternative suggestion is that the name 'axe' was due to the proximity of a stream; but for this there is no proof (see *N. and Q.* 9th ser. x. 425, xi. 110, 10th ser. i. 90). St. Mary 'Pellipariorum' occurs as a heading in the Trinity Cartulary, and occasionally elsewhere.

161, l. 10. *Grey a Pothecarie.* Presumably Balthasar Gwercye, or Guersye, the physician (*Dict. Nat. Biog.* xxiii. 316), who at his death in 1557 owned 'the house of preistes of the brotherhed of the Holy Trinite', and messuages in St. Mary Axe (*Inq. p. m. Lond.* i. 144).

162, l. 5. *iust boundes of Aldgate*—see note on p. 290.

l. 15. *grounde letten.* In 1539 the Churchwardens of St. Martin's paid 2*l.* 13*s.* 4*d.* 'to the Masters of Pappe, for the porchase of the churche y[r]de'. Nichols, *Illustrations of Manners*, &c., p. 247.

[1] geason.

l. 21. *the fraternity of Papie.* The 'Liber Papie' consists only of eleven leaves, now *Cotton MS.*, Vitellius, F. xvi, ff. 113–23, which suffered terribly in the fire of 1731; the loss is in part made good by a partial transcript written about 1550 in *Harley MS.* 604, f. 12. (Both the MSS. seem to have been in Stow's possession.) The grant from the mayor on f. 119 of the Cotton MS., though imperfect, corrects Stow's transcript: 'Be hit remembered that where nowe late the maister and wardeyns of the ffraternitee of Pappey haue made a bryke walle closyng in the Chapell of Seint Austyn called Pappey Chapell sette in the paroch' of all saintes in the walle in the warde of lymestrete of the citee of London. ffrom the south est corner of the which brike wall is a Skuncheon of xxj fote of assise from the said corner westward. And from the same Skuncheon there to a mesurage of lv. fote and di. westward. The forsaid Skunchon brekith oute of lyneright southward betwixe the mesures aforesaid three fote and v. ynches of assise vpon the comyn ground of the Citee aforsaid. Rauf Verney maire and thaldermen of the same Citee the xxij[th] day of Octobre the yere of the reigne of Kyng Edward the fourth the sixth granted vnto John Hede, Prest, maister, John Bolt and Thomas Pachette, also Preestes, wardeyns of the ffraternitee of Pappey aforsaid and their successours for euermore, the said Skuncheon which brekith oute of the Brike walle aforsaid and is sette thre foote and v. ynches vpon the comyn grounde like as it is abouesaid. To haue and to holde the same withoute any interupcion of the said maire and aldermen or their successours . . .' The 'skuncheon' or triangular projection of the wall is clearly shown in Agas's map. From f. 120 it appears that the master and wardens employed Thomas Hardyng, citizen and Scrivener, to write the book in Sept. 1477. Additions carrying on the history, with lists of the brethren, were afterwards made. The chief documents with two facsimiles are given in Hugo's account—see p. 293 above.

163, l. 5. *one large message.* The hostel of the Earl of Oxford near Bishopsgate street is mentioned in 1348 (*Cal. Wills*, i. 513). Richard de Vere, 11th Earl of Oxford, had a messuage 'in parochia S. Augustini Pavy' in 1417, as also his mother in 1401 (*Cal. Inq. p. m.* iii. 277, iv. 26). John, 13th Earl (*d.* 1513), had a house described as 'Bevesmarkes' in ward of Lime Street (*Inq. p. m. Lond.* i. 30). John, 14th Earl, died in 1526; his second sister and co-heiress, Elizabeth, married Sir Anthony Wingfield (*d.* 1552), father of Sir Robert (*d.* 1597), who was living here in 1587 (*Cal. State Papers*, 1581–90, p. 395).

164, l. 24. *the ditch.* On Agas's map the ditch appears clearly, and is shown to widen here to a point where a stream flows into it from the north. On Faithorne's map (prepared 1643–7) the ditch has completely disappeared. See further *Archaeologia*, lx. 197–200 with illustrations. Recent excavations have proved the accuracy of Stow's statement as to the filling up of the ditch with soilage and other filthiness (*id.* lx. 202).

l. 37. *purchased the patronage.* From a document in *Letter-book* F,

154, it appears that on Oct. 15, 1346, the House and Order 'Fratrum milicie beate Marie de Bethlem' were taken under the protection and patronage of the Mayor, Aldermen, &c., of the City of London. See also *Letter-books* F, 163, and H, 338, where it is claimed in answer to a royal writ that the patronage and appointment of a keeper rested with the Mayor and citizens. In 1406 Henry IV again claimed the patronage and right of visitation (*C. P. R.* Henry IV, iii. 231).

165, l. 10. *banke of deepe ditch.* In the foundation charter of Bethlehem Hospital mention is made of the 'fossatum quod vocatur Depediche' (*Mon. Angl.* vi. 622). Recent excavations revealed a part of its course near Blomfield Street, and showed it as a deep, sluggish, stagnant stream. It was ten feet below the base of the original Walbrook, which was somewhat further west. It is the stream referred to in the last note but one. See *Archaeologia*, lx. 206–7 with plan.

166, l. 1. *Fishers folly.* It is to this large and sumptuously-built house that Fletcher must refer in *The Nice Valour*, Act V. sc. iii. :—

> *Moulbazon.* Is't possible such virtue should lie hid,
> And in so little paper?
> *Lapet.* How! . . .
> Your *Herring*[1] proved the like, able to buy
> Another Fisher's Folly.

The commentators have, however, interpreted this as an allusion to a tract written in 1624 by the Puritan George Walker, in his controversy with Piercy, a Jesuit, who was known as Father Fisher, and entitled: *Fisher's Folly unfolded, or The Vaunting Jesuites Vanity discovered.* Partly on this ground Dyce and others have held that *The Nice Valour* was left incomplete by Fletcher, who died in 1625, and finished by another hand (Dyce, *Works of Beaumont and Fletcher*, x. 363, and A. H. Bullen, ap. *Dict. Nat. Biog.* xix. 309). But clearly Walker was punning on Jasper Fisher's notorious building.

Jasper Fisher, son of John Fisher, was warden of the Goldsmiths' Company in 1567 (Prideaux, *Memorials of the Goldsmiths*, i. 68). He purchased six gardens of Sir Martin Bowes, on which he built his house. He died on February 28, 1579 (*Inq. p. m. London*, iii. 20). In 1588 William, son of Thomas Cornwaleys, purchased Fisher's Folly from the Earl of Oxford (*Cal. Hatfield MSS.*, iii. 376–7). In May, 1594, Mr. Cornwallis of Fisher's Folly was suspect of Popery (*Cal. State Papers*, 1591–4, p. 503). He was still living there in 1598 (see p. 241 above). Sir Roger Manners purchased it before 1603. After him the Earl of Argyll dwelt there: 'the Lord of Argyll's house, called Fisher's Folly, offered to the East India Company—held unfit for their service' (*Cal. East Indies*, p. 368—Jan. 10, 1615). Then it passed to the Marquis of Hamilton, who died in March, 1625: 'His body was carried to Fisher's

[1] The name of a book. Perhaps an allusion to *A Herrings Tayle* printed in 1598.

Folly, his house without Bishopsgate' (*Cal. State Papers*, 1623–5, p. 697). After this it was the residence of William Cavendish, second Earl of Devonshire, who died there in 1628 (*Survey*, p. 175, ed. 1633), and of his widow, Christiana (*d.* 1675), who entertained Charles II there in 1660 (*Gent. Mag. Library*, xv. 171). Part of the site was occupied by a Baptist meeting-house, whence Samuel Butler (*Hudibras*, Pt. III, canto ii. 894) refers to 'The Rump' as representing: 'But Fisher's Folly congregation.' Fisher's Folly stood on the site of Devonshire Square, Finsbury. See Wheatley, *London Past and Present*, i. 503, and ii. 47–8.

For 'Spinilas pleasure' see note on p. 288 above.

'Kirkebyes Castell' is explained by a letter from William Fleetwood to Burghley, in which he wrote, on July 21, 1578: 'John Kirby that buylded the fayre howse upon Bednall Greene is ded, so is Fairfax and Bower, all riche men. They died of surrfaite' (*Lansdowne MS.* 26, f. 191vo). Strype identifies it with 'that now called the Blind Beggars House' (*Survey*, iv. ch. ii). Kirby may be the Kirkbie named on vol. i. p. 228 above. 'Megses glorie' was probably a house in the same neighbourhood, for the Meggs family were connected with St. Mary Matfellon (Strype, *u. s.*).

171, l. 26. *William Basing Deane of paules was the first founder.* Stow has made some confusion. About 1212 Alard, the dean, and the chapter of St. Paul's, made a grant to William, son of William, the Goldsmith, to establish Nuns at St. Helen's. The Canons of St. Paul's had held the Church of St. Helen's for many years previously (Cox, *Annals of St. Helen's*, 4–6, 359). There was no dean called William Basing. On the monuments at St. Helen's see Cox, *Annals, &c.*, 57–74. John Langthorpe should be John Leenthorp (or Leventhorpe). The date of William Bond's death was 1576.

l. 38. *purchased by the Companie of the Lethersellers.* Henry VIII granted it in 1542 to Sir Richard Williams, *alias* Cromwell (nephew of Thomas Cromwell, and great-grandfather of the Protector), who sold it to Thomas Kendall in 1544. Kendal was a leatherseller, and no doubt purchased for his company, to whom he at once demised the property (*Inq. p. m. Lond.* iii. 143; *Letters and Papers*, xvii. 220 (95)). On Leathersellers Hall see *Gent. Mag. Library*, xv. 296–8.

173, l. 18. *since the which time*, &c. Sir Bartholomew Rede dwelt in Crosby Place in 1501–2, and Sir John Best in 1516. After him Sir Thomas More, who, on Jan. 20, 1523, sold his lease to his friend Antonio Bonvisi of Lucca (see *Dict. Nat. Biog.* v. 365). Bonvisi acquired the reversion in 1542 (*Letters and Papers*, xvii. 881 (17)), and on April 1, 1547, demised Crosby Place to William Rastell and William Roper, who in turn surrendered their interest to Benedict Bonvisi and German Ceo or Cyoll. Rastell, Roper, the Bonvisis, and Cyoll all left England in 1549–50. Crosby Place was thereupon seized to the King's use (Wriothesley's *Chronicle*, ii. 34). Afterwards it was occupied by Thomas, Lord Darcy. Bonvisi returned in the reign of Queen Mary, and died seized of Crosby's

Place on Dec. 7, 1558. German Cyoll and his wife Cicely, daughter of Sir John Gresham, lived there from 1560 to 1567, when he sold it to William Bond (*d.* 1576). The French ambassador was living there in 1592. Bond's sons sold it in 1594 to Sir John Spencer. In Feb. 1601, Crosby Place, the house of Sir John Spencer, 'being very large and he seldom using it,' was suggested as suitable for the reception of the Earl of Mar. Sir Walter Ralegh was living there in the following September (*Hist. MSS. Comm.* Hatfield MSS. xi. 88, 382). It was prepared for the reception of the Duc de Biron in the same year (*Acts Privy Council*, xxxii. 190). See *Inq. p. m. London*, i. 114–6, 183, ii. 200, iii. 133–4; *A Memoir of Crosby Place*, by T. Hugo, ap. *Trans. Lond. and Midd.* i. 35–55; *Gent. Mag. Library*, xv. 249–66. For an account of seven original documents relating to Crosby Hall see *N. and Q.* 10th ser. viii. 30; they are dated 1552–67, the last being the sale by German Cyoll to William Bond.

174, l. 20. *Alice Smith.* The notice of her benefactions was inserted in the edition of 1603 on p. 580 as an *addendum.* It is now put in its intended place.

l. 38. *well with two buckets.* See note on p. 301 below.

175, l. 24. *grate of Iron.* See note on p. 334.

176, l. 17. *as large an house, builded,* &c. It had been lately built by Sir William Paulet, when in April, 1540, he obtained a grant of part of Austinfriars. Another part of the site had belonged to Thomas Cromwell, and was granted in 1543 to Sir Thomas Wriothesley. Paulet eventually acquired the whole, receiving a grant of the upper part of the church in 1550 (*Inq. p. m. Lond.* iii. 283–6).

177, l. 39. *There lye buried in this Fryers church.* An article on Austinfriars by T. Hugo, in *Trans. Lond. and Midd.* ii. 1–20, includes a list of burials compiled from *Harley MSS.* 544, ff. 66 and 68vo, and 6033. It furnishes the following variants from Stow's list, p. 178, l. 5, Hyndercke or Hynndemole (for Lindericle); l. 11, Graynsers or Greynfers; l. 17, Walter Maynell; l. 19, Sir Bartholomew Badlesmere (probably correct); l. 21, Merventon; l. 28, Talmache; l. 35, Chybury; l. 35, Peter Morowes; l. 36, Berland; Chitting; l. 37, Chornott; l. 38, Howche; p. 179, l. 1, Attepole (i. e. de la Pole); l. 7, Boell; l. 7, Mawney (Mauny is correct); l. 7, Deskay. A third list is in *Harley MS.* 6069, f. 23. *Harley MSS.* 544 and 6033 give the epitaph of Lucia de Visconti, beginning:—

> Magnifice nata Bernabensis ecce Lucia,
> Mediolanensis olim clarissima proles.

179, ll. 38–9. *that . . . to forget themselues.* Stow wrote in *Harley MS.* 538, f. 62vo: 'Of this unconscionable dealynge of hym, wherein he forgate hymselfe.'

180, ll. 14, 15. *Lethbury . . . now corruptly called Lothbury.* See the longer passage on i. 277, and note on p. 334.

ll. 22, 23. *an house pertayning to the Abbot of S. Albons.* Edward

Keacher or Ketcher, pewterer, purchased the Abbot of St. Alban's Inn from the grantee at the dissolution, and when he died in Jan. 1563, left it to his son John, the Alderman Catcher of Stow's text (*Inq. p. m. London*, ii. 38).

l. 29. *saint Martin called Oteswich.* John de Oteswich founded a chantry here in Dec. 1331, for his father William and others (*C.P.R.* Edw. III, ii. 230; cf. *id.* Henry IV, iii. 56). A Martin de Ottewich occurs in connexion with the church about 1246 (*Anc. Deeds*, A. 2683). But the name is much older; St. Martin Otteswich occurs in 1216 (see note on 'Finkes Lane' below), and Otheswych in 1222 (*Anc. Deeds*, A. 2698). The Alfwin Fink who held land in St. Martin Otteswich (*id.* A. 2658) may be the same as the alderman of 1180 (Madox, *Hist. Exchequer*, i. 562). Machyn (*Diary*, 175, 211, &c.) refers habitually to St. Martin Oteswich as 'Sant Martin's with the well and ij bokettes'; see also vol. i. pp. 164, 174. For a similar list of burials see *Harley MS.* 6069, f. 54, reading 'Wodehouse' for 'Woodroffe' (p. 181, l. 2). For the tomb of John de Oteswich see Gough, *Sepulchral Monuments*, and for inscriptions, *Gent. Mag. Libr.* xvi. 42. For extracts from Churchwardens' Accounts see J. Nichols, *Illustrations of Manners*, &c., 270–4. The site is now 39 Threadneedle Street.

182, l. 2. *after some Record.* See *Memorials*, 183–5; *Letter-Book* E, 269. The date was 10 May, 1331, i.e. the fifth (not the *sixth*) of Edward III. Yakesley is a better form than Yakley.

l. 38. *Finkes lane*, &c. Stow gets his information from a series of Charters in *Cotton MS.*, Faustina, B. II, f. 80—the Cartulary of the Nuns' Priory at Clerkenwell. Rosamond, daughter of James Finke, gave to the Priory in 1216–7 her stone house in the parish of St. Benet Finck, and tenements in St. Martin Oteswich. The Priory regranted them to Robert, son of Robert Finke.

183, l. 11. *William Coolby.* The list in *Harley MS.* 6069, f. 55, reads 'Welbye'.

l. 15. *the little Conduit, called the pissing Conduit.* So Middleton in *A Chaste Maid in Cheapside*, Act III. sc. ii:

Come along presently by the Pissing-conduit,
With two brave drums and a standard-bearer.

In *Henry VI*, Pt. 2, Act IV. sc. vi, Cade says: 'Now is Mortimer lord of this city. And here sitting upon London-stone, I charge and command, that of the City's cost, the pissing-conduit run nothing but claret wine this first year of our reign.'

184, l. 21. *one of the Proctors for saint Anthonies*, &c. The pigs of St. Anthony were privileged. But the Renter of the Hospital had to swear that he would not claim any pigs wandering in the City, nor hang bells round the necks of any which had not been given to the hospital in pure alms. Other pigs were such a nuisance that at an early date men were appointed to kill all that were found loose in the streets (*Mun. Gild.* I. 590–1, and Preface, p. xlii; *Letter-Book* D, 251).

185, l. 24. *sir John Lepington.* Apparently the same person as the Sir John Lenthaine of vol. ii. p. 83.

l. 25. *Alderban a Gascoyne.* No doubt the 'Aldebrand Gascone, Lombard' of 1376 (*Letter-Book* H, 27).

ll. 26 and 34. *Capell* and *Barne.* The dates of death, viz. 1519 and 1557, are added in *Harley MS.* 538.

186, l. 3. *Margaret Norford.* Margery de Nerford founded a chantry here in 1407 (*C. P. R.*, Henry IV, iii. 292, 316).

l. 4. *John Clauering, 1421.* His will, dated 8 Jan., enrolled 31 May, 1422, includes donations to St. Christopher's Church, but no bequest of lands (*Cal. Wills*, ii. 429).

l. 7. *had taken the Mantell and ring.* It was a common custom for a widow to take a vow of chastity, and thereon to receive in church the mantle and ring. Cf. *Cely Papers*, p. 88: 'On the xxvij day [27 March, 1482] whos Byfelde berryd, and the morrow Herby hys whyfe toke the mantell and the rynge.' For a description of the ceremony at the taking of the mantle and ring, see *Liber Pontificalis of Edmund Lacy, Bishop of Exeter*, ed. R. Barnes.

l. 16. *John Norryholme.* The list in *Harley MS.* 6069, f. 55, reads: 'John Norrye,—Holme.'

187, l. 14. *Rippers of Rye.* In 1384 an ordinance was made concerning foreigners called 'Ripieres' bringing sea-fish to the city for sale; they then occupied the Stocks. Elsewhere there is reference to 'les Ripiers qi amesnent pessoun del mier a la cite', distinguishing them from the 'Peters' or fishers in the Thames (*Letter-Book* H, 234).

188, l. 25. *but now no such matter*, &c. In *Harley MS.* 538, f. 65vo: 'A great comoditie, if the sayd water were mayntayned to come at every tyde some reasonable quantitee as at the first it dyd; but since the same is almoaste altogether ceased, through whose defaute I know not.' The text of 1598 stopped short at 'Stockes Market' (see p. 243 above). The notice in the *Annales* (p. 1171, ed. 1605) agrees very nearly with the *Harley MS.* In another place (*Harley MS.* 540, f. 123) Stow writes: 'The Standart at Ledenhall is to be reformed or pulled downe; it standeth as a shadow, or rathar a playne mockery yildinge no comodytie to the Citie, suche as was promised, but contrarywise it comberith the strete with the let of cariage.'

Middleton in *Michaelmas Term* writes: 'I tell you what I ha' done. Sometimes I carry my water all London over only to deliver it proudly at the Standard.'

189, ll. 18, 19. *brake vp . . . the Tunne.* On 18 April, 1299, pardon was granted to the persons of the City of London who broke the Tun (*tonelli*) erected for the punishment of suspected persons wandering about the city at night (*C. P. R.* Edw. I, iii. 408). The breaking of the Tun seems to have taken place in the previous summer (*Letter-Book* B, 74–5); the fine of 20,000 marks was remitted on payment of 1000*l.* (*id.* C, 38). It is curious that the original in B has 'cuiusdam dolei', and in C 'pro condonatione rancoris sui pro factione (*fractione*) cuiusdam doley.' The Tun is called *dolium* in *Letter-Book* H, 339. Neither Stow nor his authorities explain the incident; the persons concerned were all aldermen.

190, l. 10. *punishment of Priests in my youth.* One may suspect here a covert allusion to the different treatment of a minister in later times. In 1563 the minister of St. Mary Abchurch was caught in adultery with another man's wife and taken to Bridewell, 'his breche hangynge aboute his knes, his gowne and his (kyvar knave) hatt borne afftar hym with myche honor; but he lay not longe ther, but was delyveryd with owt punishment and still injoyed his beneffyssis. They were greatly blamed that apprehended hym and comitted him' (*Memoranda*, 127). On this latter incident see also Machyn, *Diary*, p. 310. At the end of *Letter-Book* I, there is a long list of the punishment of priests taken in adultery. See also *Letter-Book* H, 339, for a record of the custom in 1388–9.

191, ll. 4, 5. *prison . . . called a Cage.* So Dick the butcher said of Jack Cade: 'his father had never a house but the cage.' *Henry VI*, Pt. 2, Act IV. sc. ii.

l. 20. *saith Robert Fabian.* This passage does not appear in the printed continuation of Fabyan's *Chronicle*, and must have been derived by Stow from his manuscript. See *Introduction*, p. xxxv.

margin. *a man . . . that had sworn foolishly against his brother.* Referring to John Stow's quarrel with his brother Thomas. See *Introduction*, pp. xviii, xix.

192, l. 25. *the Royall Exchange.* Stow in his *Memoranda* (pp. 134–5) has this note: 'The xxij day of February, 1565, beynge Friday, the howsys nere to ye Conduit in Cornhylle, abowt ye nombar of lx housholds, poore and ryche, were cryed by the bell man abowte ye citie of London to be solde to them that wowld gyve moaste for them, and remeve the same from theñs, that in the place ye marchaunts mowght buyld theyr bursse. Thos howsys were dyverse tymes so cryed and at ye last solde, and they begane to pull downe ye same shortly aftar owr Lady day in Lent. In ye pullynge downe wherof dyverse persons were sore hurt and ij in great peryll of deathe; and by Whitsontyde next followynge in 1566 ye same howsys were all pullyd downe and ye grownd clearyd; all whiche chargis was borne by ye citizens of London, and then possessyon given by sertayn aldarmen to Syr Thomas Gressham, who layed ye fyrst stone (beynge bryke) of ye fowndacion on ye vij day of June, beynge Friday, in ye aftar none next aftar Whitson halydays, betwen 4 and 5 of ye cloke.' On lands in St. Michael, Cornhill, taken for the site of the Royal Exchange, see *Churchwardens' Accounts*, pp. 213, 217, 233.

193, l. 17. *the Pawne.* It was a covered walk on the south side of the Exchange. The word is derived from the Dutch *pandt*, originally meaning a covered cloister, and now used for a store or shop. In the *Remembrancia* (p. 520) there is reference to the Pawne or Exchange built at Durham House in the Strand in 1608. The Exchange, and the Pawne in particular, was famous for the sale of fine silks and draperies. Webster, *Westward Ho!* Act II. sc. i: 'You must go to the Pawn to buy lawn.' Rowlands, in *A Crew of Kind Gossips*, p. 13:

One of them gave me this same ruffe of Lawne,
It cost three pound, but laste week in the Pawne.

Middleton, *A Chaste Maid in Cheapside*, Act I. sc. ii: 'As if she lay with all the gaudy-shops in Gresham's Burse about her.'

194, l. 14. *a table.* The inscription is given by Weever in his *Funeral Monuments*, p. 413, by Strype, and in *Trans. Lond. and Midd.* iv. 301. According to Strype the original dated from the time of Edward IV. It was destroyed in the Great Fire. The story of the foundation of St. Peter's by Lucius appears, in *Letter-Book* I (*Memorials*, 651–3), in 1417, when it was decided that the Rector should have precedence among the City clergy, because his church was for four hundred years and more the Metropolitan See. On 'Archbishops of London' see Stubbs, *Reg. Sacrum Anglicanum*, pp. 214–5. The Lucius legend (which Stow describes at more length on ii. 125) first appears in the *Liber Pontificalis* not later than 700 A.D. Thence it found its way into general circulation through Nennius, and Bede's *Ecclesiastical History*. See art. by Prof. Haverfield ap. *Eng. Hist. Rev.* xi. 419. The church of St. Peter 'binnon Lunden' is mentioned in a charter of Bishop Ælfric about 1040 (Kemble, *Cod. Dipl.* dcclix).

l. 30. *This Library.* Leland in his *Collectanea*, iv. 48, has a note of four manuscripts 'in bibliotheca Petrina Londini'.

l. 39. *foure Grammar schooles.* See *Rot. Parl.* v. 137, and note on William Lichfield on p. 321 below.

195, l. 6. *William Kingston.* The reference to the Horsemill makes it clear that William Kingston, fishmonger, who left tenements to St. Peter's in 1375, is intended (*Cal. Wills*, ii. 173; compare i. 153 and note on p. 295 above, and *Hist. MSS. Comm.* 6th Rep. 409).

l. 13. *A Brotherhoode of Saint Peter.* For a register of the Fraternity of the Guild of St. Peter on Cornhill see *Hist. MSS. Comm.* 6th Rep. 407–18. The grant, on April 26, 1403, was to William Aghton, parson of St. Peter's, Richard Rybrede, John Bury, and Peter Mason; Askham and Brampton took part in the establishment of the Fraternity, but there is nothing to connect it with the Fishmongers. The Ordinances are printed in the Report, *u.s.* Mason died Dec. 20, 1412. Foxton founded his chantry in 1391. Richard Manhale (see i. 195, l. 6), who died in 1410, was another benefactor. See also *Cal. Wills*, ii. 286, 384, 397, 494, and *C.P.R.* Henry IV, ii. 260.

l. 20. *Elrington.* According to the inscription given by Strype 'Erlington', *ob.* Feb. 16, 1558.

l. 23. *Alnothus.* See *Chron. Evesham*, 75: 'Alnod, sacerdos, dedit ecclesiam beati Michaelis in Cornehalle London.' This was in 1055.

l. 34. *Elizabeth Peake.* The records of the Drapers' Company under date Aug. 14, 1518, note the burial 'this day of Mistress Elizabeth Peke, widow, from the Crane in the Vintre'; the Company lent their 'best beryall clothe' and 'every of the vj berers had a sylver spone for his labor' (*London Past and Present*, iii. 377).

196, l. 2. *blemished by the building*. In 1548 the Wardens of St. Michael's sold the Church plate, weighing 322 ounces, for 84*l*. 5*s*. 4*d*., and with the proceeds bought ten chambers or dwellings in the Churchyard. The sale of vestments and ornaments in the two following years realized 151*l*. 5*s*. 7*d*., and in 1551 there was a further sale of 660 oz. of plate for 222*l*. 17*s*. 10*d*. These sacrilegious gains were then spent in building the new houses in the Churchyard, of which Stow justly complains. The entry to the church from Cornhill was through one of the houses, and the use of back-doors and windows proved such a nuisance that in 1855, when new leases were granted, openings in the south wall were prohibited (*Churchwardens' Accounts of St. Michael's, Cornhill*, ed. Overall, pp. 69–70, 77–80, 90, 91, 98, 217–18, 231, 290).

l. 10. *Bell named 'Rus'*. In 1587 'Rus' was recast by Lawrence Wright at a total cost of 65*l*.,[1] to weigh 31 *cwt*. 56 *lb*. The bell soon wanted repairs, and did not give satisfaction. Next year it was decided that 'Rus' should be recast, though 'to stay tell somer come y^{t} she may be conveniently cast'. A new founder, Mr. Motte, was employed, and the bell recast at the cost of 21*l*. 17*s*. 5*d*. There was also paid 3*l*. 2*s*. for copper for 'Rus', and 3*l*. 12*s*. 9*d*. for tin, besides smaller items such as a shilling 'for a company of musicions to take a noate of the same bell'. 'Rus' now weighed 34 *cwt*. 42 *lb*. Ten years later it was proposed to recast 'the great bell Rous', but agreed to 'let it rest a while and use it as it is'. Ultimately in 1600 Motte recast the bell again to weight 30 *cwt*. 108 *lb*.; after allowing for the old metal the cost was 11*l*. 2*s*. 2*d*., 'and so we are content to make it up xij li. by reason he casted it so often.' An unsatisfactory bell seems to have been cast in 1599. As Stow hints, the fault was not entirely with the founders; in 1597 orders were given 'for the bells with fewer men to be rong' (*Churchwardens' Accounts*, 176–80, 245, 252–4). From the statement on pp. 244–5 above it will be seen that in 1598 'Rus' was broken, and 'therefore not rong as heretofore'. The charge for 'a knyll w^{t} Rus' was 8*s*. (*id*. 178–9). On Robert Mot, the bell-founder of Whitechapel, see Stahlschmidt, *Surrey Bells and London Bell-founders*, 91–2.

l. 36. *William Comerton*. Probably identical with the William Combarton of vol. i. p. 228. Cf. *Cal. Wills*, ii. 385–6.

197, l. 24. *Robert Fabian*. He died on 28 February, 1513 (*Inq. p. m. Lond.* i. 29). The original draft in *Harley MS*. 538, f. 67vo, reads: 'Robart fabian, draper, one of the shryves and alderman of London in the year 1491 (*sic*). He wrote a chronicle of London, England, and of France, beginning at the creation and endynge in the third of Henry the 8, which both I have in written hand.' Dr. Busch has suggested

[1] There seems to have been some dispute over this, see p. 245.

that Stow must, by speaking of 'both', have intended to distinguish the 'Chronicle of London' and the 'Chronicles of England and France'. If so, the former may have been the lost work coming down to 1512, and omitting the extraneous portions of the original. It should, however, be noted that a line has been drawn through the word 'London' in the *Harley MS.* Fabyan styled his original work, which ends at 1485, *The Concordance of Chronicles.* Richard Pynson published it in 1516 as *The new Chronicles of England and of France.*

See further, *Introduction*, p. xxxv and notes on pp. 275, 280, 283, 303 and 365–6. See also the *Introduction* to my *Chronicles of London*, pp. xxviii–xxxi and Busch, *England under the Tudors*, i. 410.

l. 34. *Richard Garnam*, &c. The original draft in *Harley MS.* 538, f. 67vo, reads: 'Elizabeth Peke, widow, who gave the patronage or gyfte of benefice to the drapars of London, buried vnder a tombe of marble in the belfrey, 1518. Richard Garnam, Skynner, in the belfrey, 1527. Edmond Trindle, draper, and Robert Smythe, clothworker, my godfathers at the font. William dixson, draper, and Margaret his wyfe, which Margaret was my godmother. In the cloyster: Thomas Stowe my graundfather, and his wife my graundmother; Thomas Stowe my father and Elizabeth my mother.' See *Introduction*, pp. vii, xlvi, xlvii. The *Churchwardens' Accounts* (p. 146) have under 1559 the entry: 'Res. of Mrs Stowe for here husbandes grave in the Cloyster, ij*s*.'

198, l. 2. *John Tolus.* In 1548, Lodge, Heade and Bolde record the receipt of 6*l.* 10*s.* from 'Mr Tolloz, Allderman', for half a year's rent. There is no record in the *Churchwardens' Accounts* of any charity of his, but in 1563 the Vestry ordered 'a certaine brasse potte which was in the keping of the late Mr. Tolorge' to be demanded of his executor (pp. 231, 87).

l. 13. *Philip Gonter.* Gonter or Gunter, skinner, was elected Alderman of Portsoken Ward in 1569, but discharged at the request of the Earl of Leicester and Cecil, not 'only from serving the office of Alderman but also from that of sheriff and collector of any fifteenths or subsidies upon payment of £400.' He died on Feb. 15, 158⅔ (City Records, ap. *Churchwardens' Accounts*, p. 231). See also below.

ll. 38–9. *Burcheouer lane . . . now corruptly called Birchin lane.* The most usual form from 1260 and a century after was Bercherverelane, but it appears also as Bercheners lane and Berchernerelane (*Cal. Wills*, i. 7, 74, 286). Berchenes-lane occurs in 1301 (*Mun. Gild.* I. 242), and Berchen-lane in 1430 (*Cal. Wills*, ii. 489).

For drapers in Berchin Lane see Middleton, *Blackbook* (*Works*, viii. 29). 'Passing through Berchin Lane amid a camp-royal of hose and doublets.'

Rowlands, *The Melancholie Knight*, p. 21:

> Come traveler from Turkey, Roome, or Spaine,
> And take a sute of trust in Birchin Lane.

199, l. 29. *one great house*, &c. Philip Gunter at his death owned three tenements in Cornhill, in one of which 'commonly called the Sarazens Heade he dwelt, being on the west part of the Back Alley or approach of the tenement or wine tavern commonly called the Popesheade'. He lived here before 1538, and purchased the property of George Monox in 1553. (*Inq. p. m. London*, i. 52, iii. 58.) The tenement next 'le Popyshed' in Lombard Street was the property of Sir William Eastfield, mayor in 1436-7 (*Anc. Deeds*, A. 644, 12276). The Popes Head was bought by George Monox from Sir Henry Owen in 1517 (*Letters and Papers*, xv. 806). John Wolfe, who published the first edition of the *Survey*, had his shop in Pope's Head Alley.

200, l. 9. *Langborne warde.* Stow's 'long borne' is a myth based on the supposed meaning of the name. Mr. J. E. Price (*Safe Deposit*, 25) has shown that the levels alone make it impossible that such a stream should have existed. Like other wards Langbourn took its name from its chief street. Geoffrey the alderman of 'Langebord' occurs in the twelfth century (*Anc. Deeds*, A. 5853). St. Edmond in 'Longbord strete' is mentioned in a document of the fourteenth century, which may, however, have followed one of the twelfth century (*Lansdowne MS.* 448, f. 8). In 1252 some property opposite to the cemetery of St. Mary de Neucherch (Woolchurch) is described as lying between the street running to 'Longebrod' on the north and a lane on the south (*Cal. Charter Rolls*, i. 407). In 1285 and 1312 the street is called 'Langburnestrate' (*Cal. Wills*, i. 74, 226). The ward appears as 'Langeford' about 1285, but 'Langeburn' in 1293 (*id.* i. 702-3). The name 'Lombard Street' first appears in 1318, when a tenement there was granted to the merchants of the society of the Bardi at Florence (*C.P.R.* Edw. II, iii. 246) as described by Stow in vol. i. p. 201. Lombards or Langeberdes were resident in London in the twelfth century; Meinbod and his son Picot the Lombard are mentioned in documents at St. Paul's (*Hist. MSS. Comm.* 9th Rep. 67). 'Lombard' was used at an early date as a generic name for bankers or money-dealers.

l. 14. *Share borne lane.* Like the 'Lang borne', the 'Share borne' rests solely on Stow's conjectural etymology. The name first occurs in 1272 as 'Shitteborwelane', and so continues for two centuries with variations like 'Schiteboroulane', and 'Shiteburgh lane' (Watney, *Account of St. Thomas Acon*, 289; *Cal. Wills*, i. 13, 162, 171, 220). 'Shirboruelane' appears in 1467, and 'Sherborne Lane' in 1556 (*id.* ii. 586, 666). See also vol. i. p. 14 above.

l. 21. *for suspition of theeues.* See note on pp. 290-1.

l. 24. *Fenne-church.* The derivation is obscure. There cannot well have been any fen here, though the statement in *Lansdowne MS.* 448 f. 11 that the 'Ecclesia de Fancherche' had belonged to the Knighten-guild may conceivably suggest some connexion with the Fen or Moor outside the city. There may, on the other hand, have been a hay-market (*faenum*) here, as well as near Allhallows ad Faenum in Dowgate. The form Fanchurch is common both in early deeds and in the sixteenth century. See also *N. and Q.* 8th ser. xii. 201, and 10th ser. iii. 181.

201, l. 3. *Lombard streete.* See note on Langborne, on p. 307.

ll. 29-31. *John Darby . . . buried about the yeare 1466.* In his will, dated 17 Feb. 1478, and enrolled in Oct. 1480, he directed that he should be buried in the Chapel of St. John at St. Dionis, lately built by him, and bequeathed his hostel 'le Belle and le Chekyr on the hoop' in Fenchurch St. for the endowment of chantries there. (*Cal. Wills*, ii. 580; cf. ii. 195 above.) There is a note of him *sub anno* 1468, in Fabyan's *Chronicle*.

202, l. 7. *Alhallowes Grasse church.* Brithmer, a citizen, gave it as All Hallowes 'Gerscherche' to Christchurch, Canterbury, in 1054 (*Mon. Angl.* i. 97). It is called All Hallows 'Graschurch' in the Trinity Cartulary in 1251 (*Guildhall MS.* 122, f. 257). *Harley MS.* 538 reads: 'The register bokes and monuments sometyme belonging to the late dissolued priory of the Holy Trinity within Aldgate so calleth it, bycause the Grasse market went downe that way, and was there kepte, but the strete was then broder.'

l. 27. *the George.* It is clearly identical with 'our great hospice in Lombard Street', which Edward III granted to St. Stephen's, Westminster, on 6 Aug. 1348 (*Mon. Angl.* vi. 1350, compare *Hist. MSS. Comm.* 9th Rep. 56 *a*, and *Anc. Deeds*, A. 13428). In 1402 the Greek ambassadors were entertained at the sign of St. George in Lombard St. (*Q. R. Wardrobe Accounts*—ap. Wylie, *Henry IV*, iv. 203). 'The George' Inn is several times mentioned in the *Paston Letters* between 1472 and 1505 (viz. v. 144, vi. 11, 172). For the inn in 1596 see *Inq. p. m. Lond.* iii. 238. For Earl Ferrers see i. 100 and note on p. 283 above; 'Lombard Street' is not mentioned either in the *Gesta Henrici* or by Hoveden. William de Ferrers, Earl of Derby (*d.* 1249), had his house in St. Lawrence Jewry Lane (*Cal. Charter Rolls*, ii. 38).

203, l. 10. *one other.* For the house of Sir Michael de la Pole in Lombard Street in 1364 see *Anc. Deeds*, D. 411.

l. 36. *Stane Church.* The name is explained by a reference to 'parochia de Stanenetha' (stone-hithe) at London in 1194. (*Cartularium de Colchester*, 298. Roxburgh Club.) 'Stonwarf' in All Hallows, Barking, occurs in 1304 (*Cal. Wills*, i. 163). See also note on 'Cradocks lane' below.

204, l. 3. *John Costin, Girdler . . . 1244.* No doubt an error for John Costyn, girdler, who by will made in 1442 and proved in 1447 left property charged with religious and charitable uses for the poor of All Hallows Stane Church (*Cal. Wills*, ii. 513).

l. 9. *Stiward.* The list in *Harley MS.* 6069, f. 30, reads 'Steward'.

l. 17. *the Writhsleys*, &c. The list of burials at St. Giles was revised accordingly. See i. 299-300 and ii. 245, 253 above. Another correction as to the burial-place of a Writhsley appears on ii. 39, see p. 260 above.

l. 20. *Cradocks lane.* In a deed of Stephen (1170-87), prior of

Trinity, there is reference to 'Stanenchirche in Cradocheslane' (*Anc. Deeds*, A. 2406).

l. 24. *Saint Nicholas Acon, or Hacon.* The church of St. Nicholas was given by Godwyn to Malmesbury Abbey in 1083; in a later deed, about 1190, it is called 'St. Nicholas Achim'—probably an error for 'Achun' (*Reg. Malmesburiense*, i. 5, ii. 12). St. Nicholas 'Hacun' occurs in 1246 (*Cal. Charter Rolls*, i. 309) and St. Nicholas 'Acun' in 1280 (*Cal. Wills*, i. 43). Possibly the name is due to some person like Haco the Alderman of 1130 (*Hist. MSS. Comm.* 9th Rep. 63, 66). Hacun was a not uncommon London surname in the twelfth and thirteenth centuries—see *Anc. Deeds*, A. 1070, 1075, 1078.

l. 27. *Francis Boyer . . . 1580.* Munday (p. 233) gives the date from his tomb as 14 June, 1581.

l. 31. *Saint Marie Woolnoth*, &c. Probably, as suggested by Mr. J. H. Round (*Athenaeum*, 31 March, 1888), the name was due to some person called Wulfnoth. Perhaps to the Wulfnoth de Walebroc of 1114–33 (*Chron. Ramsey*, p. 248; *Cartulary of Ramsey*, i. 139). Mr. Round has noted the form 'Wlnot maricherche' in 1191; 'Wollenothe Maricherche' (*Cotton MS.*, Faust., B. II, f. 71vo) and 'St. Mary Wulnothe Mariecherche' (*Anc. Deeds*, A. 2461) occur not much later. See also note on p. 317 below.

205, l. 5. *Cardinals Hat.* This tavern was demised by Simon Eyre on trust for the purpose stated, to Hugh Brice, who at his death bequeathed it with other property for pious uses in St. Mary Woolnoth (*Cal. Wills*, ii. 600, Brice's will dated 17 September, 1492, enrolled 25 Jan. 1498). 'Le Cardinals hat' is mentioned in 1364 (*id.* ii. 88).

l. 11. *John Moager.* Called 'Megre' in his will, dated 6 Aug. 1429, and proved 7 July, 1420. Apparently he was a Cornishman (*Cal. Wills*, ii. 422).

l. 12. *Perciuall . . . about 1504.* He died 19 April, 1503 (*Inq. p. m. London*, i. 21).

l. 19. *Sir Martin Bowes, Maior, buried about 1569.* His will, dated 10 August, 1565, was proved in the prerogative Court of Canterbury 21 Jan. 156 6/7. Another will was dated 29 July, 1566 (*Cal. Wills*, ii. 694–6, 728–9). The inscription on his tomb gave the date of his death as 4 August, 1566 (*Survey*, ed. 1633, p. 224).

207, l. 11. *this Epitaph.* In *Harley MS.* 538 the full epitaph is given, ending:

> Unto this citie in givinge so liberally
> Greate substaunce of livelode, wherfore now agre
> To pray unto God that reynethe eternally
> His soule to embrace and take to his mercy.
> He died in October the xxiij
> Of the reigne of the noble sixt Herry.

l. 22. *he gaue landes*, &c. The will of John Raynwell, dated 18 September, 1443, is recited at length in a deed of 2 May, 1466, printed in the *Report on Foedera*, Appendix C, pp. 22–7. See also *Cal. Wills*,

ii. 576–7. In connexion with his bequest for the relief of fifteenths the following note from the London Memoranda for 1539, ap. *Harley MS.* 530, f. 119, is of interest:—

'Memorandum. That M. Wyllm. Forman, yt tyme beyng maior of London, at ye Counsell of the Chamberleyn and of the Allderman of the Warde of Dowgate, whyche he was yt tyme allderman of, hys name ys M. Cottys, and they concluded yt the seyd ward schuld pay for a nede dude (*sic*) whyche was left one-payd in ye bookys of the Exchekar many yeres afore, the some of viij li. st., the whyche they wolde haue made thys warde of Dowgate for to haue pd. hyt. And they of ye seyd ward seyd playnly they wolde pay none, in so moche yt the meare commaundyd sertyn of them to ye tower, and ther they ware a day and a nyȝght. They made aunswer yt they wolde styke to ye will of Master Raynwell, for yt ys hys wyll yt the warde of dowgat shall pay none money for no fyveten exsep ther be above iij fyvetens in one yere, and so by ye help of god they [paid] none. Deo gracias.'

Alderman Cottys was, I suppose, John Cotes, who was mayor in 1542–3.

208, l. 27. *so called of a Bosse.* In Samuel Rowlands' *Humors Looking Glasse*, p. 29, the country fool goes to see:

> The Bosse at Billingsgate, and Londonstone,
> And at Whitehall the monstrous great Whales bone.

l. 39. *as Robert Fabian writeth.* This, again, comes from the MS. The printed *Continuation* (p. 685) is bald. In the Vitellius Chronicle the notice is rather briefer than that quoted by Stow, but is clearly from the same source (*Chron. London*, p. 209). Richard de Hakeneye died in 1342, and his wife Alice in 1349 (*Cal. Wills*, i. 467, 625). For expenses 'for the obyt and settyng upe of the tombe, and buryenge of Richard Hackney and Alys his wyff' in March, 1496–7, see Nichols, *Illustrations of Manners and Expences of Antient Times*, p. 88. (Extracts from the Churchwardens' accounts of St. Mary Hill.)

209, l. 16. *Robert Reuell.* He gave 200 marks. Nichols, *u. s.*

l. 20. *Queenes shippes.* This is the reading of *Harley MS.* 538, and is clearly right. Holstocke was comptroller for many years under Elizabeth, see *Cal. State Papers*, 1581–90, and Stow's *Annales*, 1121, 1141, ed. 1605.

l. 23. *S. Margaret Pattens.* Stow's derivation seems to be purely conjectural: if there were ever any patten-makers here, they were clean worn out in his time (vol. i. p. 81). St. Margaret Patynz occurs in the time of King John (*Mon. Angl.* vi. 624), St. Margaret de Patins in 1272, and del Patynes in 1291 (*Cal. Wills*, i. 20, 96). In the list of 1303 it is S. Margaret Patynes. It is doubtful how far pattens were in common use so early: Ducange has a quotation of 'patina' in 1256, but the first notice of patten-makers in London seems to be in 1379 (*Letter-Book* H, 135). The name might be due to a benefactor, as in so many other cases: Ranulph and Robert Patin are mentioned in twelfth-century deeds at St. Paul's (*Hist. MSS. Comm.* 9th Rep. 62, 63). See also *N. and Q.* 9th ser. xii. 170, 253.

210, ll. 7–9. *Roape Lane . . . Loue Lane.* It occurs as 'Love Lane formerly called Roppelane' in 1393, and as 'Roperelane now Love Lane' in 1455. In 1428 there is reference to 'le Stuehous' in Love-lane, in St. Mary Hill parish (*Cal. Wills*, ii. 311, 464, 536). The last instance indicates that in this case, as in that of Love Lane, Cripplegate, the name was due to wantons (cf. i. 296, above). I have not found 'Lucas-lane'; but Walter Lucas, baker, of St. Botulph Lane occurs in 1310 (*Letter-Book* B, 230). See also *N. and Q.* 10th ser. v. 302.

l. 22. *Marpor.* In *Harley MS.* 538, his Christian name, Nicholas, is given.

l. 29. *Southuckenton*, i.e. South Ockendon in Essex.

l. 37. *Rother Lane, or Red Rose Lane.* 'Rederesgate' is mentioned on a deed of Prior Norman (*d.* 1147) of Trinity (*Anc. Deeds*, A. 7309). Later instances are the lane called 'Rederisgate' in 1279, 'Rede Rose lane' in 1318, 'Retheresgates lane' in 1322, 'Puddyng lane otherwise Retherlane' in 1372 (*Cal. Wills*, i. 44, 278, 299, ii. 153). 'Finches Lane' called Pudding Lane in 1398 (*Cal. Inq. p. m.* iii. 255). 'Fynkes lane now called Puddyng lane' in 1449 (*Anc. Deeds*, A. 1723); cf. *Cal. Wills*, ii. 535). 'Retherhethe Lane *alias* Podding Lane' in 1553 (*Inq. p. m. Lond.* ii. 51). Simon Puddynglane, a baker, occurs in 1375 (*Mun. Gild.* III. 423).

211, l. 25. *Mercers and Haberdashers.* For a list of tenants on the bridge in 1633, see *Gent. Mag. Library*, xv. 308–9. They were chiefly Haberdashers, with some Mercers and Silkmen.

212, l. 5. *Henry Yeuele Freemason.* In his will, dated 25 May, and enrolled 28 October, 1400, he is described as 'mason, citizen and freeman of London' (*Cal. Wills*, ii. 346). For accounts of Yevele or Yevely, the greatest English architect of his day, see *Trans. Lond. and Midd.* ii. 259–66, *Dict. Nat. Biog.* lxiii. 321, and Lethaby, *Westminster Abbey*.

l. 7. *William Brampton*, stockfishmonger, February 1407 (*Cal. Wills*, ii. 368–9).

l. 12. *Robert Blanch.* Robert Braunche in his will; he died June 4, 1567 (*Inq. p. m. Lond.* ii. 64). *Harley MS.* 538, f. 70vo, reads: 'Robert, Braunche, 1567, with this epitaph following:

As nature yelds vs birth and lyf, so death draws on by kynde:
By deathe ageyne through faythe in Christ eternall lyfe we fynde.
A profe behold by me that ded enioy my mortal breathe
Full 50 yeres and 8 therto, and then gave place to deathe.
Of the company of girdelars fre I was, and Robert Braunch by name;
I was lyke yow and now am erthe, and you shall be the same.
Six children now supply my place, my soule is in the skye;
God send to them and the good life, and eke in Christ to dye.'

l. 13. *Iohn Couper*, &c. Stow corrects an error of his first edition (see p. 246 above). In *Harley MS.* 538, f. 71vo, he wrote: 'Also Iohn

Cowper, fishmonger, one of the shrives of London in the year of Christ 1551, was put by his tyme of maioraltie upon some private displeasure of his brethren, the aldermen, deceased 1584, and was there buried. Sir William Garrard, haberdasher, maior of London in the year of Christ 1555, deceased 1571, in the parishe of Seint Christofer by the Stok Market, but was buried in this parishe churche of Seint Magnus, because he was borne in that parishe, and there babtized.'

l. 27. *William Melker.* Presumably the William Melker of Eastcheap, whose will was proved in 1273 (*Cal. Wills*, i. 15).

l. 31. *Walter Dogget.* Strype gives the epitaph of Walter Dogget, vintner, *ob.* July 19, 1480, and of Alice his wife. Walter Dogget, the sheriff of 1380, by his will enrolled January 25, 1388, founded a chantry here for himself and his wife, another Alice (*Cal. Wills*, ii. 263–4). Walter's son John, whose wife was also called Alice, died and was buried here in 1403 (*id.* ii. 354).

213, l. 1. *Grasse Church.* St. Benedict de Garcherche in 1181–1204 (*Hist. MSS. Comm.* 9th Rep. 4).

214, l. 8. *Recordes.* See note on p. 357 below.

l. 16. *Fishmongers were greatly troubled.* These troubles were a part of the conflict between the victualling and clothing guilds, round which civic history centred during the reign of Richard II. The victualling guilds, whose leader was Nicholas Brembre, supported the King and Court party, whilst the clothing guilds headed by John Northampton sided with the opposition. See Dr. Sharpe's *Introduction* to *Letter-Book* H. The fishmonger referred to in l. 24 was Walter Sibyle. See also references on p. 393 below.

215, l. 29. *that he slue Jacke Straw.* The London Chronicles (e.g. Nicolas, 73–4, and Gregory's *Chronicle*, p. 91) state that Jack Straw was the leader of the rebels in London, and was killed by Walworth. This is also the account of Adam of Usk (*Chron.* pp. 1–2) and Hardyng (p. 339). The continuation of Knighton (ii. 137) states definitely that Jack Straw was only a nickname for Wat Tyler. It is possible that neither of the names was genuine, but they certainly represent two distinct persons; this is shown clearly in the *Rolls of Parliament* and in the *Chronicon Angliae*, 308–9. (See also *Anom. Chron.* 519–20; Walsingham, *Hist. Angl.* ii. 9–14.) The man who passed by the name of Jack Straw was arrested and tried, as Stow states, some days after the killing of Wat Tyler. See Professor Oman's *Great Revolt of* 1381, pp. 44–5. Dr. F. W. Brie has, however, maintained in *Eng. Hist. Rev.* xxi that Straw and Tyler were really the same person.

216, l. 30. *Eastcheape . . . a flesh Market of Butchers.* So Ben Jonson in *Every Man out of his Humour*, Act II, sc. i: 'Well, an e'er I meet him in the City, I'll have him jointed; I'll pawn him in Eastcheap among the butchers else.'

217, l. 4. *the kings sonnes . . . being in Eastcheape.* This narrative probably comes from one of the London Chronicles, but none of the extant copies are so full (see *Chron. Lond.* 341). The Vitellius Chronicle (*id.* 268) adds that as a consequence 'it was ordeyned that neither Tavern ne Cook shuld hold open their hous no more after ix of the clok'. (Probably in allusion to the regulation made in 1412 as to closing cook-shops on St. John's Eve, ap. *Memorials*, 581.) The incident helped to give rise to the legends of Henry V's riotous youth, and in that connexion Stow's note of the intervention of Chief Justice Gascoyne and the King's pardon is interesting.

l. 25. *he speaketh of no silks.* This is an oversight. Lydgate writes:

Then to the Cheap I began me drawne,
Where much people I saw for to stande:
One offered me velvet, sylke, and lawne.

For *London Lickpenny* see Lydgate's *Minor Poems* (Percy Soc.) and Nicolas, *London Chron.* 260 sqq.

ll. 36, 37. *Candlewright . . . or Candlewicke streete.* It appears as 'Candelwrich strete' in 1180–7 (*Hist. MSS. Comm.* 9th Rep. App. 16 *b*), 'Candelwiccestrate' in 1259, 'Candelwrihttestrate' in 1272 (*Cal. Wills*, i. 4, 14). Later it was called Candelwyke Street, and this was corrupted to Canwick Street, and ultimately to Cannon Street. The transition of the name is shown in *Nobody and Somebody*: 'If my breeches had as much cloth in them as ever was drawne betwixt Kendal and Canning Street' (Simpson, *School of Shakespeare*, i. 292). Long before Edward III's time it was occupied by workers of cloth, and especially by 'burellers', or makers of the coarse stuff called 'burel'. In 1279 there is note of a 'bureller of Candlewystrate' (*Cal. Wills*, i. 39; and see numerous instances in the Mercers Cartulary, ap. Watney, *Hospital of St. Thomas of Acon*, 286–8). In 1335 the burellers of Candelwykstrete were in controversy with the Weavers (*Letter-Book* E, 291, 297). Cloth of Candelwykstrate is mentioned in 1322 and 1372 (*id.* 172; *Cal. Wills*, ii. 145), and Lydgate, in *London Lickpenny*, writes:—

Throughout all Canwyke Street
Drapers much cloth offered me anon.

But there were also Wax-chandlers in Candlewick Street from an early date. In 1311 mention occurs of 'John le Cierger de Kandelwikstrate', and chaundelers of Candelwykstrete in 1305 and 1326 (*Letter-Books* B, 163, D, 137, E, 210). In 1371 Thomas de Weston, chandler, refers in his will to a tenement in St. Swithin's, which he had bought of Robert de Hatfield, bureller; and wax-chandlers of Candelwykstrete occur in 1402 (*Cal. Wills*, ii. 141, 353).

For protection granted to foreign clothworkers in 1344 see *Letter-Book* F, 111; and *Foedera*, iii. 23.

218, l. 30. *saint Marie Abchurch, Apechurch or Upchurch.* 'Robert the priest of Habechirce' occurs in a deed of the twelfth century (*Anc. Deeds*, A. 7821). Abchurch, which occurs as 'Abbechurche' in 1211 (*id.* A. 1449) is the normal form, but 'Apecherche lane' occurs in 1327, and 'Appecherche' in 1369 (*Cal. Wills*, i. 328, ii. 121). Riley says that

Upchurch is found in early documents, citing *Mun. Gild.* I. 100—date 1240, where, however, Upchurch near Chatham is clearly intended.

For the chantries of Winchcomb and Littleton (*d.* 1457) see *Cal. Wills*, ii. 340, 532.

219, l. 7. *the leaden porch.* 'Le Leden Porche' in Crooked Lane occurs in 1398–9 (*Cal. Inq. p. m.* iii. 255). Afterwards it was held by William Philip, Lord Bardolf, for life, and on June 11, 1441, was granted to John Merston, who still held it in 1461 (*C.P.R.* Henry VI, iii. 544; Edw. IV, i. 43). In 1485 it was granted to Thomas Freeman on the attainder of John, Duke of Norfolk (Campbell, *Mat. Hist. Henry VII*, ii. 319, 449). Taylor the Water-poet, writing in 1636 (*Travels through London*), mentions four houses that sell Rhenish wine and are inhabited by Dutchmen only, viz. 'The Stilliyard, the Swan in Thames Street, The Swan in Crooked Lane, and The Sun at St. Mary Hill.'

l. 15. *William de Burgo gaue*, &c. Under the will of Edmund Horn, who left them for a chantrie (*Cal. Wills*, i. 254).

l. 23. *tombe of Loueken was remoued.* No doubt one of those defaced by bad people in the reign of Edward VI (vol. i. p. 220). The brass plate was taken away, and used for another tomb at Walkerne in Hertfordshire, where the original inscription was discovered on the hidden side in 1870. The Fishmongers had restored Loueken's and Walworth's tombs in 1562. The name is sometimes spelt Lofkin, but is Lovekyn on the brass and in his will (*Cal. Wills*, ii. 117). See notice by J. G. Nichols, ap. *Trans. London and Middlesex*, iii. 133–7, and also vi. 341–70. For list of monuments at St. Michael's (similar to that on pp. 221–2) see *Harley MS.* 6069, f. 29.

l. 31. *arrested Wat Tyler.* Stow's account is based on Knighton, ii. 138, *Chron. Angliae*, 297, and *Anom. Chron.* 519–20. The squire's true name was Ralph Standish; 'John Cavendish' or 'Candish' is an error, which appears also in the *Annales*, p. 463, ed. 1605. The knighting of Walworth is taken almost word for word from *Anom. Chron.*, where, however, a blank is left for the third name. The City record (*Memorials*, 451) shows that Stow is correct in naming Sir Robert Launde.

221, l. 32. *Crosse and sworde of Saint Paul.* Stow is right. See the description of The Banner of St. Paul (on i. 63 above), which was the ancient banner of the City. Stow translates from the record in *Letter-Book* H. See *Memorials*, 447. The fable of Walworth's dagger got currency in Holinshed's *Chronicles*, ii. 747.

l. 37. *John Radwell.* Richard in his will (*Cal. Wills*, ii. 411).

222, l. 16. *Sir John Brudge.* In *Harley MS.* 538, 'maior of London 1520, deceased 1530.'

l. 32. *Beachamps Inne.* Reference to the tenement of Robert Beauchamp in St. Martin Orgar occurs in 1361 (*Letter-Book* G, 133).

l. 35. *saint Martin Orgar.* The name may be due to Orgar the deacon, who granted the church to St. Paul's in the twelfth century (*Hist. MSS. Comm.* 9th Rep. 63).

223, l. 18. *Alderman Beswicke.* William Beswicke, *d.* May 5, 1567 (*Inq. p. m. Lond.* ii. 102).

l. 32. *Licence . . . to new build.* In 1408 Richard Thorpe, the parson, had licence for alienation in mortmain of a plot of land for the enlargement of St. Swithin's and making of a new belfry (*C. P. R.* Henry IV, iii. 414).

224, l. 6. *Chaunteries.* Thomas Aylesby (*circa* 1470), William Neve (*d.* 1392), and Matilda Caxton (*d.* 1342) (*Cal. Wills*, i. 458, ii. 295, 584).

l. 9. *William White.* In *Harley MS.* 538, 'sheriff 1482, alderman, was there buried about 1500.'

l. 12. *prior of Tortington.* In Feb., 1286, Sir Robert Aguylon bequeathed his mansion, with courtyard and garden, in the parish of St. Swithin, to the prior of Tortington (*Cal. Wills*, i. 75). Robert had inherited it from his mother Joan, grand-daughter of Henry Fitz-Alwin, the first mayor, who lived here, and is in consequence called 'Henricus filius Eylwini de Londene-stane' (*Lib. de Ant. Legg.* 1, and Preface, pp. ix–xi, lxxiv–vi). In 1490 Henry Eburton, draper, left some adjoining tenements, called 'Draper's Halle', formerly belonging to Robert Auguylem, to his company (*Cal. Wills*, ii. 601). The Aguylons had land at Edburton in Sussex.

The above probably explains the statement made by Munday (*Survey*, 247, ed. 1633) under St. Mary Boathaw: 'The most memorable monument of all other there was that of Sir Henry Fitz-Alwine, Draper, the first Lord Mayor of London that ever was, and continued (by several elections) in the Maioraltie above 24 yeeres. His dwelling-house remaineth yet in the Parish, divided now into two or three houses. His Monument can be proved to be in that Church, as his Armes on the glasse windows and Gravestones doe sufficiently shew. Besides those houses were his gift to the Drapers, and they pay a quit-rent in his name yeerely for ever. All which are sufficient to testify that he was not buried in the Priorie of the holy Trinity within Ealdgate (now called the Dukes Place) as formerly hath been avowched by Mr. Stowe.'

Strype observed sagaciously: 'All this is not evidence enough against Stow's own eyes.' It is finally disposed of by the Trinity Cartulary (*Guildhall MS.* 122, ff. 337–8), where against the record of a quit-rent of 5*s.* on lands in St. Mary Boathaw, given by Henry Fitz-Alwin for the commemoration of his obit, is set the note: 'Iste Henricus, Maior primus London., obiit xiij Kal. Octobris [19 Sept.] et sepultus est infra introitum capituli in medio sub lamina[1] marmorea.' Henry died in 1212; his lands were taken into the king's hands by a writ dated 5 Oct. of that year (*Rot. Pat.* 14 John). There is nothing to connect him with the Drapers. Stow calls him a goldsmith (i. 306), perhaps from the belief that his father was Alwine, son of Leofstanus the goldsmith (i. 122). In

[1] The transcript has 'lan'a'. Hearne suggests 'lamina', ap. Wm. of Newborough, iii. 727.

a deed of 1196 he is called 'Henry son of Ailwin, son of Leofstan, mayor of London', and in a deed of Henry II's time he is described as 'one of the nobles of the city' (*Anc. Deeds*, A. 2103, A. 2507). This supports Dr. Stubbs' suggestion that he was an hereditary baron of London (*Const. Hist.* i. 674). Henry the Alderman, son of Ailwin, occurs in 1177 (*Anc. Deeds*, A. 7295).

The prior of Tortington's house in Candlewick Street was granted to John de Vere (*d.* 1540), fifteenth Earl of Oxford, on June 8, 1539 (*Letters and Papers*, xiv. 1192 (8)). John (*d.* 1562), sixteenth earl, kept great state here (see i. 89 above). Edward, seventeenth earl, moved to Fisher's Folly (see p. 298). Anne, daughter of Sir John Hart (*d.* 1603), married Humphrey Smith, Alderman, who was living at Oxford Place in 1633 (*Survey*, p. 243, ed. 1633). In 1641 the Salters' Company purchased 'the great house called London Stone or Oxford House' of Captain George Smith. This fixes the house of Henry Fitz-Alwin on the site of Salters Hall. See Lethaby, *London before the Conquest*, 177–9.

l. 18. *Edmond Dudley.* For Dudley's house in the parish of St. Swithin, beside London Stone, see *Letters and Papers*, i. 425, 4231.

l. 24. *London stone.* Camden first suggested that it was 'a miliary like that in the Forum of Rome'. Wren (*Parentalia*, 265) at the time of the Great Fire formed the opinion, based on the discovery of extensive Roman remains, that 'by reason of the large foundation, it was rather some more considerable monument in the Forum'. The position 'neare vnto the channel' described by Stow would have been in the middle of the street. In 1742 it was removed to the kerb against the buildings on the north, and in 1798, being then reduced to a mere stump, was built into a niche in the wall of St. Swithin's Church. For the history of London Stone and theories as to its origin and significance see Lethaby *u.s.* pp. 179–84; J. E. Price, *Roman Pavement in Bucklersbury*, 55–65; and Gomme, *Governance of London*. In Stow's time London Stone was one of the countryman's sights in the capital; see p. 310.

225, l. 10. *Font in Poules Church.* James Pilkington, bishop of Durham, denouncing the abuses of St. Paul's, wrote thus in 1561 (ap. *Works*, p. 210): 'The south alley for Popery and usury, the north for simony, and the horse fair in the midst for all kinds of bargains, meetings, brawlings, murders, conspiracies, and the font for ordinary payment of money, as well known to all men as the beggar knows his bush.' For a payment to be made at St. Paul's in 1362 see *Anc. Deeds*, A. 5869; one recognized place was 'the Rode' by the north door (*id.* C. 913); for a payment at the Font in 1537 (*id.* A. 693).

l. 11. *now . . . at the Royall Exchange.* See agreement in 1571 for an annuity to be payable 'at the Tendring House within the Ryall Exchaunge' (*Anc. Deeds*, A. 13489), and in 1597 for a payment to be made 'att or in the Telling howse usuallie appointed for receiptes and paimentes' (*id.* A. 13297).

l. 30. *tooke name of these Stockes.* In 1282 Henry le Waleis built 'domos apud Wolchirchehawe, quae vocantur Hales, anglice Stockes' (*Ann. Lond.* 90). This fixes the identity of the house called 'le Hales' which is recorded in the *Liber Custumarum* to have been given by Waleis for the support of the Bridge (*Mun. Gild.* II. i. 95; *Letter-Book* B, 217).

226, l. 5. *This Stockes market*, &c. Fabyan (p. 575) mentions only that it was begun. But see Nicolas, *London Chronicle*, p. 93, *sub anno* 1410: 'Also in this yere the stokkes betwen the Cornhull and the Pultrye was begone to make, and in the yere next folwnge it was ful complet and made.' The 'Stocks market' was on the site of the present Mansion House.

l. 18. *S. Mary Wool church.* An alleged charter of William I professed to confirm the gift to Westminster Abbey of St. Mary 'Newcirke' by Alfward 'cognomento Grossus' (*Cotton Charter*, vi. 3; it is a forgery, probably of the reign of Henry I). However, about 1104, Eudo 'dapifer' gave to Colchester Abbey, with the assent of Ailward Grossus the priest, the church of St. Mary 'de Westcheping, quae vocatur Niewechirche', which his father Hubert de Rie had bestowed on Ailward (*Cart. de Colchester*, 3-15, Roxburghe Club: cf. i. 253-4 above). The possession of the church by Colchester was disputed by the monks of Westminster (see *Eng. Hist. Review*, xvi. 726-8). As 'Newchurch' it was commonly known till about 1300, and even in 1410 it is described as 'St. Mary Newechirche otherwise Wolchirchehawe' (*Anc. Deeds*, A. 1958, B. 2110, 2112; *Mun. Gild.* II. i. 236). But it appears as St. Mary of 'Wollechurchehawe' in 1260 (*Cal. Charter Rolls*, ii. 33); and the market at Wollechirchehawe is mentioned in 1268 (Madox, *Hist. Exchequer*, i. 779). Mr. J. H. Round (*Athenaeum*, 17 Aug. 1889), on the strength of the form 'Wlnotmaricherche', and the analogous 'Wolmaricherche', which occurs in 1281, has argued that 'Woolchurch-haw' is a corruption of 'Wulnothmaricherch-haw', or the churchyard belonging to St. Mary Wolnoth (assuming that this was the mother-church of St. Mary Newchurch). This, however, is conjectural, and Stow may after all be right as to the derivation. Walbrook was a centre of the wool-trade in the latter half of the thirteenth century, when the name 'Woolchurch' first appears, and William de Wulcherchhawe was interested in that trade in 1293 (see note on p. 324 below). The sale of wool at St. Mary Woolchurch was regulated by *La Custome de Wollchirchawe* about 1300 (*Mun. Gild.* I. 246, from the *Liber Horne*).

227, l. 13. *fayre Church of Saint Stephen.* See history of the Church in *Trans. London and Middlesex*, v. 327-402. The documents there quoted show that Stow's account was accurately taken from the old church book written in the time of Edward IV. Henry Chichele was rector of St. Stephen's 1396-7. The patronage was given to Colchester Abbey by Eudo about 1100 (*Cart. Colchester*, p. 3).

228, l. 13. *Sir Richard Baker.* The uncle of the historian. He died in 1594. Thomas Gore, grocer, left his two messuages in Gracechurch Street and Lombard Street to the Grocers by will dated 11 July, 1586 (*Cal. Wills*, ii. 723).

l. 21. *a street so called of Buckle.* More accurately of the great city family of the Bukerels or Buckerells. A deed of 1270 shows that Thomas Buckerel had lately held property in Bukerelesbury (Watney, *Hospital of St. Thomas of Acon*, p. 262). The name occurs again as 'Bokerelesberi' in 1277, as 'Bokeleresbury' in 1376 and 1449, and as 'Boclersbury' in 1496 (*Cal. Wills*, i. 29, ii. 522, 599). See also notes on pp. 329–30.

229, l. 7. *S. Mary Bothaw.* Peter the priest gave his church of St. Mary Bothage to Christchurch, Canterbury, about 1150 (*Litterae Cantuarienses*, iii. 357).

l. 15. *Armes in the Windowes.* Munday identified some of them with the supposed arms of Henry Fitz-Ailwin, whom he alleged to have been buried here. See note on p. 315.

230, l. 20. *Copped hall.* It is mentioned in 1285; in 1292 Roger de Dreyton left his houses called 'La Coppedhalle' in the parish of St. John Walbrook, to be sold for the poor (*Cal. Wills*, i. 71, 106). For Ralph Cobham see *Cal. Inq. p. m.* ii. 328.

231, l. 26. *the Erber.* John de Hatfield, pepperer, dated his will on 12 August, 1368, at his house near *lerber* (*Cal. Wills*, ii. 122). His widow, Elena, in 1373 transferred to William, Lord Latimer, 'totum tenementum meum in London vocat.' le Erber'. Latimer's son-in-law, John Neville, of Raby, held it in 1384 (deeds in *Husting Rolls*, 101 (174), 106 (34), 112 (126), 117 (131); see also *Cal. Inq. p. m.* iii. 31). There was a Common-beam at the house called 'la Herber' in Walbrook in 1392 (*Letter-Book* H, 385). The Erber came into the possession of Geoffrey Scrope's grand-nephew William, Earl of Wiltshire, at whose forfeiture in December, 1399, it was granted to John Neville's son Ralph, Earl of Westmorland (*C. P. R.* Henry IV, i. 149). Ralph's son Richard, Earl of Salisbury, was lodged there in 1458 (*Chron. Lond.* 168). It came to George, Duke of Clarence, as part of his share of the Neville inheritance (*C. P. R.* Edw. IV, ii. 346, 457, 488). On his execution it fell to the crown, and on 22 July, 1486, was granted to John de Vere, thirteenth Earl of Oxford, who held it till 1513 (Campbell, *Materials Hist. Henry VII*, i. 11, 527; *Letters and Papers*, i. 1774). It was then restored to Clarence's daughter Margaret Pole, Countess of Salisbury, who lived there till her execution in 1541 (*id.* ii. 1563; xvi. p. 459). In consequence it was sometimes called Salisbury Place.

l. 35. *Bush lane*, &c. Carter Lane and the Chequer are both named in 1541 (*Letters and Papers*, xvi. 459).

232, l. 4. *Granthams lane.* In 1343 it was reported that Grantham had blocked it with two great stones and two iron bars (*Mun. Gild.* II. ii. 449). It is now called Brewers Lane. For Dodmer see *Anc. Deeds*, A. 12629.

l. 17. *Lambards messuage.* As belonging to John Lambard, father of William Lambard, the Kentish antiquary (*Inq. p. m. Lond.* i. 134).

l. 21. *the Steleyard.* In the edition of 1598 Stow wrote, 'Stelehouse or Steleyard,' preserving the old alternative, which in his time had gone out of use. The origin and meaning of the name have been so much discussed that it will be well to give its history.

The merchants of Cologne had their house in London as early as 1157. This was probably identical with the *Gilda Aula* or *Gildehalda Teutonicorum*, which is the regular description of the house of the Hanse merchants in early deeds (see note on p. 278). The *Gildehalda Teutonicorum*, at the corner of Cosin Lane and Thames Street, was distinct from the original Stalhof or Steelyard proper, which was on the east of Windgoose Lane (Lappenberg, *Urkundliche Geschichte des Hansischen Stahlhofes*, II. 96, 142). But though the Hanse did not come into possession of the Steelyard till 1475, they were in occupation of it before 1320, when their earliest extant ordinance refers specifically to the booths and chambers in the *Stalhof* (*id.* I. 24, II. 119). The earliest instance of the name 'Steelyard' which I have found is in 1382, 'quedam terre et redditus apud le Steelyerde' (*Cal. Inq. p. m.* iii. 71). In 1384 there is a reference to 'Styleyerd Lane' (*C. P. R.* Rich. II, ii. 516). In a bond executed by Sir Stephen Scroop at Dantzig in 1394 there is reference to the 'Curia Calibis' in London (*Hansisches Urkundenbuch*, v. 151, ed. Hohlbaum). During the early part of the fifteenth century I have no note of English references to the Steelyard, but in the Statutes of the London Hanse there is an order as to the closing of the door leading to the 'Stalhof' in 1410, and as to chambers therein in 1460 (Lappenberg, II. 120). Under their agreement with Edward IV the Hanse obtained possession of tenements between the old *Gilda Aula* and Windgoose Lane, and also of the '*Stilehof* otherwise called the *Stileyerd*' (*id.* II. 142–3, Act of 1475; and in other deeds 'le Stolehof' *alias* 'le Styleyerd' *id.* II. 138–9). Up to this time the house of the Hanse had been called in English 'Easterlings Hall'; now *Styleyerd* came into use as a name for the whole curtilage (see *Chron. Lond.* 198, *sub anno* 1493). Still, in 1509 we get mention of 'tenements betweene the *hall of Estlande* called *Guildehalda Theutonicorum*, and the *Stalehalfe*, whych is theire dynyng hall' (Lappenberg, II. 170). But in Acts of Henry VIII 'Stilliard' and 'Gyldehalda Teutonicorum' are used as synonymous (cf. citations ap. *N. and Q.* 10th ser. vi. 331). At the end of the sixteenth century the regular form of the name was *Stillyard* or *Stilliard*.

The instances of 1382–94 are conclusive as to the meaning attached to the name 'Steelyard' or 'Stahlhof' in England at that time; but they do not prove that this interpretation was correct. It is true that the Hanse Merchants brought some steel to England (for a trifling instance in 1408 see *Hansische Geschichtsquellen*, vi. 300, ed. Kunze); but the trade was not of sufficient importance to explain or justify the name. Moreover, if the name were of English origin it should on the analogy of 'Tymberhawe' and 'Woolcherchehawe' have been 'Steel-hawe'; I have not found 'yard' in any other early London place-name. So it seems probable that 'Steelyard' is simply an erroneous translation of 'Stahlhof', a name which dates from 1320.

The meaning of 'Stahlhof' is itself obscure. Lappenberg (I. 174) suggests that it was a stall-place or market-place, where goods were exposed for which there was no room in the old Guildhall. Thus it would closely have resembled Blackwell Hall, or Winchester-seld and Tanners-seld (see pp. 324, 337). This interpretation is supported by the reference to chambers and booths in 1320. But 'Staal-hof' in Dutch anciently meant 'a pattern office where samples of cloth were stamped' (Calisch, *Dutch Dictionary*). Cloth was one of the chief articles of Hanseatic trade in London. One of the principal tenements comprised in the original Steelyard was called 'le Dyhouse' in 1386, and this led Lappenberg (I. 70, cf. II. 68, 138–40) to suggest that there might be some connexion with the *Stahle* or dye test-cloths of the merchants.

The connexion of 'Steelyard' the place with 'Steelyard' a beam or balance has been much debated. In 1531 there is reference to the 'great scales and balance, and of the Iron Beam, and of the beam of 'le Hanzes Hangis' called 'the Stilliarde Beme' (*Letters and Papers*, v. p. 104). For a discussion on this point see *N. and Q.* 10th ser. vi. 282, 369, 412.

In Stow's time the Steelyard was famous for its winehouse in Thames Street, which was a popular resort: 'I come to entreat you to meet him this afternoon at the Rhenish Winehouse in the Stilliard. Will you steal forth and taste of a Dutch bun and a keg of sturgeon?' (Webster, *Westward Ho!* Act II. sc. i.)

For other copies of deeds relating to the *Gildhalla Teutonicorum* and the *Steelyard* see *Mun. Gild.* I. 485–8, and *Report on Foedera*, App. A. 150, and App. C. 16–32.

233, l. 7. *the said marchants.* Stow's list of names is not quite accurate. The *Liber Albus* has: 'Gerardus Merbode, aldermannus Hanse predicte, Ludulphus de Cussard, civis Coloniensis, Luderus de Dunevare, burgensis Tremoniae, Johannes de Areste, burgensis Tremoniae, Bertramus de Hamburgh, Godescalcus de Hudendale, burgensis Tremoniae, Johannes de Dole, burgensis Monasterii.' In the copy from the Hamburg archives (*Rep. on Foedera*, C. 18) there are a few variations, viz.: 'Ludulphus de Cuffelde,' 'Luderus de Dunenar;' 'Trevirensis' for 'Tremoniae'.

234, l. 13. *Richard Lions.* His house and quay on the east side of the quay and garden of Easterlings Hall passed through various hands to the Abbey of St. Albans in 1456; the Hanse obtained full ownership in 1475 (Lappenberg, I. 59–66, with numerous deeds in the *Urkunden*).

l. 19. *Windgoose Alley*, 'Wendegoslane' in 1343 (*Mun. Gild.* II. 449). The name suggests a German origin; a Benedict Wandegos occurs in the 13th century (*Anc. Deeds*, A. 1623). It is called Wendegayne Lane in Rainwell's will. In 1475 the Hanse acquired all the tenements on both sides of the lane, and closed the north end with a wall of stone (Lappenberg, II. 169).

l. 21. *Abbot of S. Albons.* See above, and Lappenberg, *Urkunden* xcv–civ.

l. 23. *John Rainwell.* His house and other tenements were on the east side of Windgoose lane, including the original Stahlhof or Steelyard, and bounded on the south by the Thames and on the north by the land of Robert Combarton; thus Rainwell's land did not reach as far as Thames Street. The property consisted of a mansion with 'le Dyehouse', and two mansions on steps, and a wine-cellar: it had belonged to John Northampton—mayor in 1381–3. See Lappenberg, I. 68–72 and *Urkunden*, xliii, cv, cxxvii, and cl, with a plan of the whole site.

235, l. 11. *William Lichfield.* Thomas Gascoigne (*Loci e Libro Veritatum*, 189) mentions him along with Gilbert Worthyngton of St. Andrew's, Holborn, amongst the famous preachers of his day. Lichfield and Worthyngton were two of the promoters of schools in London in February, 1447 (*Rot. Parl.* v. 137, see vol. i. p. 73 above). Lichfield's 'Complaint of God to Sinful man and the answer of Man', together with a 'Dialogue of the Passion between God and the Penitent Soul' are extant in Gonville and Caius Coll. MS. 174, ff. 469–82. In a deed relating to property in All Hallows parish, and dated 12 Dec. 1447, William Lichfield, clerk, is nominated as an attorney (Lappenberg, *u. s.* II. 73). The date of his death was given by Stow and Strype as 24 Oct. 1447; but this is clearly an erroneous reading of his epitaph:

Luce bis x, quater i, migrat Octobris sine panno,
C. quater, x quater, v semel, ter i, M. Karus.

which gives xxiiii Oct. M cccc xxxx viii, or 1448.

Similarly the date of John Brickle's death was printed in error as 1451 instead of 1437, his epitaph reading:

C. quater, x, ter, v, semel, i, bis, et M. sociatis,

which gives M. cccc. xxxvii.

Strype reads for '*C. quater*' in both cases *Equater*, which is meaningless.

l. 24. *one Pot.* Henry Pott, about 1550, as tenant of Sir Ralph Dodmer (*Anc. Deeds*, A. 12629). See vol. i. 232 above. The site is now occupied by the City of London Brewery.

236, l. 1. *Cold Harbrough.* Stow's account is not quite accurate: see paper by Mr. Philip Norman in *Archaeologia*, lvii. 257–84. Poultney by his will directed the Cold Harbour to be sold. A deed of 1 Nov. 1353 shows that at his death the Earl of Hereford held two parts for life, and the third part was held by Sir Nicholas Loveyn (not Lovell as on p. 236), who had married Poultney's widow, as part of her dower; Poultney's executors sold the reversion of the whole to Loveyn. Afterwards it belonged to Edward the Black Prince. Henry IV granted it to his son Henry in 1410. Later it was owned by Sir John Cornwall, Lord Fanhope, after whose death, in 1443, it passed to his step-son John Holland, Duke of Exeter. The grant of Richard III to the Heralds (*C. P. R.* Edward IV, &c. iii. 422) was cancelled by Henry VII (cf. Campbell, *Mat. Hist. Henry VII*, i. 475–6), who gave the Cold Harbour to his mother Margaret Beaufort for life. On her death Henry VIII gave it, in July 1509, to George Talbot, Earl of Shrewsbury. (*Letters and Papers*, i. 253.) Presumably on Shrewsbury's death, in 1538, it reverted to the Crown, and was about that time bestowed on Cuthbert Tunstal, who held it till 1553, when it was restored to the then Earl of Shrewsbury.

For the lease to Henry Stow see *Letter-Book* E, 108, and for the Charter of 1347 *Letter-Book* F, 158.

l. 33. *the lesse.* It is All Hallows 'ad Fenn. in Roperia' in *Cal. Inq. p. m.* iii. 211.

237, l. 3. *H. Holland, duke of Excester, and he was lodged there in the yeare 1472.* In *Harley MS.* 538, f. 80 'Ro. Fabian' is written in the margin. This statement is not found in the printed Fabyan. The date seems to be wrong : cf. the Vitellius Chronicle under 1471 :—'And the xiiij^th^ day of ffebruary the Duke of Exceter cam to London from beyond the see, . . . and after to his place in Tamystrete' (*Chron. Lond.* 183).

l. 19. *a great number of smal tenements.* The Cold Harbour became notorious as the dwelling-place of needy persons, and a sanctuary for debtors and vagabonds. So Ben Jonson in *The Silent Woman*, Act. II, sc. iii :—'It knighthood shall do worse, take sanctuary in Cole Harbour and fast. It shall fright all it friends with borrowing letters; and when one of the fourscore hath brought it ten shillings, it knighthood shall go to the Cranes or the Bear at the Bridge-foot and be drunk in fear.'

And Webster, *Westward Ho!* Act IV, sc. ii :—'Swore you would build me a lodging by Thames side with a watergate to it, or else take me a lodging in Cole Harbour.'

l. 38. *Mannor of the Rose.* Originally it belonged to Sir John Poultney, and is perhaps the house which he had licence to crenellate in 1341 (*C. P. R.* Edw. III, v. 331). It was called his principal messuage in his will. In 1384 Richard, Earl of Arundel acquired 'Pulteneyesyn' from the Master and chaplains of St. Lawrence College (*Anc. Deeds*, D. 805). It is called 'My Lady's Inne of Arundel' in 1422 (Lappenberg, *Stahlhof*, II. 63). In 1450 it is described as 'Messuagium sive hospicium vocatum Poultenaysin'. It had been sold by John Holland, Duke of Exeter, to William de la Pole, Duke of Suffolk, who was living there about 1446 (*Hist. MS. Comm.*, 9th Rep. 52). Suffolk's heirs retained it, with some vicissitudes, till 1506, when on the attainder of Edmund de la Pole it was granted to Edward, Duke of Buckingham (*d.* 1521) (*Inq. p. m. Lond.* i. 76). In *Henry VIII*, Act I. sc. ii, reference is thus made to Buckingham: 'The Duke being at the Rose, within the parish St. Lawrence Pountney.' In 1526 it was granted to Henry Courtenay, Earl of Devon, after whose execution in 1538 it was granted in 1539 to Robert Ratcliffe, Earl of Sussex (*Letters and Papers*, xiv. 867, c. 17), whose son sold the greater part to the Merchant Taylors, and the rest to Alderman Beswicke. See *Archaeologia*, lvii. 268–9.

238, l. 32. *a common cookerie or Cookes row.* FitzStephen has simply *publica coquina.* But Stow is probably right in his interpretation of this as a Cooks' Row, and not merely a solitary cook-shop. The building Assize drawn up after the Great Fire in 1212 ordered all the cook-shops on Thames to be whitewashed and plastered inside and out (*Mun. Gild.* II. i. 86; see also Mr. Riley's Preface, p. xxxii). There is a reference to 'coquinae Vinetrie' in 1221 (*Anc. Deeds*, A. 1647).

239, l. 27. *Herber lane or Brikels lane.* Herbier lane in Vintry is mentioned in a fourteenth-century deed (*Hist. MSS. Comm.*, 9th Rep. 16), and as late as 1448 (*Cal. Wills*, ii. 516). John Brikels is probably the John Brickles who died in 1437 (see p. 321 above). It is now Brickhill lane.

l. 31. *three Cranes.* Anciently there was only one Crane, and the inn was called 'The Crane in Vintry' (*Chron. Lond.* p. 81, *sub anno* 1425). Sir Walter Scott in *Kenilworth* (ch. ii) refers to it as 'the most topping tavern in London'. If not that, it was a well-known inn. Ben Jonson, in *Bartholomew Fair*, Act I, sc. i, associates it with the more famous 'Mermaid' and 'Mitre': 'A pox o' these pretenders to wit! Your Three Cranes, Mitre, and Mermaid men! not a corn of true salt, not a grain of right mustard amongst them all.' Pepys in Jan., 1662, had 'a sorry poor dinner' there in a 'narrow doghole of a room' (*Diary*, ii. 177). 'Le Peynted Aley' occurs in 1442 (*Cal. Wills*, ii. 513).

240, l. 1. *Iohn Gisers, Vintner.* This is the John Gisors who died in 1351. His grand-daughter Margaret married Henry Pycard, and inherited all his lands and tenements in St. Martin in the Vintry (*Cal. Wills*, i. 643–4). See further note on p. 354 below.

l. 19. *The Vintners.* On the history of the Company and their muniments see an article by J. G. Nichols in *Trans. Lond. and Middlesex*, iii. 432–47, with special reference to Stodie's bequest.

l. 32. *sweet wines.* By a patent dated Nov. 26, 1373, John Peachie or Pecche obtained a monopoly for the sale of sweet wines by retail (*Letter-Book* G, 318, 320). For this and his extortion in connexion therewith he was accused in the Good Parliament of 1376, and imprisoned (*Rot. Parl.* ii. 328). As a consequence he was, along with Richard Lions and Adam Bury, removed from his aldermanry and deprived of the freedom of the City (*Letter-Book* H, 38, 44). It was an incident in the political rivalry between the victualling and clothing Guilds. See note on p. 312 above.

241, l. 10. *the Church booke.* Unfortunately it no longer exists.

l. 17. *so much for Wines.* 'In the time of Henry the Eight, and Edward the Sixt, Vinteners and Taverners houses were not in any such measure, maner, nor plenteous store and variety of wines of all Nations in any one man's house, as now at this time there is in every Vintener's house; for in those days whosoever drew White, Claret, and red Wine, sold no more kindes of Wine; the Dutch then sold only Reinish wine, as now they doe; and at that time, when an Argosey came with Greeke and Spanish Wines, viz. Muscadell, Malmsey, Sacke, and Bassard, the Apothecaries of London then went unto those merchants, and every man bought such Rundlets, vessels, and quantities of those rich wines, as they thought they should Retayle, unto such as usually bought of them only for Physicke and for the Communion Table' (*Annales*, p. 867, ed. 1631). This is an addition made by Howes, but it looks so like a reminiscence of Stow's that it may very probably have been derived from his Collections.

242, l. 3. *Palmers lane, now called Anchor lane.* 'Palmereslane' in 1343 (*Mun. Gild.* II. ii. 450), and in 1439 and 1448 (*Cal. Wills*, ii. 487, 516).

l. 5. *Worcester house.* Worcester Place in St. James, Garlickhithe, was granted on May 6, 1551, by William Somerset, Earl of Worcester, to Thomas Parrys, who died seized thereof in 1563 (*Inq. p. m. Lond.*, ii. 27).

l. 11. *of olde time called Arches.* The deed, dated 1276, is calendared in *Ancient Deeds*, A. 7823; there, and in Stow's own note from a Cartulary of St. Mary Overy (ap. *Harley MS.* 544, f. 100), it reads 'Walter de Forda' and 'seld called Wynchestre seld'. A little lane called 'Le Arche' in the parish of Paternoster cherche occurs in 1299 (*Letter-Book* C, 35).

For the *Selda Wyntoniae* at Queenhithe in 1244, see *Mun. Gild.* III. 448. In 1275–80 it belonged to the Hardels (*Cal. Wills*, i. 24, 46). In 1299 William de Wulcherchehawe owned 'la Wyncestreselde', where the merchants of Andover came to deal in wool (*Mun. Gild.* II. i. 115; cf. *Letter-Book* C, 13, for 1293), 'Andovreseld' and 'le Stonhous' adjoining thereto belonged to John le Blund in 1316. (*Anc. Deeds*, C. 586). John Stodeye had a lease of 'Wynchestre Seld' in Allhallows the Great in 1347 (*Letter-Book* F, 112). I have not found any reference to 'Stendenbridge'; but William de Staundon was patron of St. Mary Somerset in 1273 (*Cal. Wills*, i. 15), and William Stondon had land in Walbrook in 1428 (see i. 227 above).

243, l. 20. *Sir Heere Tanke, or Hartancleux.* This is Sir Hartank Van Clux, a Silesian knight, who entered the service of Henry IV about 1400, and was afterwards employed by Henry V as a diplomatic agent at the court of Sigismund.

There is a list of burials in *Harley MS.* 6069, f. 29, which reads: Thomas Wandefforde, Sir Edmond Moulso, Sir William Houldhall, William Bernok and Robert Shreuyngham (for 'Sherington').

ll. 36, 37. *this Tower . . . so called, of pertayning to the kinges.* Stow is in error. 'The Royal' was a corruption of 'la Ryole', a name which was due to occupation by wine-merchants from La Reole in Gascony. At the end of the reign of Henry III, Thomas Bat demised his tenement 'la Riole' to Simon de Beauvais (Stow's 'Beawmes'), who was surgeon to Edward I and had it confirmed to him in 1275 (*Cal. Charter Rolls*, ii. 202). At the great Iter in 1320 Simon's grandson failed to maintain his right to 'La Riole' (*Placita de Quo Warranto*, 461). Edward III, in 1331, gave 'La Real' for a wardrobe to Queen Philippa, who was building there in 1349–53 (*C. P. R.* Edw. III, vii. 537, viii. 393, ix. 136, 342, 518). For grant of *hospitium vocatum le Reole* to St. Stephens in 1369, see *Mon. Angl.* vi. 1350.

244, l. 38. *Richard de Wilehale*, &c. Stow obtained this from the Cartulary of St. Mary Overy, cf. his note in *Harley MS.* 544, f. 100vo.

245, l. 13. *Forgers of Blades, and therefore called Bladers.* Presumably 'blader' was used in Stow's time as the equivalent of bladesmith. But when he employs 'blader' to translate 'bladarius', as he does in the case of Walter Nele, and of William Palmer on i. 347, there is no doubt that he was in error. In the Middle Ages 'bladarius' meant a cornmonger or dealer in corn (*bladum*). So in the Ordinances of the Crafts catalogued in the *Liber Albus*, *Bladarii et Portitores bladi* appear together, and other ordinances are for *Cultellarii et Bladsmithes*, and for *Cultellarii et Vaginarii* (sheath makers—*Mun. Gild.* I. 734–5, and III. 412, where 'bladarii' are called to give evidence on the price of corn). Walter Nele, as shown by Stow's citation from his will, had a wide agricultural connexion; of other bladers, William Palmer in 1349, and William de Thame in 1357 make bequests of granaries, and John de Eneveld in 1361 of a quantity of bread, corn, and malt (*Cal. Wills*, i. 538, 673, ii. 33). It is, however, noteworthy that in 1382 one William Warde, a 'cuteller' of York, complained that he had been admitted as a blader instead of as a cutler: here the word must surely mean bladesmith (*Memorials*, 474). Hamo le Barber (*Cal. Wills*, i. 533) was, like Palmer, connected with Henley; probably he was a cornmonger by profession, and a barber only by name. See for both Nele and Barber, *Letter-Book* E, 233.

ll. 36–8. *H. Causton . . . 1396.* Henry Causton, mercer, founded a chantry here in 1350 (*Cal. Wills*, i. 638).

246, l. 18. *William Shipton.* William Brampton by his will, dated 1456, founded a chantry here for William Shepton (*Cal. Wills*, ii. 559, 567).

l. 28. *the king was then lodged.* See notes on pp. 280 and 324.

247, l. 28. *Ringed hall.* In 1352 it occurs as the property of Benedict de Folsham, grocer (*Anc. Deeds*, C. 189). His company had met there in 1349 (Kingdon, *Grocers' Archives*, 38). Afterwards it belonged to Rewley Abbey, Oxford. Henry VIII granted it on February 11, 1541, to Morgan Phelippe *alias* Wolfe, his goldsmith, who at once sold it to Sir Thomas Mildmay (*Letters and Papers*, xvi. 580). Later owners were Sir James Croft, and Stephen Woodroffe, who died seized thereof in 1576 (*Inq. p. m. Lond.* iii. 4).

248, l. 4. *Kerion lane.* 'Kyrune lane' in 1259, afterwards usually 'Kyron' or 'Kirone' lane (*Cal. Wills*, i. 3, 24, 80, ii. 64). John Kerion held land in St. Laurence, Candlewick St., in 1284 (*Cotton MS.*, Faustina, A. viii, f. 164). There was a 'Kyrone lane' at Kingston (*Anc. Deeds*, B. 1612, 1651).

l. 9. *saint Martin de Beremand.* 'Bærmanne cyrc' is mentioned in an alleged charter of William I to Westminster in 1067 (*Cotton Chart.* vi. 3; this is, however, a fabrication, probably of the time of Henry I). Ranulph Peverel gave it to Gloucester Abbey in the time of William II

(*Cart. S. Pet. Glouc.* i. 94, 390–1). It is called 'S. Martin de Baremannes chirche apud coquinas Vinetrie' in 1221 (*Anc. Deeds*, A. 1647). The name must be connected with O.E. 'bærman', a porter, or carrier. It can hardly be connected with the neighbouring 'Wermanecher' which Edward the Confessor gave to St. Peter Ghent in 1044 (Kemble, *Cod. Dipl.* dcclxxi), unless that name is a graphic error for 'Bermanecherche', which is somewhat improbable; in later deeds this place appears as 'Wermanacre' (*Cal. French Documents*, 502–3, ed. Round), and at the Iter of 1320 as 'Terra de Wermenatra' (*Placita de Quo Warranto*, 462).

l. 10. *Mathew Columbars.* The only person of the name whom I have found is Sir Matthew de Columbars (*d.* 1282), a prominent citizen, who was the King's Chamberlain in London and taker of wines throughout England (*Letter-Book* B, 280; *Cal. Wills*, i. 59).

l. 14. *Sir Iohn Gisors.* On the Gisors family see note on pp. 354–5.

l. 20. *Bartholomew de la vauch.* The list in *Harley MS.* 6069 reads 'de la Vernha'.

l. 23. *Robert Dalusse.* In *Harley MS.* 538 the epitaph is completed thus:—

> The 29 day of September he toke the way.
> Pray for us, we yow pray.
> Lyke as you would be prayed for another day.

l. 33. *Bartrand, wife to Grimond Descure.* The Latin inscription preserved by Strype is: '*Hic jacet corpus* Bertrandae *quondam Uxoris* Ormondi Descure, *Armig. unius Hostiariorum Camerae inclytissimi* Angliae *et* Franciae *Regis* Henrici VII. *Quae obiit* 1° *die* Aprilis 1494.'

249, l. 1. *Chantries there.* Gilbert atte Merssh founded a chantry for himself and William de Stokesby and their wives in 1396 (*Cal. Wills*, ii. 328).

l. 3. *S. Iames, called at Garlick hith.* For a notice of St. James Garlickhithe see *Trans. Lond. and Midd.* iii. 392–403. The list of chantries returned in 1547–8 does not agree with Stow's, but John Rodyng, or Rothyng, appears as the principal benefactor; he was the son of Richard de Rothyng (*Letter-Book* F, 233). For chantries of John de Oxenford, John de Whitthorne, 1349, Walter Nele, and Henry Montkoy 1362, see *Cal. Wills*, i. 460, 586, 673; ii. 66. Whitthorne commemorated Goodcheape and Cressingham. St. James 'versus vinitariam' occurs about 1170 (*Hist. MSS. Comm.*, 9th Rep. 13). For the lands of Oxenford's chantry see *Inq. p. m. London*, ii. 40. Stow's authority for Galfrid Moncley is the *Liber S. Mariae Overy* (cf. *Harley MS.* 544, f. 100).

l. 20. *Nicholas Staham.* So in all the early editions, but perhaps Nicholas Statham (*d.* 1472) the lawyer is meant. See *Dict. Nat. Biog.* liv. 112, and Errata, p. 258. The list in *Harley MS.* 6069, f. 29, has 'Stathum'. The same authority gives 'Stonor' for 'Stonarde' in l. 31.

250, l. 9. *Corney streete.* 'Corneysere strate' occurs in 1274 (*Cal.*

Wills, i. 17). 'Corveyseres' street (*Anc. Deeds*, A. 2024) for Cordwainers Street is a better form.

l. 11. *Budge Row.* Budge was a kind of fur. See references to 'Furres of Budge' on i. 86 above. Milton has: 'those budge doctors of the Stoic fur' (*Comus*, 707) in allusion to the lambskin fur on graduates' hoods. Ben Jonson writes: 'Like the coneyskin woman of Budge Row' (*Bartholomew Fair*, Act I, sc. i).

l. 14. *as Leyland termeth it.* See note on p. 352.

l. 15. *the red Lion*, &c. No doubt the house called 'þe lyoun atte Dore' in Watling Street, which is mentioned 1362–66 (*Letter-Book* G, 151, 218).

l. 26. *Turnebase lane.* It is 'Tornebaston lane' in 1328, but 'Turnebast lane' in 1436 (*Cal. Wills*, i. 341; ii. 481).

251, l. 14. *Sopers lane.* Stow is in error. The name occurs as early as 1259 (*Cal. Wills*, i. 4), and was, no doubt, due to Sopers or soapmakers, who dwelt there. See *Mun. Gild.* II. i. 97. Aleyn le Soper was a disreputable person, without any obvious connexion with Sopers lane (*Memorials*, 118). Sopers lane is now Queen Street.

l. 36. *with Epitaphes.* In *Harley MS.* 538, 85vo, the epitaphs are completed as follows:

Now be they gon and we them misse.
Christ bringe theyr sowles to heven's blisse.
On the yonger thus:
Thomas Knoles lieth vnder this stone,
And his wife Isabell fleshe and bone.
They were together XIX yere,
X children they had in fere.
His father and he to this chirche
Many good dedes they ded wirche.
Example by them here ye may see,
That the world is but a vanitie.
For whether ye be smale or greate,
All shall turne to wormes meate.
This sayde Thomas was layde on bere
The viij day of the moneth of feverer
The date of Jhesu Christ truly
A M.CCCC fyve and forty.
We may not pray, hartely pray ye
For our sowles pater noster et ave;
The sonner owre paynes lessed may be,
Graunt vs the Holy Trinitie.

252, ll. 7–12. *Thomas Windout*, &c. In *Harley MS.* 538, f. 86, several corrections are contained: 'Windout one of the shrives . . .; Hind . . . and also to the steeple of Bow then in building; Hugh Acton . . . steeple of St. Anthonie's Chirche, he also glazed the west window of Aldermary Chirche, every fote of glass price xii*d*.'

l. 25. *a thousand foure hundred it was, &c.* Street died in 1460 (*Cal. Wills*, ii. 540).

l. 31. *Henrie Halton.* In *Harley MS.* 538: 'and Robert Halton his son, 1433. John Wodiam merchaunt-taylor, 1513.'

l. 33. *Iohn Grantham.* The mayor of 1328; founded a chantry in 1345 (*Cal. Wills*, i. 476).

l. 37. *Aldemarie.* The priory of Christchurch, Canterbury, held it by the gift of Living, the priest, in the reign of William I. (*Mon. Angl.* i. 109, cf. *Litterae Cantuarienses*, ii. 175.)

253, l. 6. *building vp of that Church.* In *Harley MS.* 538 the narrative continues: 'Besydes that he gave liberally to the prisons, hospitalls, lazar-houses, and to pore householders; to the mending of highe wayes betwixt London and Coventrye 200 *li.* To Rochester bridge 10 *li.* To Dover 10 markes. To pore maydes mariages 100 markes. To pore husbondmen in Oxfordshire and Warwikeshire 140 shares and 140 coultars of yron. Two serplars of his best woole to by a jewell for the Stapelers Hall. He gave to seven almsmen of the grocers company in London 6*d.* the pece wekely for ever; and to the pore of Aldermary parishe 13 shillings and four pence yerely for ever.'

The substance of this appears in the chapter on 'Honour of Citizens' (i. 111).

l. 9. *Richard Chawcer.* He occurs as a Vintner as early as 1320; he died in 1349. He was not, however, Geoffrey Chaucer's father, though in 1323 he married as her third husband the widow of Robert Chaucer, the poet's grandfather. Richard and Robert were possibly cousins. See Skeat, *Chaucer*, I. pp. xi-xv. Richard Chaucer's will, dated April 12, 1349, mentions Mary his wife and her son, Thomas Heyroun (*Cal. Wills*, i. 590).

l. 17. *Aldermarie Church.* In *Harley MS.* 558 here is inserted: 'Hewghe Acton, merchaunt-taylor, buried Seint Antonin's 1530, glazed the west window of this Aldermary chirche xii*d.* every fote of glasse. And these were the benefactors to this chirche the last that I can reade of. The foundation of a fayre steple or bell tower was layde and reysed up some xvi or xx fote above the ground, and so it restethe.'

l. 36. *newe Marie Church.* Stow is in error in identifying this with St. Mary-le-Bow. See note on p.317 above. It will be observed that he has corrected his explanation of 'de Arcubus' given in 1598 (see p. 248 above). There is a St. Mary Arches Church at Exeter, of which Freeman (*Exeter*, p. 63, Historic Towns) wrote: 'The origin of St. Mary Arches is uncertain, but it has Norman columns, and is the only parish church [in Exeter] with regular aisles.' Florence of Worcester (ii. 29), in describing the storm of 1090, refers to Bow Church as 'ecclesia quae ad Arcum dicitur'.

254, l. 34. *for his preferment.* In *Harley MS.* 538 Stow has added the words: 'Such a brother have I. God make hym penitent.' See *Introduction*, p. xix.

255, l. 36. *Bowe-bell.* Stow does not connect Bow-bell with cockney, but Rowlands in his *Letting of Humours, &c.*, p. 65, has: 'To let a Bow-bell cockney put me downe.' There is a reference to the curfew at 'nostre dame des Arches' in 1363 (*Letter-Book* G, 150).

256, l. 27. *Grammar schoole.* See vol. i. 73, and note on p. 321 above.

l. 36. *Richard Lambert.* He died on April 4, 1567, during his year of shrievalty. Stow's *Memoranda*, p. 141.

257, ll. 15, 16. *this sild . . . for himselfe.* The tradition was so strong that when Bow Church was rebuilt by Wren, a royal gallery overlooking the street was provided.

l. 25. *Crounsilde, or Tamarsilde.* Tamarsilde is no doubt a corruption of Tanners-seld, the building in Friday Street to which all 'foreign' tanners had to bring their hides (*Letter-Book* G, 260; *Memorials*, 343). The Tanners-seld in Westchepe, parish of St. Mary-le-Bow, occurs in 1280, and references to it are common down to 1370 (*Cal. Wills*, i. 46, ii. 135). In 1309–10 there was also a Tanners Seld in St. Lawrence, Jewry (*Letter-Book* C, 162, 169). 'La Selde Coronata' or Crowned Seld occurs in 1384 (*Cal. Wills*, ii. 242).

l. 37. *the Kinges head.* On June 18, 1498, Perkin Warbeck was stood on 'a scaffold made in Chepyssyde, foreagayn the Kynges hede' (*Chron. Lond.* 223).

258, l. 11. *I read of three shops.* Given to Trinity in the time of Prior John (1250–8) by Laurence de S. Michael, who held them at the rents named (*Guildhall MS.* 122, f. 410).

259, l. 26. *Buckles berie, so called*, &c. See note on p. 318 above. Mr. W. H. Stevenson (*Engl. Hist. Rev.* xii. 491) has pointed out that in London 'bury' meant little more than a large house. This is clearly so in the case of Bucklersbury.

l. 31. *the olde Barge.* Documents dealing with the history of this house from 1276 to 1440, when it became the property of the Hospital of St. Thomas Acon are calendared in Watney's *Account of St. Thomas Acon*, pp. 263–8 (see also *C.P.R.* Henry VI, iii. 511). For its later history see *Inq. p. m. London*, i. 149, ii. 74, 77. It is first called 'le Barge' in a deed of 1414. It was at one time the house of Henry le Waleis.

260, l. 2. *Cernettes towre.* The earliest reference I have found is to 'la Tower Servat' in 1331 (*Anc. Deeds*, A. 10948). This suggests some connexion with William Servat, who was an alderman in 1312 (*Memorials*, 94). In the grant to St. Stephen's of 1358 it is called 'Sewtes Tour in Bokelesbury' (*Mon. Angl.* vi. 1350). In 1365 it is described under the name of Surnetes-tour as the mansion of William Holbech, whose widow, Matilda, bequeathed it in 1393 as Sernetes-tour to John Clee, Draper (*Cal. Wills*, ii. 104, 303). Elsewhere it is called Servers tour, and Sylvestre tour in 1455 (*Hist. MSS. Comm.*, 9th Rep. 56*a*). In the edition of 1598 Stow calls it Seruesse or Seruice Tower (see p. 250 above).

l. 18. *possessed of Grocers and Apothecaries.* So in Webster's *Westward Ho!* Act I, sc. ii: 'Go into Bucklersbury and fetch me two ounces of preserved melons: look there be no tobacco taken in the shop when he weighs it.' And *Merry Wives of Windsor*, Act III, sc. iii: 'Lisping hawthorn buds, that come like women in men's apparel, and smell like Bucklersbury in simple time.'

Thomas Becon writes in 1563: 'If one devil be in so little porcion of incense, what a number of divells be there in all the apothecaries shops that are in Bucklersbury.'

Walsingham wrote in 1581 to Burghley 'hoping that his absence will do him more good than all the drugs in Bucklersbury' (*Cal. State Papers*, 1581–90, p. 21).

l. 25. *Bennet shorne, or Shrog, or Shorehog.* The name is very much older than Stow supposed. 'Alfwinus, sacerdos Scerehog' occurs in a deed dated 1111–31 (*Hist. MSS. Comm.* 9th Rep. 61 *b*). A wether is called a 'sherehog' when it has been once shorn. The name as applied to the church may be due to some person like William Serehog, or Alwin Serehog, who appear in early twelfth-century deeds (*id.* 63, 65). The church is called St. Bennet Sorhog before 1248 (*Anc. Deeds*, A. 1621).

l. 32. *buried in this church.* The list in *Harley MS.* 6069, f. 62, reads: 'Hooe' for Hold, and 'Warmyngton' for Warrington.

261, l. 11. *In this Church.* The list in *Harley MS.* 6069, f. 62, reads: John 'Bernes'; John 'Boston'; John 'Legage' (for 'Gage'); Robert Marshall alderman, 'and Elizabeth his wife'; 'Borhford' (for 'Corcheforde'); 'Nicholas Wyfolde twyse mayor of London, and Thomas his son.'

l. 29. *Pepperers in Sopers lane*, &c. In 1365 there is reference to the Misteries of Grossers, Pepperers, and Apothecaries, both in Sopers-lane and in Bokeleresbury (*Letter-Book* G, 204). See note on above. For an ordinance on Pepperers of Soperslane in 1316 see *Letter-Book* E, 67, *Memorials*, 120.

262, l. 18. *Salomon Lanuare.* Presumably Salomon de Lanvare, Cutler, who founded a chantry here by his will in 1312 (*Cal. Wills*, i. 227; Milbourn, *Hist. of St. Mildred's*, 19).

l. 19. *Hugh Game.* In 1436 (*id.* 19, 20; *Cal. Wills*, ii. 479).

l. 35. *On the north side.* In *Harley MS.* 538: 'On the north syde of the chirche remayne two tombes of marble; but the plates of inscriptions beinge taken from them, no man can tell who were buried vnder them, excepte only by the reporte of one man, who saythe they were the tombes of Thomas Monshampe and William Brothers: which William Brothers lived and was chirchewarden there in the yere 1519, and deceased 1547, as apereth by the chirche boke.' Brothers was buried here on 2 Aug. 1547 (Milbourn, *u. s.* 16, 20).

263, l. 3. *Counter in the Poultrie.* In 1441 'le Compter' in the parish of St. Mildred belonged to Thomas Haseley; it was bequeathed to the Mayor and Commonalty by Walter Hunt in 1477 (*Cal. Wills*, ii. 501, 575).

l. 7. *saint Marie at Conie hope lane ende.* Reference to St. Mary Conyhope occurs as early as 1279, when Thomas de Mymmes founded a chantry there. John Mymmes, 'ymaginour,' or image-maker, left money for a chaplain in 1348, and subsequently a Brotherhood was established there. 'Ion yrunnes' is no doubt a blunder for 'Io. mymmes'. The purchaser of the chapel was not *Thomas* but *William* Hobson, who died in Jan. 1582, seized of a 'messuage newly built called Corpus Christi Chappel, wherein he dwelt, with two shops thereto adjoining' (*Inq. p. m. London*, iii. 51; *Cal. Wills*, i. 41, 558; Milbourn, *History of St. Mildred's*, pp. 22-6.) Conyhope Lane is now called Grocers Hall Court.

l. 27. *new common hall.* See vol. i. 278, and note on pp. 334–5 below.

264, l. 16. *Bordhangly lane.* Probably a mistake for Bordhaugly lane. 'La Bordhawe in S. Mary de Colecherche' occurs in 1257 (*Hist. MSS. Comm.*, 9th Rep. p. 17) and again in 1275; the name appears as 'Bordhawelane' in 1305, 'Burdellane' in 1405, and 'Barthawlane' in 1434 (*Cal. Wills*, i. 25, 170; ii. 365, 470); 'Brodhawlane' occurs in 1557 (*Inq. p. m. London*, ii. 68). Bordhawe would most likely be a timber-yard. Dr. Sharpe suggests as an alternative derivation 'bordel', a brothel; this may be supported by the form 'Burdellane'.

l. 30. *about the yeare 1285.* The conduit in St. Mary Colechurch in West Cheap is mentioned in 1261 (*Cal. Charter Rolls*, ii. 38), and the Fraternity of St. Thomas the Martyr at the Conduit of London in 1278 (*Cal. Wills*, i. 29, 70). The first building of the Conduit, authorized in 1236 (see i. 16 above), was begun in 1245 (*Ann. Lond.* 44).

265. l. 24. *In the yere 1351.* This probably refers to the disturbances between the Fishmongers and Skinners, as a consequence of which two men were executed at the Cross in Chepe in 1340. An indemnity was granted to the Mayor on 18 March, 1346, and Stow may have taken his information from some later document, and so have made an error in the date. (See *Letter-Book* F, 58, 96–7, 138; *Memorials*, 210, 211; and Herbert, *Livery Companies*, ii. 306.)

266, l. 16. *In the yere 1533,* &c. The misprint of '1553', which appears in the edition of 1603, was repeated by Munday. Strype made a foolish correction by substituting 'Mary' for 'Anne'. The reference is to the coronation of Anne Boleyn, of whom Stow writes in his *Annales*, p. 952, ed. 1605: 'she went forward by the cross which was newly gilt.'

l. 32. *againe fastned and repaired.* This was done under an express order from the queen. See *Remembrancia*, pp. 65–6 (the document there given was before 1595).

Ben Jonson, writing in 1599 or 1600, refers to the mutilation of Cheap Cross in *Cynthia's Revels*, Act 1, sc. i:—'To frame some encomiastic speech upon this our metropolis, or the wise magistrates thereof? Descend into a particular admiration of their justice, for the due measure of coals, burning of cans and such like? As also their religion in pulling down a superstitious cross and advancing a Venus or Priapus in place of it.'

267, l. 8. *counsellers directed their letters,* &c. Stow gives the gist of the letters very accurately. The first letter, dated 2 Feb. 1600, was signed by 'the Lord Archbishop and Mr. Secretary only'; it refers to the cross having been taken away, and to 'an intent instead thereof to sett up some other devise'. The second is 'signed by all their Lordships and the rest at this sitting excepting Mr. Comptroler', but dated 14 Dec. 1600; it repeats the order as given by Stow, 'not approving that weakness in any men that will take offence at the historicall and civill use of such an ancyent ensigne of Christianitie. In the discharge of your duety herein wee are of opinion that the lesse alteracion you make the better it is.' *Acts of Privy Council*, xxx. 27, and xxxi. 44.

l. 34. *This old crosse.* Erected by the Earl of Gloucester in the reign of Henry III; also called 'The Broken Cross'. Provision was made for the erection of a conduit in its place in 1390. See *Memorials*, 397, 435, 521; *Letter-Book* H, 343, 354, 358; and vol. i. 342 above.

268, l. 32. *for the most part possessed of Mercers.* For Mercers in Cheapside see Rowlands, *Letting of Humours*, &c., p. 45:—

> Who have we here? Behold him and be mute.
> Some mightie man I'll warrant by his sute.
> If all the Mercers in Cheap side shew such,
> Ile give them leave to give me twice as much.

269, l. 4. *S. Thomas of Acon.* For its history see *Some Account of the Hospital of St. Thomas of Acon*, by Sir John Watney, F.S.A. The founder's name should be given as Thomas, son of Theobald de Helles. The list of monuments is nearly identical with one in *Harley MS.* 6069, f. 30, which, however, reads 'Gernon' for 'Ganon'.

ll. 31, 32. *Locke* and *Allen.* In *Harley MS.* 538: 'Sir W. Locke, Mercer, sheriff 1548, deceased 1550; Sir John Allen, mercer, mayor 1525 and 1535, deceased 1544' (1545 new style).

l. 39. *sir Iohn Allen . . . being founder.* Allen did not build the Mercers Chapel, but contributed 300*l.* towards the total of 2735*l.* on condition that he was buried there. In 1549 his tomb was moved to the converted Church of St. Thomas. (*Account*, *u.s.* pp. 102–5.)

270, l. 29. *S. Martin called Pomary.* In early deeds it is simply St. Martin in Ironmongers' Lane—as on i. 280. It is called St. Martin Pomer in 1252 (Watney, *Account of St. Thomas Acon*, 257), and St. Martin *in Pomerio* in 1303 (*Mun. Gild.* II. i. 237). After this St. Martin de Pomerio is usual. In mediaeval Latin *pomerium* means an apple-orchard. The suggestion adopted by Mr. Gomme (*Governance of London*, pp. 84–5) that *pomerium* has its classical meaning of the open space within and without the walls of a town, and that 'Pomary' preserves the memory of the old Roman city lacks confirmation.

271, l. 1. *Blossoms Inne, but corruptly Bosoms Inne.* The name is from the family of Blosme. 'Blosmes-hyn' and 'Blossemesin' occur in 1374–5 (*Letter-Book* F, 136), and 'Bosum-is-Inne' in 1466 (*Cal. Wills*, ii. 540). The name survives in Blossom Inn Yard.

ll. 4, 5. *Honey lane.* The name was probably due to the sale of honey; 'Huni lane' occurs as early as 1207 (*Hist. MSS. Comm.*, 9th Rep. p. 18).

l. 16. *Catte-street, corruptly called Catteten streete*, occurs as Catte-strete in 1281 (*Cal. Charter Rolls*, ii. 253), and throughout the fourteenth century; as Catton Lane (cf. i. 259 above) in 1438 and 1483 (*Cal. Wills*, ii. 523, 585). Now Gresham Street. Catte Streets occur in Oxford and many other towns, see *N. and Q.* 10th ser. v and vi.

Margin. *Liber Fletwod.* It was compiled by the Recorder, William Fleetwood, and presented by him to the City on July 31, 1576. Probably its preparation was the occasion of Fleetwood being in possession of the *Liber Custumarum* and other City records (see *Introduction*, p. xxxii).

272, l. 15. *William Elderton.* A notorious tippler and writer of ballads from 1559 onwards. The description of him as an attorney in the Sheriff's Courts is peculiar to Stow. He may be the Master Elderton whom Machyn (*Diary*, 290) mentions as a magistrate at the Guildhall in 1562. He was also an actor and master of a company of comedians, and died about 1592. To Nash in *Pierce Penilesse* (*Works*, ii. 67) he is Elderton, who 'consumed his ale-crammed nose to nothing, in bear bayting with whole bundels of ballets'.

273, l. 1. *had of the Fellowshippes.* Stow's authority is clearly the London Chronicles (*Chron. Lond.* 257). The full list of contributions is printed in Price's *Account of the Guildhall*, p. 64, from 'Repertory, I. ff. 181–2'.

l. 13. *hanging of Tapestrie.* The record in the City *Journal*, xi. f. 28, shows that Alwyn's intention was that the 'iij Clothes of Arrays' which he left for the use of the commonalty should be kept by the Mercers, and his representatives made provision accordingly. (See Price, *Account*, p. 57.)

l. 34. *to build of new.* In April, 1430, the mayor, aldermen, &c., represented that the chapel of St. Mary by the Guildhall was small, ruinous, inconvenient, and dangerous, and except the site of the Guildhall, which had long been building, there was no site near whereon a larger chapel could be built, save the messuage given by Fanelore and Frauncis. Licence was therefore granted to pull down the old chapel, and build a larger on this site; and to refound the college with Sir John Bernard as warden. (*C. P. R.* Henry VI, ii. 57–8.)

274, l. 20. *by him both builded and glased.* John Wells, who in his will directed that he should be buried at St. Anthony's, made no such provision. But his executors covenanted with the City to build a great window at the east end of the Guildhall chapel, a presbytery, two niches for images, and an altar with marble steps (City Record, ap. *Cal. Wills*, ii. 499).

275, l. 17. *the shanke bone of a man.* William Harrison, in his *Description of Britain* (Holinshed, *Chronicles*, i. 19), writes of the bone thus: 'which in times past was 28 inches in length, but now it beginneth to decaie, so that it is shorter by foure inches than it was in the time of King Edward.'

l. 35. *William Melrith*, or Melreth, died in Jan.-Feb., 1446 (*Cal. Wills*, ii. 506). He gave an illuminated missal to St. Lawrence Church; now *Arundel MS.* 109 in the British Museum. There is a similar list of names in *Harley MS.* 6069, f. 30, which, however, reads 'Chayham' for 'Chayhee' (p. 276, l. 10).

ll. 37–9. *Richard Rich . . . 1469.* Strype says his will was proved in 1464.

276, l. 12. *Iohn Marshal . . . 1493.* Munday gives the inscription with date to Jan. 1498 (*Survey*, 286, ed. 1633).

l. 36. *the Iron grates.* The arch or sluice by which the Walbrook passed under the wall. Roach Smith describes its discovery thus: 'Opposite Finsbury Circus, at a depth of 19 feet, a well-turned Roman arch was discovered, at the entrance of which on the Finsbury side were iron bars placed apparently to restrain the sedge and weeds from choking the passage' (*Archaeological Journal*, i. 111). See also *Archaeologia*, lx. 177, and compare vol. i. 175 above.

277, l. 2. *Lothberie.* It has been suggested that the name may be due to the Albert Lotering who held land about 1130 in 'Warda Haconis' (*Hist. MSS. Comm.*, 9th Rep. 66). But there is no proof that 'Warda Haconis' is Broad Street. Moreover, St. Margaret 'de Lodebure' occurs 1181–1204 (*id.* 15), and 'Lohdeber' and 'Lothbery' occur 1222–48 (*Anc. Deeds*, A. 10391–2). The form 'Lothyngebire', which appears in 1275, is exceptional; though Broad Street ward was called 'Lodingeberi' in the list of 1285, it is 'Lotheberi' in 1293 (*Cal. Wills*, i. 20, 703).

For founders and candlesticks of Lothbury see Rowlands, *A Foole's Bolt is soone shot*, p. 9:—

And swore he had found out old Raymond's tricke,
To make good Gold of a brass Candlesticke:
Lothburie, where the Brasiers doe abide,
He would make ten times richer than Cheapside.

l. 28. *Elianor . . . wife to Edward the first.* An error for Eleanor of Provence, *mother* of Edward I, to whom Henry III had granted the custody of London Bridge in 1265 (see *Hundred Rolls*, i. 403 sqq.). Dr. Sharpe informs me that the original of the document in *Letter-Book* C, 61, is headed, 'Carta Alianore quondam Regine Anglie, &c.'

278, l. 10. *their chappell.* On March 8, 1305, the friars of the Sack assigned to Robert FitzWalter their chapel in Colemanstrete, lately a synagogue of Jews, for him and his heirs to find two chaplains there (*C. P. R.* Edw. I, iv. 317; *Rot. Parl.* i. 162). FitzWalter apparently absorbed it in his mansion. Stow seems to have confused it with St. Stephen's, see p. 336 below.

l. 12. *place of the same Robert.* In the *Grocers' Archives* (p. 162, ed. Kingdon) there is record of a payment made in 1427 'pur le purchas de nostre place appelle le Seignour VitzWater'. On Nov. 1, 1429,

William Cambridge, Thomas Knolles the younger, and other grocers, had licence to grant in mortmain to the wardens their Inn in the Old Jewry, which lately was of Walter, Lord FitzWauter (*C. P. R.* Henry VI, ii. 78). Robert FitzWalter (*d.* 1234) had his house here (Madox, *Hist. Excheq.* i. 235).

l. 22. *hath to signe a Windmill.* The Windmill was a famous tavern in the time of Queen Elizabeth. One of the scenes of Ben Jonson's *Every Man in his Humour* is placed there.

279, l. 30. *Semayne or Balaster,* &c. Stow has given the facts correctly enough, but has corrupted the names, which should be Semane the cross-bowman (*balistarius*); Bonevia Mitun, Thomas Bukerell, John de Gyse ('Guso'); Lewis the painter; Walter Avener ('Turnar'); Hugh Hareman; Mose de Cantabrigia (i.e. Cambridge); Ernard Ruffus ('Arnold le Reus'). The date is July, 1227. (*Cal. Charter Rolls,* i. 54–5; see also *Cal. Close Rolls,* Henry III, i. 41, 55—reading 'Mosse Bugus'—and Watney, *Account of St. Thomas of Acon,* pp. 256, 276—reading 'Molseus Bugis de Grauntebrige'.) For the house of Bonevie, son of Samuel Muton, in Westcheap in 1221, see *Anc. Deeds,* A. 13423.

280, l. 35. *a Iewe at Tewkesbery.* The story comes from the London Chronicles (*Chron. Lond.* 5). Camden (*Remains,* p. 304) gives three lines in reference thereto:—

Tende manus, Salomon, ego te de stercore tollam.
Sabbata nostra colo; de stercore surgere nolo.
Sabbata nostra, quidem, Salomon, celebrabis ibidem.

281, l. 34. *Fereno.* Presumably a mistake for 'ferronarius', or 'ferroun', an ironmonger.

282, l. 10. *Richard Chamberlaine.* In *Harley MS.* 538: 'Richard Chamberlaine, ironmonger, one of the shrives of London in the yere 1562, deceased 1566, and was there buried with this epitaphe:—

To the pore he was liberall and gave for God's sake,
But now his fame is plentifull and he a hevenly make.
He was lyke to[1] one of us, accordinge to our moulde,
But now he is unlyke to[1] us according to herroulde[2].
His tyme was short, in sycknes rare, as to all is knowne,
But now his tyme shall longe endure, and never be overthrowne.'

Richard Chamberlain was father of John Chamberlain the letter-writer.

l. 23. *principall palace.* The grant, on March 27, 1438, was to John Stout and Robert Savage of the office of porter within the palace of the principality [of Wales] in the Old Jewry (*C. P. R.* Henry VI, iii. 196). Stout held his office by a grant of Henry V (*id.* i. 64).

l. 38. *first builder or owner of Coleman streete.* Riley suggested that the name was due to coalmen or charcoal burners, who settled there in convenient proximity to the Moor (*Memorials,* p. xix). But the name may be traced back to the 'Ceolmundingehaga' or farm of Ceolmund,

[1] Munday *omits* to *in both places.*
[2] Munday *reads*: in heaven where he would.

near the Westgate, which is mentioned in a charter of Burhred of Mercia (*circa* 857, ap. Thorpe, *Diplomatarium*, 118). Stow himself gives an instance of Coleman Street in 1227: see vol. i. 279. 'Coleman cheriche' occurs in a charter of Agnes Becket to the nuns of Clerkenwell (*Cotton MS.*, Faustina, B. II. f. 72). Reginald Coleman's will is dated Nov. 11, 1383 (*Cal. Wills*, ii. 246). For the church see below.

284, l. 2. *Rahere de Sopars lane.* No doubt Richard de Refham, who was mayor in 1310–11. He is called Richard de Soperslane in the *Short English Chronicle*, ap. *Three Fifteenth Century Chronicles*, and Richer de Refham in his will; he had property in Coleman Street and Bassishaw (*Cal. Wills*, i. 339). Stow's authority is the church-book of St. Stephen, Coleman Street, cf. *Archaeologia*, l. 53.

l. 32. *This Church.* In Newcourt's *Repertorium*, i. 535, it is shown that St. Stephen, Coleman Street, existed in the time of Ralph de Diceto (1181–1204), and that it was a chapel of St. Olaves in 1322, and finally constituted an independent parish church in 1456 (not in 1467 as stated by Stow). In describing it as at one time a Synagogue Stow seems to have confused it with the Chapel of the Friars of the Sack, see p. 334 above. For the church-books see *Archaeologia*, vol. l. pp. 17–57.

285, l. 9. *Bassings hall*, &c. The oldest note I find is of the parish of 'Bassingshage' in 1160–81 (*Hist. MSS. Comm.* 9th Rep. 20). It appears both as 'Basyngyshawe' and 'Bassishagthe' in 1246 (Watney, *Account of St. Thomas Acon*, 274–5), 'Bassieshawe' in 1278, and 'Bassinghawe' in 1284 (*Cal. Wills*, i. 36, 70). Basings Haw means the enclosure of the Basings. Riley (*Memorials*, p. xix) is clearly mistaken in distinguishing 'Bassishaw', the ward, as the haw of the Bassets, from Basinghall (the later Blackwell Hall), or the house of the Basings. Basinghall is a corruption. The ward is called 'Bassingeshol' and 'Bassyeshaw' in the *Hundred Rolls*, i. 403, 431. The connexion of the Basings with Blackwell Hall is doubtful (see note below).

l. 22. *a Charter of Henrie the second.* This charter appears in two places in the *Liber Custumarum* (*Mun. Gild.* II. i. 33, 48), in the first in its original form, in the latter as confirmed by Henry III in 1243. Stow translates the former. The second witness appears in the original as 'Warino filio Gerardi, Camerario', and in the confirmation as 'Waltero, filio Gerin, Comite'. The Charter in the possession of the Weavers Company is attested by T. Canc. (i. e. Thomas—Becket—Cancellarius) and Warino Filio Geroldi Camerario; the date can be fixed as Sept. 1155. See *Letter-Book* D, 221.

286, l. 28. *Bakewell hall.* In 1280 Sir Roger Clifford gave to the City his great hall, next to the Guildhall in the parish of St. Michael Bassishaw (*Ann. Lond.* 89; *Letter-Book* A, 227, 229). From the *Hundred Roll* (i. 403 *b*, 431) it would appear that this house previously belonged to John FitzJohn, who built it on the site of Jews' houses destroyed during the war. In 1293 the City transferred this tenement, except for a part previously sold, to John de Bauquell (*Cal. Charter Rolls*,

ii. 434; *Letter Book* C, 12). To the family of Bauquell or Backwell it owed its later name. In 1337 there is mention of the chamber of the late John de Baukewell (*id.* E, 304). Robert Bakwell held it some time before 1395 (*Cal. Wills*, ii. 536 *n.*). Stow seems to be mistaken in connecting it with the Basings. The only Basing arms I have found were: 'Or, five eagles displayed sable, two, two, and one, a canton ermine' (as given by Munday, ed. 1633, p. 539). The Clifford arms were: 'Chequer, azure and or.' I suspect it was these latter which Stow saw and described from memory, incorrectly, as: 'Gerond (gyronny) of twelve points, gold, and azure,' which were, it is true, used by some of the Bassingbornes (Papworth, *Ordinary*, ii. 901). Blackwell Hall was acquired by the City in 19 Richard II (1395–6, not 20 Richard II, as on i. 288). See *Cal. Inq. p. m.*, iii. 195.

287, l. 39. *Vnto this Adam de Bassing*, &c. Confirmation to him of the dwelling-house of Gervase de Aldermanbury, and advowsons of S. Michael Bassishaw and other churches (*Hist. MSS. Comm.*, 9th Rep. 17; *Cal. Charter Rolls*, i. 313). Adam and his son Thomas had lived in Aldermanbury for some years before 1275, when complaint was made of encroachments there (*Hundred Rolls*, i. 403 *b* sqq.).

292, l. 10. *Touching the antiquitie.* 'Aldresmanesberi' is mentioned in a document drawn up about 1130 (*Hist. MSS. Comm.*, 9th Rep. 66). The *Terra Gialle* mentioned in the same place is probably the oldest reference to the Guildhall. 'Bury' in London meant little more than a large house, as notably in the case of Bucklersbury (see p. 329). So Stow's explanation of Aldermanbury, as the bury or Court-hall of the aldermen, now called the Guildhall, seems sound. Mr. Price (*Account of the Guildhall*, 34–40) has shown that the old Guild Hall was near the west end of the present one, as Stow describes. The Osney Register is now at Christ Church, Oxford; a facsimile of 'Richard Renery's grant' is given in Price's *Account of the Guildhall*, p. 35.

l. 22. *I my selfe haue seene the ruines*, &c. An early memory of Stow's. In August, 1531, was begun the 'clensyng of certeyn olde ruinouse houses and grounde lying in Aldermanbury, sumtyme the Place of Sainct Aethelbert kyng' (*Hist. MSS. Comm.*, 9th Rep. 44).

l. 36. *a shanke bone of a man.* William Harrison, writing of the bones of giants in his *Description of Britain* (ap. Holinshed, *Chronicles*, i. 19), says: 'Another also is to be seene in Alderman burie . . . of 32 inches and rather more, whereof the symmetrie hath beene taken by some skilfull in that practise, and an image made according to that proportion, which is fixt on the east end of the cloister of the same church, not farre from the said bone, and sheweth the person of a man full ten or eleven feet high, which as some say was found in the closter of Poules, that was neere to the librarie, at such time as the Duke of Somerset did pull it doune to the verie foundation, and carried the stones thereof to the Strand, where he did build his house.'

293, l. 17. *Simon Winchcombe, Esquier, 1391.* A Simon Winchcombe was buried here in 1399 (*Cal. Wills*, ii. 340). He was an armourer: Stow may have confused *armurarius* and *armiger*.

l. 18. *Iohn Wheatley.* Whatele in his will (*id.* ii. 458). Cf. i. 257, 270.

294, l. 20. *Henry Frowike.* Died 1378. *Cal. Wills*, ii. 201.

l. 26. *conuerted into a parrish Church.* On the remains of this later St. Alphage, see articles by Mr. Philip Norman in *Architectural Review*, March, 1907, and *Archaeologia*, lx. 169.

l. 35. *sir Iohn Williams.* He had a grant of Elsing Spittal in 1540 (*Letters and Papers*, xv. 612 (7)). For the fire see Wriothesley, *Chron.* i. 133.

295, l. 6. *houses for wealthy Marchantes.* Milk Street was an important residential quarter: see Dekker, *Jests to make you Merry* (ap. *Works*, ii. 323):—'Conjecturing that at that time our worthiest citizens are from home, they goe into Milk Street, Bread Street, Lime Street, S. Mary Axe, or the most priviest places where they kept their residence.'

l. 26. *Woodstreete.* Probably so called from the sale of wood there. The name is ancient. St. Michael 'de Wodestrate' occurs 1160–81 (*Hist. MSS. Comm.*, 9th Rep. 21).

296, l. 2. *Goldsmithes row.* See note on p. 351.

l. 16. *monuments.* There is a list in *Harley MS.* 6069, f. 58, which specifies Ralph, Thomas, Ralph, and Richard as the four sons of Ralph Illingworth, and reads 'Thomas Pipehurst' and 'Richard Tuke'.

297, l. 6. *Simon de Berching.* In *Harley MS.* 538, f. 105, the following is here inserted: 'Olde epitaphes on stones, where the names of the parties buried are gone, these:—

The world's worshipe and honor with favour and fortune wanyth day by day.
Who may withstand death's stowre, when riche and powre she closeth in clay.
Wherefore to God hartely we pray, to pardon us of our misdede,
And help us now in our moaste nede.
Amen.

Another thus:—

Eche for other little syster and brother, to God we pray,
That you here and I els where may synge and say,
That God Almighty for his greate pitie mercy will have
On vs wretches, and from payne fetche vs, to make vs save.'

l. 22. *Huggen lane.* The name is older than Stow supposed. 'Hoggenelane' occurs in 1275, and 'S. Michael de Hoggenelane in Vodestrate' in 1288 (*Cal. Wills*, i. 25, 83). As Hoggeslane it occurs in 1234 (*Cotton MS.*, Faustina, B. II. f. 89vo).

l. 36. *monumentes.* The list in *Harley MS.* 6069, f. 58, is: 'William sonne of Thomas Bamburgh, squyre; William Mauf, squyre; William Tavener, squyre; John Coraunt.'

298, l. 1. *John Nash.* In *Harley MS.* 538, f. 105vo, the epitaph is given :—

For Jhesus love pray for me,
Such as I am so shall ye be.
John Nashe, citizen of London, sometyme was I,
More then yere forty and thre.
I pray yow for some charitie,
Remember hym and his wyves thre,
Which hight Elizabeth, Margaret, and Margerye.
I parted to God in the yere of grace
A thousand foure hundred six and sixty,
  That day trewly.
God of his goodnes grant vs his mercy.
And in the worshipe of the Trinitye
For owre soules say a pater noster and ave.

l. 4. *William Lambarde.* The author of the *Perambulation of Kent*, which suggested to Stow the form of the *Survey*.

l. 29. *Blacke Hall.* 'Le Blakegate' is mentioned in 1348, and a tenement called 'Blackhalle' in 1361; both of St. Michael, Wood St. (*Cal. Wills*, i. 514, ii. 67). As 'le Blake halle' it appears in 1384, in 1388, and again in 1410 when it was conveyed to William Sevenoke (*Archaeologia*, lviii. 206; *Cal. Inq. p. m.*, iii. 102).

299, l. 9. *was called Monks Wel and the street of the Wel.* Stow is in error. Algarus de Muchewella is named in a deed of the early 12th century, and 'Mukewellestrate' occurs not much later (*Hist. MSS. Comm.*, 9th Rep. 23, 61). It is Mukewellestrate in 1277, and Mugwell Street as late as 1578 (*Cal. Wills*, i. 30; ii. 693).

l. 29. *the monuments.* There is a list in *Harley MS.* 6069, f. 54, which is fuller for the Wrothesleys. For 'Cherley' (l. 38) it reads Chorley.

300, l. 21. *Robert Crowley.* Stow, in his *Memoranda*, 139, writes of him under date 1567 as 'Somtym a boke sellar, now redar at Sent Antholyns, person of S. Petar ye Powre, prebend of Pawlls, vickar of S. Gills withowt Criplegate, and deane of Harfford[1] in Wales', and says that at the time of the order on the use of Surplices he compiled a book called 'Y^{e} Unffoldynge of ye Popyshe atyr'. This book does not appear amongst Crowley's numerous printed works. Crowley died in 1588. See *Dict. Nat. Biog.* xiii. 241.

l. 21. *foure vnder one olde stone.* According to the Latin inscription given by Munday (*Survey*, p. 313, ed. 1633) the stone was for three persons only, viz. William Bullen (*d.* 1576) physician, Richard Bullen (*d.* 1563) preacher, and John Foxe (*d.* 1587). The inscription is dated 1587; Stow's reference to a 'W. Bolene, physician, 1587', is probably due to a misreading.

301, l. 38. *Beech lane.* The street called 'la beche' in St. Giles with-

[1] He was really archdeacon of Hereford.

out Crepelgate occurs in 1257 (*Anc. Deeds*, A. 2263), 'Bechestrete' in 1285, and 'Beche lane' in 1333 (*Cal. Wills*, i. 74, 402). The name is therefore older than Nicholas de la Beech. It may be connected with the spring called 'Wittewellebech' mentioned in a charter of Henry II in 1182 (*Cotton MS.*, Faustina, B. II. f. 6; the 'Witebek' of *Feet of Fines* in 1197), and as 'Whittewellebeche' in 1381 (*Memorials*, 451).

302, l. 6. *Abbot of Ramsey.* There is mention of the Abbot's house in London in 1114–30 (*Cart. de Rameseia*, i. 140, 242; ii. 133). The Abbot's lodging of Ramsey in Whitecross Street was granted to John Gates (*d.* 1553) on 5 July, 1545 (*Letters and Papers*, xix (i). p. 623). Sir Drewe Drewrie (1531?–1617) was a wealthy courtier of Elizabeth and friend of his neighbour, Lord Willoughby. See *Dict. Nat. Biog.* xvi. 54.

l. 31. *Base court.* 'Le Bas Court by Crypelgate' was granted to Robert Ufford on the treason of John Maltravers in 1331 (*C. P. R.* Edw. III, ii. 73). On the death of William Ufford, second and last earl, in 1382, it passed to his nephew Robert, Lord Willoughby d'Eresby (*Cal. Inq. p. m.* iii. 40, 209). As 'Barrecan', otherwise 'Barbycane' or 'Bascourt', William, Lord Willoughby d'Eresby, held it in 1519 (Hardy and Page, *Fines*, ii. 24–5). His daughter and heiress, Katherine, Duchess of Suffolk, was mother by her second marriage of Peregrine Bertie (*d.* 1601), who refers in his will to his 'great mansion-house called Willoughby House or Barbican' (*Five Generations of a Loyal House*, i. 439).

'Barbican' has nothing to do with 'burgh-kenning'; the word came to English through the O. F. *barbacane* and Low Latin *barbacana*, an outwork. It is of uncertain, but possibly Oriental, origin. See *N. E. D.*

303, l. 36. *Shelly house.* The rents and houses of Thomas Shelly, between the church of St. Mary at the end of Stanynglaneend and Adlyngstrete, were forfeited in Feb. 1400 (*C. P. R.* Henry IV, i. 193). Sir John Colepepper owned the tenement called 'Shelles' in 1482 (*Cal. Inq. p. m.* iv. 408).

304, l. 4. *Sergeant Fleetwoods house.* He commonly dated his letters as from Bacon house (cf. *Lansdowne MSS.* 24 and 26, for 1576–78).

l. 32. *Stayning lane.* Professor Maitland suggested that the name was due to the fact that it once contained the haws of the men of Staines (*Domesday and Beyond*, 181). The Confessor had granted to St. Peter, Westminster, the manor of Staines, with the land called 'Stæningehaga' within London and all other things that had belonged to Staines (Kemble, *Codex*, dccclv). St. Mary Stayning is called 'Ecclesia de Staningehage' in 1189 in the Clerkenwell Chartulary (*Cotton MS.*, Faustina, B. II. f. 9).

305, l. 7. *Engaine lane, or Mayden lane.* 'Englenelane' in 1282 (*Letter Book* A, 154) and 'Ingenlane' in 1382 (*Cal. Wills*, ii. 236). Cf. vol. i. 298.

l. 8. *S. Iohn Sachary*, or Zachary, from the Zachary to whom the Canons of St. Paul's granted the church of St. John the Baptist in the twelfth century (*Hist. MSS. Comm.*, 9th Rep. 13 *b*, 64).

l. 19. *Iohn Adis . . . 1400.* Munday (*Survey*, p. 322, ed. 1633) gives the date from his tomb as Feb. 28, 1461; Strype as 1470.

l. 20. *Iohn Francis*, &c. According to the inscriptions given by Munday he died on Dec. 13, 1405, and his wife on Oct. 11, 1432. He was also called Godman (*Cal. Wills*, ii. 364).

l. 21. *I*[*ohn*] *Sutton . . . 1413*. Munday gives the date from his tomb July 6, 1450, which shows that he was the alderman killed on London Bridge in Cade's rebellion (*Chron. Lond.* 161), not the sheriff of 1413.

l. 22. *Bartholomew Seman*. He founded a chantry here, but directed that he should be buried at St. Andrew, Cornhill (*Cal. Wills*, ii. 456, 459).

l. 25. *Christopher Eliot . . . 1505*. Strype gives 1509, which is correct. Cf. i. 24.

l. 31. *Iohn Cornish*. In *Harley MS.* 538, f. 108vo, the epitaph is given:—

When I alyve was, bothe more and lesse, even in lyke case right so be ye,
In piteous array, as ye se may, it is no nay, so shall ye be.
Yourselfe make mone, or ye have gon, I pray eche one to pray for me
Without delay; past is the day, I may not pray, now pray ye.
Remembre your charitie, eueryche one for the soule of John Cornishe
 hens gon,
 a pater noster and ave.
The whiche in the monthe of June deceased the seventene day serteynly,
In the Yere of our Lord M.cccc four and seventy, with de profundis clamavi.

l. 36. *as some haue fabuled*. This is hardly fair to Grafton, who gives the story for what it is worth (*Abridgment of Chronicles*, p. 136, ed. 1572). Stow himself took the pains to copy it out as follows (*Harley MS.* 367, f. 19):

'The aforsayd maior Syr Bartilmew Rede kept his maioralty in the golde smiths hall in London. And it happened on that tyme that the admirall and certeyn other noble men came as Ambassadors from the Frenche Kynge to the Kynge of England; whom the Kynge did very honourably feaste and entertayne, and comanded also the mayor to entertayne them in the citie of London in the best maner that he might. Whereupon he desired them to dinner. At whiche dinner the ambassadors, beinge accompanied with many lords and gentlemen to the nomber of an hundered persons and mo, were placed in the Goldsmiths Hall, where they filled thre longe tables, and were served with thre courses of all meates that might be gotten for money. At the first course everye messe was served with xv dishes. At the second xii dishes. At the third x dishes. So that in the whole there was servyd in the Hall xv messes and to every messe xxxvii dishes of meate. The first course was served all in vessels of new white silvar, the second in new silvar parcell gilt, the third in new silvar all gilt; beinge all marked newly with his owne marke. And no dishe nor meate was caried out of the hall untill the dyner was done, for as they were taken of the table, so they were set within a parke finely paled, and coningly dressed and garnished with all maner of swete and goodly flowers in the midste of the hall. And after diner the same meate was caried out at the gate, and immediatly given to the pore, that were orderly placed in the strete ready to receyve the same. After diner amonge the other gestes was an Italyan, a Jeweller, and he shewed forthe a stone of greate vallue, and sayd that he had oferyd the same to the Emperour, the Frenche Kynge, and the Kynge of England, but none of them would give the vallue thereof. The maior hard hym, and sayd: "Have ye ofered it to our Sovereigne lord the Kynges grace?" The Straunger aunswered: "Ye." Then sayth the Maior: "Thinke you the kynges grace refused it for want of treasure; let me see it," sayd he, and askyd hym what he valued at. The straunger sayd a thousand markes. "And will that buy it," sayth the maior. "Ye," sayth the straunger. Then the maior toke the jewell, and comanded one to bring him a spice mortar and a pestle, and willed his officer to beate it to powder, and so he did. Then the maior called for a cup of wyne, and put it in the cup and dranke it of clene, and sayd to the Straunger: "Speke honorably of the kynge of England, for thou hast now sene one of his pore subjects drinke a thousand markes at a draught." And then comanded his money to be payd hym. This I found writen in the maner that I have told it in the ende of an olde booke in the Grey friars library in London, writen by one friar Jones.'

306, l. 35. *Epitaph.* It is completed in *Harley MS.* 538 thus:

Wherfore Jhesu, that of Mary spronge,
Set theyr sowles thy payntes amonge,
Thoughe it be undeserved on theyr syde,
Yet good lord let them evermore thy mercy abyde.
And of your charitie say a pater noster and a ave mary.

307, l. 15. *these verses.* To be read thus:

Quos anguis tristi diro cum vulnere stravit,
Hos sanguis Christi miro tum munere lavit.

Similar verses occur elsewhere, as on the church at Champéry in Switzerland, and in Weever's *Ancient Funeral Monuments.*

l. 19. *William Gregory.* This is the possible author of part of *Gregory's Chronicle.* In his principal will he describes himself as of St. Mary Aldermary parish, and provides for his obit to be kept there (*Collections of a London Citizen*, pp. xlii–xlix). However, by another will he endowed a chantry at the church of SS. Anne and Agnes within Aldersgate for the souls of Margaret Holmhegge and others (*Cal. Wills*, ii. 557; see also, 556–7, 567, 573).

l. 27. *This colledge.* See A. J. Kempe's *Historical Notices of St. Martin le Grand*, where the Charter of William I (see note on pp. 270–1 above) is given on pp. 174–6, and other documents relating to the dispute in 1440 on pp. 117–33, together with the ordinance of 1457 on pp. 146–50 (the last is also given by Munday, pp. 327–30). The privileges of the Sanctuary had long been abused. Early in the sixteenth century Sir T. More (*Hist. of Richard III*) wrote of the sanctuaries at Westminster and

St. Martin's: 'What a rabble of theves, murtherers, and malicious heyghnous Traitours, and that in twoo places specyallye. The tone at the elbowe of the Citie, the tother in the very bowelles.' Complaint of the disorders in St. Martin's was made to Burghley in 1593 (Kempe, *u. s.* pp. 168–70). The privileges were abolished in the reign of James I.

l. 31. *in the yeare aforesaid.* That is in 19 Henry VI, which began on Sept. 1, 1440, shortly before the end of Malpas's and Marshall's year of office. For a full exemplification of the record see *C. P. R.* Henry VI, iii. 569–70.

309, l. 5. *straungers borne.* In Elizabeth's time the Liberty was occupied chiefly by foreigners, French, Dutch, and Germans, who worked as shoemakers (see i. 81 and ii. 281), and manufacturers of counterfeit plate, sham jewellery, embroideries and lace. Hence Stow's covert description of it as a den of thieves. So Dekker and Webster in *Westward Ho!* Act II. sc. i: 'You must to St. Martin's to buy lace.' Richard Braithwaite, in 1658, in *The Honest Ghost*, p. 167:—

By this he travells to Saint Martin's lane,
And to the shops he goes to buy a chaine.'

Butler, in *The Lady's Answer to Hudibras*, ll. 59, 60, refers to:

false St. Martin's beads
Which on our lips you lay for reds.

l. 13. *Northumberland house.* Henry Percy, second Lord, had his house here in 1352 (*Cal. Inq. p. m.* ii. 174, 288). Henry Percy, first Earl of Northumberland, gave it to his son Henry (Hotspur), at whose death in 1403 his two Inns in 'Aldrichgate strete' were granted to Richard, lord Grey (*C. P. R.* Henry IV, ii. 408; iii. 214). By other grants on July 22, 1405, and April 8, 1406, they were given to Queen Joanna, who held them till her death (*id.* iii. 34, 169). On July 11, 1437, the King's place, formerly called 'Queen Johanne Wardrobe', was granted to Thomas Aldenham (*id.* Henry VI, iii. 68, 152, 240). The Percies were endeavouring to recover it in 1435 (*id.* ii. 530–2), and eventually succeeded; for, on the attainder of the third Earl, this and the other Northumberland house in Aldgate were granted to George, Duke of Clarence (*id.* Edw. IV, i. 48, 199).

311, l. 21. *Nicholas Farendon son to the said William.* Stow's account of the Farringdon family is inaccurate. William died in 1294, leaving his property to his wife Isabella for life, and at her death to Nicholas his son-in-law and Isabella his daughter. This Nicholas Farringdon, who was mayor in 1308, 1313, 1320, and 1323, was probably the Nicholas, son of Ralph le Fevre, to whom, according to a deed cited by Antony Munday (*Survey*, p. 336, ed. 1633), William granted the aldermanry in 1293. Nicholas died in 1334, and was buried before the altar of St. Dunstan at St. Paul's Cathedral (*Hist. MSS. Comm.*, 9th Rep. 3). Through his daughter Roysia, or Rosia, he was grandfather of a second Nicholas Farringdon, who was never alderman, and dying in 1361 was buried at

St. Peter's in Cheap (*Cal. Wills*, i. 112, 397, ii. 18). The undivided Farringdon Ward was called the Ward of Ludgate and Newgate in 1285–6, but Farndon Infra and Farndon Extra in 1319–20 (*id.* i. 702–4). Nicholas de Farndon bequeathed it in 1334 to John de Pulteney as the 'Aldermanry of Farndon within Ludgate and Newgate and without'.

314, l. 2. *John Sha.* In his will he gave direction for the performance of the will of 'myn uncle Sir Edmonde Shaa knyght concernyng the continuance of dayly servyce to be songe and done withyn the parish church of St. Peter in Chepe. . . . I wyll that my executors shall cause ye said churche of Saint Petur to be bylded and made with a flat roofe. And also the Stepull there to be made up in a gode and convenient manner.' *Trans. Lond. and Midd.* iii. 348. The exact relationship of John and Edmond Shaw is given here alone.

l. 8. *buried in this Church.* Strype corrects the dates for Thomas Atkyns, *ob.* Aug. 15, 1486, and Richard Hadley, *ob.* Jan. 21, 1492, quoting the inscriptions. For Palmer he gives 1513, for Warley 1524, for Munday 1527. The Nicholas Farendon, who was buried here, was not the mayor but his grandson (see note above).

William Rus in his will (*Cal. Wills*, ii. 483) directed that he should be buried at St. Michael, Cornhill. See i. 196, ii. 305 above. The list for St. Peter's in *Harley MS.* 6069, f. 58, reads 'William Bowse'.

l. 33. *Fauster lane.* A corruption of St. Vedast's. It appears as 'Seint Fastes lane', and 'Venella Sancti Vedasti' in the fourteenth century (*Hist. MSS. Comm.*, 9th Rep. 13).

315, l. 1. *William Trist, Selerar.* Meaning William Tristour, saddler, who died in 1425. Another William Trystour, saddler, was buried here in 1439 (*Cal. Wills*, ii. 442, 489).

l. 15. *Seale.* The common seal still bears the inscription 'Sigillum Baronum Londoniarum'; the City arms were substituted for the figure of Thomas Becket in 1539. See Price, *Account of the Guildhall*, 12–13.

l. 20. *one great house.* Ralph Neville had tenements in Silver Street at the corner of Mugwell (Monk's Well) Street in 1367. John Neville (*d.* 1388) of Raby was his son. John's second wife, Elizabeth (*d.* 1395), heiress of William, Lord Latimer, was mother of John Neville (*d.* 1430), Lord Latimer. John, Lord Latimer, sold his barony to his half-brother, Ralph (*d.* 1425), first Earl of Westmorland, who died seized of 'Nevils Inn' in St. Olave parish in Farringdon Ward. Ralph (*d.* 1484), second Earl, held 'Neville Inn' in Silver Street (*Cal. Inq. p. m.* ii. 281, iii. 102, 192; iv. 103, 419). Dorothy Neville, daughter of Ralph (*d.* 1550), fourth Earl, married John de Vere, sixteenth Earl of Oxford; her only child, Katherine, married Edward, Lord Windsor (*d.* 1574), whose tomb is in the church of SS. Giovanni e Paolo at Venice; Lady Windsor died in 1600.

l. 25. *Monks well street.* See note on p. 339.

316, l. 19. *he deceased in the yeare 1577.* William Lambe died April 30, 1580. He was seized of 'le St. Jaemes Chappell at London Wall', and left it with other property to the Clothworkers for charitable and pious uses (*Inq. p. m. London*, iii. 99–101; *Cal. Wills*, ii. 703). See *Gent. Mag. Library*, xv. 288–93, describing the ruins in 1825.

l. 37. *stinking lane.* No doubt the 'Stukandelane' or 'Stigandes-lane' which was obstructed by the Grey Friars in 1275 (*Hundred Rolls*, i. 404).

319, l. 37. *Monuments.* Stow's list is based on that in the Register of Greyfriars in *Cotton MS.*, Vitellius, F. xii, which is printed in *Collectanea Topographica et Genealogica*, v. 275–90, 385–98. The original contains many names and dates not given by Stow, and supplies some corrections, viz.: p. 321, l. 5, Bartholomew de Castro (or de Castle, see *Cal. Wills*, i. 128); l. 22, 'two *daughters* of Alleyne Cheyny' (*due filie*); l. 29, 'Thomas Ap (à Parr) et Johannes Mylwater'; l. 31, John Water probably died in 1502; l. 34, William Huddy was not buried here, the entry refers to his wife Anne, who was widow of John Moyle. P. 322, l. 8, Chyrcheerd; l. 11, Philip Pettys; l. 13, Henry Reston; l. 17, John Treszawell.

'Patar, bishop of Carbon' (p. 320, l. 12) is Peter, bishop of Corbavia in Dalmatia, who was suffragan of London, Canterbury, and Winchester (Stubbs, *Reg. Sacr. Angl.* 195, ed. 1897; *Ann. Paul.* 340). Henry Frowike (p. 322, l. 10) is the sheriff of 1275, who died in 1284 (*Hist. MSS. Comm.*, 9th Rep. 46).

323, ll. 36–7. *H. Reade . . . 1450.* A misprint. His will, dated Sept. 6, 1420, was enrolled March 2, 1421 (*Cal. Wills*, ii. 423).

324, l. 7. *Aedelbertus Rex*, &c. This charter is contained in a register at St. Paul's, whence it has been printed in Dugdale, *History of St. Paul's*, p. 288, Kemble, *Cod. Dipl.* dcccclxxxii, Haddan and Stubbs, *Councils*, iii. 60, and Birch, *Cartularium Saxonicum*, i. 14. It is marked as spurious or questionable both by Kemble and by Stubbs.

l. 15. *Stortford*, &c. This grant is an O.E. charter of William I, printed in Dugdale, *St. Paul's*, p. 304.

l. 16. *He also confirmed*, &c. These two charters are printed in Dugdale, *St. Paul's*, p. 298; viz. a Latin charter confirming the grant of Æthelberht, and the other appearing to be a Latin translation of a writ drawn up in O.E. The latter is given from Charter Roll, 9 Edw. II, No. 37, and Pat. 1 Henry V. Earlier and better texts occur in *Cartae Antiquae*, C. C. No. 14 (*circa* 1200), and A 1, and BB. No. 9 (slightly later).

325, l. 28. *place of assembly.* For early (twelfth century) regulations on the chief folkmotes, viz. at Michaelmas to hear the sheriff's charge, at Christmas to keep the wards, and at Midsummer for watch against fire, see *Eng. Hist. Rev.* xvii. 502, and *Mun. Gild.* I. 118–9. The folkmote was to be summoned by the great bell at St. Paul's. See also note on p. 278 above. For the pleas in 1320 see *Mun. Gild.* II. i. 338–43. For Folkmotes at Paul's Cross see i. 331, and note on next page.

327, l. 10. *The height*, &c. Wren measured the tower as 260 feet high, but estimated that the spire had been no more than 200 (*Parentalia*,

274). The dimensions of old St. Paul's are given variously. See Sparrow-Simpson's *Documents illustrating the History of St. Paul's*, pp. 191–3.

l. 32. *dance of death.* Sir Thomas More (*Works*, p. 77, ed. 1557) alludes to the paintings at St. Paul's: 'But if we not only hear this word Death, but also let sink into our hearts the very fantasy and deep imagination thereof, we shall perceive thereby that we wer never so gretly moved by the beholding of *The Daunce of Death pictured on Pawles* as we shal fele ourself stered and altered by the feling of that imaginacion in our hearts. And no mervel. For those pictures expresse only the lothely figure of our ded bony bodies.' Lydgate's verses were printed at the end of Tottell's edition of *The Falls of Princes* in 1554; also in Dugdale's *History of St. Paul's*, 419–27, and in Douce's *The dance of death.* See also vol. i. p. 109 above.

328, l. 3. *a fayre Librarie.* Leland (*Collectanea*, iv. 47–8) gives a list of twenty-one manuscripts; there is a full list drawn up in 1458 in Dugdale's *History of St. Paul's*, 393–9. Only three can now be traced: (1) A MS. of Avicenna; (2) The *Chronicle* of Ralph de Diceto in the Lambeth Palace Library; (3) The Miracles of the Virgin in the Aberdeen University Library. A *Psalterium* now in the Cathedral Library was probably one of the Service-books of old St. Paul's. See Sparrow-Simpson, *Gleanings from Old St. Paul's*, 37–9.

331, l. 8. *The very antiquity of which Crosse.* It is mentioned in *Lib. de Ant. Legg.* 9, under date 1241, when Henry III took leave of the citizens for his journey to Gascony 'ad crucem Sancti Pauli'. Stow's instance in 1259 was on a like occasion, when Henry met the citizens 'populo in Folkesmoto congregato' (*Lib. de Ant. Legg.* 42). On the early history of Paul's Cross see Sparrow-Simpson, *Hist. of Old St. Paul's*, 149–72.

l. 27. *the steeple of Saint Paules.* Stow's narrative is an abbreviation of his original *Memorandum*: 'Anno 1561, ye 4 day of June, between 4 and 5 of ye cloke in ye aftär nonne, beynge Wedynsday and Corpus Cristi eve, ye stepull of Powlles was fyeryd by lyghtnynge, ye whiche lytenynge dyd take ye stepulle, as it dyd seme to ye beholders, ye space of ij or iij yardes benethe ye crosse and so byrnt round abought in ye same place that ye toppe felle of with ye cross wnperyshed (or wnbyrnt) and ye crosse fell southe, and so the sphere byrnt downe ward lyke as a candil consumyng, to ye stone werke and ye bells and so to ye rouffe of ye churche, and thorow ye rouffes of ye churche all fowre ways, east, west, northe, and sowthe. Within ye qwiers or chawnsylls was brynt no thyng but only ye communion table, and in ye rest of ye churche was brynt nothing but a sartayn tymber werke whiche stode at ye northe-west pyllar of ye stepull, which was fyered with ye tymber that fell in to ye churche owt of ye steple; whiche was a lamentable syghte and pytyfull remembraunce to all people that have ye feare of God before theyr eyes, consyderynge it was ye hous of owre Lord, erectyd to prays hym and pray to hym, ye beawty of ye syte of London, ye beawty of ye holle Reallme.

A mynster of suche worthy, stronge, and costly buldynge, so large, so pleasant and delectable, it passyd all comparyson, not only of mynstyrs within thys realme but ells where, as sure as travayll hathe taught ws in other realmes ethar Cristyn or hethyn. Wherfore feare we God that so sore hathe chatysyd us, and let ws well know that he whiche hathe not spayrd his owne hous wyll not spare owres, exsept we repent owr formor wykyd lyffe and serve hym in holynys and newenys of lyffe, with a parfytt faythe in God and parfytt charytye to owr neyghbour, y[e] whiche our Lorde for his byttar passyon grawnt. Amen.' (*Memoranda*, p. 116.)

The account in the *Survey* is reproduced almost verbatim from that in the *Annales*, p. 1095, ed. 1605. See for very similar accounts, Machyn, *Diary*, p. 259, and Hayward, *Annals of Queen Elizabeth*, p. 87, and three other contemporary accounts in Dr. Sparrow-Simpson's *Documents illustrating the History of St. Paul's*, pp. 113–27, Camd. Soc.; and *History of Old St. Paul's*, 134–42.

332, l. 22. *through whose default God knoweth.* The reference to Grindal in the 1598 edition (see p. 256 above) has been supposed to hint at some blame on his part. But this is unfounded. Hayward (*Annals*, p. 89) says that Grindal spent 720*l*. 'out of his proper estate.' Grindal was only too zealous, for if allowed he would have stripped the lead from St. Bartholomew's to cover St. Paul's (Strype, *Life of Grindal*, 93–6). The neglect of the Cathedral was, however, a scandal, and in 1581 the Lord Mayor wrote to Grindal, then Archbishop, 'that the walls were laid open and greatly spoiled with rain,' and prayed for his intervention, understanding that while bishop he 'not only gave of his own, but like his predecessors, had liberally borne some ordinary and yearly charge', and asking for his advice and that 'the yearly accounts of himself, his predecessors, and their officers might be seen for the city's information'. Grindal in reply wrote 'that he did in his time as much, or more, than either by law or reason he was bound' (*Remembrancia*, 322–7). If Grindal could clear himself it seems less certain that Aylmer (or Elmer), his successor, with whom, in 1581, the Corporation was in controversy, was blameless. Aylmer's son had to pay in 1597 over £4,000 for dilapidation of the church and bishop's houses. The misappropriation of the money is referred to in the play, *Nobody and Somebody* (Simpson, *School of Shakespeare*, i. p. 306):—

Nobody. I'le bring the tems through the middle of it, empty Mooreditch at my own charge, and build up Paules-steeple without a collection. I see not what becomes of these collections.

Clowne. Why, Nobody receives them.

Nobody. I, knave?

Clowne. You, knave: or, as the world goes, Somebody receives all, and Nobody is blamed for it.

Nobody and Somebody was probably written in 1592, when the question was revived in Richard Rowland or Verstegen's *Declaration of the True*

Causes of the Great Troubles. Bacon, replying in *Observations on a Libel*, wrote of 'the gathering of Paul's steeple' as 'being but a voluntary collection of that men were freely disposed to give, never grew to so great a sum as was sufficient to finish the work, for which it was appointed, and so I imagine was converted to some better use'. (*Life and Letters*, i. 176, ed. Spedding.)

l. 25. *Monumentes.* See Kalendar and Lists of Obits observed in St. Paul's, *temp.* Richard II, ap. Sparrow-Simpson, *Documents*, &c., pp. 61–106, and pp. 194–202; Holland, *Monumenta Sepulchraria Sancti Pauli*, and Dugdale, *History of St. Paul's Cathedral.*

Stow's lists contain numerous errors, especially of dates. Note the following corrections:—

Hingham, 1311; Robert Monden, 1338 (*Cal. Wills*, i. 430—his brother John was already dead); Melford, 1336; Gilbert Brewer (or Bruer), 1353; Richard Wendover, 1252; Adam de Bery (or Bury), 1386; Roger Holmes, 1395; Thomas Euers (or Eure), 1400; Thomas More, 1421. Also: Ralph Donion (or Dongon), was Canon in the time of Edward II; Richard Newport, Archdeacon of Middlesex 1309, is the bishop, who died in 1318; Swereford is a better form than Swarford.

334, l. 25. *what I haue heard by report, and haue partly seene.* Stow might have witnessed this ceremony in his youth, or he may refer only to its revival in 1557, of which Machyn (*Diary*, 141) writes thus:—'The last day of June, Saint Pauls day, was a goodly procession at Saint Pauls. There was a priest of every parriche of the dyosses of Londun with a cope, and the bishop of Londun wayreng ys myter: and after came a fat buck, and ys hed with the hornes borne a-pone a baner-pole, and xl hornes blohyng afor the boke and behynd.'

For a longer account of the grants of William and Walter Baud see Dugdale, *History of St. Paul's*, p. 12 (ed. Ellis). Camden mentions that he had seen the procession in his youth, no doubt referring to the revival of 1557 (*Britannia*, ii. 81, ed. Gough).

335, l. 37. *to serue Duke Humfrey.* Munday, in his edition of the *Survey* (p. 642, ed. 1633), adds: 'In idle and frivolous opinion of whom, some men, of late times, have made a solemn meeting at his tomb, upon St. Andrew's Day in the morning, before Christmas, and concluded on a breakfast or dinner; as assuring themselves to be servants, and to hold diversity of offices under the Good Duke Humphrey. Likewise on May Day, tankard-bearers, watermen, and some other of like quality besides, would use to come to the same tombe early in the morning, and (according to the other) have delivered serviceable presentation at the same monument, by strewing hearbes, and sprinkling faire water on it, as in the dutie of servants, and according to their degrees and charges in office. But as Master Stow hath discreetly advised such as are so merrily disposed, or simply professe themselves to serve Duke Humphrey in Pauls, if punishment of losing their dinners dayly there be not sufficient for them, they should be sent to S. Albon's, to answere there for their disobedience and long absence from their so highly well-deserving lord and master, because in their merrie disposition they please so to call him.'

St. Paul's was used regularly as a meeting-place to transact business (see note on p. 316 above). Fleetwood, writing to Cecil, speaks as a matter of course about going 'to Powles to learn some news', and of gossip, which had 'occupied Powles all last week' (*Lansdowne MS.* 24, ff. 22, 196). The aisles, and especially the neighbourhood of 'Duke Humphrey's Tomb', were the recognized haunts of loiterers, needy adventurers, and broken-down gallants. In Ben Jonson's *Every Man in his Humour* Captain Bobadil is called a 'Paul's man', and in *Every Man out of his Humour* (Act III. sc. i) another such rogue is described as: 'The most strange piece of military profession that ever was discovered in Insula Paulina.' This last jest is paralleled by Samuel Rowlands's satire on the traveller in conceit, whose 'journey is in Paules, in the back Isles' (*Letting of Humours*, &c., p. 46). From the loitering at St. Paul's of these knights of industry, who hoped there to earn a meal by their wits, 'to dine with Duke Humphrey' became a proverb for to go dinnerless. Rowlands begins a tale in his *Knave of Clubs*, p. 10, thus:—

> Two hungry sharks did travell Paules,
> Untill their guts cried out,
> And knew not how with both their wits,
> To bring one meal about.

Thomas Nashe in *Pierce Pennilesse* (*Works*, ii. 18, ed. Grosart) writes:—'I hearing of this colde comfort . . . like a careles malecontent, that knew not which way to turne, retired me to Paules to seeke my dinner with Duke Humfrey.'

Similar references abound. The third chapter of Dekker's *Guls Hornbooke* is entitled 'How a Gallant should behave himself in Powles Walkes', and is full of curious information (*Non-Dramatic Works* ii. 229–37, ed. Grosart). See also Milman's *Annals of St. Paul's*, pp. 283–8, and Sparrow-Simpson's *History of Old St. Paul's*, 235–50.

338, l. 11. *a merry poet.* Holland, in his *Monumenta Sepulchraria Sancti Pauli*, which appeared in 1614, after quoting Stow, adds: 'And no doubt but the merry poet was the merry old man Stow himself.' The lines do not appear in the original draft in *Harley MS.* 538. Stow, of course, alludes to the mediaeval legend which made St. Christopher a giant. In a note on 'the longitude of men' in *Lambeth MS.* 306 one entry is: 'Crystoferus, xvij fote & viij ynches.'

Hatton's tomb was one of the sights of London, and others than Stow commented on its excessive size. So Corbet in his *Iter Boreale*:

> Nor need the Chancellor boast, whose pyramis
> Above the host and altar is.

John Davies has an epigram:

> Titus, the brave and virtuous young gallant,
> Three years together in the town hath been,

Yet my Lord Chancellor's tomb he hath not seen,
Nor the new waterwork, nor the elephant.
I cannot tell the cause without a smile,
He hath been in the Counter all the while.

339, l. 8. *Pembrooks Inne.* John of Britanny, Earl of Richmond, had a house near Ivy Lane and Eldedenes lane (Warwick Lane) in 1312 (*Letter Book* D, 291; but see also vol. i. p. 342 above). Then Mary de St. Pol (*d.* 1377), Countess of Pembroke and widow of Aymer de Valence (*d.* 1324), lived there (*Letter Book* G, 132; *Cal. Wills*, ii. 195). In 1352 she is described as owning 'unum turellum, aedificatum cum cameris et cellario' (*Mun. Gild.* II. ii. 455). Her husband's heirs, the Hastings Earls of Pembroke, were lords of Bergavenny, and were represented in the female line by Henry Neville (*d.* 1587), Lord Bergavenny. William Beauchamp, Lord Bergavenny, held 'Pembrokes Inn' in 1411, and Johanna his widow in 1436 (*Cal. Inq. p. m.* iii. 332, iv. 167).

340, l. 29. *Margaret Queene of Scots.* Clearly meant for Margaret of Scotland, who married first Hubert de Burgh and then Gilbert Marshal. See ii. 89.

l. 30. *Robert de Attabeto.* Robert of Artois, Count of Beaumont-le-Roger, who died at London on Aug. 16, 1343. Stow's MS. list of the burials at Blackfriars is in *Harley MS.* 544, f. 68, where he writes 'Attrabeto'; also 'Hothe' (Howth) for 'Lioth' (p. 341, l. 4), and 'Nicholas Carre' for 'Nicholas Eare' (p. 341, l. 21). The list in *Harley MS.* 6033, f. 12, has 'the lord Hothe' and 'Nicholas Carrw'.

341, l. 13. *John Cornwall.* He founded a 'Cornewaill Chapel' at Blackfriars in 1437 for himself and his wife Elizabeth of Lancaster, Countess of Huntingdon (*C.P.R.* Henry VI, iii. 55–6); see Corrigenda.

l. 30. *sir Thomas Carden.* Carden or Cawarden had a grant of Blackfriars on March 12, 1550. He died on Aug. 29, 1559 (*Inq. p. m. Lond.*, i. 191–5). He was Master of the Revels and appropriated St. Anne's Church on the ground that it was required 'to lay in his Ma[ties] pavylyons, tentes, maskes, and reuels'. It was only under compulsion that he provided a room in its place (Chambers, *Tudor Revels*, 14, 15).

l. 39. *saint Michaell ad Bladum.* The meaning is shown clearly in the description of it in the reign of Henry III as St. Michael *ubi bladum venditur* (*Hist. MSS. Comm.*, 9th Rep. 20; *Cal. Wills*, i. 3). In the list of 1303 it is St. Michael 'in Foro ad Bladum' (*Mun. Gild.* II. i. 229). Sometimes it is called simply St. Michael, Cheap, or St. Michael at Paul's gate. For Ælfgar, and his son Nicholas, priests of St. Michael about 1100, see Round, *Geoffrey de Mandeville*, 309–10.

342, l. 29. *a small passage.* In 1378 complaint was made that the common passage which had existed time out of mind had been blocked, and order was given that the doorway should be reopened (*Memorials*, 417–18; *Letter Book* H, 89).

l. 37. *the prerogatiue court.* Robert de Avesbury, the historian, who was Registrar of the Court of Canterbury, lived in Ivy Lane (*Cal. Wills*, ii. 7).

343, l. 4. *Louels Inne.* It was Lovell property in 1433 (*Cal. Inq. p. m.*, iv. 73), but was forfeited by Francis, Viscount Lovell, in 1486, and granted in 1488 by Henry VII to Sir John Risley (Campbell, *Mat. Hist. Henry VII*, ii. 260), and by Henry VIII in 1513 to William Compton (*Letters and Papers*, i. 3761). Now represented by Lovell's Court.

l. 5. *Eldenese lane.* The original form was Elde-denes-lane, i.e. Old Dean's Lane, and there is reference to *Venella Veteris Decani* in the time of Henry III (*Hist. MSS. Comm.*, 9th Rep. 9) and in 1286 (*Cal. Wills*, i. 78). In the next two centuries Oldedeneslane 1365, Eldeneslane 1379, and Eldedeneslane 1442, occur (*id.* ii. 85, 209, 497). In the sixteenth century it is Warwick lane, formerly called Alden's Lane. 'Werwyk lane' occurs as early as 1475 (*Paston Letters*, v. 223), and 'Warwicke lane' in 1506 (*Chron. Lond.* 261). Thomas de Beauchamp (*d.* 1369), Earl of Warwick, had his house in Eldeneslane, as also his son Thomas in 1401, and his grandson Richard in 1439, and Richard's daughter-in-law, Cicely, Duchess of Warwick, in 1450 (*Cal. Inq. p. m.* ii. 294, iii. 277, iv. 191, 241).

345, l. 13. *Thomas Tomlinson*, &c. Stow's account is based on a note furnished by a friend, and now preserved in *Harley MS.* 367, f. 47vo:—

'A description of a vaute made for Thomas Tomlinson at the corner of Bredstreete in Cheapside.

'The vaute being digged fifteene feete deepe there was found the said pavement like vnto that of Cheapside now, and at the farther ende of the vaute in Cheapside at ye channel was found a tree sawed into fiue steppes which were, as it shuld seme, to steppe over some brooke, and vppon the edge of the seid brooke (as it seemeth) there were found lying along the bodies of two greate trees, the endes whereof were then sawed, and were as firme timber then as at the first, when they fell; part also of the said trees remaine yet in the ground vndigged. It was all forced ground vntill they went past the trees aforesaid.'

Stow wrote a note at the side, but the margin has been cut. Thomas Tomlinson, skinner, died in 1612 (*Cal. Wills*, ii. 735).

When the Saracen's Head in Cheapside was rebuilt in 1844 a Roman tessellated pavement was found 16 to 18 feet below the street level (*London Topographical Record*, iv. 56).

l. 29. *Goldsmithes Rowe.* The goldsmiths had long occupied this part of Cheap. The *Orfaveria in foro London* is mentioned in the time of Henry III (*Cal. Inq. post mortem*, i. 917, new ed.), and in 1290 there is reference to a shop in the Goldsmithery opposite St. Peter, Wood Street (*Cal. Wills*, i. 94). For Stow's time see Webster and Marston, *The Malcontent*, Induction: 'I'll walk but once down by the Goldsmith's Row in Cheap, take notice of the signs and tell you them with a breath instantly. They begin as the world did, with Adam and Eve. There's in all just five and fifty.' Paul Hentzner, the German, in his

Travels in England during the Reign of Elizabeth (p. 31, ed. Horace Walpole), writes: 'The streets in this city are very handsome and clean; but that which is named from the goldsmiths who inhabit it, surpasses all the rest; there is in it a gilt tower, with a fountain that plays. Near it on the further side is a handsome house, built by a goldsmith and presented by him to the City. There are besides to be seen in this street, as in all others where there are goldsmiths' shops, all sorts of gold and silver vessels exposed to sale, as well as ancient and modern medals, as must surprise a man the first time he sees and considers them.'

346, l. 6. *Watheling streete*, &c. See Leland, *Collectanea*, ii. 361–2: 'Nobilium via Athelingstreate, Watelingstreate corrupte.' Athelingestrate occurs in 1212 (*Anc. Deeds*, A. 1499), and instances during the thirteenth century are common, though some may refer to Addle Street (*Hist. MSS. Comm.*, 9th Rep. 2, 4; *Cal. Wills*, i. 13, 46, 157, 419—date 1336). The London 'Watling Street' seems to occur first in 1307 (*id.* i. 186). For drapers of Watling Street in Stow's time see Greene's *Tu Quoque* (*Old Plays*, xi. 207, ed. Hazlitt):—'He fills his belly and never asks what's to pay: wears broad-cloth, and yet dares walk Watling St. without any fear of his draper.'

l. 26. *Walter Turke*, &c. This comes from a Cartulary of St. Mary Overy, as shown by Stow's note in *Harley MS.* 544, f. 100.

347, l. 7. *two priests of this church*, &c. This is reproduced *verbatim* from the London Chronicle in *Harley MS.* 540, f. 8vo.

l. 22. *little damnified thereby*. Wriothesley gives an almost identical account, except that he concludes: 'But the steeple was so perished that there was no mendinge of it but to take it downe' (*Chronicle*, ii. 146). Machyn (*Diary*, 209) says the dog was a spaniel.

l. 32. *the yeare 1300 and odde*, &c. The edition of 1598 reads 'Cornishe gentleman'; that of 1603 'Cornishe gentlemen'; the latter with its faulty punctuation led Munday to read '1300, and certaine Cornish gentlemen 1312'. The true meaning appears in *Harley MS.* 538:—'about the yere of Christ 1300 and odd yeres. Cornishe, a gentleman, was buried there in the yere 1312.'

l. 33. *William Palmer*. Died 1349 (*Cal. Wills*, i. 538).

ll. 34–6. *Iohn Shadworth . . . 1428*. This is the date of his first will; he made a second in Jan. 1429. They were not proved till Oct. 1430 (*Cal. Wills*, ii. 452–3).

l. 37. *Stephen Bugge*, a draper, founded a chantry at St. Mildred's in 1430 (*id.* ii. 450).

348, l. 13. *Basing lane*. In spite of Stow's statement that he had not read of Basing 'to have anything there to do', the lane no doubt owed its name to an early owner. In 1275 Peter de Basinges made bequest of his house in Basing Lane (*Cal. Wills*, i. 20).

l. 22. *On the South side*, &c. This passage on Gerrard the Giant affords interesting illustrations of Stow's methods of composition, of his connexion with Holinshed's *Chronicles*, and of his rivalry with Grafton. The original draft in *Harley MS.* 538, f. 127, differs materially from the printed versions:—

'On the south syde of this lane is one greate house, of olde tyme builded of stone vpon arched vaultes vnder ground, with arched gates also of stone: but I haue not red who was the first builder thereof, neythar when the same was builded. It is at this present a comon Inn for recepte of travaylers, greatly frequented of carriers and of others: it is called Gerrard's Hall and sayde to be of a giaunte that ther dwelled, so named, but no authoritie is shewed, more than that of olde tyme the sayd howse hauinge a large and highe roofed hall, there stode in the midste thereof a mighty staffe, armed at the fore end with iron and stele; it reached from the grownde or flowre to the very toppe of the hall, even as it were to towche or pierce it. This staffe is sayde to be one of them, that the sayde Gerard the Giaunt vsed to runne withal in his warres. Sure he had nede of a very greate horse to cary hym, that should wild suche a staffe, but I thinke he was no horseman but went all on his fete. There stode also a lathar of the same height iust by the staffe. I have sene them ofte, and inquired of the tenaunts the cawse of theyr being there, but they could make to me none other aunswere than that the one was Gerar's staffe (as ye have herd) and the laddar to ascend to the toppe thereof, to se the same staffe to be saffe, and not decayed. Of late yeres this hall is altered in buildinge, and dyvers romthes made of it. Notwithstondinge the staffe is removed to one corner of the hawle, whiche remayneth of height as afore, save that the poynt is broken off, but the laddar is broken or sawd shortar almoste by the one halfe, and the remenaunt thereof hanged on to a wall in the yarde. A servaunt of that howse (more curtise than his master) showed me the lengthe of the staffe by a wall's syde, where the sayd staffe was layde, whiles the romthes ouer the hall were in buildinge. I measured the ground and found it 50 foot in lengthe. But the master of the howse saythe the same to lak halfe a foote of 40 foote, which worde of his I must take for curraunt, for reason cowde he gyve me none. Neyther would he rise from his sete to show me eny ferther, but bad me rede the Chronicles, for there he had hard. This muche for the east syde of Bread Street.'

For the host's reference to the great Chronicles see William Harrison's *Description of Britain*, ap. Holinshed, *Chronicles*, i. 21: 'I could speake also of Gerard's staffe or lance, yet to be seene in Gerard's Hall at London in Basing lane, which is so great and long that no man can beweld it, neither go to the top thereof without a ladder, which of set purpose and for greater countenance of the wonder is fixed by the same.'

349, l. 3. *John Leyland his Comentaries.* As to Stow's transcripts of Leland, made in 1576, see *Introduction*, p. xxv. 'Reyne Wolfe's Chronicle' refers to Holinshed's *Chronicles*, to which was prefixed William Harrison's *Description of the Island of Britain.* Harrison charged Leland with having 'made his notes intricate of set purpose', being 'loth that anie man should easilie come to that knowledge by reading which he with his great charge and no less travell atteined unto by experience'. Hearne (ap. Leland, *Collectanea*, i. p. lv) censured Harrison for his 'unbecoming reflexions upon so great a man, from whom he borrowed the most valuable and judicious passages in his Description of Britain, his own Remarks being generally very mean and trivial.'

John Bagford, in his *Letter relating to the Antiquities of London* (*id.* i. p. lxix), wrote: ''Tis my opinion that Stow had in his possession Leland's Antiquities of London, and for want of Learning most grievously mangled the Work on purpose to make it his own.' The suggestion is quite unfounded; Stow's *Collections* prove how fully his work was based on his own research; he sometimes follows Leland without express acknowledgement, but sometimes also corrects him silently; compare vol. i. p. 137 with vol. ii. p. 143, and see note on p. 290. Most of the references to Leland in the *Survey* appear to be to the extant *Collectanea* and not to any lost work, though the note on the Library at St. Peter's, Cornhill (vol. i. p. 194), does imply something more explicit than the bald reference in *Collectanea*, iv. 48.

l. 9. *R. G. in his briefe collection of Histories*. On f. ii of the *Manuell* published in 1565. For Stow and Grafton's quarrel see *Introduction*, pp. viii to xii.

l. 26. *I reade that John Gisors*, &c. Stow's account of the Gisors family here and on i. p. 248 is not clear. I cannot solve all difficulties, but some notes will be of service. The first John Gisors of importance was mayor in 1245 and 1259, and was prominent in civic history for many years after. He is probably the John, son of Peter de Gysors, whose will was proved in 1282 (*Cal. Wills*, i. 57). For Peter, son of Laurence Gisors see i. p. 245 above. John (*d.* 1282) was probably father of John Gisors, who was alderman of Vintry Ward *circa* 1283–93 (*id.* i. 702–3) and died in 1296, leaving by his wife Margery four sons, John, Anketin, Thomas, and Henry (*id.* i. 128). Margery died in 1305, when her son John was twenty-six years old and more (*Calendarium Genealogicum*, ii. 678). The third John Gisors became Alderman of Vintry Ward in 1307 (*Letter Book* C, 178). He was Mayor in 1311, 1312, and 1314, but as a consequence of the charge of having wrongfully admitted one guilty of felony to the freedom of the city—see i. 51 above—was removed from his Aldermanry in March, 1321 (*Letter Book* E, 138). He was a supporter of the Mortimers and of Queen Isabel, and was joint constable of the Tower in Nov. 1326 (*Ann. Paulini*, 305, 318), but took no further part in civic government. He died in Jan. 1351, and was buried at St. Martin in the Vintry. In his will he mentions John, his grandfather, his parents John and Margery, and two wives, Isabella and Alice. His heirs were his granddaughters Margaret (wife of Henry Picard) and Felicia (who married Thomas Travers—see i. 299), daughters of Thomas Gisors (apparently the Sir Thomas of i. 299); and two sons, Edward and Nicholas, and a daughter, Juliana (*Cal. Wills*, i. 643–5). In his will he is described as vintner (like most of his family), but is elsewhere called a pepperer. Anketin de Gisors was alderman of Aldgate from Jan. 1312 (*Letter Book* D, 15), and died before 1343 (*id.* G, 3). Henry de Gisors (*d.* 1343), vintner, was alderman of Cornhill in 1330–4 (*Letter Book* E, 256, 281); it was he, and not William de Gisors (as stated on p. 349), who was sheriff in 1329 (*id.* F, 284; see also ii. 164, above). References to a Thomas Gisors, vintner, occur in the latter part of the reign of Edward III (*Letter Book* G, 286), and to John and Henry de Gisors under Richard II (*C. P. R.* Rich. II, iv. 3, 458). I have not been able to trace their relationship.

l. 36. *Gerrards hall for Gisors hall.* John de Gisors (*d.* 1296) left to his son Thomas his New Hall in the parish of St. Mildred, Bread Street. John de Gisors (*d.* 1351) left to his granddaughter, Felicia, his tenement called 'Gysors halle' in St. Mildred, Bread Street (*Cal. Wills*, i. 128, 645). The Cartulary of St. John's, Clerkenwell (*Cotton MS.*, Nero, E. vi. f. 35), contains some deeds headed 'Gysorshall'; but they relate to tenements in St. Mildred, Bread Street, which James Gysors held in 1365 as heir of Anketin Gysors. The feoffment, which Stow describes as having been made in 1386, does not appear to have been enrolled in the Court of Husting (*Cal. Wills*, i. 643 *n.*); but in that year Paul Gisors and others executed a release of certain shops and chambers by the Conduit of London lately belonging to John Gisors (*Anc. Deeds*, A. 2049); this indicates that the family property was then being sold. 'Gisoreshalle' is mentioned in 1429 (*Cal. Wills*, ii. 453). It was an inn before 1479, when there is reference in the *Paston Letters* (vi. 34) to, 'The Crown, wich as I conseive is called Gerardes Hall, in Bred Stret.' There was still an inn called Gerrard's Hall in 1784. The crypt survived till 1852. The stonework was then removed to the Crystal Palace to be there set up; but this design was never fulfilled, and the stones were used for other purposes. See *Gent. Mag. Libr.* xv. 270–1. For an architectural account of Gisors Hall with illustrations see Turner and Parker *Domestic Architecture of the Middle Ages*, ii. 186.

350, l. 14. *howses for Merchants.* See quotation from Dekker's *Jests* on p. 338.

l. 17. *the prisoners were remoued.* For an Act of the Common Council ordering the removal, and dated 19th Sept. 1556, see Munday, *Survey*, 937, ed. 1633. The Bread Street Compter had been hired by the keepers from the Goldsmiths' Company. The letting of the new Compter was expressly forbidden. See also Wriothesley's *Chronicle*, ii. 42.

351, l. 10. *S. I. Euangelist.* Anciently it was called St. Werburga, viz. in 1249, 1278, 1303, and 1321 (*Cal. Charter Rolls*, i. 339; *Cal. Wills*, i. 34, 290; *Mun. Gild.* II. i. 230). In 1349 it is St. John Evangelist and St. Wereburga (*Cal. Wills*, i. 596). In *Harley MS.* 538 Stow adds dates of death, viz. Doggett, 1524; Askew, 1534; Dobbes, 1556; Dane, 1573; Allet 'deceased in his mayoralitie.'

l. 15. *S. Margaret Moyses.* The name may be due to 'Moyses

sacerdos', who occurs in deeds at St. Paul's about 1142. The church is called St. Margaret Moses in 1256 (*Hist. MSS. Comm.*, 9th Rep. 15, 62, 68). Nicholas Bray founded a chantry here in 1449 (*Cal. Wills*, ii. 516).

l. 23. *Distaffe lane.* 'Distar' is an error of Stow's. The record of 1438 is a grant of 'Le Lambe' in 'Distaflane' to Robert Prik and Richard Stanes (*C. P. R.* Henry VI, iii. 160, 193; for later grants see *id.* Edw. IV, i. 297, 437, and iii. 422; Campbell, *Mat. Hist. Henry VII*, i. 21; *Letters and Papers*, i. 1070). 'Distavlane' occurs in 1260 and 1295, and 'Distaflane' in 1301 (*Cal. Wills*, i. 9, 123, 154), and so commonly thereafter.

VOL. II

1, l. 16. *Spuren lane.* 'Sporuneslane' in 1271 (*Anc. Deeds*, C. 1910), 'Sporounelane' in 1295, and 'Sporenlane' in 1406 (*Cal. Wills*, i. 120, ii. 562). 'Hoggenelane' in the parish of Trinity the Less occurs in 1329 and 1375 (*id.* i. 357, ii. 181).

l. 20. *Finimore lane.* 'Fynamoures lane' in 1316 (*Cal. Wills*, i. 263). It is now called Fyefoot Lane.

l. 24. *Desboorne lane.* Stow's authority is clearly *Letter Book* F, 184. The lane was granted to John de Gildisburgh under licence from the king, with permission to build over it subject to leaving a gutter to carry off the water. It lay between the tenements of Sir Edward de Montacute and Walter (*not* William) Gladewyn, and is described as containing in length 215 feet from the king's highway to the Thames, and seven feet wide at the commencement and in the middle, but only an ell at the bottom (*C. P. R.* Edw. III, viii. 149). Five years before, in 1343, complaint was made that the lane was blocked up and impassable (*Mun. Gild.* II. ii. 452). It would seem to be identical with the 'venella que vocatur Deneburȝate', or 'Denebureghlane', which was alleged to be obstructed in 1275 (*Hundred Roll*, i. 418–9, 433).

2, l. 27. *S. Nicholas Cold Abbey.* It is St. Nicholas Coldhabey in 1378, and usually appears as Coldabbey in various spellings (*Cal. Wills*, i. 32, 195, 640). Stow's last derivation connecting it with Cold Harbour is probably correct. There are similar instances in the manor of Coldabbeye in Surrey, and the tenement called 'le Coldabbeye' in Windagain Lane (*id.* ii. 45, 373). The church is sometimes called 'atte Coldeabbey' (*id.* ii. 198, 522).

3, l. 16. *Nicholas Wolberge . . . 1407.* His will, dated 1407, was not proved till 1420 (*Cal. Wills*, ii. 419–20).

l. 28. *Barnard Randolph.* See note on p. 285.

4, l. 11. *Thomas Lewen.* In *Harley MS.* 538, 'deceased 1554' is added.

l. 18. *Blitheman.* In *Harley MS.* 538 the epitaph is given:—

Here Blitheman lies a worthy wight,
  Who feared God above;
A friend to all, a foe to none,
  Whome riche and pore did love.

Of Princes' chaple gentleman
  Unto his dieinge day,
Wher all toke greate delight to heare
  Hym on the organs play.

Whose passing skill in musyke's arte
  A scholar left behind;
John Bull, by name, his master's veyne
  Expressing in eche kynde.

But nothing here continuethe longe,
  Nor resting place can have;
His sowle departed hence to heven,
  His body here in grave.

This epitaph is given in Munday's edition of the *Survey*, p. 399, where it is stated that he died on Whitsunday, 1591. A few of William Blitheman's compositions are extant; they show that he was a master of his art, and that Bull owed much to his influence (*Dict. Nat. Biog.* v. 222).

5, l. 1. *John Glocester Alderman, 1345.* In *Harley MS.* 538 'deceased 1355' is added. This is correct (*Cal. Wills*, i. 687). But Salt Wharf was given to the church by his son John, who died in 1362 (*id.* ii. 64).

l. 16. *a Record.* See the writ and patents in *Letter Book* H, 447–8: providing, however, for Hallmotes twice a year as of old accustomed, and for the election of six persons, viz. two each from Bridge Street, Old Fish Street, and Stockfishmonger Row to govern the mistery. Compare i. 214 above. See also *Mun. Gild.* II. i. 397–408.

l. 32. *Richard Marlowe.* In *Harley MS.* 538 'deceased 1422'. This is shown to be correct by his will, where his name is spelt 'Merlawe'; but he was a native of Marlow (*Cal. Wills*, ii. 428).

6, l. 1. *Saint Mary Summerset.* In a deed of Prior Stephen (1170–87) there is mention of Ernald the priest of St. Mary Sumerset (*Anc. Deeds*, A. 2423). The name may be derived from Ralph de Sumery, who occurs about the same date (*id.* A. 2364, 2406). For the church and its monuments see *Trans. Lond. and Midd.*, iii. 253–84.

l. 5. *Edreds Hithe.* The name 'Ætheredys Hythe' occurs in 899 in a Charter of Alfred (Kemble, *Cod. Dipl.* mlxxiv). Henry I gave it to his queen Matilda. Matilda, queen of Stephen, gave rents from Edreds hythe to Trinity (*Cotton Charter*, xvi. 35). In a charter of Henry II it is described as 'Ripa Reginae que appellatur Atheres hithe' (*Mon. Angl.*, vi. 635). Isabel, queen of John, gave it to her son Richard of Cornwall (*Hundred Roll*, i. 414). For William of Ypres' charter, see *Ancient*

Charters, No 32 (Pipe Roll Soc.). See also Madox, *Hist. Exchequer*, i. 781. St. Michael, Queenhithe, is called St. Michael de 'Ædredes huda' about 1148, and 'de Hutha Regina' about 1220 (*Hist. MSS. Comm.* 9th Rep. 22, 63).

The charter of Alfred, above referred to, is a grant to Plegmund, archbishop of Canterbury, which was no doubt the origin of the later Canterbury soke. (*Mun. Gild.* I. 241; cf. i. 41 and ii. 7 above.)

7, l. 22. *woorepath and Anede Hith.* See the record from the *Liber Memorandorum* on the Customs of Queenhithe, ap. *Mun. Gild.* III. 445–8, where a note is quoted from the *Liber Horne* stating that Werepath or Worpath is in the east part of the Flete of Barking, seven miles east of London, and Anedehithe near Westminster.

8, l. 30. *Witnesses.* The names are very corrupt. The Charter in *Mun. Gild.* II. i. 47 reads: 'Hiis testibus, Radulpho filio Nicholai, Ricardo de Grey, Johanne et Willelmo, fratribus ejus, Paulino Peyvre, Radulpho de Waunci, Johanne Gumbaud et aliis.'

l. 38. *customs of this Queene Hithe.* They are given in the *Liber Albus*, see *Mun. Gild.* I. 241–3. Strype gives an English translation from the *Liber Horne.* The original has 'Wolsiesgate in Corderia' (the Ropery) for 'Wolsey Street in the parish of All hallowes the Less', and 'Berchenes lane' instead of Stow's 'Bircheovers'. For complaints as to abuses at Queenhithe see *Hundred Rolls*, i. 403 sqq.

9, l. 22. *Roomeland.* The name given to an open space near a dock where ships could discharge. There was a 'Rome land' at Billingsgate, described in the *Husting Rolls* as 'a platt of grounde raylled abowte called Rome lande on the west parte of Byllyngesgate'. In 1347 there is reference to 'le Roumland' near Crutched Friars (*Letter Book* F, 175, with note by Dr. Sharpe). For cleansing of 'Roumeland' at Queenhithe in 1368, see *Letter Book* G, 221. 'La Roumlonde' at Queenhithe is mentioned in 1311 and 1373 (*Cal. Wills*, i. 222; ii. 161).

10, l. 17. *John Cooke.* By will, dated October 16, 1542, and proved January 13, 1544, he bequeathed to the city his capital messuage called the Duke of Norfolk's place and other messuages at Broken Wharf (*Cal. Wills*, ii. 648). See Stow's subsequent statement on ii. 11. For the lane called 'le Tymber hith prope le Brokene Wharf' and 'Timber hythe otherwise called Broken Wharf' see *Hist. MSS. Comm.* 9th Rep., 17–18—14th century. For 'le Brokenewharf' in 1274, see *Anc. Deeds*, A. 1875.

11, l. 19. *Chartsey . . . and was their Inne.* In the Chertsey Register (*Cotton MS.*, Vitellius, A. xiii. f. 31) it is described as a court 'in urbe Londonia sitam super ripam Thamisie fluminis in occidentali parte urbis ipsius contra austrum uergens prope portum quod ipsi urbani *fishchuþe* uocant, id est porta piscis'. For *le Fisshwharf* in St. Mary, Somerset, see *Cal. Wills*, i. 496, and *Mun. Gild.* II, i. 406, ii. 453.

13, l. 1. *Bewmounts Inne.* As 'Newe Inne' it belonged in 1397 to William de Montagu, Earl of Salisbury (*Cal. Inq. p. m.* iii. 203, 259).

On the attainder of his nephew John in 1400 it fell to the king. Then it seems to have been held by Edward, Duke of York, and by Queen Joanna (*C.P.R.* Henry IV, iii. 2) and later by Sir Thomas Erpingham (*Cal. Inq. p. m.* iv. 125). On October 28, 1440, Henry VI granted it to William Phelip, Lord Bardolf, with remainder to John, Viscount Beaumont, who had married his only daughter and heiress (*C. P. R.* Henry VI, iii. 120, 473). After the forfeiture in 1462 of John's son William it was granted as 'Newe Inne *alias* Beaumontes Inne' in June, 1475, to William Hastings (*id.* Edw. IV, ii. 517, cf. *Cal. Inq. p. m.* iv. 322). Hastings was ancestor of the Earls of Huntingdon.

l. 9. *Scrupes Inne.* So held by Sir William FitzHugh in 1453. His father Henry, who seems to have held it in 1425, was son of Joan daughter of Henry, first Lord Scrope of Masham. Stephen Scrope, second lord, held it in 1406 (*Cal. Inq. p. m.* iii. 307, iv. 84, 256).

l. 21. *of Baynard*, &c. See i. 61 above. In *Harley MS.* 538 the history of the FitzWalters is placed here.

l. 27. *Legates Inne.* 'Legates place juxta Baynards Castle' belonged to Margaret Talbot, Countess of Shrewsbury, in 1467 (*Cal. Inq. p. m.* iv. 341).

15, l. 11. *S. Benet Hude.* St. Benet 'super Tamisiam' in 1111, and S. Benet 'super Heþam' at the end of the twelfth century (*Hist. MSS. Comm.* 9th Rep. 63, 67). Afterwards very commonly called S. Benet Woodwharf, see p. 279 *n.* above.

l. 19. *Barklies Inne.* Thomas, Lord Berkeley, held it in 1416; his daughter Elizabeth married Richard de Beauchamp, Earl of Warwick, who held it in 1439 (*Cal. Inq. p. m.* iv. 31, 191).

16, l. 28. *Woodmongers Hall.* David Smith, mentioned just above, had purchased it of Edmund Helles, woodmonger, shortly before his death in 1587, when he left it with other property to the Mayor and Commonalty on trust for Christ's Hospital (*Inq. p. m. Lond.* iii. 108-9).

l. 33. *Queene Mary gaue it*, &c. The Earl of Derby had exchanged it with Edward VI for lands in Lancashire. Cf. *Acts Privy Council*, iv. 70.

17, l. 13. *Powles Brewhouse.* The bracinum' or brewhouse of St. Paul's is mentioned in 1162, and the 'Paules hede' opposite the bakehouse in 1456 (*Hist. MSS. Comm.* 9th Rep. 12, 27). It is called 'Pouleshede' near Poulescheyne in 1444 (*Cal. Wills*, ii. 503).

l. 17. *somtime letten to the Blunts.* 'The capital house lately called Mountjoye place, and now *anglice* called the Doctors' Commons' (*Inq. p. m. London*, iii. 106—date 1587).

18, l. 18. *Do Little lane.* Now Knightriders Court. The name occurs as 'Do lyttle' or 'Do lite' lane in 1294 (*Hist. MSS. Comm.* 9th. Rep. 19).

l. 21. *Sermon lane, for Sheremoniers lane.* It occurs as Sarmoneres lane in deeds from the reign of Henry III onwards, and in 1279 there is reference to a tenement of Adam le Sarmoner (*id.* 13, 19).

19, l. 3. *a tempest of wind.* Stow in his *Memoranda* (p. 134) writes thus: 'The xxiij day of Decembar, beynge Sondaye, at nyghte, in anno 1565, was a greate tempest of wynde where thrwghe many persons were drownyd on the Thams and other placis, and the great gattes at the West ende of S. Pawls churche in London, wher is the brasen pilar, was blowne wyde open, the wynd beynge in ye west was of suche force.'

l. 15. *the Lowlardes Tower.* Often confused with the Lollards Tower at Lambeth, where the use of the name appears to be inaccurate and of much later date. For the history of the Lollards Tower see Sparrow-Simpson, *Documents illustrating the History of St. Pauls*, pp. 214–18, Camden Soc.; and *History of Old St. Paul's*, 113–26.

21, l. 29. *windagaine Lane.* 'Wandayenes lane' in 1309, and Wandageynes lane' in 1337 (*Cal. Wills*, i. 204, 422). 'Turnagayne' Lane in 1430 (*Cal. Inq. p. m.* iv. 126).

22, l. 3. *which house is also of this ward.* Stow is in error; the Liberty of the Rolls is not now, and never has been in the City. Similarly he includes the liberty of St. Martin's in Aldersgate Ward, though it was not incorporated in the City till somewhat later.

l. 28. *in the yeare 1102.* According to the *Liber Fundacionis S. Bartholomei*, cap. vii, the real date was 1123; but the same authority speaks of it as 'Henrico primo anno xxx et circiter tercium regni eius'. See Dr. Norman Moore's edition of the English *Book of Foundation*, p. liv, and *Mon. Angl.*, vi. 292. *Cotton MS.*, Vesp., B. ix contains a copy of the Latin original composed about 1180, together with an English version made about 1400.

l. 29. *Alfune*, &c. Stow is following the *Liber S. Bartholomei* (*u. s.* cap. xxii) where Alfune is described as an old man, who had not long before built the church of St. Giles. But in a deed at St. Paul's it is stated that in the reign of Henry I, Aelmund, the priest, granted to the chapter the church of St. Giles, which he had built outside the wall of the City (*Hist. MSS. Comm.* 9th Rep. 62).

23, l. 11. *John Coke,* Treasurer of the Hospital, compiled a Rental, which he began in the 'thirty-seventh year of his profession and sixty-fourth of his age' in 1456, and completed in 1468 (Morley, *Memoirs of Bartholomew Fair*, 25–6; *Dict. Nat. Biog.*, xi. 223). Wakering was master from 1422 to 1466.

l. 14. *Walter Cope.* He was a member of the old Society of Antiquaries before Feb., 1590, was knighted April 20, 1603, made Chamberlain of the Exchequer in 1609, and died in 1614. He was the original builder of Holland House, which he called Cope Castle; it passed with his only daughter to Henry Rich, afterwards first Earl of Holland. See Hearne, *Curious Discourses*, ii. 427; *Dict. Nat. Biog.* xii. 168.

l. 15. *Monumentes.* There is a list in *Harley MS.* 6069, f. 57, which supplies the following variants: Adam Hore (l. 16); Sir Thomas Palefant, baron of Winva, Lord St. George, Oncketon, and Pille (l. 21);

Shipley (l. 26); Wesbye (l. 27); Robert Caldecote (l. 29) William Brokas (l. 32).

l. 32. *John Shirley.* Shirley's transcripts of Chaucer, Lydgate, and other poets are of great value and importance. Nothing is known of his life except what Stow here records, save that in 1440 he was living in London. Translations by him of 'The Lamentable Cronycle of the dethe and false murdere of James Stewarde, late kynge of Scotys' and of two other small pieces are contained in *Additional MS.* 5467. Shirley's MSS. are *Harley*, 78, 2251, 7333, and *Additional* 16165, in the British Museum; *Ashmole* 59, in the Bodleian Library; Trinity College, Cambridge, R. 3, 20; and the Sion College MS. In *Additional MS.* 29729 are some poems of Lydgate's 'copyed out of ye boke of John Shirley by John Stowe'. See Skeat, *Chaucer*, i. 25, 53–9 and *Dict. Nat. Biog.* lii. 133.

27, l. 19. *priuiledge of fayre.* The fair existed before 1133, when Henry I granted a charter of protection (*Mon. Angl.*, vi. 296). The charter of Henry II, granted *circa* 1156–62, was confirmed by Henry III in 1253 (*Cal. Charter Rolls*, ii. 368–70). For the history of the fair see Morley, *Memorials of Bartholomew Fair*; for a description of the fair in Stow's time see Ben Jonson's *Bartholomew Fair*, and in the early part of the nineteenth century Hone, *Everyday Book*, i. 1166–1251. The fair was held for the last time in 1855.

28, l. 36. *brokers*, &c. See Webster, *Northward Ho!* Act II, sc. i: 'All the brokers in Long Lane had rifled their wardrobe.' Taylor, the Water-poet, writes in *Three Weeks from London to Hamburgh*, p. 1:— 'Like a desperate pawn had lain seven years in lavender on sweeting in Long Lane, or amongst the dogged inhabitants of Houndsditch.'

Long Lane was perhaps called after William le Long of Portepul, who held land here before 1249 (*Anc. Deeds*, B. 2330). Richard le Lung 'feleper' (fripper or broker) is mentioned in 1279 (*Letter Book* A, 30).

29, l. 4. *Horse-poole.* So called in 1384 (*Letter Book* H, 236).

l. 14. *Prior of Semperingham.* As last master of the order Robert Holgate, Archbishop of York, owned it, and died there on Nov. 15, 1555 (*Inq. p. m. Lond.* i. 142).

l. 21. *markets of horses and cattle.* In *Henry IV*, Pt. 2, Act I, sc. ii, Falstaff says of Bardolph: 'I bought him in Paul's, and he'll buy me a horse in Smithfield: if I could get me a wife in the stews, I were manned, horsed, and wived.' So Burton (*Anatomy of Melancholy*, Part 3, Sec. 3, Mem. 4, subs. 2): 'He that marries a wife out of a suspected inn or alehouse, buys a horse in Smithfield, and hires a servant in Paul's, as the diverb is, shall likely have a jade to his horse, a knave for his man, an arrant honest woman to his wife.'

33, l. 25. *Chamberlaine gate.* Stow follows Leland: 'Parochia S. Sepulchri extra Chamberlaingate, quae nunc ut videtur Newgate appellatur (*Collectanea*, ii. 361). 'Newgate . . . formerly Chamberlain gate' (Camden, *Britannia*, ii. 80, ed. Gough). From *Domesday* (i. 127) it appears that William the Chamberlain paid 6*s*. a year for his vineyard at Holeburn. This shows that the Chamber had property outside Newgate in 1086, and explains the name. Stow calls the Old Bailey the 'court of the Chamberlaine' on ii. 21, 37.

l. 31. *one of the Pophames.* Sir John Popham (*d.* 1463); he was chancellor of Anjou and Maine, and captain of St. Suzanne. The Popham referred to on p. 34 was his cousin Stephen (*d.* 1445–6), whose daughters were Sir John's co-heiresses. See ii. 47 above and *Dict. Nat. Biog.*, xlvi. 146–7.

34, l. 12. *Clamparde.* The list in *Harley MS.* 6069, f. 55, has Clampberd.

l. 38. *Scropes Inne.* It belonged to Richard, first Lord Scrope of Bolton (*d.* 1403), and in 1459 to Henry, fourth lord (*Cal. Inq. p. m.*, iv. 284). Afterwards it was Sergeants Inn till its restoration to John the fifth lord in 1494 (*Inq. p. m. Lond.*, i. 7). John Cottyngham (*d.* 1560) and Henry Gaynsford (*d.* 1574) were later owners (*id.* ii. 90, iii. 7).

35, l. 16–17. *William de Luda . . . gaue this house.* Stow gives the terms of William de Luda's will correctly (see *Cal. Wills*, i. 138). But William's immediate predecessor, John de Kirkeby, had in 1290 left the bishopric of Ely his houses at Holborn, together with his vines and gardens (*id.* i. 90). The validity of Kirkeby's will was disputed. The rights of the Bishop of Ely against Kirkeby's heirs were only established in 1321 (*Hist. MSS. Comm.*, 6th Rep., 295 *b*, 298 *b*).

ll. 35–6. *feastes . . . by the Sergeants at the law.* See Pulling, *Order of the Coif*, 234–7. Stow's account of the feast of 1464 adds some details to the longer narrative in *Gregory's Chronicle*, 222. For a feast kept at Ely Place by the Sergeants on Nov. 21, 1495, see *Chron. Lond.*, 207–8. On Nov. 23, 1503, the feast was kept at Lambeth, *id.* 260.

37, l. 19. *Furniualles Inne.* It occurs as an Inn of Chancery in the reign of Henry IV. The heiress of the Furnivals brought it to John Talbot, first Earl of Shrewsbury, whose descendant sold it to the society in 1546 (Herbert, *Inns of Court*, 324–8).

l. 35. *Chamberlaines . . . kept their courts.* This seems to be an unwarranted conjecture on Stow's part. The deed of 1356 is simply a lease to John Cambridge (cf. *Letter Books* G, 121, 279, and I, f. ccxxxi) relating to property of the corporation here. See R. R. Sharpe, *Memorials of Newgate Gaol*, p. 9.

38, l. 22. *Seacole lane, I thinke called Limeburners lane.* Seacole Lane and Limeburners Lane were distinct. In 1308 John Hereward left his daughter 'shops in Secollane and Lymbarnereslane' (*Cal. Wills*, i. 204).

l. 33. *Shooe lane.* It occurs as 'Vicus de Solande' in the time of King John (e. g. *Cotton MS.*, Faustina, B. II, f. 83vo), and as 'Sholonde' in 1272. In 1283 Roger de Scholond had tenements in Scholane (*Cal. Wills*, i. 12, 67).

l. 36. *Oldborne Hall.* See note on p. 372 below.

l. 39. *a Grammer schoole.* See vol. i. 73 and note on p. 321.

39, l. 26. *Thaues Inne.* In early records it is always 'Davyesinne', as in 1419 when it belonged to Robert Plesyngton (*Cal. Inq. p. m.*, iv. 40). But in the will of John Tavy (*d.* 1348) there is mention of his hospice in St. Andrew, Holborn, 'ubi apprenticii habitare solebant' (*Letter Book* F, 102; *Cal. Wills*, i. 619). A John Davy occurs as holding lands in Holborne in 1398 (*id.* ii. 332). See Herbert, *Inns of Court*, 322–4.

l. 29. *so called of Fewters (or idle people).* Stow is no doubt correct. Fetter Lane is probably the Viter lane without Newgate which occurs in 1294 and 1299 (*Cal. Wills*, i. 119, 139). Faitereslane appears in 1312, the new lane called Faitur Lane in 1352; other forms in the fourteenth and fifteenth centuries are Faytores lane, Faitours lane, Faytours lane and Faitour-lane (*id.* i. 230, 252, 698; ii. 44, 167, 591). Faitour, faytor, or fayter, means an impostor, a cheat, *especially* a vagrant, who shams illness or pretends to tell fortunes (*N. E. D.*). Such persons, no doubt, infested the western suburb, as the wise-women and fortune-tellers of Stow's own time did the north-eastern suburbs of Shoreditch and Hoxton (cf. Heywood's *Wise Woman of Hogsdon*). The suggestion that the name is due to fewters or fetters (the rests for a spear) made here by armourers (Mr. Loftie in *N. and Q.*, 8th ser. xii. 161) is untenable. 'Fewter' Lane occurs commonly in Elizabeth's reign (*Inq. p. m. London*, iii. 94, 150, 153).

40, l. 15. *Staple Inne.* It is mentioned as 'le Stapled halle' in St. Andrew, Holborn, in 1333, when it belonged to Richard Starcolf, Mercer (*Cal. Wills*, i. 394). There were two other Stapled halls; one in All-hallows, Barking, mentioned in 1330 (*id.* i. 363); the other in St. Botolph's without Bishopsgate, mentioned 1330–46 (*Letter Book* E, 251). In this connexion the name meant no more than a wholesale storehouse. Staple Inn in Holborn is stated to have become an Inn of Chancery in 1413. It was rebuilt 1580–92. For its history see *Staple Inn* by E. Williams.

l. 32. *Roberte Leueland.* He claimed, in 1198, to have custody of the King's house, and Fleet prison by inheritance since the Conquest (Madox, *Hist. Exchequer*, i. 514).

42, l. 17. *returned againe to the Cliffordes.* Probably it was only leased, for it appears as Clifford property in 1390, 1422, and 1455 (*Cal. Inq. p. m.* iii. 114, iv. 67, 266). It was acquired by the Society at a rental of 4*l.* soon after the last date (Herbert, *Inns of Court*, 274).

l. 21. *Sergeantes Inne.* Anciently called Farringdon Inne (Herbert, *Inns of Court*, 352–5).

l. 39. *William Burstall.* The grant of 1377 is printed in full in Holinshed, *Chronicles*, iv. 365.

43, l. 13. *Nocton Parke.* The house in Chancery Lane, formerly called Harflu Inn, part of the possessions of Nocton Park Priory, was assured to the Six Clerks in 1539 (*Letters and Papers*, xiv. 867, c. 27). For references in 1454, see *Mon. Angl.* vi. 341, and *Cal. Inq. p. m.* iv. 261.

l. 36. *Bridewell.* It was surely from Stow that Dekker borrowed his description, in *The Honest Whore*, Part 2 (*Works*, ii. 167):—

Duke. Your Bridewell? that the name? for beauty, strength
Capacity and forme of ancient building,
(Besides the Rivers neighbourhood) few houses
Wherein we keep our Court can better it.
1st Master. Hither from forraigne Courts have Princes come,
And with our Duke did Acts of State commence,
Here that great Cardinall had first audience,
(The grave Campayne); that Duke dead, his Sonne
(That famous Prince) gaue free possession
Of this his Palace, to the Cittizens,
To be the poore man's ware-house; and endowed it
With Lands to th' valew of seven hundred marke,
With all the bedding and the furniture,
Once proper (as the Lands then were) to an Hospitall
Belonging to a Duke of Savoy. Thus
Fortune can tosse the World, a Princes Court
Is thus a prison now.

The grant of Edward VI is printed in *Gent. Mag. Library*, xv. 182–9.

45, l. 28. *Chauntries.* Ulsthorpe in 1432, Evesham in 1351, and Wigan in 1360 (*Cal. Wills*, i. 652, ii. 25, 469).

46, l. 2. *Iohn Bale.* He describes the introduction of the Carmelites to England, and the foundation of their first house at Aylesford in Kent by Richard Grey of Codnor in 1241, in his *Heliades*, ap. *Harley MS.* 3838, ff. 13, 14, 20.

l. 22. *There were buried*, &c. The names in the printed list are somewhat corrupt. A manuscript list of Stow's (*Harley MS.* 544 ff. 67–8), and another contemporary list ap. *Harley MS.* 6033, f. 9, give some help; the latter appears to have been consulted by Strype. 'John Mowbery . . . 1398,' probably means John IV (*d.* 1383); there is no date in either of the MSS. Bayholt is 'Bayllhot' in 544, and 'Baylhott' in 6033. 'Elizabeth, Countess of Athole' is probably the wife of David de Strabolgi, and afterwards of John Malwayn; she died in 1374 (*Cal. Inq. p. m.* ii. 337). 'Sir Pence Castle' is 'Sir Pons Castle, Baron of ——' in 6033; perhaps Pontius, Lord of Castelhon in Gascony (Wylie, *Henry IV*, iii. 276). 'Sir Richard Derois' is 'Deroys' in 544, and 'de Royes' in 6033. 'Ashley' is 'Asteley' and 'Call' is 'Cawlle' in 544. 'Neddow' is 'Meddow' both in 544 and 6033. For 'Dame Margaret' Strype suggests Margaret Grey (*d.* 1540), Countess of Kent. Peter Wigus is in 544 Peter Wigñs (? Wigornensis), and in 6032 Peter Wygich. 'Robert Mathew' is Metham in 544, and 'Matham' in 6033. 'Norice' is 'Norres', and 'Terwit' Tirwhit in 544. 'Robert Brocket' is Brockas ('Brocas') in both MSS. 'Chanlowes' is Chalouns, 'Dabby' Dalby, and 'Bampton' Lampton in 6033. For 'Thomas Federinghey' both MSS. have Dame — Foderinghey, and for 'Eldsmere' Elsmere; also *William* Hart and *John* Heron. 'Archer' is 'Awcher' in 6033. For 'Peter de Mota' 544 has Peter de Muta, and 6033 Peter de Mora. 'Hugh Bromflete' is Henry Bromflete (*d.* 1469), lord Vessey; Stow seems to have confused him with John de Vesci (*fl.* 1250), who was associated with Richard de Grey in introducing the Carmelites to England.

Both MSS. add: Joan Wollasell, Gentlewoman, Elizabeth, wife of Robert Tanfield, John Ynglowe, Henry Bedle, and Richard Beynton.

50, l. 9. *Fabian.* Apparently in his MS.

l. 12. *the new Temple.* It was granted in 1313 to Aymer de Valence, who released it to Thomas, Earl of Lancaster, in 1314 (*Letter Book* E, 229; *C. P. R.* Edw. II, ii. 184). On Lancaster's death it was regranted to Aymer de Valence (*Foedera*, ii. 480), but again lapsed to the crown in 1324, and was then granted to Hugh le Despenser. See Williams, *Staple Inn*, p. 53.

51, l. 2. *crosse legged as men vowed to the holy land.* This is a popular notion unsupported by fact. Effigies of known Crusaders are found with the legs uncrossed, and cross-legged effigies of knights (and even ladies) who never went to Palestine, or died long after the Crusades were over. See Hartshorne, *Recumbent Monumental Effigies in Northants*, p. 119. For the tombs in the Temple Church see *Vetusta Monumenta* V, xix–xxv, Gough, *Sepulchral Monuments*, i. 24, 50; and Baylis, *The Temple Church*, 94–115. The ascription of them is open to question.

l. 23. *by Sir Amias Paulet.* Cf. *Annales*, p. 835, ed. 1605. In *Harley MS.* 538 the story is repeated at length. Briefly it is as follows: Paulet, for some offence, when Wolsey was but a schoolmaster, put him in the stocks. When Wolsey became chancellor he forbade Paulet to leave London. Paulet then rebuilt the gate-house of the Middle Temple, and adorned it with Wolsey's arms, hoping thus to appease his wrath.

52, l. 6. *Hauing treated of Wardes*, &c. In *Harley MS.* 544, ff. 96–9, there is a rough and early draft of this chapter: 'Of the Borough of Southwarke in the County of Southrey.' 'Now leauinge the City of Westminster, the farthest west part of suburbes without the Citye of London, I am to pase ovar the Thames & to say some what of Southwarke, a borughe so called for that the same lyeth on the south syde of the Ryvar of Thamis directly agaynst the citye of London, and at the south syde of the bridge. This broughe beinge in the county of Sothorey consisteth of dyvars stretes, wayes, &c.' The narrative then continues with only slight variations to 'bad men to lyke women' on p. 54. Then it proceeds: 'The originall of this privilege I have not red, but I have sene a patent thereof dated the 19 of E. 3'; and so continues with little variation to 'before that any bridge was builded' (on p. 56). Then a long passage (pp. 56–60) is lacking. The events of 1376–7 are given rather more in detail. The notice of the Tabard and Chaucer is omitted. The account of St. Thomas Hospital is shorter and differently arranged, and the subsequent narrative down to 'diuided into sundrie tenements' (p. 65) does not appear. There is an important addition on Sir John Throston (see below), and after this the narrative continues nearly as printed to 'Earles of Sussex' (p. 67), where it stops. Stow then states that having treated of the suburbs, &c., he is next to enter the city: compare note on pp. 285–6 above.

53, l. 22. 5. *prisons or Gaoles.* Taylor, the Water-poet, writes:

Five jayles or prisons are in Southwarke placed,
The Counter once St. Margaret's church defaced,
The Marshalsea, the King's Bench, and White Lyon,
Then there 's the Clinke where handsome lodgings be.

54, l. 5. *two Beare gardens.* The two rings are shown in Hofnagel's and Agas's maps, and marked separately as 'The bolle-bayting' and 'The Beare-bayting'. They were a little to the east of the landing-place at Paris-Garden (see *Introduction*, p. xl above).

l. 15. *In a Parliament*, &c. For a transcript of 'Ordinances touching the governance of the Stew-houlders in Southwarke vnder the direction of the bishope of Winchester, instituted in the tyme of Henry the Second', see *Harley MS.* 293, ff. 62–7.

55, l. 9. *Also I find*, &c. In *Harley MS.* 544 this reads: 'More I find in one olde boke fayre writen in parchement in the reigne of Richard the Second that in the 4 yere of his reigne, &c.' This is interesting, as showing that Stow used the original of the *Liber S. Mariae Ebor.* or *Anominalle Chronicle* (see *Introduction*, p. xxxiii), and was not dependent on Thynne's transcript.

l. 15. *Fabian writeth.* This does not appear in the printed continuation, and must come from Stow's manuscript. See *Introduction*, p. xxxv.

57, l. 36. *speculum meditantis.* This work, long believed to have been lost, was identified by Mr. G. C. Macaulay in 1895, with a poem entitled *Mirour de l'Omme*, contained in the Cambridge University Library *Additional MS.* 1891, and was printed by him in his edition of Gower's *Works*, vol. i. pp. 1–334.

For the inscriptions on Gower's tomb see *id.* iv. pp. xxii sqq., viz.:

Charitée.	En toy qu'es fitz de dieu le pere,
	Sauvé soit que gist souz cest piere.
Mercye.	O bon Jesu, fai ta mercy
	Al alme dont le corps gist ci.
Pité.	Pur ta pité, Jesu, regarde,
	E met cest alme in sauve garde.

58, l. 27. *monumentes.* There is a list in *Harley MS.* 6069, f. 27, which reads Robert Hilyeard (l. 27); Katheren wife of John Stocker (l. 31); Lorde of Paryed Ferrar for 'Lord Ospay Ferar' (l. 32); and John Brome (l. 33). 'Ospay Ferar' may perhaps conceal some Italian noble of Ferrara, who died and was buried in England.

61, l. 39. *sir John Imworth.* Stow's authority (*Anom. Chron.* 518) has 'Johne de Imworthe'. But his real name was Sir Richard Imworth (*C. P. R.* Richd. II, i. 556).

62, l. 13. *many fayre Innes.* See Rendle and Norman, *Inns of Old Southwark*, and Norman, *London Vanished and Vanishing*, pp. 1–27.

63, l. 22. *Monuments in this Hospitall Church*, &c. Strype corrects thus: Adam Attewod, William Weston, and John Every. These come from a list in *Harley MS.* 6069, f. 27, which has also Roger Chamber, Richarde Chaunder, John Wode, Michael Enebrigge, and Thomas Knynton.

65, ll. 35–9. *Sir John Throstone*, &c. This is a curtailed version of the original draft in *Harley MS.* 544, f. 98vo, which reads: 'Gaue by his Testament towardes this purpos 200 *li.* Thes were begone to be made by his lady and othar his executors in the yere of Christ 1521, and ended in the yere 1522, Sir John Monday beinge then Maior of London, and therefore by some thowght to be builded at the charges of the said maior: but that was mistaken, for before as behynde every the sayde ovens the goldsmithes armes are fayre engraven in stone, so ovar every ovene are likewise ingraven the armes of the sayd sir Iohn Throstone, and his ladies in one escutchen. There is of late taken &c.'

70, l. 36. *Wapping in the Woze.* 'West,' the reading of the 1603 edition, is a printer's error, foolishly altered by Munday to 'East' (*Survey*, p. 461). A woze, or ooze, is a low marshy place. For the hanging of ten pirates at Wapping in the Woze in August, 1583, see *Annales*, 1175, ed. 1605.

Samuel Rowlands, in his *Knave of Hearts*, p. 48, writes:—

For though Pyrates exempted be
From fatall Tyburne's wither'd tree,
They have an Harbour to arrive
Call'd Wapping, where as ill they thrive
As those that ride up Holbourne Hill,
And at the Gallows make their Will.

71, l. 17. *Radcliffe it selfe hath beene also encreased*, &c. Howes in an addition to the *Annales*, p. 868, *sub anno* 1605, and possibly using material left by Stow, writes thus: 'The undiscernable and new building of goodly houses, shoppes, sheds, and lodgings within the City, in many vacant places, with the converting of the Citie Bulwarkes into houses of pleasure, to the great and wondrous enlarging of the suburbs and skirts thereof, namely Ratcliffe, Limehouse, Rederiffe, Southwarke, Shoreditch, Whitechappell and Saint Katherines.' In the same place he writes that before 1563 'faire houses in London were plenteous, and very easie to be had at low and small rents, and by reason of the late dissolution of Religious houses many houses in London stood vacant, and not any man desirous to take them.' Howes ascribes the growth of London to the great immigration of foreigners through the troubles in France and the Netherlands. Compare with this the quotation on vol. i. p. 208 of a presentment made as to the increase of alien residents in Billingsgate. From his frequent reference to the pestering of the suburbs, and open places in the City with filthy small tenements it is clear that Stow sympathized with the anxiety of Elizabeth's government about the growth of the capital. In 1580 a royal proclamation (see Birch, 128–31) forbade any new buildings within three miles of the gates of the City. Three years later the Council directed attention to the great increase of building 'to danger of pestilence and riot', and to the practice of dividing single tenements. Nevertheless, in spite of repeated complaints by the Council, the mischief continued. In addition to the previous objections it was pointed out that the growth of London caused the decay of other towns, and increased the difficulty of provisioning the Capital (a matter which caused Elizabeth's government much anxiety). Finally, in 1593 a statute—35 Eliz. c. 3—was passed, declaring that 'great mischiefs daily grow and increase by reason of pestering the houses with diverse families, harbouring of inmates, and converting great houses into several tenements, and the erecting of new buildings in London and Westminster'. But the statute was no more easy to enforce than the previous proclamations. In 1596 the Council again addressed the Middlesex magistrates on the 'multitudes of base tenements and houses of unlawfull and disorderly resort in the suburbs', calling attention to the 'great number of dissolute, loose, and insolent people harboured in such and the lyke noysom and disorderly howses, as namely poor cottages, and habitacions of beggars and people without trade, stables, ins, alehowses, tavernes, garden-houses converted to dwellings, ordinaries, dicyng-howses, bowling-allies, and brothel houses' (*Acts of Privy Council*, xxv. 230). Naturally the growth of London could not be checked thus, though regulation was no doubt needed. More or less vain attempts to restrain the increase of buildings continued throughout the seventeenth century (see *Remembrancia*, 41–51; *Acts of Privy Council*, xii. 94, 155, 213; xiii. 201; xiv. 356; xix. 278–81, 324 (for St. Katherine's to Blackwall), 348, 350 (Tower Hamlets); xx. 326; xxii. 70, 145 (near Moorgate); xxv. 230; xxviii. 427 (Shoreditch, St. Giles, Cripplegate, and Clerkenwell), 435 (Southwark); and xxix. 5.

The present passage furnishes a convenient place for a general note. See Index III under 'Bowling Alleys', 'Building', 'Dicing houses', 'Tenements'.

73, l. 8. *saint Mary Matfellon.* Stow's reference is to *Cal. Inq. p. m.*, iii. 186; but the name is much older, and appears as 'Mantefelune' in 1280, and 'Mattefelon' or 'Matrefelun' in 1282 (*Cal. Wills*, i. 48, 58, 59). 'Matfellon' or 'Matrefillen' is Old-French for the centaury or knapweed. Probably, as in other cases, the church owed its distinctive name to some benefactor. 'Matfelon' and 'Materfeloun' occur as surnames in the fourteenth century (*N. and Q.*, 9th ser., viii. 337–8). John de Knopwed, a mercer, died in 1341 (*Cal. Wills*, i. 448; see also *Letter Book* F, 79).

l. 37. *From Holy well*, &c. The omission here of the reference to the Theatre and The Curtain (see p. 262 above) is noteworthy. It may perhaps be explained in part by the fact that The Curtain was pulled down in 1600. But probably it was intentional, and due to lack of interest; for the slight reference in the chapter on Sportes and Pastimes was also omitted in 1603 (see p. 236 above). The original notice in

Harley MS. 538, was as follows: 'Neare adjoyning are builded two houses for the shewe of Activities, Comedies, tragedies and histories, for recreation. The one of them is named the Curtayn in Holy Well, the other The Theatre. There are on the bak-syde of Holywell towards the filde from Holywell a continuall &c.'

In both of Howes's editions of the *Annales* (p. 698, ed. 1631) there is an often-quoted passage under date 1583, on how comedians and stage-players were grown exquisite actors, and praising Thomas Wilson and Richard Tarleton for their wit. But in Stow's own editions there is nothing whatever to correspond.

74, l. 6. *Ealdestreete.* Or Old Street: it was certainly a Roman way, and as 'Ealde Street' occurs in the twelfth century (Lethaby, *London before the Conquest*, 58).

margin. *Soerditch, . . . as I can proue by record.* Stow is probably referring to the late legend, which connected Shoreditch with Jane Shore, and is adopted by Heywood, *Edward IV*, Part 2, Act v, sc. iii:—

> The people from the love they bear to her
> And her kind husband, pitying his wrongs,
> For ever after mean to call the ditch
> Shore's ditch, as in the memory of them.

The name is, of course, much older. St. Leonard de Soreditch occurs in a deed *circa* 1218 (vol. i. 166 above, and *Monasticon*, vi. 625), and in the list of 1303 (*Mun. Gild.* II. i. 229); for other references in the thirteenth century see *Hist. MSS. Comm.* 9th Rep. 14, 15.

l. 25. *small and base tenements.* Alluding no doubt to the gambling-houses, brothels, and other disreputable places which made the district notorious. Middleton, in *Father Hubbard's Tales* (*Works*, viii. 96), calls 'Spital and Shoreditch the only Cole-harbour and sanctuary for wenches and soldiers'.

75, l. 28. *of late one Vicker there.* Meredith Hanmer, vicar of St. Leonard's, 1581–92; Fleetwood described him as 'a very bad man' and 'not regarding an oath'. See *Dict. Nat. Biog.* xxiv. 297.

76, l. 4. *this iustice was done.* Alluding to the old quarrel with Thomas Stow. See *Introduction*, pp. xiii–xix.

l. 14. *the More.* Stow's references to William's Charter and to Fitz-Stephen show the state of the Moor in the eleventh and twelfth centuries. But recent excavations have proved that the marsh did not exist in the early Roman period. Roman remains are found on the gravel underneath the marsh deposit. It was apparently the building of the wall (see p. 269 above), and the obstruction of the Walbrook, that converted the land on the north to a swamp, and set up the difficulties of drainage described in the subsequent passage. See *Archaeologia*, lx. 181–3.

l. 38. *all the Gardens.* From *Memorials*, 614 (see p. 274 above). They seem to have been first made in 1415. For their destruction see *Chron. Lond.* 224.

77, l. 3. *Roger Atchley.* On Jan. 14, 1512, it was 'agreed that the Chamberleyn of this Citie shall cause a grounde callid the Mooreffelde to be levellid by the oversight of my lorde Maier and of the Shrevys of this Citie, and over that to provide a convenyent place for the dogge hous of the Comen Hunte of this Citie, and that the olde hous be removed' (*Repertory*, 2, f. 126 *b*).

l. 9. *diuers sluces.* From the London Chronicle in *Harley MS.* 540, f. 7:—'In ye same yere in Julii and in August was ye slewcys made in Fynsbery fylde to convaye ye yll watars ovar ye towne diche by pypes of lede in to ye Temes.'

l. 16. *three windmilles.* In a Survey of the Manor of Finsbury (ap. *Survey*, 913, ed. 1633) taken in 1567, there is reference to the 'High Field or Meadow ground, where the three windmills stand, commonly called Finsbury Field'. Four windmills are shown on Agas's map a little later: but one of them stands rather to the west of the others; see Map in this volume. Others were afterwards added; so Middleton writes, about 1617, in *A Fair Quarrel*, Act IV. sc. i.: 'I have heard 'em roar from the six windmills to Islington.' Six mills are shown on Faithorne's map in 1658. Windmill Street, now re-named Tabernacle Street, preserved their memory.

l. 18. *inclosures of common grounds.* From Hall (*Chron.* 568), whose narrative stops at 'were never hedged'. The rest is an addition of Stow's.

78. l. 13. *many fayre summer houses.* The building of garden-houses, or summer-houses in the rural suburbs, was very popular in the sixteenth century. They are often referred to in the old dramatists as favourite places for assignations. One of the scenes in Webster's *Northward Ho!* (Act III. sc. ii) is laid at 'my master's garden-house here in Moorfields'. Samuel Rowlands, in his *Knave of Clubs*, p. 7, describes how 'a countrie blew-coate serving-man' wandering about London

> got into More fieldes
> Viewing the Walkes and Trees,
> And thence to Garden-Alley goes.

The Moorfields were set in better order with new and pleasant walks soon after Stow's death (see *Annales*, p. 1021 *b*, ed. Howes). To their previous unsatisfactory condition Dekker alludes in *The Guls Hornbooke*: 'To purge it will be a sorer labour than the cleansing of Augeas stable or scouring of Moreditch' (*Non-Dramatic Works*, ii. 212, ed. Grosart).

79, l. 19. *Grubstreete.* It was convenient for bowyers, since it lay near the Archery-butts in Finsbury Fields. Randolph in *Hey for Honesty*, ap. *Works*, ed. 1651, p. 475, writes:—

> Her eyes are Cupid's Grub-Street: the blind archer
> Makes his love-arrows there.

On the later history of Grub Street (now Milton Street) see *Trans. Lond. and Middlesex*, iii. 223–44.

81, l. 21. *no mans land.* Probably the 12½ acres called 'nanes maneslande' which the king held in 1087 (*Domesday*, i. 127).

82, l. 36. *Monuments.* Stow's manuscript list in *Harley MS.* 544, f. 67, supplies the correction, 'John Dorewentwatar, knight.' It adds 'Katheren wyfe to William Lowe', 'Joane' wife of John Peake, and 'the wife of William Ardlestone'.

83, l. 14. *in place whereof.* Edward, Lord North, entertained Elizabeth here in 1558 and 1561. His son Roger sold the Charterhouse to Thomas, Duke of Norfolk, on May 31, 1565 (Nichols, *Progresses of Queen Elizabeth*, i. 31).

l. 24. *Turnemill streete.* Stow does not mention the houses of ill-fame which account for so many references to Turnmill or Turnbull Street in the Elizabethan dramatists, e.g. *Henry IV*, Pt. 2, Act III. sc. ii, where Falstaff says of Shallow: 'This same starved justice hath done nothing but prate to me of the wildness of his youth, and the feats he hath done about Turnbull Street.'

l. 29. *Priorie of saint John.* Stow's account is taken from the Cartulary of the Hospital in *Cotton MS.*, Nero, E. vi, f. 3.

84, l. 33. *a storehouse.* The King's tents were housed at the Charterhouse in 1543–4. They may then have been kept for a time at St. John's. But in the autumn of 1545 the Tents and Revels were removed to Blackfriars. However, the Masters of the Tents, the Toils, and the Revels all appear to have had their storehouses at the 'late Hospital of St. John' before June 1560 (Chambers, *Tudor Revels*, 13–20).

85, l. 9. *buried in this Church.* There is a list in *Harley MS.* 6069, f. 43vo, which supplies the following variants: Panclay for 'Vanclay'; Lanncolen; Radington; Walshall for 'Marshall'; Ouldhall for 'Gondall'. The first fifteen are described as 'ffryars'. 'Hilles or Hayles' is distinguished from 'William Hulles'.

86, l. 3. *Ralph Timbleby.* The list in *Harley MS.* 6069, f. 57vo, has 'Ralphe Thrimbye'. It adds 'Dame Katherin Grene' and 'Agnes wife of Thomas Batman, squyre.'

l. 32. *other welles.* See notes on pp. 272–3.

87, l. 3. *Porte Poole or Grayes Inne.* Simon de Gardino de Purtepole left his house within Holeburne bar to his son-in-law Richard de Chygewelle or Chigwell (*Cal. Wills*, i. 48). Chygewelle in 1294 enfeoffed the Dean and Chapter of St. Paul's with the property, and they enfeoffed Reginald de Grey, who held it of them in 1307. The Greys retained their connexion till 1506. But before 1397 Henry Grey de Wilton had made a feoffment of 'Portpole maner' called 'Grey's Inn' to certain persons in trust. See E. Williams, *Staple Inn*, 22, 38–44, and Douthwaite, *Gray's Inn*, 3–18.

l. 16. *Richard Alington.* Amongst Stow's *Memoranda*, 117–21, is 'The confessyon of Master Rychard Allington, esquere, the xxij of Novembre, 1561, abowte viij of ye clocke at nyght'. He accused himself of having made much money by usury, and says in his confession that he never thought his death 'wolde have cum to passe by this dessease, consideryinge it is but ye smalle pockes'. Machyn describes him as son of Sir Giles Alington (*Diary*, p. 274).

89, l. 35. *This olde Fryer house.* Stow places the original Blackfriars outside the City. But it seems clear that it was in the parish of St. Andrew, Holborn, in Shoe Lane, both from grants to the friars between 1224 and 1260, and from the will of Henry de Lacy, Earl of Lincoln, where his place that belonged to the Preaching Friars is mentioned; as the conveyance to Lincoln in 1288 and his will were both enrolled in the Court of Husting (*Cal. Wills*, i. 218), they must have related to property within the City. Probably this is the Oldborne Hall mentioned on ii. 38 above. Henry de Lacy's daughter married, as her first husband, Thomas, Earl of Lancaster, and in her right Earl of Lincoln. As Earl of Lancaster he was Lord of the manor of the New Temple, including Ralph Neville's house in Chancery Lane on part of the site of the modern Lincoln's Inn. See E. Williams, *Staple Inn*, 45–54.

90, l. 19. *encreased with fayre buildinges.* There was much building at Lincoln's Inn during Elizabeth's reign. See Herbert, *Inns of Court*, 290–5.

l. 37. *a sell to Burton Lager of Jerusalem.* The reference is to the Hospital of lepers of St. Lazarus of Jerusalem at Burton Lazars in Leicestershire. But St. Giles was not annexed thereto till 1299, an arrangement which was confirmed in 1354 (Tanner, *Notitia Monastica*, i. 304; *Monast. Angl.* vi. 632, 635; *Letter Book* G, 27–9).

91, l. 7. *Gote on the Hope.* It was bequeathed to the Drapers by William Calley in 1517; it is mentioned in 1432 (*Cal. Wills*, ii. 473, 602, 625). Ancient tavern signs were nearly always 'on the hoop'. See 'Griffon on the hope' on i. 323, and many instances in the *Calendar of Wills*, as 'Le Castell on the hoop' and 'Le Moone on the hoop'. The 'hoop' seems to have 'originated in the highly ornamented bush or crown, which latterly was made of hoops covered with evergreens' (Larwood and Hotten, *History of Signboards*, pp. 503–5, 3rd ed.).

l. 10. *a great Bowle of Ale.* John Chamberlain wrote to Dudley Carleton on Oct. 31, 1618, thus: 'The morning that he [Ralegh] went to execution there was a cup of excellent sack brought him, and being asked how he liked it, "As the fellow," saith he, "that drinking of St. Giles's bowl as he went to Tyburn said: 'That were good drink, if a man might tarry by it'"' (*Court and Times of James I*).

92, l. 10. *Walter Stapleton.* According to the account in the *Annales Paulini*, p. 317, his body was refused burial at St. Clement Danes, and then laid temporarily in the waste church of the Innocents close by.

l. 38. *Chesters Inne.* Hoccleve's reference to his residence at 'Chestres Inne right fast by the Stronde' (*De Regimine Principum*, 1) is all that is known of it. (Herbert, *Inns of Court*, 284.)

95, l. 35. *Bedford house.* Acquired by John, Lord Russell, afterwards first Earl of Bedford, in exchange in 1539 (*Letters and Papers*, xiv. 867, c. 26).

l. 36. *Iuie bridge.* On its history and that of Ivy-bridge Lane, which was destroyed by the extension of the Hotel Cecil, see *N. and Q.*, 10th ser., v. 81, 136, 175. Sir Robert Cecil writes on Oct. 24, 1602, of 'My new howse (called Cecyll howse) by Ivye bridge' (*Letters*, Camd. Soc.).

96, l. 25. *a fayre leager Booke.* Stow is clearly quoting the Chertsey

Register in *Cotton MS.*, Vitellius, A. xiii, f. 35, though not perhaps from his own knowledge. It is there stated that in the time of Æthelred I (866–71) the Danes arrived at Chertsey and summoned the monks to come out: 'Illis autem exire nolentibus, nec eorum obsecundare preceptis, omnes gladio interfecti sunt uidelicet xc., quorum corpora in uno loco iuxta uetus monasterium condita sunt. Postea ecclesiam et omnes officinas predicti monasterii igni combusserunt, res, terras, uillulas, et omnes eorum possessiones depredauerunt. Illi autem in malicia sua perdurantes, repatriare cupientes iusto dei iudicio apud Londoniam omnes interfecti sunt, in loco qui dicitur ecclesia Danorum.' The burial-place of the slaughtered monks was discovered after the refounding of Chertsey Abbey by Bishop Æthelwold of Winchester. The remains were then transferred to a shrine, 'sicut in cronicis predicti monasterii anglico ideomate inuenitur: "On[1] Certeseye in þe munstre þer restet seint Beccan abbod, and seint Edor messe prest, and seint Fritheuuold king þat staþelede erest þat munstre, mid seint Erkenuualde abbod, þat est werþ Bissup on Londone suuiþe holi: and hundniȝenti moneches of slaȝene mid heþene men." Acta sunt hec anno dominice incarnacionis octogintesimo octogesimo quarto, tempore Ethelredi regis filii regis Etheluulfi.'

The Chertsey record was written about 1260. The greater part is based on William of Malmesbury, Abbo *Passio S. Edmundi*, and Bede. But the account of the destruction of Chertsey is peculiar; Malmesbury (*Gesta Pontificum*, 143) refers simply to its destruction by the Danes—'qui, ut cetera, locum illum pessundedere, ecclesia succensa cum monachis et abbate.' The English fragment is based on the early eleventh century Anglo-Saxon list of Saints (see Liebermann, *Die Heiligen Englands*, p. 19; and the *Hyde Liber Vitae*, p. 94), with an interpolation from Bede of the notice of St. Erkenwald.[2] The incorrect date, '884' (Æthelred I died in 871), and the fact that the whole passage is a late compilation from various sources, make it untrustworthy. Very probably the punishment of the Danes refers to the massacre in the time of Æthelred II. As for the name St. Clement Danes, the street there was called 'Denchemen's street' early in the thirteenth century.

97, l. 30. *three Innes of Chancery.* On these small Inns see Herbert, *Inns of Court*, 276–83. Stow has given the history of the establishment of New Inn on ii. 38 above. See *Anc. Deeds*, B. 2135–62.

98, ll. 28, 29. *house . . . doth yet remaine.* J. T. Smith (*Antiquities of Westminster*, 12), writing in 1807: 'the spot was where a part of the stable of the Golden Cross Inn, and some of the houses at the south end of St. Martin's Lane now stand.'

l. 30. *the Mewse.* The site of Trafalgar Square.

99, l. 8. *Durham house.* Originally built by Antony Bek (*d.* 1310), Bishop of Durham. (Pennant, *London*, 192.) The site is the present Adelphi.

l. 14. *triumphant Iusting.* See the Challenge and note of open

[1] The MS. has '*N*' simply.

[2] I am indebted for these references to Mr. W. H. Stevenson.

house kept from April 30 to May 7, ap. *Letters and Papers*, xv. 617, and account of the Justing in Wriothesley's *Chronicle*, i. 116–18.

100, l. 31. *S. Marie Rounciuall.* Founded by William Marshal, Earl of Pembroke, in 1222, suppressed as an alien priory after 1432 (*C. P. R.* Henry VI, ii. 247), and revived for a fraternity in 1476 (*Mon. Angl.* vi.' 677; *C. P. R.* Edw. IV, ii. 542). It was on the site of the present Northumberland Avenue.

l. 36. *Hermitage*, &c. 'The hermitage of St. Katherine between St. Mary Rouncivall and the King of Scottis ground'—i.e. Scotland Yard (*C. P. R.* Edw. IV, i. 213–4).

101, l. 3. *an Hospitall of saint James.* Turold was warden of the Hospital of St. James by Charing (*Cherringam*) in the reign of Richard I (*Anc. Deeds*, A. 7822).

102, l. 13. *built by king Henry the eight.* Thomas Cromwell drew up in 1536 a memorandum of 'Things done by the King's highness sythyn I came to his service'. He has purchased 'St. James in the Fields and all the ground, whereof the new park of Westminster is now made: all the old tenements in Westminster where now is builded the new garden, the tennis plays, and cockfight' . . . 'He has newly builded . . . the place at Westminster with the tennis plays and cockfight, and walled the park with a sumptuous wall; and St. James in the Fields, a magnificent and goodly house' (*Letters and Papers*, x. 1231). The gate by the gallery is said to have been designed by Holbein; it was removed in 1750. The other gate near the north end of the former King Street, and end of Downing Street, was pulled down in 1723. See Smith, *Antiquities*, 20, 21, with views (facing p. 24) showing the Gallery, Gate, and Tiltyard. See *Anc. Deeds*, A. 13406, 13446–8 for lands purchased for these improvements.

l. 16. *From this gate*, &c. Ben Jonson, who knew Westminster well, gives a summary of its topography in his *Staple of News*, Act III. sc. ii.

'*Tattle.* I have better news from the bakehouse in ten thousand parts in a morning: or the conduits in Westminster: all the news of Tuttle Street, and both the Alm'ries, the two Sanctuaries, Long and Round Woolstaple, with King Street and Cannon Row to boot.

'*Mirth.* Ay! my gossip Tattle knew what fine slips grew in Gardener's Lane; who kist the butcher's wife with the cow's breath: what matches were made in the Bowling-alley, and what bets were won and lost; how much grist went to the Mill, and what besides; who conjured in Tuttle fields and how many.'

l. 16. *Kings streete.* Till long after Stow's time it was the only way to Westminster from the north. The last part of it has now been covered by the new Government offices in Parliament Street.

l. 16. *Long ditch.* A watercourse ran from the Thames by Canon Row to the end of Gardener's Lane. 'From the west end of Gardener's Lane it turned southward, and after passing down what is now called Prince's Street, but was then Long Ditch, crossed Tothill Street a little westward of the Gatehouse; then taking an eastern direction, it ran along by the south wall of the Abbey garden, where College Street now stands, to the Thames; and this is still the exact course of the common sewer which was erected over it' (see Maitland, *London*, 1328; Smith, *Antiquities*, 2, 102). Prince's Street was known as Long Ditch till about 1750. For houses on 'Langediche' between 1331 and 1367 see Samuel Bentley, *Abstract of Westminster Charters*, 67-8.

l. 18. *Chanon Row.* It is called 'Chanen Row' in 1501 (Gairdner, *Letters*, &c., *Richard III and Henry VII*, i. 406). Howel (*Londinopolis*, 350) says it is corruptly called 'Channel Row'. Smith argues that the latter form is the original, and connects it with the channel or cut from the Thames, referred to in the previous note (*Antiquities*, 3). However, the name 'Channel Row' does not seem to occur before 1557 (Machyn, *Diary*, 126; see also *London Past and Present*, iii. 325). An alternative name, as Stow notes in the margin, and on p. 122, was St. Stephen's Alley.

l. 27. *high Tower.* See p. 122 and note on p. 379.

l. 31. *the Woolestable.* The Long Staple extended from the south end of Canon Row to King Street, whilst the Round Staple, at right angles to it, was about in the position of Parliament Street. For the history of the Woolstable see Hall, *History of the Custom Revenue in England*, and Cunningham, *Growth of English Industry and Commerce*, vol. i, 4th ed., 1905. For the Merchants of the Staple see Gross, *Gild-Merchant*, i. 140–7.

104, l. 13. *vpon Enirode.* This is obscure. Possibly it may be a corruption of 'eny rode' (any riding or raid) as suggested by the reading of 1633. Or it may refer to the 'roade' which Stow in his *Annales* (p. 437, ed. 1605) relates to have been made by Sir Hugh Calveley in 1377. The passage does not appear in the 1598 edition: that edition has, however, the marginal note 'Manuscript French' which must consequently belong to the next paragraph. The Staple had been fixed once more at Calais in 1376 (*Foedera*, iii. 1057).

l. 27. *sixe wooll houses*, &c. Granted on Nov. 16, 1442, and confirmed by Edward IV on July 16, 1461 (*C. P. R.* Edw. IV, i. 163; cf. Smith, *Antiquities*, 111-12). See further note on p. 378 below.

l. 33. *Theeuing lane.* Smith describes it as 'a turning still existing' on the west side of King Street, 'very near its south end' (*Antiquities*, 27). If the thieves had entered the Sanctuary, they must have been liberated. Maitland (*London*, 1342) describes it as on the north of the Clochard.

105, l. 8. *Sulcardus.* He was a monk of Westminster about 1075, and author of a treatise, *De Constitutione Ecclesiae Westmonasteriensis*. It is merely by way of introduction to the Cartulary which he had prepared at the command of his abbot, and of which two extended copies are preserved in *Cotton MSS.*, Titus, A. viii (early fourteenth century), and Faustina, A. iii (late thirteenth century). The reference to the Temple of Apollo appears in the latter MS. on f. 19vo.

l. 17. *T. Clifford.* See note on pp. 281–2 above.

l. 34. *Charter.* Stow's version of the charter, which is given in facsimile, is manifestly incorrect. Some of the errors are probably typographical, but others are due to the omission or addition of final *e*, most of the early antiquaries having no idea that this letter meant any more in Anglo-Saxon than it did in the orthography of their own day. The words *seo gifta* in line three are redundant; the second word perhaps arises from anticipation by the copyist of the immediately following *gyfen*. The charter is printed by Kemble, *Cod. Dipl.* dccclxi, from the thirteenth-century copy in *Cotton MS.*, Faustina, A. III, f. 110vo, where the text is corrupt. Stow's text is superior in having the correct Anglo-Saxon *longaþ* in l. 6 against the Middle-English *longen* of the *Cotton MS.*, and in some other minor details. It is possible that he may have derived his text from the original charter, or from a better copy than that contained in the *Cotton MS.*; but these superior readings in his text may be due to corrections by some one moderately versed in Anglo-Saxon. The Cotton text, derived from the MS. itself and without Kemble's accents and normalizations, is as follows:—

Edward king gret Willem bisceop *and* Leofstan *and* Alfsy porterefen *and* alle mine burhtheynes on Lundene frendlice. *And* icc ciþe eow þæt icc habbe segifen (*sic*) *and* unnen Crist *and* Sainte Petre þam halegen apostle into Westminstre fulne fredom ofer alle þa land þe longen into þare halagen stowe.

Stow omits two-thirds of the text of the charter. I have to thank Mr. W. H. Stevenson for this note.

107, l. 13. *the White Rose.* In the Vitellius Chronicle (*Chron. Lond.* 258) it is stated that 'the tavern of the Sun' was pulled down. More than one inn may have been destroyed.

l. 27. *Peter a Painter.* Pietro Torregiano, who came to England in the reign of Henry VII, and remained till at least 1518. He contracted in 1512 to make 'well, surely, cleanly, workmanly, curiously, and substantially' for the sum of £1,500 a tomb of marble with 'images, figures, beasts, and other things, of copper gilt'. (Lethaby, *Westminster Abbey*, 236–7.)

108, l. 29. *buried in this Church.* Stow's printed list is based in part on one of which he has preserved a copy in *Harley MS.* 544, ff. 65 and 67vo; this latter list seems to have been compiled after 1499, for it includes John, Viscount Welles, but before 1506, for it gives Catherine of Valois as buried in the Lady Chapel. The burials are described under the several chapels. Early printed lists are those in Camden's *Reges, Reginae*, &c., published in 1603, Weever's *Funerall Monuments* (1631), and Henry Keepe's *Monumenta Westmonasteriensia* (1682). For some critical notes see Mr. Lethaby's *Westminster Abbey and the King's Craftsmen*, pp. 332–50, giving extracts from the list in *Harley MS.* 544.

109, l. 10. *Henry the fift.* His tomb was plundered in 1546 (*Acts of the Privy Council*, i. 328; Kingsford, *Henry V*, 386–7).

l. 18. *remayneth aboue ground.* Katherine's body remained unburied till 1778, when it was removed to the Percy vaults. Finally, through the care of Dean Stanley, she was buried in her husband's chantry in 1878 (*Archaeologia*, xlvi. 281–93).

110, l. 27. *Johane Tokyne*, &c. The list in *Harley MS.* 544, f. 67, reads 'the lady Joane Tokayne daughter of dabridgecourte'. Probably the true reading is 'Cokayne'; for Joan, daughter of Sir John Dabridgecourt (*d.* 1415), married John Cokayne (*d.* 1447), though her tomb has been supposed to exist at Ashbourne in Derbyshire (A. E. Cockayne, *Cockayne Memoranda*, i. 20, ii. 195–6).

l. 38. *in the Cloyster.* According to Caxton, Chaucer was buried before St. Benet's Chapel, close to the monument which Brigham set up in 1555.

111, l. 6. *mine owne paynefull labors.* The edition of Chaucer was Stow's first production. See *Introduction*, vol. i. pp. ix and lxxxvi. On p. cccxl of his edition Stow writes thus: 'Here foloweth certaine woorkes of Geoffrey Chauser, whiche hathe not heretofore been printed, and are gathered and added to this booke by Iohn Stowe.' Of twenty pieces thus added three are admittedly genuine, and Professor Skeat accepts two others; of the remainder some are obviously by Lydgate or other later poets. Professor Skeat writes: 'It is clear that Stow had no better reason for inserting pieces in his edition of Chaucer than their occurrence in this MS. (Trin. Coll. Camb. R. 3, 19), to which he had access.' 'Stow in 1561 added more pieces to the collection, but he suppressed nothing. Neither did he himself exercise much principle of selection.' See Skeat, *Chaucer*, i. pp. 31–43, 56, and v. p. x; and *The Chaucer Canon*, 117–26.

l. 31. *Charter.* The privileges of Sanctuary here set out are to be found incorporated in the spurious Charter of Edward the Confessor, professedly granted to Westminster in 1066. See Kemble, *Codex*, dccccxxv, vol. iv. pp. 181–90, and especially pp. 186 and 188. I have not been able to trace a more exact original.

113, margin. *Liber Woodbridge.* Now apparently perished (*Mon. Angl.* vi. 600).

116, l. 24. *noted by Robert Fabian.* From the lost manuscript. See vol. i. p. xxxv above. The corresponding passage in the Vitellius Chronicle (*Chron. Lond.* 200) is somewhat different.

119, l. 39. *the Starre Chamber.* Smith (*Antiquities*, 29) has an engraving of the Elizabethan ceiling decorated with roses, portcullises, and fleurs-de-lys. The name is much older than the Court (established in 1488); it occurs in 1378 (*C. P. R.* Richd. II, i. 276).

120, l. 7. *a great Chamber.* This White Hall, in which the Court of Wards and Liveries, and Court of Requests were held in Stow's time, was one of the rooms of the old palace of Westminster, and had of course no connexion with the later Whitehall Palace. As the 'White chamber' in the palace of Westminster it occurs in 1341 (*Cal. Close Rolls*, Edw. III, vi. 339; see also *Chron. Lond.* 47, for 'White Hall' in 1399). The House of Lords sat here from 1801 to 1834.

l. 10. *S. Stephens Chappell.* There are frequent references to it during the reign of Henry III. It was refounded by Edward I in 1292, and work was in progress there from time to time down to 1352. For the history of the chapel and its decoration see Smith, *Antiquities*, 72–101, 144–64, and 171–250, with elaborate illustrations. See also

Lethaby, *Westminster Abbey*, 180–2, 188–91. For the foundation Charter of Edward III, dated Aug. 6, 1348, see *Mon. Angl.* vi. 1349.

l. 19. *He builded for those.* Munday (*Survey*, 523, ed. 1633) altered this to 'He builded it for them', which led Smith (*Antiquities*, 81–2, 101) to censure Stow, since the chapel did not stand 'from the house of Receipt, along nigh to the Thames, but this was actually the situation of houses for the vicars'. The latter was clearly Stow's own meaning.

l. 21. *there was also builded*, &c. What Stow means here is not clear; but probably he depends on a grant by Henry VI in 1438, which, after explaining that the ground appointed for the dean's dwelling had not been and could not be built on, confirmed to the Dean rooms 'situated within and on the wall of the king's said palace, adjoining "le Wolbrigge" of the king's staple there on the east, and the Clock-Tower of the palace on the west, and the palace wall on the south running along from the said clock-tower to the Thames, and bounded on the north by the way which runs between "le Weyhous" of the said staple and the said "Wolbrigge"' (*C. P. R.* Henry VI, iii. 192). This grant itself is somewhat obscure. The way from the Weyhouse to the Woolbridge was on the line of the modern Bridge Street. On its north side were the six wool-houses referred to on p. 104. The ultimate additional buildings ran north and south along the Thames and formed Cannon Row. See Smith, *Antiquities*, 82, 101–6, 111, with plan facing p. 124.

l. 25. *a strong Clochard.* Stow's ascription of this building to Edward III was probably due to some confusion with the Clock-house (see pp. 379–80 below). It did not belong to St. Stephen's; J. T. Smith describes another tower, which appears to have been the bell-tower of that Chapel, and formed before 1834 the state staircase of the Speaker's house. The Clochard at the west end of the Little Sanctuary was an isolated belfry, and was built in 1249–53. It was a massive tower about sixty feet high, surmounted with a leaded spire. The spire was probably destroyed before Stow wrote, but the tower survived till 1750. John Norden, about 1600, wrote of: 'the Little Sanctuary, wherein is a very ancient and old building and strong, now made a dwelling-house, sometime a tower, wherein was a bell of wonderful bigness weighing, as is reported, 33,000 wt. and was rung only at coronations, which bell King Henry VIII employed to other uses at his going to Boulogne' (Lethaby, *Westminster Abbey*, 56–60, 155–6; Smith, *Antiquities*, 89–92). In Maitland's time the ruined building was used as a tavern or wine-vault; he describes it as 'a prodigious strong stone-building of two hundred and ninety feet square, or seventy-two feet and a half the length of each side, and the walls in thickness [at the base] no less than twenty-five feet' (*London*, 1342). Stukely contributed an account of the building at the time of its destruction to *Archaeologia*, i. 39–44, with plans; he regarded it as the ruin of an asylum, connected with the Sanctuary, and described the interior as two chapels, one above the other; his error has since been often repeated.

121, l. 10. *John Chambers,* or Chamber, was appointed Dean in 1526, and died in 1549 (see *Dict. Nat. Biog.* x. 30). He gave lands to St. Stephen's (Wood, *Fasti Oxonienses*, i. 89, ed. Bliss). For his cloisters, which were on the north side of the Chapel, see Smith, *Antiquities*, 128, 148, 232. The College was dissolved in 1546. From that date till its destruction in 1834 the Chapel was used for the House of Commons. Its site is now St. Stephen's Hall.

l. 18. *our Lady of the Piew.* In his first edition Stow incorrectly described the chapel of the Pew as a part of the house of Bethlehem Hospital near St. Martin-in-the Fields (see p. 264 above). The Chapel of the Pew was probably situated on the north side of St. Stephen's, for at the creation of Henry, Duke of York, to be a Knight of the Bath in 1494, the knights 'toke their waye secretly by our ladie of Pieu, thorough St. Stephen's Chapell on to the steyr foote of the Ster Chambre end' (Gairdner, *Letters, &c., Richard III and Henry VII*, i. 391). Maitland (*London*, 1341) cites a reference to Our Lady of the Pew in 1369. The chapel occurs as 'the king's closet of St. Mary de la Pewe' in the reign of Richard II. Froissart (ix. 409, ed. Luce), when describing the king's visit to Westminster on June 15, 1381, says that 'Richard went to a little chapel, with an image of Our Lady, that worked great miracles, wherein the Kings of England have great trust.' The latest notice which I have found is the record in Henry VIII's Privy Purse Expenses for 1531 of the payment of 8*l.* 1*s.* 8*d.* 'to the clerk of the closet for money in charity at our Lady of the Pewe' (*Letters and Papers*, v. p. 756). These instances suggest that 'our Lady of the Pewe' owed its name to the fact that the king's closet or pew was there (cf. *N. E. D. s. v.* pew). As the king's private chapel its usefulness ceased with the abandonment of the old palace; probably it was destroyed when Chambers built his cloisters. Anthony, Earl Rivers, bequeathed his heart to be buried at our Lady of Pue, and provided for a priest to pray there one year (*Excerpta Historica*, 246-7). The 'keeper of the chapel', named on ii. 120, l. 18 above, was keeper of 'la Pew'. Smith thought that the name was connected with the French *puits*, since there was a well close by. See *Antiquities*, 11, 101, 112-3, 116, 123-7.

l. 35. *a Tower of stone.* According to tradition this Clock-house was built with the fine imposed on Ralph Hingham, the judge, in 1290, for falsifying the record in order to reduce the fine on a poor man. This story appears first in Coke's *Institutes* (iv. 255), published in 1628. But Justice Southcote (*d.* 1585) is reported on a like occasion to have 'said openly that he meant not to build a clock-house' (*Anecdotes and Traditions*, 119, Camd. Soc.; Strype, *Survey*, vi. 55; *Archaeologia*, v. 427, xxxiii. 10). As a matter of fact the Clock-house was built for Edward III in 1365-6—'Turris infra palatium pro quodam orlogio facta' (*Archaeologia*, xxxvii. 23-6, giving an account of the expenses, but confusing it with the Clochard). The dimensions of the Clock-Tower were 24 feet by 17 feet 6 inches. The bell, which was called 'Edward of Westminster' or 'Great Tom', was presented by William III to St. Paul's. It then weighed 9,261 lb., but it was cracked in the process of removal and has since been twice recast with additional metal. The original bell had the inscription :—

Tercius aptavit me Rex, Edwardque vocavit,
Sancti decore Edwardi signarentur ut hore.

The Clock-Tower was granted to the parish of St. Margaret in 1698, and soon afterwards pulled down (Smith, *Antiquities*, 28, 261; Walcote, *Memorials of Westminster*, 197–9). The grant to Walesby on June 23, 1453, was confirmed by Edward IV on July 16, 1461 (*C. P. R.* Edw. IV, i. 163; for earlier grants of the office of keeper of the Clock-Tower see *id.* Richd. II, i. 134, v. 648; Henry IV, i. 84, iii. 385; Henry VI, ii. 184, 540, iii. 131). Both Clock-Tower and fountain are shown in Hollar's print of New Palace Yard, date 1643.

122, l. 12. *a verie faire gate.* 'Highgate (a very beautiful and stately edifice) having occasioned great obstructions to the members of Parliament in their passage to and from their respective houses, was taken down in 1706' (Maitland, *London*, 1341; see also Smith, *Antiquities*, 54).

123, l. 10. *first Presse of booke printing . . . about . . . 1471.* Stow's account is very inaccurate. John Islip only entered the abbey in 1480, and did not become abbot till 1500. Caxton's first book, *The Recuyell of the Histories of Troy*, was printed at Bruges in 1474. His first book printed at Westminster was *The Dictes and Sayings of the Philosophers* on Nov. 18, 1477. He rented of the abbey in the ordinary way of business a house in the Almonry called 'The Red Pale' (Blades, *Life of Caxton*, i. 60, 65–8).

l. 19. *Anne sister to Thomas the Lorde Buckhurst.* She was *the* daughter of Sir Richard Sackville, and married Gregory (not *Gyles*) Fiennes, tenth and last Lord Dacre of the South. Dacre died in 1594, and his widow on May 14, 1595. Her almshouse was for twenty poor persons, ten of each sex, with a school for twenty children (*Dict. Nat. Biog.* xviii. 427–8). It continued till recently as Emmanuel Hospital. The name of Stourton House survives in Strutton Ground, close by.

l. 26. *Petty France.* Renamed York Street in honour of Frederick, Duke of York, who lived at Dover House from 1789 to 1792.

l. 26. *S. Hermits hill.* Now St. Ermin's Hill, a blind-alley out of Great Chapel Street. It occurs as St. Armin's Hill in 1610 (*Cal. State Papers*, 1603–10, p. 582). In the eighteenth century it was called Torment Hill, or St. Torment's Hill. Van Dun's almshouses, also known as Red Lion almshouses, are placed by Strype in Petty France, backing on St. Ermin's Hill; they are now abolished (*N. and Q.*, 7th ser. v. 449–50, vi. 88, 213; 8th ser. ix. 242–3; *London Past and Present*, ii. 467, iii. 424).

125, l. 21. *Lucius.* See note on p. 304.

l. 27. *of the London Bishops.* Stow clearly took some pains over his list: but the result in its earlier part is not satisfactory. The British archbishops are purely legendary, as Stow recognized (see Stubbs, *Reg. Sacr. Anglicanum*, 2nd ed., pp. 215–16). The subsequent list down to Swithulf is fairly correct, but for Ingwald's three successors read 'Ecgwulf, Sigheah, and Aldberht'; the dates are also inaccurate. Deorwulf was bishop as late as 862. From Swithulf to Robert, Stow's list is quite wrong. The true succession with the approximate dates was: Ælfstan (*d.* 898), Wulfsige (898–910), Heahstan, Theodred (926–51), Wulfstan, Brihthelm (953–9), Dunstan (959–61), Ælfstan (961–95), Wulfstan II (996–1003), Ælfwin (1004–12), Elfwig (1014–35), Elfweard (1035–44). Stow himself refers elsewhere to Elfweard or Alfward, viz. on ii. 148 above. See further, Stubbs, *u. s.* pp. 220–1.

128, l. 21. *confirmed.* A spurious Charter of Æthelbald. (*Cod. Dipl.* lxvi.)

l. 31. *Charter.* Of Wiglaf of Mercia, spurious. (*Cod. Dipl.* ccxxxiii.)

l. 37. *Charter.* Of Berhtuulf of Mercia, spurious. (*Cod. Dipl.* cclxv.)

129, l. 7. *buried.* In the *Flores Historiarum*, i. 332—whence Stow seems to get his list to this point—it is expressly said that their tombs are unknown.

l. 9. *Theodricus.* Theodred, bishop of London, witnessed a charter of Edred in 947. (*Cod. Dipl.* ccccxiii.)

l. 19. *he confirmed.* Stow has assigned to 'Edgare' acts which should belong to Ælfstan. 'Ædelstanus' or 'Ælfstanus' of London witnesses spurious charters to Winchester and Croyland in 966 (*Cod. Dipl.* dxxiii, dxxviii). 'Eadgar presbyter' appears as witness to genuine charters for 'Wulfrinton' (Wolverton) in 977 and 984 (*id.* dcxii, dcxlv).

l. 32. *sate* 17. *yeares.* Stow is in manifest error. William was consecrated in 1051, in place of Spearhafoc, whom archbishop Robert had rejected, and lived till 1075, when he was succeeded by Hugh de Orivalle, or Orwell, who died in 1086. Bishop William's epitaph from St. Paul's is given in Godwin, *De Praesulibus*, 174–5.

130, l. 11. *Gilbertus Vniversalis.* Consecrated Jan. 22, 1128, died Aug. 10, 1134.

l. 13. *Robert de Sigillo.* Consecrated 1141, died 1151.

l. 20. *deceased 1186.* Should be Feb. 18, 1187.

132, l. 11. *1241. Fulco Basset.* Though Roger Niger died on Sept. 29, 1241, Basset was not consecrated till Oct. 9, 1244.

l. 15. *Henry Wingham.* Consecrated Feb. 15, 1260.

l. 20. *Richard Talbot.* Not given by Stubbs; Sandwich was consecrated May 27, 1263.

l. 24. *1273. John Cheshul.* Consecrated April 29, 1274, died Feb. 8, 1280.

133, l. 5. *yeare 1307.* Should be Jan. 30, 1306.

l. 13. *Stephen Grauesend.* Consecrated Jan. 14, 1319.

l. 17. *Raph Stratford.* Consecrated Mar. 12, 1340.

l. 23. *Michaell Norbroke.* Better *Northburgh*; consecrated July 12, 1355.

l. 25. *Simon Sudbery.* Consecrated Mar. 20, 1362.

l. 30. *Robert Breybrooke.* Consecrated Jan. 5, 1382.

134, l. 22. *Robert Fitzhugh.* Consecrated Sept. 16, 1431.

l. 26. *Robert Gilbert.* Consecrated Oct. 28, 1436.

l. 28. *Thomas Kempe.* Consecrated Feb. 8, 1450.

l. 35. *John Marshal.* There was no such bishop of London. A John Marshall was bishop of Llandaff 1478–96.

l. 37. *Richard Hill.* Consecrated Nov. 15, 1489, died Feb. 20, 1496.

135, l. 13. *deceased 1521.* Should be Jan. 15, 1522.

l. 18. *Cuthbert Tunstal.* Consecrated Oct. 19, 1522.

l. 24. *Edmond Boner.* Consecrated April 4, 1540.

137, l. 16. *John Elmere.* Or Aylmer; consecrated March 24, 1577.

138, l. 7. *parish churches.* Stow's list may be compared with the list of churches in the City proper in 1303 in the *Liber Custumarum*, ap. *Mun. Gild.* II. i. 228–38. All the churches named by Stow appear in the older list except St. Katherine's by the Tower, Trinity in the Minories, St. Peter in the Tower, The Chapel in Guildhall, St. Anne at the Blackfriars, and St. James by Cripplegate; the absence of these is easily explained. Most of the remainder can be traced back to the twelfth century, and many even further. See references in notes above, and for churches belonging to St. Paul's see *Hist. MSS. Comm.* 9th Report.

140, l. 14. *New Mary Church.* See notes on pp. 317, 328.

147, l. 30. *diuers old Registers.* One was no doubt the London Chronicle in *Harley Roll*, C. 8, which, unlike any other version with which I am acquainted, begins with a Latin notice of the early government of the City from the time of Edward the Confessor to 1189; the Roll contains some notes in Stow's writing. I have not been able to trace the St. Albans book; but like the *Harley Roll* it probably derived its information from the account given in the Trinity Cartulary, which was printed by Hearne in the notes to his edition of William of Newburgh (iii. 724–6). Under the reign of William II the Roll has 'G. de Magum Vicecomes' (see i. 121, 287 above) and 'R. de Pere, prepositus'; Hearne has 'G. de Magnavilla' and 'R. del Parc.' Under Henry I the Roll has Hugo de Boche (Hearne, 'Boch'), this is no doubt the well-known Hugh de Bocland; and 'Rob. de Berquereola', Stow's 'Bar Querel', who may possibly be one of the Bockerels; Aubrey de Vere, who was sheriff in 1125, was killed in 1141 (Round, *Geoff. de Mandeville*, 81, 309). Under Stephen, Stow's 'Andrew Bucheuet' is the 'Andreas Buchuynt' of the Roll, who was 'Justiciar of London' (*id.* 373, and *Commune of London*, 99, 108–13).

For the charter naming Alfward and Wolfgar see *Letter Book* C, 218; the date must be 1042–4. Swetman is named in a Chertsey Charter (*Cod. Dipl.* dccclvi), Leofstan and Aelfsi in two Westminster Charters of Edward the Confessor (*id.* dccclvii, and dccclxi, see also ii. 105 above).

For a facsimile of William's London Charter see Sharpe, *London and the Kingdom*, vol. i.

For a list of the early sheriffs see *Record Office Lists* 9, p. 200. Of those named by Stow, Peter FitzWalter, who held office 1174–6, was strictly speaking 'custos' or 'bailiff', not sheriff; FitzNigel was sheriff in 1177, Buchell or Buzell in 1178, and FitzIsabel in 1156, 1162, 1176, 1178, and 1181.

149, l. 18. *In the first yeare of king Richard the first*, &c. This is erroneous. Richard did not grant a Commune to London. That privilege was not obtained till 1191, when the citizens took advantage of the quarrel between John, the king's brother, and William Longchamp the Chancellor, to extort this privilege from the former as the price of their support. Round, *Commune of London*, 219–25; see also *Eng. Hist. Rev.*, xix. 702–6.

l. 29. *The names*, &c. Stow probably based his list of Mayors and Sheriffs on the current lists, of which examples are found in the London Chronicles and in Fabyan. But these lists had in process of time been much confused and corrupted. A chief cause of error was the numbering of the civic officers under each king's reign separately. Regnal and Mayoral years did not, however, coincide: thus the Mayor and Sheriffs elected in the last year of Henry III (i. e. in Sept.–Oct. 1272) held office during nearly the whole of the first year of Edward I; this may help to explain the misdating by Stow of the Mayors and Sheriffs for the greater part of Edward's reign. Other difficulties were caused by the removal or death of Mayors and Sheriffs during their term of office. In consequence, the lists in the Chronicles and in Stow are hopelessly inaccurate down to 1300. For the Sheriffs an authoritative list has been compiled from records of the Exchequer in *Record Office: Lists and Indexes*, 9. The names in this list agree so well with those in the *Liber de Antiquis Legibus* (covering the period 1189–1274), that we may accept the latter as a trustworthy guide for the names of the Mayors; I have checked it by the attestation of documents in the *Catalogue of Ancient Deeds*. A list of mayors and sheriffs from 1276 to 1320, prepared at the great Iter of 1320, is given in the *Liber Custumarum* (*Mun. Gild.* II. i. 291–4; another list on pp. 239–46 is not free from error). There is a list of Mayors and Sheriffs in *Letter Book* F (pp. 276–303), which was originally compiled in 1354, subsequent names being added from time to time down to 1548. In its earliest part this list presents similar errors to those of Stow; but from about the end of the reign of Edward I it may be accepted as an authoritative record. In addition to the foregoing there is a nearly contemporary list of sheriffs for the reigns of Richard I and John in *Additional MS.* 14252, f. 107. A similar list of Mayors and Sheriffs, coming down to 1222, is printed from the Trinity Cartulary by Hearne in his notes to William of Newburgh, iii. 726–8. Both the latter resemble Stow in giving Henry de Cornhill and Richard filius Reneri as sheriffs for 1 Richard I, though they really vacated office early in that regnal year at Michaelmas, 1189. Hearne's list, like Stow's, gets the later dates right by omitting Serlo le Mercer and Henry of St. Albans under 1206–7; this list seems to represent the original of the lists in the *Chronicles.* In *Add. MS.* 14252 the Sheriffs are a year too late down to 'Martinus Aliz' and 'Petrus Bat' in the '16th' year; then comes the note: 'Sal. et hug. de bar̄. Discidium inter regem et barones. Andr. Neū. et Johes. trauers. Aduentus lodowici primus. Will's. Albus trauers, B. Seint.'

Dr. Gairdner printed an annotated list from 1199 to 1470 in *Collections of a London Citizen*, pp. 242–58, giving the chief variations of the lists in the London Chronicles, and in Fabyan.

In revising the list on pp. 149–86 above, Stow's spelling has been preserved, wherever possible; and also his system of dating, the year A.D. being always that in which the Mayor and Sheriffs named took office; thus under 1400, John Francis is the Mayor who held office from Oct. 29, 1400, to Oct. 28, 1401, being the second mayoral year of Henry IV. Throughout the whole period the Sheriffs took office on Sept. 29 and the Mayor on Oct. 29; this overlapping sometimes causes confusion, e.g. in 1247-8 both Peter FitzAlan and Michael Tovy occur as Mayor, with William Vyel and Nicholas Bat, Sheriffs. (For an account of how the Lord Mayor's day was changed to Nov. 9 see *N. and Q.*, 10th ser., v. 30.)

The errors of date in Stow's list have affected his notices of events. I have endeavoured to put these notices under their appropriate years; thus the notes on Walter Brune, Henry FitzAlwin, and William Joyner, which in the edition of 1603 appear under 1203, 1212, and 1239, are put back to 1202, 1211, and 1238. Similarly the notices for Alen de la Souch (1266), Gregory Rocksley (1274), and Henry Walleis (1281) are all put back one year, in order that they may appear where these persons are first mentioned, as they do in the text of 1603. For other notices see notes below.

In the footnotes on pp. 149–86 the following abbreviations are used:—

A. = *Additional MS.* 14252.
F. = The list in *Letter Book* F.
G. = Dr. Gairdner's list.
H. = Hearne's list from the *Trinity Cartulary.*
L. = *Liber de Antiquis Legibus.*
O. = Official list in *Record Office List*, 9.
S. = Stow's list in the *Survey* for 1603.

149, l. 34. *Their* 1. *Maior.* It is probable that Henry FitzAlwin's term of office dated from the recognition of the Commune in 1191. But the earliest mention of the Mayor of London seems to occur in 1193 (Round, *Commune of London*, pp. 225–35). 'Fifteenth of King John' is an error; FitzAlwin died on Sept. 19, 1212, in the fourteenth regnal and thirteenth mayoral year.

151, l. 23. *to chuse . . a Maior.* I leave this under the date to which Stow assigns it; but there was no charter in 1208–9, and the reference must be to the Charter of May 9, 1215 (Birch, 12). It is noteworthy that the London Chronicles allege that the first mayor held office in 10 John (see *Gregory's Chronicle*, 60; *Chron. Lond.* 2).

152, l. 11. *the ditch.* I leave this under 1213–14; but see vol. i, p. 19.

153, l. 9. *Constantine FitzAlulf.* Stow places under 1222–23; but the true date was July–August, 1222. See *Lib. de Ant. Legg.* 5; *Gregory's Chronicle*, 63; M. Paris, iii. 71.

156, l. 13. *The King graunted*, &c. Stow places under 1250–1; but see *Lib. de Ant. Legg.* 19.

l. 19. *The Liberties*, &c. Stow places under 1252–3; but see *Lib. de Ant. Legg.* 21.

l. 21. *The Maior, &c.* I leave under 1254–5; but it would refer better to 1257–8, cf. *Lib. de Ant. Legg.* 22, and 29–36.

157, l. 3. *the walles.* Stow places under 1257–8, and it may refer to M. Paris, v. 697; but more probably it refers to v. 634 and belongs to 1256–7.

158, l. 12. *Thomas FitzTheobald.* I leave this note under the year where Stow gave it. But FitzTheobald and his wife Agnes, sister of Thomas Becket, of course founded their hospital much earlier. See i. 269.

l. 22. *Bow Church.* Stow places under 1271–2; but the date was Jan. 1271 (*Ann. Lond.* 81).

160, l. 3. *Lawrence Ducket.* Stow places under 1284–5; but it was in the year that Goodcheape was sheriff. Cf. i. 254 and *Ann. Lond.* 81. For some light on the murder see references to another affair in which Ducket and Crepin had been concerned in *Hundred Rolls*, i. 403 sqq.

l. 19. *Raph Barnavars.* In the *Cotton MS.* Julius, B. II (*Chron. London* 7), Ralph de Sandwich is said to have been Custos 'usque in crastinum Sancti Barnabi Apostoli, anno xxii°'. (So also the list in *Letter-Book*, F, 282.) However, from the *Liber Custumarum* (*Mun. Gild.* II. 292) it appears that in 1289 Sandwich was removed 'ante festum Purificationis Beatae Mariae', and Ralph de Berners, deputy-Constable of the Tower, was appointed in his place; but within a few days Berners was succeeded as Custos by John le Breton. Then in 19 Edward I Berners and Breton were removed, and Sandwich again made both Custos and Constable of the Tower. See also *Ann. Lond.* 97.

l. 28. *Three men.* Stow places under 1293–4; but see *Ann. Lond.* 102.

161, l. 13. *the Tunne.* Stow places under 1298–9; but it was before August, 1298 (*Letter-Book*, B, 75). See note on pp. 302–3 above.

165, l. 9. *Walter Nele, Bladesmith.* It should be 'blader', i.e. corn-monger, see note on p. 325 above.

l. 12. *The king graunted.* The date of this grant was June 10, 1354. (Birch, 63.)

166, l. 26. *Aldermen.* Edward II granted in 1319 that they should be removeable every year on March 12, and not be re-elected (*Mun. Gild.* II. i. 269). There was some doubt whether this meant that they must be removed, or only that they might be removed. On November 12, 1376, it was ordained that all the aldermen should vacate office on that day, and not be re-elected. But on March 8, 1384, it was ordered that they should not be removed except for some reasonable cause (*id.* I. 36, II. ii. 436; cf. *Letter-Book*, H, 58).

169, ll. 16–17. *Brember . . . beheaded.* An error. Brembre was hanged at Tyburn (*Rot. Parl.* iii. 238). Stow repeats the mistake in the *Annales.*

186, l. 26. *James Dalton.* Stow in his *Annales*, p. 1217, ed. 1605, under date 1586, writes of a letter from the Queen 'read openly in a great assembly of the Commons in the Guildhall, August 22, before the reading whereof, master James Dalton, one of the Counsellers of the City, in the absence of the Recorder made this speech hereafter following, &c.' James Dalton was made under-sheriff of London through Burghley's favour in March, 1594 (*Lansdowne MSS.* 77 (31); and 34 (18), 77 (51) and 79 (75)—three other letters from Dalton).

195, l. 37. *the new fashion of flatte caps.* Howes in 1631, with reference to the time of Queen Mary and beginning of the reign of Elizabeth, writes of the London apprentices: 'They also wore flat caps, both then and many yeares after, as well Apprentices as Journey-men, and others, both at home and abroad, whom the Pages of the Court in derision called Flat-caps', *Annales*, p. 1041. Ben Jonson, in *Every man in his Humour*, Act II, Sc. i, writes:—

> Make their loose comments upon every word,
> Gesture, or look I use; mock me all over,
> From my flat-cap unto my shining shoes.

And Dekker in *The Honest Whore*, Pt. 2:—

> Flat Caps as proper are to Citty Gownes,
> As to Armors Helmets, or to kings their Crownes.
> Let then the City Cap by none be scorn'd
> Since with it Princes heads have been adornd.

196, l. 5. *Sir John White wore it.* Stow in his *Memoranda* (pp. 127–8) writes: 'Ser John Whit, beynge mayre, wore bothe a longe beard and allso a round cape that wayed not iiij ounces, whiche semyd to all men, in consideracyon of ye auncient bonyt, to be very uncomly.' Dekker in *The Honest Whore*, Pt. 2, comments both on caps and shaving (*Works*, ii. 110):—

> For Caps are emblems of humility;
> It is a citizens badge, and first was worne
> By th' Romans; for when any Bondmans turne
> Came to be made a Freeman: thus 'twas said,
> He to the Cap was call'd; that is, was made
> Of Rome a Freeman, but was first close shorne,
> And so a Citizen's haire is still short worne.

In 1543 the Court of Aldermen had actually ordered that no one wearing a beard 'of more notable prolyxyte or length than that worn by other citizens should be admitted by redemption to the liberties and freedom of the City as long as he should wear any such beard' (*Repertory*, 10, f. 343, ap. *Letter-Book*, D, p. xi).

196, l. 33. *The author.* Stow expressly conceals his name, whilst stating that he was a Londoner born. From a reference at the head of p. 202 it appears that the writer was a young scholar at Oxford during the reign of Queen Mary, and from another on p. 208 to have been a lawyer, familiar with London constitutional government. The facts might suit James Dalton, who was at Christ Church in 1551 (*Reg. Univ. Oxford*, i. 217). The occasion for writing seems to have been the proclamation against new building in 1580 (see note on pp. 367–8 above).

220. *Descriptio Londoniae* was written in 1174 by William Fitz-Stephen as a prelude to his life of Thomas Becket. It is not, however, found in all the extant copies of that work, and of the manuscripts used for the edition in *Materials for the History of Thomas Becket*, vol. iii (Rolls Series), *Lansdowne* 398 (in the British Museum) alone has it in full, whilst *Douce*, 287 (in the Bodleian Library) has an imperfect copy. Other copies are contained in *Marshall MS.* 75 (in the Bodleian Library), and in the *Liber Custumarum*, preserved at the Guildhall and edited by H. T. Riley in *Mun. Gild.* II. i. 1–15. Stow might presumably have had access to the last; but his discussion on London Schools (vol. i. 71–3) shows that he had not made use of it. His original more nearly resembled the *Douce MS.* which belonged to Lessness Abbey, near Erith, and the *Marshall MS.* which Hearne thought Stow had used.

The Description of London has been several times printed, viz. by Strype in his *Survey* (Appendix, pp. 9–11), using the *Liber Custumarum*; by Thomas Hearne in vol. viii of Leland's *Itinerary* from the *Marshall MS.*; by Samuel Pegge in 1772 with notes; and by W. J. Thoms in his edition of the *Survey*, where the previous printed editions are collated with the *Lansdowne MS.* The present text is based on a comparison of Stow's text with the two versions in the Rolls Series, which I have collated anew with the *Lansdowne MS.* I have further given some references to Hearne's text and to the *Douce MS.*

The copy in the *Liber Custumarum*, though somewhat late in date, is of peculiar interest for its civic origin. On the whole it agrees with Stow's text more closely than does the *Lansdowne MS.* It has the peculiarity of being divided into twenty-five chapters, as against the eleven of Stow's version; the chapter *De Pascuis et Sationalibus* is divided into two; the chapter *De Dispositione Urbis* has four divisions, and that *De Ludis* no less than ten. In the *Lansdowne MS.* there is no division into chapters. In the present edition Stow's division (which is also that of Hearne) is retained. As a rule the text follows that of Stow, where he is supported by either of the chief MSS. No MS. appears to be entitled to pre-eminent authority.

In the footnotes on pp. 219–29 above,

C.=*Liber Custumarum.*
D.=Douce MS. 287.
H.=Hearne's edition.
L.=*Lansdowne MS.* 398.
S.=Stow's text of 1603.

FitzStephen adorned his narrative with an extraordinary display of classic learning (much of it no doubt second-hand). I have given as many references as I could find in previous editions or trace elsewhere.

ADDENDA

i. **217,** l. 25. *no silks.* See ii. 313, where the note should be that the best version of *London Lickpenny* does mention silk, though Stow's own copy has simply 'Paris thred, coton, and vmple'. Nicolas, *Lond. Chron.*, 263 and 267; and Skeat, *Specimens of English Literature* (ed. 1879, p. 26).

i. **336,** l. 13. *Beatrix his wife.* Stow has made a confusion here. Sir Richard Burley (*d.* 1387) married, as her third husband, Beatrix, daughter of Ralph, Earl of Stafford, and widow of Thomas, Lord Ros of Hamelake, who died in 1383. Beatrix died on April 14, 1415 (G. E. C. *Complete Peerage*, iii. 84, vi. 401; Beltz, *Memorials of the Garter*, 293).

i. **339,** l. 7. *Pembrooks Inne.* See ii. 350. John of Brittany, Earl of Richmond, had licence on May 5, 1331, to grant to Mary, Countess of Pembroke, the castles, towns, manors, and lands which he held in England (*C.P.R.* Edw. III, ii. 110).

i. **347,** l. 28. *parish church of St. Mildred.* On Faithorne's map the church is shown on the *north* side of Basing Lane, and this seems to be the position indicated by Stow, cf. i. 348, l. 13. But the existing church is on the *south* side, and there does not seem to be any record of a change of site when the church was rebuilt after 1666.

ii. **102,** l. 18. *Chanon Row.* See ii. 375. 'The Chanon Row' is mentioned in a letter of Anthony, Earl Rivers (*d.* 1483), ap. *Additional MS.*, 25459, f. 316.

ii. **104,** l. 28. *six wooll houses.* See ii. 375 and 378. On Dec. 15, 1437, Henry VI granted to John Beket and Thomas Carre, the six houses called the houses of the king's wools. The houses were part of the foundation of the College of St. Stephen, but had been lately returned to the king for a certain compensation. This grant was surrendered, when on Nov. 16, 1443, the king granted the houses to the Dean and Canons of St. Stephen's in frank almoign (*C.P.R.* Henry VI, iii. 123, 125).

SUPPLEMENT TO THE NOTES

THE purpose of this Index is to give references to modern editions of authors cited or used by Stow; and to Collections and Calendars, where documents so used or cited may be found. I have endeavoured, where possible, to give the actual source of Stow's information. But it must not be assumed that he had always made use of the authority here given. Thus whilst it is certain that he had used the *Liber Albus* and *Liber Custumarum*, it is not so clear that he was acquainted with the *Liber de Antiquis Legibus*. The references are unavoidably imperfect; some are difficult to trace; some come from sources still unprinted and uncalendared. Stow had, moreover, made use of manuscripts which seem now to have perished; such are his *Liber S. Mariae Overy* and *Liber Woodbridge*. For the minor religious foundations in London, the editors of the *Monasticon Anglicanum* could often add nothing to the information preserved in the *Survey*.

When the sources of any statement have been discussed in the Notes, they are not here repeated. Whenever possible, references to mediaeval historians are to the editions in the Rolls Series. The following abbreviations are used both in the Notes and in this Index.

Anc. Deeds.] Descriptive Catalogue of Ancient Deeds preserved in the Public Record Office, vols. i to v. (The deeds are arranged in four classes lettered A, B, C, and D.)

Ann. Lond. } *Ann. Paul.* } Annales Londonienses and Annales Paulini, ap. *Chronicles of the reigns of Edward I and Edward II.* (Rolls Series.)

Ann. Mon.] Annales Monastici. (Rolls Series.)

Anom. Chron.] An Anominalle Chronicle belonging to the abbey of St. Maries in York, ap. *English Historical Review*, xiii. 509–22. (Stow's *Liber S. Mariae Eborum.*)

Birch.] The Historical Charters and Constitutional Documents of the City of London, ed. W. de G. Birch.

Cal. Inq. p. m.] Calendarium Inquisitionum post mortem. 4 vols. folio. (Record Commission.)

C. P. R.] Calendars of the Patent Rolls, prepared under the superintendence of the Deputy-Keeper of the Records. (Cited by the sovereign, and number of the volume in each reign.)

Cal. Wills.] Calendar of Wills in the Court of Husting, London. 2 vols., ed. R. R. Sharpe.

Chron. Angliae.] Chronicon Angliae, 1328–88, ed. Sir E. M. Thompson. (Rolls Series.)

Chron. Lond.] Chronicles of London, ed. C. L. Kingsford.

Cod. Dipl.] Codex Diplomaticus Aevi Saxonici, ed. J. M. Kemble. (English Hist. Soc.)

Flor. Wig.] Florentii Wigorniensis Chronicon. 2 vols. (English Hist. Soc., with the continuations by John Taxter and John Eversden, ii. 136–279.)

Gent. Mag. Libr.] The Gentleman's Magazine Library, ed. G. L. Gomme.

Gregory Chron.] Gregory's Chronicle of London, ap. *Collections of a London Citizen.* (Camden Soc.)

Hall.] Edward Hall's *Chronicle*, ed. 1809.

Hist. MSS. Comm. 9th Rep.] Ninth Report of the Royal Historical Manuscripts Commission. Appendix A. Manuscripts of the Dean and Chapter of St. Paul's.

Inq. p. m. Lond.] Inquisitiones post mortem relating to the City of London. vols. i–iii. (British Record Soc.)

Letters and Papers.] Calendar of Letters and Papers of the Reign of Henry VIII, ed. J. S. Brewer and James Gairdner.

Letter-Book, A, &c.] Calendars of Letter-Books of the City of London, ed. R. R. Sharpe. (The several volumes are distinguished by letters. Only the calendars for A to H have as yet appeared. Dr. Sharpe has kindly allowed me to consult his MS. calendar for I ; its interest is, however, chiefly for general English history. The early publication of a calendar to K, which was used by Stow, and is of great value for London history, is much to be desired.)

Lib. de Ant. Legg.] Liber de Antiquis Legibus. (Camden Soc. The earliest of London chronicles.)

Maitland.] *The History and Survey of London*, by W. Maitland. 2 vols., folio, 1756.

Memoranda.] John Stow's Memoranda of contemporary occurrences, 1561–67, ap. *Three Fifteenth Century Chronicles*, pp. 115–47. (Camden Soc.)

Memorials.] Memorials of London and London Life, ed. H. T. Riley. (A translation of documents from *Letter-Books* A to I, between 1272 and 1420.)

Mon. Angl.] Monasticon Anglicanum, ed. Caley, Ellis, and Baudinell.

Mun. Gild.] Munimenta Gildhallae Londoniensis, ed. H. T. Riley. (Rolls Ser. The *Liber Albus* with Appendices is contained in vols. I and III, the *Liber Custumarum* in vol. II, i. and ii.)

Nicolas, *Lond. Chron.*] A Chronicle of London, ed. Sir N. H. Nicolas and E. Tyrrel, 1827.

N. and Q.] Notes and Queries.

Rot. Parl.] Rotuli Parliamentorum (Rolls of Parliament), 6 vols.

Remembrancia.] Index to the Remembrancia preserved among the archives of the City of London, 1878.

Trans. Lond. and Midd.] Transactions of the London and Middlesex Archaeological Society.

VOLUME I

1. 3, Geoff. Monmouth, *Hist. Britt.* i. 17; 16, *id. ib.*

6. 23, Wittekind, *Res Gestae Saxonicae*, i. 8, ap. Migne, *Patrologia*, cxxxvii.

7. 5, W. Malmesbury, *Gesta Regum*, i. 7; 20, Bede, *Hist. Eccl.* i. c. 14; 29, *id. Vita Benedicti*, ap. *Op.* i. 368, ed. Plummer.

8. 22, W. Malm. *Gesta Regum*, i. 187, Asser, 83, Marianus Scotus, 153, (ed. 1559,) Flor. Wig. i. 151; 27, W. Malm. *Gesta Regum*, i. 216; 32, *id.* i. 243.

9. 17, Rog. Wendover, ii. 116, M. Paris, ii. 587, R. Coggeshall, 171; 22, M. Paris, v. 634; 26, *Letter-Book*, A, 223–4; 36, *id.* D, 244, E, 63.

10. 2, *C.P.R.* Richd. II, iii. 210; 6, *Chron. Lond.* 187.

13. 18, *id.* 258.

14. 6, *Mun. Gild.* II. i. 409, *Memorials*, 43.

16. 33, *Letter-Book*, A, 14.

17. 18, Maitland, i. 191.

18. 20, *Mun. Gild.* II. i. 64–6.

19. 3, *Ann. Mon.* iii. 34; 29, *Letter-Book*, G, 27; 34, *id.* H, 116, 137.

20. 3, *Memorials*, 615; 5, *Chron. Lond.* 187.

21. 20, W. Malm. *Gesta Regum*, i. 208; 28, *id.* i. 216; 34, *id.* i. 243.

22. 4, *Ann. Mon.* iii. 432; 10, *id.* iii. 433; 14, *Foedera*, i. 8; 27, *Ann. Mon.* iii. 435.

23. 11, *id.* ii. 240.

24. 10, Walter of Coventry, ii. 205–6; 31, *Ann. Lond.* 89, *Ann. Mon.* iv. 483; 34, *C. P. R.* Edw. II, iii. 502, 517.

25. 11, *Chron. Lond.* 18: 27, *id.* 160; 32, *id.* 185.

27. 16, *Letter-Books*, **A**, 178, C, 71, *Memorials*, 615.

28. 20, *Letter-Book*, C, 217.

29. 1, *Letter-Book*, H, 2; 5, *id.* H, 443; 28, M. Paris, ii. 587; 39, Coggeshall, 171.

30. 11, *Chron. Lond.* 185, *Arrivall of Edward IV*, 33–7 (Camd. Soc.).

31. 31, *Mon. Angl.* vi. 624; 39, *id.* vi. 622.

32. 3, *Mun. Gild.* I. 485–8; 25, *Memorials*, 614.

33. 20, *Engl. Hist. Review*, xi. 740; 30, cf. *C. P. R.* Edw. I, iii. 434.

35. 5–18, *Nova Legenda Angliae*, i. 395–6, ed. Horstman.

36. 5, *Rot. Claus.* i. 398; 10, M. Paris, iv. 30–31.

37. 2, *Gregory Chron.* 116; 14, *Chron. Lond.* 97, 134; 25, *id.* 167.

38. 12, Rog. Wendover, ii. 116, M. Paris, ii. 587.

39. 10, *Letter-Book*, H, 97; 12, *id.* H, 208, 213, 292.

41. 25, *Mun. Gild.* I. 240.

42. 27, *Chron. Lond.* 142; 33, *id.* 185.

43. 20, Geoff. Monmouth, *Hist. Britt.* iii. 10.

44. 11, M. Paris, v. 697.

45. 11, *Textus Roffensis*, 212; 24, W. Malm. *Gesta Regum*, ii. 375; 30, H. Huntingdon, *Hist. Angl.* 230.

46. 5, Trivet, *Annals*, 13, cf. Round, *Geoffrey de Mandeville*, 117–18; 16, Rog. Wendover, i. 190, *Gesta Henrici II*, ii. 106; 24, *Letter-Book*, C, 217; 32, *C. P. R.* Edw. III, vi. 84.

47. 7, M. Paris, iii. 532; 30, *id.* iv. 94, 374, 510, 603, v. 22, 47, 100, 128, 367, 409, 568.

48. 9, *Letter-Book*, E, 52; 20, M. Paris, iii. 324; 26, Madox, *Hist. Exchequer*, i. 381; 31, *C. P. R.* Edw. III, v. 302.

49. 33, M. Paris, ii. 419, 446.

50. 1, *Rot. Claus.* i. 154 b; 7–10, Nicolas, *Lond. Chron.* 6, 11, 15; 11, M. Paris, iii. 73; 21, Nicolas, *Lond. Chron.* 16; 35, *Flores Historiarum*, ii. 482.

51. 6, *Ann. Lond.* 90; 10, Flor. Wig. ii. 241; 15, *Mun. Gild.* II. i. 371–4; 19, *Ann. Paul.* 305; 25, *id.* 318; 29, *id.* 352; 33, *Letter-Book*, F, 107.

53. 9, Nicolas, *Lond. Chron.* 29.

54. 11, cf. *C. P. R.* Henry VI, iii. 421; 24, Madox, *Hist. Exchequer*, i. 290; 32, *Letter-Book*, C, 39, 42; 36, *Foedera*, iii. 223.

55. 13, *Chron. Lond.* 68; 17, *id.* 73; 32, *id.* 179.

57. 22, Commines, *Memoires*, V. xviii.; 37, *Anom. Chron.* 517–18.

58. 13, *Chron. Lond.* 73, 80; 15, Amundesham, *Annales*, i. 7; 23, *Chron. Lond.* 168; 29, *id.* 182; 35, *id.* 188; 37, *id.* 191.
59. 6, *id.* 258.
60. 24, *id.* 142; 28, *id.* 185; 33, Gervase of Tilbury, *Otia Imperialia*, ap. Coggeshall, 425.
61. 26, *Ann. Lond.* 15.
66. 4, *Chron. Lond.* 168; 5, *id.* 173–4; 34, More, *Life of Richard III*, 74 (ed. Lumby).
67. 1, *Chron. Lond.* 250; 4, *id.* 259.
68. 11, Birch, 3; 18, *Letter-Book*, C, 71, *Cal. Charter Rolls*, ii. 211, *C.P.R.* Edw. I, i. 147; 30, *Letter-Book*, B, 55.
69. 9, *Nova Legenda Angliae*, i. 395–6; 31, M. Paris, ii. 530.
71. 6, Froissart, x. 112, 117, 123–4, ed. Luce; 8, *Anom. Chron.* 521; 12, *Chron. Angliae*, 367, 373; 26, *Mon. Angl.* vi. 1350.
72. 21, M. Paris, ii. 311.
73. 19, *Mon. Angl.* vi. 677; 22, *Rot. Parl.* v. 137.
76. 4, *Cal. Wills*, ii. 698–700.
77. 38, Fortescue, *De Legibus Angliae*, ch. xlix.
82. 23, W. Malm. *Gesta Pont.* 140; 32, *Mun. Gild.* II. i. 64–6; 35, *id.* I. 228.
83. 11, *id.* I. 319; 33, *Letter-Books*, A, 217, H, 352.
89. 34, Malmesbury, *Gesta Pontificum*, 169.
90. 3, M. Paris, v. 638; 7, *Anglia Sacra*, i. 12–13; 36, *Hist. Dunelm. Scriptores*, 128 (*Surtees Soc.*).
93. 25, Higden, *Polychronicon*, ix. 47; 28, Nicolas, *Lond. Chron.* 91.
94. 7, M. Paris, v. 367; 39, *id.* iii. 71.
95. 4, *Chron. Lond.* 164 *n.* (a note of Stow's); 22, M. Paris, iii. 336.
97. 5, Nicolas, *Lond. Chron.* 87; 29, *Chron. Lond.* 156.
98. 10, Hall, 515.
99. 3, Lydgate, ap. Nicolas, *Lond. Chron.* 257; 25, Hall, 588–90; 31, cf. Freeman, *Norman Conquest*, iii. 185.
101. 3, M. Paris, v. 368–9.
105. 22, *Materials for History of T. Becket*, iii. 14–17; 34, *Mon. Angl.* vi. 624.
106. 1, M. Paris, iii. 26–9; 5, *Mon. Angl.* vi. 622; 8, *Mun. Gild.* II. i. 274; 15, *Cal. Wills*, i. 562; 19, *Archaeologia*, lvii. 281; 27, *Trans. Lond. and Midd.* iii. 432–47; 31, Stow, *Annales*, p. 415, ed. 1605 (adding something), S. Bentley, *Westminster Charters*, 43, 74.
107. 4, *Mon. Angl.* vi. 1380; 5, *Cal. Wills*, ii. 180; *Letter-Book*, H, 63 *n.*, *C. P. R.* Henry VI, ii. 217; 11, *Chron. Angliae*, 199; 21, Walsingham, *Hist. Angl.* ii. 115.
108. 4, *C. P. R.* Richd. II, ii. 149; 17, Nicolas, *Lond. Chron.* 93; 20, *Cal. Wills*, ii. 474; 30, *Memorials*, 614.
109. 20, *Cal. Wills*, ii. 489–92; 26, *id.* ii. 577; 29, *id.* ii. 499; 33, *id.* ii. 509–11.
110. 3, Orridge, *Illustrations of Jack Cade's Rebellion*, 8.
111. 1, Leland, *Itinerary*, iv. 69–70; 31, *Cal. Wills*, ii. 640.
112. 3, *Chron. Lond.* 226, 234; 21, *id.* p. xviii. *n.*
113. 3, *Cal. Wills*, ii. 651, 677; 8, *id.* ii. 668; 16, *id.* ii. 677, *Inq. p. m. Lond.* ii. 105; 39, *Cal. Wills*, ii. 699, *Wills from Doctors Commons*, 59 (Camden Soc.).
114. 8, *Cal. Wills*, ii. 686; 15, *id.* ii. 693.
116. 11, *Cal. Wills*, ii. 654.
117. 5, *Chron. Lond.* 115.
119. 20, *Rot. Parl.* iii. 317–18, *Letter-Book*, H, 407–8; 27, Maitland, i. 242–7.
124. 5, Leland, *Collectanea*, i. 113; 27, *C. P. R. Edw. III*, viii. 484, 560.
125. 2, *id.* ix. 488; 16, cf. *Statutes at Large*, ii. 682 (on Queen's Storehouse of Minories); 38, *Mon. Angl.* vi. 1553.
130. 36, Leland, *Collectanea*, i. 110; 39, *C. P. R.* Edw. IV, i. 428.
132. 38, *Rot. Parl.* iv. 69.
133. 12, *Chron. Lond.* 161.
135. 23, *C. P. R.* Richd. II, ii. 149.
137. 33, *Cal. Inq. p. m.* iv. 283.
139. 34, *Letter-Book*, C, 219.
146. 39, *C. P. R.* Edw. IV, i. 297.
147. 16, *C. P. R.* Edw. III, vi. 115.
149. 12, *Cal. Inq. p. m.* iv. 267; 34, *id.* i. 87; 36, *id.* iii. 61.
151. 9, cf. *Inq. p. m. Lond.* iii. 224.

152. 17, *Chron. Lond.* 161.
153. 18, Maitland, i. 191.
155. 4, Birch, 85, *C. P. R.* Edw. IV, i. 285; 18, *id.* i. 516; 33, Arnold, *Customs of London*, 82–4.
163. 21, *Letter-Book*, G, 284.
164. 29, *Mon. Angl.* vi. 622; Leland, *Collectanea*, i. 113.
166. 23, *Mon. Angl.* vi. 625.
167. 14, *Cal. Wills*, ii. 313.
168. 8, Walsingham, *Hist. Angl.* ii. 227; 10, Orridge, *Illustrations of Jack Cade's Rebellion*, 8.
173. 11, *C. P. R.* Henry IV, ii. 54.
176. 13, *id.* Edw. IV, iii. 41.
180. 4, *id.* Henry VI, iii. 244.
181. 7, *id.* Henry IV, iii. 56, Clode, *Memorials of the Merchant Taylors*, 102.
182. 11, *id.* 96–7; 18, *id.* 194–8.
184. 13, *Mon. Angl.* vi. 1359; 31, *Chron. Lond.* 226.
186. 3, *Cal. Wills*, ii. 296; 16, *Chron. Lond.* p. xviii.
189. 1, *Mun. Gild.* II. i. 213; 25, Walsingham, *Hist. Angl.* ii. 65.
192. 20, *Cal. Wills*, ii. 635.
193. 35, *Mun. Gild.* II. i. 86–8.
199. 9, Lydgate, *London Lickpenny*, ap. Nicolas, *Lond. Chron.* 264; 35, M. Paris, *Historia Anglorum*, ii. 350.
201. 21, *C. P. R.* Edw. IV, ii. 424.
206. 25, *Mun. Gild.* I. 237–8.
213. 7, *Mun. Gild.* I. 247; 36, *C. P. R.* Edw. I, ii. 306, 377.
214. 13, *Letter-Book*, H, 176; 18, *Rot. Parl.* iii. 143.
215. 4, Walsingham, *Hist. Angl.* ii. 110, 116, *Chron. Angliae*, 360, Higden, *Polychronicon*, ix. 46; 18, *C. P. R.* Richd. II, iv. 296, 311, *Rot. Parl.* iii. 282, 292, *Letter-Book*, H, 359, 370.
218. 12, *Letter-Book*, G, 265.
219. 20, *Cal. Inq. p. m.* iii. 159; 35, Walsingham, *Hist. Angl.* ii. 9–14; Knighton, ii. 137–8, *Anom. Chron.* 519–20.
220. 28, Leland, *Collectanea*, i. 110, *Mon. Angl.* vi. 1380.
223. 13, *C. P. R.* Edw. III, vi. 489; Leland, *Collectanea*, i. 110.
225. 32, *C. P. R.* Edw. I, ii. 23; 34, *id.* Edw. II, iv. 425.
229. 1, *Cal. Wills*, ii. 385–6.
230. 17, *C. P. R.* Edw. IV, i. 237; 25, *id.* Edw. III, i. 34, cf. *id.* Henry VI, iii. 190–1.
231. 20, *Mon. Angl.* vi. 172.
236. 31, *Cal. Inq. p. m.* iii. 211.
237. 22, *C. P. R.* Edw. IV, ii. 236.
238. 21, *Letter-Book*, C, 75, 80; Delpit, *Collection*, &c. xxxiii, lxx, lxxix.
240. 20, *C. P. R.* Edw. II, iii. 355, Edw. III, iii. 120; 31, *Letter-Book*, G, 4; 36, Amundesham, *Annales*, i. 18, *Chron. Lond.* 273.
242. 2, *C. P. R.* Henry VI, iii. 80; 38, *Memorials*, 578.
243. 2, *C. P. R.* Henry VI, i. 259; 4, *id.* ii. 214–17.
244. 2, Froissart, x. 112, ed. Luce; 12, *Anom. Chron.* 521; 27, *Chron. Angliae*, 367, 373.
245. 9, *Cal. Wills*, ii. 76; 21, *Memorials*, 568–70.
246. 18, Watney, *Account of St. Thomas Acon*, 280.
247. 6, *Chron. Angliae*, 123–4; 36, *C. P. R.* Edw. IV, i. 433–4, *Rot. Parl.* v. 625.
251. 27, *C. P. R.* Edw. III, ix. 242.
253. 8, *Cal. Wills*, i. 238, *C. P. R.* Henry IV, iii. 159.
254. 11, W. Malm. *Gesta Regum*, ii. 375; 20, Hoveden, iv. 6, R. de Diceto, ii. 143; 35, *Ann. Lond.* 81; 37, *id.* 92, Nicolas, *Lond. Chron.* 31.
255. 20, *Cal. Wills*, ii. 578; 31, *id.* ii. 583.
258. 10, *Letter-Book*, A, 221; 15, *id.* E, 134.
261. 22, Hall, 824.
262. 17, Milbourn, *Hist. S. Mildred's*, 12.
263. 28, *C. P. R.* Henry VI, ii. 78; 32, *Cal. Wills*, ii. 474.
264. 13, *C. P. R.* Henry IV, i. 284, Milbourn, *Hist. S. Mildred's*, 39, 46–8.
265. 19, *Ann. Lond.* 102; 21, *Ann. Paul.* 316–17; 28, *Three Fifteenth-Century Chronicles*, 52 (Camden Soc.); 30, *Chron. Lond.* 161; 31, *id.* 176.
266. 7, *Ann. Paulini*, 354, G. le Baker, *Chron.* 48; 8, Maitland, i. 191.
267. 29, Higden, *Polychronicon*, viii. 320.

269. 6, *C.P.R.* Edw. III, v. 12, *Mon. Angl.* vi. 646.
270. 5, *C.P.R.* Richd. II, v. 425; 18, *id.* Henry VI, i. 280.
271. 10, *Cal. Wills*, ii. 564, 578; 28, Fabyan, 576, Nicolas, *Lond. Chron.* 93; 30, *Memorials*, 589.
273. 21, *C.P.R.* Edw. III, ix. 478, *Memorials*, 288, *Letter-Books*, G, 67, H, 178, 339; 28, *Cal. Inq. p. m.* iii. 194.
274. 3, *Cal. Wills*, ii. 477.
277. 16, *Lib. de Ant. Legg.* 62, *Flores Historiarum*, ii. 489; 21, M. Paris, v. 612.
278. 37, *Gesta Ricardi I*, ii. 83.
279. 13, M. Paris, ii. 528; 25, Coggeshall, 171.
280. 18, M. Paris, iii. 262; 21, *id.* iii. 305; 25, *id.* iv. 260; 27. *id.* v. 136; 32, *id.* v. 516.
281. 3, Flor. Wig. ii. 214; 7, *id.* ii. 221, *Ann. Lond.* 88; 13, Peckham, *Registrum*, i. 213; 16, *Ann. Lond.* 96; 19, *id.* 99, Flor. Wig. ii. 243; 30, *C.P.R.* Edw. II, iv. 302.
286. 13, M. Paris, ii. 442; 18, *C.P.R.* Henry III, i. 155; 21, *id.* Richd. II, i. 452, *Letter-Book*, H, 94, 151.
288. 18, *Cal. Inq. p. m.* iii. 195; 33, *Memorials*, 550, *Letter-Book*, H. 449.
293. 19, *Cal. Wills*, ii. 509–11.
294. 8, *id.* i. 362, 562, *Mon. Angl.* vi. 703–4; 9, *Cal. Wills*, i. 637.
295. 3, *Inq. p. m. Lond.* iii. 203; 15, *Cal. Wills*, ii. 640.
297. 16, *C.P.R.* Henry VI, iii. 142; 17, *id.* Edw. IV, iii. 168; 34, *id.* Richd. II, v. 171, *Cal. Inq. p. m.* iii. 166.
300. 27, Leland, *Collectanea*, i. 111.
301. 9, *id. ib.* i. 114; 14, *C.P.R.* Richd. II, iv. 458; 30, Hoveden, ii. 137.
305. 10, *Cal. Wills*, i. 154, ii. 621; 12, *id.* ii. 283.
306. 22, *C.P.R.* Richd. II, v. 219.
309. 20. *id.* Edw. IV, iii. 318; 28, Leland, *Collectanea*, i. 111; 32, *id. ib.*; 38, *Cal. Inq. p. m.* iii. 211.
310. 11, Maitland, ii. 1319; 25, *Rot. Parl.* iii. 317–18, *Letter-Book*, H, 407.
315. 35, *C.P.R.* Edw. IV, i. 109.
316. 7, Leland, *Collectanea*, i. 112; 8, *C.P.R.* Edw. III, v. 145; 12, *Memorials*, 553, *Letter-Book*, F, 180.
317. 1, *Memorials*, 357, *Letter-Book*, H, 372, 375–6; 7, *Monumenta Franciscana*, i. 493; 13, *id.* i. 494; 16–22, *id.* i. 508; 23–39, *id.* i. 513–15.
318. 1–12, *id.* i. 518; 17, *id.* i. 509; 18, *id.* i. 518.
319. 26, cf. Wriothesley, *Chron.* ii. 80, 82.
323. 7, *C.P.R.* Henry III, i. 366; 30, *Mun. Gild.* II. i. 338–44.
325. 2, *Nova Legenda Angliae*, i. 395–6; 23–35, *Mun. Gild.* II. i. 338–44.
326. 10, *Ann. Lond.* 232; *Ann. Paul.* 276; 16, *id.* 274; 22, *Chron. Lond.* 156.
327. 20, Sparrow-Simpson, *Reg. Statutorum S. Pauli*, 326–9.
329. 13, Leland, *Collectanea*, i. 111; 30, *Letter-Book*, C, 6, *Hist. MSS. Comm.* 9th Rep. 50; 37, *C.P.R.* Henry VI, ii. 56–7.
330. 32, *Monumenta Franciscana*, ii. 235, cf. Wriothesley, *Chron.* ii. 67.
331. 15, *Lib. de Ant. Legg.* 53.
338. 27, *Letter-Book*, A, 213–14.
339. 32, *id.* C, 71.
340. 3, *Chron. Lond.* 158, *Rot. Parl.* v. 171; 5, Hall, 640; 6, *id.* 652; 16, *id.* 756; 23, *id.* 760, 764.
342. 5, *Memorials*, 521.
344. 19, *Mun. Gild.* I. 356–8, II. i. 104.
351. 27, cf. *C. P. R.* Henry VI, iii. 308, *Memorials*, 571; 33, *Rot. Parl.* v. 566, *Gregory Chron.*, 238.

VOLUME II

2. 21, *Cal. Wills*, i. 328, 573.
3. 4, *C. P. R.* Edw. III, ix. 239–40.
4. 11, *Cal. Wills*, ii. 663.
5. 8, *C. P. R.* Richd. II, iii. 479, 492; 28, *Cal. Wills*, ii. 418.
7. 14, *Mun. Gild.* III. 445–9.
8. 3, *id.* II. i. 46–7; 36, Fabyan, 336; 39, *Mun. Gild.* I. 241–3, II. i. 379.

9. 21, *Letter-Books*, C, 65–6, E, 75, *C.P.R.* Edw. II, i. 187, Edw. III, i. 560.
10. 36, *Cal. Inq. p. m.* i. 38.
11. 5, *Cal. Charter Rolls*, ii. 16; 8, *Cal. Inq. p. m.* iv. 145.
14. 3, *C.P.R.* Henry VI, iii. 522; 6, *Rot. Chart.* 2; 21, See i. 64, above; 35, *Letter-Book*, A, 222.
15. 1, *Rot. Parl.* i. 200.
16. 23, *Inq. p. m. Lond.* iii. 147.
19. 16, Foxe, *Acts and Monuments*, vol. viii; 32, *Hist. MSS. Comm.* 9th. Rep. 12.
20. 28, *Rot.Parl.*iii.317–18, *Letter-Book*, H, 407.
25. 33, M. Paris, v. 121–4.
27. 3, Hall, 675.
29. 26, Fabyan, 467; 31, *Chron. Angliae*, 51; 38, Nicolas, *Lond. Chron.* 70.
30. 5, *id.* 76; 11, Froissart, xiv. 258–61; ed. Kervyn de Lettenhove. See also Higden, *Polychronicon*, ix. 241, and *Letter-Book*, H, 353.
31. 19, Nicolas, *Lond. Chron.* 91, 22, *id. ib.* Leland, *Collectanea*, i. 486; 31, *Gregory's Chron.* 171, *C.P.R.* Henry VI, ii. 38.
32. 1, *Chron. Lond.* 150; 15, Fabyan, 618; 25, *Chron. Lond.* 156–7; 31, *id.* 179, Bentley, *Excerpta Historica*, 176–222.
35. 24, *C.P.R.* Edw. III, iii. 94, 107.
36. 2, *Gregory Chron.* 222–3.
37. 22, *Cal. Inq. p. m.* iii. 48.
38. 8, *Anc. Deeds*, B, 2135–62.
39. 33, *Cal. Inq. p. m.* iv. 261.
40. 25, Madox, *Hist. Exchequer*, i. 514; 29, *Rot. Litt. Pat.* i. 5; 35, *Harley MS.* 540, ff. 68–9, see vol. i. p. lxxxix.
41. 31, *Cal. Wills*, ii. 429; 32, *id.* i. 221, 503, 515, ii. 406, 519.
42. 6, *C.P.R.* Edw. II, i. 211; 24, *Cal. Charter Rolls*, i. 143, *Mon. Angl.* vi. 683.
43. 8, cf. *C.P.R.* Henry VI, iii. 157.
44. 6, Hall, 640; 11, *id.* 703; 25, *id.* 753–5.
46. 8, Leland, *Collectanea*, i. 108; 17, *Chron. Lond.* 64–5.
48. 29, M. Paris, iii. 232, cf. *C.P.R.* Henry III, iii. 2, 5.
49. 17, M. Paris, iv. 302, vi. 476; 24, *Ann. Mon.* iii. 222; 32, *Flores Historiarum*, iii. 331–4.
50. 21, *Cal. Close Rolls*, Edw. II, i. 532, *Letter-Book*, E, 255; 31, Baylis, *Temple Church*, 56–7.
51. 16, *Anom. Chron.* 515.
55. 10, *id.* 514.
56. 25, *Mon. Angl.* vi. 171; 37, *Ann. Mon.* iii. 430.
57. 5, *Mon. Angl.* vi. 172; 10, *Ann. Mon.* iii. 451.
58. 23, *Letters and Papers*, xv. 498 (iii).
60. 28, *Flores Historiarum*, iii. 104; Hemingburgh, ii. 232; 31, Knighton, ii. 235; 38, *id.* ii. 321.
61. 7, *Chron. Angliae*, 122; 18, *id.* 138; 36, *Anom. Chron.* 518.
62. 3–7, *C.P.R.* Edw. IV, ii. 85; 8, Holinshed, iii. 532.
63. 5, Leland, *Collectanea*, i. 113.
64. 9, *Gent. Mag. Libr.* xv. 182–9; 26, *Letter-Book*, E, 243; 34, Thorne ap. Twysden, *Scriptores Decem*, 1932.
65. 18, *Letters and Papers*, xv. 942 (36).
66. 24, *Ann. Mon.* iii. 425; 25, *id.* iii. 427; 31, *id.* iii. 428; 35, *id. ib.*
67. 1, *id.* iii. 433; 4, *id.* iii. 442; 8, *id.* iii. 478; 13, *id.* iii. 480; 16, *id.* iii. 483; 19, *id.* iii. 485.
68. 11, *Mun. Gild.* II. ii. 435, *C.P.R.* Edw. III, i. 36; 14, *id.* i. 377, *Letter-Book*, F, 37–8; 16, *Mun.Gild.*I.169, II.ii.433, *C.P.R.* Henry IV, iii. 207; 17, Birch, 80, Maitland, i. 202; 18, *id.* i. 242–7.
70. 30, *Mun. Gild.* I. 136, II. i. 44.
71. 14, *Cal. Inq. p. m.* iii. 165; 26, *Chron. Lond.* 147, 153, *Three Fifteenth Century Chronicles*, 63.
72. 32, *Chron. Lond.* 132.
73. 26, *Mon. Angl.* iv. 391; 28, cf. Machyn, *Diary*, 215.
76. 15, *Engl. Hist. Review*, xi. 740; 24, *Letter-Book*, E, 165; 25, *Memorials*, 614; 34, *Chron. Lond.* 187.
78. 33, *Liber S. Bartholomei*, cap. xxii.
80. 25, Leland, *Collectanea*, i. 113.
81. 9, Bearcroft, *Historical Account of Charterhouse*, 167–73, *Cal. Wills*, ii. 62; 20, G. le Baker, *Chron.* 99.
82. 17, *Mon. Angl.* vi. 9.

83. 18, *C.P.R.* Henry VI, ii. 105.
84. 14, *Anom. Chron.* 516.
85. 32, *Mon. Angl.* iv. 81.
88. 8, Holinshed, iv. 365; 18, *Cal. Charter Rolls*, i. 51, *Cal. Close Rolls*, 1227–30, p. 21, cf. *Lib. de Ant. Legg.* 5.
89. 5, M. Paris, iv. 243; 18, *id.* v. 127; 28, *C.P.R.* Edw. I. i. 147.
90. 3, M. Paris, iv. 287; 13, *Cal. Wills*, i. 218 *n.*; 32, Leland, *Collectanea*, i. 112, cf. *C.P.R.* Edw. IV, i. 136.
91. 35, *Cal. Charter Rolls*, i. 292.
93. 2, *C.P.R.* Edward II, i. 286; 24, *Flores Historiarum*, iii. 87; 33, *Cal. Charter Rolls*, i. 292.
94. 21, Knighton, ii. 118; 25, *id.* ii. 134.
95. 1, *Anom. Chron.* 515.
96. 2, *C.P.R.* Richd. II, ii. 476.
98. 2, Roper, *Life of More*, 3, ed. Hearne; 32, *C.P.R.* Richd. II, i. 78; 37, Hall, 816.
99. 9, *Hist. Dunelm. Scriptores*, 138 (Surtees Soc.).
100. 31, Leland, *Collectanea*, i. 113.
101. 3, *id. ib.* i. 111; 9, *Cal. Charter Rolls*, i. 269; 15, *id.* ii. 353.
102. 7, Nichols. *Progresses of Queen Elizabeth*, iii. 45.
103. 1, *Rot. Parl.* ii. 253; 3, *Statutes at Large*, i. 275–84; 14, Avesbury, 431; 23, *Rot. Parl.* ii. 268–9; 37, *id.* ii. 301, Hall, *Hist. Custom-Revenue*, i. 223.
104. 11, *Foedera*, iii. 1068; 19, *Rot. Parl.* iii. 279, 368.
105. 13, Walsingham, *Hist. Angl.* i. 114.
106. 9, S. Bentley, *Westminster Charters*, 42; 14, M. Paris, iii. 59; 17, *id.* iv. 427; 20, *id.* v. 29, 49; 31, *Flores Historiarum*, iii. 104.
112. 15, *Statutes at Large*, ii. 281; 17, Bentley, *Westminster Charters*, 42; 37, Gale, *Scriptores*, i. 62.
113. 7, M. Paris, ii. 110; 20, *Materials for Hist. of T. Becket*, iii. 19; 37, M. Paris, iii. 470; 39, *id.* iv. 83.
114. 5, *id.* iv. 177; 6, *id.* iv. 263; 12, *Lib. de Ant. Legg.* 23; 25, *Flores Historiarum*, iii. 17, 19; 27, *id.* iii. 18, Flor. Wig. ii. 203; 34, M. Paris, iii. 339.
115. 3, *id.* iv. 230; 7, *Flores Historiarum*, iii. 104; 12, *Flores Historiarum*, iii. 115–7; *Ann. Lond.* 132; 20, Trokelowe, *Annals*, 98; Walsingham, *Hist. Angl.* i. 149.
117. 10, *Vita Ricardi II*, 131–3, ed. Hearne; 22, *Rot. Parl.* iii. 415.
120. 11, *Rot. Chartarum*, 161.
122. 27, Maitland, ii. 1311.
123. 32, M. Paris, v. 575.
124. 11, *Statutes at Large*, ii. 645–7, 27 Eliz. c. 13; 30, Gale, *Scriptores*, iii. 292–3.
125. 13, *Mun. Gild.* II, ii. 630–2; Bede, *Hist. Eccl.* i. 4.
126. 25, Labbé, *Concilia*, ii. 476; 33, Bede, *Hist. Eccl.* i. 23.
128. 6, *Flores Historiarum*, i. 331; 22, Hoveden, i. 6; 29, *id.* i. 18; 38, Gale, *Scriptores*, i. 15.
130. 5, M. Paris, ii. 134; 38, Coggeshall, 188.
131. 2, *id. ib.* M. Paris, iii. 66; 17, *id.* iii. 193; 36, *id.* iii. 331.
132. 14, Flor. Wig. ii. 189; 16, *id.* ii. 190; 21, *id. ib.*; 23, *id.* ii. 212; 26, *id. ib.*; 28, *id.* ii. 223; 30, *Letter-Book*, C, 4, *Memorials*, 28.
133. 25, Murimouth, Cont. 195 (Engl. Hist. Soc.).
134. 17, *Mon. Angl.* vi. 704.
145. 22, Hoveden, iv. 135–6; 36, *Memorials*, 230, *Letter-Book*, F, 138.
146. 16, cf. *Letter-Books*, G, 27–31, H, 343; 25, *Memorials*, 384.
147. 10, Asser, 83, Flor. Wig. i. 151, Marianus Scotus, 154; 20, Fabyan, 293.
150. 23, *Mun. Gild.* II. i. 249, Birch, 13–15.
151. 7, *Mon. Angl.* vi. 624.
153. 1, *Mun. Gild.* I. 136; 23, *id.* II. i. 44, Birch, 26, 28–31.
154. 23, *Monumenta Franciscana*, ii. 18.
155. 22, *Mon. Angl.* vi. 622; 23, *Mun. Gild.* I. 136, Birch, 32.
156. 13, *id.* 34.
157. 17, *Lib. de Ant. Legg.* 56; 24, *id.* 78–9, Flor. Wig. ii. 195.
158. 6, *Ann. Lond.* 81; 8, *Lib. de Ant. Legg.* 90.
159. 8, *Ann. Lond.* 88.
160. 7, *Mun. Gild.* II. i. 328–9.

162. 19, *Letter-Books*, D. 244, E. 63; 24, *id.* D, 282; 31, *Mun. Gild.* II. ii. 678.

163. 3, *Gregory Chron.* 75, Nicolas, *Lond. Chron.* 45; 20, *Mun. Gild.* II. i. 371–4; 28, *Letter-Book*, E, 179–80.

164. 1, *Ann. Paul.* 316–17; 9, *Mun. Gild.* II. ii. 438–44, Birch, 52–9; *Ann. Paul.* 325–32; 25, G. le Baker, *Chron.* 48; 33, *Mon. Angl.* vi. 703–4.

165. 5, *C.P.R.* Edw. III, vi. 489; 9, *Cal. Wills*, i. 674; 23, *Letter-Book*, F. 83.

166. 18. *Memorials*, 267; 32, Bentley, *Westminster Charters*, 43.

167. 34, *Cal. Wills*, ii. 180, *Letter-Book*, H, 63 *n*, *C.P.R.* Henry VI, ii. 217.

168. 11, *Chron. Angliae*, 123; 12, *Letter-Book*, H, 38, 60; 19, *Chron. Angliae*, 199; 23, *Cal. Wills*, ii. 275–6; 30, *Mon. Angl.* vi. 1380.

169. 2, *Chron. Angliae*, 360; 8, *C.P.R.* Richd. II, ii. 149; 13, *Chron. Angliae*, 370; 24, Nicolas, *Lond. Chron.* 79; 28, Walsingham, *Hist. Angl.* ii. 208, *Letter-Book*, H. p. liii, 379–81; 33, *id.* 407, *Rot. Parl.* iii. 317–18.

170. 28, *Chron. Lond.* 64; *Gregory Chron.* 104; 32, Walsingham, *Hist. Angl.* ii. 276.

171. 7, Nicolas, *Lond. Chron.* 91; 12, *id.* 93; 25, *Memorials*, 513–14.

172. 3, *Letter-Book*, H, 439; 20, See Note on p. 315 above; 26, See Note on p. 277 above; 35, See Note on pp. 309–10 above.

173. 14, *Cal. Wills*, ii. 499; 30, Fabyan, 612, cf. *C.P.R.* Henry VI, iii. 163, 232, 345; 34, Orridge, *Illustrations of Jack Cade's Rebellion*, 8.

174. 4, *C.P.R.* Henry VI, ii. 369; 13, *Chron. Lond.* 156; 34, *Chron. Lond.* 164 *n*.

175. 3, *id.* 164; 10, *id.* 166.

176. 5, Fabyan, 656; 13, *Chron. Lond.* 182; 17, *id.* 185; 32, Fabyan, 663.

177. 8, *Chron. Lond.* 187; 12, *id. ib.*; 16, *id.* 188.

178. 2, *id.* 193; 29, *id.* 198.

179. 3, *id.* 215; 6, *id.* 224; 21, *id.* 234.

193. 3, M. Paris, iii. 336; 13, *Lib. de Ant. Legg.* 249; 21, *Gesta Henrici Quinti*, 61–8; 26, *Chron. Lond.* 97–115, *Mun. Gild.* III. 457–64.

194. 1, *Chron. Lond.* 193.

GLOSSARY

A

abashed, afraid : 'the Queene remayned right sore abashed,' i. 244.
abbeyes, abbess, i. 126.
ABC or **absey**; primer, hornbook (*N.E.D.*, quoting Shaks. *K. John*, I. i. 196), ii. 256.
abiding house: 'this was the Abbot's abiding house when he came to London,' ii. 16.
aboundance, abundance: 'He prouided from beyond the seas Corne in great aboundance, so that the Citie was able to serue the countrie,' ii. 169.
abstinencie, i. 83.
aburn, auburn: 'the hair of his head aburn,' ii. 57.
achates (cates), provisions, i. 350; *lit.* 'things purchased.'
acquit: 'The Queene was to acquite her Church therof,' i. 139. Cf. i. 199.
Actiuities, acrobatic performances, Comedies, &c., ii. 369.
— to show, i. 245.
adhorting, i. 4.
adiudged, sentenced, i. 51.
aduenture, *v.*, venture, i. 100.
aduertized: 'whereof when the Earle was aduertized,' i. 67.
aduouterie, adultery, i. 189.
advowsion, advowson, i. 131. Lat. *advocationem.* Cf. *Auotion.*
afterclappes, later surprises; i.e. unwelcome contingencies in the shape of expense of upkeep, i. 142.
against, again, ii. 196.
agast, *p. pple.*; also **agasted,** i. 97.
alablaster, i. 330.
alay, alloy, i. 55.
aldermanry, ward, i. 117; office of alderman, i. 310–11.
ale-cunners, -conners, 'examiners or inspectors of ale; earliest known use in *Liber Albus*' (*N.E.D.*), ii. 97.
Alhallon Eve, All Saints' Eve (Oct. 31), i. 97.
allayed (of coins), i. 55.
of alliance to, related to, i. 36.
Almaine, Haunce of, i. 136. See *Hanse* in Index III.
almaine rivets, i. 102; 'a kind of light armour, first used in Germany, in which great flexibility was obtained by overlapping plates sliding on rivets' (*N.E.D.*).
Almerie: 'the Almerie, or house of Almes for conuarts and poore children,' ii. 63.
almesehouses, i. 299, 302.
ambergris, amber, i. 80.
amblers, i. 80; trotters, *ib.*
amerce, *v. a.*, ii. 7.
amerciaments, fines, ii. 119; **amercements,** i. 271.
ancris, ankeress, i. 164.
angelets (vis. viii*d.*), **half angels,** and **farthings** (vs. vi*d.*) coined, 1465, i. 56.
angell noble, the, sixth part of an ounce troy, i. 56.
annoyances, nuisances, ii. 124.
annoyed, injured, i. 196.
'**Anthonie pigges**' and '**pigeons of Paules**' (schoolboy amenities), i. 75. See i. 184 and note on p. 301; and Halliwell. 'St. Anthonie was always figured with a pig following him' (Stow).
Apernes of Mayle, i. 103.
appeached, impeached, accused, i. 100.
appeached of treason, ii. 75.
appellators, i. 189. See *Articuli Cleri Anglicani oblati Edw.* 2 *Regi an.* 1316 *cap.* 10: *Placet etiam Domino Regi ut Latrones et Appellatores, quandocumque voluerint, possint sacerdotibus sua facinora confiteri.*
appendant, *adj.*, vnto the said soken, i. 64.
apposers and answerers, i. 74.
apprehend, arrest, ii. 49.
appurtenances, i. 65.
— of a manor, i. 153 and *passim.*
— 'the manor of Charlton, with the appurtenances,' ii. 66.
Arches, Court of the, i. 254.
'**Archers** in coats of white fustian, **signed** on the breast and back with the armes of the Cittie,' i. 102.
argent, Easterling money so called, i. 52.

aristocritie, the, aristocracy, ii. 199.
armors, armament, i. 158.
armour, sets of arms, i. 107.
arriue, *v.n.*, to come to shore, i. 6.
arrows : standard, broad arrow, and **flight** ; '**broad arrow,** an arrow with a broad head for cleaving ; **flight,** a long and well-feathered arrow for long-distance shooting' (*N.E.D.*). Cf. 'a good flight shoot,' ii. 74.
artificial, skilfully constructed, i. 18.
ascendings vp, staircases, ii. 118.
assay, *v.*, essay, i. 100.
assesse, *subs.*, assessment, ii. 213.
assise, law fixing the price of bread, meat, &c. The regulation or assessment of the weight or price of bread, &c. The ordinance in which such regulation is embodied. Cf. 'Assize of weights and measures,' ii. 97.
— inches of, i. 162.
— perches of, i. 10.
— tailor's yards of, i. 102.
assise of bread, the, ii. 156. See Index III.
assurance, to take of, i. 9.
attaint, *p.p.*, attainted, ii. 76.
Auerell, April, i. 157.
auoid, *v.n.*, depart, ii. 263; 'that all leprose persons should auoid within 15 daies.' Cf. ii. 146, and 'auoyd dyvel,' *Introduction*, p. liii.
— *v.a.*, *ib.*, remove from ; 'all leprose persons to be voided the citie & suburbs.' Cf. i. 214, 'which ⟨charge⟩ the Chancellor by oath on the Sacrament auoideth.'
auotion, advowson, i. 131 ; also *avoweson*. Cf. *Advowsion*.

B

backsyde, ii. 369.
banck[it]ing ⟨Stow's error⟩ on the Riuer Thames, standing on bank of, i. 68, 336; ii. 13.
banketting, banqueting, ii. 131.
'**Banqueting houses,** like Banqueroutes, bearing great show and little worth,' ii. 78 *marg.*
Bannerer of London, chief, i. 62.
barbican, i. 70, 302 ; 'an outer fortification or defence to a city or castle ; of uncertain origin, perhaps from Arabic or Persian' (*N.E.D.*).
baronry of Little Dunmow, the, i. 61.
barons ⟨freemen⟩, Londoners so called, i. 94, 315, 339. Cf. the Barons of the Cinque Ports, and see *N.E.D.*
barres, the, 'a marke shewing how farre the liberties of the Citie do extend,' i. 127.
baselard, a sort of dagger, *pugio*, (Stratmann), i. 219. 'The Mayor having received his stroke, drew his basiliard ⟨dagger, *sica* or *pugio* : '*traha sa baselarde*,' Anom. Chron. 520⟩, and grievously wounded *Wat*.'
basons, an offender rung with = 'rough music,' i. 190–1.
Bassenet, a light helmet, worn sometimes with a movable front (Halliwell) : 'The Maior had on his head a **Basonet,**' i. 219.
baston, club, bat. 'The scholars of every school have their ball, or baston, in their hands,' i. 92. Cf. Swift's 'hugeous battoons' (*J. to S.*).
battailes, battalions, i. 103.
battle, a light river boat, i. 206 ; *dimin.* of Fr. *bateau*.
Bawdrike, a, of gold about his ⟨the Mayor's⟩ necke trilling ⟨trailing⟩ down behind him, ii. 193.
bayled, having a half-hoop to support the cover of a wagon, &c., ii. 82 (of the Fraerie Cart).
Baylie, the Old, ii. 38, from Lat. *balium* or *ballium*. The Old Bailey was so called from the ancient *bailey* or *ballium* of the city wall between Ludgate and Newgate. Cf. Stow on 'Old Bayly,' ii. 37, and note on p. 362.
Baylywicke, Bailiff-wick, ii. 146. '**Bailie, baillie** (Lat. *balliva*), **bailiwick,** the limit of the authority of a sheriff, bailiff, or other officer' (Nichols' *Britton*, Glossary).
beam, the common, i. 156; supportation and charges of, *ib.*; farmer of it, *ib.* '*The Common or King's Beam* was the public standard balance formerly in the custody of the Grocers Company' (*N.E.D.*). See Index III.
beame-light and lamp, i. 271.
beasts of venery, of the chase, i. 306.
beautify, i. 103, 306 : a word hated of Shakespeare : 'the most beautified Ophelia' ; 'that's an ill phrase, a vile phrase ; "beautified" is a vile phrase' (*Hamlet*, II. ii. 110).
became, came, i. 119.
bedred, bedridden, i. 128.
belike, possibly, ii. 49.
bell : 'That faire steeple hath but one bell, as Friers were wont to use,' i. 202.
beneficially, i. 43.
benevolence : 'The citizens gave first a great benevolence, and after that the fifteenes to be speedily paid,' i. 332.

beseechers, petitioners, i. 159.
bestow much, spend much, i. 80.
bestowing, contributing, i. 101.
bet, *pret.* of beat, *Introd.* p. liv; i. 279.
beweld, wield: 'no man can beweld it ⟨Gerard's staff⟩,' ii. 353.
bewray, to betray, i. 266.
bin, been, ii. 70 and *passim.*
Biscay, Bay of, salt from, ii. 10; see *N.E.D.*, and Kingsford, *Chronicles of London*, Glossary, *s.v.* 'baysalt.'
Bishops' alms dishes given to the poor, i. 89, 91.
bisket, to serue H.M. Shippes, i. 125.
Blacke Parliament, i. 340.
Blanch Charters, i.e. *blank*, i. 265.
blanks (coining term): 'round plates, called blanks, deliuered by weight,' i. 52.
blowed: 'the Keeper blowed the death of the Bucke, and then the horners presently answered him,' i. 334. Cf. Madden's *Diary of Master Silence* (ed. 1907), pp. 49, 57.
bolion, bullion, i. 54.
boltas mootes, and putting of cases, i. 78; 'readinges, meetings, boltinges, and other learned exercises,' *ib.*, l. 16. See note on p. 281.
bonefiers: 'called as well of good amitie amongest neighbours, as also for the virtue that a great fire hath to purge the infection of the ayre,' i. 101. The obvious derivation (*bone-fire*) is now generally accepted.
Books in use formerly sold by Stationers in Paternoster Row: viz. *A.B.C.* with *Paternoster*, *Aue*, *Creede*, *Graces*, &c.
boorde, began the, i. 36. Cf. Chaucer, ed. Skeat, vol. v, Notes to *C. T.*, *The Knight*, p. 6, 'had been placed at the head of the daïs, or table of state.'
bosse, a head or reservoir of water, i. 208 and *passim.*
bottelers, butlers, i. 95.
Bouche of Court, ii. 117. 'An allowance of victual granted by a king or noble to his household, his attendants on a military expedition, &c. Only with reference to the phrase *avoir bouche à* (*en, cour*)' (*N.E.D.*).
bounder, i. 291: prob. a corruption of *boundure* (*N.E.D.*), boundary.
bows and arrows of silver (school prizes), i. 75.
bowyers, i. 81, almost *worne out* with the Fletchers. The phrase recurs constantly in the *Survey*, e.g. i. 336. See Index III.
brabble, quarrel, ii. 55.
brake (of a gun), burst, i. 222.
braky = broke (of Sir Thomas Lodge, *Introd.*, xl), near bankruptcy.
Branched, damaske, i. 249: 'adorned with a figured . . . pattern in embroidery,' &c. (*N.E.D.*).
brast, *p. t.* burst, i. 148.
break up: 'Certaine Cittizens of London brake vp the Tunne vppon Cornhill, and took out prisoners,' ii. 161 (A.D. 1297). Cf. Matt. xxiv. 43 (A.V.).
brent, burnt, ii. 51.
bridge, a landing-stage. See 'Strand bridge'; and 'a fayre bridge and landing-place', ii. 122.
bridgemaisters, i. 60.
bringers-in, of patients to a hospital, i. 165.
broad cloath rowed or striped thwart, ii. 190; **broad cloathes**, i. 250.
brokers, sellers of old apparel, and such like, i. 129.
bruited: 'many fables have been bruted,' i. 292.
budge, i. 86: 'A kind of fur, consisting of lamb's skin, with the wool dressed outwards' (*N.E.D.*).
budget, ii. 19: 'a pouch, bag, or wallet, usually of leather' (*N.E.D.*).
bulworkes, of the Tower, &c., i. 9, 47–8.
Burdious, Burdeous, Bordeaux, i. 240, 243.
burel: 'burels or cloth listed,' i. 286; var. of **borrell**, *adj.*, **buret**, obs.; cf. Fr. *burac*, 'stuff that's halfe silke and half worsted' (Cotgrave); but this may be a dim. of *bure*. See *French Book of Rates* (1714), 36, 'Bures and Burets Stuff per 100 weight.' Cf. *Bureau* (*N.E.D.*).
burellers, or makers of the coarse stuff called 'burel', ii. 313.
burgage, to hold in, i. 35, 270: 'a form of Socage,' Cowell's *Interpreter*; 'A tenure whereby lands or tenements in cities and towns were held of the king or other lord for a certain yearly rent' (*N.E.D.*).
— 'Lands held of the King in burgage,' i. 288.
burganets, i. 102: 'burgonet, a very light casque or steel cap' (*N.E.D.*).
Burgh-Kenning, i. 70, 302: (acc. to Stow) = 'Barbican, as a *bikenning* is called *a Beacon*,' i. 302 [ghost-word].
burial, burial-place, i. 114 and *passim.*
burnt tile, i. 193.

C

called down (of coins), value diminished by proclamation, i. 57; 'called to a lower rate,' *ib.*

calling, name, i. 43.

'**came in with** the Conqueror,' i. 68.

Candlemas, Feast of the Purification (Feb. 2), i. 55, 97.

Cane-stone, i.e. from Caen in Normandy, i. 137.

canons, secular, ii. 307; **regular**, i. 140; ii. 47.

cap or pot verses, to, i. 72: see *N.E.D.* The *pot* was a light helmet worn later in the Civil Wars.

Cappers and **Hurrers** form company of Haberdashers, i. 298.

carack: a Spanish carrack; a large ship of burden, also fitted for warfare; a galleon, i. 75. This refers to the *Madre de Dios*—taken off the Azores in 1592. A prize of extraordinary value—after much plunder yielded £150,000. The cargo was stored at Leadenhall.

cariage, traffic, i. 35.

carit (carat), i. 56.

carriage, goods carried, i. 49; traffic, i. 34; cf. 'we took up our cariages, and went up to Jerusalem,' Acts xxi. 15 (A.V.).

carrie-load, i. 293: **carrie**, a small two-wheeled vehicle.

carted, carried in a cart through the streets by way of punishment, i. 190.

Carts of the Franchise of the Temple and S. Martin's le Grand; and of S. John of Jerusalem, i. 213.

carts, shodde, having iron rims to the wheels, i. 83, 169.

cast a trench, i. 8, &c. Cf. St. Luke xix. 43.

castellated, of a conduit, i. 300.

Castillon (Castellan), Robert, of London, ii. 14.

cattes lions, lion cubs, i. 48.

causeys, causeways, i. 112: Fr. *chaussée*, from *via calciata*, and Milton *P.L.* x. 415; so in Berners's trans. of Froissart (Skeat).

ceiled, provided with a ceiling, i. 145, 318.

'**Celerer**' to the Monastery, ii. 122.

cellarage, i. 138; cf. *Hamlet*, I. v. 151 (*selleredge*).

certaine, fixed: 'A certaine rent of x pound by the yeare,' ii. 50.

cessed, assessed, i. 129: **cess**, *subs.*, assessment, tax, or levy; cf. Shaks. 1 *Hen. IV*, II. i. 8 (and see *N.E.D.*).

chafron, i. 33: 'the frontlet of a barded horse' (*N.E.D.*).

chanons, canons, i. 140.

chaplen, chaplain, i. 137.

chaptered, arranged in chapters: 'I had long since gathered notes to haue chaptered,' ii. 187.

chare coale, charcoal, i. 148.

chargeable, costly, i. 60; 'large summes of monies,' *ib.*; also ii. 118. Cf. *Introduction*, lxvi.

charges, to the, at the cost of, i. 317.

charges and discharges, incomings and outgoings, i. 24. Cf. *Introduction*, lxvii.

charnell: 'before the chernell and Chappel of S. Edmond the Bishop,' i. 167.

charter warren, ii. 132: 'Warren, a franchise or place privileged, either by prescription, or grant from the King, to keep beasts and fowl of Warren; which are Hares and Conies, Partridges and Pheasants' (Cowell).

Chastilarie (for Chastellanie), i. 62.

chatysyd, chastised, ii. 347.

chaunteries, i. 41.

cheared, treated: 'they cheared all the Knightes and the Burgesses,' ii. 100.

checke roll, i. 88: 'A *Roll* or Book containing the Names of such as are Attendants in Pay to great Personages, as their Household Servants, 19 Car. 2, cap. 1. It is otherwise called *The Chequer Roll*, and seems to take its etymology from the Exchequer' (Cowell's *Interpreter*).

chest with three lockes, ii. 167.

Chief Butler of England, i. 143.

chirographer, i. 310: 'The officer appointed to engross fines in the Court of Common Pleas (abolished 1833)' (*N.E.D.*).

Church of England: 'Edward IV began his raigne the fourth of March in the yeare 1460 after the account of the Church of England,' ii. 175.

cider (also **sidar**), i. 87: in M.E. *sicer*, *cyder*, *syder* (*N.E.D.*); 'lit. strong drink (Judges xiii. 7), not necessarily from apples' (Skeat).

cistern, *v.a.*, i. 17; **cistern** (sestern), *subs.*, i. 17.

Citizen and paynter stayner of London, i. 302, 304; Serjeant Painter, i. 314.

City Courts enumerated, i. 271; Court of Requests commonly called the Court of Conscience, *ib.*

clapboord, i. 137: 'a smaller size of split oak, imported from N. Germany, and used by coopers for making barrel-staves, &c.' (*N.E.D.*).

clarkes, scholars, learned men, i. 99.
cleane decayed, i. 300; clean worn out, i. 81; a gate clean taken downe, i. 39.
clearke conuict, ii. 122: '*convict* not used in this sense till convict, *ppl. adj.*, began to go out of use' (*N.E.D. s.v.*).
Clearkes of the Greene Cloathe, i. 131. One of the departments of the Royal Household, having control of various matters of expenditure, discipline, &c. (see *N.E.D.*); so called from the green-covered table at which its business was originally transacted.
'**clipping**' or '**washing**' of coin, i. 55.
Cloath, coloured Mustard villars (a colour now out of vse), and two yeardes of Cloath coloured blew, price two shillinges the yeard, in all eight shillings. More, paied to *John Pope*, Draper, for two Gowne clothes eight yards of two colours, *lux ambo deux de roug* (or red) *medley brune* and porre (or purple) colour price the yeard 2*s.*, ii. 190.
clochard, a bell tower, ii. 120; **clochier**, i. 330; **clochiarde**, i. 331.
clocke house, ii. 121.
cloystry, cloister, i. 319.
coaped: 'the spring was coaped in, and arched over with hard stone,' i. 301. See also *cooped.*
cofferer, i. 85. 'An officer of the royal ⟨or other great⟩ household next under the Controller' (*N.E.D.*).
coffin, siluer, case, casket, i. 86; cf. Plat, *Delightes for Ladies* (in *N.E.D.*), 'Coffins of white plate.'
cognisance of the Blew Bore, i. 89.
combe, a, of corn, i. 206: 'a dry measure = 4 bushels' (*N.E.D.*).
combersome, awkward, i. 35.
— tangled, i. 2, 3.
commaunded, commended: 'This Schoole was commaunded in the raigne of H. the sixt, and sithence also aboue other,' i. 185.
comminaltie of London, i. 153 (also **communalitie**, i. 319).
commoditie, advantage, i. 54: 'Commodity, the bias of the world' (Shaks. *K. John* II. 573).
commodity, convenience, ii. 169.
commons, to keep, i. 231: 'diuers Judges and Sergeants at the law keep a Commons there,' ii. 47.
commune, commonalty, i. 157.
competently, adequately, i. 101.
composition, agreement, i. 237.
composition, arrangement, i. 166.

Compter (more recently **Counter**). 'The prison attached to a City Court... In this sense, the official spelling from the 17th century was *Compter*' (*N.E.D.*).
Compters, The, i. 37, 115, 308. See Index III.
concluded, determined: 'it was concluded, the Image of Iesus to be curiously painted on the wall in Paules Church,' i. 337.
conduct, i. 146: 'a salaried chaplain' (*N.E.D.*).
conductes, conduits, i. 80.
Conduit vpon Cornhill was this yere ⟨1401⟩ made of an old prison house called the *Tunne*, ii. 170.
conference, comparison, i. 81.
confidence, in, i.e. in trust, i. 116.
Congregations against the Fishmongers, i. 214–15.
conseruer, generall of the ... Recordes (i. e. the Tower), i. 59.
continuall, continuous (*passim*).
continuation, continuance, i. 254.
controuersies, to take vp, settle, ii. 97.
conuented before certain commissioners at Lambeth, ii. 135.
conuey, to appropriate: 'He first dissolued the Quire, conueyed the plate and ornaments, then the bells,' i. 185. Cf. 'conuey, the wise it call' (Shaks. *Merry Wives*, I. iii. 32).
conuict, *p.p.*, convicted, i. 215.
cookerie or cookes row, i. 79.
cooped: 'the spring is cooped about with stone,' i. 16; 'a bridge of stone faire coaped,' i. 25, 26; coping, i. 26; curbed, i. 34.
cope, *v. n.*: 'the Champions coaped together,' i. e. contended, i. 33.
copy: 'S. Eyre, sometime an Vpholster, then by *changing of his copie* a Draper,' i. 153 *marg.*
coriars, curriers, ii. 191.
corrected: 'Basset corrected (i. e. reformed) the Bakers,' &c., ii. 177.
cottage: the Guildhall anciently a little cottage, i. 271.
Cotton, umple, 'fine lawne, Paris threed, Cotton, Vmple, and other linnin clothes,' i. 217.
couched, put away, hidden, i. 38.
couent, convent, i. 35.
couerture ⟨covering⟩ of mens heads was then hoodes, ii. 195.
counsell vnto, of: 'Sir John Allen, sometime ... of counsell vnto King Henry the eight,' i. 132.

countenance: 'for greater countenance of the wonder,' ii. 353; cf. ii. 203.
counters, nails, and **points,** played for at cards on festivals, i. 97 (all mentioned as things of little intrinsic value).
courses: 'the Justes began, and many commendable courses were run,' ii. 30–1.
Coursitors, ii. 88: 'The 34 Clerks of the Court of Chancery, whose office it was to make out all original writs *de cursu*' (*N.E.D*).
Court and Leete, ii. 97: *T. of S.*, Induction, ii. 89; cf. 'Keep courts and law days', *Othello*, III. iii. 140, and **Leet,** *inf.*
Court of the Arches: 'the Court of the Arches is kept in this (Bow) Church, and taketh name of the place, not the place of the Court,' i. 254.
coynes: 'Pophame dyed rich, leauing great treasure of strange coynes,' ii. 33.
coyning irons, i. 54: 'viz. Standard or Staple, and two Trussels or Punchons.'
cramping, pricking, cause to be seized with cramp, i. 59.
cranage up, drawing up by cranes, i. 135.
— of wares and merchandise, i. 135.
crane, *v.*: 'the marchants of Bordeaux craned their wines out of Lighters,' i. 238.
cresset, an iron vessel containing materials for burning, i. 102: *N.E.D.* quotes Milton, *P. L.* i. 728.
crest and vent: 'the Conduit of sweet water castellated with crest and vent,' i. 211.
Cross, the, on coins, i. 52.
— 'An ancient ensigne of Christianitie', i. 267.
— an ancient, called 'The Standart without the north doore of S. Paul's Church,' *ib.*
— 'a cross, double to the ring, between fower rowals of sixe poyntes,' i. 52.
Crowched Friars, crutched friers, so called from wearing a cross, i. 139.
Crowdes (crypt) of the Cathedral Church of Pauls, i. 329; also **Shrowdes.**
Crown, pleas of the, i. 50.
Crowner, a, of the Lord Mayor's house, ii. 188; cf. *Hml.* v. i. 4.
Crownsilde *or* **Tamarsilde,** i. 257: selda = *taberna mercatoria* (Ducange).
cultars of iron, i. 111; ploughshares; Lat. *culter.*
currall (coral), i. 169.
curraunt, ii. 353.
cursing by the Cleargie, excommunication, i. 351.
curtelarge, curtilage, i. 200.
curtise, courteous, ii. 353.
curtoled, curtailed, ii. 125.
custom, of, customarily, i. 117.
customer, customs officer, i. 135.
customer of London outward, a custom-house officer for exports, i. 114.
Customers Key (Quay), i. 43.
custos set over the City, i. 51.
custos, as *plur.*: 'Nic. Marshall & Ri. Coxe were Custos (*sic*) or Wardens,' i. 147; 'Vnder flat stones do lye diuers Custos of the chappel,' i. 274.
cutlars: 'Three Artes or sortes of workmen in Cutlars' Company; viz. (1) Bladers; (2) Haftmakers; (3) Sheathmakers, later forming one fraternity,' i. 245.

D

Dairie houses, or Cottages, wherein they make butter and cheese, are vsually called **Wickes,** i. 218 ⟨?⟩.
damasked: 'an habit of purple damasked down to his feet,' ii. 57.
damnified, injured, i. 101, 347.
Dance of Death (or of Paules), i. 109.
Deepe Ditch by Bethlehem, i. 165.
Defendants or **Undertakers,** opponents at Turney, ii. 99.
delators, informers, ii. 119.
delectable, ii. 347.
delicatenesse, delicacies, i. 79.
Demilaunces on great horses; light horsemen armed with demi-lances, i. 102, 103.
Demise, ii. 14; 'conveyance or transfer of an estate by will or lease' (*N.E.D.*).
Democratie, or **Aristocratie,** ii. 206.
denarii, Latin, i. 53.
denison (denizen), a, or free English, ii. 67.
denting in (of a wall), i. 9; opposed to 'as straight as the string of a bow.'
departed, parted, i. 33; 'how the . . . heraulds departed therewith I have not read,' i. 237.
depict, depicted, ii. 62.
deriue, to divert: 'deriue the river of Thames, with her tides, to haue flowed about it,' i. 28.
dilicately, i. 80.
dirte, dearth, i. 157.
disarmed, of launces, i. 84, 92.
discease, decease, i. 289 (*bis*).
discharged of assise and warde, i. 113.

discommoditie, inconvenience, i. 46.
disdainly, disdainfully, ii. 252.
disguisings, masques and masquerades, i. 97 ; ii. 116.
dispatch, to effect hastily, i. 44.
dispend, to spend, i. 340 ; 'This Hospital . . . was valued to dispend 478. pounds,' i. 167.
dispense, expense, ii. 225.
dispensed with : 'Dr. Bull is dispensed with to read the Musick lecture in English only,' i. 76.
dissimule, *v.a.*, ii. 78.
distracted : 'an hospital for distracted people,' i. 164.
distraight, i. 165.
distraine : 'to distraine the said parishioners,' i. 14; ii. 114.
domesmen, or judges of the King's Court, ii. 149.
Doomesday book, the, ii. 147.
Dortar (-er, -our), dormitory, i. 319.
dowked, ducked, i. 94.
drawne : 'a new foundation was drawne,' i. 60 ; a Porter of the Tower drawne, hanged, and headed, i. 58.
Draye man : 'the Draye man sitteth . . . on his Drea,' i. 83.
drown (of ships), sink, ii. 71.
drowned with : 'Duke of Clarence drowned with Malmsey in the Tower,' i. 58.
drowning in Thames, execution by, i. 65.
dubbing the Maior knight, ii. 116.

E

easements, conveniences, accommodations, i. 135.
Eastarling pence, first made by the Easterlings in England, *temp.* Henry II, i. 53; other derivations of the name, i. 54; cf. i. 178.
edified, built, i. 39.
eftsoones, again; forthwith, immediately, i. 6.
eldarne (elder) trees, i. 34.
Elemosinary or **Almory**, at Westminster, now corruptly the **Aumbry**, ii. 123.
Elmes in Smithfield, the, place of execution, i. 48, 49, 51, 65 ; ii. 29.
eln, iron, the King's : containing in length 83, half, quarter, and half quartern of, i. 140.
embattoled, embattled, i. 66.
embezzled (imbeseled), stolen.
embrotherer, embroiderer, ii. 65.
emortising and **propriation** ; amortising = alienation in mortmain (*N.E.D.*), i. 166.
encounter companion : 'I will not fayle an encounter companion,' ii. 33.
encroachment, i. 119.
endamaged, i. 60.
engine, mechanism, i. 41.
engrosse : 'merchants engrosse old florins or nobles,' i. 55; 'coins of gold enhaunced, and allayed,' *ib.*
enhanced, *p.p.*; **enhauncing**, *v.s.*, to enhance, to raise the value of a coin, commodity, &c., i. 56.
Enirode [?], ii. 104.
enormities, abuses needing reformation, i. 83.
— crimes of violence, i. 101.
enterlaced, ii. 208.
enterludes, i. 15.
Enthimems . . . imperfect sillogismes; a syllogism in which one premiss is suppressed, i. 72 ; see *N.E.D.*
erect, erected, i. 130.
Ermony, Armenia, i. 71.
Escheator, ex-, an officer who received the escheats of the Crown (Stubbs), i. 35.
Esses, a collar of, ii. 57.
Estates of England, great personages, ii. 71.
esteemation, estimation, i. 319.
Esterling pence, plates to be coined into, ii. 259.
Esterlings, a riot made upon the, i. 178.
euerie ⟨one⟩ of these foure, i. 60.
euery ⟨one of⟩ these Wardes, i. 120.
Euil May Day, insurrection of prentices, &c., against aliens, May Day 1517, i. 99, 143, 152. See Index III.
Exchaunger, the King's, i. 49.
Exchetor, i. 35; from *Escheat* : 'an officer that taketh notice of the escheats of the King in the county whereof he is *Escheator*, and certifieth them into the Exchequer' (Cowell's *Interpreter*). See also **Escheator.** Lands and goods of Jews *excheated* to the king, i. 279.
Exchetre, the King's, i. 39; **Escaetor**, i. 42 ; the King's exchetes, i. 280.
exhibited : 'a petition exhibited by the commons to the common councell, and by them allowed' (approved), i. 157.
exhibition, i. 77.
— funds supplied by parents and friends, i. 77.
exhibitors of petitions, i. 214.
expulsed : 'the number of Jews then expulsed were 15,060 persons,' i. 281.

F

fabule, to, i. 34, 305, 348.

fabulous book, a, i. 220.

fact, crime, i. 190; 'his detestable facts,' crimes, deeds, i. 90, 254.

Faculty, i. e. the King of Armes, Heraults, and Purseuantes, &c., ii. 17.

fadome, fathom, i. 160.

fall-gate, ii. 73: 'a gate across a public road' (*N.E.D.*).

false packing, conspiracy (in collections of money), ii. 216.

false roof against the weather, i. 332.

fantasied, as some have, i. 286.

far-fetch, *v.*, i. 14.

fastnes, a fortress, i. 4; see *N.E.D.*

fautor, friend and, ii. 215.

fealty in free socage, ii. 69: Free socage, also called common socage, is opposed to base socage = villenage.

feared ⟨terrified⟩ by Prognostications, which declared that in the year of Christ 1524, there should be such Eclipses in watrie signes, and such **conjunctions** that by waters and floudes many people should perish ... all things necessary within him ⟨i. e. in his own house⟩, ii. 27.

feast folower: 'I [Stow] was neuer feast folower,' ii. 191.

fee farme⟨s⟩: 'Lands held in fee by rendering for them yearly the true value, or more or less; which rent if the feoffes cease to pay for two years together, an action thereby accrues to the feoffors their heirs, to demand the tenements in demesne; for which tenements neither homage, wardship, marriage, nor relief can be demanded without specialty in writing' (*Britton*, ed. Oxford, 1865, ii. 5, 6).

fee ferme (Lat. *feodi firma*), 'a free tenure, the services of which were rendered in money' (Nichols's *Britton*, Glossary). Fee-farm rent of a borough (Gross).

feere: 'in feere,' in company, i. 252.

feet, of St. Paul, i. 318.

feffement, i. 115, 349: 'the act of investing a person with a fief or fee' (*N.E.D.*).

feffles, feoffees, i. 115.

feleper, broker, ii. 361.

fellowship or **companie incorporate,** i. 158, 273.

Fellowships of the cittie (Companies), i. 273.

felmongers, skinners, i. 132.

fels, skins, i. 156.

feoffment, i. 349.

feoffment, feoffor, feoffee: see Stephen, quoted in Earle's *L.C.* p. xvii.

fereno, ironmonger, i. 281; see note, p. 335.

ferling, farthing, i. 53: 'the fourth part of a sterling' (Bp. Fleetwood in *N.E.D.*); 'the quarter of a denarius' (Gross).

ferrer, a shoer of horses, a worker in iron, ii. 172.

feruently: 'The fire burst out again more feruently,' i. 326.

fewters (or idle people, *lit.* 'keepers of greyhounds' (*N.E.D.*)), ii. 39. See note, p. 363.

flered out (of William Longbeard), ii. 216.

fifteene, a, a tax formerly imposed on all kinds of personal property, i. 13, 128.

filed, defiled, ii. 13.

finding ⟨i. e. support⟩ of 13 poor people for euer, ii. 168 and *passim*.

fishfull: 'the fishfull riuer of Thames,' i. 8.

Flanders tile brought from Normandy, i. 30; Britain or Roman Tile, i. 160.

floren of gold, called of the Florentines, makers thereof, i. 53; 'The old Floren or noble [*c.* 1351] ... worth much above the taxed rate of the new,' i. 55.

florences, gold, i. 51, 57 *bis*.

fodder, fother, i. 153: 'a definite weight of some specified substance, *e. g.* lead; now usually 19½ cwt.' (*N.E.D.*).

Folke Mootes, i. 325, 331: 'a general assembly of the people of a town, city, or shire' (*N.E.D.*).

follilie, foolishly, i. 241.

follower, technical term for a mode of scouring the channel of Fleet dike into the Thames, i. 13.

Font in Poules, the, i. 225.

fooles whoode, a, i. 157.

foond, found, ii. 35.

foranenst, opposite to, facing, ii. 44.

forced ground, opp. to **the mayne,** i. 345.

forcier, *n.*, contrivance for propelling water (*N.E.D.*), i. 18; 'an engine or **forcier,** for the winding up of water to serue the cittie,' i. 42.

foreigner (*forinsecus*), a person not enjoying the privileges of a borough (Gross); 'out of the manor,' ii. 69.

forreigns, i. 155; all maner f., i. 156.

forreins, outsiders, i. 156, ii. 69; 'decreed that no forrein or stranger should sell any wollen cloth,' i. 288.

forthright, straightforward, ii. 74.
fortuned, it, i. 100.
foyle, fine silver made into, i. 53 (called *temp.* Edw. I 'siluer of Guthuron's Lane').
foystor, a saddle-tree maker (*N.E.D.*), ii. 192.
Fraerie Cart, the, of the Priory of S. John of Jerusalem, ii. 82.
frame, i. 34: 'a structure of timbers, joists, &c., fitted together to form the skeleton of a building' (*N.E.D.*, quoting *Prompt. Parv.*, &c.); 'a large strong frame of timber and brick,' i. 131; 'a fair large frame of timber, containing [several] tenements,' i. 151.
franches, soke or court, i. 29.
franchises, privileges, i. 308.
Frankpledge, ii. 69: 'the French and Latin terms *fraunceplege, francus plegius*, appear to have arisen from a misunderstanding of the A.S. *Friðbohs* or *Fribohs* = pledge of peace' (Nichols's *Britton*).
Fratres de sacca *or* **de penitentia**, i. 277; Friars of the Sack.
Fratrie, the, refectory, i. 317, 319.
fray: '1401. Souldiers made a fray against the Maior,' ii. 174; '1452. This yeare was a great fray at the wrastling,' ii. 174.
free quitted: 'that all men of the Realme should be free quitted and discharged of all Toll,' i. 207.
freese, i. 110; 'ye kyveringe which was but frise,' *Introd.* p. lix; 'coarse woollen cloth, with a nap, usually on one side only' (*N.E.D.*).
frequent, populous, ii. 206.
fripperers or vpholders, i. 199: '**fripper**, a broker' (*N.E.D.*); cf. *Introd.* p. lxxxvii, 'broker and fripper': upholder means broker or auctioneer (see Skeat).
Froes of Flaunders, ii. 55 (i.e. Frows = loose women).
fullage, refuse, street sweepings, ii. 270.
furniture: 'for furniture of the Quire in divine service, and ministration of the sacraments, a College of 12 pety Chanons, &c.,' ii. 137.
furtherer: 'a great furtherer of the new work of Powles,' ii. 133.

G

gailekeeping: 'so that both the old and new worke of Ludgate aforesaid, be one prison, *gailekeeping*, and charge for euermore,' i. 39.
galley halfpence, forbidden 13 Henry IV and 4 Henry V, i. 132.
gallows were erect⟨ed⟩, i. 130.
galory, gallery, *passim.*
gardian or Warden, and a communaltie, i. 237.
garland, i.e. victory, or its reward, i. 74.
garner, granary: 'the common Garner called Leaden Hall,' ii. 180.
gate, got, i. 128.
geason, scarce, ii. 296.
geld, the Flemish, i. 234.
gentlemanlike disposition, a, ii. 218.
Gerond, *gironné*, i. 287.
gersum, i. 311: 'a premium or fine paid to a feudal superior on entering upon a holding' (*N.E.D.*). See also Cowell, *s.v.*
gild, 'to gild withal;' for gilding purposes, i. 57.
gilliflowers, the clove pink: 'paying yearely one cloue of Gereflowers at Easter,' i. 245; 'one cloue or slip of Gilliflowers,' i. 311.
gin, contrivance, engine: 'a gin to convey Thames water to Dowgate conduit,' i. 232 *marg.*
glasier: 'Launcelot Young, Maister Glasier to her Majestie,' i. 298.
glass house: 'a . . . wherein was made glass of divers sorts to drink in,' i. 148.
goddards: 'from OF. *Godart* (1397), F. *Godet*, a drinking-cup; still so called in N. Wales' (*N.E.D.*), i. 343.
Goldyng Lyon, the, i. 312.
Gote on the Hope, Goat on the Hoop, ii. 91: 'Fr. *cerceau, sercle*, the hoop of a barrel, the sign of a brewster's occupation' (Gross, *G.M.*).
goutes, *plur.*, i. 152.
grant to, i. 121: 'granted *to* their request,' i. 120.
grayners, granaries, ii. 65.
Greene yard of the Leaden Hall, i. 151. Cf. green churchyard, *Introd.* p. vii.
grithe, sanctuary, refuge, shelter: 'took grithe of,' i. 308. Cf. **Grithbriche**, violation of sanctuary, i. 324.
groate and halfe groate, i. 55.
ground, made (*opp.* to **main, natural**), i. 43.
groundsell, i. 137: 'a doorsill, threshold' (*N.E.D.*).
g⟨u⟩arded, trimmed or turned up with some material, i. 88, 89 (*v. N.E.D.*).
Guildhall Teutonicorum: 'the Companie called the Guildhall Teutonicorum (or the **Flemish Geld**),' i. 234.

H

habiliments of war: munitions of war, warlike implements, weapons, equipment, &c., i. 126.
hability: 'euery man graunted liberally according to his hability,' ii. 25.
had rather than much good: 'the new serjeants had rather than much good it had not so happened,' ii. 36.
halfe-hakes, half-hackbuts, i. 102.
Hallmotes, i. 344.
Hanaper, the King's, in the Chancery, ii. 67: 'The department of the Chancery into which fees were paid for the sealing and enrolment of charters and other documents. Abolished, 1832' (*N.E.D.*). (Lat. *hanaperium*, hamper): 'The *Hanaper* of the Chancery, anno 10 R. 2, seems to signify the same that *Fiscus* doth originally in the Latin' (Cowell's *Interpreter*).
happened upon: 'a great fire happened upon . . . Leaden Hall,' i. 155.
happily, haply, i. 43; possibly, i. 82.
harbenger to the Queen, purveyor of lodgings, &c., i. 133.
harborow of . . . leprous persons, ii. 146.
harbouring: 'the blessed work of harbouring the harbourlesse,' i. 198.
hard beneath (cf. *hard by*), ii. 135.
harnised men, accoutred, equipped, i. 103.
harth, 'made of Britain, or rather Roman, tile,' i. 160.
haw, yard: 'Wooll Church Haw,' i. 226.
haw yard, or garden, a great, i. 149.
hazard, to, to game, i. 149.
henchman, i. 102–3: 'a squire or page of honour to a great man, who walked or rode beside him in pageants, processions, &c.' (*N.E.D.*). See also *Henxemen*, ii. 193.
herebefore, i. 157.
heuenly make ⟨mate⟩, ii. 335.
hide, hyde, 'the hyde or territory of Southwarke,' ii. 67.
hithertowardes, hitherto, ii. 132.
Hoisting, Husting, i. 292: a Court held in the Guildhall of London by the Lord Mayor, Recorder, and Sheriffs; long the Supreme Court of the City. For its etymology and history, see article in *N.E.D.*, and Index III. 'A full hoystings,' i. 189.
holbard, halbert, i. 102.
holdefast's hands, a close-fisted person: 'that money being in holdefast's hands,' i. 114. Cf. Shaks., *Henry V*, II. iii. 54 (Holdfast is the only dog); and the proverb, 'Bray is a good dog, but Holdfast is better.' See Schmidt's *Shakespeare-Lexicon*, *s. v.*
Hole, i. 115: 'The worst ward in the Counter Prisons.' See note on p. 285.
holme, holly, i. 97.
holydome, holiness, i. 115: 'The substitution of -dam, -dame was apparently due to popular etymology, the word being taken to denote "Our Lady"' (*N.E.D.*).
honestly, honourably: '⟨He⟩ was honestly buried in the churchyard,' i. 255.
honor: 'Euery man's house of Honor or Worship,' i. 98.
honor of Baynards Castell, the, i. 61; 'honor was "a seignory of several manors held under one baron or lord paramount"' (*N.E.D.*).
hood or head attire, who might not wear, except of reied or striped cloth, ii. 166.
Hoop, the Griffon on the, i. 323.
Horne, Sir *W. Littlesbery, alias Horne*: 'for K. Ed. the 4 so named him because he was a most excellent blower in a horne,' i. 246.
Horners of London: 'the horners that were about the cittie, presently aunswered in like manner,' i. 334. There were at least three classes of Horners: (1) a worker in horn; (2) a maker of musical horns; (3) a blower or winder of the horn. See Munday (1633, p. 638).
horse (*plur.*): '160 drawing horse,' i. 87.
horse-coursers, jobbing dealers in horses, i. 82.
Horsemill, the, in Grasse Street, i. 153.
hospitall: 'an Hospitall of great relief,' i. 167.
Hospitelar: 'the first Hospitelar or Proctor, for the poor of S. Bartilmew,' ii. 22.
Hostelar, the, innkeeper, i. 348.
hostery, hostelry, i. 38.
hourded up, hoorded, i. 57.
houses, religious: 'by whose wealth and **haunt** (=resort) many of those places were chiefly fedde and nourished,' ii. 211.
housing: 'much housing was there destroyed,' i. 155, 227.
hoysting, husting, i. 65, 189.
hurly burly, ii. 216.
Hurrer, i. 298: 'a dealer in, or maker of hats and caps; a haberdasher' (*N.E.D.*).
Husband, economist, ii. 210.

I

'idol' (the Maypole at S. Andrew Undershaft), sawn in pieces and burnt, i. 144. Philip Stubbs, *ap.* Strutt (ed. J. C. Cox, p. 277), calls the Maypole 'a stinking idol.'

images of Kings defaced under Edward VI, by such as judged every image to be an Idoll, i. 38.

imbeseled: 'Many jewels were burned, and more imbeseled,' i. 295.

impeach, to hinder, ii. 206.

impoysoning, i. 164.

in perpetual alms, in frank almoigne, ii. 65.

incastellate, *v.*, i. 45.

— '[water] incastellated in sufficient cisterns,' i. 293.

incorporate(d), i. 180.

increased, enlarged: 'He increased the parish church of Saint *Michael*,' ii. 168. Cf. p. 177.

indighted: 'Cross in Cheap indighted' (i.e. 'presented by Juries or quests of Wardmote'), i. 266 *marg.*; cf. i. 350 *marg.*

(1) **Infangethef** (2) **Outfangethef**: '(1) a liberty granted from the King to some lords of a manor to try all thieves, their tenants, within their own court; (2) a liberty of trying foreigners apprehended for theft within their own fee' (Kennett, *Glossary*): see also Stubbs, *Select Charters*, ed. 1900, p. 78.

infirmitorie, infirmary, i. 317.

infranchised: 'This sir R. Knoles, thus worthily infranchised ⟨to be⟩ a citizen,' i. 107.

inmates: 'subtenants or lodgers tending to increase the number of paupers locally chargeable' (*N.E.D.*), ii. 124.

inned, gathered in: 'from the first of Aprill till new corne was inned,' i. 90. From *v.* 'to inn'; cf. *innings* (Skeat).

inquest, i. 303.

instinction, a godly, a divine impulse, ii. 126.

instore, to, the Grayners of the City with wheat, i. 208.

insulate: 'Long Ditch almost insulateth the City of Westminster,' ii. 102.

interdiction, interdict, ii. 130.

intermit, interfere: 'so that none but they intermit within the Citie of their craft but he be of their Guild,' i. 285.

inuesture, investiture, i. 45.

inwall, *v. a.*, i. 5.

Iseldon, Islington, i. 31.

isle, aisle, i. 294. See note on p. 349.

J

jebit, obs. form of gibbet, i. 144.

jornet, i. 102: 'a loose travelling cloak; in 15-16th cent. worn over armour' (*N.E.D.*).

judgment by water, water-dome (marg. *ordalii*), i. 100.

Jurie, the poor (of Jews dwelling there), i. 149.

Jurors, forsworn, ride to the pillory on Cornhill, with Miters of paper on their heads, i. 191.

just, to, *v.*, a course or twaine, i. 61.

justes (1458), jousts, i. 58.

Justicer, i. 50: from med. Lat. *iustitiarius*, a judge, magistrate.

K

keddles, large fixed nets (stake nets?), *A. Fr. Kidel*, Act xii. Edw. IV (1472), O.F. *Quidel, engin à pêcher* (Lacurne) (*Dialect Dict.*), ii. 153.

kept, attended: 'This Mayor *kept* the Market so well that he would be at the Leaden hall by foure a clocke in the Sommers mornings,' i. 157; = remained, ii. 36.

Kiuerings, mentioned with *Wolsteds, Stayes, Staimus*, &c., i. 155; *Introd.*, p. lix. See Index II.

Knape: Church of S. Andrew the Apostle, i. 143, called of the *Knape* or *Undershaft*, from the May-pole set up there yearly on May day morning. 'The real meaning is S. Andrew's on the Knap or Hill.' See Index II.

Knight Marshall, i. 144.

Knighthood, conferment of, i. 220.

Kyrlie Merlie, prob. a corruption of *Kyrie eleison*, i. 252.

L

landes euicted: 'if the landes should be evicted ⟨i. e. recovered by a judicial process, &c.⟩ . . . yet he and his Heyres should accomplish the gifte,' i. 334.

lapped: 'I have been shewed the same body (that of James IV. of Scots) so lapped in lead,' i. 298.

Larder, sargeant of the, i. 134.

'largeness of room,' i. 158; cf. 146.

Lateran, Patriarchate of the, i. 72.

lathar, ladder, ii. 353.

Laton workes; **latten**: 'a mixed metal of yellow colour, either identical with, or closely resembling, brass. The word occurs not infrequently as a trans. of Lat. *orichalcum*' (*N.E.D.*).

lauer of brass, the, in the cloyster of the Hospital of Bethlehem, i. 319.

Launder, a washerman or -woman, ii. 293.

Law-worth, ii. 148: worthy of, i. e. entitled to, the laws, &c.; having a standing in the law courts, possessed of full legal rights' (*N.E.D.*); Gross compares *probi homines*, good men and true.

Law-worthy. See Charter of William I to the City of London, *apud* Stubbs, *Select Charters*, p. 83.

laye, alloy, i. 53.

laystalle, a midden, manure-heap, i. 70.

lazar houses, lepers' hospitals, i. 110.

Leaden Hall, i. 153; meant to have been made a Bursse for the assembly of merchants, but without success; part reserved for the making and resting of the Midsummer pageants, &c., i. 159. See Index II.

leades: 'faire leades to walk upon well imbatailled,' i. 40.

least, lest, i. 47.

ledgier book, i. 161: 'a book containing records, a register, a cartulary' (*N.E.D.*). Cf. 'a fayre leager booke,' ii. 96.

leese, to lose or forfeit, i. 133.

Leet, ii. 97: 'a special kind of court of record which the lords of certain manors were empowered by charter or prescription to hold annually or semi-annually. = Court-leet' (*N.E.D.*).

left, left off, ceased, i. 5, 349.

Legiance, allegiance, i. 117.

Lepers to be removed into some out-places of the fields, ii. 146. Cf. Index III.

letted, hesitated: 'men have not *letted* to speak their pleasure,' i. 166.

letten, *pt. pa.*, i. 51.

— down, i. 49.

— out, i. 137.

letters insealed, i. 82.

Letters Patentes, i. 155; **letters pattentes**, *ib.*

lewde fellowe, a (a counterfeit physician), his subtiltie, i. 58.

Liberties, &c., of the City: King Edward III grants: (1) the Mayor 'to be Justice for the Gaole deliuery at Newgate; (2) that the Cittizens should not be constrained to goe out of the Citty to any warre; (3) that the liberties and franchises of the citty should not after this time, for any cause, be taken into the Kinges hands; (4) that no Escheter should be in the citty, but the Mayor for his time,' ii. 164. Cf. i. 127.

light, alight: 'hundreds of Lampes light at once,' i. 101.

lighting the streets: 'This H. B. ordayned Lanthornes with lights to be hanged out on the Winter euening betwixt Hallontide and Candlemass,' ii. 171. Cf. i. 271.

lightly, commonly, i. 99.

— gladly, readily, i. 98.

linces, lynxes, i. 48.

Lion Tower, the, i. 48; afterwards called 'The Bulwarke,' *ib.*

liuelode, livelihood, i. 308; ii. 112.

liuings, means of living, i. 62.

lodgings for the poor *translated* into stabling for horses, i. 294.

lofted, provided with lofts or upper stories: 'this Library is now lofted through,' i. 275.

Lomsbery, Bloomsbury, i. 217.

London called 'The Kinges Chamber,' i. 117. See *Chronicles of London*, pp. 99, 268; '*Camera regis*,' ii. 202.

London Lickepennie, i. 217.

Londoners anciently called Barons, i. 94.

lordship and parish of Stebunheth, ii. 132.

lorimar, loriner or lorimer, bitmaker, i. 305: makers of bits and ornamental metal work for reins; distinct from saddlers. See Riley, *Memorials*, 156, and *N.E.D.*

louer, ii. 90.

lowsed, loosed, i. 179.

Luce of the sea, the hake, i. 96: *N.E.D.* quotes 'Luces, properly called Pikes of the Sea.'

'**Lunatike** or phrensie people,' i. 137 *marg.*

lyne right, straight, ii. 297. Ephyphanye in *Tundale* (15th cent.), 'The sterre hem brought to Beedlem And lyne right the chylde aboue' (*N.E.D.*).

M

Machabray, dance of, meters or poesie, translated from French by John Lidgate, i. 327.

main and hard ground, ii. 77. See *mayne*.

maine, great: 'maine timber posts were scrat and cleft,' i. 196.

maine tides, huge tides: 'The Thames breaketh into the French Ocean by maine tides,' i. 11.

maioralities, i. 152.

Maister of defence, i. e. fencing master, i. 276; ii. 86. This corporation was organized by Henry VIII in July 1540, under the title of 'Masters of the Noble Science of Defence' (Strutt, p. 211).
maletolt, *mala tolta*: 'evil, unjust, or burdensome tax' (*N.E.D.*). See also Hubert Hall, *Customs Revenue of England*, i. 67.
malignant spirit, the, act of, i. 97.
Malmesies, imported by the Lombards, i. 241: 'a sweet, strong wine, originally the product of *Monemvasia* in the Morea; from *Malvasia* called *Malvoisie* in French and *Malmsey* in English' (*N.E.D.*).
'**Mampudding, Mother**,' i. 137. See Index I.
marble, gray: 'a livery of marble gray,' i. 89; cf. Machyn's *Diary*, Camden Soc., p. 462, 'made with wool or silk of various colours mixed together': see *Gent. Mag.* 1835, N.S. vi. 2, 114, 226; and *N.E.D.* (variegated or mottled).
Marchandize of three sorts—(1) Nauigation; (2) Inuection; (3) Negotiation, ii. 207.
marchant of Leauaunt, i. 210.
marchants vintners of Gascoyne, i. 240.
marching watch, the, i. 102.
marrish, marsh; cf. *merse*, a marsh (Skeat, *Etym. Dict.*).
marshall (i. e. martial) **law**, i. 144.
Martin ⟨Merton⟩ **College** in Oxford, ii. 134, 135.
Martinmas, Feast of St. Martin (Nov. 11), i. 55.
mascle, ii. 90: 'three Mascles sable, between three cinquefoils argent, Lat. *macula*, also a net; in heraldry, a charge in the form of a lozenge, with a lozenge-shaped opening, through which the field appears' (*N.E.D.*).
mases ⟨= maces⟩ of siluer and guilt, ii. 165.
mayings, May festivities, i. 98.
mayne, solid or natural ground, i. 345. See *N.E.D.* 4. b.
mayor and communalty, i. 164.
Mayster of the Workes of money in the Tower of London, ii. 174.
Maze, the, Southwark, ii. 66.
measurer of the Queen's soke, i. 41: 'The Measurer (or the Meater) ought to have 8. chiefe Master porters,' ii. 9.
medley brune, and **porre** (or purple) colour, price the yeard 2*s*., ii. 190.
merced, amerced: six bakers merced in the Guild Hall for baking under the size appointed, i. 157.
Mercery in West Cheape, the, i. 257: 'The trade in mercery ware, or the place where it is carried on' (*N.E.D.*).
merchants ingrosse vp old coins, i. 55.
meyney, retinue, company; **meynie**, i. 98, 334.
middest, midst, i. 139.
minchuns, mincheons, nuns, i. 132.
minde-day, the anniversary of death, i. 109.
Misrule, Lord of, or Maister of merry disports, i. 97.
mistery, i. 305; ii. 357; Lat. *ministerium*: 'a corruption of ME. *mistere*, a trade, craft. Cf. OF. *mestier*, Ital. *mestiere*' (Skeat).
moities of Cold Harborough, i. 236.
moneys forbidden: 'galley halfepence, suskinges, or dodkins,' i. 132–3. Cf. Camden's *Remaines*, ed. 1629, pp. 171–2.
monuments, public buildings, i. 313.
more larger, i. 119.
Morian, a Moor: 'his arms three water budgets, and his crest a Morians head,' i. 201.
morish ground, ii. 25.
morrow-mass, the mass on the morning after a festival, i. 261.
Mountgodard Street, etymology of name, i. 343.
mured up, walled up: 'the other two ⟨arches⟩ mured up,' i. 234.
murren, a, of kine, ii. 163.
murrey, dark red, ii. 195; properly mulberry coloured (Skeat).
mustard-villers, *mustre-de-villiars*, ii. 189: 'a kind of mixed grey woollen cloth, which continued in use up to Elizabeth's reign' (Halliwell). The name is due to Montivilliers (anciently called Monstredevillars) in Normandy. See under **Cloath**, *supra*.

N

namely, especially, i. 22, 132; ii. 113 and *passim*.
napery, linen for the table, i. 231.
nathelesse, nevertheless, ii. 273. Cf. Milton, *P. L.* i. 299; Spenser, *Hymn to Celestial Beauty*, l. 159.
naughty packs, a pack of rascals, ii. 206; **vnthriftes**, ne'er do wells, *ib.* Fabyan is called 'a *nowghty* Cronycle', *Introd.*, p. li.
nayle: 'The nayle lying dry is by *scaling* greatly wasted,' i. 170.

near hand, well-nigh, i. 244.
'nipping and quipping their fellows,' i. 72.
no . . . no: that no Butcher should kil no flesh, i. 317.
no mo ⟨more⟩, i. 49.
nobilitating, *subs.*, i. 34.
nocked, notched: 'Arrowes nocked in their hands,' ii. 117.
note, *subs.*, mention, i. 31, 34: 'which Well is the only peculiar *note* belonging to that gate'; a note or sign, i. 38; *v.* i. 44.
noyances, injuries, i. 119.
noysance, offence, i. 209.

O

obedienciarie: 'London is but a . . . subiect, and no free estate, an obedienciarie, and no place indowed with any distinct or absolute power,' ii. 206.
Obit, funeral obsequies, annual memorial service; 'an obite, or aniuersary, to be spent on the poore,' i. 197.
of new, anew, i. 34 and *passim*.
often (*adj.*) casualties by fire, i. 83.
or, ere: 'a bye worde, such a man will be Maior, or he be shiriffe,' ii. 187.
orchyard, ii. 102: for *ortyard*, formerly supposed to be derived from Greek ὄρχατος.
order, ordering, i. 302.
original, origin, i. 48.
osterie, a common, for travellers, i. 202; cf. *hosterie*, i. 216.
othersome, others, i. 333.
ouer, outright: 'sold it over,' i. 152.
ouerhayled: 'which Bell, named *Rus*, rung by one man for 150 years, . . . of late ouerhayled by four or five at once, hath been thrice broken and new cast within . . . ten years,' i. 196.
ouerpasse, *v.a.*, i. 306 and *passim*.
ouerplus, i. 207.
ought, owed, i. 65; in Ld. Mountjoy's epitaph, i. 252.
'Our Lady of the Piew,' ii. 127.
out places of the fields, ii. 146.
outward, outer, i. 121.

P

pageant, 'an allegorical device carried on a fixed stage or car in a public show' (*N.E.D.*); 'the Mayor had besides his Giant three pageants,' i. 103.
pageants, midsummer, i. 102, 159.
paine, pecuniarie, penalty, ii. 202.
Palatine Tower, belonging to the sovereign, i. 44.
pale, paling, i. 20.
paled park, fenced in, i. 306.
papes: 'in some language Priests are called Papes,' i. 146.
parcelled, divided, i. 129.
Park, Woodstock, the first in England, i. 48. 'The word is English, being a contraction of M.E. *parrok* from A.S. *pearroc*, now also spelt *paddock*' (Skeat).
partie offender, the, ii. 120.
passed, excelled, i. 140.
passed not vpon the honor, cared not for: 'Hee said that he passed not vpon the honor, but came to visite them,' ii. 25.
pastelars, pastry-cooks, i. 81.
pastime, shewing: 'pastimes were shewed on the riuer of Thames,' i. 22; 97, 115.
Paternoster-makers, Bead-makers, and **Text-writers,** of late called **Stationers,** i. 81; one paire of Paternosters, i. 86, 338.
Patriarchie of Laterane (i. e. patriarchate), i. 72.
Patricksey, Battersea, i. 23.
Pattenmakers extinct, i. 81.
Paueline, i. 281 (*a ghost word*). 'Euery Vsurer should weare a Table on their breast, the breadth of a paueline.' i. 281, l. 6, *paueline*. This is clearly a printer's error for 'palme', which is the reading of the corresponding passage in the *Summarie Abridged* both for 1598 and for 1604, and also in the *Annales*, p. 305, ed. 1605; probably Stow wrote 'paulme'. From the *Annales* it appears that Stow's authority was the *Historia Regum* of John Rous (p. 202, ed. Hearne), which reads, 'rex eximius Judaeis in regno suo ut ab aliis noscerentur tabulare ad unius palmae longitudinem signa ferrent in exterioribus indumentis.' Rous copied the *Flores Historiarum* (iii. 45). I am indebted to Mr. Walter Worrall for indicating the solution of this difficulty.
Paul, S., feet of, i. 318.
Pawne, the, at the Old Royal Exchange, ii. 303: 'richly furnished like a bazaar with all sorts of the finest wares in the Citie,' i. 193. The name is derived from Du. *pand*, a walk. See note, p. 303.
paynted table: 'A fayre paynted Table of hir picture was placed in the

Chapple . . . which she had builded,' i. 116.

penny force, $25\frac{1}{2}$ gs.; **penny deble** or **feeble,** $22\frac{1}{2}$ gs., i. 53. See *Foedera,* x. 161–3, date 1421. 'French mercenaries were paid in money so feeble that it passeth not a good English noble a month.' See Kingsford, *Henry V*, p. 367.

Pens, the, (or **folds**) in Smithfield, ii. 21, 28–9.

pentises of one row of houses, eaves, i. 143; 'an appendix or outbuilding' (Skeat). See *Much Ado,* III. iii. 110.

Perchers: 'of lights for Paris candles, called Perchers,' i. 85. See *N.E.D.*; 'a large wax candle, generally used for the altar' (Halliwell).

perie plants, pear-trees, i. 48; so in Chaucer and *Piers Plowman* (Skeat).

perpetual alms, in, i. 181.

person, parson, i. 37 and *passim.*

persuade: 'to persuade ⟨enforce⟩ the Article of Christ's resurrection,' i. 167.

pestered: 'many houses builded with alleys backward ⟨at the back⟩ . . . too much pesterd with people (a great cause of infection),' i. 165; 'this house . . . being now of late years enclosed about or pestered with small tenements,' i. 124; a church 'pestered with loftes and seates,' i. 127; 'with diuerse Allyes,' *ib.*

Pew, Piew, Our Lady of the, ii. 121. See Index II.

phrensie: 'lunatic or phrensie people,' i. 137.

picked staff, a, pointed, i. 93.

pikes: 'A Bridge of stone faire coaped on either side with iron pikes, on the which be also certain lanthorns of stone,' i. 26.

pilgrim: 'They chose H. de Ryall to be their **pilgrim,** for the maister of this misterie (as one that trauelled for the whole companie (Merchant Taylors) was then so called . . . and the four wardens were then called Purueyors of almes (now called quarterage) of the said fraternitie,' i. 181.

pill, *v.*, to plunder: '[William Rufus] pilled and shaued the people with tribute,' i. 45.

Pix, or Boxe of Assay, i. 54: Lat. *pixis,* chest, treasury (Gross).

Place of honour: 'In . . . 1238. King Henry kepte his feast of Christmas at Westminster in the great Hall, so did he in 1241, where he placed the Legate in the most honorable place of the Table, to wit in the midest,' ii. 113–4. Cf. *begin the boord, supra.*

plashed = pleached (Shaks. *Much Ado,* III. i. 7; Skeat, *Etymol. Dict.*), i. 3.

platform: 'the very platforme thereof [St. Bride's House] remayned for great part wast,' i. 69.

playne mockery, a, ii. 302.

Pleas, Common, or **Place,** i. 78 and *passim.*

Pleas of the Crowne, pleaded in the Tower; suits in the King's name against offences committed against his Crown and dignity, i. 51.

plot, site, i. 294: 'the plot of Aldgate, and the Soke thereunto belonging,' i. 140.

pointed, appointed, i. 54.

popingey, a parrot, i. 166; here 'a mark like a parrot, put on a pole to be shot at' (Skeat).

porpentine, porcupine, i. 48: cf. *Hamlet,* I. v. 20.

porre, purple colour, ii. 190.

Port the, or entrie into the Hall, ii. 118.

portcloses, i. 29: '*portcullis,* a sliding gate' (Skeat, *Etymol. Dict.*).

portgrave, portreeve, derivation of, ii. 147.

portrature, i. 337.

pory, porous, i. 293.

Postles chappell, the, i. 321.

Pothecarie, apothecary, i. 161.

Potmaker for the Mint (W. Foxley), his long sleep, i. 59.

Poulter, poulterer, i. 262.

pound starlings, i. 317.

poundage: 'they could not sell their wines, paying poundage,' i. 238.

power, force, i. 1, 107; ii. 171.

poynting, appointing: 'the King poynting a Custos,' i. 301.

practise, to intrigue: 'Richard, Duke of Gloucester, then Protector, practised for the Crown,' ii. 235.

pralle, *app.* variant of *prolle,* prowl, Lat. *scrutor* (*N.E.D.*), i. 160.

'Premunire, the,' Premunirey, Cardinal Wolsey condemned in, i. 340.

preposterous zeal, ii. 75.

Presbeterie, chancel, sanctuary, ii. 46.

Presbytery, the quire or chancel, ii. 132.

present, immediate: 'the people did nothing else but expect present death,' i. 24.

presented: 'the Crosse in Cheape presented (= indicted) by diuers Juries, or Quests of Wardmote,' i. 266.

president, precedent, i. 130.
prest, loan, ii. 214.
Prices set on victuals, &c. (A.D. 1313), ii. 162–3.
prilling, trickling, i. 267.
Priores aliens, i. e. priories alien, i. 131.
Priories Aliens, suppressed 4 Henry V, i. 39.
Priors: 'these Priors ⟨of Christ Church⟩ have sitten and ridden amongst the Aldermen of London, in liuery like vnto them,' i. 141.
prise, price, i. 24; cf. Stratmann, *M.E.D.*
prises, goods taken from the French, i. 318.
procession-way, i. 227; 'the aisle in a cathedral or collegiate church behind the high altar, round which a procession could take its way' (Lee's *Glossary*).
procurators, or Wardens, of London Bridge, i. 31. Cf. St. Antonie's Procters, i. 184.
procurement, by, i. 272.
professed trade: 'till of late time euery man liued by his professed trade, not any one interrupting another,' i. 238.
proper, neat, handsome, i. 132 and *passim*.
prosecute, to follow up, i. 118.
protracted, wasted: 'as they stayed or protracted time,' i. 24.
Prusia: 'This man sent into Prusia, and caused to be brought from thence certaine ships laden with Rie,' ii. 173.
Purbecke, hard stone of, i. 272.
purprestures, 'enchrochmentes on highwayes, lanes, and common grounds,' i. 83.
pursiuaunt, i. 99: 'an attendant on Heralds' (Skeat); **purseuants**, i. 237.
purueyors of almes, i. 181. See *pilgrim*.
put foorth, to, ⟨i. e. to put out⟩ the lightes of this Chappel, ii. 121.
put out, evicted, i. 151.
Pye-powders, Court of, ii. 69: 'travelling men, wayfarers, esp. an itinerant merchant or trader (Fr. *pied-poudreux*, Lat. *pede pulverosus*, dusty-foot)' (*N.E.D.*). See also Ben Jonson's *Bartholomew Fair*, and H. Morley's *History*.
Pyramis, a, to be set up in place of the top of the Cross in Cheap, i. 267.

Q

quadrant, 'a proper, or squared court,' i. 134, 159; 'the large Southeast quadrant to the same gate ⟨Ludgate⟩ adioyning.'
quarterage, a quarter's wages or pension (*N.E.D.*), i. 181. See *pilgrim*.
Queen: 'The Tower Royall called the Queene's Wardrope,' i. 244.
Queen's Soke, measure and measurer of the, i. 41.
queristers, choristers, i. 154.
quinten, running at the, for prizes, i. 94.
quire *or* **queere** (of a church), i. 21, 134.
quitclaim, '*quietum clamare*, to quit-claim, release' (Gloss. to Nichols's *Britton*).

R

ray, striped, i. 86. See 'reied or striped cloth,' ii. 166; 'ray gowns' of broad cloth rowed or striped athwart, ii. 189.
Readers, i. e. Lecturers, a college of, i. 75, 174.
Reading tawney: 'a livery of Reading tawney,' i. 88–9; '*Tawny* = Tanny, a yellowish brown' (Skeat); a fabric formerly made at Reading.
ready, made himself: accoutred himself, i. 64.
rebatement of Bishops liuinges, ii. 20.
receipt, reception, i. 49.
— of travellers, also **recept**, reception, i. 164.
— capacity: 'an Hospital of great receipt,' ii. 143.
recluse or **ankorage, a**, ii. 22.
Recognition: 'since the said Recognition,' ii. 7; see Skeat *s.v.*: from recognizance, law term; Chaucer, *C. T.* 130260.
Recorder: He learnedly delivereth the sentences of the whole Court: 'G. H., Alderman, was elected to bee Recorder of London . . . and was appointed to weare his apparrell as an Alderman,' ii. 161–2.
red (*p.p.* of *read*): 'I haue not red of Basing,' i. 348 *bis*, ii. 147, and *passim*.
re-edifier, or new builder, ii. 306.
reformed, corrected, i. 215.
reforme peace, to, i. 71.
reforming, restoration: 'the reforming of that church,' i. 173.
Registers (-trars), offices kept by, i. 342.
relief and harborow of . . . leprous persons, ii. 146.
reliefe (*v.a.*) them [viz. prisons], i. 154.
Remembrancer of the office of the first-fruits, i. 293. There were three Remembrancers: (1) the King's;

(2) the Lord Treasurer's; (3) the Remembrancer of the First Fruits (see Cowell's *Interpreter*).

Remembrances, Book of, ⟨*Remembrancia*⟩ in the Guildhall, i. 123. The City Letter-books were also called 'books of Remembrances.' Here it refers to Letter-Book C.

remised and quiteclaimed, ii. 64; see Cowell's *Interpreter*, *s.vv.*, and under *quitclaim.*

remit, *subs.*, ii. 65.

remove, *subs.*, i. 351.

render, *v.*, to surrender, i. 46.

renowmed, renowned, i. 71.

repayre, to make r. to, i. 84.

repayred, resorted: 'such Market people as repayred to prayer,' i. 155.

repayrers to this Citie, i. 84.

replenished, adorned: 'replenished . . . with beautiful houses of stone,' i. 302 and *passim.*

replenished with, full of: 'replenished with strangers,' ii. 66.

reprises, in all, i. 35: 'Deductions and duties which are yearly paid out of a Manor and Lands. . . . Wherefore when we speak of the clear yearly value of a Manor, we say it is so much *per annum ultra reprisas*' (Cowell's *Interpreter*).

reuestry, sacristy, i. 347.

Rhodes, Knights of the, ii. 84 and *passim.*

rifeled: 'the Barons rifeled the Jews coffers,' i. 279.

rills or rillets, i. 14.

ring of nine bells, a, well tuned, i. 142.

Ringleaders of Inquests defined, i. 191.

Rippers or Rippiers of Rye, i. 187; so called from carrying fish for sale in a *ripp* or basket; pedlars in Kent used them in pairs and slung on each side of a horse for carrying loads, such as salt, fish, sand, &c. (*Dialect Dict.*).

rise against, to meet, i. 65: Lat. *assurgere alicui,* quoted by Steele in H. of C.

rising, accruing: 'C. li. so rising yearly,' i. 116.

roade (of ships), *v.p.t.*, 'as if they r. at Queene Hith,' i. 41.

Roane ⟨Rouen⟩, inscription on great bell at, ii. 120.

'Romish' order of sacraments, the, ii. 136.

romthes, rooms, ii. 353; see Skeat, *s.v. room.*

rood and tabernacle destroyed, i. 209.

rose nobles, i. 55.

Round walke, the, of the Temple Church '(which is the West part without the Quire) . . . the rest are coaped stones,' ii. 50, 51.

roundelets of hoods, ii. 197.

routs, tumults, ii. 120.

rowals, of six points (on coinage of William I), i. 52.

rowlocks (orelockes), boats provided with, i. 206.

royalty, royal state, i. 66; 'countenance (i. e. show) of insufficiencie,' *ib.*

rub it out, tide it over: '⟨he⟩ did rub it out,' i. 351.

rugh and clench, shipnails so called: 'rugh and clenche, i. e. rugh nayles with broad round heades, and clenched on the other side with square plates of iron: the roofe of this hall is also wrought of the like boord, . . . and seemeth as it were a Gallie, the Keele turned upwards,' i. 137.

ruinated, i. 163; ii. 123.

russet, cloth of, i. 85; clothes of medley, i. 86.

— cotton, brown, i. 319.

S

Sabbaoth, the, and principall Feasts, i. 157.

sacke and soke, toll, and **Theam,** ⟨and⟩ **infangthefe,** i. 122. See Stubbs, *Select Charters*, p. 78.

Sacraments and sacramentals, i. 319: 'Sacramentals: a term for certain rites, ceremonies, and religious observances, . . . adopted as valuable adjuncts to the sacraments' (Lee, *Glossary of Liturgical Terms*).

sacred, *pple.*, consecrated (Stratmann), ii. 216.

St. Scithen, St. Swithin, i. 108.

Sake (*or* Sach) **and Soke, toll,** and **theam,** i. 43: 'The right to hold a court for one's tenants, and to have the amercements arising from this court' (Gross, *G. M.*, ii. 417).

Sanctuary men, ii. 216.

sarpler, ii. 328. 'A sarpler of wool, a pocket or half a sack' (Halliwell).

say, serge, i. 96, 102–3.

Sayes, Stamins, Kiuerings, i. 155.

say-maister, assay-master, i. 306; ii. 159.

Scabine, *échevin,* a gild officer, alderman, judge, i. 323.

scantly, scarcely: 'four foote scantly remained above ground,' i. 254; ii. 131. Cf. *Skant,* i. 170.

schools . . . lately aduanced, set up, i. 73; decayed by suppression of religious houses whereof they were members, i. 73.

Scot and lot, i. 161: 'A customary contribution laid upon all subjects, according to their ability' (Cowell's *Interpreter*).

scour: 'Iohn Philpot sent shippes to the sea, and scoured it of Pirates,' ii. 168.

scrating, scratching, i. 277; scrat, i. 196.

scrine, screen, i. 350.

seacole forbidden to be burned in London, Southwark, &c. (A.D. 1306), ii. 162.

Seals of the Mayoralty, i. 221. See Index III.

seased, seized, i. 152.

seasor, *seizer*, i. 234.

Secondarie, a *delegate, deputy* (Todd-Johnson, quoting Wakefield's *Memoirs* for meaning of *usher*), ii. 177. The title is still held by one of the chief City officials.

seiser of liberties, seizure, ii. 216.

Seisin, corporal possession: 'they did put the ... Prior in seisine thereof,' i. 122. '*Seisin in fact* is when a corporal possession is taken; *Seisin in law*, when something is done, which the law accounteth a seisin, as an enrolment' (Cowell's *Interpreter*).

Seisin, Livery of: 'The documentary habit did not for many centuries extinguish the ceremony of personal giving and taking; the old custom survived into the period when Norman-French became the language of law, and then it was called *livery of Seisin*, and the feudal investitures were conducted with a solemn delivery of possession' (Earle, *Land Charters*, xvi-xvii, quoting also Stephen's Commentaries for *feoffment, feoffor, feoffee*).

selda, a shed, i. 257.

sell, cell: 'a sell to Burton Lager,' ii. 90.

sellar, cellar, i. 35.

Sellarer to the King, saddler (*sellarius*), i. 315. See note on p. 344.

separall, i. 41: '*separia, Separaria*, a *several*, or divided Enclosure, severed or separated from other ground. *Placia quae jacet juxta separiam Prioris et conventus de Burncestre*' (Kennett, quoted from *Paroch. Antiq.* in Cowell's *Interpreter*).

Sergeants feast at Elie house: question of precedence, ii. 36.

seruiceable: 'a serviceable Gentleman,' ii. 19; 'officious; in a good as well as a bad sense' (Schmidt, *Shakespeare-Lexicon*). 'If it be so to do good service, never let me be counted serviceable' (*Cymb.* III. ii. 15).

seruitude, opp. to 'liberty of a guild,' i. 120.

set, arranged: 'set the guests,' ii. 114. 'The mummers **set to** the Prince three jewels—a boule of gold, a cup of gold, and a ring of gold,' i. 96.

settles, double, of wainscot (for a library), i. 318.

shank bone, a, 28½ inches of assisse long, i. 292-3.

sheades, sheds, i. 330.

shearman, shereman, 'one whose occupation is to shear cloth' (2 *H. VI*, IV. ii. 145), ii. 75.

shelues, sandbanks: 'shelues, and other stoppages of . . . Thames,' i. 208.

Sheremoniers, such as cut and rounded the plates to be coyned or stamped into Estarling pence, ii. 18.

Sheremoniers' Lane, ii. 259. See Index II.

sheweth, appeareth, i. 28.

ships with tops, i. 206.

shoppes, with **solars, sellars**, &c., i. 297.

Shriuewick, office of sheriff, ii. 149, 150.

siege, house called the common, i. 25; cf. ii. 232, 'common stage.'

signioritie, lordship, i. 64.

siluer of Guthuron's Lane, i. 53.

simetery, symmetry, i. 349.

sindals, i. 63: sendal, cendal, O.F. A kind of rich thin silk used for lining, very highly esteemed. Thynne says, 'a thinne stuff, like sarcenett.' Palsgrave, however, has *cendell*, thynne lynen, sendal' (Skeat, in Notes to *Canterbury Tales*, A. 440).

Sinke Portes, the, ii. 15.

sith, i. 233.

sithence, since, i. 71.

sithens, *adv.*, since, i. 123.

sitten, *pa. part.*, 129, &c.

skuncheon, a triangular projection of a wall, i. 162; ii. 197. Stow interprets 'scutcheon', which suggests that it was a shield-shaped piece of ground. See note, p. 297.

sleepie drink, a, sleeping draught, i. 51.

slue, *pret.*, slew, i. 30.

so that, on condition that, i. 5.

soap ⟨sope⟩-making in London, i. 251.

soke, i. 29: 'Jurisdiction, the right to hold a court; a district having this privilege' (Gross, ii. 418).
soke, the Queen's, i. 41. See Index III.
sokeman, i. 64: 'tenant in ancient demesne' (Nichols's *Britton*).
sokemanrie, i. 64; **soken, or warde**, *ib.*
sole women, unmarried, i. 125: 'single; legally independent' (*Stanford Dict.*).
soler, an upper story: 'sheds or shops, with solers over them,' i. 268.
sophisters . . . flowed with words, i. 72.
sorency, astrology, i. ix.
sort, number, i. 3.
Sothorey, Southrey, Surrey, ii. 365.
soundeth, signifies, i. 120.
Southwarke, 'Manor and borough of, with all the members, rights, and appurtenances,' ii. 68. See also Index II.
soylage, dirt, sewage, i. 164.
speere, spire: 'the steeple had sometime a fair speere of stone,' ii. 257.
spoyle, spoiling, i. 20.
stall boards, their first and later use, i. 343.
standard (of spring water), i. 38.
— 'a standard of tree set up full of Holme and Iuie,' i. 265.
staple: 'Lat. *stapulum*, a scaffold for the sale of wares; afterward, a town where alone by law certain goods might be vended' (Gross, *Glossary*). See ii. 102–4.
stare, starling, i. 54.
starling penny, the, i. 52; derivation of the name, i. 53.
— **peny, starlings; Easterling, Esterling**, i. 52; marks easterlings, Easterling pence, *ib.*
state, good estate: 'for the state of the King, the Queene, and their children,' ii. 113; 'stately tyred like a Pope,' i. 96: the Pope was a 'state', but a 'state' was not a 'Pope'. See 'estate' in *Chron. Lond.* Glossary and 'estatly'.
States of Nobilitie created at Bridewell, ii. 44.
staues in meter Royall, i. 99.
— **ragged**, imbrodered on coats of Earl Warwick, i. 88.
stayning: 'that workemanship of *s.* is departed out of use in England,' ii. 4; cf. i. 302–4.
steely, like steel, i. 293.
stered chamber, the Star Chamber, i. 308; starre chamber, ii. 119.
stilts: 'it leaneth vpon proppes or stilts,' ii. 2.
sintes, meete, to be well governed ⟨a convenient limit of the population of a city if it is to be properly governed⟩, ii. 205.
stirring, prancing, i. 103.
stockes, for Gunnes, i. 155.
stockfishmongers, i. 81; opp. to wet-fishmongers, *ib.*
strake, *pret.* of strike, i. 25.
Strand Bridge, 'with the lane under it,' ii. 93; for 'Iuie bridge,' cf. p. 96 *infra*, par. 2.
Strandage, a fee for landing from a boat, i. 206.
Stratford: '1491. Hugh Clopton builded the great stone bridge at Stratford vpon Hauen in Warwicke shire,' ii. 178.
strawne hat, a, i. 102.
streightened, straitened, i. 118 and *passim.*
strikes of iron, strips, bands, i. 323.
Striuelin (Stirling), i. 54.
stud, or nail of silver, i. 57.
stulpes, stulps, short stout posts fixed in the ground as a barrier.
sturs, the seditious, of the said John, i. 215.
subtiller, more, *double comp.*, i. 54.
subtiltie, fraud, roguery, i. 58.
sufficient, competent, i. 40.
— = substantial (of a pavement), i. 43.
summarie, in, summarily, i. 59.
summer houses . . . like Midsommer Pageantes, with Towers, Turrets, and Chimney tops, ii. 78.
Suppression, the late general, i. 125.
supprior, the, ii. 26.
surceased, from *surseoir*, ceased: 'these disputations surceased,' i. 74.
surmaster, second master, i. 74.
surplesses, i. 230.
surplusage, excess, i. 55.
suskinges, or **dodkins**, i. 132–3: 'an early name for the doit, a small Dutch coin' (*N.E.D.*, which quotes Act 3 *Hen. V*, c. i. § 2, 'Les Galyhalpens, et la Moneie appelle Seskyn et Doydekin').
sute, series, i. 315.
— suit, i. 155; ii. 67 *bis.*
sweating sickness, ii. 178.

T

tabard, or herald's coat, described, ii. 62.
tables, a game at, backgammon, i. 190.
talles, i. 191: 'a supply of men impannelled upon a Jury or Inquest, and not appearing, or at their appear-

ance challenged by either party as not indifferent; in which case the judge upon motion grants a supply to be made by the Sheriff of one or more such there present; and hereupon the very act of supplying is called a *Tales de circumstantibus*' (Cowell's *Interpreter*).

Tasell Close: 'a large Close called Tasell Close . . . for that there were Tasels planted for the use of Clothworkers,' i. 166. See Index III.

Tayler's yardes, i. 327; ii. 32.

tenement with purtenance in the lane, i. 242.

Theam (Team, Them, Theim), ii. 122: 'the right of compelling the person in whose hands lost property was found "to vouch to warranty," that is, to name the person from whom he received it' (Stubbs).

thwart, crosswise, ii. 78.

'**Tintegall** (Tintagel), in the confines of Cornwall,' i. 215.

tipplers of beere, publicans, i. 137.

toft, i. 249: 'a plantation, a green knoll (*Scand.*); a place marked out for a building' (Skeat).

Touch, a kind of very hard black granite (Halliwell); basalt (Todd-Johnson): 'a tombe of Touch,' i. 203.

Tower Royal, the, called the Queenes Wardrope, i. 244.

translated: 'Lodgings for the poore are translated into stabling for horses,' i. 294; 'His body was **translated** 1140, being richly shrined aboue the Quire,' i. 332.

trauailers, travellers: (*a*) 'poore people, **trauailers** and others that were diseased,' i. 82. (*b*) 'This most noble citizen . . . that had **trauelled** (*laboraverat*) for the commoditie of the whole Realme,' i. 107.

tree, wood, i. 97.

Trespasses, common, i. 33.

Trink, ii. 170: 'a narrow, open drain for the passage of water; the bed or channel of a river or stream; the water which flows in the channel' (*Dialect Dict.*). [?]

triumph: 'If any triumph or noblenesse were to be done,' i. 158.

tronage, tronagium, payment made for weighing goods at the public beam, i. 155; so *tronare*, to weigh at the public beam or steelyard; *tronarium*, public beam or steelyard by which heavy articles were weighed. Cf. Trongate of Edinburgh (see Gross, *Glossary*).

troupe: 'one large middle row or troupe of small tenementes,' ii. 91.

tutor, governor, i. 242.

tyred like a Pope, attired, i. 96.

U

vmbray: 'the shade for the eyes placed immediately over the sight of a helmet, and sometimes attached to the vizor' (Halliwell). See Kingsford, *London Chronicles*, Glossary. (Misprinted *uniber*, ii. 32.)

vnapt: 'the old Seale being very smal, vnapt, and vncomely,' i. 221.

vnder [subject to] correction, i. 57.

vndesevered: 'of bones undesevered,' i. 209.

Vniuersity of students of the Common Law in London, i. 77.

vnneath, scarcely: 'Famine and mortality, so that the quicke might vnneath bury the dead,' ii. 163.

vnprayseable, inestimable: 'vessels of gold and silver vnprayseable,' ii. 49.

vnright: 'I forbid that any man do to them any *vnright* or *disease*' ⟨Stow's words, not those of the patent⟩, i. 286 (Patent of H. 2).

Vnwitting the Sergeants, and against their willes, ii. 36.

vpholster, broker, i. 153.

vre, kept in, practice, i. 104.

Vtter Barresters, degree of, i. 78.

vttered (of wares): 'to be shewed, sold, and vttered,' i. 156.

V

'**vagabonde**,' a common labourer, i. 20.

valour, value: 'two acres of wood . . . in valour 20*s.* and 3*d.* by yeare,' i. 249.

vawmure, an advanced wall, ii. 70; cf. *vant*-warde, &c. (Stratmann). Stow's trans. of FitzStephen's *antemurale*, i. 70.

vellem, i. 328.

verify to be true, confirm, i. 196, 226.

vertue vegitable, the, i. 99.

Vicecounties, Vicounties, or **Shiriffes**, ii. 149.

vinetree, vintry, i. 81.

Violets (violet robes): 'the Aldermen accustomed to be present in their Violets, and in their Scarlets at the Spittle,' i. 167.

Vlfrimhampton, Wolverhampton, i. 111.

void, *v. a.*, 'Leprouse persons to be voided the city,' ii. 145 *marg.*; *v. n.*, 'that all leprose persons inhabiting there should *avoid* within fifteen days next.'

voluntarie, freewill: he resigned his bishopricke of his own voluntarie, ii. 130.

W

'Waddemole, now called woadmel, in Oxfordshire woddenell, a coarse sort of stuff used for the covering of the collars of cart-horses. Mr. Ray described it to be a hairy, coarse stuffe, made of Island wool, and brought thence by our seamen to Norfolk, Suffolk,' &c. (Kennett, *Glossary, s. v.*), i. 284.

waif, O.F. *gaif, pl.* waives, weives (Stratmann).

waifs and strays: '*Waif*, a thing abandoned; also the right of a lord to appropriate such things found upon his manor' (Nichols's *Britton*).

Walling of Cities, i. 8.

wan upon: 'Knightes Hospitelars of . . . S. John of Jerusalem . . . after wan upon the sayd Turke dayly,' ii. 50.

wanne, *pret.*, won, i. 51.

warden of the . . . Marches *foranenst* Scotland, facing, i. 44.

warder, a staff, truncheon: 'the King cast down his warder,' ii. 33. Cf. Shaks. *Rich. II*, I. iii. 118.

Wardrope: 'the Tower Royal called the Queenes Wardrope, i. 244.

waste of one Cocke [of water], i. 34, 38.

wasters, cudgels used in Fence schools (Halliwell), i. 95.

Water-Bayly, the, Bailiffe, i. 189.

water-bugges, casks (heraldic): 'Stephen Bugge Gent., his Armes be three water bugges, 1419,' i. 347.

waterdome, the (*ordalii*), i. 100. For this ordeal, see Hubert Hall, *Court Life under the Plantagenets*, 94 sq.

Watheling street: acc. to Leland, Atheling or Noble street. Stow rather takes it to be so named of the great high way 'of the same calling'. See Index II, and note, p. 352.

Watmols, i. 284, woollen bays, flannels, and such like. Cf. curtains of *Wedmole lace* in Hubert Hall, *Society in the Elizabethan Age*, p. 210; Rogers, *Agriculture and Prices*, ii. 542, 'Wadmal for collars'; and Kennett, *Glossary*.

Waytes of the City, the, i. 103. The City watchmen provided with trumpets (also known as waits) to give the alarm (Riley, *Memorials*, 420). Skeat explains the word as 'one who is awake to play music at night,' and compares *wayte*, a spy, *wayte*, waker, vigil (*Prompt. Parv.*).

wealthes, *plur.*, ii. 78.

weapons ouergrown with foulness, i. 104.

weauers: 'In London formerly weauers of diuerse sorts . . . of Drapery, or Taperie, and Naperie,' i. 218.

weeke (wick), the cotton or yarn of candles, i. 218.

welbeloved to, i. 120.

were, weir, A.S. and M.E. *wer*, i. 45; 'qui dedit unum were Ecclesiae Rofen,' *ib.*

whiffler, i. 102: 'one who goes first in a procession; orig. a piper or fifer' (Skeat). Cf. *Introd.*, p. viii.

whirlicotes or chariots, i. 83–4.

white money, silver, i. 55.

whoodes, hoods, i. 98.

wiar drawers, spinners of wire, i. 150.

'widdowes almes,' the leg-irons, i. 350.

Windgoose or **Wildgoose Lane,** i. 234. See Index II.

wine tunners, i. 242.

winning, to save space: 'for the winning of ground,' i. 295.

wirche, work, ii. 327.

with, a twisted tree, i. 98; cf. Judges xvi. 11, and see Skeat's *Etym. Dict.*

woad, woades, trade in, i. 82.

wodden (wooden), i. 7.

wols, wools, i. 155.

wolsteads, to scour or calender, i. 152.

wolsted, worsted, i. 102–3. From *Worstead*, Norfolk. 'Chaucer is perhaps the earliest author who mentions it' (Skeat).

woodmen, wildmen, satyrs, fauns, i. 314.

woodmen, wildmen, houses garnished with the likeness of, i. 296, 345.

woollen cloths to be in breadth two yards within the lists, i. 286.

wool-winders and packers wound and packed their wools in Leaden Hall, i. 160.

woon, *p.p.* of win, ii. 206.

woont, wont, i. 139.

worn out, extinct, i. 81, 136, 218 and *passim.*

Woze, Wapping in the, a low marshy place, ii. 70.

wrastling: '1452, a great fray at the wrastling,' ii. 174.

Y

year, by the, yearly, i. 36.

Ymaginour, image-maker, ii. 331.

INDEX I: OF PERSONS

B

C

D

F

H

I

U

V

Y

Z

INDEX II: OF PLACES

C

N

O

INDEX III: OF SUBJECTS

C

D

MAP POCKET

ADDENDA TO GLOSSARY

Cotton, umple, *add*: *Umple* occurs also in the pseudo-Chaucerian Assembly *of Ladies* (Skeat's *Chaucerian and other Pieces*, Glossary, p. 597), where it is explained as 'fine stuff in a single fold, fine gauze or lawn.' A variant MS. reading given by Prof. Skeat is vmpylle (*op. cit.* p. 537).

lyne right: *add* i. 162.

procedure if a culprit refuse to be tried by an inquest or jury (*peine forte et dure*), i. 215; and *see* (for the case of a woman) Kingsford's *Chronicles*, p. 152. The Notes in Nichols's *Britton* (i. 26 and 102) should also be consulted, as well as the brief article in *N.E.D. s.v. peine.* The last recorded case was in 1726.

woodmen: i. 314, *add*: Wōse, *subs.*, OE. Wāsa, *satyr*; cf. wodewōse (Stratmann-Bradley).

FINIS

Oxford: Printed at the Clarendon Press by HORACE HART, M.A.